THE McGRAW-HILL READER

Themes in the Disciplines

The McGraw-Hill Reader

FIFTH EDITION

Themes in the Disciplines

GILBERT H. MULLER

The City University of New York, LaGuardia

McGraw-Hill, Inc.

New York St. Louis San Francisco Auckland Bogotá Caracas Lisbon London Madrid Mexico City Milan Montreal New Delhi San Juan Singapore Sydney Tokyo Toronto

THE McGRAW-HILL READER
Themes in the Disciplines

Acknowledgments appear on pages 705–712, and on this page by reference.

This book is printed on recycled, acid-free paper containing 10% postconsumer waste.

2 3 4 5 6 7 8 9 0 DOC DOC 9 0 9 8 7 6 5 4

ISBN 0-07-044254-1

This book was set in Plantin Light by The Clarinda Company.
The editors were Alison Husting Zetterquist, Laurie PiSierra, and David Dunham;
the designer was Joan Greenfield;
the production supervisor was Leroy A. Young.
R. R. Donnelley & Sons Company was printer and binder.

Library of Congress Cataloging-in-Publication Data

The McGraw-Hill reader: themes in the disciplines/ [edited by]
Gilbert H. Muller.—5th ed.
p. cm.
Includes index.
ISBN 0-07-044254-1
1. College readers. 2. English language—Rhetoric.
3. Interdisciplinary approach in education. I. Muller, Gilbert H., (date).
PE1417.M44 1994
808'.9427—dc20 93-20824

ABOUT THE AUTHOR

GILBERT H. MULLER, who received a Ph.D. in English and American Literature from Stanford University, is currently professor of English and Special Assistant to the President at the LaGuardia campus of the City University of New York. He has also taught at Stanford, Vassar, and several universities overseas. Dr. Muller is the author of the award-winning *Nightmares and Visions: Flannery O'Connor and the Catholic Grotesque, Chester Himes,* and other critical studies. His essays and reviews have appeared in *The New York Times, The New Republic, The Nation, The Sewanee Review, The Georgia Review,* and elsewhere. He is also a noted author and editor of textbooks in English and composition, including *The Short Prose Reader* with Harvey Wiener and, with John A. Williams, *The McGraw-Hill Introduction to Literature, Bridges: Literature across Cultures,* and *Ways In: Reading and Writing about Literature*. Among Dr. Muller's awards are National Endowment for the Humanities Fellowships, a Fulbright Fellowship, and a Mellon Fellowship.

To Parisa and Darius
My favorite readers

CONTENTS

3: *MANNERS AND CUSTOMS*

4: *SCHOOL AND COLLEGE*

5: *GENDER AND HUMAN DEVELOPMENT*

6: *SOCIAL PROCESSES AND INSTITUTIONS*

7: *WORK, BUSINESS, AND ECONOMICS*

10: PHILOSOPHY AND ETHICS

11: RELIGIOUS THOUGHT AND EXPERIENCE

12: NATURE AND THE ENVIRONMENT

13: SCIENCE, MEDICINE, AND MATHEMATICS

14: CIVILIZATION

CONTENTS OF ESSAYS BY RHETORICAL MODE

NARRATION

DESCRIPTION

ILLUSTRATION

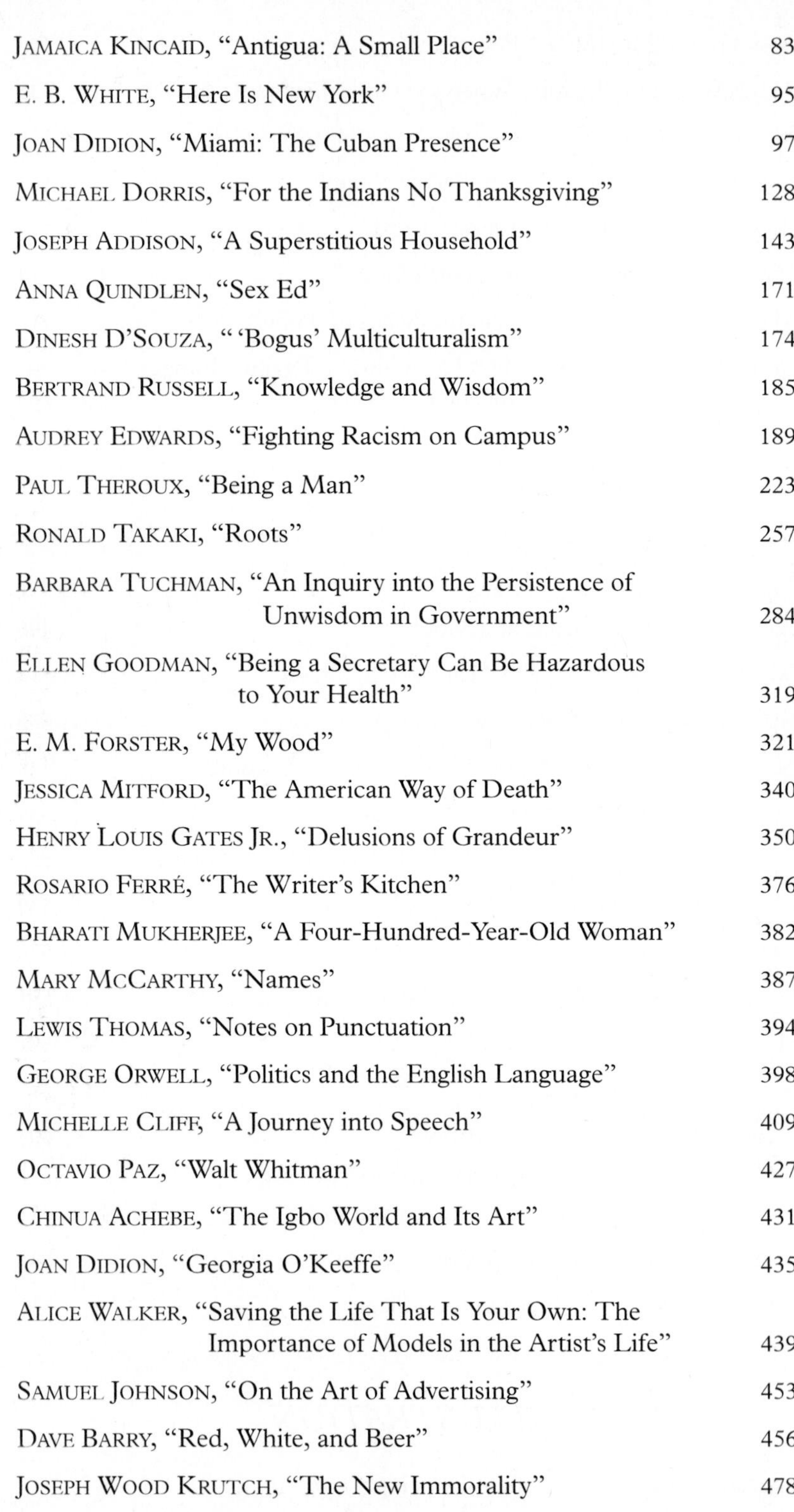

COMPARISON AND CONTRAST

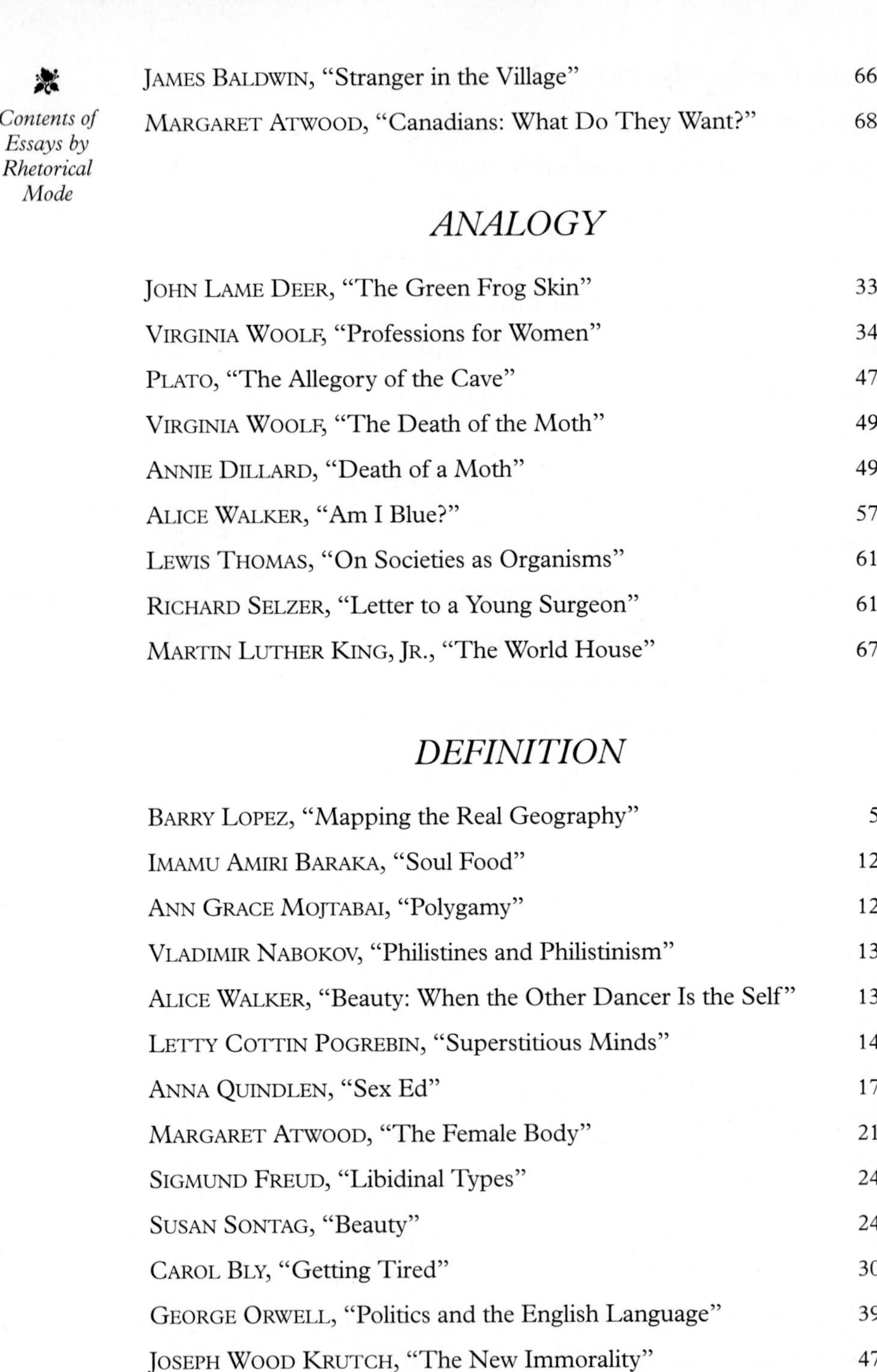

ANALOGY

DEFINITION

CLASSIFICATION

PROCESS ANALYSIS

CAUSAL ANALYSIS

ARGUMENT AND PERSUASION

LOGIC

HUMOR, IRONY, AND SATIRE

PREFACE

Any college reader reaching its fifth edition has traveled many miles to hundreds of colleges, and deserves an overhaul rather than a tune-up. For the fifth edition of *The McGraw-Hill Reader,* a great deal of care has gone into the creation of a text for the 1990s. The original features that have made the reader a success are still present, but the aim has been to develop an anthology that meets the needs and expectations of a new generation of college students.

The fifth edition of *The McGraw-Hill Reader* preserves the form and spirit of earlier editions. It continues to present the finest classic and contemporary essays for today's college students. Addressing the continuing national interest in core liberal arts programs, interdisciplinary themes, and multicultural perspectives, this text offers students and teachers a full range of prose models important to writing courses, reading sequences, and key undergraduate disciplines. All the selections, consisting of complete essays, chapters, and self-contained sections of chapters, have been selected for their significance, vitality, and technical precision. With its high caliber of material, its consistent humanistic emphases, and its clear organization, *The McGraw-Hill Reader* is lively, sophisticated, and eminently usable for college composition and reading programs.

The organization of *The McGraw-Hill Reader* is one of its most significant features. Composed of fourteen chapters, the text embraces all major modes of writing and most disciplines that college students encounter as undergraduates. Chapters 1 to 3, dealing with childhood and family, the sense of place, and manners and morals, provide students with prose models largely of a personal, experiential, narrative, descriptive, or reflective nature—essays that enhance the acquisition of basic language skills while encouraging students to construct their own versions of social reality, a reality rooted in knowledge of cross-cultural perspectives. Following chapters cover core liberal arts disciplines, including education, the social sciences, business and economics, the humanities, and the sciences, and culminate in a final interdisciplinary chapter on civilization that is integral to the scope and method of *The McGraw-Hill Reader.* While reinforcing earlier modes of writing presented in the text, these disciplinary chapters offer prose models that

provide practice in techniques of analysis, criticism, argumentation, and persuasion. As an integrated text, *The McGraw-Hill Reader* seeks to reconcile expressive and abstract varieties of thought in order to treat the total reading and writing process. An alternate table of contents, listing carefully selected essays in each of twelve rhetorical categories, adds to the flexibility of the text.

A second distinct advantage of *The McGraw-Hill Reader,* perhaps the primary one for teachers who prefer to create their own approaches to composition and reading courses, is the wide range of material and the varied constituencies represented in the text. The essays in this book have been selected carefully to embrace a rich international assortment of authors, to achieve balance among constituencies, to cover major historical periods, and to provide prose models and styles for class analysis, discussion, and imitation. The authors in this text—whether Plato or Maya Angelou, Swift or Joan Didion—have high visibility as writers and thinkers of value. Some of these authors are represented by two or three essays. All the authors—writing from such vantage points as literature, journalism, anthropology, sociology, art history, biology, and philosophy—presuppose that ideas exist in the world, that we should be alert to them, and that we should be able to deal with them in our own discourse. Because the selections extend from very simple essays to the most abstract and complex modes of prose, teachers and students will be able to use *The McGraw-Hill Reader* at virtually all levels of a program. Containing 128 complete essays, *The McGraw-Hill Reader* thus is a flexible companion for composition courses. It can be used from any of the major pedagogical perspectives common to the practice of composition today: as a writing-across-the-curricula text; as the basis for a rhetorically focused course; as a thematic reader; as a multicultural anthology; as an in-depth reader. Above all, teachers can develop their own sequence of essays that will contribute not only to their students' reading and writing proficiency but also to growing intellectual power.

The third major strength of *The McGraw-Hill Reader* is in the uniform apparatus that has been designed for every essay. Much can be learned from any well-written essay, especially if the apparatus is systematic in design. For each selection in this text there is a brief introduction. After each essay, there are questions organized in a common format created to reinforce essential reading, writing, and oral communication skills. Arranged in three categories—Comprehension, Rhetoric, and Writing—these questions reflect current compositional theory as they move students from audience analysis to various modes and processes of composition. All specialized terms used in the questions are defined for students in an extensive Glossary of Terms at the end of the text. The integrated design of these questions along with additional features that are new to the fifth edition makes each essay—simple or complex, short or long, old or new—accessible to college students who possess mixed reading and writing abilities.

New to the Fifth Edition

Teachers planning a composition course around *The McGraw-Hill Reader* will discover that the fifth edition has several new features:

- approximately sixty new selections—many on such topics as sex education, the death penalty, and searching for one's roots—that elicit provocative student writing;
- the addition of even more women writers than in previous editions, so that now 50 percent of all selections are by women;
- the creation of a multicultural anthology through the addition of writers like Judith Ortiz Cofer, Jamaica Kincaid, Pico Iyer, Michael Dorris, Ronald Takaki, V. S. Naipaul, Richard Rodriguez, and others;
- the appearance of an introductory chapter on the reading and writing process;
- two new chapters on gender and on the environment, along with several reconstituted chapters such as "Childhood and Family" that make academic disciplines more comprehensible for students;
- introductions to all chapters, with previewing sections that alert students to possibilities for reading, discussion, and writing;
- a "Classic and Contemporary" set of essays for each chapter, matching an older essayist with a more recent one so that students can gain fresh perspectives on influence and the essay tradition;
- a "Connections" section at the end of each chapter that helps students to make comparative assessments of various groups of essays;
- a new design and format, created to make the anthology even more inviting for today's students.

All of these new features appear in response to suggestions made by composition teachers across the country whose reviews and advice have shaped the fifth edition of *The McGraw-Hill Reader.*

Supplementing *The McGraw-Hill Reader* is a comprehensive instructor's manual. Unlike many manuals, this one is a complete teacher's guide. *A Guide to the McGraw-Hill Reader* offers sample syllabi, well-considered strategies for teaching individual essays, sample rhetorical analyses, answers to questions, additional thought-provoking questions, comparative essay discussion formats, and tips for prewriting and guided writing activities. There is also a bibliography of criticism and research on the teaching of composition.

Eudora Welty, whose work appears in *The McGraw-Hill Reader,* speaks of reading as "a sweet devouring." This anthology alerts students to the vast and varied pleasures of reading *and* writing, while offering them opportunities to experience numerous perspectives on academic discourse. It is a reader that encourages students to make intelligent choices as they handle assignments for composition.

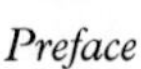

Acknowledgments

It is a pleasure to acknowledge the support, assistance, and guidance of numerous individuals who helped to create *The McGraw-Hill Reader.* Foremost among these people are the many McGraw-Hill sales representatives who obtained teacher responses to questionnaires when the text was in its formative stages. I also want to thank the excellent McGraw-Hill family of assistants, editors, and executives who participated enthusiastically in the project from the outset and who encouraged me at every step.

The final design and content of *The McGraw-Hill Reader,* Fifth Edition reflects the expertise and advice offered by college teachers across the country who gave generously of their time when asked to respond to questionnaires submitted to them by McGraw-Hill sales representatives. These include: Jean Bauso, Peace College; Roberta Bienvenu, Johnson State College; Alvin W. Bowker, University of Maine at Machias; Alan Brown, Livingston University; Teresa Dalle, Memphis State University; Miriam Espinosa, Texas Wesleyan University; Florence Halle, Memphis State University; Vanessa Lynn Kerns, West Virginia University; MaryKay Mahoney, Merrimack College; Frank Micklewright, San Joaquin Delta College; Meredith Morgan, Landmark College; Beth A. Rauer, West Virginia University; David Rogner, Concordia University; Edwina Romero, New Mexico Highlands University; Philip J. Skerry, Lakeland Community College; Lolly Smith, Everett Community College; Maria Solheim, Dawson Community College; Randall A. Wells, Coastal Carolina College; and Thomas Zolnay, Harold Washington College.

Warm appreciation is also extended to those college and university English professors who carefully read the manuscript in part or in its entirety and who made many constructive suggestions for improvement of the first and second editions. I am most grateful to David Bartl, New Mexico Military Institute; Kathleen Bell, University of Miami; Robert L. Brown, University of Minnesota; Irene Clark, University of Southern California; David Fite, University of Santa Clara; Dennis R. Gabriel, Cuyahoga Community College; Alan Golding, University of California, Los Angeles; Lillian Gottesman, Bronx Community College; Eugene Hammond, University of Maryland; John Hanes, Duquesne University; Pamela Howell, Midland College; James Mauch, Foothill College; Mary McFarland, Fresno Community College; Susan Miller, University of Wisconsin; Albert Nicolai, Middlesex Community College; Patricia Owen, Nassau Community College; Robert J. Pelinski, University of Illinois; Linda H. Peterson, Yale University; Rosentine Purnell, California State University, Northridge; Carl Quesnell, Iowa State University; Grayce F. Salerno, Seton Hall University; Margaret A. Strom, George Washington University; Beverly Thorsen, Central State University; Randall Wells, University of South Carolina; Jack Wilson, Old Dominion University; Mary Ann Wilson, Georgia State Univesity; and Carl Wooton, University of Southwestern Louisiana.

Special recognition must also be given to those specialists in various liberal arts fields who provided advice: Jane S. Zembaty, Department of Philosophy, University of Dayton; Linda Davidoff, Department of Psychology, Essex Community College; Curtis Williams, Department of Biology, The State University of New York; and Diane Papalia-Finlay, Department of Psychology, University of Wisconsin.

For the fourth edition, I thank the following reviewers for their supportive and most helpful evaluations: Susan Aylworth, California State University; Lynette Black, Memphis State University; Mary Edge Blevetty, Cardinal Stritch College; Nadia Creamer, Columbia-Greene Community College; Paula Friedman, Cardinal Stritch College; James Fuller, Midland College; LaVerne Gonzalez, San Jose State University; Peter Hardon, Bradley University; Elyce Rae Helford, University of Iowa; Glenda Linsey Hicks, Midland College; Katherine Kernberger, Linfield College; Diane Koenig, Columbia-Greene Community College; Mary Kay Mahoney, Merrimack College; Ross Primm, Mount Senario College; Audrey Schmidt, Cardinal Stritch College; Patrick Shaw, Texas Tech University; Kathy Sheldon, Iowa University; Emma Johanne Thomas, Prairie View A&M University; Jeanne Wescott, Miami Dade Community College; Clifford Wood, University of Wisconsin; and Robert J. Wurster, Western Kentucky University.

For the fifth edition, I appreciate the assistance of the following scholars: Tuzyline Allan, Baruch College; Michael Cochran, Santa Fe Community College; Valerie Giroux, Miami Dade Community College; Lawrence Griffin, Midland College; Lee Hammer, Culver-Stockton College; Mary Katzif, University of South Carolina; Thomas Long, Thomas Nelson Community College; Alan Powers, Bristol Community College; Barbara Sloan, Santa Fe Community College; Theodore Tasis, Northeastern University; and Jeanne Wescott, Miami Dade Community College.

Finally, I am pleased to acknowledge support from the Mellon Foundation, the Graduate Center of The City University of New York, and the United States Office of Education (Title III) that enabled me to concentrate on the development of this text.

Gilbert H. Muller

THE McGRAW-HILL READER

Themes in the Disciplines

INTRODUCTION

Reading and Writing Essays

For much of your college career, you will be reading and writing essays. An essay, as the eighteenth-century English wit Samuel Johnson observed, is "a loose sally of the mind; an irregular, undigested piece; not a regular and orderly performance." College essays that follow Dr. Johnson's prescription receive failing grades. However, if you reverse Johnson's advice, composing essays that are carefully and logically constructed, limited and clear in execution, and grammatically correct, you will produce passing—perhaps even commendable—papers.

You never know for certain what will happen when you sit down to read or write, for the nature of these reciprocal processes is complex. In both instances, words flow on paper (or on a computer screen). The eye and the brain—and the hand when writing, typing, or keyboarding—work in almost magical unison to move the reading and writing processes along. When reading critically, you absorb new ideas, develop perspectives on various bodies of knowledge, contend with competing viewpoints, learn something about yourself and your world. You also generate the raw stuff for writing, sifting information and also learning from significant authors the tricks of the trade that can help you become an effective essayist.

Critical reading *can* help produce sound critical writing, the sort of writing that college professors (and employers) like to see. The Renaissance philosopher Francis Bacon stresses the unity of reading and writing in his famous essay "Of Studies," where he asserts that "Reading maketh a full man, conference a ready man, and writing an exacting man." (In this era of gender-neutral usage, we would add "woman" to Bacon's remark in order to create a more truthful rendering of reality.)

Through critical reading, discussion, and writing—the essential method used in this anthology—you can learn to communicate effectively in essay form.

Reading and Responding to Texts

When you read an essay or any type of text, you are creating meaning out of the material the author has presented. If the essay is relatively simple, clear, and concise, the experience that you construct from your reading may be very similar to what the author intended. Nevertheless, the way that you interact with even the most comprehensible texts will never be identical to the way another reader interacts.

Consider the first essay that you will encounter in this anthology, Langston Hughes's "Salvation." A chapter from his autobiography, *The Big Sea* (1940), this essay tells of a childhood incident in which the young Hughes's faith was tested. The narrative focuses on a church revival meeting that Hughes was taken to and the increasing pressure he sensed at the meeting to "testify" to the presence of Jesus in his life. At first the young Hughes holds out against the fervor of the congregation, but ultimately he pretends to be converted, or "saved." That night, however, he weeps and then testifies to something entirely unexpected: the loss of faith he experienced because Jesus did not "save" him in a time of need.

As your class reads this essay, individuals among you may be struck by the compressed energy of the narration and the description of the event; by the swift characterization and revealing dialogue; or by the conflict and mounting tension. Moreover, the heightened personal and spiritual conflict will force class members to consider the sad irony inherent in the title "Salvation."

Even if your class arrives at a broad consensus on the intentions of the author, individual reader responses to the text will vary. Readers who have ever attended a revival meeting will respond differently from those who have not. Evangelical Christians will see the text from a different perspective than will Catholics, Muslims, or Jews. African-American readers (Hughes himself was black) will respond differently than will white readers. Women may respond differently than men, and so on.

In this brief assessment of possible reader responses, we are trying to establish meaning from a shifting series of critical perspectives. Although we can establish a consensus of meaning over what Hughes probably intended, our own interpretation and evaluation of the text will be conditioned by our personal experiences, backgrounds, attitudes, biases, and beliefs. In other words, even as the class attempts to construct a common reading, each member of the class is also constructing a somewhat different meaning, one based on the individual's own interaction with the text.

Reading Essays Critically

As you read an essay, think critically about the meanings and perspectives the author is creating. When you think critically, you interact with the text to create your own meanings. Here are some key questions you should ask yourself about the text:

• Who is the author? What is the author's background—his or her age, education, ethnic and class affiliation, ideology? What credentials does the author bring to the subject? What authority does the author have to write about the subject? Does George Orwell, for example, possess a special authority to write about British imperialism because he experienced it firsthand?

• Who is the audience? Authors often address an essay to an intended group of readers. What information or knowledge does the author assume that the audience possesses? What other assumptions does the author make about the audience? What are the audience's expectations? Perri Klass, for instance, who writes the "Hers" column for *The New York Times,* is writing for women but also for all relatively literate readers of this publication.

• What is the writer's purpose? Why did the author write this essay? What is his or her thesis, or main idea? An author creates a text in order to inform, explain, entertain, educate, argue, evaluate, persuade, warn, justify, narrate, or describe. Often a combination of these purposes motivates a single text. What specifically does the writer hope to achieve? Is this purpose stated directly, as in Virginia Woolf's "Professions for Women," or must it be inferred, as in another essay by Woolf, "The Death of the Moth"?

• What strategies does the author use? Authors make basic stylistic and rhetorical choices as they compose essays. Often a particular form—narration, description, illustration, comparison and contrast, classification, definition, process analysis, causal analysis, or argumentation and persuasion—is selected. Which form predominates in any given essay, and why? Why does the subject lend itself to this form or forms? How does the author sustain the reader's attention? How does the essay develop? Why, for example, does J. B. Priestley employ classification in his essay "Wrong Ism"?

• What is your experience of the text? Ultimately, you have to clarify your relationship to the text. What personal experiences do you bring to the essay? How much do you know about the subject? What is your moral or ethical position on the subject? What biases or beliefs intervene as you read the text? How have your opinions been challenged or changed—as in Deborah Salazar's "My Abortion" or Martin Luther King Jr.'s "I Have a Dream"?

Preparing to Write

Thinking critically about the essays you read prepares you for writing. College writing is often a translation process in which you convert into your own words the knowledge, perceptions, and stylistic skills of established authors. If this translation process is effective, readers will

be able to understand your own ways of thinking as well as appreciate your writing abilities.

The McGraw-Hill Reader has several distinctive features designed to facilitate this translation process. Every chapter contains a cluster of essays arranged around academic subject areas and key themes that you will encounter in the course of a standard college education. Thus the first chapter, "Childhood and Family," includes narratives by nine major authors dealing with the formative stages of human development from several multicultural perspectives. The sixth chapter, "Social Processes and Institutions," contains essays that encourage you to think about the significance of history and political science, while the last chapter, "Civilization," places a cluster of essays—and, indeed, the entire text—in a global, intercultural frame of reference.

Critical thinking about these readings is also facilitated by brief chapter introductions, followed by "Previewing the Chapter" questions that help you develop overviews of the essays. This attempt to establish critical overviews is reinforced by a comparative section of questions, entitled "Connections," at the end of each chapter. By utilizing these materials and your own critical powers, you develop an inquiring attitude about all of the essays in any given section. You discover fresh relationships among essays as well as an understanding of numerous forms of academic inquiry as they are defined by such disciplines as literature, psychology, anthropology, and science. A unique feature in each chapter is a paired set of readings entitled "Classic and Contemporary." This section pairs an established older author (typically deceased) with a present-day author for purposes of comparative assessment. For example, Virginia Woolf's "The Death of the Moth" is paired with Annie Dillard's "Death of a Moth" in the chapter on philosophy and ethics. Such comparative assessment will help you understand more clearly those influences that exist upon authors from age to age and generation to generation.

Every essay in this anthology is followed by a three-part set of exercises designed to take you from critical reading to directed writing. This set—"Comprehension," "Rhetoric," and "Writing"—stresses critical reflection and response. Critical reflection is typified by a willingness to test assertions and examine evidence, by a consistency in your viewpoints, by the detection and avoidance of faulty reasoning, by an understanding of relationships, by the creation of hypotheses (and theses), and by the prediction of outcomes. Through this active process of creating and forming ideas, you will be able to discover what you wish to say and write.

There is no one approach to reading and writing that will automatically solve your composing problems. Nevertheless, you *can* learn to model your writing after other authors, and many of the greatest essayists—from Swift to Orwell to Joan Didion—appear in this anthology. These authors engage you in a dialogue across centuries and numerous cultures. They encourage you to develop your own stylistic skills, rhetorical abilities, and intellectual positions. By following the course of readings in this text, you can identify and define a topic, develop methods to order your thoughts, and then translate these thoughts into print—an essay—for others to see.

CHAPTER ONE

Childhood and Family

Families and friendships are the two networks that nourish us during childhood. Essayists have always been aware of the rich subject of family life, and have created many superb narratives capturing the sweetness and innocence, as well as the terror and crazy logic, of children, families, and friends. Tolstoy wrote that "Happy families are all alike; every unhappy family is unhappy is its own way." In the opening chapter of this anthology, we will encounter both happy and unhappy families. We shall also discover that Tolstoy must have been wrong because our finest essayists can recreate or reimagine even happy families in decidedly unique ways.

The family, of course, is one of the few institutions that we find in virtually every society throughout the world. Anthropologists and sociologists tell us that family patterns are exceedingly diverse even in the same societies. The broad fact is that historically and today, children grow up in many ways: in "nuclear" and in nontraditional households; in single-parent and in dual-parent arrangements; in extended families and kinship networks; and in patriarchal and matriarchal, heterosexual and homosexual, monogamous and polygamous situations. And the dynamics of family life assume added dimensions as we move across cultures, studying European families, African-American families, Hispanic families, Asian families, and so forth.

Ultimately it is the emotional life of children as they relate to their families and friends that interest us the most when we read about them. It is easy to agree with the nineteenth-century English novelist Jane Austin, who, in *Emma,* wrote that "Nobody who has not been in the interior of a family can say what the difficulties of any individual of that family may be." This chapter contains vivid accounts of the interior lives—typically of narrators who as children confronted numerous difficulties as well as numerous possibilities for growth. We see the love that cuts across families, cultures, and generations in E. B. White's "Once More to the Lake," Judith Ortiz Cofer's "Silent Dancing," and Maya Angelou's "Momma, the Dentist, and Me." We witness family conflicts in essays such as Maxine Hong Kingston's "The Woman Warrior" and Isaac Bashevis Singer's "Why the Geese Shrieked." We confront children trying to make sense of a complex and contradictory adult world in Langston Hughes's "Salvation" and Mark Twain's "A Boy's Life."

All of the writers in this chapter write from the vantage point of adults looking backward on their youth. They replay scenes from their childhoods involving family and friends. Some of them, like White and Angelou, seem haunted by the events that they narrate; others, like McCullers and Welty, are nostalgic in their memoirs; still others are amused by childhood events. These essayists objectify childhood memories sufficiently so that we, as readers, understand the importance of the tales they tell. They range over what Mark Twain in his essay terms the "comedy and tragedy" of life. In these narratives of childhood, we encounter young people coming to terms with their families and with the larger world unfolding for them.

Previewing the Chapter

As you read the essays in this chapter and respond to them in discussion and writing, consider the following questions:

- Where does the narrative take place? How important is the setting to the action?
- What are the strengths and weaknesses of the families and friendships described?
- Why is the culture of the family—its ethnic, racial, social, or economic background—important to your understanding of the narrative?
- How does the author present himself or herself to you? Is the author likable or not? Do you find the narrator to be honest and reliable? On what evidence do you base your response?
- Is the author subjective or objective in developing the narrative? How do you know?
- What stylistic devices does the author employ to recreate childhood memories as vividly as possible?
- What similarities and differences do you encounter in the family patterns the author presents? Are all families alike in certain ways and different in others?
- What does the author learn in the course of the narrative of childhood that has been presented?
- What have you learned or discovered about children, families, and friendships from reading these essays?

LANGSTON HUGHES James Langston Hughes (1902–1967), poet, playwright, fiction writer, biographer, and essayist, was for more than fifty years one of the most productive and significant modern American authors. In *The Weary Blues* (1926), *Simple Speaks His Mind* (1950), *The Ways of White Folks* (1940), *Selected Poems* (1959), and dozens of other books, he strove, in his own words, "to explain the Negro condition in America." This essay, from his 1940 autobiography, *The Big Sea,* reflects the sharp, humorous, often bittersweet insights contained in Hughes's examination of human behavior.

LANGSTON HUGHES

Salvation

I was saved from sin when I was going on thirteen. But not really saved. 1
It happened like this. There was a big revival at my Auntie Reed's church. Every night for weeks there had been much preaching, singing, praying, and shouting, and some very hardened sinners had been brought to Christ, and the membership of the church had grown by leaps and bounds. Then just before the revival ended, they held a special meeting for children, "to bring the young lambs to the fold." My aunt spoke of it for days ahead. That night I was escorted to the front row and placed on the mourners' bench with all the other young sinners, who had not yet been brought to Jesus.

My aunt told me that when you were saved you saw a light, and 2
something happened to you inside! And Jesus came into your life! And God was with you from then on! She said you could see and hear and feel Jesus in your soul. I believed her. I had heard a great many old people say the same thing and it seemed to me they ought to know. So I sat there calmly in the hot, crowded church, waiting for Jesus to come to me.

The preacher preached a wonderful rhythmical sermon, all moans 3
and shouts and lonely cries and dire pictures of hell, and then he sang a song about the ninety and nine safe in the fold, but one little lamb was left out in the cold. Then he said: "Won't you come? Won't you come to Jesus? Young lambs, won't you come?" And he held out his arms to all us young sinners there on the mourners' bench. And the little girls cried. And some of them jumped up and went to Jesus right away. But most of us just sat there.

A great many old people came and knelt around us and prayed, old 4
women with jet-black faces and braided hair, old men with work-gnarled hands. And the church sang a song about the lower lights are burning, some poor sinners to be saved. And the whole building rocked with prayer and song.

Still I kept waiting to *see* Jesus. 5

Finally all the young people had gone to the altar and were saved, 6

but one boy and me. He was a rounder's son named Westley. Westley and I were surrounded by sisters and deacons praying. It was very hot in the church, and getting late now. Finally Westley said to me in a whisper: "God damn! I'm tired o' sitting here. Let's get up and be saved." So he got up and was saved.

Then I was left all alone on the mourners' bench. My aunt came and knelt at my knees and cried, while prayers and song swirled all around me in the little church. The whole congregation prayed for me alone, in a mighty wail of moans and voices. And I kept waiting serenely for Jesus, waiting, waiting—but he didn't come. I wanted to see him, but nothing happened to me. Nothing! I wanted something to happen to me, but nothing happened. 7

I heard the songs and the minister saying: "Why don't you come? My dear child, why don't you come to Jesus? Jesus is waiting for you. He wants you. Why don't you come? Sister Reed, what is this child's name?" 8

"Langston," my aunt sobbed. 9

"Langston, why don't you come? Why don't you come and be saved? Oh, Lamb of God! Why don't you come?" 10

Now it was really getting late. I began to be ashamed of myself, holding everything up so long. I began to wonder what God thought about Westley, who certainly hadn't seen Jesus either, but who was now sitting proudly on the platform, swinging his knickerbockered legs and grinning down at me, surrounded by deacons and old women on their knees praying. God had not struck Westley dead for taking his name in vain or for lying in the temple. So I decided that maybe to save further trouble, I'd better lie, too, and say that Jesus had come, and get up and be saved. 11

So I got up. 12

Suddenly the whole room broke into a sea of shouting, as they saw me rise. Waves of rejoicing swept the place. Women leaped in the air. My aunt threw her arms around me. The minister took me by the hand and led me to the platform. 13

When things quieted down, in a hushed silence, punctuated by a few ecstatic "Amens," all the new young lambs were blessed in the name of God. Then joyous singing filled the room. 14

That night, for the last time in my life but one—for I was a big boy twelve years old—I cried. I cried, in bed alone, and couldn't stop. I buried my head under the quilts, but my aunt heard me. She woke up and told my uncle I was crying because the Holy Ghost had come into my life, and because I had seen Jesus. But I was really crying because I couldn't bear to tell her that I had lied, that I had deceived everybody in the church, that I hadn't seen Jesus, and that now I didn't believe there was a Jesus any more, since he didn't come to help me. 15

COMPREHENSION

1. What does the title tell you about the subject of this essay? How would you state, in your own words, the thesis that emerges from the title and the essay?

2. How does Hughes recount the revival meeting he attended? What is the dominant impression?
3. Explain Hughes's shifting attitude toward salvation in this essay. Why is he disappointed in the religious answers provided by his church? What does he say about salvation in the last paragraph?

RHETORIC

1. Key words and phrases in this essay relate to the religious experience. Locate five of these words and expressions, and explain their connotations.
2. Identify the level of language in the essay. How does Hughes employ language effectively?
3. Where is the thesis statement in the essay? Consider the following: the use of dialogue; the use of phrases familiar to you (*idioms*); and the sentence structure. Cite examples of these elements.
4. How much time elapses, and why is this important to the effect? How does the author achieve narrative coherence?
5. Locate details and examples in the essay that are especially vivid and interesting. Compare your list with what others have listed. What are the similarities? The differences?
6. What is the tone of the essay? What is the relationship between tone and point of view?

WRITING

1. Describe a time in your life when you suppressed your feelings before adults because you thought they would misunderstand.
2. Recount an event in your life during which you surrendered to group pressures.
3. Write a narrative account of the most intense religious experience in your life.
4. Narrate an episode in which you played a trick on people simply to win their approval or satisfy their expectations.

EUDORA WELTY Eudora Welty (1909–) was born and raised in Mississippi. She attended the University of Wisconsin, from which she received a B.A. in 1929, and Columbia University, where she studied advertising. Rejecting a career in advertising, Welty turned to writing, publishing her first short story in 1936. After a decade of writing short fiction, she published her first novel, *Delta Wedding,* in 1946. Welty is considered one of our most important regional writers and one of the few contemporary masters of both the short story and the novel. Among her major works are *The Optimist's Daughter* (1972), which won a Pulitzer Prize, and *One Writer's Beginnings* (1984). She is a recipient of the National Medal for literature (1980) and the Presidential Medal of Freedom (1980). In this vivid reminiscence, Welty explores the relationship between reality and the imagination as she attempts to trace her origins as a writer.

EUDORA WELTY

One Writer's Beginnings

I had the window seat. Beside me, my father checked the progress of our train by moving his finger down the timetable and springing open his pocket watch. He explained to me what the position of the arms of the semaphore meant; before we were to pass through a switch we would watch the signal lights change. Along our track, the mileposts could be read; he read them. Right on time by Daddy's watch, the next town sprang into view, and just as quickly was gone. 1

Side by side and separately, we each lost ourselves in the experience of not missing anything, of seeing everything, of knowing each time what the blows of the whistle meant. But of course it was not the same experience: what was new to me, not older than ten, was a landmark to him. My father knew our way mile by mile; by day or by night, he knew where we were. Everything that changed under our eyes, in the flying countryside, was the known world to him, the imagination to me. Each in our own way, we hungered for all of this: my father and I were in no other respect or situation so congenial. 2

In Daddy's leather grip was his traveler's drinking cup, collapsible; a lid to fit over it had a ring to carry it by; it traveled in a round leather box. This treasure would be brought out at my request, for me to bear to the water cooler at the end of the Pullman car, fill to the brim, and bear back to my seat, to drink water over its smooth lip. The taste of silver could almost be relied on to shock your teeth. 3

After dinner in the sparkling dining car, my father and I walked back to the open-air observation platform at the end of the train and sat on the folding chairs placed at the railing. We watched the sparks we made fly behind us into the night. Fast as our speed was, it gave us time enough to see the rose-red cinders turn to ash, each one, and disappear from sight. Sometimes a house far back in the empty hills showed a light no bigger than a star. The sleeping countryside seemed itself to open a way through for our passage, then close again behind us. 4

The swaying porter would be making ready our berths for the night, pulling the shade down just so, drawing the green fishnet hammock across the window so the clothes you took off could ride along beside you, turning down the tight-made bed, standing up the two snowy pillows as high as they were wide, switching on the eye of the reading lamp, starting the tiny electric fan—you suddenly saw its blades turn into gauze and heard its insect murmur; and drawing across it all the pair of thick green theaterlike curtains—billowing, smelling of cigar smoke—between which you would crawl or dive headfirst to button them together with yourself inside, to be seen no more that night. 5

When you lay enclosed and enwrapped, your head on a pillow parallel to the track, the rhythm of the rail clicks pressed closer to your body as if it might be your heart beating, but the sound of the engine seemed to come from farther away than when it carried you in daylight. The whistle was almost too far away to be heard, its sound wavering back from the engine over the roofs of the cars. What you listened for was the different sound that ran under you when your own car crossed on a trestle, then another sound on an iron bridge; a low or a high bridge—each had its pitch, or drumbeat, for your car. 6

Riding in the sleeper rhythmically lulled me and waked me. From time to time, waked suddenly, I raised my window shade and looked out at my own strip of the night. Sometimes there was unexpected moonlight out there. Sometimes the perfect shadow of our train, with our car, with me invisibly included, ran deep below, crossing a river with us by the light of the moon. Sometimes the encroaching walls of mountains woke me by clapping at my ears. The tunnels made the train's passage resound like the "loud" pedal of a piano, a roar that seemed to last as long as a giant's temper tantrum. 7

But my father put it all into the frame of regularity, predictability, that was his fatherly gift in the course of our journey. I saw it going by, the outside world, in a flash. I dreamed over what I could see as it passed, as well as over what I couldn't. Part of the dream was what lay beyond, where the path wandered off through the pasture, the red clay road climbed and went over the hill or made a turn and was hidden in trees, or toward a river whose bridge I could see but whose name I'd never know. A house back at its distance at night showing a light from an open doorway, the morning faces of the children who stopped still in what they were doing, perhaps picking blackberries or wild plums, and watched us go by—I never saw with the thought of their continuing to be there just the same after we were out of sight. For now, and for a long while to come, I was proceeding in fantasy. 8

COMPREHENSION

1. At the end of the second paragraph, the narrator says, "Each in our own way, we hungered for all of this." Do father and child hunger for the same thing? Describe what each one is enjoying. In what way do they crave the same thing?
2. According to the author, what constitutes a writer's "beginnings"?
3. What does the narrator mean when she says that regularity and predictability were the gifts her father gave her "in the course of our journey"?

RHETORIC

1. The author makes vivid use of sensory language. Give instances where she employs her senses of touch, sound, taste, and smell.

2. Why is the "flying countryside" an important image? What other images of movement and acceleration can you find?
3. Is the time frame of this story one day or several? Why is the author compressing experience? What effect does this achieve?
4. Is the narrator writing this from the point of view of a child or an adult? Is there any place where the narrator judges something in retrospect? How is Welty's handling of point of view similar to that of Langston Hughes in "Salvation"?
5. What is the purpose of this narrative? Is the thesis overstated? Explain your answer.
6. In what sense is this trip a metaphor for the relationship between father and child?

WRITING

1. Discuss what qualities life had for you as a child. In what ways have your perceptions of the world changed over time?
2. In a narrative essay, describe an experience you had that served as a metaphor for your relationship to the world.
3. Select a particularly memorable childhood trip that you took with your family or a member of your family. As Welty does, try to recapture the event by using vivid sensory language.
4. Compare and contrast what we learn about Welty and Hughes from their respective essays about childhood events.

JUDITH ORTIZ COFER Judith Ortiz Cofer (1952–) was born in Puerto Rico and immigrated to the United States in 1956. Once a bilingual teacher in Florida public schools, Cofer has written collections of poetry, including *Native Dancer,* as well as plays, among them *Latin Women Pray* and *Reaching for the Mainland.* Her shorter work has appeared in anthologies, including *Hispanics in the United States.* One of the themes Cofer explores in her writing is the clash between Hispanic and American cultures. In the following autobiographical piece, she evokes the pain of assimilation.

JUDITH ORTIZ COFER

Silent Dancing

We have a home movie of this party. Several times my mother and I have watched it together, and I have asked questions about the silent revelers coming in and out of focus. It is grainy and of short duration, but it's a great visual aid to my memory of life at that time. And it is in color—the only complete scene in color I can recall from those years. 1

We lived in Puerto Rico until my brother was born in 1954. Soon after, 2
because of economic pressures on our growing family, my father joined the United States Navy. He was assigned to duty on a ship in Brooklyn Yard—a place of cement and steel that was to be his home base in the States until his retirement more than twenty years later. He left the Island first, alone, going to New York City and tracking down his uncle who lived with his family across the Hudson River in Paterson, New Jersey. There my father found a tiny apartment in a huge tenement that had once housed Jewish families but was just being taken over and transformed by Puerto Ricans, overflowing from New York City. In 1955 he sent for us. My mother was only twenty years old, I was not quite three, and my brother was a toddler when we arrived at El Building, as the place had been christened by its newest residents.

My memories of life in Paterson during those first few years are all 3
in shades of gray. Maybe I was too young to absorb vivid colors and details, or to discriminate between the slate blue of the winter sky and the darker hues of the snow-bearing clouds, but that single color washes over the whole period. The building we lived in was gray, as were the streets, filled with slush the first few months of my life there. The coat my father had bought for me was similar in color and too big; it sat heavily on my thin frame.

I do remember the way the heater pipes banged and rattled, star- 4
tling all of us out of sleep until we got so used to the sound that we automatically shut it out or raised our voices above the racket. The hiss from the valve punctuated my sleep (which has always been fitful) like a nonhuman presence in the room—a dragon sleeping at the entrance of my childhood. But the pipes were also a connection to all the other lives being lived around us. Having come from a house designed for a single family back in Puerto Rico—my mother's extended-family home—it was curious to know that strangers lived under our floor and above our heads, and that the heater pipe went through everyone's apartment. (My first spanking in Paterson came as a result of playing tunes on the pipes in my room to see if there would be an answer.) My mother was as new to this concept of beehive life as I was, but she had been given strict orders by my father to keep the doors locked, the noise down, ourselves to ourselves.

It seems that Father had learned some painful lessons about preju- 5
dice while searching for an apartment in Paterson. Not until years later did I hear how much resistance he had encountered with landlords who were panicking at the influx of Latinos into a neighborhood that had been Jewish for a couple of generations. It made no difference that it was the American phenomenon of ethnic turnover which was changing the urban core of Paterson, and that the human flood could not be held back with an accusing finger.

"You Cuban?" one man had asked my father, pointing at his name 6
tag on the navy uniform—even though my father had the fair skin and light brown hair of his northern Spanish background, and the name Ortiz is as common in Puerto Rico as Johnson is in the United States.

"No," my father had answered, looking past the finger into his ad- 7
versary's angry eyes. "I'm Puerto Rican."

"Same shit." And the door closed. 8

My father could have passed as European, but we couldn't. My 9
brother and I both have our mother's black hair and olive skin, and so we lived in El Building and visited our great-uncle and his fair children on the next block. It was their private joke that they were the German branch of the family. Not many years later that area too would be mainly Puerto Rican. It was as if the heart of the city map were being gradually colored brown—*café con leche* brown. Our color.

The movie opens with a sweep of the living room. It is "typical" immigrant 10
Puerto Rican decor for the time: the sofa and chairs are square and hard-looking, upholstered in bright colors (blue and yellow in this instance) and covered with the transparent plastic that furniture salesmen then were so adept at convincing women to buy. The linoleum on the floor is light blue; where it had been subjected to spike heels, as it was in most places, there were dime-size indentations all over it that cannot be seen in this movie. The room is full of people dressed up: dark suits for the men, red dresses for the women. When I have asked my mother why most of the women are in red that night, she has shrugged and said, "I don't remember. Just a coincidence." She doesn't have my obsession for assigning symbolism to everything.

The three women in red sitting on the couch are my mother, my eighteen- 11
year-old cousin, and her brother's girlfriend. The novia *is just up from the Island, which is apparent in her body language. She sits up formally, her dress pulled over her knees. She is a pretty girl, but her posture makes her look insecure, lost in her full-skirted dress, which she has carefully tucked around her to make room for my gorgeous cousin, her future sister-in-law. My cousin has grown up in Paterson and is in her last year of high school. She doesn't have a trace of what Puerto Ricans call* la mancha *(literally, the stain: the mark of the new immigrant—something about the posture, the voice, or the humble demeanor that makes it obvious to everyone the person has just arrived on the mainland). My cousin is wearing a tight, sequined, cocktail dress. Her brown hair has been lightened with peroxide around the bangs, and she is holding a cigarette expertly between her fingers, bringing it up to her mouth in a sensuous arc of her arm as she talks animatedly. My mother, who has come up to sit between the two women, both only a few years younger than herself, is somewhere between the poles they represent in our culture.*

It became my father's obsession to get out of the barrio, and thus we 12
were never permitted to form bonds with the place or with the people who lived there. Yet El Building was a comfort to my mother, who never got over yearning for *la isla*. She felt surrounded by her language: the walls were thin, and voices speaking and arguing in Spanish could be heard all day. *Salsas* blasted out of radios, turned on early in the morning and left on for company. Women seemed to cook rice and beans perpetually—the strong aroma of boiling red kidney beans permeated the hallways.

Though Father preferred that we do our grocery shopping at the 13
supermarket when he came home on weekend leaves, my mother insisted that she could cook only with products whose labels she could read. Consequently, during the week I accompanied her and my little brother to La Bodega—a hole-in-the-wall grocery store across the street from El Building. There we squeezed down three narrow aisles jammed with various products. Goya and Libby's—those were the trademarks that were trusted by her *mamá,* so my mother bought many cans of Goya beans, soups, and condiments, as well as little cans of Libby's fruit juices for us. And she also bought Colgate toothpaste and Palmolive soap. (The final *e* is pronounced in both these products in Spanish, so for many years I believed that they were manufactured on the Island. I remember my surprise at first hearing a commercial on television in which "Colgate" rhymed with "ate.") We always lingered at La Bodega, for it was there that Mother breathed best, taking in the familiar aromas of the foods she knew from Mamá's kitchen. It was also there that she got to speak to the other women of El Building without violating outright Father's dictates against fraternizing with our neighbors.

Yet Father did his best to make our "assimilation" painless. I can 14
still see him carrying a real Christmas tree up several flights of stairs to our apartment, leaving a trail of aromatic pine. He carried it formally, as if it were a flag in a parade. We were the only ones in El Building that I knew of who got presents on both Christmas and *día de Reyes,* the day when the Three Kings brought gifts to Christ and to Hispanic children.

Our supreme luxury in El Building was having our own television 15
set. It must have been a result of Father's guilt feelings over the isolation he had imposed on us, but we were among the first in the barrio to have one. My brother quickly became an avid watcher of Captain Kangaroo and Jungle Jim, while I loved all the series showing families. By the time I started first grade, I could have drawn a map of Middle America as exemplified by the lives of characters in *Father Knows Best, The Donna Reed Show, Leave It to Beaver, My Three Sons,* and (my favorite) *Bachelor Father,* where John Forsythe treated his adopted teenage daughter like a princess because he was rich and had a Chinese houseboy to do everything for him. In truth, compared to our neighbors in El Building, *we* were rich. My father's navy check provided us with financial security and a standard of living that the factory workers envied. The only thing his money could not buy us was a place to live away from the barrio—his greatest wish, Mother's greatest fear.

In the home movie the men are shown next, sitting around a card table set 16
up in one corner of the living room, playing dominoes. The clack of the ivory pieces was a familiar sound. I heard it in many houses on the Island and in many apartments in Paterson. In Leave It to Beaver, *the Cleavers played bridge in every other episode; in my childhood, the men started every social occasion with a hotly debated round of dominoes. The women would sit around and watch, but they never participated in the games.*

Here and there you can see a small child. Children were always brought 17

to parties and, whenever they got sleepy, were put to bed in the host's bedroom. Babysitting was a concept unrecognized by the Puerto Rican women I knew: a responsible mother did not leave her children with any stranger. And in a culture where children are not considered intrusive, there was no need to leave the children at home. We went where our mother went.

Of my preschool years I have only impressions: the sharp bite of the wind in December as we walked with our parents toward the brightly lit stores downtown; how I felt like a stuffed doll in my heavy coat, boots, and mittens; how good it was to walk into the five-and-dime and sit at the counter drinking hot chocolate. On Saturdays our whole family would walk downtown to shop at the big department stores on Broadway. Mother bought all our clothes at Penney's and Sears, and she liked to buy her dresses at the women's specialty shops like Lerner's and Diana's. At some point we'd go into Woolworth's and sit at the soda fountain to eat. 18

We never ran into other Latinos at these stores or when eating out, and it became clear to me only years later that the women from El Building shopped mainly in other places—stores owned by other Puerto Ricans or by Jewish merchants who had philosophically accepted our presence in the city and decided to make us their good customers, if not real neighbors and friends. These establishments were located not downtown but in the blocks around our street, and they were referred to generically as La Tienda, El Bazar, La Bodega, La Botánica. Everyone knew what was meant. These were the stores where your face did not turn a clerk to stone, where your money was as green as anyone else's. 19

One New Year's Eve we were dressed up like child models in the Sears catalogue: my brother in a miniature man's suit and bow tie, and I in black patent-leather shoes and a frilly dress with several layers of crinoline underneath. My mother wore a bright red dress that night, I remember, and spike heels; her long black hair hung to her waist. Father, who usually wore his navy uniform during his short visits home, had put on a dark civilian suit for the occasion: we had been invited to his uncle's house for a big celebration. Everyone was excited because my mother's brother Hernan—a bachelor who could indulge himself with luxuries—had bought a home movie camera, which he would be trying out that night. 20

Even the home movie cannot fill in the sensory details such a gathering left imprinted in a child's brain. The thick sweetness of women's perfumes mixing with the ever-present smells of food cooking in the kitchen: meat and plantain *pasteles,* as well as the ubiquitous rice dish made special with pigeon peas—*gandules*—and seasoned with precious *sofrito* sent up from the Island by somebody's mother or smuggled in by a recent traveler. *Sofrito* was one of the items that women hoarded, since it was hardly ever in stock at La Bodega. It was the flavor of Puerto Rico. 21

The men drank Palo Viejo rum, and some of the younger ones got 22 weepy. The first time I saw a grown man cry was at a New Year's Eve party: he had been reminded of his mother by the smells in the kitchen. But what I remember most were the boiled *pasteles,* plantain or yucca rectangles stuffed with corned beef or other meats, olives, and many other savory ingredients, all wrapped in banana leaves. Everybody had to fish one out with a fork. There was always a "trick" *pastel*—one without stuffing—and whoever got that one was the "New Year's Fool."

There was also the music. Long-playing albums were treated like 23
precious china in these homes. Mexican recordings were popular, but the songs that brought tears to my mother's eyes were sung by the melancholy Daniel Santos, whose life as a drug addict was the stuff of legend. Felipe Rodríguez was a particular favorite of couples, since he sang about faithless women and brokenhearted men. There is a snatch of one lyric that has stuck in my mind like a needle on a worn groove: *De piedra ha de ser mi cama, de piedra la cabezera . . . la mujer que a mi me quiera . . . ha de quererme de veras. Ay, Ay, Ay, corazón, porque no amas. . . .* I must have heard it a thousand times since the idea of a bed made of stone, and its connection to love, first troubled me with its disturbing images.

The five-minute home movie ends with people dancing in a circle—the 24
creative filmmaker must have set it up, so that all of them could file past him. It is both comical and sad to watch silent dancing. Since there is no justification for the absurd movements that music provides for some of us, people appear frantic, their faces embarrassingly intense. It's as if you were watching sex. Yet for years, I've had dreams in the form of this home movie. In a recurring scene, familiar faces push themselves forward into my mind's eye, plastering their features into distorted close-ups. And I'm asking them: "Who is *she?* Who is the old woman I don't recognize? Is she an aunt? Somebody's wife? Tell me who she is."

> "See the beauty mark on her cheek as big as a hill on the lunar land- 25
> scape of her face—well, that runs in the family. The women on your father's side of the family wrinkle early; it's the price they pay for that fair skin. The young girl with the green stain on her wedding dress is *la novia*—just up from the Island. See, she lowers her eyes when she approaches the camera, as she's supposed to. Decent girls never look at you directly in the face. *Humilde,* humble, a girl should express humility in all her actions. She will make a good wife for your cousin. He should consider himself lucky to have met her only weeks after she arrived here. If he marries her quickly, she will make him a good Puerto Rican-style wife; but if he waits too long, she will be corrupted by the city, just like your cousin there."

> "She means me. I do what I want. This is not some primitive island 26
> I live on. Do they expect me to wear a black mantilla on my head and go to mass every day? Not me. I'm an American woman, and I will do

as I please. I can type faster than anyone in my senior class at Central High, and I'm going to be a secretary to a lawyer when I graduate. I can pass for an American girl anywhere—I've tried it. At least for Italian, anyway—I never speak Spanish in public. I hate these parties, but I wanted the dress. I look better than any of these *humildes* here. *My* life is going to be different. I have an American boyfriend. He is older and has a car. My parents don't know it, but I sneak out of the house late at night sometimes to be with him. If I marry him, even my name will be American. I hate rice and beans—that's what makes these women fat."

"Your *prima* is pregnant by that man she's been sneaking around 27
with. Would I lie to you? I'm your *tiá política,* your great-uncle's common-law wife—the one he abandoned on the Island to go marry your cousin's mother. I was not invited to this party, of course, but I came anyway. I came to tell you that story about your cousin that you've always wanted to hear. Do you remember the comment your mother made to a neighbor that has always haunted you? The only thing you heard was your cousin's name, and then you saw your mother pick up your doll from the couch and say: 'It was as big as this doll when they flushed it down the toilet.' This image has bothered you for years, hasn't it? You had nightmares about babies being flushed down the toilet, and you wondered why anyone would do such a horrible thing. You didn't dare ask your mother about it. She would only tell you that you had not heard her right, and yell at you for listening to adult conversations. But later, when you were old enough to know about abortions, you suspected.

"I am here to tell you that you were right. Your cousin was growing 28
an *americanito* in her belly when this movie was made. Soon after, she put something long and pointy into her pretty self, thinking maybe she could get rid of the problem before breakfast and still make it to her first class at the high school. Well, *niña,* her screams could be heard downtown. Your aunt, her *mamá,* who had been a midwife on the Island, managed to pull the little thing out. Yes, they probably flushed it down the toilet. What else could they do with it—give it a Christian burial in a little white casket with blue bows and ribbons? Nobody wanted that baby—least of all the father, a teacher at her school with a house in West Paterson that he was filling with real children, and a wife who was a natural blonde.

"Girl, the scandal sent your uncle back to the bottle. And guess 29
where your cousin ended up? Irony of ironies. She was sent to a village in Puerto Rico to live with a relative on her mother's side: a place so far away from civilization that you have to ride a mule to reach it. A real change in scenery. She found a man there—women like that cannot live without male company—but believe me, the men in Puerto Rico know how to put a saddle on a woman like her. *La gringa,* they call her. Ha, ha, ha. *La gringa* is what she always wanted to be. . . ."

The old woman's mouth becomes a cavernous black hole I fall into. 30
And as I fall, I can feel the reverberations of her laughter. I hear the

echoes of her last mocking words: *la gringa, la gringa!* And the conga line keeps moving silently past me. There is no music in my dream for the dancers.

When Odysseus visits Hades to see the spirit of his mother, he 31
makes an offering of sacrificial blood, but since all the souls crave an audience with the living, he has to listen to many of them before he can ask questions. I, too, have to hear the dead and the forgotten speak in my dream. Those who are still part of my life remain silent, going around and around in their dance. The others keep pressing their faces forward to say things about the past.

My father's uncle is last in line. He is dying of alcoholism, shrunken 32
and shriveled like a monkey, his face a mass of wrinkles and broken arteries. As he comes closer I realize that in his features I can see my whole family. If you were to stretch that rubbery flesh, you could find my father's face, and deep within *that* face—my own. I don't want to look into those eyes ringed in purple. In a few years he will retreat into silence, and take a long, long time to die. *Move back, Tío,* I tell him. *I don't want to hear what you have to say. Give the dancers room to move. Soon it will be midnight. Who is the New Year's Fool this time?*

COMPREHENSION

1. How did Cofer's parents differ in their views about life in the United States? Explain. Give concrete examples.
2. What is the attitude of those born or raised in the United States toward those Puerto Ricans still carrying *"la mancha"?* Cite evidence from the essay to support your opinion.
3. Cofer refers to learning "painful lessons about prejudice." What examples from the narrative illustrate these lessons?

RHETORIC

1. To what end does Cofer employ the italicized portions of the essay? How does this device contribute to the overall power of the narrative?
2. What is the mood of the essay? What phrases or passages reveal the narrator's point of view?
3. Cofer uses powerful images and sensory details in her narration. Which of these are especially evocative? Give examples, and explain how they enhance the emotional impact of her story.
4. What is the function of the Spanish idioms and phrases Cofer uses? Does she employ them successfully?
5. Toward the end of the essay, Cofer uses disembodied voices to recount the Latino experience in the United States. Is this an effective method? How do these voices affect the mood of the story?
6. Explain the overall pattern of essay development that emerges from this essay. In other words, how does Cofer unify the various scenes and episodes that constitute the narrative?

WRITING

1. There were many family gatherings in the Ortiz household. Write a narrative essay about a memorable family gathering you experienced as a child. Use sensory images to enrich your essay.
2. Write an essay recounting a time when you or someone you know experienced rejection or humiliation because of race, color, religion, or economic status. What happened, how did you feel, and what effect has it had on you?
3. As you read the next selection, consider Cofer's connotative labels of *"humilde"* and *"gringa"* and decide which category Maxine Hong Kingston, although Asian American, might fall under. Analyze this connection in the context of ethnic identity in the United States.

MAXINE HONG KINGSTON Maxine Hong Kingston (1940–) has written three books on the Chinese-American experience that have established her as a major contemporary prose stylist. *The Woman Warrior* (1976) and *China Men* (1980) are brilliant explorations of personal and ethnic consciousness. Her newest work, a novel, is entitled *Tripmaster Monkey* (1989). This selection from her first book is filled with the mysteries, family tales, and legends that she uses to create the tapestry of her complex cultural identity.

MAXINE HONG KINGSTON

The Woman Warrior

My American life has been such a disappointment. 1

"I got straight A's, Mama." 2

"Let me tell you a true story about a girl who saved her village." 3

I could not figure out what was my village. And it was important that I do something big and fine, or else my parents would sell me when we made our way back to China. In China there were solutions for what to do with little girls who ate up food and threw tantrums. You can't eat straight A's. 4

When one of my parents or the emigrant villagers said, "Feeding girls is feeding cowbirds," I would thrash on the floor and scream so hard I couldn't talk. I couldn't stop. 5

"What's the matter with her?" 6

"I don't know. Bad, I guess. You know how girls are. 'There's no profit in raising girls. Better to raise geese than girls.' " 7

"I would hit her if she were mine. But then there's no use wasting all that discipline on a girl. 'When you raise girls, you're raising children for strangers.' " 8

"Stop that crying!" my mother would yell. "I'm going to hit you if 9 you don't stop. Bad girl! Stop!" I'm going to remember never to hit or to scold my children for crying, I thought, because then they will only cry more.

10 "I'm not a bad girl," I would scream. "I'm not a bad girl. I'm not a bad girl." I might as well have said, "I'm not a girl."

11 "When you were little, all you had to say was 'I'm not a bad girl,' and you could make yourself cry," my mother says, talking-story about my childhood.

12 I minded that the emigrant villagers shook their heads at my sister and me. "One girl—and another girl," they said, and made our parents ashamed to take us out together. The good part about my brothers being born was that people stopped saying, "All girls," but I learned new grievances. "Did you roll an egg on *my* face like that when *I* was born?" "Did you have a full-month party for *me*?" "Did you turn on all the lights?" "Did you send *my* picture to Grandmother?" "Why not? Because I'm a girl? Is that why not?" "Why didn't you teach me English?" "You like having me beaten up at school, don't you?"

13 "She is very mean, isn't she?" the emigrant villagers would say.

14 "Come, children. Hurry. Hurry. Who wants to go out with Great-Uncle?" On Saturday mornings, my great-uncle, the ex-river pirate, did the shopping. "Get your coats, whoever's coming."

15 "I'm coming. I'm coming. Wait for me."

16 When he heard girls' voices, he turned on us and roared, "No girls!" and left my sisters and me hanging our coats back up, not looking at one another. The boys came back with candy and new toys. When they walked through Chinatown, the people must have said, "A boy—and another boy—and another boy!" At my great-uncle's funeral I secretly tested out feeling glad that he was dead—the six-foot bearish masculinity of him.

17 I went away to college—Berkeley in the sixties—and I studied, and I marched to change the world, but I did not turn into a boy. I would have liked to bring myself back as a boy for my parents to welcome with chickens and pigs. That was for my brother, who returned alive from Vietnam.

18 If I went to Vietnam, I would not come back; females desert families. It was said, "There is an outward tendency in females," which meant that I was getting straight A's for the good of my future husband's family, not my own. I did not plan ever to have a husband. I would show my mother and father and the nosey emigrant villagers that girls have no outward tendency. I stopped getting straight A's.

19 And all the time I was having to turn myself American-feminine, or no dates.

20 There is a Chinese word for the female *I*—which is "slave." Break the women with their own tongues!

21 I refused to cook. When I had to wash dishes, I would crack one or two. "Bad girl," my mother yelled, and sometimes that made me gloat rather than cry. Isn't a bad girl almost a boy?

22 "What do you want to be when you grow up, little girl?"

"A lumberjack in Oregon." 23

Even now, unless I'm happy, I burn the food when I cook. I do not 24
feed people. I let the dirty dishes rot. I eat at other people's tables but won't invite them to mine, where the dishes are rotting.

If I could not-eat, perhaps I could make myself a warrior like the 25
swordswoman who drives me. I will—I must—rise and plow the fields as soon as the baby comes out.

Once I get outside the house, what bird might call me; on what 26
horse could I ride away? Marriage and childbirth strengthen the swordswoman, who is not a maid like Joan of Arc. Do the women's work; then do more work, which will become ours too. No husband of mine will say, "I could have been a drummer, but I had to think about the wife and kids. You know how it is." Nobody supports me at the expense of his own adventure. Then I get bitter: no one supports me; I am not loved enough to be supported. That I am not a burden has to compensate for the sad envy when I look at women loved enough to be supported. Even now China wraps double binds around my feet.

When urban renewal tore down my parents' laundry and paved 27
over our slum for a parking lot, I only made up gun and knife fantasies and did nothing useful.

From the fairy tales, I've learned exactly who the enemy are. I eas- 28
ily recognize them—business-suited in their modern American executive guise, each boss two feet taller than I am and impossible to meet eye to eye.

I once worked at an art supply house that sold paints to artists. 29
"Order more of that nigger yellow, willya?" the boss told me. "Bright, isn't it? Nigger yellow."

"I don't like that word," I had to say in my bad, smallperson's voice 30
that makes no impact. The boss never deigned to answer.

I also worked at a land developer's association. The building indus- 31
try was planning a banquet for contractors, real estate dealers, and real estate editors. "Did you know the restaurant you chose for the banquet is being picketed by CORE and the NAACP?" I squeaked.

"Of course I know." The boss laughed. "That's why I chose it." 32

"I refuse to type these invitations," I whispered, voice unreliable. 33

He leaned back in his leather chair, his bossy stomach opulent. He 34
picked up his calendar and slowly circled a date. "You will be paid up to here," he said. "We'll mail you the check."

If I took the sword, which my hate must surely have forged out of 35
the air, and gutted him, I would put color and wrinkles into his shirt.

It's not just the stupid racists that I have to do something about, but 36
the tyrants who for whatever reason can deny my family food and work. My job is my own only land.

To avenge my family, I'd have to storm across China to take back 37
our farm from the Communists; I'd have to rage across the United States to take back the laundry in New York and the one in California. Nobody in history has conquered and united both North America and Asia. A descendant of eighty pole fighters, I ought to be able to set out

confidently, march straight down our street, get going right now. There's work to do, ground to cover. Surely, the eighty pole fighters, though unseen, would follow me and lead me and protect me, as is the wont of ancestors.

Or it may well be that they're resting happily in China, their spirits 38
dispersed among the real Chinese, and not nudging me at all with their poles. I mustn't feel bad that I haven't done as well as the swordswoman did; after all, no bird called me, no wise old people tutored me. I have no magic beads, or water gourd sight, no rabbit that will jump in the fire when I'm hungry. I dislike armies.

I've looked for the bird. I've seen clouds make pointed angel wings 39
that stream past the sunset, but they shred into clouds. Once at a beach after a long hike I saw a seagull, tiny as an insect. But when I jumped up to tell what miracle I saw, before I could get the words out I understood that the bird was insect-size because it was far away. My brain had momentarily lost its depth perception. I was that eager to find an unusual bird.

The news from China has been confusing. It also had something to 40
do with birds. I was nine years old when the letters made my parents, who are rocks, cry. My father screamed in his sleep. My mother wept and crumpled up the letters. She set fire to them page by page in the ashtray, but new letters came almost every day. The only letters they opened without fear were the ones with red borders, the holiday letters that mustn't carry bad news. The other letters said that my uncles were made to kneel on broken glass during their trials and had confessed to being land-owners. They were all executed, and the aunt whose thumbs were twisted off drowned herself. Other aunts, mothers-in-law, and cousins disappeared; some suddenly began writing to us again from communes or from Hong Kong. They kept asking for money. The ones in communes got four ounces of fat and one cup of oil a week, they said, and had to work from 4 A.M. to 9 P.M. They had to learn to do dances waving red kerchiefs; they had to sing nonsense syllables. The Communists gave axes to the old ladies and said, "Go and kill yourself. You're useless." If we overseas Chinese would just send money to the Communist bank, our relatives said, they might get a percentage of it for themselves. The aunts in Hong Kong said to send money quickly; their children were begging on the sidewalks and mean people put dirt in their bowls.

When I dream that I am wire without flesh, there is a letter on blue 41
airmail paper that floats above the night ocean between here and China. It must arrive safely or else my grandmother and I will lose each other.

My parents felt bad whether or not they sent money. Sometimes 42
they got angry at their brothers and sisters for asking. And they would not simply ask but have to talk-story too. The revolutionaries had taken Fourth Aunt and Uncle's store, house, and lands. They attacked the house and killed the grandfather and oldest daughter. The grandmother escaped with the loose cash and did not return to help. Fourth Aunt picked up her sons, one under each arm, and hid in the pig house,

where they slept that night in cotton clothes. The next day she found her husband, who had also miraculously escaped. The two of them collected twigs and yams to sell while their children begged. Each morning they tied the faggots on each other's back. Nobody bought from them. They ate the yams and some of the children's rice. Finally Fourth Aunt saw what was wrong. "We have to shout 'Fuel for sale' and 'Yams for sale,'" she said, "We can't just walk unobtrusively up and down the street." "You're right," said my uncle, but he was shy and walked in back of her. "Shout," my aunt ordered, but he could not. "They think we're carrying these sticks home for our own fire," she said. "Shout." They walked about miserably, silently, until sundown, neither of them able to advertise themselves. Fourth Aunt, an orphan since the age of ten, mean as my mother, threw her bundle down at his feet and scolded Fourth Uncle, "Starving to death, his wife and children starving to death, and he's too damned shy to raise his voice." She left him standing by himself and afraid to return empty-handed to her. He sat under a tree to think, when he spotted a pair of nesting doves. Dumping his bag of yams, he climbed up and caught the birds. That was when the Communists trapped him, in the tree. They criticized him for selfishly taking food for his own family and killed him, leaving his body in the tree as an example. They took the birds to a commune kitchen to be shared.

It is confusing that my family was not the poor to be championed. 43
They were executed like the barons in the stories, when they were not barons. It is confusing that birds tricked us.

What fighting and killing I have seen have not been glorious but 44
slum grubby. I fought the most during junior high school and always cried. Fights are confusing as to who has won. The corpses I've seen had been rolled and dumped, sad little dirty bodies covered with a police khaki blanket. My mother locked her children in the house so we couldn't look at dead slum people. But at news of a body, I would find a way to get out; I had to learn about dying if I wanted to become a swordswoman. Once there was an Asian man stabbed next door, words on cloth pinned to his corpse. When the police came around asking questions, my father said, "No read Japanese. Japanese words. Me Chinese."

I've also looked for old people who could be my gurus. A medium 45
with red hair told me that a girl who died in a far country follows me wherever I go. This spirit can help me if I acknowledge her, she said. Between the head line and heart line in my right palm, she said, I have the mystic cross. I could become a medium myself. I don't want to be a medium. I don't want to be a crank taking "offerings" in a wicker plate from the frightened audience, who, one after another, asked the spirits how to raise rent money, how to cure their coughs and skin diseases, how to find a job. And martial arts are for unsure little boys kicking away under fluorescent lights.

I live now where there are Chinese and Japanese, but no emigrants 46
from my own village looking at me as if I had failed them. Living

among one's own emigrant villagers can give a good Chinese far from China glory and a place. "That old busboy is really a swordsman," we whisper when he goes by, "He's a swordsman who's killed fifty. He has a tong ax in his closet." But I am useless, one more girl who couldn't be sold. When I visit the family now, I wrap my American successes around me like a private shawl; I *am* worthy of eating the food. From afar I can believe my family loves me fundamentally. They only say, "When fishing for treasures in the flood, be careful not to pull in girls," because that is what one says about daughters. But I watched such words come out of my own mother's and father's mouths; I looked at their ink drawing of poor people snagging their neighbor's flotage with long flood hooks and pushing the girl babies on down the river. And I had to get out of hating range. I read in an anthropology book that Chinese say, "Girls are necessary too"; I have never heard the Chinese I know make this concession. Perhaps it was a saying in another village. I refuse to shy my way anymore through our Chinatown, which tasks me with the old sayings and the stories.

47 The swordswoman and I are not so dissimilar. May my people understand the resemblance soon so that I can return to them. What we have in common are the words at our backs. The ideographs for *revenge* are "report at crime" and "report to five families." The reporting is the vengeance—not the beheading, not the gutting, but the words. And I have so many words—"chink" words and "gook" words too—that they do not fit on my skin.

COMPREHENSION

1. What is the historical context of this personal narrative? What assumptions does the author make about her audience?
2. Summarize the "autobiography" that Kingston presents of herself in this selection. What are her family and its individual members like?
3. Explain the author's American life. How does she relate to Chinese culture *and* to American culture? What is her major problem? How would she overcome it?

RHETORIC

1. What connotations does Kingston explore for the words *girls* and *females?* What connotations does she bring to the word *swordswoman?*
2. Locate five Chinese expressions or sayings in this selection. What is their effect on the tone of the essay?
3. The author's introductory paragraph consists of a single sentence. Is this strategy effective? Why?
4. Analyze the author's presentation of chronology. List the scenes into which the action is divided. Where are there stories within stories? Why does Kingston present such a complex tapestry of chronology and events? How, finally, does the author use narration to advance expository or explanatory ends?

5. Why is characterization important to the development of Kingston's thesis? How does the author *create* vivid characters? Cite specific examples and techniques.
6. Which paragraphs comprise the conclusion? How do these paragraphs reflect some of the major motifs of the essay?

WRITING

1. In *China Men,* Kingston speaks of "trying to unravel the mysteries" of her family. What mysteries does she explore here? Look up the word *mystery* in your dictionary. What "mysteries" concerning your family or your origins would you like to explore? Write an essay on this topic.
2. Write an autobiographical or narrative essay tracing a particular problem that you had to face while growing up in your family.
3. Narrate an event that happened to one of your relatives or ancestors in the "old country," the nation of your family's origin.

ISAAC BASHEVIS SINGER Isaac Bashevis Singer (1904–1991) was born in Radzymin, Poland, and came to the United States in 1935. He became an American citizen in 1943. Singer, who wrote in Yiddish, is the author of several superlative short-story collections, including *Gimpel the Fool* (1957), *The Seance* (1968), and *The Spinoza of Market Street* (1961). He also wrote novels, books for children, and memoirs, notably *A Day of Pleasure* (1969) and *Lost in America* (1981). Singer received the Nobel Prize in Literature in 1975. A former rabbinical student, Singer injected elements of religion into his work, often in a comic way. "Why the Geese Shrieked" is typical of Singer's seriocomic approach to the conflicts and tribulations of this world.

ISAAC BASHEVIS SINGER

Why the Geese Shrieked

In our home there was always talk about spirits of the dead that possess the bodies of the living, souls reincarnated as animals, houses inhabited by hobgoblins, cellars haunted by demons. My father spoke of these things, first of all because he was interested in them, and second because in a big city children so easily go astray. They go everywhere, see everything, read nonreligious books. It is necessary to remind them from time to time that there are still mysterious forces at work in the world. 1

One day, when I was about eight, he told us a story found in one of 2
the holy books. If I am not mistaken, the author of that book is Rabbi Eliyahu Graidiker, or one of the other Graidiker sages. The story was about a girl possessed by four demons. It was said that they could actually be seen crawling around in her intestines, blowing up her belly, wandering from one part of her body to another, slithering into her legs. The Rabbi of Graidik had exorcised the evil spirits with the blowing of the ram's horn, with incantations, and the incense of magic herbs.

When my brother Joshua questioned these things, my father became 3
very excited. He argued: "Was then the great Rabbi of Graidik, God forbid, a liar? Are all the rabbis, saints, and sages deceivers, while only atheists speak the truth? Woe is us! How can one be so blind?"

Suddenly the door opened, and a woman entered. She was carrying 4
a basket with two geese in it. The woman looked frightened. Her matron's wig was tilted to one side. She smiled nervously.

Father never looked at strange women, because it is forbidden by 5
Jewish law, but Mother and we children saw immediately that something had greatly upset our unexpected visitor.

"What is it?" Father asked, at the same time turning his back so as 6
not to look upon her.

"Rabbi, I have a very unusual problem." 7

"What is it?" 8

"It's about these geese." 9

"What's the matter with them?" 10

"Dear Rabbi, the geese were slaughtered properly. Then I cut off 11
their heads. I took out the intestines, the livers, all the other organs, but the geese keep shrieking in such a sorrowful voice. . . ."

Upon hearing these words, my father turned pale. A dreadful fear 12
befell me, too. But my mother came from a family of rationalists and was by nature a skeptic.

"Slaughtered geese don't shriek," she said. 13

"You will hear for yourself," replied the woman. 14

She took one of the geese and placed it on the table. Then she took 15
out the second goose. The geese were headless, disemboweled—in short, ordinary dead geese.

A smile appeared on my mother's lips. "And *these geese* shriek?" 16

"You will soon hear." 17

The woman took one goose and hurled it against the other. At once 18
a shriek was heard. It is not easy to describe that sound. It was like the cackling of a goose, but in such a high, eerie pitch, with such groaning and quaking, that my limbs grew cold. I could actually feel the hairs on my earlocks pricking me. I wanted to run from the room. But where would I run? My throat constricted with fear. Then I, too, shrieked and clung to my mother's skirt, like a child of three.

Father forgot that one must avert one's eyes from a woman. He ran 19
to the table. He was no less frightened than I was. His red beard trembled. In his blue eyes could be seen a mixture of fear and vindication.

For my father this was a sign that not only to the Rabbi of Graidik, but to him too, omens were sent from heaven. But perhaps this was a sign from the Evil One, from Satan himself?

"What do you say now?" asked the woman. 20

My mother was no longer smiling. In her eyes there was something 21
like sadness, and also anger.

"I cannot understand what is going on here," she said, with a cer- 22
tain resentment.

"Do you want to hear it again?" 23

Again the woman threw one goose against the other. And again the 24
dead geese gave forth an uncanny shriek—the shriek of dumb creatures slain by the slaughterer's knife who yet retain a living force; who still have a reckoning to make with the living, an injustice to avenge. A chill crept over me. I felt as though someone had struck me with all his might.

My father's voice became hoarse. It was broken as though by sobs. 25
"Well, can anyone still doubt that there *is* a Creator?" he asked.

"Rabbi, what shall I do and where shall I go?" The woman began to 26
croon in a mournful singsong. "What has befallen me? Woe is me! What shall I do with them? Perhaps I should run to one of the Wonder Rabbis? Perhaps they were not slaughtered properly? I am afraid to take them home. I wanted to prepare them for the Sabbath meal, and now, such a calamity! Holy Rabbi, what shall I do? Must I throw them out? Someone said they must be wrapped in shrouds and buried in a grave. I am a poor woman. Two geese! They cost me a fortune!"

Father did not know what to answer. He glanced at his bookcase. If 27
there was an answer anywhere, it must be there.

Suddenly he looked angrily at my mother. "And what do you say 28
now, eh?"

Mother's face was growing sullen, smaller, sharper. In her eyes 29
could be seen indignation and also something like shame.

"I want to hear it again." Her words were half-pleading, half-com- 30
manding.

The woman hurled the geese against each other for the third time, 31
and for the third time the shrieks were heard. It occurred to me that such must have been the voice of the sacrificial heifer.

"Woe, woe, and still they blaspheme. . . . It is written that the 32
wicked do not repent even at the very gates of hell." Father had again begun to speak. "They behold the truth with their own eyes, and they continue to deny their Maker. They are dragged into the bottomless pit and they maintain that all is nature, or accident. . . ."

He looked at Mother as if to say: You take after *them*. 33

For a long time there was silence. Then the woman asked, "Well, 34
did I just imagine it?"

Suddenly my mother laughed. There was something in her laughter 35
that made us all tremble. I knew, by some sixth sense, that Mother was preparing to end the mighty drama being enacted before our eyes.

"Did you remove the windpipes?" my mother asked. 36

"The windpipes? No. . . ." 37

"Take them out," said my mother, "and the geese will stop shrieking."

My father became angry. "What are you babbling? What has this got to do with windpipes?"

Mother took hold of one of the geese, pushed her slender finger in- 40
side the body, and with all her might pulled out the thin tube that led from the neck to the lungs. Then she took the other goose and removed its windpipe also. I stood trembling, aghast at my mother's courage. Her hands had become bloodied. On her face could be seen the wrath of the rationalist whom someone has tried to frighten in broad daylight.

Father's face turned white, calm, a little disappointed. He knew 41
what had happened here: logic, cold logic, was again tearing down faith, mocking it, holding it up to ridicule and scorn.

"Now, if you please, take one goose and hurl it against the other!" 42
commanded my mother.

Everything hung in the balance. If the geese shrieked, Mother 43
would have lost all: her rationalist's daring, her skepticism, which she had inherited from her intellectual father. And I? Although I was afraid, I prayed inwardly that the geese *would* shriek, shriek so loud that people in the street would hear and come running.

But, alas, the geese were silent, silent as only two dead geese with- 44
out windpipes can be.

"Bring me a towel!" Mother turned to me. 45

I ran to get the towel. There were tears in my eyes. Mother wiped 46
her hands on the towel like a surgeon after a difficult operation.

"That's all it was!" she announced victoriously. 47

"Rabbi, what do you say?" asked the woman. 48

Father began to cough, to mumble. He fanned himself with his 49
skullcap.

"I have never before heard of such a thing," he said at last. 50

"Nor have I," echoed the woman. 51

"Nor have I," said my mother. "But there is always an explanation. 52
Dead geese don't shriek."

"Can I go home now and cook them?" asked the woman. 53

"Go home and cook them for the Sabbath." Mother pronounced 54
the decision. "Don't be afraid. They won't make a sound in your pot."

"What do you say, Rabbi?" 55

"Hmm . . . they are kosher," murmured Father. "They can be 56
eaten." He was not really convinced, but now he could not pronounce the geese unclean.

Mother went back to the kitchen. I remained with my father. 57
Suddenly he began to speak to me as though I were an adult. "Your mother takes after your grandfather, the Rabbi of Bilgoray. He is a great scholar, but a cold-blooded rationalist. People warned me before our betrothal. . . ."

And then Father threw up his hands, as if to say: It is too late now 58
to call off the wedding.

COMPREHENSION

1. Explain the conflict between the author's mother and father.
2. Where does Singer, as a child, stand in relation to the conflict? What do you think that he learns from this episode?
3. Does this essay have a thesis? Justify your answer.

RHETORIC

1. This essay contains strong *visual* and *auditory* imagery. Cite examples, and explain how such imagery contributes to the effect of the narrative.
2. Locate and analyze examples of parallel sentence structure in paragraphs 1 and 2. What effects are achieved?
3. What is the function of the first three paragraphs? How are they connected to the body of the essay?
4. Trace Singer's development of conflict, terror, and suspense in the story he narrates. How does he handle these elements successfully?
5. What is the tone of the essay? How does Singer achieve it?
6. What do the last two paragraphs contribute to the essay?

WRITING

1. Do you accept Singer's implied premise that children often get caught between the conflicting value systems of their parents? Why, or why not? Can you think of an example from your personal experience? Narrate a personal experience that grew out of a conflict of opinions or beliefs between your parents, relatives, or friends.
2. Examine the conflicts in values and family beliefs in the essays by Hughes, Kingston, and Singer.
3. Are you a "rationalist" or a believer in "mysterious forces"? Describe an episode in your life that supports your response to this question.

CARSON McCULLERS Carson McCullers (1917–1967) is the author of a small but impressive body of fiction, including *The Heart Is a Lonely Hunter* (1940), *Reflections in a Golden Eye* (1941), *A Member of the Wedding* (1946), and *The Ballad of the Sad Cafe* (1951). Although she was preoccupied in her fiction with the theme of loneliness, this selection from her autobiography reveals instead the love, joy, and sense of community permeating one episode from her Georgia childhood.

CARSON MCCULLERS

Home for Christmas

Sometimes in August, weary of the vacant, broiling afternoon, my 1
younger brother and sister and I would gather in the dense shade under the oak tree in the back yard and talk of Christmas and sing carols. Once after such a conclave, when the tunes of the carols still lingered in the heat-shimmered air, I remember climbing up into the tree-house and sitting there alone for a long time.

Brother called up: "What are you doing?" 2

"Thinking," I answered. 3

"What are you thinking about?" 4

"I don't know." 5

"Well, how can you be thinking when you don't know what you are 6
thinking about?"

I did not want to talk with my brother. I was experiencing the first 7
wonder about the mystery of Time. Here I was, on this August afternoon, in the tree-house, in the burnt, jaded yard, sick and tired of all our summer ways. (I had read *Little Women* for the second time, *Hans Brinker and the Silver Skates, Little Men,* and *Twenty Thousand Leagues under the Sea.* I had read movie magazines and even tried to read love stories in the *Woman's Home Companion*—I was so sick of everything.) How could it be that I was I and now was now when in four months it would be Christmas, wintertime, cold weather, twilight and the glory of the Christmas tree? I puzzled about the *now* and *later* and rubbed the inside of my elbow until there was a little roll of dirt between my forefinger and thumb. Would the *now* I of the tree-house and the August afternoon be the same *I* of winter, firelight and the Christmas tree? I wondered.

My brother repeated: "You say you are thinking but you don't know 8
what you are thinking about. What are you really doing up there? Have you got some secret candy?"

September came, and my mother opened the cedar chest and we 9
tried on winter coats and last year's sweaters to see if they would do again. She took the three of us downtown and bought us new shoes and school clothes.

Christmas was nearer on the September Sunday that Daddy round- 10
ed us up in the car and drove us out on dusty country roads to pick elderberry blooms. Daddy made wine from elderberry blossoms—it was a yellow-white wine, the color of weak winter sun. The wine was dry to the wry side—indeed, some years it turned to vinegar. The wine was served at Christmastime with slices of fruitcake when company came. On November Sundays we went to the woods with a big basket of fried

chicken dinner, thermos jug and coffee-pot. We hunted partridge berries in the pine woods near our town. These scarlet berries grew hidden underneath the glossy brown pine needles that lay in a slick carpet beneath the tall wind-singing trees. The bright berries were a Christmas decoration, lasting in water through the whole season.

In December the windows downtown were filled with toys, and my 11
brother and sister and I were given two dollars apiece to buy our Christmas presents. We patronized the ten-cent stores, choosing between jackstones, pencil boxes, water colors and satin handkerchief holders. We would each buy a nickel's worth of lump milk chocolate at the candy counter to mouth as we trudged from counter to counter, choice to choice. It was exacting and final—taking several afternoons—for the dime stores would not take back or exchange.

Mother made fruitcakes, and for weeks ahead the family picked out 12
the nut meats of pecans and walnuts, careful of the bitter layer of the pecans that lined your mouth with nasty fur. At the last I was allowed to blanch the almonds, pinching the scalded nuts so that they sometimes hit the ceiling or bounced across the room. Mother cut slices of citron and crystallized pineapple, figs and dates, and candied cherries were added whole. We cut rounds of brown paper to line the pans. Usually the cakes were mixed and put into the oven when we were in school. Late in the afternoon the cakes would be finished, wrapped in white napkins on the breakfast-room table. Later they would be soaked in brandy. These fruitcakes were famous in our town, and Mother gave them often as Christmas gifts. When company came thin slices of fruitcake, wine and coffee were always served. When you held a slice of fruitcake to the window or the firelight the slice was translucent, pale citron green and yellow and red, with the glow and richness of our church windows.

Daddy was a jeweler, and his store was kept open until midnight all 13
Christmas week. I, as the eldest child, was allowed to stay up late with Mother until Daddy came home. Mother was always nervous without a "man in the house." (On those rare occasions when Daddy had to stay overnight on business in Atlanta, the children were armed with a hammer, saw and a monkey wrench. When pressed about her anxieties Mother claimed she was afraid of "escaped convicts or crazy people." I never saw an escaped convict, but once a "crazy" person did come to see us. She was an old, old lady dressed in elegant black taffeta, my mother's second cousin once removed, and came on a tranquil Sunday morning and announced that she had always liked our house and she intended to stay with us until she died. Her sons and daughters and grandchildren gathered around to plead with her as she sat rocking in our front porch rocking chair and she left not unwillingly when they promised a car ride and ice cream.) Nothing ever happened on those evenings in Christmas week, but I felt grown, aged suddenly by trust and dignity. Mother confided in secrecy what the younger children were getting from Santa Claus. I knew where the Santa Claus things

were hidden, and was appointed to see that my brother and sister did not go into the back-room closet or the wardrobe in our parents' room.

Christmas Eve was the longest day, but it was lined with the glory of tomorrow. The sitting-room smelled of floor wax and the clean, cold odor of the spruce tree. The Christmas tree stood in a corner of the front room, tall as the ceiling, majestic, undecorated. It was our family custom that the tree was not decorated until after we children were in bed on Christmas Eve night. We went to bed very early, as soon as it was winter dark. I lay in bed beside my sister and tried to keep her awake.

"You want to guess again about your Santa Claus?" 15

"We've already done that so much," she said. 16

My sister slept. And there again was another puzzle. How could it 17
be that when she opened her eyes it would be Christmas while I lay awake in the dark for hours and hours? The time was the same for both of us, and yet not at all the same. What was it? How? I thought of Bethlehem and cherry candy, Jesus and skyrockets. It was dark when I awoke. We were allowed to get up on Christmas at five o'clock. Later I found out that Daddy juggled the clock Christmas Eve so that five o'clock was actually six. Anyway it was always still dark when we rushed in to dress by the kitchen stove. The rule was that we dress and eat breakfast before we could go in to the Christmas tree. On Christmas morning we always had fish roe, bacon and grits for breakfast. I grudged every mouthful—for who wanted to fill up on breakfast when there in the sitting-room was candy, at least three whole boxes? After breakfast we lined up, and carols were started. Our voices rose naked and mysterious as we filed through the door to the sitting-room. The carol, unfinished, ended in raw yells of joy.

The Christmas tree glittered in the glorious, candlelit room. There 18
were bicycles and bundles wrapped in tissue paper. Our stockings hanging from the mantlepiece bulged with oranges, nuts and smaller presents. The next hours were paradise. The blue dawn at the window brightened, and the candles were blown out. By nine o'clock we had ridden the wheel presents and dressed in the clothes gifts. We visited the neighborhood children and were visited in turn. Our cousins came and grown relatives from distant neighborhoods. All through the morning we ate chocolates. At two or three o'clock the Christmas dinner was served. The dining-room table had been let out with extra leaves and the very best linen was laid—satin damask with a rose design. Daddy asked the blessing, then stood up to carve the turkey. Dressing, rice and giblet gravy were served. There were cut-glass dishes of sparkling jellies and stateliness of festal wine. For dessert there was always sillabub or charlotte and fruitcake. The afternoon was almost over when dinner was done.

At twilight I sat on the front steps, jaded by too much pleasure, sick 19
at the stomach and worn out. The boy next door skated down the street in his new Indian suit. A girl spun around on a crackling son-of-a-gun.

My brother waved sparklers. Christmas was over. I thought of the monotony of Time ahead, unsolaced by the distant glow of paler festivals, the year that stretched before another Christmas—eternity.

COMPREHENSION

1. What, according to the author, is the essence of Christmas?
2. Trace chronologically the preparations for Christmas by the McCullers family.
3. What is the author's attitude toward time? Paraphrase the last sentence of the essay.

RHETORIC

1. This essay is rich in sensory language. Cite five words or phrases that are especially vivid, and analyze their effect. To which senses does the writing appeal?
2. Define these words: *conclave* (paragraph 1); *patronized* (paragraph 11); *blanch* (paragraph 12); *tranquil* (paragraph 13); and *festal* (paragraph 18). Use them in sentences of your own.
3. McCullers writes in paragraph 7 that she "was experiencing the first wonder about the mystery of Time." How does this theme serve as the organizing principle for the essay? How does the author convey the mystery of time? What is her dual attitude toward time, and how does this serve as a structuring device in the essay? How does the author's treatment of time resemble that of Welty in "One Writer's Beginnings"?
4. What principles of emphasis do you find in McCullers's treatment of chronology?
5. How and why does the author connect the many and varied details in the essay? How effective are her details in conveying a sense of her childhood and evolving personality? How is this reflected in point of view?
6. How does the conclusion relate to the rest of the essay? Do you find the conclusion effective? Why, or why not?

WRITING

1. Do you still look forward to special holidays or celebrations, or does the type of anticipation of which McCullers speaks exist only for children? Why do children have different perceptions of time than adults? Evaluate this matter in an essay.
2. Write a narrative account of a vivid holiday event in your childhood.
3. Analyze McCuller's use of sensory language to create a dominant impression in "Home for Christmas."

E. B. WHITE Elwyn Brooks White (1899–1985), perhaps the finest contemporary American essayist, is at his most distinctive in his treatments of people and nature. A recipient of the National Medal for literature, and associated for years with *The New Yorker,* White is the author of *One Man's Meat* (1942), *Here Is New York* (1949), and *The Second Tree from the Corner* (1954), among numerous other works. He is also one of the most talented writers of literature for children, the author of *Stuart Little* (1945), *Charlotte's Web* (1952), and *The Trumpet of the Swan* (1970). In this essay, White combines narration and description to make a poignant and vivid statement about past and present, youth and age, life and death.

E. B. WHITE

Once More to the Lake

One summer, along about 1904, my father rented a camp on a lake in 1
Maine and took us all there for the month of August. We all got ringworm from some kittens and had to rub Pond's Extract on our arms and legs night and morning, and my father rolled over in a canoe with all his clothes on; but outside of that the vacation was a success and from then on none of us ever thought there was any place in the world like that lake in Maine. We returned summer after summer—always on August 1st for one month. I have since become a salt-water man, but sometimes in summer there are days when the restlessness of the tides and the fearful cold of the sea water and the incessant wind which blows across the afternoon and into the evening make me wish for the placidity of a lake in the woods. A few weeks ago this feeling got so strong I bought myself a couple of bass hooks and a spinner and returned to the lake where we used to go, for a week's fishing and to revisit old haunts.

I took along my son, who had never had any fresh water up his nose 2
and who had seen lily pads only from train windows. On the journey over to the lake I began to wonder what it would be like. I wondered how time would have marred this unique, this holy spot—the coves and streams, the hills that the sun set behind, the camps and the paths behind the camps. I was sure the tarred road would have found it out and I wondered in what other ways it would be desolated. It is strange how much you can remember about places like that once you allow your mind to return into the grooves which lead back. You remember one thing, and that suddenly reminds you of another thing. I guess I remembered clearest of all the early mornings, when the lake was cool and motionless, remembered how the bedroom smelled of the lumber it was made of and of the wet woods whose scent entered through the

screen. The partitions in the camp were thin and did not extend clear to the top of the rooms, and as I was always the first up I would dress softly so as not to wake the others, and sneak out into the sweet outdoors and start out in the canoe, keeping close along the shore in the long shadows of the pines. I remembered being very careful never to rub my paddle against the gunwale for fear of disturbing the stillness of the cathedral.

The lake had never been what you would call a wild lake. There 3
were cottages sprinkled around the shores, and it was in farming country although the shores of the lake were quite heavily wooded. Some of the cottages were owned by nearby farmers, and you would live at the shore and eat your meals at the farmhouse. That's what our family did. But although it wasn't wild, it was a fairly large and undisturbed lake and there were places in it which, to a child at least, seemed infinitely remote and primeval.

I was right about the tar: it led to within half a mile of the shore. But 4
when I got back there, with my boy, and we settled into a camp near a farmhouse and into the kind of summertime I had known, I could tell that it was going to be pretty much the same as it had been before—I knew it, lying in bed the first morning, smelling the bedroom, and hearing the boy sneak quietly out and go off along the shore in a boat. I began to sustain the illusion that he was I, and therefore, by simple transposition, that I was my father. This sensation persisted, kept cropping up all the time we were there. It was not an entirely new feeling, but in this setting it grew much stronger. I seemed to be living a dual existence. I would be in the middle of some simple act, I would be picking up a bait box or laying down a table fork, or I would be saying something, and suddenly it would be not I but my father who was saying the words or making the gesture. It gave me a creepy sensation.

We went fishing the first morning. I felt the same damp moss cover- 5
ing the worms in the bait can, and saw the dragonfly alight on the tip of my rod as it hovered a few inches from the surface of the water. It was the arrival of this fly that convinced me beyond any doubt that everything was as it always had been, that the years were a mirage and there had been no years. The small waves were the same, chucking the rowboat under the chin as we fished at anchor, and the boat was the same boat, the same color green and the ribs broken in the same place, and under the floor-boards the same fresh-water leavings and débris—the dead hellgrammite, the wisps of moss, the rusty discarded fishhook, the dried blood from yesterday's catch. We stared silently at the tips of our rods, at the dragonflies that came and went. I lowered the tip of mine into the water, tentatively, pensively dislodging the fly, which darted two feet away, poised, darted two feet back, and came to rest again a little farther up the rod. There had been no years between the ducking of this dragonfly and the other one—the one that was part of memory. I looked at the boy, who was silently watching his fly, and it was my hands that held his rod, my eyes watching. I felt dizzy and didn't know which rod I was at the end of.

We caught two bass, hauling them in briskly as though they were mackerel, pulling them over the side of the boat in a businesslike manner without any landing net, and stunning them with a blow on the back of the head. When we got back for a swim before lunch, the lake was exactly where we had left it, the same number of inches from the dock, and there was only the merest suggestion of a breeze. This seemed an utterly enchanted sea, this lake you could leave to its own devices for a few hours and come back to, and find that it had not stirred, this constant and trustworthy body of water. In the shallows, the dark, water-soaked sticks and twigs, smooth and old, were undulating in clusters on the bottom against the clean ribbed sand, and the track of the mussel was plain. A school of minnows swam by, each minnow with its small individual shadow, doubling the attendance, so clear and sharp in the sunlight. Some of the other campers were in swimming, along the shore, one of them with a cake of soap, and the water felt thin and clear and unsubstantial. Over the years there had been this person with the cake of soap, this cultist, and here he was. There had been no years. 6

Up to the farmhouse to dinner through the teeming, dusty field, the road under our sneakers was only a two-track road. The middle track was missing, the one with the marks of the hooves and the splotches of dried, flaky manure. There had always been three tracks to choose from in choosing which track to walk in; now the choice was narrowed down to two. For a moment I missed terribly the middle alternative. But the way led past the tennis court, and something about the way it lay there in the sun reassured me; the tape had loosened along the backline, the alleys were green with plaintains and other weeds, and the net (installed in June and removed in September) sagged in the dry noon, and the whole place steamed with midday heat and hunger and emptiness. There was a choice of pie for dessert, and one was blueberry and one was apple, and the waitresses were the same country girls, there having been no passage of time, only the illusion of it as in a dropped curtain—the waitresses were still fifteen; their hair had been washed, that was the only difference—they had been to the movies and seen the pretty girls with the clean hair. 7

Summertime, oh summertime, pattern of life indelible, the fadeproof lake, the woods unshatterable, the pasture with the sweetfern and the juniper forever and ever, summer without end; this was the background, and the life along the shore was the design, the cottagers with their innocent and tranquil design, their tiny docks with the flagpole and the American flag floating against the white clouds in the blue sky, the little paths over the roots of the trees leading from camp to camp and the paths leading back to the outhouses and the can of lime for sprinkling, and at the souvenir counters at the store the miniature birch-bark canoes and the post cards that showed things looking a little better than they looked. This was the American family at play, escaping the city heat, wondering whether the newcomers in the camp at the head of the cove were "common" or "nice," wondering whether it was 8

true that the people who drove up for Sunday dinner at the farmhouse were turned away because there wasn't enough chicken.

It seemed to me, as I kept remembering all this, that those times and 9
those summers had been infinitely precious and worth saving. There had been jollity and peace and goodness. The arriving (at the beginning of August) had been so big a business in itself, at the railway station the farm wagon drawn up, the first smell of the pine-laden air, the first glimpse of the smiling farmer, and the great importance of the trunks and your father's enormous authority in such matters, and the feel of the wagon under you for the long ten-mile haul, and at the top of the last long hill catching the first view of the lake after eleven months of not seeing this cherished body of water. The shouts and cries of the other campers when they saw you, and the trunks to be unpacked, to give up their rich burden. (Arriving was less exciting nowadays, when you sneaked up in your car and parked it under a tree near the camp and took out the bags and in five minutes it was all over, no fuss, no loud wonderful fuss about trunks.)

Peace and goodness and jollity. The only thing that was wrong now, 10
really, was the sound of the place, an unfamiliar nervous sound of the outboard motors. This was the note that jarred, the one thing that would sometimes break the illusion and set the years moving. In those other summertimes all motors were inboard; and when they were at a little distance, the noise they made was a sedative, an ingredient of summer sleep. They were one-cylinder and two-cylinder engines, and some were make-and-break and some were jump-spark, but they all made a sleepy sound across the lake. The one-lungers throbbed and fluttered, and the twin-cylinder ones purred and purred, and that was a quiet sound too. But now the campers all had outboards. In the daytime, in the hot mornings, these motors made a petulant, irritable sound; at night, in the still evening when the afterglow lit the water, they whined about one's ears like mosquitoes. My boy loved our rented outboard, and his great desire was to achieve singlehanded mastery over it, and authority, and he soon learned the trick of choking it a little (but not too much), and the adjustment of the needle valve. Watching him I would remember the things you could do with the old one-cylinder engine with the heavy flywheel, how you could have it eating out of your hand if you got really close to it spiritually. Motor boats in those days didn't have clutches, and you would make a landing by shutting off the motor at the proper time and coasting in with a dead rudder. But there was a way of reversing them, if you learned the trick, by cutting the switch and putting it on again exactly on the final dying revolution of the flywheel, so that it would kick back against compression and begin reversing. Approaching a dock in a strong following breeze, it was difficult to slow up sufficiently by the ordinary coasting method, and if a boy felt he had complete mastery over his motor, he was tempted to keep it running beyond its time and then reverse it a few feet from the dock. It took a cool nerve, because if you threw the switch a twentieth of a second too soon you would catch the flywheel when it

still had speed enough to go up past center, and the boat would leap ahead, charging bull-fashion at the dock.

We had a good week at the camp. The bass were biting well and the sun shone endlessly, day after day. We would be tired at night and lie down in the accumulated heat of the little bedrooms after the long hot day and the breeze would stir almost imperceptibly outside and the smell of the swamp drift in through the rusty screens. Sleep would come easily and in the morning the red squirrel would be on the roof, tapping out his gay routine. I kept remembering everything, lying in bed in the mornings—the small steamboat that had a long rounded stern like the lip of a Ubangi, and how quietly she ran on the moonlight sails, when the older boys played their mandolins and the girls sang and we ate doughnuts dipped in sugar, and how sweet the music was on the water in the shining night, and what it had felt like to think about girls then. After breakfast we would go up to the store and the things were in the same place—the minnows in a bottle, the plugs and spinners disarranged and pawed over by the youngsters from the boys' camp, the fig newtons and the Beeman's gum. Outside, the road was tarred and cars stood in front of the store. Inside, all was just as it had always been, except there was more Coca-Cola and not so much Moxie and root beer and birch beer and sarsaparilla. We would walk out with a bottle of pop apiece and sometimes the pop would backfire up our noses and hurt. We explored the streams, quietly, where the turtles slid off the sunny logs and dug their way into the soft bottom; and we lay on the town wharf and fed worms to the tame bass. Everywhere we went I had trouble making out which was I, the one walking at my side, the one walking in my pants.

One afternoon while we were there at that lake a thunderstorm 12
came up. It was like the revival of an old melodrama that I had seen long ago with childish awe. The second-act climax of the drama of the electrical disturbance over a lake in America had not changed in any important respect. This was the big scene, still the big scene. The whole thing was so familiar, the first feeling of oppression and heat and a general air around camp of not wanting to go very far away. In midafternoon (it was all the same) a curious darkening of the sky, and a lull in everything that had made life tick; and then the way the boats suddenly swung the other way at their moorings with the coming of a breeze out of the new quarter, and the premonitory rumble. Then the kettle drum, then the snare, then the bass drum and cymbals, then crackling light against the dark, and the gods grinning and licking their chops in the hills. Afterward the calm, the rain steadily rustling in the calm lake, the return of light and hope and spirits, and the campers running out in joy and relief to go swimming in the rain, their bright cries perpetuating the deathless joke about how they were getting simply drenched, and the children screaming with delight at the new sensation of bathing in the rain, and the joke about getting drenched linking the generations in a strong indestructible chain. And the comedian who waded in carrying an umbrella.

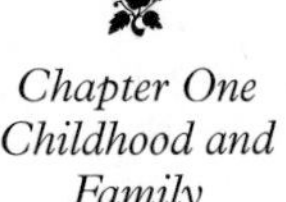

When the others went swimming my son said he was going in too. 13
He pulled his dripping trunks from the line where they had hung all through the shower, and wrung them out. Languidly, and with no thought of going in, I watched him, his hard little body, skinny and bare, saw him wince slightly as he pulled up around his vitals the small, soggy, icy garment. As he buckled the swollen belt suddenly my groin felt the chill of death.

COMPREHENSION

1. At what point in the essay do you begin to sense White's main purpose? What *is* his purpose? What type of reader might his purpose appeal to?
2. What motivates White to return to the lake in Maine? Explain the "simple transposition" that he mentions in paragraph 4. List the illustrations that he gives of this phenomenon. What change does he detect in the lake?
3. Explain the significance of White's last sentence. Where are there foreshadowings of this statement?

RHETORIC

1. Describe the author's use of figurative language in paragraphs 2, 10, and 12.
2. Identify those words and phrases that White invokes to establish the sense of mystery about the lake. Why are these words and their connotations important to the nature of the illusion that he describes?
3. Explain the organization of the essay in terms of the following paragraph units: 1 to 4; 5 to 7; 8 to 10; and 11 to 13. Explain the function of paragraphs 8 and 12.
4. There are many vivid and unusual descriptive details in this essay—for example, the dragonfly in paragraph 5 and the two-track road in paragraph 7. How does White create symbolic overtones for these descriptive details and others? Why is the lake itself a complex symbol? Explain with reference to paragraph 6.
5. Describe the persona that White creates for himself in the essay. How does this persona function?
6. What is the relation between the introductory and concluding paragraphs, specifically in terms of irony of statement?

WRITING

1. Explore in an essay the theme of nostalgia in "Once More to the Lake." What are the beauties and the dangers of nostalgia? Can the past ever be recaptured or relived? Justify your answer.
2. Write a descriptive account of a return to a favorite location and of your reaction to the experience. Explore the interrelationship of past and present.
3. Explain, in a short essay, the appeal of this classic essay by White.

4. One of White's favorite authors was Thoreau. Read Thoreau's "Economy" (pp. 584–587) and, in a brief essay, identify the influence that you see at work in "Once More to the Lake."

CLASSIC AND CONTEMPORARY

MARK TWAIN Mark Twain (1835–1910) was the pseudonym of Samuel Langhorne Clemens. In *The Adventures of Tom Sawyer* (1876), *Life on the Mississippi* (1883), and *The Adventures of Huckleberry Finn* (1885), Twain celebrated the challenge of the frontier experience and the promise of a new world. Adventurous, democratic, individualistic, hardheaded, and sentimental, he projected the image of the essential American, a role that did not always correspond to the bitter and tragic aspects of his later life. In this selection from his autobiography, Twain successfully juggles tragedy and comedy in a bittersweet exploration of guilt and faith.

MARK TWAIN

A Boy's Life

1 In 1849, when I was fourteen years old, we were still living in Hannibal, on the banks of the Mississippi, in the new "frame" house built by my father five years before. That is, some of us lived in the new part, the rest in the old part back of it and attached to it. In the autumn my sister gave a party and invited all the marriageable young people of the village. I was too young for this society and was too bashful to mingle with young ladies, anyway, therefore I was not invited—at least not for the whole evening. Ten minutes of it was to be my whole share. I was to do the part of a bear in a small fairy play. I was to be disguised all over in a close-fitting brown hairy stuff proper for a bear. About half past ten I was told to go to my room and put on this disguise and be ready in half an hour. I started but changed my mind, for I wanted to practice a little and that room was very small. I crossed over to the large unoccupied house on the corner of Main Street, unaware that a dozen of the young people were also going there to dress for their parts. I took the little black boy, Sandy, with me and we selected a roomy and empty chamber on the second floor. We entered it talking and this gave a couple of half-dressed young ladies an opportunity to take refuge behind a screen undiscovered. Their gowns and things were hanging on hooks behind the door but I did not see them; it was Sandy that shut the door but all his heart was in the theatricals and he was as unlikely to notice them as I was myself.

That was a rickety screen with many holes in it but as I did not 2
know there were girls behind it I was not disturbed by that detail. If I had known, I could not have undressed in the flood of cruel moonlight that was pouring in at the curtainless windows; I should have died of shame. Untroubled by apprehensions, I stripped to the skin and began my practice. I was full of ambition, I was determined to make a hit, I was burning to establish a reputation as a bear and get further engagements; so I threw myself into my work with an abandon that promised great things. I capered back and forth from one end of the room to the other on all fours, Sandy applauding with enthusiasm; I walked upright and growled and snapped and snarled, I stood on my head, I flung handsprings, I danced a lubberly dance with my paws bent and my imaginary snout sniffing from side to side, I did everything a bear could do and many things which no bear could ever do and no bear with any dignity would want to do, anyway; and of course I never suspected that I was making a spectacle of myself to anyone but Sandy. At last, standing on my head, I paused in that attitude to take a minute's rest. There was a moment's silence, then Sandy spoke up with excited interest and said:

"Mars Sam, has you ever seed a dried herring?" 3

"No. What is that?" 4

"It's a fish." 5

"Well, what of it? Anything peculiar about it?" 6

"Yes, suh, you bet you dey is. *Dey* eats 'em innards and all!" 7

There was a smothered burst of feminine snickers from behind the 8
screen! All the strength went out of me and I toppled forward like an undermined tower and brought the screen down with my weight, burying the young ladies under it. In their fright they discharged a couple of piercing screams—and possibly others—but I did not wait to count. I snatched my clothes and fled to the dark hall below, Sandy following. I was dressed in half a minute and out the back way. I swore Sandy to eternal silence, then we went away and hid until the party was over. The ambition was all out of me. I could not have faced that giddy company after my adventure, for there would be two performers there who knew my secret and would be privately laughing at me all the time. I was searched for but not found, and the bear had to be played by a young gentleman in his civilized clothes. The house was still and everybody asleep when I finally ventured home. I was very heavy-hearted and full of a bitter sense of disgrace. Pinned to my pillow I found a slip of paper which bore a line which did not lighten my heart but only made my face burn. It was written in a laboriously disguised hand and these were its mocking terms:

> You probably couldn't have played bear but you played bare very 9
> well—oh, very *very* well!

We think boys are rude, unsensitive animals but it is not so in all 10
cases. Each boy has one or two sensitive spots and if you can find out where they are located you have only to touch them and you can scorch

him as with fire. I suffered miserably over that episode. I expected that the facts would be all over the village in the morning but it was not so. The secret remained confined to the two girls and Sandy and me. That was some appeasement of my pain but it was far from sufficient—the main trouble remained: I was under four mocking eyes and it might as well have been a thousand, for I suspected all girls' eyes of being the ones I so dreaded. During several weeks I could not look any young lady in the face; I dropped my eyes in confusion when any one of them smiled upon me and gave me greeting; I said to myself, "That is one of them," and got quickly away. Of course I was meeting the right girls everywhere but if they ever let slip any betraying sign I was not bright enough to catch it. When I left Hannibal four years later the secret was still a secret; I had never guessed those girls out and was no longer hoping or expecting to do it.

One of the dearest and prettiest girls in the village at the time of my 11
mishap was one whom I will call Mary Wilson, because that was not her name. She was twenty years old; she was dainty and sweet, peach-blooming and exquisite, gracious and lovely in character. I stood in awe of her, for she seemed to me to be made out of angel clay and rightfully unapproachable by just any unholy ordinary kind of boy like me. I probably never suspected *her*. But—

The scene changes to Calcutta—forty-seven years later. It was in 12
1896. I arrived there on a lecturing trip. As I entered the hotel a vision passed out of it, clothed in the glory of the Indian sunshine—the Mary Wilson of my long-vanished boyhood! It was a startling thing. Before I could recover from the pleasant shock and speak to her she was gone. I thought maybe I had seen an apparition but it was not so, she was flesh. She was the granddaughter of the other Mary. The other Mary, now a widow, was upstairs and presently sent for me. She was old and gray-haired but she looked young and was very handsome. We sat down and talked. We steeped our thirsty souls in the reviving wine of the past, the pathetic past, the beautiful past, the dear and lamented past; we uttered the names that had been silent upon our lips for fifty years and it was as if they were made of music; with reverent hands we unburied our dead, the mates of our youth, and caressed them with our speech; we searched the dusty chambers of our memories and dragged forth incident after incident, episode after episode, folly after folly, and laughed such good laughs over them, with the tears running down; and finally Mary said, suddenly, and without any leading up:

"Tell me! What is the special peculiarity of dried herrings?" 13

It seemed a strange question at such a hallowed time as this. And so 14
inconsequential, too. I was a little shocked. And yet I was aware of a stir of some kind away back in the deeps of my memory somewhere. It set me to musing—thinking—searching. Dried herrings? Dried herrings? The peculiarity of dri . . . I glanced up. Her face was grave, but there was a dim and shadowy twinkle in her eye which— All of a sudden I knew and far away down in the hoary past I heard a remembered voice murmur, "Dey eats 'em innards and all!"

"At—last! I've found one of you, anyway! Who was the other girl?" 15

But she drew the line there. She wouldn't tell me. 16

But a boy's life is not all comedy; much of the tragic enters into it. 17
The drunken tramp who was burned up in the village jail lay upon my conscience a hundred nights afterward and filled them with hideous dreams—dreams in which I saw his appealing face as I had seen it in the pathetic reality, pressed against the window bars, with the red hell glowing behind him—a face which seemed to say to me, "If you had not given me the matches this would not have happened; you are responsible for my death." I was *not* responsible for it, for I had meant him no harm but only good, when I let him have the matches; but no matter, mine was a trained Presbyterian conscience and knew but the one duty—to hunt and harry its slave upon all pretexts and on all occasions, particularly when there was no sense nor reason in it. The tramp—who was to blame—suffered ten minutes; I, who was not to blame, suffered three months.

The shooting down of poor old Smarr in the main street at noonday 18
supplied me with some more dreams; and in them I always saw again the grotesque closing picture—the great family Bible spread open on the profane old man's breast by some thoughtful idiot and rising and sinking to the labored breathings and adding the torture of its leaden weight to the dying struggles. We are curiously made. In all the throng of gaping and sympathetic onlookers there was not one with common sense enough to perceive that an anvil would have been in better taste there than the Bible, less open to sarcastic criticism and swifter in its atrocious work. In my nightmares I gasped and struggled for breath under the crush of that vast book for many a night.

All within the space of a couple of years we had two or three other 19
tragedies and I had the ill luck to be too near by on each occasion. There was the slave man who was struck down with a chunk of slag for some small offense; I saw him die. And the young Californian emigrant who was stabbed with a bowie knife by a drunken comrade; I saw the red life gush from his breast. And the case of the rowdy young brothers and their harmless old uncle; one of them held the old man down with his knees on his breast while the other one tried repeatedly to kill him with an Allen revolver which wouldn't go off. I happened along just then, of course.

Then there was the case of the young Californian emigrant who got 20
drunk and proposed to raid the "Welshman's house" all alone one dark and threatening night. This house stood halfway up Holliday's Hill and its sole occupants were a poor but quite respectable widow and her blameless daughter. The invading ruffian woke the whole village with his ribald yells and coarse challenges and obscenities. I went up there with a comrade—John Briggs, I think—to look and listen. The figure of the man was dimly visible; the women were on their porch, not visible in the deep shadow of its roof, but we heard the elder woman's voice. She had loaded an old musket with slugs and she warned the man that

if he stayed where he was while she counted ten it would cost him his life. She began to count, slowly; he began to laugh. He stopped laughing at "six"; then through the deep stillness, in a steady voice, followed the rest of the tale: "Seven . . . eight . . . nine"—a long pause, we holding our breaths—"ten!" A red spout of flame gushed out into the night and the man dropped with his breast riddled to rags. Then the rain and the thunder burst loose and the waiting town swarmed up the hill in the glare of the lightning like an invasion of ants. Those people saw the rest; I had had my share and was satisfied. I went home to dream and was not disappointed.

My teaching and training enabled me to see deeper into these tragedies than an ignorant person could have done. I knew what they were for. I tried to disguise it from myself but down in the secret deeps of my troubled heart I knew—and I *knew* I knew. They were inventions of Providence to beguile me to a better life. It sounds curiously innocent and conceited now, but to me there was nothing strange about it; it was quite in accordance with the thoughtful and judicious ways of Providence as I understood them. It would not have surprised me nor even over-flattered me if Providence had killed off that whole community in trying to save an asset like me. Educated as I had been, it would have seemed just the thing and well worth the expense. *Why* Providence should take such an anxious interest in such a property, that idea never entered my head, and there was no one in that simple hamlet who would have dreamed of putting it there. For one thing, no one was equipped with it. 21

It is quite true, I took all the tragedies to myself and tallied them off in turn as they happened, saying to myself in each case, with a sigh, "Another one gone—and on my account; this ought to bring me to repentance; the patience of God will not always endure." And yet privately I believed it would. That is, I believed it in the daytime; but not in the night. With the going down of the sun my faith failed and the clammy fears gathered about my heart. It was then that I repented. Those were awful nights, nights of despair, nights charged with the bitterness of death. After each tragedy I recognized the warning and repented; repented and begged; begged like a coward, begged like a dog; and not in the interest of those poor people who had been extinguished for my sake but only in my *own* interest. It seems selfish when I look back on it now. 22

My repentances were very real, very earnest; and after each tragedy they happened every night for a long time. But as a rule they could not stand the daylight. They faded out and shredded away and disappeared in the glad splendor of the sun. They were the creatures of fear and darkness and they could not live out of their own place. The day gave me cheer and peace and at night I repented again. In all my boyhood life I am not sure that I ever tried to lead a better life in the daytime—or wanted to. In my age I should never think of wishing to do such a thing. But in my age, as in my youth, night brings me many a deep remorse. I realize that from the cradle up I have been like the rest of the race—never quite sane in the night. When "Injun Joe" died. . . . But never 23 mind. Somewhere I have already described what a raging hell of repentance I passed through then. I believe that for months I was as pure as the driven snow. After dark.

COMPREHENSION

1. Why does Twain the child feel responsible for the tragedies in his town? What role does religion play in his feelings of guilt?
2. What relation does the first episode have to the others recounted in the narrative?
3. How does the adult Twain feel about these childhood events and feelings?

RHETORIC

1. Does the essay contain a thesis? Where is it located?
2. How does Twain use dialogue and dialect in his essay? What does it add to his story?
3. Comment on the writer's use of language. Is it figurative or concrete? How does it contribute to the point the writer is making? Cite effective uses of language in the essay.
4. How does the author structure his narrative? Is there one narrative account or several? Explain why Twain's narrative approach is effective.
5. Discuss the author's use of symbolism in paragraph 18. Is this element used elsewhere in the story?
6. How does Twain's conclusion work? Does it provide a satisfactory closing to the essay? How does the writer use irony in the final phrase? Why is using a sentence fragment effective?

WRITING

1. Compose a narrative essay recounting an event in your life that was humorous, embarrassing, or tragic. Use details and dialogue to describe the situation and the people involved in it. Also consider how this event affected you later in life.
2. Write an essay exploring the effects of religion on the mind and behavior of a young person. How might young minds interpret and process religious learning? What effects might it have on them when they grow up? Use support from the essays of Twain and Hughes in your writing.

MAYA ANGELOU Maya Angelou (1928–) is an American poet, playwright, television screenwriter, actress, and singer. Taken together, her autobiographical books—*I Know Why the Caged Bird Sings* (1970), *Gather Together in My Name* (1974), *Singin' and Swingin' and Gettin' Merry Like Christmas* (1976), *The Heart of a Woman* (1981), and *I Shall Not Be Moved* (1990)—provide one of the fullest accounts of the black female experience in contemporary literature. Fluent in six languages and active in artistic, educational, and political affairs, Angelou often presents autobiographical material against the backdrop of larger cultural concerns. In the following selection from *I Know Why the Caged Bird Sings,* the physical pain of a toothache is overshadowed by the emotional pain of bigotry and humiliation.

MAYA ANGELOU

Momma, the Dentist, and Me

The angel of the candy counter had found me out at last, and was exacting excruciating penance for all the stolen Milky Ways, Mounds, Mr. Goodbars and Hersheys with Almonds. I had two cavities that were rotten to the gums. The pain was beyond the bailiwick of crushed aspirins or oil of cloves. Only one thing could help me, so I prayed earnestly that I'd be allowed to sit under the house and have the building collapse on my left jaw. Since there was no Negro dentist in Stamps, nor doctor either, for that matter, Momma had dealt with previous toothaches by pulling them out (a string tied to the tooth with the other end looped over her fist), pain killers and prayer. In this particular instance the medicine had proved ineffective; there wasn't enough enamel left to hook a string on, and the prayers were being ignored because the Balancing Angel was blocking their passage. 1

I lived a few days and nights in blinding pain, not so much toying with as seriously considering the idea of jumping in the well, and Momma decided I had to be taken to a dentist. The nearest Negro dentist was in Texarkana, twenty-five miles away, and I was certain that I'd be dead long before we reached half the distance. Momma said we'd go to Dr. Lincoln, right in Stamps, and he'd take care of me. She said he owed her a favor. 2

I knew there were a number of whitefolks in town that owed her favors. Bailey and I had seen the books which showed how she had lent money to Blacks and whites alike during the Depression, and most still owed her. But I couldn't aptly remember seeing Dr. Lincoln's name, nor had I ever heard of a Negro's going to him as a patient. However, Momma said we were going, and put water on the stove for our baths. I had never been to a doctor, so she told me that after the bath (which would make my mouth feel better) I had to put on freshly starched and ironed underclothes from inside out. The ache failed to respond to the bath, and I knew then that the pain was more serious than that which anyone had ever suffered. 3

Before we left the Store, she ordered me to brush my teeth and then wash my mouth with Listerine. The idea of even opening my clamped jaws increased the pain, but upon her explanation that when you go to a doctor you have to clean yourself all over, but most especially the part 4

that's to be examined, I screwed up my courage and unlocked my teeth. The cool air in my mouth and the jarring of my molars dislodged what little remained of my reason. I had frozen to the pain, my family nearly had to tie me down to take the toothbrush away. It was no small effort to get me started on the road to the dentist. Momma spoke to all the passers-by, but didn't stop to chat. She explained over her shoulder that we were going to the doctor and she'd "pass the time of day" on our way home.

Until we reached the pond the pain was my world, an aura that 5
haloed me for three feet around. Crossing the bridge into whitefolks' county, pieces of sanity pushed themselves forward. I had to stop moaning and start walking straight. The white towel, which was drawn under my chin and tied over my head, had to be arranged. If one was dying, it had to be done in style if the dying took place in whitefolks' part of town.

On the other side of the bridge the ache seemed to lessen as if a 6
whitebreeze blew off the whitefolks and cushioned everything in their neighborhood—including my jaw. The gravel road was smoother, the stones smaller and the tree branches hung down around the path and nearly covered us. If the pain didn't diminish then, the familiar yet strange sights hypnotized me into believing that it had.

But my head continued to throb with the measured insistence of a 7
bass drum, and how could a toothache pass the calaboose, hear the songs of the prisoners, their blues and laughter, and not be changed? How could one or two or even a mouthful of angry tooth roots meet a wagonload of powhitetrash children, endure their idiotic snobbery and not feel less important?

Behind the building which housed the dentist's office ran a small 8
path used by servants and those tradespeople who catered to the butcher and Stamps' one restaurant. Momma and I followed that lane to the backstairs of Dentist Lincoln's office. The sun was bright and gave the day a hard reality as we climbed up the steps to the second floor.

Momma knocked on the back door and a young white girl opened it 9
to show surprise at seeing us there. Momma said she wanted to see Dentist Lincoln and to tell him Annie was there. The girl closed the door firmly. Now the humiliation of hearing Momma describe herself as if she had no last name to the young white girl was equal to the physical pain. It seemed terribly unfair to have a toothache and a headache and have to bear at the same time the heavy burden of Blackness.

It was always possible that the teeth would quiet down and maybe 10
drop out of their own accord. Momma said we would wait. We leaned in the harsh sunlight on the shaky railings of the dentist's back porch for over an hour.

He opened the door and looked at Momma. "Well, Annie, what can 11
I do for you?"

He didn't see the towel around my jaw or notice my swollen face. 12

Momma said, "Dentist Lincoln. It's my grandbaby here. She got 13
two rotten teeth that's giving her a fit."

She waited for him to acknowledge the truth of her statement. He 14
made no comment, orally or facially.

"She had this toothache purt' near four days now, and today I said, 'Young lady, you going to the Dentist.'"

"Annie?" 15

"Yes, sir, Dentist Lincoln." 17

He was choosing words the way people hunt for shells. "Annie, you 18
know I don't treat nigra, colored people." 19

"I know, Dentist Lincoln. But this here is just my little grandbaby, and she ain't gone be no trouble to you. . . ."

"Annie, everybody has a policy. In this world you have to have a 20
policy. Now, my policy is I don't treat colored people."

The sun had baked the oil out of Momma's skin and melted the 21
Vaseline in her hair. She shone greasily as she leaned out of the dentist's shadow.

"Seem like to me, Dentist Lincoln, you might look after her, she 22
ain't nothing but a little mite. And seems like maybe you owe me a favor or two."

He reddened slightly. "Favor or no favor. The money has all been 23
repaid to you and that's the end of it. Sorry, Annie." He had his hand on the doorknob. "Sorry." His voice was a bit kinder on the second "Sorry," as if he really was.

Momma said, "I wouldn't press on you like this for myself but I 24
can't take No. Not for my grandbaby. When you come to borrow my money you didn't have to beg. You asked me, and I lent it. Now, it wasn't my policy. I ain't no moneylender, but you stood to lose this building and I tried to help you out."

"It's been paid, and raising your voice won't make me change my 25
mind. My policy. . . ." He let go of the door and stepped nearer Momma. The three of us were crowded on the small landing. "Annie, my policy is I'd rather stick my hand in a dog's mouth than in a nigger's."

He had never once looked at me. He turned his back and went 26
through the door into the cool beyond. Momma backed up inside herself for a few minutes. I forgot everything except her face which was almost a new one to me. She leaned over and took the doorknob, and in her everyday soft voice she said, "Sister, go on downstairs. Wait for me. I'll be there directly."

Under the most common of circumstances I knew it did no good to 27
argue with Momma. So I walked down the steep stairs, afraid to look back and afraid not to do so. I turned as the door slammed, and she was gone.

Momma walked in that room as if she owned it. She shoved that silly 28
nurse aside with one hand and strode into the dentist's office. He was sitting in his chair, sharpening his mean instruments and putting extra sting into his medicines. Her eyes were blazing like live coals and her arms had doubled themselves in length. He looked up at her just before she caught him by the collar of his white jacket.

"Stand up when you see a lady, you contemptuous scoundrel." Her 29
tongue had thinned and the words rolled off well enunciated. Enunciated and sharp like little claps of thunder.

The dentist had no choice but to stand at R.O.T.C. attention. His head 30
dropped after a minute and his voice was humble. "Yes, ma'am, Mrs. Henderson."

"You knave, do you think you acted like a gentleman, speaking to me 31
like that in front of my granddaughter?" She didn't shake him, although she had the power. She simply held him upright.

"No, ma'am, Mrs. Henderson." 32

"No, ma'am, Mrs. Henderson, what?" Then she did give him the tiniest 33
of shakes, but because of her strength the action set his head and arms to shaking loose on the ends of his body. He stuttered much worse than Uncle Willie. "No, ma'am, Mrs. Henderson, I'm sorry."

With just an edge of her disgust showing, Momma slung him back in his 34
dentist's chair. "Sorry is as sorry does, and you're about the sorriest dentist I ever laid my eyes on." (She could afford to slip into the vernacular because she had such eloquent command of English.)

"I didn't ask you to apologize in front of Marguerite, because I don't 35
want her to know my power, but I order you, now and herewith. Leave Stamps by sundown."

"Mrs. Henderson, I can't get my equipment. . . . " He was shaking ter- 36
ribly now.

"Now, that brings me to my second order. You will never again practice 37
dentistry. Never! When you get settled in your next place, you will be a vegetarian caring for dogs with the mange, cats with the cholera and cows with the epizootic. Is that clear?"

The saliva ran down his chin and his eyes filled with tears. "Yes, ma'am. 38
Thank you for not killing me. Thank you, Mrs. Henderson."

Momma pulled herself back from being ten feet tall with eight-foot arms 39
and said, "You're welcome for nothing, you varlet, I wouldn't waste a killing on the likes of you."

On her way out she waved her handkerchief at the nurse and turned her 40
into a crocus sack of chicken feed.

Momma looked tired when she came down the stairs, but who 41
wouldn't be tired if they had gone through what she had. She came close to me and adjusted the towel under my jaw (I had forgotten the toothache; I only knew that she made her hands gentle in order not to awaken the pain). She took my hand. Her voice never changed. "Come on, Sister."

I reckoned we were going home where she would concoct a brew to 42
eliminate the pain and maybe give me new teeth too. New teeth that would grow overnight out of my gums. She led me toward the drugstore, which was in the opposite direction from the Store. "I'm taking you to Dentist Baker in Texarkana."

I was glad after all that I had bathed and put on Mum and Cashmere 43
Bouquet talcum powder. It was a wonderful surprise. My toothache had

quieted to solemn pain, Momma had obliterated the evil white man, and we were going on a trip to Texarkana, just the two of us.

On the Greyhound she took an inside seat in the back, and I sat be- 44
side her. I was so proud of being her granddaughter and sure that some of her magic must have come down to me. She asked if I was scared. I only shook my head and leaned over on her cool brown upper arm. There was no chance that a dentist, especially a Negro dentist, would dare hurt me then. Not with Momma there. The trip was uneventful, except that she put her arm around me, which was very unusual for Momma to do.

The dentist showed me the medicine and the needle before he 45
deadened my gums, but if he hadn't I wouldn't have worried. Momma stood right behind him. Her arms were folded and she checked on everything he did. The teeth were extracted and she bought me an ice cream cone from the side window of a drug counter. The trip back to Stamps was quiet, except that I had to spit into a very small empty snuff can which she had gotten for me and it was difficult with the bus humping and jerking on our country roads.

At home, I was given a warm salt solution, and when I washed out 46
my mouth I showed Bailey the empty holes, where the clotted blood sat like filling in a pie crust. He said I was quite brave, and that was my cue to reveal our confrontation with the peckerwood dentist and Momma's incredible powers.

I had to admit that I didn't hear the conversation, but what else 47
could she have said than what I said she said? What else done? He agreed with my analysis in a lukewarm way, and I happily (after all, I'd been sick) flounced into the Store. Momma was preparing our evening meal and Uncle Willie leaned on the door sill. She gave her version.

"Dentist Lincoln got right uppity. Said he'd rather put his hand in a 48
dog's mouth. And when I reminded him of the favor, he brushed it off like a piece of lint. Well, I sent Sister downstairs and went inside. I hadn't never been in his office before, but I found the door to where he takes out teeth, and him and the nurse was in there thick as thieves. I just stood there till he caught sight of me." Crash bang the pots on the stove. "He jumped just like he was sitting on a pin. He said, 'Annie, I done tole you, I ain't gonna mess around in no niggah's mouth.' I said, 'Somebody's got to do it then,' and he said, 'Take her to Texarkana to the colored dentist' and that's when I said, 'If you paid me my money I could afford to take her.' He said, 'It's all been paid.' I tole him everything but the interest been paid. He said ''Twasn't no interest.' I said, ''Tis now. I'll take ten dollars as payment in full.' You know, Willie, it wasn't no right thing to do, 'cause I lent that money without thinking about it.

"He tole that little snippety nurse of his'n to give me ten dollars and 49
make me sign a 'paid in full' receipt. She gave it to me and I signed the papers. Even though by rights he was paid up before, I figger, he gonna be that kind of nasty, he gonna have to pay for it."

Momma and her son laughed and laughed over the white man's evilness and her retributive sin. 50

I preferred, much preferred, my version. 51

COMPREHENSION

1. Briefly describe the circumstances and social climate in which the narrator lived.
2. Why does the young Angelou need to imagine a different confrontation between Momma and the dentist than the one which actually took place? Why does she prefer the fantasy?
3. How would you describe the character of Angelou's grandmother?

RHETORIC

1. How does the writer structure her narrative? Why is this method effective?
2. What is the point of view of the writer? What response does it elicit from the reader?
3. Compare the diction and vocabulary Angelou's grandmother uses in the fantasy encounter to her language in the real event. How do they differ? Cite specific examples, and explain what the writer is trying to accomplish. How does the use of dialect affect the force of the narrative in general?
4. In paragraph 7, how does figurative language and the use of questions support the point of the paragraph?
5. What mood does Angelou create in her story? How does she achieve this? Use examples from the narrative.

WRITING

1. Compose a narrative essay describing an event that caused you embarrassment or humiliation. Describe what happened, who else was involved, and how you felt. Create a mood using figurative language and dialogue.
2. In an essay, explore the psychic damage caused by racism. How does it feel to be treated cruelly or thoughtlessly because of your racial or ethnic background? How might such treatment affect a child?
3. Compose an essay recounting an unpleasant event in your life that you wish had happened differently. Write what actually occurred as well as what you wish had occurred. Use Angelou's essay as a guide.

CLASSIC AND CONTEMPORARY: QUESTIONS FOR COMPARISON

1. Compare and contrast the childhood experiences of Twain and Angelou. How are they similar, and how are they different? In what ways did their childhood experiences influence their lives?

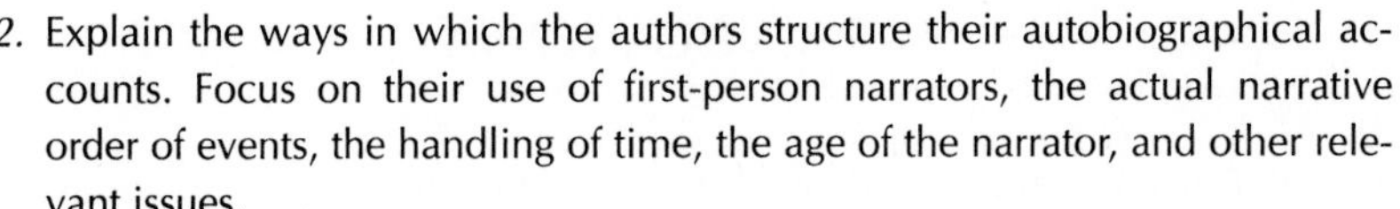

2. Explain the ways in which the authors structure their autobiographical accounts. Focus on their use of first-person narrators, the actual narrative order of events, the handling of time, the age of the narrator, and other relevant issues.

3. From one perspective, we can view these essays as reflections on the tragedy and comedy of life. How do Twain and Angelou approach this subject? What *is* their philosophy of life? Are they optimists or pessimists? Explain.

CONNECTIONS

1. Both Cofer and Angelou address the issue of the minority experience in the United States. Do they also share a common voice or mood? What is distinctive about each essay? In your opinion, which essay is more effective? Why? Consider the style and emotional impact of the writing.
2. Kingston, Cofer, and Twain are haunted by ghosts, events, rumors in their narratives. Find examples in their writing, and examine the impact of these memories on the writers' lives and their perceptions as adults.
3. Analyze the roles of women as depicted in the narratives of Angelou, Kingston, and Cofer.
4. Compare the essays of Twain and Hughes as regards childhood guilt and religion. What effect did the feeling of guilt have on the writers' religious beliefs, if any?
5. Examine the use of setting and evocative language in the works of Clemens and White. Cite examples in both essays in which language is especially effective in enriching the narrative.
6. In the essays of Angelou, Twain, and Hughes, examine the use of dialect and dialogue. How do these devices strengthen the stories being told? Use examples from the essays to support your views.
7. The issue of "family values" has provoked considerable political debate recently. Using examples from the essays in this section, write your own definition of family values.
8. Argue for or against the proposition that there is a "typical" family unit. Refer to at least three essays in this chapter to support your position.
9. Select your favorite writer from this chapter, and explain why you prefer his or her essay to others. Refer to the essays in your evaluation.

CHAPTER TWO

The Sense of Place

In his award-winning book, *Arctic Dreams* (1986), Barry Lopez asks, "How do people imagine the landscape they find themselves in?" For Lopez, whose essay "Mapping the Real Geography" appears at the start of this chapter, our sense of place should never be taken for granted. Instead, we must investigate and attempt to understand the ways in which landscape or place affects us physically, mentally, emotionally, and perhaps spiritually. Whether we love a place or hate it, feel an intimate relationship to it or feel alienated from it, we perceive that the places we inhabit mold our sense of identity.

Essayists who write about place sense that the subject is a perfect vehicle for self-discovery. Essays rooted in a sense of place also foster understanding of cultural diversity—of the complex interaction of human behavior, background, environment, and heritage. The essays in this chapter range over a broad and varied landscape: a colonial outpost in Burma; a town in rural Canada; a postwar panorama of Vietnam; an island in the Caribbean; a house in Chile; another house in Kiowa country; the cityscapes of New York and Miami. The authors of these essays invite us on voyages of discovery. The exterior landscapes that they depict so vividly tell us a great deal about the authors' own lives and values. Their essays arouse in us a desire to know more about the places that are so important to them.

"Only connect," wrote the English author E. M. Forster, whose famous essay "My Wood" appears in another chapter of this text. In many ways we spend our lives attempting to connect to a place or to a series of places. As a species, we are territorial, requiring "turf" or a "stamping ground." We know the importance of the place where we grew up; we recall the anxieties of emigration, or moving; we under-

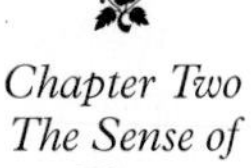

stand almost immediately the challenge of life on a new campus or in a new dormitory. We avoid or embrace certain places, mourn or celebrate others. Indeed, encountering and thinking about places inspires us, unlocks our creative impulses. And through language we attempt to capture the essence, or spirit, of a place—known or unknown, beautiful or ugly, urban or rural, settled or wild. Like the famous Chilean poet Pablo Neruda, we might want to celebrate, in exotic figurative language, the place we call home; or like George Orwell in "Shooting an Elephant," we might want to offer a cultural critique of a certain place. In short, the sense of place provokes many voices in us—sometimes in clear and sometimes in ambivalent tones.

Writing about a place may carry you from the personal to the objective. You may write about yourself, but extend the investigation outward to families, communities, regions, nations. Your memories of the past and present, understandings of your cultural legacies, may enrich your portrayal of diverse human relations nourished in one spot on Earth. In reading and writing about place, we acquire a better perception of human community and cultural cohesion. And we begin to unlock mysteries about our relationship to place for, as the American essayist, poet, and novelist Wendell Berry observes, if you don't know where you are, you don't know *who* you are.

Previewing the Chapter

As you read the essays in this chapter and respond to them in discussion and writing, consider the following questions:

- What is the writer's relationship to the place and his or her attitude toward it?
- What is the author's purpose in writing about a specific place?
- Is the place described friendly or hostile, known or unknown?
- Does the writer present an objective or a subjective picture of the place?
- What social, political, or ethical ideas does the author present?
- What are the main conflicts that the author presents?
- How well does the author know the place he or she is writing about? How do you know?
- What impact does the writer think a certain place has on culture?
- What does the author learn from his or her presentation of place?
- What have you learned from the author's presentation?

BARRY LOPEZ Barry Lopez (1945–) is a distinguished American writer on natural history, the environment, and our community obligations to the planet. He was born in Port Chester, New York; raised in rural California and New York City; and educated at the University of Notre Dame and the University of Oregon. Since the early 1970s, he has lived on the MacKenzie River in western Oregon. His award-winning books include *Of Wolves and Men* (1978), *Winter Count* (1981), *Arctic Dreams* (1986), *Crow and Weasel* (1990, winner of the Parents Choice Foundation Award), and *The Rediscovery of North America* (1991). A frequent contributor to periodicals, Lopez has collected some of his best essays and short fiction in *Crossing Open Ground* (1988). Lopez is a keen, poetic observer of landscape, by which he means "the complete lay of the land." In the following essay, Lopez warns of the dangers of viewing the American landscape as a symbol of patriotism or political agendas.

BARRY LOPEZ

Mapping the Real Geography

It has become commonplace to observe that Americans know little of the geography of their country, that they are innocent of it as a landscape of rivers, mountains, and towns. They do not know, supposedly, the location of the Delaware Water Gap, the Olympic Mountains, or the Piedmont Plateau; and, the indictment continues, they have little conception of the way the individual components of this landscape are imperiled, from a human perspective, by modern farming practices or industrial pollution. 1

I do not know how true this is, but it is easy to believe that it is truer than most of us would wish. A recent Gallup Organization and National Geographic Society survey found Americans woefully ignorant of world geography. Three out of four couldn't locate the Persian Gulf. The implication was that we knew no more about our own homeland, and that this ignorance undermined the integrity of our political processes and the efficiency of our business enterprises. 2

As Americans, we profess a sincere and fierce love for the American landscape, for our rolling prairies, free-flowing rivers, and "purple mountains' majesty"; but it is hard to imagine, actually, where this particular landscape is. It is not just that a nostalgic landscape has passed away—that Mark Twain's Mississippi is now dammed from Illinois to Louisiana and the prairies have all been sold and fenced. It is that it's *always* been a romantic's landscape. In the attenuated form in which it is presented on television today, in magazine articles, and in calendar photographs, the essential wildness of the American landscape is reduced to attractive scenery. We look out on a familiar, memorized land- 3

scape that portends adventure and promises enrichment. There are no distracting people in it and few artifacts of human life. The animals are all beautiful, diligent, one might even say well behaved. Nature's unruliness, the power of rivers and skies to intimidate, and any evidence of disastrous human land-management practices are all but invisible. It is, in short, a magnificent garden, a colonial vision of paradise imposed on a real place that is, at best, only selectively known.

The real American landscape is a face of almost incomprehensible 4
depth and complexity. If one were to sit for a few days, for example, among the ponderosa pine forests and black lava fields of the Cascade Mountains in western Oregon, inhaling the pines' sweet balm on an evening breeze from some point on the barren rock, and then were to step off onto the Olympic Peninsula in Washington, to those rain forests with sphagnum moss floors soft as fleece underfoot and Douglas firs too big around for five people to hug, and then head south to walk the ephemeral creeks and sun-blistered playas of the Mojave Desert in southern California, one would be reeling under the sensations. The contrast is not only one of plants and soils, a different array, say, of brilliantly colored beetles. The shock to the senses comes from a different shape to the silence, a difference in the very quality of light, in the weight of the air. And this relatively short journey down the West Coast would still leave the traveler with all that lay to the east to explore—the anomalous sand hills of Nebraska, the heat and frog voices of Okefenokee Swamp, the fetch of Chesapeake Bay, and the hardwood corpses and black bears of the Ozark Mountains.

No one of these places, of course, can be entirely fathomed, biologi- 5
cally or aesthetically. They are mysteries upon which we impose names. Enchantments. We tick the names off glibly but lovingly. We mean no disrespect. Our genuine desire, though we may be skeptical about the time it would take and uncertain of its practical value to us, is to actually know these places. As deeply ingrained in the American psyche as the desire to conquer and control the land is the desire to sojourn in it, to sail up and down Pamlico Sound, to paddle a canoe through Minnesota's boundary waters, to walk on the desert of the Great Salt Lake, to camp in the stony hardwood valleys of Vermont.

To do this well, to really come to an understanding of a specific 6
American geography, requires not only time but a kind of local expertise, an intimacy with place few of us ever develop. There is no way around the former requirement: If you want to know, you must take the time. It is not in books. A specific geographical understanding, however, can be sought out and borrowed. It resides with men and women more or less sworn to a place, who abide there, who have a feel for the soil and history, for the turn of leaves and night sounds. Often they are glad to take the outlander in tow.

These local geniuses of American landscape, in my experience, are 7
people in whom geography thrives. They are the antithesis of geographical ignorance. Rarely known outside their own communities, they often seem, at the first encounter, unremarkable and anonymous.

They may not be able to recall the name of a particular wildflower—or they may have given it a name known only to them. They might have forgotten the precise circumstances of a local historical event. Or they can't say for certain when the last of the Canada geese passed through in the fall, or can't differentiate between two kinds of trout in the same creek. Like all of us, they have fallen prey to the fallacies of memory and are burdened with ignorance; but they are nearly flawless in the respect they bear these places they love. Their knowledge is intimate rather than encyclopedic, human but not necessarily scholarly. It rings with the concrete details of experience.

America, I believe, teems with such people. The paradox here, be- 8
tween a faulty grasp of geographical knowledge for which Americans are indicted and the intimate, apparently contradictory familiarity of a group of largely anonymous people, is not solely a matter of confused scale. (The local landscape is easier to know than a national landscape—and many local geographers, of course, are relatively ignorant of a national geography.) And it is not simply ironic. The paradox is dark. To be succinct: The politics and advertising that seek a national audience must project a national geography; to be broadly useful that geography must, inevitably, be generalized, and it is often romantic. It is therefore frequently misleading and imprecise. Yet the same films, magazines, and television features that tout this imaginary American landscape also honor the anonymous men and women who interpret it. Their affinity for the land is lauded, their local allegiance admired. But the rigor of their local geographies, taken together, contradicts the patriotic, national vision of unspoiled, untroubled land. These men and women are ultimately forgotten, along with the details of the landscapes they speak for, in the face of more pressing national matters. It is the chilling nature of modern society to find an ignorance of geography, local or national, as excusable as an ignorance of hand tools; and to find the commitment of people to their home places only momentarily entertaining. And finally naive.

If one were to pass time among Basawara people in the Kalahari 9
Desert, or with Kreen-Akrora in the Amazon Basin, or with Pitjantjatjara Aborigines in Austrailia, the most salient impression they might leave is of an absolutely stunning knowledge of their local geography—geology, hydrology biology, and weather. In short, the extensive particulars of their intercourse with it.

In 40,000 years of human history, it has been only in the last few 10
hundred years or so that a people could afford to ignore their local geographies as completely as we do and still survive. Technological innovations, from refrigerated trucks to artificial fertilizers, from sophisticated cost accounting to mass air transportation, have utterly changed concepts of season, distance, soil productivity, and the real cost of drawing sustenance from the land. It is now possible for a resident of Boston to bite into a fresh strawberry in the dead of winter; for someone in San Francisco to travel to Atlanta in a few hours with

no worry about how formidable might be crossings of the Great Basin Desert or the Mississippi River; for an absentee farmer to gain a tax advantage from a farm that leaches poisons into its water table and on which crops are left to rot. The Pitjantjatjara might shake their heads in bewilderment and bemusement, not because they are primitive or ignorant people, not because they have no sense of irony or are incapable of marveling, but because they have not (many would say not yet) realized a world in which such manipulation of the land—surmounting the imperatives of distance it imposes, for example, or turning the large-scale destruction of forests and arable land into wealth—is desirable or plausible.

In the years I have traveled through America, in cars and on horse- 11
back, on foot and by raft, I have repeatedly been brought to a sudden state of awe by some gracile or savage movement of animal, some odd wrapping of a tree's foliage by the wind, an unimpeded run of dew-laden prairie stretching to a horizon flat as a coin where a pin-dot sun pales the dawn sky pink. I know these things are beyond intellection, that they are the vivid edges of a world that includes but also transcends the human world. In memory, when I dwell on these things, I know that in a truly national literature there should be odes to the Triassic reds of the Colorado Plateau, to the sharp and ghostly light of the Florida Keys, to the aeolian soils of southern Minnesota and the Palouse in Washington, though the modern mind abjures the literary potential of such subjects. (If the sand and floodwater farmers of Arizona and New Mexico were to take the black loams of Louisiana in their hands they would be flabbergasted, and that is the beginning of literature.) I know there should be eloquent evocations of the cobbled beaches of Maine, the plutonic walls of the Sierra Nevada, the orange canyons of the Kaībab Plateau. I have no doubt, in fact, that there are. They are as numerous and diverse as the eyes and fingers that ponder the country—it is that only a handful of them are known. The great majority are to be found in drawers and boxes, in the letters and private journals of millions of workaday people who have regarded their encounters with the land as an engagement bordering on the spiritual, as being fundamentally linked to their state of health.

One cannot acknowledge the extent and the history of this kind of 12
testimony without being forced to the realization that something strange, if not dangerous, is afoot. Year by year, the number of people with firsthand experience in the land dwindles. Rural populations continue to shift to the cities. The family farm is in a state of demise, and government and industry continue to apply pressure on the native peoples of North America to sever their ties with the land. In the wake of this loss of personal and local knowledge, the knowledge from which a real geography is derived, the knowledge upon which a country must ultimately stand, has come something hard to define but, I think, sinister and unsettling—the packaging and marketing of land as a form of entertainment. An incipient industry, capitalizing on the nostalgia

Americans feel for the imagined virgin landscapes of their fathers, and on a desire for adventure, now offers people a convenient though sometimes incomplete or even spurious geography as an inducement to purchase a unique experience. But the line between authentic experience and a superficial exposure to the elements of experience is blurred. And the real landscape, in all its complexity, is distorted even further in the public imagination. No longer innately mysterious and dignified, a ground from which experience grows, it becomes a curiously generic backdrop on which experience is imposed.

In theme parks the profound, subtle, and protracted experience of 13
running a river is reduced to a loud, quick, safe equivalence, a pleasant distraction. People only able to venture into the countryside on annual vacations are, increasingly, schooled in the belief that wild land will, and should, provide thrills and exceptional scenery on a timely basis. If it does not, something is wrong, either the land itself or possibly with the company outfitting the trip.

People in America, then, face a convoluted and ultimately destruc- 14
tive situation. The land itself, vast and differentiated, defies the notion of a national geography. Yet Americans are daily presented with, and have become accustomed to talking about, a homogenized national geography, one that seems to operate independently of the land, a collection of objects appearing in advertisements, as a background in movies, and in patriotic calendars. The suggestion is that there *can* be a national geography because the constituent parts are interchangeable and can be treated as commodities. On reflection, this is an appalling condescension and a terrible imprecision, the very antithesis of knowledge. The idea that either the Green River in Utah or the Salmon River in Idaho will do, or that the valleys of Kentucky and West Virginia are virtually interchangeable, is not just misleading. For people still dependent on the soil for their sustenance, or for people whose memories tie them to those places, it betrays a numbing casualness, a utilitarian, expedient, and commercial frame of mind. It heralds a society in which it is no longer necessary for human beings to know where they live, except as those places are described and fixed by numbers. The truly difficult and lifelong task of discovering where one lives is finally disdained.

If a society forgets or no longer cares where it lives, then anyone 15
with the political power and the will to do so can manipulate the landscape to conform to certain social ideals or nostalgic visions. People may hardly notice that anything has happened, or assume that whatever happens—a mountain stripped of timber and eroding into its creeks—is for the common good. The more superficial—or artificial—becomes a society's knowledge of the real dimensions of the land it occupies, the more vulnerable the land is to exploitation, to manipulation for short-term gain. The land, virtually powerless before political and commercial entities, finds itself finally with no defenders. It finds itself bereft of intimates with indispensable, concrete knowledge. (Oddly, or perhaps not oddly, while American society continues to value local knowl-

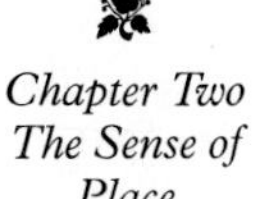

edge as a quaint part of its heritage, it continues to cut such people off from any real political power. This is as true for small farmers and illiterate cowboys as it is for American Indians, native Hawaiians, and Eskimos.)

The intense pressure of imagery in America, and the manipulation of images necessary to a society with specific goals, means the land will inevitably be treated like a commodity; and voices that tend to contradict the proffered image will, one way or another, be silenced or discredited by those in power. This is not new to America; the promulgation in America of a false or imposed geography has been the case from the beginning. All local geographies, as they were defined by hundreds of separate, independent native traditions, were denied in favor of an imported and unifying vision of America's natural history. The country, the landscape itself, was eventually defined according to dictates of progress like Manifest Destiny and laws like the Homestead Act, which reflected a poor understanding of the physical lay of the land. 16

When I was growing up in southern California, I formed the rudiments of a local geography—eucalyptus trees, February rains, Santa Ana winds. I lost much of it when my family moved to New York City, a move typical of the modern, peripatetic style of American life, responding to the exigencies of divorce and employment. As a boy I felt a hunger to know the American landscape that was extreme; when I was finally able to travel on my own, I did so. Eventually I visited most of the United States, living for brief periods of time in Arizona, Indiana, Alabama, Georgia, Wyoming, New Jersey, and Montana before settling twenty years ago in western Oregon. 17

The astonishing level of my ignorance confronted me everywhere I went. I knew early on that the country could not be held together in a few phrases, that its geography was magnificent and incomprehensible, that a man or woman could devote a lifetime to its elucidation and still feel in the end that he had but sailed many thousands of miles over the surface of the ocean. So I came into the habit of traversing landscapes I wanted to know with local tutors and reading what had previously been written about, and in, those places. I came to value exceedingly novels and essays and works of nonfiction that connected human enterprise to real and specific places, and I grew to be mildly distrustful of work that occurred in no particular place, work so cerebral and detached as to be refutable only in an argument of ideas. 18

These sojourns in various corners of the country infused me, somewhat to my surprise on thinking about it, with a great sense of hope. Whatever despair I had come to feel at a waning sense of the real land and the emergence of false geographies—elements of the land being manipulated, for example, to create erroneous but useful patterns in advertising—was dispelled by the depth of a single person's local knowledge, by the serenity that seemed to come with that intelligence. Any harm that might be done by people who cared nothing for the land, to whom it was not innately worthy but only something ultimately for sale, I thought, would one day have to meet this kind of integrity, 19

people with the same dignity and transcendence as the land they occupied. So when I traveled, when I rolled my sleeping bag out on the shores of the Beaufort Sea or in the high pastures of the Absaroka Range in Wyoming, or at the bottom of the Grand Canyon, I absorbed those particular testaments to life, the indigenous color and songbird song, the smell of sunbleached rock, damp earth, and wild honey, with some crude appreciation of the singular magnificence of each of those places. And the reassurance I felt expanded in the knowledge that there were, and would likely always be, people speaking out whenever they felt the dignity of the Earth imperiled in these places.

20 This promulgation of false geographies, which threaten the fundamental notion of what it means to live somewhere, is a current with a stable and perhaps growing countercurrent. There are people living in New York City who are familiar with the stone basements, the cratonic geology, of that island and have a feeling for birds migrating through in the fall, their sequence and number. They do not find the city alien but human, its attenuated natural history merely different from that of rural Georgia or Kansas. I find the countermeasure, too, among Eskimos who cannot read but who might engage you for days on the subtleties of sea-ice topography. And among men and women who, though they have followed in the footsteps of their parents, have come to the conclusion that they can no longer farm or fish or log in the way their ancestors did; they recognize that finite boundaries to this sort of wealth have appeared in their lifetime. Or among young men and women who have taken several decades of book-learned agronomy, zoology, silviculture and horticulture, ecology, ethnobotany, and fluvial geomorphology and turned it into a new kind of local knowledge, who have taken up residence in a place and sought, both because of and in spite of their education, to develop a deep intimacy with it. Or they have gone to work, idealistically, for the National Park Service or the fish and wildlife services or for a private institution like The Nature Conservancy. These are people to whom the land is more than politics or economics. These are people for whom the land is alive. It feeds them, directly, and that is how and why they learn its geography.

21 In the end, then, if one begins among the blue crabs of Chesapeake Bay and wanders for several years, down through the Smoky Mountains and back to the bluegrass hills, along the drainages of the Ohio and into the hill country of Missouri, where in summer a chorus of cicadas might drown out human conversation, then up the Missouri itself, reading on the way the entries of Meriwether Lewis and William Clark and musing on the demise of the plains grizzly and the sturgeon, crosses west into the drainage of the Platte and spends the evenings with Gene Weltfish's *The Lost Universe*, her book about the Pawnee who once thrived there, then drops south to Palo Duro Canyon and the irrigated farms of the Llano Estacado in Texas, turns west across the Sangre de Christo, southernmost of the Rocky Mountain ranges, and moves north and west up onto the slickrock mesas of Utah, those

browns and oranges, the ocherous hues reverberating in the deep canyons, then goes north, swinging west to the insular ranges that sit like battleships in the pelagic space of Nevada, camps at the steaming edge of sulphur springs in the Black Rock Desert, where alkaline pans are glazed with a ferocious light, a heat to melt iron, then crosses the northern Sierra Nevada, waist-deep in summer snow in the passes, to descend to the valley of the Sacramento, and rises through groves of elephantine redwoods in the Coast Range, to arrive at Cape Mendocino, before Balboa's Pacific, cormorants and gulls, gray whales headed north for Unimak Pass in the Aleutians, the winds crashing down on you, facing the ocean over the blue ocean that gives the scene its true vastness, making this crossing, having been so often astonished at the line and the color of the land, the ingenious lives of its plants and animals, the varieties of its darknesses, the intensity of the stars overhead, you would be ashamed to discover, then, in yourself, any capacity to focus on ravages in the land that left you unsettled. You would have seen so much, breathtaking, startling, and outsize, that you might not be able for a long time to break the spell, the sense, especially finishing your journey in the West, that the land had not been as rearranged or quite as compromised as you had first imagined.

After you had slept some nights on the beach, however, with that 22
finite line of the ocean before you and the land stretching out behind you, the wind first battering then cradling you, you would be compelled by memory, obligated by your own involvement, to speak of what left you troubled. To find the rivers dammed and shrunken, the soil washed away, the land fenced, a tracery of pipes and wires and roads laid down everywhere, blocking and channeling the movement of water and animals, cutting the eye off repeatedly and confining it—you had expected this. It troubles you no more than your despair over the ruthlessness, the insensitivity, the impetuousness of modern life. What underlies this obvious change, however, is a less noticeable pattern of disruption: acidic lakes, skies empty of birds, fouled beaches, the poisonous slags of industry, the sun burning like a molten coin in ruined air.

It is a tenet of certain ideologies that man is responsible for all that 23
is ugly, that everything nature creates is beautiful. Nature's darkness goes partly unreported, of course, and human brilliance is often perversely ignored. What is true is that man has a power, literally beyond his comprehension, to destroy. The lethality of some of what he manufactures, the incompetence with which he stores it or seeks to dispose of it, the cavalier way in which he employs in his daily living substances that threaten his health, the leniency of the courts in these matters (as though products as well as people enjoyed the protection of the Fifth Amendment), and the treatment of open land, rivers, and the atmosphere as if, in some medieval way, they could still be regarded as disposal sinks of infinite capacity, would make you wonder, standing face to in the wind at Cape Mendocīno, if we weren't bent on an errand of madness.

24 One afternoon on the Sīuslaw River in the Coast Range of Oregon, in January, I hooked a steelhead, as sea-run trout, that told me, through the muscles of my hands and arms and shoulders, something of the nature of the thing I was calling "the Sīuslaw River." Years ago I had stood under a pecan tree in Upson County, Georgia, idly eating the nuts, when slowly it occurred to me that these nuts would taste different from pecans growing somewhere up in South Carolina. I didn't need a sharp sense of taste to know this, only to pay attention at a level no one had ever told me was necessary. One November dawn, long before the sun rose, I began a vigil at the Dumont Dunes in the Mojave Desert in California, which I kept until a few minutes after the sun broke the horizon. During that time I named to myself the colors by which the sky changed and by which the sand itself flowed like a rising tide through grays and silvers and blues into yellows, pinks, washed duns, and fallow beiges.

25 It is through the power of observation, the gifts of eye and ear, of tongue and nose and finger, that a place first rises up in our mind; afterward it is memory that carries the place, that allows it to grow in depth and complexity. For as long as our records go back, we have held these two things dear: landscape and memory. Each infuses us with a different kind of life. The one feeds us, figuratively and literally. The other protects us from lies and tyranny. To keep landscapes intact—and the memory of them, our history in them, alive—seems as imperative a task in modern time as finding the extent to which individual expression can be accommodated, before it threatens to destroy the fabric of society.

26 If I were now to visit another country, I would ask my local companion, before I saw any museum or library, any factory or fabled town, to walk me in the country of his or her youth, to tell me the names of things and how, traditionally, they have been fitted together in a community. I would ask for the stories, the voice of memory over the land. I would ask to taste the wild nuts and fruits, to see their fishing lures, their bouquets, their fences. I would ask about the history of storms there, the age of the trees, the winter color of the hills. Only then would I ask to see the museum. I would want first the sense of a real place, to know that I was not inhabiting an idea. I would want to know the lay of the land first, the real geography, and take some measure of the love of it in my companion before I stood before the paintings or read works of scholarship. I would want to have something real and remembered against which I might hope to measure their truth.

COMPREHENSION

1. According to Lopez, what is the difference between "real" geography and "imagined" geography?
2. What does Lopez mean by the phrase "the concrete details of experience"?
3. What connection does the author make between an intimate knowledge of geography and human survival?

RHETORIC

1. What is the thesis of the essay? Where is it expressed, and what support does Lopez provide for it?
2. What is the tone of Lopez's introductory paragraph? How does it establish the writer's point of view?
3. What is the origin of the phrase "purple mountains' majesty" in paragraph 2? What associations are triggered by its use, and how does it help the writer's argument?
4. In paragraph 3, how does Lopez support his statement about the diversity of America? Do his examples aid the reader's understanding? Would you have added or substituted other examples?
5. How does Lopez use a pattern of definitions to help structure his essay? Cite examples.
6. How do the examples in paragraph 7 contribute to the point being made? Examine the arrangement of examples. What is the significance of the final example?

WRITING

1. Is it possible for technological advances and environmental concerns to coexist, or must one always be sacrificed to the other? Write an essay in which you explore this question.
2. Lopez states, "If you want to know, you must take the time." Do you be- 11
lieve most Americans "take the time" to learn about their landscape? Write an essay examining this attitude and its possible consequences.
3. What role does politics play in a country's attitude toward its land? Use current news events, as well as quotes from Lopez's essay, to develop this theme in an essay.
4. Become a local geographer. Take an hour's walk through an area in your hometown. Then, using its various sights, smells, and sounds, write a descriptive essay in which you particularize this area for the reader.

GEORGE ORWELL George Orwell (1903–1950) was the pseudonym of Eric Blair, an English novelist, essayist, and journalist. Orwell served with the Indian Imperial Police from 1922 to 1927 in Burma, fought in the Spanish Civil War, and acquired from his experiences a disdain of totalitarian and imperialistic systems. This attitude is reflected in his satiric fable, *Animal Farm* (1945), and in his bleak futuristic novel, *1984* (1949). In this essay, Orwell invokes personal experience to expose the contradictions inherent in British imperialism.

GEORGE ORWELL

Shooting an Elephant

In Moulmein, in Lower Burma, I was hated by large numbers of people—the only time in my life that I have been important enough for this to happen to me. I was subdivisional police officer of the town, and in an aimless, petty kind of way anti-European feeling was very bitter. No one had the guts to raise a riot, but if a European woman went through the bazaars alone somebody would probably spit betel juice over her dress. As a police officer I was an obvious target and was baited whenever it seemed safe to do so. When a nimble Burman tripped me up on the football field and the referee (another Burman) looked the other way, the crowd yelled with hideous laughter. This happened more than once. In the end the sneering yellow faces of young men that met me everywhere, the insults hooted after me when I was at a safe distance, got badly on my nerves. The young Buddhist priests were the worst of all. There were several thousands of them in the town and none of them seemed to have anything to do except stand on street corners and jeer at Europeans. 1

All this was perplexing and upsetting. For at that time I had already made up my mind that imperialism was an evil thing and the sooner I chucked up my job and got out of it the better. Theoretically—and secretly, of course—I was all for the Burmese and all against their oppressors, the British. As for the job I was doing, I hated it more bitterly than I can perhaps make clear. In a job like that you see the dirty work of Empire at close quarters. The wretched prisoners huddling in the stinking cages of the lock-ups, the grey, cowed faces of the long-term convicts, the scarred buttocks of the men who had been flogged with bamboos—all these oppressed me with an intolerable sense of guilt. But I could get nothing into perspective. I was young and ill-educated and I had had to think out my problems in the utter silence that is imposed on every Englishman in the East. I did not even know that the British Empire is dying, still less did I know that it is a great deal better than the younger empires that are going to supplant it. All I knew was that I was stuck between my hatred of the empire I served and my rage against the evil-spirited little beasts who tried to make my job impossible. With one part of my mind I thought of the British Raj as an unbreakable tyranny, as something clamped down, *in saecula saeculorum,* upon the will of prostrate peoples; with another part I thought that the greatest joy in the world would be to drive a bayonet into a Buddhist priest's guts. Feelings like these are the normal by-products of imperialism; ask any Anglo-Indian official, if you can catch him off duty. 2

3 One day something happened which in a roundabout way was enlightening. It was a tiny incident in itself, but it gave me a better glimpse than I had had before of the real nature of imperialism—the real motives for which despotic governments act. Early one morning the sub-inspector at a police station the other end of the town rang me up on the phone and said that an elephant was ravaging the bazaar. Would I please come and do something about it? I did not know what I could do, but I wanted to see what was happening and I got on to a pony and started out. I took my rifle, an old .44 Winchester and much too small to kill an elephant, but I thought the noise might be useful *in terrorem.* Various Burmans stopped me on the way and told me about the elephant's doings. It was not, of course, a wild elephant, but a tame one which had gone "must." It had been chained up as tame elephants always are when their attack of "must" is due, but on the previous night it had broken its chain and escaped. Its mahout, the only person who could manage it when it was in that state, had set out in pursuit, but he had taken the wrong direction and was now twelve hours' journey away, and in the morning the elephant had suddenly reappeared in the town. The Burmese population had no weapons and were quite helpless against it. It had already destroyed somebody's bamboo hut, killed a cow and raided some fruit-stalls and devoured the stock; also it had met the municipal rubbish van, and, when the driver jumped out and took to his heels, had turned the van over and inflicted violence upon it.

4 The Burmese sub-inspector and some Indian constables were waiting for me in the quarter where the elephant had been seen. It was a very poor quarter, a labyrinth of squalid bamboo huts, thatched with palm-leaf, winding all over a steep hillside. I remember that it was a cloudy stuffy morning at the beginning of the rains. We began questioning the people as to where the elephant had gone, and, as usual, failed to get any definite information. That is invariably the case in the East; a story always sounds clear enough at a distance, but the nearer you get to the scene of events the vaguer it becomes. Some of the people said that the elephant had gone in one direction, some said that he had gone in another, some professed not even to have heard of any elephant. I had almost made up my mind that the whole story was a pack of lies, when we heard yells a little distance away. There was a loud, scandalized cry of "Go away, child! Go away this instant!" and an old woman with a switch in her hand came round the corner of a hut, violently shooing away a crowd of naked children. Some more women followed, clicking their tongues and exclaiming; evidently there was something there that the children ought not to have seen. I rounded the hut and saw a man's dead body sprawling in the mud. He was an Indian, a black Dravidian coolie, almost naked, and he could not have been dead many minutes. The people said that the elephant had come suddenly upon him round the corner of the hut, caught him with its trunk, put its foot on his back and ground him into the earth. This was the rainy season and the ground was soft, and his face had scored a trench a foot deep and a couple of yards long. He was lying on his belly with arms

crucified and head sharply twisted to one side. His face was coated with mud, the eyes wide open, the teeth bared and grinning with an expression of unendurable agony. (Never tell me, by the way, that the dead look peaceful. Most of the corpses I have seen looked devilish.) The friction of the great beast's foot had stripped the skin from his back as neatly as one skins a rabbit. As soon as I saw the dead man I sent an orderly to a friend's house nearby to borrow an elephant rifle. I had already sent back the pony, not wanting it to go mad with fright and throw me if it smelled the elephant.

The orderly came back in a few minutes with a rifle and five car- 5
tridges, and meanwhile some Burmans had arrived and told us that the elephant was in the paddy fields below, only a few hundred yards away. As I started forward practically the whole population of the quarter flocked out of their houses and followed me. They had seen the rifle and were all shouting excitedly that I was going to shoot the elephant. They had not shown much interest in the elephant when he was merely ravaging their homes, but it was different now that he was going to be shot. It was a bit of fun to them, as it would be to an English crowd; besides, they wanted the meat. It made me vaguely uneasy. I had no intention of shooting the elephant—I had merely sent for the rifle to defend myself if necessary—and it is always unnerving to have a crowd following you. I marched down the hill, looking, and feeling, a fool, with the rifle over my shoulder and an ever-growing army of people jostling at my heels. At the bottom, when you got away from the huts, there was a metalled road and beyond that a miry waste of paddy fields a thousand yards across, not yet ploughed but soggy from the first rains and dotted with coarse grass. The elephant was standing eighty yards from the road, his left side towards us. He took not the slightest notice of the crowd's approach. He was tearing up bunches of grass, beating them against his knees to clean them and stuffing them into his month.

I had halted on the road. As soon as I saw the elephant I knew with 6
perfect certainty that I ought not to shoot him. It is a serious matter to shoot a working elephant—it is comparable to destroying a huge and costly piece of machinery—and obviously one ought not to do it if it can possibly be avoided. And at a distance, peacefully eating, the elephant looked no more dangerous than a cow. I thought then and I think now that his attack of "must" was already passing off; in which case he would merely wander harmlessly about until the mahout came back and caught him. Moreover, I did not in the least want to shoot him. I decided that I would watch him for a little while to make sure that he did not turn savage again, and then go home.

But at that moment I glanced round at the crowd that had followed 7
me. It was an immense crowd, two thousand at the least and growing every minute. It blocked the road for a long distance on either side. I looked at the sea of yellow faces above the garish clothes—faces all happy and excited over this bit of fun, all certain that the elephant was going to be shot. They were watching me as they would watch a conjuror about to perform a trick. They did not like me, but with the magi-

cal rifle in my hands I was momentarily worth watching. And suddenly I realised that I should have to shoot the elephant after all. The people expected it of me and I had got to do it; I could feel their two thousand wills pressing me forward, irresistibly. And it was at this moment, as I stood there with the rifle in my hands, that I first grasped the hollowness, the futility of the white man's dominion in the East. Here was I, the white man with his gun, standing in front of the unarmed native crowd—seemingly the leading actor of the piece, but in reality I was only an absurd puppet pushed to and fro by the will of those yellow faces behind. I perceived in this moment that when the white man turns tyrant it is his own freedom that he destroys. He becomes a sort of hollow, posing dummy, the conventionalised figure of a sahib. For it is the condition of his rule that he shall spend his life in trying to impress the "natives" and so in every crisis he has got to do what the "natives" expect of him. He wears a mask, and his face grows to fit it. I had got to shoot the elephant. I had committed myself to doing it when I sent for the rifle. A sahib has got to act like a sahib; he has got to appear resolute, to know his own mind and do definite things. To come all that way, rifle in hand, with two thousand people marching at my heels, and then to trail feebly away, having done nothing—no, that was impossible. The crowd would laugh at me. And my whole life, every white man's life in the East, was one long struggle not to be laughed at.

But I did not want to shoot the elephant. I watched him beating his 8
bunch of grass against his knees, with that preoccupied grandmotherly air that elephants have. It seemed to me that it would be murder to shoot him. At that age I was not squeamish about killing animals, but I had never shot an elephant and never wanted to. (Somehow it always seems worse to kill a *large* animal.) Besides, there was the beast's owner to be considered. Alive, the elephant was worth at least a hundred pounds; dead, he would only be worth the value of his tusks—five pounds, possibly. But I had got to act quickly. I turned to some experienced-looking Burmans who had been there when we arrived, and asked them how the elephant had been behaving. They all said the same thing: he took no notice of you if you left him alone, but he might charge if you went too close to him.

It was perfectly clear to me what I ought to do. I ought to walk up to 9
within, say, twenty-five yards of the elephant and test his behaviour. If he charged I could shoot, if he took no notice of me it would be safe to leave him until the mahout came back. But also I knew that I was going to do no such thing. I was a poor shot with a rifle and the ground was soft mud into which one would sink at every step. If the elephant charged and I missed him, I should have about as much chance as a toad under a steam-roller. But even then I was not thinking particularly of my own skin, only the watchful yellow faces behind. For at that moment, with the crowd watching me, I was not afraid in the ordinary sense, as I would have been if I had been alone. A white man mustn't be frightened in front of "natives"; and so, in general, he isn't frightened. The sole thought in my mind was that if anything went wrong

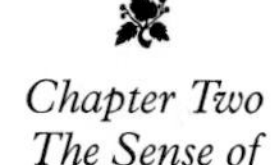

those two thousand Burmans would see me pursued, caught, trampled on and reduced to a grinning corpse like that Indian up the hill. And if that happened it was quite probable that some of them would laugh. That would never do. There was only one alternative. I shoved the cartridges into the magazine and lay down on the road to get a better aim.

The crowd grew very still, and a deep, low, happy sigh, as of people 10
who see the theatre curtain go up at last, breathed from innumerable throats. They were going to have their bit of fun after all. The rifle was a beautiful German thing with cross-hair sights. I did not then know that in shooting an elephant one should shoot to cut an imaginary bar running from ear-hole to ear-hole. I ought therefore, as the elephant was sideways on, to have aimed straight at his ear-hole; actually I aimed several inches in front of this, thinking the brain would be further forward.

When I pulled the trigger I did not hear the bang or feel the kick— 11
one never does when a shot goes home—but I heard the devilish roar of glee that went up from the crowd. In that instant, in too short a time, one would have thought, even for the bullet to get there, a mysterious, terrible change had come over the elephant. He neither stirred nor fell, but every line of his body had altered. He looked suddenly stricken, shrunken, immensely old, as though the frightful impact of the bullet had paralysed him without knocking him down. At last, after what seemed a long time—it might have been five seconds, I dare say—he sagged flabbily to his knees. His mouth slobbered. An enormous senility seemed to have settled upon him. One could have imagined him thousands of years old. I fired again into the same spot. At the second shot he did not collapse but climbed with desperate slowness to his feet and stood weakly upright, with legs sagging and head drooping. I fired a third time. That was the shot that did for him. You could see the agony of it jolt his whole body and knock the last remnant of strength from his legs. But in falling he seemed for a moment to rise, for as his hind legs collapsed beneath him he seemed to tower upwards like a huge rock toppling, his trunk reaching skyward like a tree. He trumpeted, for the first and only time. And then down he came, his belly towards me, with a crash that seemed to shake the ground even where I lay.

I got up. The Burmans were already racing past me across the mud. 12
It was obvious that the elephant would never rise again, but he was not dead. He was breathing very rhythmically with long rattling gasps, his great mound of a side painfully rising and falling. His mouth was wide open—I could see far down into caverns of pale pink throat. I waited a long time for him to die, but his breathing did not weaken. Finally I fired my two remaining shots into the spot where I thought his heart must be. The thick blood welled out of him like red velvet, but still he did not die. His body did not even jerk when the shots hit him, the tortured breathing continued without a pause. He was dying, very slowly and in great agony, but in some world remote from me where not even a bullet could damage him further. I felt that I had got to put an end to that dreadful noise. It seemed dreadful to see the great beast lying there, powerless to move and yet powerless to die, and not even to be able to finish him. I

sent back for my small rifle and poured shot after shot into his heart and down his throat. They seemed to make no impression. The tortured gasps continued as steadily as the ticking of a clock.

In the end I could not stand it any longer and went away. I heard later that it took him half an hour to die. Burmans were arriving with dahs and baskets even before I left, and I was told they had stripped his body almost to the bones by the afternoon. 13

Afterwards, of course, there were endless discussions about the shooting of the elephant. The owner was furious, but he was only an Indian and could do nothing. Besides, legally I had done the right thing, for a mad elephant has to be killed, like a mad dog, if its owner fails to control it. Among the Europeans opinion was divided. The older men said I was right, the younger men said it was a damn shame to shoot an elephant for killing a coolie, because an elephant was worth more than any damn Coringhee coolie. And afterwards I was very glad that the coolie had been killed; it put me legally in the right and it gave me a sufficient pretext for shooting the elephant. I often wondered whether any of the others grasped that I had done it solely to avoid looking a fool. 14

COMPREHENSION

1. State in your own words the thesis of this essay.
2. How does the shooting of the elephant give Orwell a better understanding of "the real nature of imperialism—the real motives for which despotic governments act" (paragraph 3)? Why does Orwell kill the elephant? What is his attitude toward the Burmese people?
3. Why does Orwell concentrate on the prolonged death of the elephant? What effect does it have?

RHETORIC

1. How would you describe the level of language in the essay? Point to specific words, sentences, and phrases to support your answer.
2. Define *supplant* (paragraph 2); *labyrinth* (paragraph 4); *jostling* (paragraph 5); *conjuror* (paragraph 7); and *senility* (paragraph 11).
3. What is the function of the first two paragraphs? Where is the thesis stated in the essay?
4. Analyze Orwell's use of dramatic techniques to develop the narrative. Examine consecutive paragraphs in the essay to determine the author's presentation of action from different perspectives. What other essays in this chapter strike you as dramatic, and why?
5. Select and analyze some of the details in the essay that are designed to impress the reader's senses and emotions. Why does Orwell rely so heavily on the presentation and accumulation of detail in the essay?
6. How is the entire essay structured by irony of situation and paradox? How do these devices relate to the ethical issues raised by Orwell?

WRITING

1. In this essay, written in 1936, Orwell declares: "I did not even know that the British Empire is dying, still less did I know that it is a great deal better than the younger empires that are going to supplant it" (paragraph 2). In what ways is Orwell's statement prophetic?
2. Write a narrative essay about an episode in your life that brought you into conflict with social or political forces.
3. For a research project, consult library sources, and then write a report, employing proper documentation, on the importance of Orwell as an essayist.

MARGARET LAURENCE Margaret Laurence (1926–) was born Jean Margaret Wemyss in Manitoba, Canada, of Scotch-Irish ancestry. Once a reporter for the *Winnipeg Citizen,* she later married and moved to Africa, where she lived for eight years. Africa was a formative influence on Laurence's literary career and provided stimulating challenge, as well as a setting for her earlier works, including *This Side Jordan* (1960). Later, while living in England, she began a series of novels set in the fictional prairie town of Manawaka: *The Stone Angel* (1964), *A Jest of God* (1966), *The Fire-Dwellers* (1969), and *The Diviners* (1974). In this essay, she recaptures a Canadian landscape—the "territory" of her youth.

MARGARET LAURENCE

Where the World Began

A strange place it was, that place where the world began. A place of incredible happenings, splendours and revelations, despairs like multitudinous pits of isolated hells. A place of shadow-spookiness, inhabited by the unknowable dead. A place of jubilation and of mourning, horrible and beautiful. 1

It was, in fact, a small prairie town. 2

Because that settlement and that land were my first and for many years my only real knowledge of this planet, in some profound way they remain my world, my way of viewing. My eyes were formed there. Towns like ours, set in a sea of land, have been described thousands of times as dull, bleak, flat, uninteresting. I have had it said to me that the railway trip across Canada is spectacular, except for the prairies, when it would be desirable to go to sleep for several days, until the ordeal is over. I am always unable to argue this point effectively. All I can say is—well, you really have to live there to know that country. The town of my childhood could be called bizarre, agonizingly repressive or cruel at times, and the land in which it grew could be called harsh in the vio- 3

lence of its seasonal changes. But never merely flat or uninteresting. Never dull.

In winter, we used to hitch rides on the back of the milk sleigh, our 4
moccasins squeaking and slithering on the hard rutted snow of the roads, our hands in ice-bubbled mitts hanging onto the box edge of the sleigh for dear life, while Bert grinned at us through his great frosted moustache and shouted the horse into speed, daring us to stay put. Those mornings, rising, there would be the perpetual fascination of the frost feathers on windows, the ferns and flowers and eerie faces traced there during the night by unseen artists of the wind. Evenings, coming back from skating, the sky would be black but not dark, for you could see a cold glitter of stars from one side of the earth's rim to the other. And then the sometime astonishment when you saw the Northern Lights flaring across the sky, like the scrawled signature of God. After a blizzard, when the snowploughs hadn't yet got through, school would be closed for the day, the assumption being that the town's young could not possibly flounder through five feet of snow in the pursuit of education. We would then gaily don snowshoes and flounder for miles out into the white dazzling deserts, in pursuit of a different kind of knowing. If you came back too close to night, through the woods at the foot of the town hill, the thin black branches of poplar and chokecherry now meringued with frost, sometimes you heard coyotes. Or maybe the banshee wolf-voices were really only inside your head.

Summers were scorching, and when no rain came and the wheat 5
became bleached and dried before it headed, the faces of farmers and townsfolk would not smile much, and you took for granted, because it never seemed to have been any different, the frequent knocking at the back door and the young men standing there, mumbling or thrusting defiantly their requests for a drink of water and a sandwich if you could spare it. They were riding the freights, and you never knew where they had come from, or where they might end up, if anywhere. The Drought and Depression were like evil deities which had been there always. You understood and did not understand.

Yet the outside world had its continuing marvels. The poplar bluffs 6
and the small river were filled and surrounded with a zillion different grasses, stones, and weed flowers. The meadowlarks sang undaunted from the twanging telephone wires along the gravel highway. Once we found an old flat-bottomed scow, and launched her, poling along the shallow brown waters, mending her with wodges of hastily chewed Spearmint, grounding her among the tangles of yellow marsh marigolds that grew succulently along the banks of the shrunken river, while the sun made our skins smell dusty-warm.

My best friend lived in an apartment above some stores on Main 7
Street (its real name was Mountain Avenue, goodness knows why), an elegant apartment with royal-blue velvet curtains. The back roof, scarcely sloping at all, was corrugated tin, of a furnace-like warmth on a July afternoon, and we would sit there drinking lemonade and looking across the back lane at the Fire Hall. Sometimes our vigil would be rewarded.

Oh joy! Somebody's house burning down! We had an almost-perfect callousness in some ways. Then the wooden tower's bronze bell would clonk and toll like a thousand speeded funerals in a time of plague, and in a few minutes the team of giant black horses would cannon forth, pulling the fire wagon like some scarlet chariot of the Goths, while the firemen clung with one hand, adjusting their helmets as they went.

The oddities of the place were endless. An elderly lady used to 8
serve, as her afternoon tea offering to other ladies, soda biscuits spread with peanut butter and topped with a whole marshmallow. Some considered this slightly eccentric, when compared with chopped egg sandwiches, and admittedly talked about her behind her back, but no one ever refused these delicacies or indicated to her that they thought she had slipped a cog. Another lady dyed her hair a bright and cheery orange, by strangers often mistaken at twenty paces for a feather hat. My own beloved stepmother wore a silver fox neckpiece, a whole pelt, *with the embalmed (?) head still on.* My Ontario Irish grandfather said, "sparrow grass," a more interesting term than asparagus. The town dump was known as "the nuisance grounds," a phrase fraught with weird connotations, as though the effluvia of our lives was beneath contempt but at the same time was subtly threatening to the determined and sometimes hysterical propriety of our ways.

Some oddities were, as idiom had it, "funny ha ha"; others were 9
"funny peculiar." Some were not so very funny at all. An old man lived, deranged, in a shack in the valley. Perhaps he wasn't even all that old, but to us he seemed a wild Methuselah figure, shambling among the underbrush and tall couchgrass, muttering indecipherable curses or blessings, a prophet who had forgotten his prophesies. Everyone in town knew him, but no one knew him. He lived among us as though only occasionally and momentarily visible. The kids called him Andy Gump, and feared him. Some sought to prove their bravery by tormenting him. They were the mediaeval bear baiters, and he the lumbering bewildered bear, half blind, only rarely turning to snarl. Everything is to be found in a town like mine. Belsen, writ small but with the same ink.

All of us cast stones in one shape or another. In grade school, 10
among the vulnerable and violet girls we were, the feared and despised were those few older girls from what was charmingly termed "the wrong side of the tracks." Tough in talk and tougher in muscle, they were said to be whores already. And may have been, that being about the only profession readily available to them.

The dead lived in that place, too. Not only the grandparents who 11
had, in local parlance, "passed on" and who gloomed, bearded or bonneted, from the sepia photographs in old albums, but also the uncles, forever eighteen or nineteen, whose names were carved on the granite family stones in the cemetery, but whose bones lay in France. My own young mother lay in that graveyard, beside other dead of our kin, and when I was ten, my father, too, only forty, left the living town for the dead dwelling on the hill.

When I was eighteen, I couldn't wait to get out of that town, away from the prairies. I did not know then that I would carry the land and town all my life within my skull, that they would form the mainspring and source of the writing I was to do, wherever and however far away I might live. 12

This was my territory in the time of my youth, and in a sense my life since then has been an attempt to look at it, to come to terms with it. Stultifying to the mind it certainly could be, and sometimes was, but not to the imagination. It was many things, but it was never dull. 13

The same, I now see, could be said for Canada in general. Why on earth did generations of Canadians pretend to believe this country dull? We knew perfectly well it wasn't. Yet for so long we did not proclaim what we knew. If our upsurge of so-called nationalism seems odd or irrelevant to outsiders, and even to some of our own people *(what's all the fuss about?),* they might try to understand that for many years we valued ourselves insufficiently, living as we did under the huge shadows of those two dominating figures, Uncle Sam and Britannia. We have only just begun to value ourselves, our land, our abilities. We have only just begun to recognize our legends and to give shape to our myths. 14

There are, God knows, enough aspects to deplore about this country. When I see the killing of our lakes and rivers with industrial wastes, I feel rage and despair. When I see our industries and natural resources increasingly taken over by America, I feel an overwhelming discouragement, especially as I cannot simply say "damn Yankees." It should never be forgotten that it is we ourselves who have sold such a large amount of our birthright for a mess of plastic Progress. When I saw the War Measures Act being invoked in 1970, I lost forever the vestigial remains of the naive wish-belief that repression could not happen here, or would not. And yet, of course, I had known all along in the deepest and often hidden caves of the heart that anything can happen anywhere, for the seeds of both man's freedom and his captivity are found everywhere, even in the microcosm of a prairie town. But in raging against our injustices, our stupidities, I do so *as family,* as I did, and still do in writing, about those aspects of my town which I hated and which are always in some ways aspects of myself. 15

The land still draws me more than other lands. I have lived in Africa and in England, but splendid as both can be they do not have the power to move me in the same way as, for example, that part of southern Ontario where I spent four months last summer in a cedar cabin beside a river. "Scratch a Canadian, and you find a phony pioneer," I used to say to myself in warning. But all the same it is true, I think, that we are not yet totally alienated from physical earth, and let us only pray we do not become so. I once thought that my lifelong fear and mistrust of cities made me a kind of old-fashioned freak; now I see it differently. 16

The cabin has a long window across its front western wall, and sitting at the oak table there in the mornings, I used to look out at the 17

river and at the tall trees beyond, green-gold in the early light. The river was bronze; the sun caught it strangely, reflecting upon its surface the near-shore sand ripples underneath. Suddenly, the crescenting of a fish, gone before the eye could clearly give image to it. The old man next door said these leaping fish were carp. Himself, he preferred muskie, for he was a real fisherman and the muskie gave him a fight. The wind most often blew from the south, and the river flowed toward the south, so when the water was wind-riffled, and the current was strong, the river seemed to be flowing both ways. I liked this, and interpreted it as an omen, a natural symbol.

A few years ago, when I was back in Winnipeg, I gave a talk at my old college. It was open to the public, and afterward a very old man came up to me and asked me if my maiden name had been Wemyss. I said yes, thinking he might have known my father or my grandfather. But no. "When I was a young lad," he said, "I once worked for your great-grandfather, Robert Wemyss, when he had the sheep ranch at Raeburn." I think that was a moment when I realized all over again something of great importance to me. My long-ago families came from Scotland and Ireland, but in a sense that no longer mattered so much, true roots were here. 18

I am not very patriotic, in the usual meaning of that word. I cannot say "My country right or wrong" in any political, social or literary context. But one thing is inalterable, for better or worse, for life. 19

This is where my world began. A world which includes the ancestors—both my own and other people's ancestors who become mine. A world which formed me, and continues to do so, even while I fought it in some of its aspects, and continue to do so. A world which gave me my own lifework to do, because it was here that I learned the sight of my own particular eyes. 20

COMPREHENSION

1. Referring to her town, Laurence claims, "My eyes were formed there." What does she mean?
2. During what time period was the writer raised? Cite details from the essay that justify your answer.
3. How does Laurence feel about her hometown and its people? Support your opinion with evidence from the essay.

RHETORIC

1. What response does Laurence set up in her introductory paragraph, and how does the next one-sentence paragraph affect the reader's expectations? Is this strategy effective?
2. What is the organizational structure of the essay? Trace the progression of ideas through the essay.

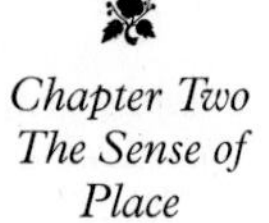

3. What is the essay's thesis? Is it stated or implied? Where in the essay is it most strongly evident?
4. Paragraph 4 is especially rich in sensory details. What emotions do these images evoke in the reader, and how do they serve the writer's purpose? Give specific examples.
5. Examine the use of the word *patriotic* in paragraph 19. What are the connotative and denotative definitions? How is Laurence using it?
6. Does the writer ultimately succeed in supporting her original description of her town? Explain.

WRITING

1. Write an essay in which you describe your earliest memory of place. Use similes and figurative language to capture the sights, sounds, and smells as you recall them. What associations do you make between the place and yourself? Consider the impact of memory on place.
2. Compose a word portrait of someone you know who embodies the qualities of a particular locale. Use metaphors to illustrate the impact of one on the other.
3. Do you think that Americans are, as a whole, "totally alienated from physical earth"? Do you believe, as Laurence seems to, that Canadians (or others) have a closer relationship with the land? Support your views with evidence from the essays of Laurence and Lopez.

PICO IYER Pico Iyer was born in Oxford, England, and educated at Eton, Oxford, and Harvard. He now lives in Santa Barbara, California. A correspondent for *Time* magazine, Iyer also contributes articles and reviews to *Partisan Review,* the *Village Voice,* and numerous other publications. His book *Video Night in Kathmandu* (1988) places Iyer in the forefront of contemporary travel writers. In the following essay, Iyer trains his camera-sharp eye on one Asian nation in order to offer a comparative assessment of culture.

PICO IYER

Vietnam: A Delicate Innocence

In Hue, the gracious, reticent capital of old Vietnam, I drifted one morning, by sampan, down to the Linh Mu pagoda, its gardens scented with orchids, frangipani, and jackfruit and scattered with a flutter of white and crimson butterflies. Monks with girlish faces ushered me into the kitchen, where eleven-year-old novices, tassel-haired, were slicing vegetables and stoking fires. Then, over tea and green bean cake, the 1 head abbot, smiling-eyed, told me about how Buddhism had long been suppressed in his country and pointed out to me the grayish Austin, sitting neatly in the temple garden, in which a monk from the pagoda had driven to Saigon to immolate himself in 1963. Later that day, I walked around the lakeside pavilion where the emperor Tu Duc had once composed poems, sipped lotus tea, and dallied with his 104 courtesans; I wandered into the shaded, pink-walled French colonial school where Ho Chi Minh, General Vo Nguyen Giap, and former prime minister Ngo Dinh Diem had all been educated (and, as ever in Hue, felt as if I were walking through an avenue of smiles); and that night I returned to the kind of lyric pleasures that I had come to expect in Vietnam—the couples gathered in cafés along the waterside, sitting on wicker chairs, their glasses balanced on stones, watching the lights on the river while a syrupy female singer softened the night.

In Hue, watching the famous local beauties, flowerlike in their tradi- 2
tional *ao dais,* bicycling with queenly serenity the bridge across the Perfume River, long hair falling to their waists and pink parasols held up against the sun, I felt that here was a scene that could move even a journalist to poetry. Just one week later, to my astonishment, I read in Morley Safer's *Flashbacks* that even this most hard-headed of investigative journalists had, he confessed, written a poem in Hue (which "mercifully [he had] both lost and forgotten").

A few days later, I found myself inside the busiest and brashest cir- 3
cus I had ever seen. Saigon could be called Scooter City, the home of the Motorcycle Revolution, a 350cc Beijing. For, every weekend night, all the bright young things of town dress up in their Sunday best, get onto their bikes, and start racing and roaring around the central streets, swerving in and out of packs, speeding along in swarms; girls in cocktail dresses, boys in white shirts and ties, whole families on a single scooter, teenagers in denim skirts, even demure old gray-haired couples, all of them roaring around and around and around, past high-rise murals that say "To Keep Money in the Bank Is Patriotic," past packs of others lined up along the sidewalks, the whole group of them enacting a kind of crazy, revved-up *thé dansant* on wheels.

The feverish carnival atmosphere was like nothing I had ever 4
known before: In Italian towns, teenagers famously promenade around the main plaza in the evenings, exchanging glances and flirtations, but here the whole ritual was speeded up, intensified, and played out at top volume, half of Saigon caught up in this surging mass, trading smiles as they went, catching the eyes of strangers, or simply exulting in a literal version of their brand-new motto of *song voi,* or "living fast." It seemed an almost perfect metaphor for the sudden explosion of energy and excitement in Saigon, as sharp as if a rubber band, stretched out for fifteen years, had suddenly snapped back, and with a vengeance.

As the night wore on, the feverish sense of abandon grew ever more 5
surreal. Somehow, in Saigon it is always 9:30 at night in some flashy, shady dive, and a chanteuse in a sequined microskirt is belting out "I'm

on the top of the world, looking down on creation . . . " to the accompaniment of violins and cellos played by girls in shocking pink miniskirts.

Vietnam, to me, seemed two distinct, almost contradictory, countries: Saigon (Ho Chi Minh City) and the rest. And almost anything I might say about the one would be contradicted by the other. In part, of course, this reflects nothing more than the universal disjunction between big city and unspoiled countryside, equally apparent around New York, Paris, Buenos Aires, and Bangkok. In part, it reflects merely the geography of a country that was divided into two—twenty years ago and two hundred years ago. Hanoi is as far north of Ho Chi Minh City as Boston is of Charleston, and the character, the pace, and even the climate of the quiet, unshowy northern capital bear little relation to the helter-skelter, anything-goes vitality of the south (in ten days in the north, I never saw the sun; in ten days in the south, I almost got charbroiled). Even now, North and South Vietnam are as different as past and future, silence and frenzy, maiden aunt and bar girl; as different, ultimately, as Beijing and Hong Kong. Ask someone in Saigon if she's ever been to Hanoi, and she'll say, "No, I've never been outside Vietnam." Her cousin in the north will say, with equal conviction, "In Saigon, you can do anything. But in Vietnam. . . ." Saigon and Vietnam are as different, almost literally, as night and day. 6

Yet both places are distinctly new to foreign eyes, and both places— 7
that of an aging bicycle and of a juiced-up Honda—have their own exhilarations. Vietnam is a smiling Southeast Asian country set amid the systems and institutions of old China, yet it is more unspoiled than Thailand and more gentle than the Middle Kingdom. Indeed, it is hard not to grow woozily romantic when enumerating the holiday seductions of the place. There are the mist-wreathed rain forests of the west and north, where you can find fifty-three distinct minority tribes—each with its own colorful costumes, customs, and tongue—hunting, still with bows and arrows, and, if asked how old they are, answering, "Ten or fifteen water buffaloes' lives."

COMPREHENSION

1. According to the essay, what sets Saigon apart from the rest of the country? What evidence does Iyer provide?
2. How does the writer feel about his subject?
3. Is Iyer promoting or condemning tourism in Vietnam?

RHETORIC

1. Iyer employs exotic words and images to help convey an impression of Vietnam. Give some examples of his use of language. How does it help you understand the subject?
2. Why has Iyer written this essay? What message is he conveying? Specifically where in the essay does his intention become clear?
3. Who is Iyer's audience? What support can you find in the essay?

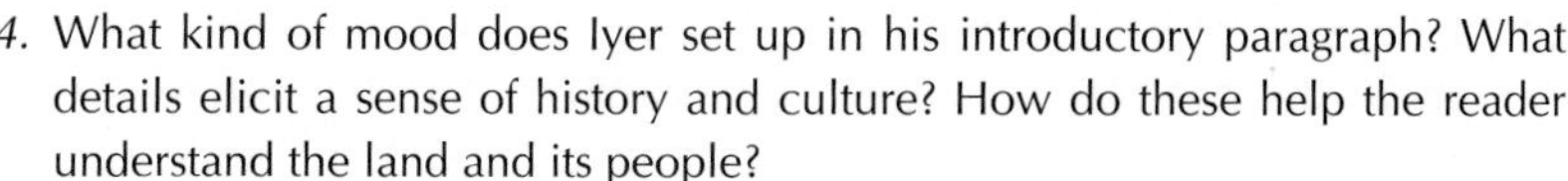

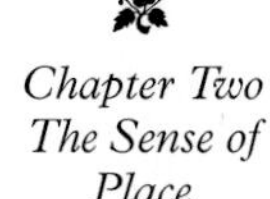

4. What kind of mood does Iyer set up in his introductory paragraph? What details elicit a sense of history and culture? How do these help the reader understand the land and its people?
5. How does Iyer use a pattern of comparison and contrast to develop his essay?
6. What transition does Iyer make in paragraph 7? What purpose do the colorful details serve?

WRITING

1. If you were planning a vacation in Asia, would you consider visiting Vietnam? Write an essay in which you develop the reasons for your answer. How would Iyer's descriptions and opinions influence your choice? Be specific.
2. Compare Lopez's view of landscape as entertainment to Iyer's views on tourism. Do they share a common view of place? In what ways do they differ? Use support from both writers.
3. Write an essay examining America's historic link to Vietnam and its impact on the people and geography. Some research may be necessary. In addition, evidence from Iyer's essay should be considered.
4. Consider in an essay the effects of tourism on a country's people, land, economy. What are the advantages of marketing a culture? How can it be detrimental to a country's resources and identity?

JAMAICA KINCAID Jamaica Kincaid (1949–) remains a citizen of Antigua, the small island in the Caribbean where she was born, though she resides in Vermont with her husband and two children. Kincaid graduated from Bennington College and has been a staff writer for the *New Yorker* since 1976. She has written a collection of short stories, *At the Bottom of the River* (1985), *Annie John* (1985), *A Small Place* (1988) and, most recently, *Lucy* (1991). Using language as sensuous and evocative as the place she's describing, Kincaid takes us to her birthplace, with its lush beauty and harsh historical realities, in the following selection.

JAMAICA KINCAID

Antigua: A Small Place

Antigua is beautiful. Antigua is too beautiful. Sometimes the beauty of it seems unreal. Sometimes the beauty of it seems as if it were stage sets for a play, for no real sunset could look like that; no real seawater could strike that many shades of blue at once; no real sky could be that shade of blue—another shade of blue, completely different from the shades of blue seen in the sea—and no real cloud 1

could be that white and float just that way in that blue sky; no real day could be that sort of sunny and bright, making everything seem transparent and shallow; and no real night could be that sort of black, making everything seem thick and deep and bottomless. No real day and no real night could be that evenly divided—twelve hours of one and twelve hours of the other; no real day would begin that dramatically or end that dramatically (there is no dawn in Antigua: one minute, you are in the complete darkness of night; the next minute, the sun is overhead and it stays there until it sets with an explosion of reds on the horizon, and then the darkness of night comes again, and it is as if the open lid of a box you are inside suddenly snaps into place). No real sand on any real shore is that fine or that white (in some places) or that pink (in other places); no real flowers could be these shades of red, purple, yellow, orange, blue, white; no real lily would bloom only at night and perfume the air with a sweetness so thick it makes you slightly sick; no real earth is that colour brown; no real grass is that particular shade of dilapidated, run-down green (not enough rain); no real cows look that poorly as they feed on the unreal-looking grass in the unreal-looking pasture, and no real cows look quite that miserable as some unreal-looking white egrets sit on their backs eating insects; no real rain would fall with that much force, so that it tears up the parched earth. No real village in any real countryside would be named Table Hill Gordon, and no real village with such a name would be so beautiful in its pauperedness, its simpleness, its one-room houses painted in unreal shades of pink and yellow and green, a dog asleep in the shade, some flies asleep in the corner of the dog's mouth. Or the market on a Saturday morning, where the colours of the fruits and vegetables and the colours of the clothes people are wearing and the colour of the day itself, and the colour of the nearby sea, and the colour of the sky, which is just overhead and seems so close you might reach up and touch it, and the way the people there speak English (they break it up) and the way they might be angry with each other and the sound they make when they laugh, all of this is so beautiful, all of this is not real like any other real thing that there is. It is as if, then, the beauty—the beauty of the sea, the land, the air, the trees, the market, the people, the sounds they make—were a prison, and as if everything and everybody inside it were locked in and everything and everybody that is not inside it were locked out. And what might it do to ordinary people to live in this way every day? What might it do to them to live in such heightened, intense surroundings day after day? They have nothing to compare this incredible constant with, no big historical moment to compare the way they are now to the way they used to be. No Industrial Revolution, no revolution of any kind, no Age of Anything, no world wars, no decades of turbulence balanced by decades of calm. Nothing, then, natural or unnatural, to leave a mark on their character. It is just a little island. The unreal way in which it is beautiful now is the unreal way in which it was always beautiful.

The unreal way in which it is beautiful now that they are a free people is the unreal way in which it was beautiful when they were slaves.

2 Again, Antigua is a small place, a small island. It is nine miles wide by twelve miles long. It was discovered by Christopher Columbus in 1493. Not too long after, it was settled by human rubbish from Europe, who used enslaved but noble and exalted human beings from Africa (all masters of every stripe are rubbish, and all slaves of every stripe are noble and exalted; there can be no question about this) to satisfy their desire for wealth and power, to feel better about their own miserable existence, so that they could be less lonely and empty—a European disease. Eventually, the masters left, in a kind of way; eventually, the slaves were freed, in a kind of way. The people in Antigua now, the people who really think of themselves as Antiguans (and the people who would immediately come to your mind when you think about what Antiguans might be like; I mean, supposing you were to think about it), are the descendants of those noble and exalted people, the slaves. Of course, the whole thing is, once you cease to be a master, once you throw off your master's yoke, you are no longer human rubbish, you are just a human being, and all the things that adds up to. So, too, with the slaves. Once they are no longer slaves, once they are free, they are no longer noble and exalted; they are just human beings.

COMPREHENSION

1. What actual facts about Antigua and its people does the reader extract from the writer's lyrical descriptions?
2. What is the significance of the title?
3. How does Kincaid define *master* and *slave?*

RHETORIC

1. What situation does the writer set up with the first two sentences of the essay? What effect does the use of "too" have on the reader? How does it help set a tone for the following images?
2. How does repetition and rhythm help to set up a mood in the first paragraph? What response is called for? Identify specific words that resonate through the passage, and explain why they're powerful.
3. Why does Kincaid break the mood of her descriptions in several places with parenthetical information? How do these interruptions serve to alert the reader?
4. Find the line in the first paragraph where the images in Kincaid's piece begin to change. What does the writer wish to convey with this change? Locate a couple of images that show the writer's shift.
5. How does the "prison" metaphor work? What is Kincaid saying about Antigua's place in the world? How does the rest of the paragraph help define "little island" in a historical context?

6. How does the juxtaposition of "real" and "unreal" elements aid in the development of Kincaid's thesis?
7. What tone and style does Kincaid adopt in the last paragraph? Contrast them to the language and mood originally set up.

WRITING

1. Write an essay in which you attempt to answer Kincaid's question: "And what might it do to ordinary people to live in this way every day?" referring to Antigua's beauty as a prison. How does such isolation help or hinder the inhabitants?
2. Using support from Kincaid's essay as well as Orwell's "Shooting an Elephant," consider the effects of slavery on the native population of a country as well as on the landscape itself.
3. Write a research paper that combines Kincaid's personal view of Antigua with factual, historical information about its geography and inhabitants. How does one approach enrich the other?

PABLO NERUDA Pablo Neruda (1904–1973), one of the greatest modern poets writing in Spanish, was born in Parral, Chile, the son of a railway worker. He studied in Santiago from 1923 to 1926, publishing five volumes of poetry. Later he served as Chilean counsel in Burma, Ceylon, Java, Spain, and Mexico. Neruda, a Communist, was elected to the Chilean senate in 1945 but was driven into hiding and eventual exile in 1948. He returned to Chile in 1952 and remained active as a poet-politician up to his untimely death twelve days after the coup that overthrew President Allende. Neruda's major volumes of poetry include *Residence on Earth* (1925–1945), *Elementary Odes* (1954–1957), *Estravagaria* (1958), and *A Hundred Love Sonnets* (1960). The following essay, in a translation by Margaret Sayers Peden, comes from *Passions and Impressions* (1982). It reflects the broad range of images, figurative language, and heightened meanings that also endow Neruda's poetry with such power.

PABLO NERUDA

The Odors of Homecoming

My house nestles among many trees. After a long absence, I like to lose myself in hidden nooks to savor my homecoming. Mysterious, fragrant thickets have appeared that are new to me. The poplar I planted in the back of the garden, so slim it could barely be seen, is now an adult tree. Its bark is patterned with wrinkles of wisdom that 1

rise toward the sky to express themselves in a constant tremor of new leaves in the treetop.

The chestnut trees were the last to recognize me. When I arrived, 2
their naked, dry branches, towering and unseeing, seemed imperious and hostile, though the pervading spring of Chile was germinating amid their trunks. Every day I went to call on them, for I understood that they demanded my homage, and in the cold of morning stood motionless beneath the leafless branches, until one day a timid green bud, high overhead, came out to look at me, and others followed. So my reappearance was communicated to the wary, hidden leaves of the tallest chestnut tree, which now greets me with condescension, tolerating my return.

In the trees the birds renew their age-old trills, as if nothing ever 3
happened beneath the leaves.

A pervasive odor of winter and years lingers in the library. Of all 4
places, this was the most suffused with absence.

There is something of mortality about the smell of musty books; it 5
assaults the nostrils and strikes the rugged terrain of the soul, because it is the odor of oblivion, of buried memory.

Standing beside the weathered window, staring at the blue and 6
white Andean sky, I sense that behind my back the aroma of spring is pitting its strength against the books. They resist being rooted out of their long neglect, and still exude signs of oblivion. Spring enters every room, clad in a new dress and the odor of honeysuckle.

The books have been unruly in my absence. None is missing, but 7
none is in its place. Beside an austere volume of Bacon, a rare seventeenth-century edition, I find Salgari's *The Captain of Yucatan,* and in spite of everything, they've got along rather well together. On the other hand, as I pick up a solitary Byron, its cover drops off like the dark wing of an albatross. Laboriously, I stitch spine and cover, but not before a puff of cold Romanticism clouds my eyes.

The shells are the most silent occupants of my house. They en- 8
dured the years of the ocean, solidifying their silence. Now, to those years have been added time and dust. Their cold, glinting mother-of-pearl, their concentric Gothic ellipses, their open valves, remind me of distant coasts, long-ago events. This incomparable lance of rosy light is the *Rostellaria,* which the Cuban malacologist Carlos de la Torre, a magus of the deep, once conferred upon me like an underseas decoration. And here, slightly more faded and dusty, is the black "olive" of the California seas, and, of the same provenance, the oyster of red spines and the oyster of black pearls. We almost drowned in that treasure-laden sea.

There are new occupants, books and objects liberated from boxes 9
long sealed. The pine boxes come from France. The boards smell of sunny noon in the Midi, and as I pry them open, they creak and sing, and the golden light falls on the red bindings of Victor Hugo. *Les Misérables,* in an early edition, arrives to crowd the walls of my house with its multitude of heartrending lives.

Then, from a large box resembling a coffin, comes the sweet face of 10
a woman, firm wooden breasts that once cleaved the wind, hands saturated with music and brine. It is the figure of a woman, a figurehead. I baptize her María Celeste, because she has all the mystery of a lost ship. I discovered her radiant beauty in a Paris *bric-á-brac,* buried beneath used hardware, disfigured by neglect, hidden beneath the sepulchral rags and tatters of the slums. Now, aloft, she sails again, alive and new. Every morning her cheeks will be covered by mysterious dew or saltwater tears.

All at once the roses are in bloom. Once I was an enemy of the rose, 11
of its interminable literary associations, of its arrogance. But as I watched them grow, having endured the winter with nothing to wear and nothing to cover their heads, and then as snowy breasts or glowing fires peered from among hard and thorny stems, little by little I was filled with tenderness, with admiration for their ox-like health, for the daring, secret wave of perfume and light they implacably extract from the black earth at just the right moment, as if duty were a miracle, as if they thrived on precise maneuvers in harsh weather. And now roses grow everywhere, with a moving solemnity I share—remote, both they and I, from pomp and frivolity, each absorbed in creating its individual flash of lightning.

Now every wave of air bears a soft, trembling movement, a 12
flowery palpitation that pierces the heart. Forgotten names, forgotten springs, hands that touched briefly, haughty eyes of yellow stone, tresses lost in time: youth, insistently throbbing with memories and ecstatic aromas.

It is the perfume of the honeysuckle, the first kisses of spring. 13

COMPREHENSION

1. What is the season? What are some of the "odors of homecoming" that Neruda detects? What do the odors and sights remind him of?
2. List the various objects that Neruda describes. What is his attitude toward them? Is it the same attitude as the one expressed by Thoreau in "Economy" (see Chapter 12)? Justify your answer.
3. What responses by Neruda to the odors of homecoming contribute to your understanding of the author?

RHETORIC

1. Analyze the sensory language in this essay. What senses does Neruda evoke? Cite examples. Describe the mood or atmosphere that the imagery creates.
2. Locate similes and metaphors in the essay. What do they contribute to the dominant impression?
3. What sentence in the introductory paragraph establishes the purpose of Neruda's description of his home? Is this the thesis statement? Why, or why not?

4. How does Neruda arrange descriptive details in paragraphs 1 to 3, 4 to 6, 7 to 10, and 11 to 13?
5. Neruda employs a considerable amount of personification in this essay. Cite and explain examples of this method. What cumulative impression is created?
6. What effect is achieved by the relatively short paragraphs 3, 4, and 5 and by the one-sentence conclusion?

WRITING

1. Is Neruda excessively impressionistic, romantic, or sentimental in this essay? Justify your response in a brief essay.
2. Describe a particularly vivid homecoming of your own. Incorporate sensory details and other poetic devices.
3. Write a descriptive paragraph that captures the dominant impression of a specific month or season.

N. SCOTT MOMADAY Navarre Scott Momaday (1934–), Pulitzer Prize-winning poet, critic, and academician, is the author of *House Made of Dawn* (1968), *The Way to Rainy Mountain* (1969), *The Names* (1976), and other works. "I am an American Indian (Kiowa), and am vitally interested in American Indian art, history and culture," Momaday has written. In this essay, he elevates personal experience to the realm of poetry and tribal myth.

N. SCOTT MOMADAY

The Way to Rainy Mountain

A single knoll rises out of the plain in Oklahoma, north and west of the Wichita Range. For my people, the Kiowas, it is an old landmark, and they gave it the name Rainy Mountain. The hardest weather in the world is there. Winter brings blizzards, hot tornadic winds arise in the spring, and in summer the prairie is an anvil's edge. The grass turns brittle and brown, and it cracks beneath your feet. There are green belts along the rivers and creeks, linear groves of hickory and pecan, willow and witch hazel. At a distance in July or August the steaming foliage seems almost to writhe in fire. Great green and yellow grasshoppers are everywhere in the tall grass, popping up like corn to sting the flesh, and tortoises crawl about on the red earth, going nowhere in the plenty of time. Loneliness is an aspect of the land. All things in the plain are isolate; there is no confusion of objects in the eye, but *one* hill or *one* tree or *one* man. To look upon that landscape in the early morning, with the sun at your back, is to lose the sense of proportion. Your imagination comes to life, and this, you think, is where Creation was begun. 1

I returned to Rainy Mountain in July. My grandmother had died in 2
the spring, and I wanted to be at her grave. She had lived to be very old and at last infirm. Her only living daughter was with her when she died, and I was told that in death her face was that of a child.

I like to think of her as a child. When she was born, the Kiowas 3
were living the last great moment of their history. For more than a hundred years they had controlled the open range from the Smoky Hill River to the Red, from the headwaters of the Canadian to the fork of the Arkansas and Cimarron. In alliance with the Comanches, they had ruled the whole of the southern Plains. War was their sacred business, and they were among the finest horsemen the world has ever known. But warfare for the Kiowas was preeminently a matter of disposition rather than of survival, and they never understood the grim, unrelenting advance of the U.S. Cavalry. When at last, divided and ill-provisioned, they were driven onto the Staked Plains in the cold rains of autumn, they fell into panic. In Palo Duro Canyon they abandoned their crucial stores to pillage and had nothing then but their lives. In order to save themselves, they surrendered to the soldiers at Fort Sill and were imprisoned in the old stone corral that now stands as a military museum. My grandmother was spared the humiliation of those high gray walls by eight or ten years, but she must have known from birth the affliction of defeat, the dark brooding of old warriors.

Her name was Aho, and she belonged to the last culture to evolve in 4
North America. Her forebears came down from the high country in western Montana nearly three centuries ago. They were a mountain people, a mysterious tribe of hunters whose language has never been positively classified in any major group. In the late seventeenth century they began a long migration to the south and east. It was a journey toward the dawn, and it led to a golden age. Along the way the Kiowas were befriended by the Crows, who gave them the culture and religion of the Plains. They acquired horses, and their ancient nomadic spirit was suddenly free of the ground. They acquired Tai-me, the sacred Sun Dance doll, from that moment the object and symbol of their worship, and so shared in the divinity of the sun. Not least, they acquired the sense of destiny, therefore courage and pride. When they entered upon the southern Plains they had been transformed. No longer were they slaves to the simple necessity of survival; they were a lordly and dangerous society of fighters and thieves, hunters and priests of the sun. According to their origin myth, they entered the world through a hollow log. From one point of view, their migration was the fruit of an old prophecy, for indeed they emerged from a sunless world.

Although my grandmother lived out her long life in the shadow of 5
Rainy Mountain, the immense landscape of the continental interior lay like memory in her blood. She could tell of the Crows, whom she had never seen, and of the Black Hills, where she had never been. I wanted to see in reality what she had seen more perfectly in the mind's eye, and traveled fifteen hundred miles to begin my pilgrimage.

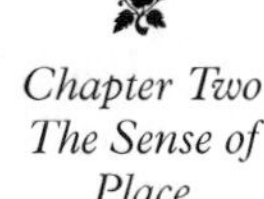

6 Yellowstone, it seemed to me, was the top of the world, a region of deep lakes and dark timber, canyons and waterfalls. But, beautiful as it is, one might have the sense of confinement there. The skyline in all directions is close at hand, the high wall of the woods and deep cleavages of shade. There is a perfect freedom in the mountains, but it belongs to the eagle and the elk, the badger and the bear. The Kiowas reckoned their stature by the distance they could see, and they were bent and blind in the wilderness.

7 Descending eastward, the highland meadows are a stairway to the plain. In July the inland slope of the Rockies is luxuriant with flax and buckwheat, stonecrop and larkspur. The earth unfolds and the limit of the land recedes. Clusters of trees, and animals grazing far in the distance, cause the vision to reach away and wonder to build upon the mind. The sun follows a longer course in the day, and the sky is immense beyond all comparison. The great billowing clouds that sail upon it are shadows that move upon the grain like water, dividing light. Farther down, in the land of the Crows and Blackfeet, the plain is yellow. Sweet clover takes hold of the hills and bends upon itself to cover and seal the soil. There the Kiowas paused on their way; they had come to the place where they must change their lives. The sun is at home on the plains. Precisely there does it have the certain character of a god. When the Kiowas came to the land of the Crows, they could see the dark lees of the hills at dawn across the Bighorn River, the profusion of light on the grain shelves, the oldest deity ranging after the solstices. Not yet would they veer southward to the caldron of the land that lay below; they must wean their blood from the northern winter and hold the mountains a while longer in their view. They bore Tai-me in procession to the east.

8 A dark mist lay over the Black Hills, and the land was like iron. At the top of a ridge I caught sight of Devil's Tower upthrust against the gray sky as if in the birth of time the core of the earth had broken through its crust and the motion of the world was begun. There are things in nature that engender an awful quiet in the heart of man; Devil's Tower is one of them. Two centuries ago, because they could not do otherwise, the Kiowas made a legend at the base of the rock. My grandmother said:

> Eight children were there at play, seven sisters and their brother. Suddenly the boy was struck dumb; he trembled and began to run upon his hands and feet. His fingers became claws, and his body was covered with fur. Directly there was a bear where the boy had been. The sisters were terrified; they ran, and the bear after them. They came to the stump of a great tree, and the tree spoke to them. It bade them climb upon it, and as they did so it began to rise into the air. The bear came to kill them, but they were just beyond its reach. It reared against the tree and scored the bark all around with its claws. The seven sisters were borne into the sky, and they became the stars of the Big Dipper.

From that moment, and so long as the legend lives, the Kiowas have kinsmen in the night sky. Whatever they were in the mountains, they could be no more. However tenuous their well-being, however much they had suffered and would suffer again, they had found a way out of the wilderness.

9 My grandmother had a reverence for the sun, a holy regard that now is all but gone out of mankind. There was a wariness in her, and an ancient awe. She was a Christian in her later years, but she had come a long way about, and she never forgot her birthright. As a child she had been to the Sun Dances; she had taken part in those annual rites, and by them she had learned the restoration of her people in the presence of Tai-me. She was about seven when the last Kiowa Sun Dance was held in 1887 on the Washita River above Rainy Mountain Creek. The buffalo were gone. In order to consummate the ancient sacrifice—to impale the head of a buffalo bull upon the medicine tree—a delegation of old men journeyed into Texas, there to beg and barter for an animal from the Goodnight herd. She was ten when the Kiowas came together for the last time as a living Sun Dance culture. They could find no buffalo; they had to hang an old hide from the sacred tree. Before the dance could begin, a company of soldiers rode out from Fort Sill under orders to disperse the tribe. Forbidden without cause the essential act of their faith, having seen the wild herds slaughtered and left to rot upon the ground, the Kiowas backed away forever from the medicine tree. That was July 20, 1890, at the great bend of the Washita. My grandmother was there. Without bitterness, and for as long as she lived, she bore a vision of deicide.

10 Now that I can have her only in memory, I see my grandmother in the several postures that were peculiar to her: standing at the wood stove on a winter morning and turning meat in a great iron skillet; sitting at the south window, bent above her beadwork, and afterwards, when her vision failed, looking down for a long time into the fold of her hands; going out upon a cane, very slowly as she did when the weight of age came upon her; praying. I remember her most often at prayer. She made long, rambling prayers out of suffering and hope, having seen many things. I was never sure that I had the right to hear, so exclusive were they of all mere custom and company. The last time I saw her she prayed standing by the side of her bed at night, naked to the waist, the light of a kerosene lamp moving upon her dark skin. Her long, black hair, always drawn and braided in the day, lay upon her shoulders and against her breasts like a shawl. I do not speak Kiowa, and I never understood her prayers, but there was something inherently sad in the sound, some merest hesitation upon the syllables of sorrow. She began in a high and descending pitch, exhausting her breath to silence; then again and again—and always the same intensity of effort, of something that is, and is not, like urgency in the human voice. Transported so in the dancing light among the shadows of her room, she seemed beyond the reach of time. But that was illusion; I think I knew then that I should not see her again.

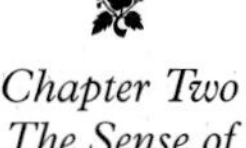

Chapter Two
The Sense of Place

Houses are like sentinels in the plain, old keepers of the weather watch. There, in a very little while, wood takes on the appearance of great age. All colors wear soon away in the wind and rain, and then the wood is burned gray and the grain appears and the nails turn red with rust. The windowpanes are black and opaque; you imagine there is nothing within, and indeed there are many ghosts, bones given up to the land. They stand here and there against the sky, and you approach them for a longer time than you expect. They belong in the distance; it is their domain. 11

Once there was a lot of sound in my grandmother's house, a lot of coming and going, feasting and talk. The summers there were full of excitement and reunion. The Kiowas are a summer people; they abide the cold and keep to themselves, but when the season turns and the land becomes warm and vital they cannot hold still; an old love of going returns upon them. The aged visitors who came to my grandmother's house when I was a child were made of lean and leather, and they bore themselves upright. They wore great black hats and bright ample shirts that shook in the wind. They rubbed fat upon their hair and wound their braids with strips of colored cloth. Some of them painted their faces and carried the scars of old and cherished enmities. They were an old council of warlords, come to remind and be reminded of who they were. Their wives and daughters served them well. The women might indulge themselves; gossip was at once the mark and compensation of their servitude. They made loud and elaborate talk among themselves, full of jest and gesture, fright and false alarm. They went abroad in fringed and flowered shawls, bright beadwork and German silver. They were at home in the kitchen, and they prepared meals that were banquets. 12

There were frequent prayer meetings, and great nocturnal feasts. When I was a child I played with my cousins outside, where the lamplight fell upon the ground and the singing of the old people rose up around us and carried away into the darkness. There were a lot of good things to eat, a lot of laughter and surprise. And afterwards, when the quiet returned, I lay down with my grandmother and could hear the frogs away by the river and feel the motion of the air. 13

Now there is funeral silence in the rooms, the endless wake of some final word. The walls have closed in upon my grandmother's house. When I returned to it in mourning, I saw for the first time in my life how small it was. It was late at night, and there was a white moon, nearly full. I sat for a long time on the stone steps by the kitchen door. From there I could see out across the land; I could see the long row of trees by the creek, the low light upon the rolling plains, and the stars of the Big Dipper. Once I looked at the moon and caught sight of a strange thing. A cricket had perched upon the handrail, only a few inches away from me. My line of vision was such that the creature filled the moon like a fossil. It had gone there, I thought, to live and die, for there, of all places, was its small definition made whole and eternal. A warm wind rose up and purled like the longing within me. 14

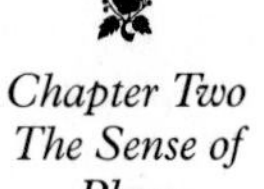

The next morning I awoke at dawn and went out on the dirt road to 15
Rainy Mountain. It was already hot, and the grasshoppers began to fill the air. Still, it was early in the morning, and the birds sang out of the shadows. The long yellow grass on the mountain shone in the bright light, and a scissortail hied above the land. There, where it ought to be, at the end of a long and legendary way, was my grandmother's grave. Here and there on the dark stones were ancestral names. Looking back once, I saw the mountain and came away.

COMPREHENSION

1. What is the significance of Momaday's title? How does the title help to explain the author's purpose?
2. Why does Momaday return to his grandmother's house and journey to her grave?
3. List the various myths and legends the author mentions in the essay. What subjects do they treat? How are these subjects interrelated?

RHETORIC

1. Locate and explain instances of sensory, metaphorical, and symbolic language in the essay. Why are these modes of language consistent with the subject and theme elaborated by Momaday?
2. How does Momaday's use of abstract language affect the concrete vocabulary in the essay?
3. What is the method of development in the first paragraph? How does the introduction serve as a vehicle for the central meanings in the essay?
4. Consider the relationship of narration to description in the organization of the essay. What forms of narrative serve to unify the selection? Are the narrative patterns strictly linear, or do they shift for other purposes? Explain. In what sense is Momaday's descriptive technique cinematic?
5. How do the land, the Kiowas, and Momaday's grandmother serve as reinforcing frames of the essay?
6. Describe in detail the creation of mood in this essay. Explain specifically the mood at the conclusion.

WRITING

1. Momaday implies that myth is central to his life and the life of the Kiowas. What *is* myth? Do you think that myth is as strong in general American culture as it is in Kiowa culture? In what ways does it operate? How can myth sustain the individual, community, and nation? Write an analytical essay on this subject.
2. Write about a person and place that, taken together, inspire a special reverence in you.

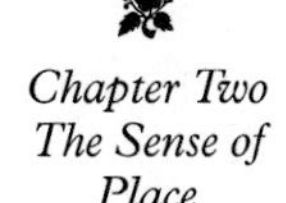

3. In an essay, explore the ways in which environment molds personality in "The Way to Rainy Mountain" and in "Wyoming: The Solace of Open Spaces" by Gretel Ehrlich (see pp. 556–561).

CLASSIC AND CONTEMPORARY

E. B. WHITE Elwyn Brooks White (1899–1985), one of the finest American essayists, is at his most distinctive when treating people and nature. A recipient of the National Medal for literature and associated for years with *The New Yorker,* White is the author of *One Man's Meat* (1942), *Here Is New York* (1949), and *The Second Tree from the Corner* (1954), among numerous other works. A selection of his essays appeared in 1977. He is also a talented writer of literature for children, including *Stuart Little* (1945), *Charlotte's Web* (1952), and *The Trumpet of the Swan* (1970). In the following essay, White brings to life the excitingly complex rhythms of one of the world's great cities.

E. B. WHITE

Here Is New York

There are roughly three New Yorks. There is, first, the New York of the 1
man or woman who was born here, who takes the city for granted and accepts its size and its turbulence as natural and inevitable. Second, there is the New York of the commuter—the city that is devoured by locusts each day and spat out each night. Third, there is the New York of the person who was born somewhere else and came to New York in quest of something. Of these three trembling cities the greatest is the last—the city of final destination, the city that is a goal. It is this third city that accounts for New York's high-strung disposition, its poetical deportment, its dedication to the arts, and its incomparable achievements. Commuters give the city its tidal restlessness; natives give it solidity and continuity; but the settlers give it passion. And whether it is a farmer arriving from Italy to set up a small grocery store in a slum, or a young girl arriving from a small town in Mississippi to escape the indignity of being observed by her neighbors, or a boy arriving from the Corn Belt with a manuscript in his suitcase and a pain in his heart, it makes no difference: each embraces New York with the intense excitement of first love, each absorbs New York with the fresh eyes of an adventurer, each generates heat and light to dwarf the Consolidated Edison Company.

The commuter is the queerest bird of all. The suburb he inhabits 2
has no essential vitality of its own and is a mere roost where he comes at day's end to go to sleep. Except in rare cases, the man who lives in Mamaroneck or Little Neck or Teaneck, and works in New York, discovers nothing much about the city except the time of arrival and departure of trains and buses, and the path to a quick lunch. He is desk-bound, and has never, idly roaming in the gloaming, stumbled suddenly on Belvedere Tower in the Park, seen the ramparts rise sheer from the water of the pond, and the boys along the shore fishing for minnows, girls stretched out negligently on the shelves of the rocks; he has never come suddenly on anything at all in New York as a loiterer, because he has had no time between trains. He has fished in Manhattan's wallet and dug out coins, but has never listened to Manhattan's breathing, never awakened to its morning, never dropped off to sleep in its night. About 400,000 men and women come charging onto the Island each week-day morning, out of the mouths of tubes and tunnels. Not many among them have ever spent a drowsy afternoon in the great rustling oaken silence of the reading room of the Public Library, with the book elevator (like an old water wheel) spewing out books onto the trays. They tend their furnaces in Westchester and in Jersey, but have never seen the furnaces of the Bowery, the fires that burn in oil drums on zero winter nights. They may work in the financial district downtown and never see the extravagant plantings of Rockefeller Center—the daffodils and grape hyacinths and birches and the flags trimmed to the wind on a fine morning in spring. Or they may work in a midtown office and may let a whole year swing round without sighting Governors Island from the sea wall. The commuter dies with tremendous mileage to his credit, but he is no rover. His entrances and exits are more devious than those in a prairie-dog village; and he calmly plays bridge while buried in the mud at the bottom of the East River. The Long Island Rail Road alone carried forty million commuters last year; but many of them were the same fellow retracing his steps.

The terrain of New York is such that a resident sometimes travels 3
farther, in the end, than a commuter. Irving Berlin's journey from Cherry Street in the lower East Side to an apartment uptown was through an alley and was only three or four miles in length; but it was like going three times around the world.

COMPREHENSION

1. What are the three New Yorks in White's essay?
2. When do you think this essay was written? What is your evidence from the text?
3. Which New York is White's favorite, and why?

RHETORIC

1. What is the writer's thesis? Is it stated explicitly? Explain.
2. How does the author support his claim that New York's "settlers give it passion"?
3. What concrete examples aid in establishing the city's reality? Which images conjure an "imagined" place?
4. Explain White's scheme of classification. Do all New Yorks get an equal share of attention?
5. Examine White's writing style, explaining how it is compatible with his subject matter.

WRITING

1. Compare and contrast New York (or any large city) with the suburbs. Do you agree with White's unflattering portrait of suburbia? Use figurative as well as concrete language to support your views.
2. If you live in or near a big city, which of White's categories do you fit into? Describe your relation to the city and its people. How do you experience the city?
3. Write your own classification essay, entitled "The Three ______." Focus on a specific place as the subject of this classification essay.

JOAN DIDION Joan Didion (1934–) grew up in California and graduated from the University of California at Berkeley in 1956. She began writing for national magazines such as *Mademoiselle, The Saturday Evening Post,* and *Life.* She published her first novel, *Run River,* in 1963. Although she has continued to write novels and has written several screenplays, her most acclaimed work is nonfiction. This includes *Slouching Towards Bethlehem* (1968), *The White Album* (1979), *Salvador* (1983), *Democracy* (1984), *Miami* (1987), and her latest collection, *After Henry* (1992). In the following selection from *Miami,* Didion describes a city rich in ethnic diversity yet torn along lines of mistrust and fear.

JOAN DIDION

Miami: The Cuban Presence

On the 150th anniversary of the founding of Dade County, in February of 1986, the *Miami Herald* asked four prominent amateurs of local history to name "the ten people and the ten events that had the most impact on the county's history." Each of the four submitted his or her own list of "The Most Influential People in Dade's History," and among the names mentioned were Julia Tuttle ("pioneer business- 1

woman"), Henry Flagler ("brought the Florida East Coast Railway to Miami"), Alexander Orr, Jr. ("started the research that saved Miami's drinking water from salt"), Everest George Sewell ("publicized the city and fostered its deepwater seaport"). . . . There was Dr. James M. Jackson, an early Miami physician. There was Napoleon Bonaparte Broward, the governor of Florida who initiated the draining of the Everglades. There appeared on three of the four lists the name of the developer of Coral Gables, George Merrick. There appeared on one of the four lists the name of the coach of the Miami Dolphins, Don Shula.

On none of these lists of "The Most Influential People in Dade's 2
History" did the name Fidel Castro appear, nor for that matter did the name of any Cuban, although the presence of Cubans in Dade County did not go entirely unnoted by the *Herald* panel. When it came to naming the Ten Most Important "Events," as opposed to "People," all four panelists mentioned the arrival of the Cubans, but at slightly off angles ("Mariel Boatlift of 1980" was the way one panelist saw it), and as if the arrival had been just another of those isolated disasters or innovations which deflect the course of any growing community, on an approximate par with the other events mentioned, for example the Freeze of 1895, the Hurricane of 1926, the opening of the Dixie Highway, the establishment of Miami International Airport, and the adoption, in 1957, of the metropolitan form of government, "enabling the Dade County Commission to provide urban services to the increasingly populous unincorporated area."

This set of mind, in which the local Cuban community was seen as 3
a civic challenge determinedly met, was not uncommon among Anglos to whom I talked in Miami, many of whom persisted in the related illusions that the city was small, manageable, prosperous in a predictable broad-based way, Southern in a progressive Sunbelt way, American, and belonged to them. In fact 43 percent of the population of Dade County was by that time "Hispanic," which meant mostly Cuban. Fifty-six percent of the population of Miami itself was Hispanic. The most visible new buildings on the Miami skyline, the Arquitectonica buildings along Brickell Avenue, were by a firm with a Cuban founder. There were Cubans in the board rooms of the major banks, Cubans in clubs that did not admit Jews or blacks, and four Cubans in the most recent mayoralty campaign, two of whom, Raul Masvidal and Xavier Suarez, had beaten out the incumbent and all other candidates to meet in a runoff, and one of whom, Xavier Suarez, a thirty-six-year-old lawyer who had been brought from Cuba to the United States as a child, was by then mayor of Miami.

The entire tone of the city, the way people looked and talked and 4
met one another, was Cuban. The very image the city had begun presenting of itself, what was then its newfound glamour, its "hotness" (hot colors, hot vice, shady dealings under the palm trees), was that of prerevolutionary Havana, as perceived by Americans. There was even in the way women dressed in Miami a definable Havana look, a more distinct emphasis on the hips and décolletage, more black, more veiling,

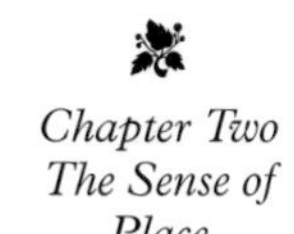

a generalized flirtatiousness of style not then current in American cities. In the shoe departments at Burdine's and Jordan Marsh there were more platform soles than there might have been in another American city, and fewer displays of the running shoe ethic. I recall being struck, during an afternoon spent at La Liga Contra el Cancer, a prominent exile charity which raises money to help cancer patients, by the appearance of the volunteers who had met that day to stuff envelopes for a benefit. Their hair was sleek, of a slightly other period, immaculate pageboys and French twists. They wore Bruno Magli pumps, and silk and linen dresses of considerable expense. There seemed to be a preference for strictest gray or black, but the effect remained lush, tropical, like a room full of perfectly groomed mangoes.

This was not, in other words, an invisible 56 percent of the popula- 5
tion. Even the social notes in *Diario Las Americas* and in *El Herald,* the daily Spanish edition of the *Herald* written and edited for *el exilio,* suggested a dominant culture, one with money to spend and a notable willingness to spend it in public. La Liga Contra el Cancer alone sponsored, in a single year, two benefit dinner dances, one benefit ball, a benefit children's fashion show, a benefit telethon, a benefit exhibition of jewelry, a benefit presentation of Miss Universe contestants, and a benefit showing, with Saks Fifth Avenue and chicken *vol-au-vent,* of the Adolfo (as it happened, a Cuban) fall collection.

One morning *El Herald* would bring news of the gala at the Pavillon 6
of the Amigos Latinamericanos del Museo de Ciencia y Planetarium; another morning, of an upcoming event at the Big Five Club, a Miami club founded by former members of five fashionable clubs in prerevolutionary Havana: a *coctel,* or cocktail party, at which tables would be assigned for yet another gala, the annual "Baile Imperial de las Rosas" of the American Cancer Society, Hispanic Ladies Auxiliary. Some members of the community were honoring Miss America Latina with dinner dancing at the Doral. Some were being honored themselves, at the Spirit of Excellence Awards Dinner at the Omni. Some were said to be enjoying the skiing at Vail; others to prefer Bariloche, in Argentina. Some were reported unable to attend (but sending checks for) the gala at the Pavillon of the Amigos Latinamericanos del Museo de Ciencia y Planetarium because of a scheduling conflict, with *el coctel de* Paula Hawkins.

Fete followed fete, all high visibility. Almost any day it was possible 7
to drive past the limestone arches and fountains which marked the boundaries of Coral Gables and see little girls being photographed in the tiaras and ruffled hoop skirts and maribou-trimmed illusion capes they would wear at their *quinces,* the elaborate fifteenth-birthday parties at which the community's female children come of official age. The favored facial expression for a *quince* photograph was a classic smolder. The favored backdrop was one suggesting Castilian grandeur, which was how the Coral Gables arches happened to figure. Since the idealization of the virgin implicit in the *quince* could exist only in the presence of its natural foil, *machismo,* there was often a brother around, or a

boyfriend. There was also a mother, in dark glasses, not only to protect the symbolic virgin but to point out the better angle, the more aristocratic location. The *quinceanera* would pick up her hoop skirts and move as directed, often revealing the scuffed Jellies she had worn that day to school. A few weeks later there she would be, transformed in *Diario Las Americas*, one of the morning battalion of smoldering fifteen-year-olds, each with her arch, her fountain, her borrowed scenery, the gift if not exactly the intention of the late George Merrick, who built the arches when he developed Coral Gables.

Neither the photographs of the Cuban *quinceaneras* nor the notes 8
about the *coctel* at the Big Five were apt to appear in the newspapers read by Miami Anglos, nor, for that matter, was much information at all about the daily life of the Cuban majority. When, in the fall of 1986, Florida International University offered an evening course called "Cuban Miami: A Guide for Non-Cubans," the *Herald* sent a staff writer, who covered the classes as if from a distant beat. "Already I have begun to make some sense out of a culture, that, while it totally surrounds us, has remained inaccessible and alien to me," the *Herald* writer was reporting by the end of the first meeting, and, by the end of the fourth:

> What I see day to day in Miami, moving through mostly Anglo corridors of the community, are just small bits and pieces of that other world, the tip of something much larger than I'd imagined. . . . We may frequent the restaurants here, or wander into the occasional festival. But mostly we try to ignore Cuban Miami, even as we rub up against this teeming, incomprehensible presence.

Only thirteen people, including the *Herald* writer, turned up for the 9
first meeting of "Cuban Miami: A Guide for Non-Cubans" (two more appeared at the second meeting, along with a security guard, because of telephone threats prompted by what the *Herald* writer called "somebody's twisted sense of national pride"), an enrollment which suggested a certain willingness among non-Cubans to let Cuban Miami remain just that, Cuban, the "incomprehensible presence." In fact there had come to exist in South Florida two parallel cultures, separate but not exactly equal, a key distinction being that only one of the two, the Cuban, exhibited even a remote interest in the activities of the other. "The American community is not really aware of what is happening in the Cuban community," an exiled banker named Luis Botifoll said in a 1983 *Herald* Sunday magazine piece about ten prominent local Cubans. "We are clannish, but at least we know who is whom in the American establishment. They do not." About another of the ten Cubans featured in this piece, Jorge Mas Canosa, the *Herald* had this to say:

> He is an advisor to U.S. senators, a confidant of federal bureaucrats, a lobbyist for anti-Castro U.S. policies, a near unknown in Miami. When his political group sponsored a luncheon speech in Miami by Secretary of Defense Caspar Weinberger, almost none of the American business leaders attending had ever heard of their Cuban host.

The general direction of this piece, which appeared under the cover 10
line "THE CUBANS: *They're ten of the most powerful men in Miami. Half the population doesn't know it,*" was, as the *Herald* put it,

> to challenge the widespread presumption that Miami's Cubans are not really Americans, that they are a foreign presence here, an exile community that is trying to turn South Florida into North Cuba. . . . The top ten are not separatists; they have achieved success in the most traditional ways. They are the solid, bedrock citizens, hard-working humanitarians who are role models for a community that seems determined to assimilate itself into American society.

This was interesting. It was written by one of the few Cubans then 11
on the *Herald* staff, and yet it described, however unwittingly, the precise angle at which Miami Anglos and Miami Cubans were failing to connect: Miami Anglos were in fact interested in Cubans only to the extent that they could cast them as aspiring immigrants, "determined to assimilate," a "hard-working" minority not different in kind from other groups of resident aliens. (But had I met any Haitians, a number of Anglos asked when I said that I had been talking to Cubans.) Anglos (who were, significantly, referred to within the Cuban community as "Americans") spoke of cross-culturalization, and of what they believed to be a meaningful second-generation preference for hamburgers, and rock-and-roll. They spoke of "diversity," and of Miami's "Hispanic flavor," an approach in which 56 percent of the population was seen as decorative, like the Coral Gables arches.

Fixed as they were on this image of the melting pot, of immigrants 12
fleeing a disruptive revolution to find a place in the American sun, Anglos did not on the whole understand that assimilation would be considered by most Cubans a doubtful goal at best. Nor did many Anglos understand that living in Florida was still at the deepest level construed by Cubans as a temporary condition, an accepted political option shaped by the continuing dream, if no longer the immediate expectation, of a vindicatory return. *El exilio* was for Cubans a ritual, a respected tradition. *La revolución* was also a ritual, a trope fixed in Cuban political rhetoric at least since José Martí, a concept broadly interpreted to mean reform, or progress, or even just change. Ramón Grau San Martín, the president of Cuba during the autumn of 1933 and from 1944 until 1948, had presented himself as a revolutionary, as had his 1948 successor, Carlos Prío. Even Fulgencio Batista had entered Havana life calling for *la revolución,* and had later been accused of betraying it, even as Fidel Castro was now.

This was a process Cuban Miami understood, but Anglo Miami did 13
not, remaining as it did arrestingly innocent of even the most general information about Cuba and Cubans. Miami Anglos for example still had trouble with Cuban names, and Cuban food. When the Cuban novelist Guillermo Cabrera Infante came from London to lecture at Miami-Dade Community College, he was referred to by several Anglo

faculty members to whom I spoke as "Infante." Cuban food was widely seen not as a minute variation on that eaten throughout both the Caribbean and the Mediterranean but as "exotic," and full of garlic. A typical Thursday food section of the *Herald* included recipes for Broiled Lemon-Curry Cornish Game Hens, Chicken Tetrazzini, King Cake, Pimiento Cheese, Raisin Sauce for Ham, Sauteed Spiced Peaches, Shrimp Scampi, Easy Beefy Stir-Fry, and four ways to use dried beans ("Those cheap, humble beans that have long sustained the world's poor have become the trendy set's new pet"), none of them Cuban.

This was all consistent, and proceeded from the original construction, that of the exile as an immigration. There was no reason to be curious about Cuban food, because Cuban teenagers preferred hamburgers. There was no reason to get Cuban names right, because they were complicated, and would be simplified by the second generation, or even by the first. "Jorge L. Mas" was the way Jorge Mas Canosa's business card read. "Raul Masvidal" was the way Raul Masvidal y Jury ran for mayor of Miami. There was no reason to know about Cuban history, because history was what immigrants were fleeing. 14

Even the revolution, the reason for the immigration, could be covered in a few broad strokes: "Batista," "Castro," "26 Julio," this last being the particular broad stroke that inspired the Miami Springs Holiday Inn, on July 26, 1985, the thirty-second anniversary of the day Fidel Castro attacked the Moncada Barracks and so launched his six-year struggle for power in Cuba, to run a bar special on Cuba Libres, thinking to attract local Cubans by commemorating their holiday. "It was a mistake," the manager said, besieged by outraged exiles. "The gentleman who did it is from Minnesota." 15

There was in fact no reason, in Miami as well as in Minnesota, to know anything at all about Cubans, since Miami Cubans were now, if not Americans, at least aspiring Americans, and worthy of Anglo attention to the exact extent that they were proving themselves, in the *Herald's* words, "role models for a community that seems determined to assimilate itself into American society"; or, as George Bush put it in a 1986 Miami address to the Cuban American National Foundation, "the most eloquent testimony I know to the basic strength and success of America, as well as to the basic weakness and failure of Communism and Fidel Castro." 16

The use of this special lens, through which the exiles were seen as a tribute to the American system, a point scored in the battle of the ideologies, tended to be encouraged by those outside observers who dropped down from the Northeast corridor for a look and a column or two. George Will, in *Newsweek,* saw Miami as "a new installment in the saga of America's absorptive capacity," and Southwest Eighth Street as the place where "these exemplary Americans," the seven Cubans who had been gotten together to brief him, "initiated a columnist to fried bananas and black-bean soup and other Cuban contributions to the 17 tanginess of American life." George Gilder, in *The Wilson Quarterly,* drew pretty much the same lesson from Southwest Eighth Street, finding it "more effervescently thriving than its crushed prototype," by which he seemed to mean Havana. In fact Eighth Street was for George Gilder a street that seemed to "percolate with the forbidden commerce of the dying island to the south . . . the Refrescos Cawy, the Competidora and El Cuño cigarettes, the *guayaberas,*[1] the Latin music pulsing from the storefronts, the pyramids of mangoes and tubers, gourds and plantains, the iced coconuts served with a straw, the new theaters showing the latest anti-Castro comedies."

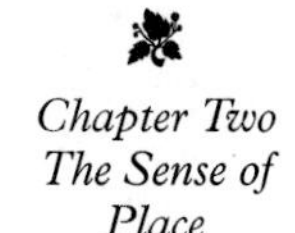

There was nothing on this list, with the possible exception of the "anti-Castro comedies," that could not most days be found on Southwest Eighth Street, but the list was also a fantasy, and a particularly *gringo* fantasy, one in which Miami Cubans, who came from a culture which had represented western civilization in this hemisphere since before there was a United States of America, appeared exclusively as vendors of plantains, their native music "pulsing" behind them. There was in any such view of Miami Cubans an extraordinary element of condescension, and it was the very condescension shared by Miami Anglos, who were inclined to reduce the particular liveliness and sophistication of local Cuban life to a matter of shrines on the lawn and love potions in the *botanicas,* the primitive exotica of the tourist's Caribbean. 18

Cubans were perceived as most satisfactory when they appeared most fully to share the aspirations and manners of middle-class Americans, at the same time adding "color" to the city on appropriate occasions, for example at their *quinces* (the *quinces* were one aspect of Cuban life almost invariably mentioned by Anglos, who tended to present them as evidence of Cuban extravagance, i.e., Cuban irresponsibility, or childishness), or on the day of the annual Calle Ocho Festival, when they could, according to the *Herald,* "samba" in the streets and stir up a paella for two thousand (ten cooks, two thousand mussels, two hundred and twenty pounds of lobster, and four hundred and forty pounds of rice), using rowboat oars as spoons. Cubans were perceived as least satisfactory when they "acted clannish," "kept to themselves," "had their own ways," and, two frequent flash points, "spoke Spanish when they didn't need to" and "got political"; complaints, each of them, which suggested an Anglo view of what Cubans should be at significant odds with what Cubans were. 19

This question of language was curious. The sound of spoken Spanish was common in Miami, but it was also common in Los Angeles, and Houston, and even in the cities of the Northeast. What was unusual about Spanish in Miami was not that it was so often spoken, but that it was so often heard: In, say, Los Angeles, Spanish remained a language only barely registered by the Anglo population, part of the ambient noise, the language spoken by the people who worked in 20

[1]guayaberas: summer shirts. (Ed.)

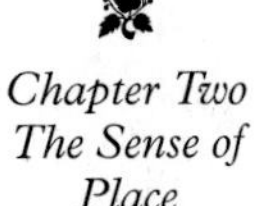

the car wash and came to trim the trees and cleared the tables in restaurants. In Miami Spanish was spoken by the people who ate in the restaurants, the people who owned the cars and the trees, which made, on the socio-auditory scale, a considerable difference. Exiles who felt isolated or declassed by language in New York or Los Angeles thrived in Miami. An entrepreneur who spoke no English could still, in Miami, buy, sell, negotiate, leverage assets, float bonds, and, if he were so inclined, attend galas twice a week, in black tie. "I have been after the *Herald* ten times to do a story about millionaires in Miami who do not speak more than two words in English," one prominent exile told me. "'Yes' and 'no.' Those are the two words. They come here with five dollars in their pockets and without speaking another word of English they are millionaires."

The truculence a millionaire who spoke only two words of English 21
might provoke among the less resourceful native citizens of a nominally American city was predictable, and manifested itself rather directly. In 1980, the year of Mariel, Dade County voters had approved a referendum requiring that county business be conducted exclusively in English. Notwithstanding the fact that this legislation was necessarily amended to exclude emergency medical and certain other services, and notwithstanding even the fact that many local meetings continued to be conducted in that unbroken alternation of Spanish and English which had become the local patois ("I will be in Boston on Sunday and *desafortunadamente yo tengo un compromiso en* Boston *qu no puedo romper y yo no podre estar con Vds.*," read the minutes of a 1984 Miami City Commission meeting I had occasion to look up. "*En espiritu, estaré, pero* the other members of the commission I am sure are invited . . . "),[2] the very existence of this referendum was seen by many as ground regained, a point made. By 1985 a St. Petersburg optometrist named Robert Melby was launching his third attempt in four years to have English declared the official language of the state of Florida, as it would be in 1986 of California. "I don't know why your legislators here are so, how should I put it?—spineless," Robert Melby complained about those South Florida politicians who knew how to count. "No one down here seems to want to run with the issue."

Even among those Anglos who distanced themselves from such ef- 22
forts, Anglos who did not perceive themselves as economically or socially threatened by Cubans, there remained considerable uneasiness on the matter of language, perhaps because the inability or the disinclination to speak English tended to undermine their conviction that assimilation was an ideal universally shared by those who were to be assimilated. This uneasiness had for example shown up repeatedly during the 1985 mayoralty campaign, surfacing at odd but apparently irrepressible

[2]"I will be in Boston on Sunday and unfortunately I have an appointment in Boston that I can't break and I won't be able to be with you. In spirit, I will be, but the other members of the commission I am sure are invited. . . . "

angles. The winner of that contest, Xavier Suarez, who was born in Cuba but educated in the United States, a graduate of Harvard Law, was reported in a wire service story to speak, an apparently unexpected accomplishment, "flawless English."

A less prominent Cuban candidate for mayor that year had unset- 23
tled reporters at a televised "meet the candidates" forum by answering in Spanish the questions they asked in English. "For all I or my dumbstruck colleagues knew," the *Herald* political editor complained in print after the event, "he was reciting his high school's alma mater or the ten Commandments over and over again. The only thing I understood was the occasional *Cubanos vota Cubano* he tossed in." It was noted by another *Herald* columnist that of the leading candidates, only one, Raul Masvidal, had a listed telephone number, but: " . . . if you call Masvidal's 661-0259 number on Kiaora Street in Coconut Grove—during the day, anyway—you'd better speak Spanish. I spoke to two women there, and neither spoke enough English to answer the question of whether it was the candidate's number."

On the morning this last item came to my attention in the *Herald* I 24
studied it for some time. Raul Masvidal was at that time the chairman of the board of the Miami Savings Bank and the Miami Savings Corporation. He was a former chairman of the Biscayne Bank, and a minority stockholder in the M Bank, of which he had been a founder. He was a member of the Board of Regents for the state university system of Florida. He had paid $600,000 for the house on Kiaora Street in Coconut Grove, buying it specifically because he needed to be a Miami resident (Coconut Grove is part of the city of Miami) in order to run for mayor, and he had sold his previous house, in the incorporated city of Coral Gables, for $1,100,000.

The Spanish words required to find out whether the number listed 25
for the house on Kiaora Street was in fact the candidate's number would have been roughly these: *"¿Es la casa de Raul Masvidal?"* The answer might have been *"Si,"* or the answer might have been *"No."* It seemed to me that there must be very few people working on daily newspapers along the southern borders of the United States who would consider this exchange entirely out of reach, and fewer still who would not accept it as a commonplace of American domestic-life that daytime telephone calls to middle-class urban households will frequently be answered by women who speak Spanish.

Something else was at work in this item, a real resistance, a balki- 26
ness, a coded version of the same message Dade County voters had sent when they decreed that their business be done only in English: WILL THE LAST AMERICAN TO LEAVE MIAMI PLEASE BRING THE FLAG, the famous bumper stickers had read the year of Mariel. "It was the last American stronghold in Dade County," the owner of the Gator Kicks Longneck Saloon, out where Southwest Eighth Street runs into the Everglades, had said after he closed the place for good the night of Super Bowl Sunday, 1986. "Fortunately or unfortunately, I'm not alone in my inability," a *Herald* columnist named

Charles Whited had written a week or so later, in a column about not speaking Spanish. "A good many Americans have left Miami because they want to live someplace where everybody speaks one language: theirs." In this context the call to the house on Kiaora Street in Coconut Grove which did or did not belong to Raul Masvidal appeared not as a statement of literal fact but as shorthand, a glove thrown down, a stand, a cry from the heart of a beleaguered raj.

COMPREHENSION

1. What are the two Miamis depicted in Didion's essay?
2. How do Cubans view the issue of assimilation?
3. What stereotypical perceptions do Anglos in Miami have about their Cuban neighbors? What differences do the Anglos find most threatening?
4. In your opinion, where do the writer's sympathies lie? Justify your answer.

RHETORIC

1. Examine Didion's opening paragraph. Why did she choose to begin this way? Does it prepare the reader for her views? Why does she also mention the accomplishments of the people in the introduction?
2. What is Didion's thesis? Where is it stated or implied? What support does she give?
3. How does the writer use language to bring the Cuban community to life in her essay? Cite specific images, words, phrases; and show how they contribute to her exposition.
4. Is Didion stating her case objectively? What indications are there in the piece that demonstrate this?
5. How does Didion's use of quotes from various sources strengthen her credibility? Give examples.
6. In paragraph 6, Didion lists Cuban social and charity events, using specific names and places. What point is she making?
7. Consider Didion's use of the term "beleaguered raj" in her final paragraph. What connection is she making between the social climate in the two Miamis and a more global perspective? Does the image hold?

WRITING

1. Conduct an interview with an older member of your community, and discuss the changing face of the community in terms of racial or cultural differences. What impact has immigration had on your state, town, or city? How are this person's views representative of others in the community?
2. In an argumentation essay, give your views on assimilation. Consider its benefits to immigrants and natives as well as its drawbacks.
3. Write a personal essay in which you describe the ethnic and racial diversity of your community. How comfortable do you feel with the differences?

Have you made any attempts to interact with members of other nationalities? Why, or why not? Do you sense any conflicts within yourself similar to the ones in Didion's essay? Use your personal experience to support your views.

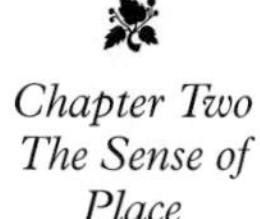

CLASSIC AND CONTEMPORARY: QUESTIONS FOR COMPARISON

1. White and Didion both discuss life in big cities. How do their visions differ? Examine the strategies they use. What moods do they establish in their essays, and how? Do they have similar goals? Discuss in an essay.
2. When were these essays written? What details provide a sense of time? What impact did the prevailing political and social realities of the time have on the writers? Write an essay addressing these questions.
3. Consider the level of language in both essays. How does the presence or absence of abstract or concrete images help to advance the writers' views? How appropriate or effective are they?
4. Write an essay in which you either "update" White's portrait of New York or describe Didion's Miami of two or three decades ago. Research your subject, choose an effective strategy, and use quotes from either or both writers in your own piece.

CONNECTIONS

1. Using the essays of Iyer, Lopez, and Kincaid as support, consider the ramifications of imposing a foreign consciousness on a country's people and geography.
2. Laurence, Momaday, and Neruda write about going home. How do they establish mood in their works? Do they share similar feelings about their homes? How are their aims similar, and how do they differ? Use examples from the essays to support your views.
3. Both Orwell and Kincaid deal with the influences of foreign domination on a country's landscape. How do the writers approach this theme? How do they establish a mood? Are they equally effective? Is there a historical link between the two? Compare and contrast.
4. Titles play an important part in establishing an essay's theme and setting a mood. Pick three of the writers in this section, and discuss why these writers chose the particular titles for their pieces and how appropriate their choices were.
5. The link between human beings and the land is crucial. Using the essays of Lopez, Iyer, and White, discuss the writers' attitudes. How do these writers see humanity's impact on the landscape?
6. Discuss the contribution made by figurative language and details in an essay. Consider the level of language in the works of Momaday, Kincaid, and Neruda in your discussion.
7. Some essays in this section are expository while others are of a more personal nature. Choose two writers using dissimilar strategies, and consider why the strategy used works for that writer.
8. Select one of the specific places or landmarks mentioned in any of the essays and research it. How did the writer spark your interest in the place? How did the place in the essay compare to the information you found?
9. Compare and contrast Didion's and White's vision of city life.
10. Select the essay in this section that most satisfied you as a reader. What feelings and ideas did it evoke? How did it accomplish this? What personal connections did it make? Compare it to an essay in this section that you feel was less effective.

CHAPTER THREE

Manners and Customs

Every society lives by certain rituals and rules, and observes certain tastes and fashions. These manners and customs help us to understand our culture and the traditions that mold it. In fact, manners and customs—such as handing down your great-grandmother's wedding ring from bride to bride, following a favorite family recipe faithfully, and celebrating a holiday in a specific way—are our inheritance.

The way in which we behave in a culture is determined by manners and customs. Sometimes these customs cut across cultures; at other times they conflict. Moreover, in modern times, it is increasingly difficult to find manners and customs that are unchanging, for social life today is characterized by innovation and transformation. Take as an example the culture of food. On or near any typical college campus, you can find Chinese, Italian, Mexican, Greek, and Japanese restaurants and more, including the ubiquitous American diner. As Imamu Amiri Baraka tells us in his essay "Soul Food," the habits we bring to the simple act of eating define our values, lifestyles, and cultural identity. And when we experience the cuisines of other cultures, we learn something about the social patterns of those cultures.

Our ability to understand the manners and customs of other people is one of the best antidotes to cultural ignorance. As Julia Alvarez and Jade Snow Wong observe in their essays in this chapter, immigrants to this nation are under special challenges to comprehend new manners and customs while preserving their own traditions. Conversely, when we encounter other customs at home or abroad, we often have our own notions of "heritage" challenged. We might have set notions about marriage customs, but as Ann Grace Mojtabai reminds us in "Polygamy," other patterns of marriage exist around the world. Similarly, Alice Walker reminds us that notions of beauty are often gender- and culture-specific, adhering to unspoken but understood rules of the cultural game.

People who parade their manners and customs are often blind to other perspectives. What, for example, is your favorite holiday? How do you celebrate it? Would everyone else necessarily find this holiday as appealing as you do? What if you were a Native American, like Michael Dorris, and you were asked to celebrate Thanksgiving? You might discover, as Dorris does in "For the Indians No Thanksgiving," that a holiday that you celebrate actually might offend the traditions or heritage of others.

Some customs and cultural habits might seem strange to us and even defy logic—read the essays on superstition by Addison and Pogrebin—but if we are fair-minded, we make an effort to comprehend them and perhaps even to honor them. Thomas Carlyle wrote, "Good breeding differs, if at all, from high breeding only as it gracefully remembers the rights of others, rather than insisting on its own rights." In learning to understand others' manners and customs, we gain wisdom about other cultures and learn to structure our social relations in new and more useful ways.

Previewing the Chapter

As you read the essays in this chapter and respond to them in discussion and writing, consider the following questions:

- What is the author's purpose? Does the author have a personal motive in addressing the topic in the way he or she does?
- Does the writer present a negative or a positive picture of the manners and customs under consideration? How do you know?
- What cultural problems and conflicts are raised by the author in his or her treatment of the subject?
- What is the writer's tone? Is it serious, humorous, critical, biased, unbiased, or what?
- Which writers focus simply on the need to understand certain customs and manners, and which authors advocate changing rather than preserving them?
- What strengths and weaknesses does the author find in the customs under discussion?
- Does the author have a broad or narrow focus on the relationship of manners to the larger society?
- What is your position or perspective on the subjects and themes raised by each author?
- Which authors altered your position on a topic, and why?

JULIA ALVAREZ Julia Alvarez (1950–) was raised in the Dominican Republic and immigrated to the United States in 1960. She received undergraduate and graduate degrees in literature and writing. Alvarez taught poetry for many years and is currently an English professor at Middlebury College. *Homecoming* (1984) is a volume of poetry, and her novel, *How the Garcia Girls Lost Their Accents,* won the 1991 PEN Oakland/Josephine Miles Book Award. In the essay below, Alvarez puts a humorous slant on food, stepmotherhood, and ethnic identity.

JULIA ALVAREZ

Hold the Mayonnaise

"If I die first and Papi ever gets remarried," Mami used to tease when we were kids, "don't you accept a new woman in my house. Make her life impossible, you hear?" My sisters and I nodded obediently, and a filial shudder would go through us. We were Catholics, so of course, the only kind of remarriage we could imagine had to involve our mother's death. 1

We were also Dominicans, recently arrived in Jamaica, Queens, in the early 60's, before waves of other Latin Americans began arriving. So, when we imagined who exactly my father might possibly ever think of remarrying, only American women came to mind. It would be bad enough having a *madrastra,* but a "stepmother." . . . 2

All I could think of was that she would make me eat mayonnaise, a food I identified with the United States and which I detested. Mami understood, of course, that I wasn't used to that kind of food. Even a madrastra, accustomed to our rice and beans and tostones and pollo frito, would understand. But an American stepmother would think it was normal to put mayonnaise on food, and if she were at all strict and a little mean, which all stepmothers, of course, were, she would make me eat potato salad and such. I had plenty of my own reasons to make a potential stepmother's life impossible. When I nodded obediently with my sisters, I was imagining not just something foreign in our house, but in our refrigerator. 3

So it's strange now, almost 35 years later, to find myself a Latina stepmother of my husband's two tall, strapping, blond, mayonnaise-eating daughters. To be honest, neither of them is a real aficionado of the condiment, but it's a fair thing to add to a bowl of tuna fish or diced potatoes. Their American food, I think of it, and when they head to their mother's or off to school, I push the jar back in the refrigerator behind their chocolate pudding and several open cans of Diet Coke. 4

5 What I can't push as successfully out of sight are my own immigrant childhood fears of having a *gringa* stepmother with foreign tastes in our house. Except now, I am the foreign stepmother in a gringa household. I've wondered what my husband's two daughters think of this stranger in their family. It must be doubly strange for them that I am from another culture.

6 Of course, there are mitigating circumstances—my husband's two daughters were teen-agers when we married, older, more mature, able to understand differences. They had also traveled when they were children with their father, an eye doctor, who worked on short-term international projects with various eye foundations. But still, it's one thing to visit a foreign country, another altogether to find it brought home—a real bear plopped down in a Goldilocks house.

7 Sometimes, a whole extended family of bears. My warm, loud Latino family came up for the wedding: my *tia* from Santo Domingo; three dramatic, enthusiastic sisters and their families; my papi, with a thick accent I could tell the girls found it hard to understand; and my mami, who had her eye trained on my soon-to-be stepdaughters for any sign that they were about to make my life impossible. "How are they behaving themselves?" she asked me, as if they were 7 and 3, not 19 and 16. "They're wonderful girls," I replied, already feeling protective of them.

8 I looked around for the girls in the meadow in front of the house we were building, where we were holding the outdoor wedding ceremony and party. The oldest hung out with a group of her own friends. The younger one whizzed in briefly for the ceremony, then left again before the congratulations started up. There was not much mixing with me and mine. What was there for them to celebrate on a day so full of confusion and effort?

9 On my side, being the newcomer in someone else's territory is a role I'm used to. I can tap into that struggling English speaker, that skinny, dark-haired, olive-skinned girl in a sixth grade of mostly blond and blue-eyed giants. Those tall, freckled boys would push me around in the playground. "Go back to where you came from!" *"No comprendo!"* I'd reply, though of course there was no misunderstanding the fierce looks on their faces.

10 Even now, my first response to a scowl is that old pulling away. (My husband calls it "checking out.") I remember times early on in the marriage when the girls would be with us, and I'd get out of school and drive around doing errands, killing time, until my husband, their father, would be leaving work. I am not proud of my fears, but I understand—as the lingo goes—where they come from.

11 And I understand, more than I'd like to sometimes, my stepdaughters' pain. But with me, they need never fear that I'll usurp a mother's place. No one has ever come up and held their faces and then addressed me, "They look just like you." If anything, strangers to the remarriage are probably playing Mr. Potato Head in their minds, trying to figure out how my foreign features and my husband's fair Nebraskan

features got put together into these two tall, blond girls. "My husband's daughters," I kept introducing them.

Once, when one of them visited my class and I introduced her as such, two students asked me why. "I'd be so hurt if my stepmom introduced me that way," the young man said. That night I told my stepdaughter what my students had said. She scowled at me and agreed. "It's so weird how you call me Papa's daughter. Like you don't want to be related to me or something."

"I didn't want to presume," I explained. "So it's O.K. if I call you 13
my stepdaughter?"

"That's what I am," she said. Relieved, I took it for a teensy inch of 14
acceptance. The takings are small in this stepworld, I've discovered. Sort of like being a minority. It feels as if all the goodies have gone somewhere else.

Day to day, I guess I follow my papi's advice. When we first came, 15
he would talk to his children about how to make it in our new country. "Just do your work and put in your heart, and they will accept you!" In this age of remaining true to your roots, of keeping your Spanish, of fighting from inside your culture, that assimilationist approach is highly suspect. My Latino students—who don't want to be called Hispanics anymore—would ditch me as faculty adviser if I came up with that play-nice message.

But in a stepfamily where everyone is starting a new life together, 16
it isn't bad advice. Like a potluck supper, an American concept my mami never took to. ("Why invite people to your house and then ask them to bring the food?") You put what you've got together with what everyone else brought and see what comes out of the pot. The luck part is if everyone brings something you like. No potato salad, no deviled eggs, no little party sandwiches with you know what in them.

COMPREHENSION

1. What was Alvarez's greatest fear as a child when confronted with the possibility of acquiring a stepmother?
2. How does the writer feel about her stepdaughters? Cite examples from the essay where her attitude seems clear.
3. What connection does Alvarez make between being a stepmother and being a member of a minority?

RHETORIC

1. Does the title "Hold the Mayonnaise" seem fitting? Does the essay's tone follow through with the title's lightheartedness? Explain.
2. What point is Alvarez making in her essay?
3. What role does irony play in Alvarez's piece? Find evidence of irony in the essay, and explain how it functions.

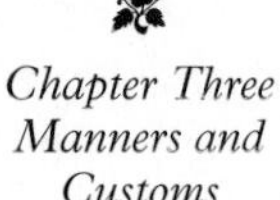

4. Consider the relevance of fairy tales in strengthening the writer's thesis. What fairy tale is directly mentioned, and how does Alvarez change it? Do these changes help to depict the author's situation?
5. What distinction is Alvarez making between "stepmother" and *madrastra?* How is this distinction pertinent to her point of view? What other comparative strategies does the author employ?
6. Does the simile Alvarez employs in her final paragraph illustrate her frame of mind? Does her conflict seem resolved? Justify your response.

WRITING

1. Write an essay in which you describe the first time you ate a particular food or meal. Explain the circumstances surrounding that event: your age; the setting; the taste, smell, and feel of the food; your feelings about it. How do you feel about that food now?
2. Write a letter to Ms. Alvarez advising her on how to bridge the gap between stepmothers and stepdaughters. Use your own experience or observations when relevant.
3. Argue for or against this statement: Cultural or ethnic differences run too deep for a multicultural household to survive happily; one side must inevitably compromise more than the other.

JADE SNOW WONG Jade Snow Wong (1922–), the daughter of a manufacturer father, was born in San Francisco. Wong has been a secretary, co-owner of a travel agency, and owner of a ceramics gallery. She has won prizes for her work in pottery and enamel. As a writer, she is known best for her autobiography, *Fifth Chinese Daughter,* and has contributed to periodicals such as *Holiday* magazine. Through her life and work, Wong hopes to bridge the gap between Chinese and Americans. In the following narrative, she develops the theme of mainstreaming and its effects on her family.

JADE SNOW WONG

Pilgrims from the Orient

From infancy to my sixteenth year, I was reared according to nineteenth-century ideals of Chinese womanhood. I was never left alone, though it was not unusual for me to feel lonely, while surrounded by a family of seven others, and often by ten (including bachelor cousins) at meals. 1

My father (who enjoyed our calling him Daddy in English) was the unquestioned head of our household. He was not talkative, being pre- 2 occupied with his business affairs and with reading constantly otherwise. My mother was mistress of domestic affairs. Seldom did these two converse before their children, but we knew them to be a united front, and suspected that privately she both informed and influenced him about each child.

In order to support the family in America, Daddy tried various oc- 3
cupations—candy making, the ministry to which he was later ordained—but finally settled on manufacturing men's and children's denim garments. He leased sewing equipment, installed machines in a basement where rent was cheapest, and there he and his family lived and worked. There was no thought that dim, airless quarters were terrible conditions for living and working, or that child labor was unhealthful. The only goal was for all in the family to work, to save, and to become educated. It was possible, so it would be done.

My father, a meticulous bookkeeper, used only an abacus, a brush, 4
ink, and Chinese ledgers. Because of his newly learned ideals, he pioneered for the right of women to work. Concerned that they have economic independence, but not with the long hours of industrial home work, he went to shy housewives' apartments and taught them sewing.

My earliest memories of companionship with my father were as his 5
passenger in his red wheelbarrow, sharing space with the piles of blue-jean materials he was delivering to a worker's home. He must have been forty. He was lean, tall, inevitably wearing blue overalls, rolled shirt sleeves, and high black kid shoes. In his pockets were numerous keys, tools, and pens. On such deliveries, I noticed that he always managed time to show a mother how to sew a difficult seam, or to help her repair a machine, or just to chat.

I observed from birth that living and working were inseparable. My 6
mother was short, sturdy, young looking, and took pride in her appearance. She was at her machine the minute housework was done, and she was the hardest-working seamstress, seldom pausing, working after I went to bed. The hum of sewing machines continued day and night, seven days a week. She knew that to have more than the four necessities, she must work and save. We knew that to overcome poverty, there were only two methods: working and education.

Having provided the setup for family industry, my father turned his 7
attention to our education. Ninety-five percent of the population in his native China had been illiterate. He knew that American public schools would take care of our English, but he had to nurture our Chinese knowledge. Only the Cantonese tongue was ever spoken by him or my mother. When the two oldest girls arrived from China, the schools of Chinatown received only boys. My father tutored his daughters each morning before breakfast. In the midst of a foreign environment, he clung to a combination of the familiar old standards and what was permissible in the newly learned Christian ideals.

My eldest brother was born in America, the only boy for fourteen 8
years, and after him three daughters—another older sister, myself, and my younger sister. Then my younger brother, Paul, was born. That

older brother, Lincoln, was cherished in the best Chinese tradition. He had his own room; he kept a German shepherd as his pet; he was tutored by a Chinese scholar; he was sent to private school for American classes. As a male Wong, he would be responsible some day for the preservation of and pilgrimages to ancestral graves—his privileges were his birthright. We girls were content with the unusual opportunities of working and attending two schools. By day, I attended American public school near our home. From 5:00 P.M. to 8:00 P.M. on five weekdays and from 9:00 A.M. to 12 noon on Saturdays, I attended the Chinese school. Classes numbered twenty to thirty students, and were taught by educated Chinese from China. We studied poetry, calligraphy, philosophy, literature, history, correspondence, religion, all by exacting memorization.

9 Daddy emphasized memory development; he could still recite fluently many lengthy lessons of his youth. Every evening after both schools, I'd sit by my father, often as he worked at his sewing machine sing-songing my lessons above its hum. Sometimes I would stop to hold a light for him as he threaded the difficult holes of a specialty machine, such as one for bias bindings. After my Chinese lessons passed his approval, I was allowed to attend to American homework. I was made to feel luckier than other Chinese girls who didn't study Chinese, and also luckier than Western girls without a dual heritage.

10 There was little time for play, and toys were unknown to me. In any spare time, I was supplied with embroidery and sewing for my mother. The Chinese New Year, which by the old lunar calendar would fall sometime in late January or early February of the Western Christian calendar, was the most special time of the year, for then the machine stopped for three days. Mother would clean our living quarters very thoroughly, decorate the sitting room with flowering branches and fresh oranges, and arrange candied fruits or salty melon seeds for callers. All of us would be dressed in bright new clothes, and relatives or close friends, who came to call, would give each of us a red paper packet containing a good luck coin—usually a quarter. I remember how my classmates would gleefully talk of *their* receipts. But my mother made us give our money to her, for she said that she needed it to reciprocate to others.

11 Yet there was little reason for unhappiness. I was never hungry. Though we had no milk, there was all the rice we wanted. We had hot and cold running water—a rarity in Chinatown—as well as our own bathtub. Our sheets were pieced from dishtowels, but we had sheets. I was never neglected, for my mother and father were always at home. During school vacation periods, I was taught to operate many types of machines—tacking (for pockets), overlocking (for the raw edges of seams), buttonhole, double seaming; and I learned all the stages in producing a pair of jeans to its final inspection, folding, and tying in bundles of a dozen pairs by size, ready for pickup. Denim jeans are heavy—my shoulders ached often. My father set up a modest nickel-

and-dime piecework reward for me, which he recorded in my own notebook, and paid me regularly.

My mother dutifully followed my father's leadership. She was extremely thrifty, but the thrifty need pennies to manage, and the old world had denied her those. Upon arrival in the new world of San Francisco, she accepted the elements her mate had selected to shape her new life: domestic duties, seamstress work in the factory-home, mothering each child in turn, church once a week, and occasional movies. Daddy frowned upon the community Chinese operas because of their very late hours (they did not finish till past midnight) and their mixed audiences.

Very early in my life, the manners of a traditional Chinese lady were 13
taught to me: how to hold a pair of chopsticks (palm up, not down); how to hold a bowl of rice (one thumb on top, not resting in an open palm); how to pass something to elders (with both hands, never one); how to pour tea into the tiny, handleless porcelain cups (seven-eighths full so that the top edge would be cool enough to hold); how to eat from a center serving dish (only the piece in front of your place, never pick around); not to talk at table, not to show up outside of one's room without being fully dressed; not to be late, ever; not to be too playful. In a hundred and one ways, we were molded to be trouble-free, unobtrusive, cooperative.

We were disciplined by first being told, and then by punishment if 14
we didn't remember. Punishment was instant and unceremonious. At the table, it came as a sudden whack from Daddy's chopsticks. Away from the table, punishment could be the elimination of a privilege or the blow on our legs from a bundle of cane switches.

Only Daddy and Oldest Brother were allowed individual idiosyn- 15
crasies. Daughters were all expected to be of one standard. To allow each one of many daughters to be different would have posed enormous problems of cost, energy, and attention. No one was shown physical affection. Such familiarity would have weakened my parents and endangered the one-answer authoritative system. One standard from past to present, whether in China or in San Francisco, was simpler to enforce. My parents never said "please" and "thank you" for any service or gift. In Chinese, both "please" and "thank you" can be literally translated as "I am not worthy" and naturally, no parent is going to say that about a service which should be their just due.

Traditional Chinese parents pit their children against a standard of 16
perfection without regard to personality, individual ambitions, tolerance for human error, or exposure to the changing social scene. It never occurred to that kind of parent to be friends with their children on common ground.

During the Depression, my mother and father needed even more 17
hours to work. Daddy had been shopping daily for groceries (we had no icebox) and my mother cooked. Now I was told to assume both those duties. My mother would give me fifty cents to buy enough fresh food for dinner and breakfast. In those years, twenty-five cents could

buy a small chicken or three sanddabs, ten cents bought three bunches of green vegetables, and fifteen cents bought some meat to cook with these. After American school I rushed to the stores only a block or so away, returned and cleaned the foods, and cooked in a hurry in order to eat an early dinner and get to Chinese school on time. When I came home at 8:00 P.M., I took care of the dinner dishes before starting to do my homework. Saturdays and Sundays were for housecleaning and the family laundry, which I scrubbed on a board, using big galvanized buckets in our bathtub.

I had no sympathetic guidance as an eleven-year-old in my own reign in the kitchen, which lasted for four years. I finished junior high school, started high school, and continued studying Chinese. With the small earnings from summer work in my father's basement factory (we moved back to the basement during the Depression), I bought materials to sew my own clothes. But the routine of keeping house only to be dutiful, to avoid tongue or physical lashings, became exasperating. The tiny space which was the room for three sisters was confining. After I graduated from Chinese evening school, I began to look for part-time paying jobs as a mother's helper. Those jobs varied from cleaning house to baking a cake, amusing a naughty child to ironing shirts, but wearying, exhausting as they were, they meant money earned for myself. 18

As I advanced in American high school and worked at those jobs, I was gradually introduced to customs not of the Chinese world. American teachers were mostly kind. I remember my third-grade teacher's skipping me half a year. I remember my fourth-grade teacher—with whom I am still friendly. She was the first person to hold me to her physically and affectionately—because a baseball bat had been accidentally flung against my hand. I also remember that I was confused by being held, since physical comfort had not been offered by my parents. I remember my junior high school principal, who skipped me half a grade and commended me before the school assembly, to my great embarrassment. 19

In contrast, Chinese schoolteachers acted as extensions of Chinese parental discipline. There was a formal "disciplinarian dean" to apply the cane to wayward boys, and girls were not exempt either. A whisper during chapel was sufficient provocation to be called to the dean's office. No humor was exchanged; no praise or affection expressed by the teachers. They presented the lessons, and we had to learn to memorize all the words, orally, before the class. Then followed the written test, word for word. Without an alphabet, the Chinese language requires exact memorization. No originality or deviation was permitted and grading was severe. One word wrong during an examination could reduce a grade by 10 percent. It was the principle of learning by punishment. 20

Interest and praise, physical or oral, were rewards peculiar to the American world. Even employers who were paying me thanked me for a service or complimented me on a meal well cooked, and sometimes 21 helped me with extra dishes. Chinese often said that "foreigners" talked too much about too many personal things. My father used to tell me to think three times before saying anything, and if I said nothing, no one would say I was stupid. I perceived a difference between two worlds.

By the time I was graduating from high school, my parents had 22
done their best to produce an intelligent, obedient daughter, who would know more than the average Chinatown girl and should do better than average at a conventional job, her earnings brought home to them in repayment for their years of child support. Then, they hoped, she would marry a nice Chinese boy and make him a good wife, as well as an above-average mother for his children. Chinese custom used to decree that families should "introduce" chosen partners to each other's children. The groom's family should pay handsomely to the bride's family for rearing a well-bred daughter. They should also pay all bills for a glorious wedding banquet for several hundred guests. Then the bride's family could consider their job done. Their daughter belonged to the groom's family and must henceforth seek permission from all persons in his home before returning to her parents for a visit.

But having been set upon a new path, I did not oblige my parents 23
with the expected conventional ending. At fifteen, I had moved away from home to work for room and board and a salary of twenty dollars per month. Having found that I could subsist independently, I thought it regrettable to terminate my education. Upon graduating from high school at the age of sixteen, I asked my parents to assist me in college expenses. I pleaded with my father, for his years of encouraging me to be above mediocrity in both Chinese and American studies had made me wish for some undefined but brighter future.

My father was briefly adamant. He must conserve his resources for 24
my oldest brother's medical training. Though I desired to continue on an above-average course, his material means were insufficient to support that ambition. He added that if I had the talent, I could provide for my own college education. When he had spoken, no discussion was expected. After his edict, no daughter questioned.

But this matter involved my whole future—it was not simply asking 25
for permission to go to a night church meeting (forbidden also). Though for years I had accepted the authority of the one I honored most, his decision that night embittered me as nothing ever had. My oldest brother had so many privileges, had incurred unusual expenses for luxuries which were taken for granted as his birthright, yet these were part of a system I had accepted. Now I suddenly wondered at my father's interpretation of the Christian code: was it intended to discriminate against a girl after all, or was it simply convenient for my father's economics and cultural prejudice? Did a daughter have any right to expect more than a fate of obedience, according to the old Chinese standard? As long as I could remember, I had been told that a female followed three men during her lifetime: as a girl, her father; as a wife, her husband; as an old woman, her son.

My indignation mounted against that tradition and I decided then that my past could not determine my future. I knew that more education would prepare me for a different expectation than my other female schoolmates, few of whom were to complete a college degree. I, too, had my father's unshakable faith in the justice of God, and I shared his unconcern with popular opinion. 26

So I decided to enter junior college, now San Francisco's City College, because the fees were lowest. I lived at home and supported myself with an after-school job which required long hours of housework and cooking but paid me twenty dollars per month, of which I saved as much as possible. The thrills derived from reading and learning, in ways ranging from chemistry experiments to English compositions, from considering new ideas of sociology to the logic of Latin, convinced me that I had made a correct choice. I was kept in a state of perpetual mental excitement by new Western subjects and concepts and did not mind long hours of work and study. I also made new friends, which led to another painful incident with my parents, who had heretofore discouraged even girlhood friendships. 27

The college subject which had most jolted me was sociology. The instructor fired my mind with his interpretation of family relationships. As he explained to our class, it used to be an economic asset for American farming families to be large, since children were useful to perform agricultural chores. But this situation no longer applied and children should be regarded as individuals with their own rights. Unquestioning obedience should be replaced with parental understanding. So at sixteen, discontented as I was with my parents' apparent indifference to me, those words of my sociology professor gave voice to my sentiments. How old-fashioned was the dead-end attitude of my parents! How ignorant they were of modern thought and progress! The family unit had been China's strength for centuries, but it had also been her weakness, for corruption, nepotism, and greed were all justified in the name of the family's welfare. My new ideas festered; I longed to release them. 28

One afternoon on a Saturday, which was normally occupied with my housework job, I was unexpectedly released by my employer, who was departing for a country weekend. It was a rare joy to have free time and I wanted to enjoy myself for a change. There had been a Chinese-American boy who shared some classes with me. Sometimes we had found each other walking to the same 8:00 A.M. class. He was not a special boyfriend, but I had enjoyed talking to him and had confided in him some of my problems. Impulsively, I telephoned him. I knew I must be breaking rules, and I felt shy and scared. At the same time, I was excited at this newly found forwardness, with nothing more purposeful than to suggest another walk together. 29

He understood my awkwardness and shared my anticipation. He asked me to "dress up" for my first movie date. My clothes were limited but I changed to look more graceful in silk stockings and found a bright ribbon for my long black hair. Daddy watched, catching my 30 mood, observing the dashing preparations. He asked me where I was going without his permission and with whom.

I refused to answer him. I thought of my rights! I thought he surely would not try to understand. Thereupon Daddy thundered his displeasure and forbade my departure.

I found a new courage as I heard my voice announce calmly that I was no longer a child, and if I could work my way through college, I would choose my own friends. It was my right as a person. 32

My mother heard the commotion and joined my father to face me; both appeared shocked and incredulous. Daddy at once demanded the source of this unfilial, non-Chinese theory. And when I quoted my college professor, reminding him that he had always felt teachers should be revered, my father denounced that professor as a foreigner who was disregarding the superiority of our Chinese culture, with its sound family strength. My father did not spare me; I was condemned as an ingrate for echoing dishonorable opinions which should only be temporary whims, yet nonetheless inexcusable. 33

The scene was not yet over. I completed my proclamation to my father, who had never allowed me to learn how to dance, by adding that I was attending a movie, unchaperoned, with a boy I met at college. 34

My startled father was sure that my reputation would be subject to whispered innuendos. I must be bent on disgracing the family name; I was ruining my future, for surely I would yield to temptation. My mother underscored him by saying that I hadn't any notion of the problems endured by parents of a young girl. 35

I would not give in. I reminded them that they and I were not in China, that I wasn't going out with just anybody but someone I trusted! Daddy gave a roar that no man could be trusted, but I devastated them in declaring that I wished the freedom to find my own answers. 36

Both parents were thoroughly angered, scolded me for being shameless, and predicted that I would some day tell them I was wrong. But I dimly perceived that they were conceding defeat and were perplexed at this breakdown of their training. I was too old to beat and too bold to intimidate. 37

COMPREHENSION

1. How were boys and girls treated in the Wong family? What was expected of each?
2. What kind of child was Jade? What precipitated her change?
3. What values were instilled in the Wong children?

RHETORIC

1. Who are the "pilgrims" in Wong's title? Does the title effectively convey the thematic content of the essay? What is Wong's thesis? Where is it stated?

2. What is Wong emphasizing by the capitalization of "Daddy"? Is there any evidence of irony in the word? Explain.
3. What comparative strategy does Wong employ in her essay?
4. What specific examples does the writer use to illustrate the clash between Chinese and American values and customs?
5. How does the writer present the confrontation with Daddy at the end of the essay? Does this approach work to intensify or dilute the drama of the scene?
6. What is the significance of the essay's final line: "I was too old to beat and too bold to intimidate"? What resolution does the writer seem to have come to?

WRITING

1. Write an essay in which you argue for or against the necessity of rejecting your parents' values and traditions in order to develop independence and selfhood. Use examples from Wong's essay as well as personal experience in your development.
2. Wong's essay explores some of the ways in which Chinese traditions defined her role as a girl and, later, as a woman. What restrictions does American society place on sexual identity? What were the messages (subtle or overt) sent by your family as you were growing up?
3. Wong spends some time in her essay comparing the educational system in China to the American system. Using the information she provides, which method seems more effective to you? Write an essay in which you explore what one could learn from the other.

IMAMU AMIRI BARAKA Imamu Amiri Baraka (1934–) is a playwright, novelist, editor, poet, essayist, and community leader. Baraka's most famous work, the play *Dutchman* (1964), is about the often destructive relations between black and white Americans. During his career, Baraka has, through the powerful use of the black idiom, introduced the public to the richness of African-American culture.

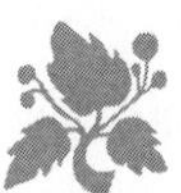

IMAMU AMIRI BARAKA

Soul Food

Recently, a young Negro novelist writing in *Esquire* about the beauties of America mentioned that one of the things wrong with Negroes was that, unlike the Chinese, boots have neither a language of their own nor a characteristic cuisine. And this to me is the deepest stroke, the un- 1 kindest cut, of oppression, especially as it has distorted Black Americans. America, where the suppliant, far from rebelling or even disagreeing with the forces that have caused him to suffer, readily backs them up and finally tries to become an honorary oppressor himself.

No language? No characteristic food? Oh, man, come on. 2

Maws are things ofays seldom get to peck, nor are you likely ever to 3
hear about Charlie eating a chitterling. Sweet potatoe pies, a good friend of mine asked recently, "Do they taste anything like pumpkin?" Negative. They taste more like memory, if you're not uptown.

All those different kinds of greens (now quick frozen for anyone) 4
once were all Sam got to eat. (Plus the potlikker, into which one slipped some throwed away meat.) Collards and turnips and kale and mustards were not fit for anybody but the woogies. So they found a way to make them taste like something somebody would want to freeze and sell to a Negro going to Harvard as exotic European spinach.

The watermelon, friend, was imported from Africa (by whom?) 5
where it had been growing many centuries before it was necessary for some people to deny that they had ever tasted one.

Did you ever hear of a black-eyed pea? (Whitey used it for forage, 6
but some folks couldn't.) And all those weird parts of the hog? (After the pig was stripped of its choicest parts, the feet, snout, tail, intestines, stomach, etc., were all left for the "members," who treated them mercilessly.) Is it mere myth that shades are death on chickens? (Deep fat frying, the Dutch found out in 17th century New Amsterdam, was an African speciality: and if you can get hold of a fried chicken leg, or a fried porgie, you can find out what happened to that tradition.)

I had to go to Rutgers before I found people who thought grits were 7
meant to be eaten with milk and sugar, instead of gravy and pork sausage . . . and that's one of the reasons I left.

Away from home, you must make the trip uptown to get really 8
straight as far as a good grease is concerned. People kill chickens all over the world, but chasing them through the dark on somebody else's property would probably insure, once they went in the big bag, that you'd find some really beautiful way to eat them. I mean, after all the risk involved. The fruit of that tradition unfolds everywhere above 100th Street. There are probably more restaurants in Harlem whose staple is fried chicken, or chicken in the basket, than any other place in the world. Ditto, barbecued ribs—also straight out of the South with the West Indians, *i.e.,* Africans from farther south in the West, having developed the best sauce for roasting whole oxen and hogs, spicy and extremely hot.

Hoppin' John (black-eyed peas and rice), hushpuppies (crusty 9
cornmeal bread cooked in fish grease and best with fried fish, especially fried salt fish, which ought to soak overnight unless you're over fifty and can take all that salt), hoecake (pan bread), buttermilk biscuits and pancakes, fatback, *i.e.,* streak'alean-streak'afat, dumplings, neck bones, knuckles (both good for seasoning limas or string beans), okra (another African importation, other name gumbo), pork chops—some more sta-

ples of the Harlem cuisine. Most of the food came North when the people did.

10 There are hundreds of tiny restaurants, food shops, rib joints, shrimp shacks, chicken shacks, "rotisseries" throughout Harlem that serve "soul food"—say, a breakfast of grits, eggs and sausage, pancakes and Alaga syrup—and even tiny booths where it's at least possible to get a good piece of barbecue, hot enough to make you whistle, or a chicken wing on a piece of greasy bread. You can *always* find a fish sandwich: a fish sandwich is something you walk with, or "Two of those small sweet potato pies to go." The Muslim temple serves bean pies which are really separate. It is never necessary to go to some big expensive place to get a good filling grease. You *can* go to the Red Rooster, or Wells, or Joch's, and get a good meal, but Jennylin's, a little place on 135th near Lenox, is more filling, or some place like the A&A food shop in a basement up in the 140's, and you can really get away. I guess a square is somebody who's in Harlem and eats at Nedicks.

COMPREHENSION

1. Who is Baraka's primary audience for this essay? What is the author's attitude toward this audience? Cite evidence to support your answer.
2. According to Baraka, what foods and cooking styles originated in African or African-American culture?
3. The theme of white oppression and the black response to it recurs frequently in the essay. Identify some of the different ways in which the theme is put forth. Why does the author state and restate the theme?

RHETORIC

1. List the various words that come from the black language, and define them. There are also several references to "uptown" in the essay, references which can be considered examples of metonymy. Explain.
2. Why is slang so effective in this essay?
3. What are the two opinions Baraka sets out to disprove? He uses two different methods of refuting these opinions. What are they?
4. How does the essay use inductive reasoning?
5. Why does Baraka present historical information in parentheses?
6. Analyze the way that Baraka develops his concluding paragraph.

WRITING

1. Write an essay that develops your own definition of *soul food, ethnic food,* or *junk food.*
2. Write an argumentative essay on the value of the "separate" language used by a particular ethnic, social, or professional group.
3. Develop an appreciative essay on your favorite national cuisine.

ANN GRACE MOJTABAI Ann Grace Mojtabai (1938–) spent several years living in Iran. She has written several novels, including *Mundome* (1974), *The Four Hundred Eels of Sigmund Freud* (1976), and *A Stopping Place* (1979). In the following essay, Mojtabai tries to look clearly at a particularly disturbing—from our perspective—aspect of Iranian culture.

ANN GRACE MOJTABAI

Polygamy

Teheran, 1960. A warm evening. The courtyard in which we were sitting was not very beautiful. There was a narrow strip of ground that ran along the edge of the wall, spotted with shrubbery and some insignificant roses; the rest was flagstone surrounding the customary small pool for ablutions, set like a turquoise in the center. 1

I had come to Iran expecting nightingales and roses, but had not yet heard a nightingale above the sounds of streets hawkers and traffic, and the famed rose gardens of Persia were nowhere in evidence; they remained out of sight, if they ever existed, sealed off by high proprietary walls. 2

But my interest of the moment was not in the garden; my eyes were fixed on my father-in-law. He was a large, imposing man in his mid-90's, with high color, still-black eyebrows and the scrub of a heavy beard. He might have passed for a much younger man and, in fact, claimed to be in his young, vigorous 70's. 3

"What do you think of this?" he asked, pointing to his wives, one large, one small, on either side of him. His wives smiled in my direction, then at each other. My father-in-law continued to stare at me and to wait; he really wanted to know what I thought. 4

For the few separate moments it took to translate his question and my reply (with what distortion I shall never know), we gazed coolly at each other, each an anthropologist confronting opacity—the mind of a stranger. I thought I could hear him taking notes. I, for my part, was certainly jotting things down—but only impressions. I would see; I wasn't going to judge prematurely. My judgment, when it came, wouldn't be narrow, biased or culture-bound. "Customs differ," I said. 5

Long before meeting my father-in-law, I had been prepared for this—or, rather, I had been briefed, and imagined that I was prepared. It had been a briefing full of history (polygamy as a practical solution to the decimation of the male population in warfare and the resulting disproportionate preponderance of females over males); it had been a briefing on principle as well (the Koranic requirement that the husband distribute his affection equally among the co-wives). 6

But, of course, I was not ready to confront the live instance—three 7
individuals who would bear an intimate family relation to me. Mother, father and what—aunt? mother-surrogate? I decided that the other party would simply be my Other Mother-in-Law. At that moment, the language barrier turned out to be an opportune cover for, really, I did not know what I thought.

The happy threesome sat cross-legged on a takhte, a low wooden 8
platform, covered with a rug. My particular mother-in-law, the tiny one, was the junior wife, chosen, I later learned, by the older woman as someone agreeable to herself, someone she thought the old man would like, too. The senior wife's passion was for talking, and her husband's silence had long been wearing her down. She wanted someone in the house willing to hear her out and, she hoped, to respond from time to time.

I was left to imagine the precise formalities, but it seemed to me to 9
be a marriage welcome to all the parties concerned. It was an arrangement not without its share of bickerings and quarrels, for however well-disposed the women were to each other, their respective children were rivals, and the wives were partisan for their children.

Still, as marriages go, theirs seemed to be a reasonably happy one. 10

When it grew chilly, we moved indoors. The sitting room was also 11
my father-in-law's bedroom. He sat on a fine, ancient rug, with bolsters at his back, a bay of windows on his left and, in front of him, an array of small vials: vitamins, elixirs, purges. He didn't believe in modern medicine, but was taking no chances.

Stiff, wooden chairs of mismatching shapes were lined against the 12
walls of the room. I eyed them, but, noticing that they were mantled in dust, furred with a thin, unbroken velvet, decided they were not really for use, and sat on the floor instead. In fact, the chairs were chiefly ceremonial, a reluctant concession to the times, to the imposition of Westernization around the world. Not like the television set, which was an ecstatic testimony to the march of *universal* human progress, and which held, along with the samovar, pride of place among the old man's possessions.

The wives stepped out to bring refreshments. With a sinking sense, 13
I noticed my husband getting up to speak to his mother in private. I was utterly adrift, alone with my father-in-law, a total stranger. The old man turned to me and said what I later learned was: "When hearts speak, no language is necessary." I recognized none of the words, but I guessed from his face and tone that whatever it was he had said was meant to be comforting and, trusting in a language of gesture and sign, I ventured a smile by way of reply.

Even today, I do not know what I think about polygamy. Or, per- 14
haps, I know what I think—it's only that my feelings are mixed. Abstractly, I oppose the custom. These bonds ought to be reciprocal, one-to-one. Sexual favors *may* be distributed equally as required (a night with A, a night with B), but I doubt whether affection can be distributed so neatly. And, of course, the custom speaks of the poverty of opportunities for women.

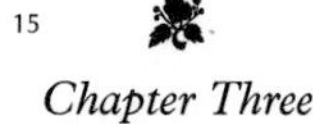

On the other hand, the custom of mut'a, or temporary marriage, 15
practiced by Shiites, though not by Sunnites, seems to me to be possessed of some merits and, on the whole, somewhat more enlightened than prostitution, or the vaguely polygamous custom of balancing wife (with legal rights) with mistress (having no rights), which is so widely prevalent in the West.

In the mut'a marriage, a term is stipulated—a night, a year, a 16
decade, an hour, whatever. A set term, a mehr—a wedding endowment for the woman—mutual consent and a contract specifying all this are required. The children of such unions are legitimate and entitled to a share of the father's inheritance, although the sigheh, the temporary wife, has no claim to maintenance beyond the initial marriage endowment.

But polygamy is meant to be more than a mere alternative to such 17
clearly deficient institutions as prostitution. And my feelings for polygamy as a true and viable form of marriage remain contrary, held in suspension. My opposition in theory is muffled by my observation of one palpable contrary fact. I saw a polygamous marriage work, and work well. That my mothers-in-law were deeply attached to each other, I have no doubt. I tend to question rather more their devotion to the husband who brought them together.

As for two mothers-in-law in one household, an old proverb would 18
seem to apply: "Better two tigers in one cage than two mistresses in one household." But, in point of fact, the laws of addition don't always apply. After all, one shark and one codfish equal one shark; one raindrop and one raindrop equal one raindrop. The two women worked off their intensities on each other, with less energy left for me. So, actually, I had one mother-in-law, which, as all the proverbs of all nations attest, was quite sufficient.

COMPREHENSION

1. How do paragraphs 1 to 5 serve the author's purpose?
2. What effects of Westernization appear in the essay? Of which ones do the Iranians approve? Of which ones do they disapprove?
3. What academic-sounding reasons for polygamy has Mojtabai been given? Do they help her to confront the reality of it? Why, or why not? What is her final attitude toward polygamy?

RHETORIC

1. Identify Iranian words in the essay, and explain what they mean.
2. What does Mojtabai mean when she describes her first meeting with her father-in-law as "each an anthropologist confronting opacity" (paragraph 5)? What level of language does that suggest Mojtabai uses in the essay? Can these words be used by Westerners to describe aspects of Western culture?
3. What is the function of the opening narrative? Why is it effective?

4. In this essay, the narrator is both actor and observer. How does this affect the tone of the essay? Where else in the anthology have we seen this strategy?
5. Why does Mojtabai spend considerable time describing *mut'a?* What elements of contrast does she utilize here? For what purpose?
6. One paragraph is considerably shorter than the others. How does this contribute to the structure and meaning of the essay?

WRITING

1. Discuss a custom you have confronted that was alien to your own values. Compare your response to Mojtabai's response.
2. Write your own evaluation of polygamy.
3. Does the United States have a more enlightened perspective on women and marriage than does the Iran depicted by Mojtabai? Discuss this question in an essay.

MICHAEL DORRIS Michael Dorris (1945–), a member of the Modoc tribe and a native of Washington, is a professor of anthropology and Native-American studies at Dartmouth College. He has written, among other works, *The Broken Cord: A Family's Ongoing Struggles with Fetal Alcohol Syndrome* (1987). He has also written about the Native-American experience in books such as *Native Americans: Five Hundred Years After Cromwell* (1975). He and his wife, Louise Erdrich, coauthored a novel, *The Crown of Columbus* (1991). In this essay, Dorris wonders how the first Thanksgiving might have been seen through the eyes of non-Pilgrims.

MICHAEL DORRIS

For the Indians No Thanksgiving

Maybe those Pilgrims and Wampanoags actually got together for a November picnic, maybe not. It matters only as a facile, ironical footnote. 1

For the former group, it would have been a celebration of a precarious hurdle successfully crossed on the path to the political domination first of a continent and eventually of a planet. For the latter, it would have been, at best, a naïve extravaganza—the last meeting as equals with invaders who, within a few years, would win King Philip's War and decorate the city limits of their towns with rows of stakes, each topped with an Indian head. 2

The few aboriginal survivors of the ensuing violence were either sold into Caribbean slavery by their better armed, erstwhile hosts, or 3 were ruthlessly driven from their Cape Cod homes. Despite the symbolic idealism of the first potluck, New England—from the emerging European point of view—simply wasn't big enough for two sets of societies.

4 An enduring benefit of success, when one culture clashes with another, is that the victorious group controls the record. It owns not only the immediate spoils but also the power to edit, embellish and concoct the facts of the original encounter for the generations to come. Events, once past, reside at the small end of the telescope, the vague and hazy antecedents to accepted reality.

5 Our collective modern fantasy of Thanksgiving is a case in point. It has evolved into a ritual pageant in which almost everyone of us, as children, either acted or were forced to watch a 17th century vision that we can conjure whole in the blink of an eye.

6 The cast of stock characters is as recognizable as those in any Macy's parade: long-faced Pilgrim men, pre-N.R.A. muskets at their sides, sitting around a rude outdoor table while their wives, dressed in long dresses, aprons and linen caps, bustle about lifting the lids off steaming kettles—pater and materfamilias of New World hospitality.

7 They dish out the turkey to a scattering of shirtless Indian invitees. But there is no ambiguity as to who is in charge of the occasion, who could be asked to leave, whose protocol prevails.

8 Only good Indians are admitted into this tableau, of course: those who accept the manifest destiny of a European presence and are prepared to adopt English dining customs and, by inference, English everything else.

9 These compliant Hollywood extras are, naturally enough, among the blessings the Pilgrims are thankful for—and why not? They're colorful, bring the food and vanish after dessert. They are something exotic to write home about, like a visit to Frontierland. In the sound bite of national folklore, they have metamorphosed into icons, totems of America as evocative, and ultimately as vapid, as a flag factory.

10 And these particular Indians did not all repair to the happy hunting grounds during the first Christmas rush. They lived on, smoking peace pipes and popping up at appropriate crowd-pleasing moments.

11 They lost mock battles from coast to coast in Wild West shows. In 19th century art, they sat bareback on their horses and watched a lot of sunsets. Whole professional teams of them take the home field every Sunday afternoon in Cleveland or Washington.

12 They are the sources of merit badges for Boy Scouts and the emblem of purity for imitation butter. They are, and have been from the beginning, predictable, manageable, domesticated cartoons, inventions without depth or reality apart from that bestowed by their creators.

13 These appreciative Indians, as opposed to the pesky flesh and blood native peoples on whom they are loosely modeled, did not question the

enforced exchange of their territories for a piece of pie. They did not protest when they died by the millions of European diseases.

They did not resist—except for the "bad" ones, the renegades—when solemn pacts made with them were broken or when their religions and customs were declared illegal. They did not make a fuss in courts in defense of their sovereignty. They never expected all the fixings anyway. 14

As for Thanksgiving 1988, the descendants of those first partygoers sit at increasingly distant tables, the pretense of equity all but abandoned. Against great odds, native Americans have maintained political identity—hundreds of tribes have Federal recognition as "domestic, dependent nations." 15

But, in a country so insecure about heterogeneity that it votes its dominant language as "official," this refusal to melt into the pot has been an expensive choice. 16

A majority of reservation Indians reside in among the most impoverished counties in the nation. They constitute the ethnic group at the wrong peak of every scale: most undernourished, most short-lived, least educated, least healthy. 17

For them, that long ago Thanksgiving was not a milestone, not a promise. It was the last full meal. 18

COMPREHENSION

1. Where in the essay does Dorris state his main idea? Would you say that he is arguing his point or simply presenting it? How do you know?
2. In your own words, state what Dorris explains about the myth and reality of the Native American.
3. How does Dorris explain the "collective modern fantasy" of Thanksgiving?

RHETORIC

1. Which paragraphs constitute the author's introduction? How does the author unify these paragraphs?
2. At what point does the body of the essay actually begin? What is the position of the thesis in relation to the body?
3. Explain Dorris's style, tone, and approach to paragraph development. What do these elements tell us about his intended audience?
4. How does Dorris develop an extended example of the "collective modern fantasy of Thanksgiving"? Which paragraphs constitute this extended example?
5. How does Dorris employ definition and comparison and contrast to advance his point?
6. Where does the conclusion of this essay begin? How do you know? Does the conclusion satisfy the reader's earlier expectations? Explain your response.

WRITING

1. Write a letter to Michael Dorris defending Thanksgiving. In the course of your argumentative essay, rebut the issues raised by the author.
2. Write an essay about your favorite holiday. Provide examples and details, narration and description.
3. In an explanatory essay, examine why it is desirable to be able to approach holidays from various perspectives and at least to understand why some people might not want to celebrate certain holidays the way you do.

VLADIMIR NABOKOV Vladimir Nabokov (1899–1977) was born into an aristocratic family in czarist Russia. Following the Russian Revolution, he went into exile in England in 1919. In 1922, he graduated with honors from Cambridge University. Subsequently he lived in Germany and France, writing in Russian, giving tennis lessons, and collecting butterflies—all recounted in his poignant autobiography, *Speak Memory* (1966). He came to the United States in 1940. Nabokov taught at Wellesley College from 1944 to 1948 and at Cornell University from 1948 to 1958. Nabokov, who once termed himself the greatest Russian novelist writing in English, gained enormous success with *Lolita* (1956). His later novels include *Pale Fire* (1962) and *Ada* (1969). He died in Montreux, Switzerland. With stylistic grace and satiric precision, Nabokov in the following essay defines both a state of mind and a social condition of our times.

VLADIMIR NABOKOV

Philistines and Philistinism

A philistine is a full-grown person whose interests are of a material and commonplace nature, and whose mentality is formed of the stock ideas and conventional ideals of his or her group and time. I have said "full-grown person" because the child or the adolescent who may look like a small philistine is only a small parrot mimicking the ways of confirmed vulgarians, and it is easier to be a parrot than to be a white heron. "Vulgarian" is more or less synonymous with "philistine": the stress in a vulgarian is not so much on the conventionalism of a philistine as on the vulgarity of some of his conventional notions. I may also use the terms *genteel* and *bourgeois*. *Genteel* implies the lace-curtain refined vulgarity which is worse than simple coarseness. To burp in company may be rude, but to say "excuse me" after a burp is genteel and thus worse than vulgar. The term *bourgeois* I use following Flaubert, not Marx. *Bourgeois* in Flaubert's sense is a state of mind, not a state of pocket. A bourgeois is a smug philistine, a dignified vulgarian. 1

2 A philistine is not likely to exist in a very primitive society although no doubt rudiments of philistinism may be found even there. We may imagine, for instance, a cannibal who would prefer the human head he eats to be artistically colored, just as the American philistine prefers his oranges to be painted orange, his salmon pink, and his whisky yellow. But generally speaking philistinism presupposes a certain advanced state of civilization where throughout the ages certain traditions have accumulated in a heap and have started to stink.

3 Philistinism is international. It is found in all nations and in all classes. An English duke can be as much of a philistine as an American Shriner or a French bureaucrat or a Soviet citizen. The mentality of a Lenin or a Stalin or a Hitler in regard to the arts and the sciences was utterly bourgeois. A laborer or a coal miner can be just as bourgeois as a banker or a housewife or a Hollywood star.

4 Philistinism implies not only a collection of stock ideas but also the use of set phrases, clichés, banalities expressed in faded words. A true philistine has nothing but these trivial ideas of which he entirely consists. But it should be admitted that all of us have our cliché side; all of us in everyday life often use words not as words but as signs, as coins, as formulas. This does not mean that we are all philistines, but it does mean that we should be careful not to indulge too much in the automatic process of exchanging platitudes. On a hot day every other person will ask you, "Is it warm enough for you?" but that does not necessarily mean that the speaker is a philistine. He may be merely a parrot or a bright foreigner. When a person asks you "Hullo, how *are* you?" it is perhaps a sorry cliché to reply, "Fine"; but if you made to him a detailed report of your condition you might pass for a pedant and a bore. It also happens that platitudes are used by people as a kind of disguise or as the shortest cut for avoiding conversation with fools. I have known great scholars and poets and scientists who in the cafeteria sank to the level of the most commonplace give and take.

5 The character I have in view when I say "smug vulgarian" is, thus, not the part-time philistine, but the total type, the genteel bourgeois, the complete universal product of triteness and mediocrity. He is the conformist, the man who conforms to his group, and he also is typified by something else: he is a pseudo-idealist, he is pseudo-compassionate, he is pseudo-wise. The fraud is the closest ally of the true philistine. All such great words as "Beauty," "Love," "Nature," "Truth," and so on become masks and dupes when the smug vulgarian employs them. In *Dead Souls* you have heard Chichikov. In *Bleak House* you have heard Skimpole. You have heard Homais in *Madame Bovary.* The philistine likes to impress and he likes to be impressed, in consequence of which a world of deception, of mutual cheating, is formed by him and around him.

6 The philistine in his passionate urge to conform, to belong, to join, is torn between two longings: to act as everybody does, to admire, to use this or that thing because millions of people do; or else he craves to belong to an exclusive set, to an organization, to a club, to a hotel pa-

tronage or an ocean liner community (with the captain in white and wonderful food), and to delight in the knowledge that there is the head of a corporation or a European count sitting next to him. The philistine is often a snob. He is thrilled by riches and rank—"Darling, I've actually talked to a duchess!"

7 A philistine neither knows nor cares anything about art, including literature—his essential nature is anti-artistic—but he wants information and he is trained to read magazines. He is a faithful reader of the *Saturday Evening Post,* and when he reads he identifies himself with the characters. If he is a male philistine he will identify himself with the fascinating executive or any other big shot—aloof, single, but a boy and a golfer at heart; or if the reader is a female philistine—a philistinette—she will identify herself with the fascinating strawberry-blond secretary, a slip of a girl but a mother at heart, who eventually marries the boyish boss. The philistine does not distinguish one writer from another; indeed, he reads little and only what may be useful to him, but he may belong to a book club and choose beautiful, *beautiful* books, a jumble of Simone de Beauvoir, Dostoevski, Marquand, Somerset Maugham, *Dr. Zhivago,* and Masters of the Renaissance. He does not much care for pictures, but for the sake of prestige he may hang in his parlor reproductions of Van Gogh's or Whistler's respective mothers, although secretly preferring Norman Rockwell.

8 In his love for the useful, for the material goods of life, he becomes an easy victim of the advertisement business. Ads may be very good ads—some of them are very artistic—that is not the point. The point is that they tend to appeal to the philistine's pride in possessing things whether silverware or underwear. I mean the following kind of ad: just come to the family is a radio set or a television set (or a car, or a refrigerator, or table silver—anything will do). It has just come to the family: mother clasps her hands in dazed delight, the children crowd around all agog: junior and the dog strain up to the edge of the table where the Idol is enthroned; even Grandma of the beaming wrinkles peeps out somewhere in the background; and somewhat apart, his thumbs gleefully inserted in the armpits of his waistcoat, stands triumphant Dad or Pop, the Proud Donor. Small boys and girls in ads are invariably freckled, and the smaller fry have front teeth missing. I have nothing against freckles (in fact I find them very becoming in live creatures) and quite possibly a special survey might reveal that the majority of small American-born Americans *are* freckled, or else perhaps another survey might reveal that all successful executives and handsome housewives had been freckled in their childhood. I repeat, I have really nothing against freckles as such. But I do think there is considerable philistinism involved in the use made of them by advertisers and other agencies. I am told that when an unfreckled, or only slightly freckled, little boy actor has to appear on the screen in television, an artificial set of freckles is applied to the middle of his face. Twenty-two freckles is the minimum: eight over each cheekbone and six on the saddle of the pert nose. In the comics, freckles look like a case of bad rash. In one series of

comics they appear as tiny circles. But although the good cute little boys of the ads are blond or redhaired, with freckles, the handsome young men of the ads are generally dark haired and always have thick dark eyebrows. The evolution is from Scotch to Celtic.

The rich philistinism emanating from advertisements is due not to their exaggerating (or inventing) the glory of this or that serviceable article but to suggesting that the acme of human happiness is purchasable and that its purchase somehow ennobles the purchaser. Of course, the world they create is pretty harmless in itself because everybody knows that it is made up by the seller with the understanding that the buyer will join in the make-believe. The amusing part is not that it is a world where nothing spiritual remains except the ecstatic smiles of people serving or eating celestial cereals, or a world where the game of the senses is played according to bourgeois rules, but that it is a kind of satellite shadow world in the actual existence of which neither sellers nor buyers really believe in their heart of hearts—especially in this wise quiet country. 9

Russians have, or had, a special name for smug philistinism—*poshlust. Poshlism* is not only the obviously trashy but mainly the falsely important, the falsely beautiful, the falsely clever, the falsely attractive. To apply the deadly label of *poshlism* to something is not only an esthetic judgment but also a moral indictment. The genuine, the guileless, the good is never *poshlust.* It is possible to maintain that a simple, uncivilized man is seldom if ever a *poshlust* since *poshlism* presupposes the veneer of civilization. A peasant has to become a townsman in order to become vulgar. A painted necktie has to hide the honest Adam's apple in order to produce *poshlism.* 10

It is possible that the term itself has been so nicely devised by Russians because of the cult of simplicity and good taste in old Russia. The Russia of today, a country of moral imbeciles, of smiling slaves and poker-faced bullies, has stopped noticing *poshlism* because Soviet Russia is so full of its special brand, a blend of despotism and pseudoculture; but in the old days a Gogol, a Tolstoy, a Chekhov in quest of the simplicity of truth easily distinguished the vulgar side of things as well as the trashy systems of pseudo-thought. But *poshlists* are found everywhere, in every country, in this country as well as in Europe—in fact *poshlism* is more common in Europe than here, despite our American ads. 11

COMPREHENSION

1. What does Nabokov reveal of his own background, beliefs, and behavior in this essay?
2. What, according to the author, is a philistine? Explain the representative characteristics of a philistine.
3. What does philistinism tell us about the state of society? Why is philistinism international? What does Nabokov say about the degrees of philistinism in Europe and in America?

RHETORIC

1. Nabokov employs several synonyms for *philistine* and *philistinism.* List them, and explain their shades of meaning.
2. Identify and explain the effectiveness of the various literary allusions in the essay.
3. Identify the topic sentence in each paragraph. Why are they so consistently placed? Relate their placement to the movement from general or abstract to specific and concrete in three representative paragraphs.
4. Does the author use actual examples or hypothetical examples in the essay? Explain.
5. How does Nabokov use definition? For what purpose does he employ it? What instances of comparison and contrast and causal analysis do you find?
6. What is the tone of the essay? What effect does that tone have on the way that Nabokov describes the philistine?

WRITING

1. What is your opinion of Nabokov's assertion that philistinism is rampant in the modern world? Respond to this question in an argumentative essay.
2. Write an extended definition of *philistinism,* using examples drawn from personal experience, reading, and the media.
3. Write an essay that uses definition to make a comic or satiric point about manners or social behavior.

ALICE WALKER Alice Walker (1944–) was born in Eatonton, Georgia, and now lives in San Francisco and Mendocino County, California. A celebrated poet, short-story writer, and novelist, she is the author of *Revolutionary Petunias and Other Poems, In Love and Trouble: Stories of Black Women,* and *Meridian,* among other works. Her 1983 novel, *The Color Purple,* won the American Book Award and the Pulitzer Prize in fiction. Her latest book, *Possessing the Secret of Joy,* was published in 1992 and continues the story of the characters introduced in *The Color Purple.* In the following narrative, Walker writes of a childhood accident that almost destroyed her self-esteem.

ALICE WALKER

Beauty: When the Other Dancer Is the Self

It is a bright summer day in 1947. My father, a fat, funny man with beautiful eyes and a subversive wit, is trying to decide which of his 1 eight children he will take with him to the county fair. My mother, of course, will not go. She is knocked out from getting most of us ready: I hold my neck stiff against the pressure of her knuckles as she hastily completes the braiding and then beribboning of my hair.

My father is the driver for the rich old white lady up the road. Her 2 name is Miss Mey. She owns all the land for miles around, as well as the house in which we live. All I remember about her is that she once offered to pay my mother thirty-five cents for cleaning her house, raking up piles of her magnolia leaves, and washing her family's clothes, and that my mother—she of no money, eight children, and a chronic earache—refused it. But I do not think of this in 1947. I am two and a half years old. I want to go everywhere my daddy goes. I am excited at the prospect of riding in a car. Someone has told me fairs are fun. That there is room in the car for only three of us doesn't faze me at all. Whirling happily in my starchy frock, showing off my biscuit-polished patent-leather shoes and lavender socks, tossing my head in a way that makes my ribbons bounce, I stand, hands on hips, before my father. "Take me, Daddy," I say with assurance: "I'm the prettiest!"

Later, it does not surprise me to find myself in Miss Mey's shiny 3 black car, sharing the back seat with the other lucky ones. Does not surprise me that I thoroughly enjoy the fair. At home that night I tell the unlucky ones all I can remember about the merry-go-round, the man who eats live chickens, and the teddy bears, until they say: that's enough, baby Alice. Shut up now, and go to sleep.

It is Easter Sunday, 1950. I am dressed in a green, flocked, scal- 4 loped-hem dress (handmade by my adoring sister, Ruth) that has its own smooth satin petticoat and tiny hot-pink roses tucked into each scallop. My shoes, new T-strap patent leather, again highly biscuit-polished. I am six years old and have learned one of the longest Easter speeches to be heard that day, totally unlike the speech I said when I was two: "Easter lilies/pure and white/blossom in/the morning light." When I rise to give my speech I do so on a great wave of love and pride and expectation. People in the church stop rustling their new crinolines. They seem to hold their breath. I can tell they admire my dress, but it is my spirit, bordering on sassiness (womanishness), they secretly applaud.

"That girl's a little *mess*," they whisper to each other, pleased. 5

Naturally I say my speech without stammer or pause, unlike those 6 who stutter, stammer, or, worst of all, forget. This is before the word "beautiful" exists in people's vocabulary, but "Oh, isn't she the *cutest* thing!" frequently floats my way. "And got so much sense!" they gratefully add . . . for which thoughtful addition I thank them to this day.

It was great fun being cute. But then, one day, it ended. 7

I am eight years old and a tomboy. I have a cowboy hat, cowboy 8 boots, checkered shirt and pants, all red. My playmates are my brothers, two and four years older than I. Their colors are black and green, the only difference in the way we are dressed. On Saturday nights we all go to the picture show, even my mother; Westerns are her favorite kind of movie. Back home, "on the ranch," we pretend we are Tom Mix, Hopalong Cassidy, Lash LaRue (we've even named one of our dogs Lash LaRue); we chase each other for hours rustling cattle, being outlaws, delivering damsels from distress. Then my parents decide to buy my brothers guns. These are not "real" guns. They shoot "BBs," copper pellets my brothers say will kill birds. Because I am a girl, I do not get a gun. Instantly I am relegated to the position of Indian. Now there appears a great distance between us. They shoot and shoot at everything with their new guns. I try to keep up with my bow and arrows.

One day while I am standing on top of our makeshift "garage"—pieces of tin nailed across some poles—holding my bow and arrow and looking out toward the fields, I feel an incredible blow in my right eye. I look down just in time to see my brother lower his gun. 9

Both brothers rush to my side. My eye stings, and I cover it with my hand. "If you tell," they say, "we will get a whipping. You don't want that to happen, do you?" I do not. "Here is a piece of wire," says the older brother, picking it up from the roof; "say you stepped on one end of it and the other flew up and hit you." The pain is beginning to start. "Yes," I say, "Yes, I will say that is what happened." If I do not say this is what happened, I know my brothers will find ways to make me wish I had. But now I will say anything that gets me to my mother. 10

Confronted by our parents we stick to the lie agreed upon. They place me on a bench on the porch and I close my left eye while they examine the right. There is a tree growing from underneath the porch that climbs past the railing to the roof. It is the last thing my right eye sees. I watch as its trunk, its branches, and then its leaves are blotted out by the rising blood. 11

I am in shock. First there is intense fever, which my father tries to break using lily leaves bound around my head. Then there are chills: my mother tries to get me to eat soup. Eventually, I do not know how, my parents learn what has happened. A week after the "accident" they take me to see a doctor. "Why did you wait so long to come?" he asks, looking into my eye and shaking his head. "Eyes are sympathetic," he says. "If one is blind, the other will likely become blind too." 12

This comment of the doctor's terrifies me. But it is really how I look that bothers me most. Where the BB pellet struck there is a glob of whitish scar tissue, a hideous cataract, on my eye. Now when I stare at people—a favorite pastime, up to now—they will stare back. Not at the "cute" little girl, but at her scar. For six years I do not stare at anyone, because I do not raise my head. 13

Years later, in the throes of a mid-life crisis, I ask my mother and sister whether I changed after the "accident." "No," they say, puzzled. "What do you mean?" 14

15 *What do I mean?*

16 I am eight, and, for the first time, doing poorly in school, where I have been something of a whiz since I was four. We have just moved to the place where the "accident" occurred. We do not know any of the people around us because this is a different county. The only time I see the friends I knew is when we go back to our old church. The new school is the former state penitentiary. It is a large stone building, cold and drafty, crammed to overflowing with boisterous, ill-disciplined children. On the third floor there is a huge circular imprint of some partition that has been torn out.

17 "What used to be here?" I ask a sullen girl next to me on our way past it to lunch.

18 "The electric chair," says she.

19 At night I have nightmares about the electric chair, and about all the people reputedly "fried" in it. I am afraid of the school, where all the students seem to be budding criminals.

20 "What's the matter with your eye?" they ask, critically.

21 When I don't answer (I cannot decide whether it was an "accident" or not), they shove me, insist on a fight.

22 My brother, the one who created the story about the wire, comes to my rescue. But then brags so much about "protecting" me, I become sick.

23 After months of torture at the school, my parents decide to send me back to our old community, to my old school. I live with my grandparents and the teacher they board. But there is no room for Phoebe, my cat. By the time my grandparents decide there *is* room, and I ask for my cat, she cannot be found. Miss Yarborough, the boarding teacher, takes me under her wing, and begins to teach me to play the piano. But soon she marries an African—a "prince," she says—and is whisked away to his continent.

24 At my old school there is at least one teacher who loves me. She is the teacher who "knew me before I was born" and bought my first baby clothes. It is she who makes life bearable. It is her presence that finally helps me turn on the one child at the school who continually calls me "one-eyed bitch." One day I simply grab him by his coat and beat him until I am satisfied. It is my teacher who tells me my mother is ill.

25 My mother is lying in bed in the middle of the day, something I have never seen. She is in too much pain to speak. She has an abscess in her ear. I stand looking down on her, knowing that if she dies, I cannot live. She is being treated with warm oils and hot bricks held against her cheek. Finally a doctor comes. But I must go back to my grandparents' house. The weeks pass but I am hardly aware of it. All I know is that my mother might die, my father is not so jolly, my brothers still have their guns, and I am the one sent away from home.

26 "You did not change," they say.

Did I imagine the anguish of never looking up? 27

I am twelve. When relatives come to visit I hide in my room. My cousin Brenda, just my age, whose father works in the post office and whose mother is a nurse, comes to find me. "Hello," she says. And then she asks, looking at my recent school picture, which I did not want taken, and on which the "glob," as I think of it, is clearly visible, "You still can't see out of that eye?"

"No," I say, and flop back on the bed over my book. 29

That night, as I do almost every night, I abuse my eye. I rant and 30
rave at it, in front of the mirror. I plead with it to clear up before morning. I tell it I hate and despise it. I do not pray for sight. I pray for beauty.

"You did not change," they say. 31

I am fourteen and baby-sitting for my brother Bill, who lives in 32
Boston. He is my favorite brother and there is a strong bond between us. Understanding my feelings of shame and ugliness he and his wife take me to a local hospital, where the "glob" is removed by a doctor named O. Henry. There is still a small bluish crater where the scar tissue was, but the ugly white stuff is gone. Almost immediately I become a different person from the girl who does not raise her head. Or so I think. Now that I've raised my head I win the boyfriend of my dreams. Now that I've raised my head I have plenty of friends. Now that I've raised my head classwork comes from my lips as faultlessly as Easter speeches did, and I leave high school as valedictorian, most popular student, and *queen,* hardly believing my luck. Ironically, the girl who was voted most beautiful in our class (and was) was later shot twice through the chest by a male companion, using a "real" gun, while she was pregnant. But that's another story in itself. Or is it?

"You did not change," they say. 33

It is now thirty years since the "accident." A beautiful journalist 34
comes to visit and to interview me. She is going to write a cover story for her magazine that focuses on my latest book. "Decide how you want to look on the cover," she says. "Glamorous, or whatever."

Never mind "glamorous," it is the "whatever" that I hear. Suddenly 35
all I can think of is whether I will get enough sleep the night before the photography session: if I don't, my eye will be tired and wander, as blind eyes will.

At night in bed with my lover I think up reasons why I should not 36
appear on the cover of a magazine. "My meanest critics will say I've sold out," I say. "My family will now realize I write scandalous books."

"But what's the real reason you don't want to do this?" he asks. 37

"Because in all probability," I say in a rush, "my eye won't be 38
straight."

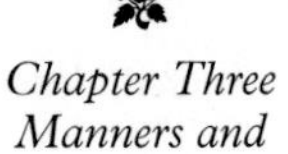

"It will be straight enough," he says. Then, "Besides, I thought 39
you'd made your peace with that."

And I suddenly remember that I have. 40

I remember: 41

I am talking to my brother Jimmy, asking if he remembers anything unusual about the day I was shot. He does not know I consider that day the last time my father, with his sweet home remedy of cool lily leaves, chose me, and that I suffered and raged inside because of this. "Well," he says, "all I remember is standing by the side of the highway with Daddy, trying to flag down a car. A white man stopped, but when Daddy said he needed somebody to take his little girl to the doctor, he drove off."

I remember: 42

I am in the desert for the first time. I fall totally in love with it. I am so overwhelmed by its beauty, I confront for the first time, consciously, the meaning of the doctor's words years ago: "Eyes are sympathetic. If one is blind, the other will likely become blind too." I realize I have dashed about the world madly, looking at this, looking at that, storing up images against the fading of the light. *But I might have missed seeing the desert!* The shock of that possibility—and gratitude for over twenty-five years of sight—sends me literally to my knees. Poem after poem comes—which is perhaps how poets pray.

On Sight 43

I am so thankful I have seen
The Desert
And the creatures in the desert
And the desert Itself.

The desert has its own moon
Which I have seen
With my own eye.
There is no flag on it.

Trees of the desert have arms
All of which are always up
That is because the moon is up
The sun is up
Also the sky
The stars
Clouds
None with flags.
If there were flags, I doubt
the trees would point.
Would you?

But mostly, I remember this: 44

I am twenty-seven, and my baby daughter is almost three. Since her birth I have worried about her discovery that her mother's eyes are different from other people's. Will she be embarrassed? I think. What will she say? Every day she watches a television program called "Big Blue Marble." It begins with a picture of the earth as it appears from the moon. It is bluish, a little battered-looking, but full of light, with whitish clouds swirling around it. Every time I see it I weep with love, as if it is a picture of Grandma's house. One day when I am putting Rebecca down for her nap, she suddenly focuses on my eye. Something inside me cringes, gets ready to try to protect myself. All children are cruel about physical differences, I know from experience, and that they don't always mean to be is another matter. I assume Rebecca will be the same.

But no-o-o-o. She studies my face intently as we stand, her inside 45
and me outside her crib. She even holds my face maternally between her dimpled little hands. Then, looking every bit as serious and lawyer-like as her father, she says, as if it may just possibly have slipped my attention: "Mommy, there's a *world* in your eye." (As in, "Don't be alarmed, or do anything crazy.") And then, gently, but with great interest: "Mommy, where did you get that world in your eye?"

For the most part, the pain left then. (So what, if my brothers grew 46
up to buy even more powerful pellet guns for their sons and to carry real guns themselves. So what, if a young "Morehouse man" once nearly fell off the steps of Trevor Arnett Library because he thought my eyes were blue.) Crying and laughing I ran to the bathroom, while Rebecca mumbled and sang herself off to sleep. Yes indeed, I realized, looking into the mirror. There was a world in my eye. And I saw that it was possible to love it: that in fact, for all it had taught me of shame and anger and inner vision, I *did* love it. Even to see it drifting out of orbit in boredom, or rolling up out of fatigue, not to mention floating back at attention in excitement (bearing witness, a friend has called it), deeply suitable to my personality, and even characteristic of me.

That night I dream I am dancing to Stevie Wonder's song "Always" 47
(the name of the song is really "As," but I hear it as "Always"). As I dance, whirling and joyous, happier than I've ever been in my life, another bright-faced dancer joins me. We dance and kiss each other and hold each other through the night. The other dancer has obviously come through all right, as I have done. She is beautiful, whole and free. And she is also me.

COMPREHENSION

1. Describe Walker's self-image before and after the accident.
2. How do the adults' perceptions differ from Walker's when she confronts them years later?
3. How does Walker's daughter react to her mother's deformity? What effect does this have on the writer?

RHETORIC

1. Why does Walker go into detail when describing clothing and appearance in paragraphs 2, 4, and 8? How do these descriptions underscore the thesis of her essay?
2. Examine the use of the word *mess* (paragraph 5); look it up in the dictionary, and compare its meaning to the way it is used in the paragraph.
3. What device does Walker utilize to take us through the key points in the narrative? How does this device help to "ground" the story for the reader?
4. Why is paragraph 7 italicized and set apart from surrounding paragraphs? What is Walker trying to emphasize here? What effect does this paragraph have on the reader?
5. Identify the devices and strategies that Walker uses to divide her essay into sections.
6. What point is Walker making toward the end of paragraph 32, where she recounts the tragic end of the girl voted "most beautiful"? What is its value to the narrative?

WRITING

1. Write an essay in which you analyze the emphasis placed on physical beauty in American society. Is the pressure placed equally on males and females? Would a man write an essay similar to Walker's? Why, or why not?
2. Write an essay defining *beauty*. Consider both the denotative and connotative meanings. Where does human physical beauty fit in your definition?
3. Write a personal narrative describing your own body image. What positive or negative messages did you receive from your family and environment as a child? How did other people's opinions help shape your current body image?

CLASSIC AND CONTEMPORARY

JOSEPH ADDISON Joseph Addison (1672–1719) was an essayist, poet, dramatist, statesman, and journalist. As a playwright, he wrote one of the most successful tragedies of the eighteenth century (*Cato,* in 1713). As a statesman, he served as secretary of state under George I. As an essayist, he wrote with reason and wit in the *Tatler* (1710–1711) and the *Spectator* (1711–1712, and 1714). Just as he excelled as a statesman and tragedian, he excelled as an essayist; he is often considered one of the best English essayists. Here, Addison examines one of the great foibles of his age—and ours.

JOSEPH ADDISON

A Superstitious Household

Somnia, terrores magicos, miracula, sagas,
*Nocturnos, lemures, portentaque Thessala rides?** —Horace

Going yesterday to dine with an old acquaintance, I had the misfortune to find his whole family very much dejected. Upon asking him the occasion of it, he told me that his wife had dreamt a very strange dream the night before, which they were afraid portended some misfortune to themselves or to their children. At her coming into the room, I observed a settled melancholy in her countenance, which I should have been troubled for, had I not heard from whence it proceeded. We were no sooner sat down, but, after having looked upon me a little while, "My dear," says she, turning to her husband, "you may now see the stranger that was in the candle last night." Soon after this, as they began to talk of family affairs, a little boy at the lower end of the table told her that he was to go into join-hand on Thursday. "Thursday?" says she, "no, child, if it please God, you shall not begin upon Childermas Day, tell your writing master that Friday will be soon enough." I was reflecting with myself on the oddness of her fancy, and wondering that anybody would establish it as a rule to lose a day in every week. In the midst of these my musings, she desired me to reach her a little salt upon the point of my knife, which I did in such a trepidation and hurry of obedience, that I let it drop by the way; at which she immediately startled, and said it fell towards her. Upon this I looked very blank; and, observing the concern of the whole table, 1

*"Can you make sport of portents, gipsy crones, Hobgoblins, dreams, raw head and bloody bones?" John Conington (translator)

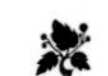

began to consider myself, with some confusion, as a person that had brought a disaster upon the family. The lady however recovering herself, after a little space, said to her husband with a sigh, "My dear, misfortunes never come single." My friend, I found, acted but an under part at his table, and being a man of more good nature than understanding, thinks himself obliged to fall in with all the passions and humors of his yoke-fellow. "Do not you remember, child," says she, "that the pigeon-house fell the very afternoon that our careless wench spilt the salt upon the table?" "Yes," says he, "my dear, and the next post brought us an account of the battle of Almanza." The reader may guess at the figure I made, after having done all this mischief. I despatched my dinner as soon as I could, with my usual taciturnity; when, to my utter confusion, the lady seeing me cleaning my knife and fork, and laying them across one another upon my plate, desired me that I would humor her so far as to take them out of that figure, and place them side by side. What the absurdity was which I had committed I did not know, but I suppose there was some traditionary superstition in it; and therefore, in obedience to the lady of the house, I disposed of my knife and fork in two parallel lines, which is the figure I shall always lay them in for the future, though I do not know any reason for it.

It is not difficult for a man to see that a person has conceived an 2
aversion to him. For my own part, I quickly found, by the lady's looks, that she regarded me as a very odd kind of fellow, with an unfortunate aspect: for which reason I took my leave immediately after dinner, and withdrew to my own lodgings. Upon my return home, I fell into a profound contemplation on the evils that attend these superstitious follies of mankind; how they subject us to imaginary afflictions, and additional sorrows, that do not properly come within our lot. As if the natural calamities of life were not sufficient for it, we turn the most indifferent circumstances into misfortunes, and suffer as much from trifling accidents as from real evils. I have known the shooting of a star spoil a night's rest; and have seen a man in love grow pale and lose his appetite upon the plucking of a merry-thought. A screech owl at midnight has alarmed a family more than a band of robbers; nay, the voice of a cricket hath struck more terror than the roaring of a lion. There is nothing so inconsiderable, which may not appear dreadful to an imagination that is filled with omens and prognostics. A rusty nail, or a crooked pin, shoot up into prodigies.

I remember I was once in a mixed assembly, that was full of noise 3
and mirth, when on a sudden an old woman unluckily observed there were thirteen of us in company. This remark struck a panic terror into several who were present, insomuch that one or two of the ladies were going to leave the room; but a friend of mine taking notice that one of our female companions was big with child, affirmed there were fourteen in the room, and that, instead of portending one of the company should die, it plainly foretold one of them should be born. Had not my friend found this expedient to break the omen, I question not but half the women in the company would have fallen sick that very night.

An old maid, that is troubled with the vapors, produces infinite dis- 4
turbances of this kind among her friends and neighbors. I know a maiden aunt of a great family, who is one of these antiquated Sibyls, that forebodes and prophesies from one end of the year to the other. She is always seeing apparitions, and hearing death-watches, and was the other day almost frightened out of her wits by the great house-dog, that howled in the stable at a time when she lay ill of the tooth-ache. Such an extravagant cast of mind engages multitudes of people not only in impertinent terrors, but in supernumerary duties of life; and arises from that fear and ignorance which are natural to the soul of man. The horror with which we entertain the thoughts of death (or indeed of any future evil) and the uncertainty of its approach, fill a melancholy mind with innumerable apprehensions and suspicions, and consequently dispose it to the observation of such groundless prodigies and predictions. For as it is the chief concern of wise men to retrench the evils of life by the reasonings of philosophy; it is the employment of fools to multiply them by the sentiments of superstition.

For my own part, I should be very much troubled were I endowed with this divining quality, though it should inform me truly of every thing that can befall me. I would not anticipate the relish of any happiness, nor feel the weight of any misery, before it actually arrives.

I know but one way of fortifying my soul against these gloomy presages and terrors of mind, and that is, by securing to myself the
friendship and protection of that Being who disposes of events, and 6
governs futurity. He sees, at one view, the whole thread of my existence, not only that part of it which I have already passed through, but that which runs forward into all the depths of eternity. When I lay me down to sleep, I recommend myself to his care; when I awake, I give myself up to his direction. Amidst all the evils that threaten me, I will look up to him for help, and question not but he will either avert them, or turn them to my advantage. Though I know neither the time nor the manner of the death I am to die, I am not at all solicitous about it; because I am sure that he knows them both, and that he will not fail to comfort and support me under them.

COMPREHENSION

1. Compare the attitude of Addison toward superstition with the attitude of his acquaintance's wife.
2. According to Addison, what is the difference between wise men and fools?
3. Even if he could foretell the future, Addison would choose not to. Why?

RHETORIC

1. Who was the Sibyl? Why is the allusion to her in paragraph 4 appropriate?
2. Define these words: *join-hand* (paragraph 1); *Childermas* (paragraph 1); *merry-thought* (paragraph 2); *death-watches* (paragraph 4).

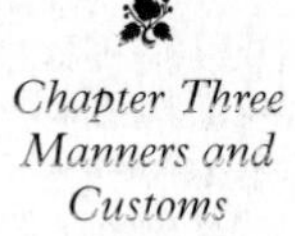

3. How are superstitions examples of the logical fallacy *post hoc ergo propter hoc* in this essay?
4. Explain shifts of tone in the essay. What function does the shifting serve?
5. How does comparison and contrast function in this essay?
6. What assumptions about reason and superstition underlie this essay?

WRITING

1. What superstitions described in the essay are still prevalent today? Why do you think superstitions remain popular?
2. Write an argumentative essay on the value of superstition. Write from the first-person point of view, and cite examples.
3. Classify the main types of superstition encountered in society today.

LETTY COTTIN POGREBIN Letty Cottin Pogrebin (1939–) is deeply committed to women's issues, family politics, and the nonsexist rearing and education of children. A native of New York, she graduated from Brandeis University and, from 1971–1987, was the editor of *Ms.* magazine, for which she remains a contributing editor. She has also contributed to such publications as the *New York Times* and *The Nation* and has written a number of books, among them *Among Friends* (1986); *Debra, Golda and Me: Being Female and Jewish in America* (1991); and *Family Politics* (1983). Pogrebin lectures frequently and is a founder of the Women's Political Caucus. In the following essay, she reminisces about her fearful, superstitious mother, whom she understands much better since becoming a mother herself.

LETTY COTTIN POGREBIN

Superstitious Minds

I am a very rational person. I tend to trust reason more than feeling. But I also happen to be superstitious—in my fashion. Black cats and rabbits' feet hold no power for me. My superstitions are my mother's superstitions, the amulets and incantations she learned from her mother and taught me. 1

I don't mean to suggest that I grew up in an occult atmosphere. On the contrary, my mother desperately wanted me to rise above her immigrant ways and become an educated American. She tried to hide her superstitions, but I came to know them all: Slap a girl's cheeks when she first gets her period. Never take a picture of a pregnant woman. Knock wood when speaking about your good fortune. Eat the ends of bread if you want to have a boy. Don't leave a bride alone on her wedding day. 2

When I was growing up, my mother often would tiptoe in after I seemed to be asleep and kiss my forehead three times, making odd 3 noises that sounded like a cross between sucking and spitting. One night I opened my eyes and demanded an explanation. Embarrassed, she told me she was excising the "Evil Eye"—in case I had attracted its attention that day by being especially wonderful. She believed her kisses could suck out any envy or ill will that those less fortunate may have directed at her child.

By the time I was in my teens, I was almost on speaking terms with 4
the Evil Eye, a jealous spirit that kept track of those who had "too much" happiness and zapped them with sickness and misery to even the score. To guard against this mischief, my mother practiced rituals of interference, evasion, deference, and above all, avoidance of situations where the Evil Eye might feel at home.

This is why I wasn't allowed to attend funerals. This is also why my 5
mother hated to mend my clothes while I was wearing them. The only garment one should properly get sewn *into* is a shroud. To ensure that the Evil Eye did not confuse my pinafore with a burial outfit, my mother insisted that I chew a thread while she sewed, thus proving myself very much alive. Outwitting the Evil Eye also accounted for her closing the window shades above my bed whenever there was a full moon. The moon should only shine on cemeteries, you see; the living need protection from the spirits.

Because we were dealing with a deadly force, I also wasn't sup- 6
posed to say any words associated with mortality. This was hard for a 12-year-old who punctuated every anecdote with the verb "to die," as in "You'll die when you hear this!" or "If I don't get home by ten, I'm dead." I managed to avoid using such expressions in the presence of my mother until the day my parents brought home a painting I hated and we were arguing about whether it should be displayed on our walls. Unthinking, I pressed my point with a melodramatic idiom: "That picture will hang over my dead body!" Without a word, my mother grabbed a knife and slashed the canvas to shreds.

I understand all this now. My mother emigrated in 1907 from a 7
small Hungarian village. The oldest of seven children, she had to go out to work before she finished the eighth grade. Experience taught her that life was unpredictable and often incomprehensible. Just as an athlete keeps wearing the same T-shirt in every game to prolong a winning streak, my mother's superstitions gave her a means of imposing order on a chaotic system. Her desire to control the fates sprung from the same helplessness that makes the San Francisco 49ers' defensive more superstitious than its offensive team. Psychologists speculate this is because the defense has less control; they don't have the ball.

Women like my mother never had the ball. She died when I was 8
15, leaving me with deep regrets for what she might have been—and a growing understanding of who she was. *Superstitious* is one of the things she was. I wish I had a million sharp recollections of her, but when you don't expect someone to die, you don't store up enough memories. Ironically, her mystical practices are among the clearest

impressions she left behind. In honor of this matrilineal heritage—and to symbolize my mother's effort to control her life as I in my way try to find order in mine—I knock on wood and I do not let the moon shine on those I love. My children laugh at me, but they understand that these tiny rituals have helped keep my mother alive in my mind.

A year ago, I awoke in the night and realized that my son's window blinds had been removed for repair. Smiling at my own compulsion, I got a bed sheet to tack up against the moonlight and I opened his bedroom door. What I saw brought tears to my eyes. There, hopelessly askew, was a blanket my son, then 18, had taped to his window like a curtain. 9

My mother never lived to know David, but he knew she would not want the moon to shine upon him as he slept. 10

COMPREHENSION

1. What is the function of superstition in the writer's life? What purpose did it serve in her mother's life?
2. What was Pogrebin's reaction to her mother's behavior while she was growing up? How does the adult feel?
3. How does the writer use superstitions now as an adult? Has she passed on these beliefs to her children? Explain.

RHETORIC

1. Examine Pogrebin's first sentence. How does it prepare the reader for the content of the essay? How does its simplicity add to its force?
2. How do the accumulated examples in paragraph 2 illustrate the point of the paragraph?
3. What is the writer's tone? Justify your answer.
4. What is the point of paragraph 7? How does the metaphor work to support Pogrebin's point?
5. What is the purpose of the essay? Where does it become apparent? How do the other paragraphs reinforce it?
6. Comment on the author's final sentence. What effect does it have on the reader? How does it help to hold the essay together?

WRITING

1. Children are often annoyed or embarrassed by their parents' behavior or beliefs. Write an essay describing something your parents repeatedly said or did that caused you discomfort or confusion. Include how you now feel about their actions and any insight you may have since gained about their motives or feelings.
2. Write an essay about superstition. Consider the meaning of the word. What

connection, if any, does it have with religion? How do superstitions affect the people who believe in them? Why do they believe? What is the role of superstition in your family? Provide examples of superstitions.

3. Write an essay in which you consider how your parents raised you—the values, opinions, beliefs they instilled in you. Would you want to pass these on to your children? Why, or why not?

CLASSIC AND CONTEMPORARY: QUESTIONS FOR COMPARISON

1. How do Addison and Pogrebin view superstitions? Cite examples from both that support their views. What particular views are held in common by both writers? Where do their opinions differ?
2. Examine the use of language in both essays. Pick particular phrases or passages that exemplify the styles of each. What expressions or ideas are illustrative of the time the essays were written?
3. Using support from either author, write an essay in which you explore the role of superstition in your own family. Which particular superstitions mentioned in the essays were believed in your family, and which are unknown to you?
4. According to Pogrebin and Addison, how important are family and community in upholding and promulgating superstitions?

CONNECTIONS

1. Baraka and Alvarez write about food in their essays. What connections do they make between food and cultural alienation? How do they present their ideas? How does Baraka's tone differ from that of Alvarez? Consider the use of humor in both pieces.
2. Write an essay exploring the role of the father in the essays of Walker and Wong. Compare the impact these men had on the writers' lives. How strong is the maternal presence in these essays?
3. How do Alvarez, Walker, and Pogrebin use experiences with their children to support or illustrate their respective points of view? Give examples from all three writers.
4. Consider the current position of women in the world. What determines beauty or desirability in a woman? Do women own their own bodies? Explore these issues, using support for your views from Mojtabai, Wong, and Walker.
5. What role have manner and custom played in shaping contemporary American culture? Mention specific customs you're familiar with, and describe the lessons they teach about life in America today. Make a connection between your views and those of Michael Dorris.
6. Consider the use of dialogue, slang, and syntax in the essays of Walker and Baraka. How does language help to promote the writers' points of view? Are they using language in a similar manner? Who are they writing for?
7. How does one's experience of being an "outsider," or stranger to a culture, affect one's understanding of that culture? Use the essays by Alvarez, Wong, and Mojtabai as a basis for your discussion.

CHAPTER FOUR

School and College

In "Learning to Read and Write," a chapter from his autobiography, Frederick Douglass offers a spirited affirmation of the rights we all should have to pursue an education. For Douglass, who began his life in slavery, knowledge began with experience but also with the need to articulate that experience through literacy. The ability to read and write should be the possession of all human beings, and Douglass was willing to risk punishment—even death—to gain that ability.

Perhaps the struggle for an education always involves a certain amount of effort and risk, but the struggle also conveys excitement and the deep, abiding satisfaction that derives from achieving knowledge of oneself and of the world. Time and again in the essays comprising this chapter, we discover that there is always a price to be paid for acquiring knowledge, developing intellectual skills, and attaining wisdom. However, numerous task forces and national commissions tell us that students today are not willing to pay this price and that, as a consequence, we have become academically mediocre. Is it true that we no longer delight in educating ourselves through reading, as Richard Rodriguez recounts in "The Lonely Good Company of Books"? Is it true that we take libraries for granted but never visit them, a thought that would have been anathema to Richard Wright, who educated himself through them? A democratic society requires an educated citizenry, people who refuse to commit intellectual suicide. The writers in this chapter, who take many pathways to understanding, remind us that we cannot afford to be passive or compliant when our right to an education is challenged.

Today we are in an era of dynamic change in attitudes toward education. Such issues as sex education, multiculturalism, and racism on

campus—subjects treated by three of the essayists in this chapter—suggest the liveliness of the educational debate. Any debate over contemporary education touches on the themes of politics, economics, religion, or the social agenda, forcing us to recognize that configurations of power are at the heart of virtually all educational issues in society today.

Mark Twain, whom you encountered in an earlier chapter, called "petrified opinion" the opposite of true knowledge and the enemy of democratic processes. Indeed, if we judge the tenor of the essayists in this section, we discover that many of them are subversives, waging war against both ignorance *and* received dogma. These writers treat education as the key vehicle to upset the status quo and effect change. Operating from diverse backgrounds and cultural traditions, they reveal many pathways to knowledge and wisdom, inviting us to think critically about the purpose of education.

Previewing the Chapter

As you read the essays in this chapter and respond to them in discussion and writing, consider the following questions:

- What is the main educational issue that the author deals with?
- What tone does the author establish in treating the subject? Does the author take a positive or a negative approach to the topic?
- How does the author define *education?* How closely is the definition tied to the author's own experience?
- Which problems and conflicts influence the writer's attitude toward education? How did the writer overcome these problems?
- What is the impact of race, ethnicity, class, and gender on the educational issues discussed?
- How does education change the writer's view of himself or herself?
- According to the author, what is the purpose or end of education?
- Do you share the writer's viewpoint on education, or do you oppose it?
- How closely does the author's educational experience or attitude parallel your own?
- What have you learned about the value of education from reading these selections?

E. B. WHITE Elwyn Brooks White (1899–1985), perhaps the finest contemporary American essayist, is at his most distinctive in his treatments of people, nature, and social conventions. A recipient of the National Medal for literature, and associated for years with *The New Yorker,* White is the author of *One Man's Meat* (1942), *Here Is New York* (1949), and *The Second Tree from the Corner* (1954), among numerous other works. He is also one of the most talented writers of literature for children, the author of *Stuart Little* (1945), *Charlotte's Web* (1952), and *The Trumpet of the Swan* (1970). Most writers and lovers of language have read and reread his witty, cogent explanation of English grammar in his revision of William Strunk Jr.'s *The Elements of Style* (1959). In the following essay, White reveals his abiding love for the country experience as he muses on the comparative values of urban and rural, private and public education.

E. B. WHITE

Education

I have an increasing admiration for the teacher in the country school where we have a third-grade scholar in attendance. She not only undertakes to instruct her charges in all the subjects of the first three grades, but she manages to function quietly and effectively as a guardian of their health, their clothes, their habits, their mothers, and their snowball engagements. She has been doing this sort of Augean task for twenty years, and is both kind and wise. She cooks for the children on the stove that heats the room, and she can cool their passions or warm their soup with equal competence. She conceives their costumes, cleans up their messes, and shares their confidences. My boy already regards his teacher as his great friend, and I think tells her a great deal more than he tells us. 1

The shift from city school to country school was something we worried about quietly all last summer. I have always rather favored public school over private school, if only because in public school you meet a greater variety of children. This bias of mine, I suspect, is partly an attempt to justify my own past (I never knew anything but public schools) and partly an involuntary defense against getting kicked in the shins by a young ceramist on his way to the kiln. My wife was unacquainted with public schools, never having been exposed (in her early life) to anything more public than the washroom of Miss Winsor's. Regardless of our backgrounds, we both knew that change in schools was something that concerned not us but the scholar himself. We hoped it would work out all right. In New York our son went to a medium-priced private institution with semi-progressive ideas of education, 2

and modern plumbing. He learned fast, kept well, and we were satisfied. It was an electric, colorful, regimented existence with moments of pleasurable pause and giddy incident. The day the Christmas angel fainted and had to be carried out by one of the Wise Men was educational in the highest sense of the term. Our scholar gave imitations of it around the house for weeks afterward, and I doubt if it ever goes completely out of his mind.

His days were rich in formal experience. Wearing overalls and an 3
old sweater (the accepted uniform of the private seminary), he sallied forth at morn accompanied by a nurse or a parent and walked (or was pulled) two blocks to a corner where the school bus made a flag stop. This flashy vehicle was as punctual as death: seeing us waiting at the cold curb, it would sweep to a halt, open its mouth, suck the boy in, and spring away with an angry growl. It was a good deal like a train picking up a bag of mail. At school the scholar was worked on for six or seven hours by half a dozen teachers and a nurse, and was revived on orange juice in mid-morning. In a cinder court he played games supervised by an athletic instructor, and in a cafeteria he ate lunch worked out by a dietitian. He soon learned to read with gratifying facility and discernment and to make Indian weapons of a semi-deadly nature. Whenever one of his classmates fell low of a fever the news was put on the wires and there were breathless phone calls to physicians, discussing periods of incubation and allied magic.

In the country all one can say is that the situation is different, and 4
somehow more casual. Dressed in corduroys, sweatshirt, and short rubber boots, and carrying a tin dinner-pail, our scholar departs at crack of dawn for the village school, two and a half miles down the road, next to the cemetery. When the road is open and the car will start, he makes the journey by motor, courtesy of his old man. When the snow is deep or the motor is dead or both, he makes it on the hoof. In the afternoons he walks or hitches all or part of the way home in fair weather, gets transported in foul. The schoolhouse is a two-room frame building, bungalow type, shingles stained a burnt brown with weather-resistant stain. It has a chemical toilet in the basement and two teachers above stairs. One takes the first three grades, the other the fourth, fifth, and sixth. They have little or no time for individual instruction, and no time at all for the esoteric. They teach what they know themselves, just as fast and as hard as they can manage. The pupils sit still at their desks in class, and do their milling around outdoors during recess.

There is no supervised play. They play cops and robbers (only they 5
call it "Jail") and throw things at one another—snowballs in winter, rose hips in fall. It seems to satisfy them. They also construct darts, pinwheels, and "pick-up sticks" (jackstraws), and the school itself does a brisk trade in penny candy, which is for sale right in the classroom and which contains "surprises." The most highly prized surprise is a fake cigarette, made of cardboard, fiendishly lifelike.

The memory of how apprehensive we were at the beginning is still 6
strong. The boy was nervous about the change too. The tension, on

that first fair morning in September when we drove him to school, almost blew the windows out of the sedan. And when later we picked him up on the road, wandering along with his little blue lunch-pail, and got his laconic report "All right" in answer to our inquiry about how the day had gone, our relief was vast. Now, after almost a year of it, the only difference we can discover in the two school experiences is that in the country he sleeps better at night—and *that* probably is more the air than the education. When grilled on the subject of school-in-country vs. school-in-city, he replied that the chief difference is that the day seems to go so much quicker in the country. "Just like lightning," he reported.

COMPREHENSION

1. How does White define his subject in this essay? Does he present a limited or comprehensive view of his subject? Justify your answer.
2. Why were the Whites "quietly" worried about the shift from private to public school? What were the two schools like? Which school does the author prefer? How do you know?
3. Explain the connections between the city and private schools and the country and public schools.

RHETORIC

1. White refers to his son as the "scholar" several times in this essay. What are the purpose and effect of this strategy?
2. What is the significance of the word "Education" as used in the title? Is this significance a matter of connotation or denotation? Explain.
3. What is White's thesis? Is it ever explicitly stated? Why, or why not?
4. What standard means of exposition does the author employ in the introduction? Why is the introductory paragraph especially effective?
5. How does the author develop his pattern of comparison and contrast in this essay? What major and minor points in the contrast does he develop?
6. How are the rhetorical strategies of narration, description, and argumentation reflected in this essay?

WRITING

1. Debate this proposition: Rural schools cannot provide the educational advantages of urban private schools.
2. Write a comparative essay on the type of school that you prefer—public or private.
3. Compare and contrast the relative advantages and disadvantages of urban and rural (or, if you wish, suburban) education.
4. In a comparative essay, examine the father-son relationship in this essay and in White's "Once More to the Lake."

MAYA ANGELOU Maya Angelou (1928–) is an American poet, playwright, television screenwriter, actress, and singer. Her autobiographical books, notably *I Know Why the Caged Bird Sings* (1970), from which the following selection is taken, provide one of the fullest accounts of the black female experience in contemporary literature. Fluent in six languages and active in artistic, educational, and political affairs, Angelou often presents autobiographical material against the backdrop of larger cultural concerns. In this vivid reminiscence of her 1940 graduation from grade school in Stamps, Arkansas, she provides insights into a community of young scholars who gain inspiration and wisdom from their experience during commencement ceremonies.

MAYA ANGELOU

Graduation

The children in Stamps trembled visibly with anticipation. Some adults were excited too, but to be certain the whole young population had come down with graduation epidemic. Large classes were graduating from both the grammar school and the high school. Even those who were years removed from their own day of glorious release were anxious to help with preparations as a kind of dry run. The junior students who were moving into the vacating classes' chairs were tradition-bound to show their talents for leadership and management. They strutted through the school and around the campus exerting pressure on the lower grades. Their authority was so new that occasionally if they pressed a little too hard it had to be overlooked. After all, next term was coming, and it never hurt a sixth grader to have a play sister in the eighth grade, or a tenth-year student to be able to call a twelfth grader Bubba. So all was endured in a spirit of shared understanding. But the graduating classes themselves were the nobility. Like travelers with exotic destinations on their minds, the graduates were remarkably forgetful. They came to school without their books, or tablets or even pencils. Volunteers fell over themselves to secure replacements for the missing equipment. When accepted, the willing workers might or might not be thanked, and it was of no importance to the pregraduation rites. Even teachers were respectful of the now quiet and aging seniors, and tended to speak to them, if not as equals, as beings only slightly lower than themselves. After tests were returned and grades given, the student body, which acted like an extended family, knew who did well, who excelled, and what piteous ones had failed. 1

Unlike the white high school, Lafayette County Training School distinguished itself by having neither lawn, nor hedges, nor tennis court, nor climbing ivy. Its two buildings (main classrooms, the grade 2

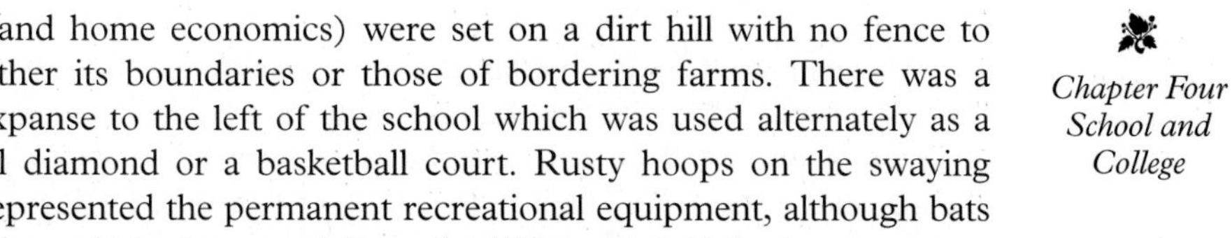

school and home economics) were set on a dirt hill with no fence to limit either its boundaries or those of bordering farms. There was a large expanse to the left of the school which was used alternately as a baseball diamond or a basketball court. Rusty hoops on the swaying poles represented the permanent recreational equipment, although bats and balls could be borrowed from the P.E. teacher if the borrower was qualified and if the diamond wasn't occupied.

Over this rocky area relieved by a few shady tall persimmon trees 3
the graduating class walked. The girls often held hands and no longer bothered to speak to the lower students. There was a sadness about them, as if this old world was not their home and they were bound for higher ground. The boys, on the other hand, had become more friendly, more outgoing. A decided change from the closed attitude they projected while studying for finals. Now they seemed not ready to give up the old school, the familiar paths and classrooms. Only a small percentage would be continuing on to college—one of the South's A & M (agricultural and mechanical) schools, which trained Negro youths to be carpenters, farmers, handymen, masons, maids, cooks and baby nurses. Their future rode heavily on their shoulders, and blinded them to the collective joy that had pervaded the lives of the boys and girls in the grammar school graduating class.

Parents who could afford it had ordered new shoes and ready-made 4
clothes for themselves from Sears and Roebuck or Montgomery Ward. They also engaged the best seamstresses to make the floating graduating dresses and to cut down secondhand pants which would be pressed to a military slickness for the important event.

Oh, it was important, all right. Whitefolks would attend the ceremo- 5
ny, and two or three would speak of God and home, and the Southern way of life, and Mrs. Parsons, the principal's wife, would play the graduation march while the lower-grade graduates paraded down the aisles and took their seats below the platform. The high school seniors would wait in empty classrooms to make their dramatic entrance.

In the Store I was the person of the moment. The birthday girl. The 6
center. Bailey had graduated the year before, although to do so he had had to forfeit all pleasures to make up for his time lost in Baton Rouge.

My class was wearing butter-yellow piqué dresses, and Momma 7
launched out on mine. She smocked the yoke into tiny crisscrossing puckers, then shirred the rest of the bodice. Her dark fingers ducked in and out of the lemony cloth as she embroidered raised daisies around the hem. Before she considered herself finished she had added a crocheted cuff on the puff sleeves, and a pointy crocheted collar.

I was going to be lovely. A walking model of all the various styles of 8
fine hand sewing and it didn't worry me that I was only twelve years old and merely graduating from the eighth grade. Besides, many teachers in Arkansas Negro schools had only that diploma and were licensed to impart wisdom.

The days had become longer and more noticeable. The faded beige 9
of former times had been replaced with strong and sure colors. I began

to see my classmates' clothes, their skin tones, and the dust that waved off pussy willows. Clouds that lazed across the sky were objects of great concern to me. Their shiftier shapes might have held a message that in my new happiness and with a little bit of time I'd soon decipher. During that period I looked at the arch of heaven so religiously my neck kept a steady ache. I had taken to smiling more often, and my jaws hurt from the unaccustomed activity. Between the two physical sore spots, I suppose I could have been uncomfortable, but that was not the case. As a member of the winning team (the graduating class of 1940) I had outdistanced unpleasant sensations by miles. I was headed for the freedom of open fields.

Youth and social approval allied themselves with me and we trammeled memories of slights and insults. The wind of our swift passage remodeled my features. Lost tears were pounded to mud and then to dust. Years of withdrawal were brushed aside and left behind, as hanging ropes of parasitic moss. 10

My work alone had awarded me a top place and I was going to be one of the first called in the graduating ceremonies. On the classroom blackboard, as well as on the bulletin board in the auditorium, there were blue stars and white stars and red stars. No absences, no tardiness, and my academic work was among the best of the year. I could say the preamble to the Constitution even faster than Bailey. We timed ourselves often: "WethepeopleoftheUnitedStatesinordertoformamoreperfectunion. . . ." I had memorized the Presidents of the United States from Washington to Roosevelt in chronological as well as alphabetical order. 11

My hair pleased me too. Gradually the black mass had lengthened and thickened, so that it kept at last to its braided pattern, and I didn't have to yank my scalp off when I tried to comb it. 12

Louise and I had rehearsed the exercises until we tired out ourselves. Henry Reed was class valedictorian. He was a small, very black boy with hooded eyes, a long, broad nose and an oddly shaped head. I had admired him for years because each term he and I vied for the best grades in our class. Most often he bested me, but instead of being disappointed, I was pleased that we shared top places between us. Like many Southern black children, he lived with his grandmother, who was as strict as Momma and as kind as she knew how to be. He was courteous, respectful and softspoken to elders, but on the playground he chose to play the roughest games. I admired him. Anyone, I reckoned, sufficiently afraid or sufficiently dull could be polite. But to be able to operate at a top level with both adults and children was admirable. 13

His valedictory speech was entitled "To Be or Not to Be." The rigid tenth-grade teacher had helped him write it. He'd been working on the dramatic stresses for months. 14

The weeks until graduation were filled with heady activities. A group of small children were to be presented in a play about buttercups and daisies and bunny rabbits. They could be heard throughout the building practicing their hops and their little songs that sounded like sil- 15 ver bells. The older girls (non-graduates, of course) were assigned the task of making refreshments for the night's festivities. A tangy scent of ginger, cinnamon, nutmeg and chocolate wafted around the home economics building as the budding cooks made samples for themselves and their teachers.

In every corner of the workshop, axes and saws split fresh timber as the woodshop boys made sets and stage scenery. Only the graduates were left out of the general bustle. We were free to sit in the library at the back of the building or look in quite detachedly, naturally, on the measures being taken for our event. 16

Even the minister preached on graduation the Sunday before. His subject was, "Let your light so shine that men will see your good works and praise your Father, Who is in Heaven." Although the sermon was purported to be addressed to us, he used the occasion to speak to backsliders, gamblers and general ne'er-do-wells. But since he had called our names at the beginning of the service we were mollified. 17

Among Negroes the tradition was to give presents to children going only from one grade to another. How much more important this was when the person was graduating at the top of the class. Uncle Willie and Momma had sent away for a Mickey Mouse watch like Bailey's. Louise gave me four embroidered handkerchiefs. (I gave her three crocheted doilies.) Mrs. Sneed, the minister's wife, made me an underskirt to wear for graduation, and nearly every customer gave me a nickel or maybe even a dime with the instruction "Keep on moving to higher ground," or some such encouragement. 18

Amazingly the great day finally dawned and I was out of bed before I knew it. I threw open the back door to see it more clearly, but Momma said, "Sister, come away from that door and put your robe on." 19

I hoped the memory of that morning would never leave me. Sunlight was itself still young, and the day had none of the insistence maturity would bring it in a few hours. In my robe and barefoot in the backyard, under cover of going to see about my new beans, I gave myself up to the gentle warmth and thanked God that no matter what evil I had done in my life He had allowed me to live to see this day. Somewhere in my fatalism I had expected to die, accidentally, and never have the chance to walk up the stairs in the auditorium and gracefully receive my hard-earned diploma. Out of God's merciful bosom I had won reprieve. 20

Bailey came out in his robe and gave me a box wrapped in Christmas paper. He said he had saved his money for months to pay for it. It felt like a box of chocolates, but I knew Bailey wouldn't save money to buy candy when we had all we could want under our noses. 21

He was as proud of the gift as I. It was a soft-leather-bound copy of a collection of poems by Edgar Allan Poe, or, as Bailey and I called him, "Eap." I turned to "Annabel Lee" and we walked up and down the garden rows, the cool dirt between our toes, reciting the beautifully sad lines. 22

Momma made a Sunday breakfast although it was only Friday. After we finished the blessing, I opened my eyes to find the watch on 23

my plate. It was a dream of a day. Everything went smoothly and to my credit. I didn't have to be reminded or scolded for anything. Near evening I was too jittery to attend to chores, so Bailey volunteered to do all before his bath.

Days before, we had made a sign for the Store, and as we turned out the lights Momma hung the cardboard over the doorknob. It read clearly: CLOSED. GRADUATION. 24

My dress fitted perfectly and everyone said that I looked like a sunbeam in it. On the hill, going toward the school, Bailey walked behind with Uncle Willie, who muttered, "Go on, Ju." He wanted him to walk ahead with us because it embarrassed him to have to walk so slowly. Bailey said he'd let the ladies walk together, and the men would bring up the rear. We all laughed, nicely. 25

Little children dashed by out of the dark like fireflies. Their crepe-paper dresses and butterfly wings were not made for running and we heard more than one rip, dryly, and the regretful "uh uh" that followed. 26

The school blazed without gaiety. The windows seemed cold and unfriendly from the lower hill. A sense of ill-fated timing crept over me, and if Momma hadn't reached for my hand I would have drifted back to Bailey and Uncle Willie, and possibly beyond. She made a few slow jokes about my feet getting cold, and tugged me along to the now-strange building. 27

Around the front steps, assurance came back. There were my fellow "greats," the graduating class. Hair brushed back, legs oiled, new dresses and pressed pleats, fresh pocket handkerchiefs and little handbags, all homesewn. Oh, we were up to snuff, all right. I joined my comrades and didn't even see my family go in to find seats in the crowded auditorium. 28

The school band struck up a march and all classes filed in as had been rehearsed. We stood in front of our seats, as assigned, and on a signal from the choir director, we sat. No sooner had this been accomplished than the band started to play the national anthem. We rose again and sang the song, after which we recited the pledge of allegiance. We remained standing for a brief minute before the choir director and the principal signaled to us, rather desperately I thought, to take our seats. The command was so unusual that our carefully rehearsed and smooth-running machine was thrown off. For a full minute we fumbled for our chairs and bumped into each other awkwardly. Habits change or solidify under pressure, so in our state of nervous tension we had been ready to follow our usual assembly pattern: the American national anthem, then the pledge of allegiance, then the song every Black person I knew called the Negro National Anthem. All done in the same key, with the same passion and most often standing on the same foot. 29

Finding my seat at last, I was overcome with a presentiment of worse things to come. Something unrehearsed, unplanned, was going to happen, and we were going to be made to look bad. I distinctly re- 30 member being explicit in the choice of pronoun. It was "we," the graduating class, the unit, that concerned me then.

The principal welcomed "parents and friends" and asked the Baptist minister to lead us in prayer. His invocation was brief and punchy, and for a second I thought we were getting back on the high road to right action. When the principal came back to the dais, however, his voice had changed. Sounds always affected me profoundly and the principal's voice was one of my favorites. During assembly it melted and lowered weakly into the audience. It had not been in my plan to listen to him, but my curiosity was piqued and I straightened up to give him my attention.

He was talking about Booker T. Washington, our "late great leader," 32
who said we can be as close as the fingers on the hand, etc. . . . Then he said a few vague things about friendship and the friendship of kindly people to those less fortunate than themselves. With that his voice nearly faded, thin, away. Like a river diminishing to a stream and then to a trickle. But he cleared his throat and said, "Our speaker tonight, who is also our friend, came from Texarkana to deliver the commencement address, but due to the irregularity of the train schedule, he's going to, as they say, 'speak and run.'" He said that we understood and wanted the man to know that we were most grateful for the time he was able to give us and then something about how we were willing always to adjust to another's program, and without more ado—"I give you Mr. Edward Donleavy."

Not one but two white men came through the door offstage. The 33
shorter one walked to the speaker's platform, and the tall one moved over to the center seat and sat down. But that was our principal's seat, and already occupied. The dislodged gentleman bounced around for a long breath or two before the Baptist minister gave him his chair, then with more dignity than the situation deserved, the minister walked off the stage.

Donleavy looked at the audience once (on reflection, I'm sure that 34
he wanted only to reassure himself that we were really there), adjusted his glasses and began to read from a sheaf of papers.

He was glad "to be here and to see the work going on just as it was 35
in the other schools."

At the first "Amen" from the audience I willed the offender to im- 36
mediate death by choking on the word. But Amens and Yes, sir's began to fall around the room like rain through a ragged umbrella.

He told us of the wonderful changes we children in Stamps had in 37
store. The Central School (naturally, the white school was Central) had already been granted improvements that would be in use in the fall. A well-known artist was coming from Little Rock to teach art to them. They were going to have the newest microscopes and chemistry equipment for their laboratory. Mr. Donleavy didn't leave us long in the dark over who made these improvements available to Central High. Nor were we to be ignored in the general betterment scheme he had in mind.

He said that he had pointed out to people at a very high level that 38
one of the first-line football tacklers at Arkansas Agricultural and
Mechanical College had graduated from good old Lafayette County
Training School. Here fewer Amens were heard. Those few that did 39
break through lay dully in the air with the heaviness of habit.

He went on to praise us. He went on to say how he had bragged
that "one of the best basketball players at Fisk sank his first ball right
here at Lafayette County Training School."

The white kids were going to have a chance to become Galileos and 40
Madame Curies and Edisons and Gauguins, and our boys (the girls
weren't even in on it) would try to be Jesse Owenses and Joe Louises.

Owens and the Brown Bomber were great heroes in our world, but 41
what school official in the white-goddom of Little Rock had the right to
decide that those two men must be our only heroes? Who decided that
for Henry Reed to become a scientist he had to work like George
Washington Carver, as a bootblack, to buy a lousy microscope? Bailey
was obviously always going to be too small to be an athlete, so which
concrete angel glued to what country seat had decided that if my brother wanted to become a lawyer he had to first pay penance for his skin
by picking cotton and hoeing corn and studying correspondence books
at night for twenty years?

The man's dead words fell like bricks around the auditorium and 42
too many settled in my belly. Constrained by hard-learned manners I
couldn't look behind me, but to my left and right the proud graduating
class of 1940 had dropped their heads. Every girl in my row had found
something new to do with her handkerchief. Some folded the tiny
squares into love knots, some into triangles, but most were wadding
them, then pressing them flat on their yellow laps.

On the dais, the ancient tragedy was being replayed. Professor 43
Parsons sat, a sculptor's reject, rigid. His large, heavy body seemed devoid
of will or willingness, and his eyes said he was no longer with us. The other
teachers examined the flag (which was draped stage right) or their notes,
or the windows which opened on our now-famous playing diamond.

Graduation, the hush-hush magic time of frills and gifts and con- 44
gratulations and diplomas, was finished for me before my name was
called. The accomplishment was nothing. The meticulous maps, drawn
in three colors of ink, learning, and spelling decasyllabic words, memorizing the whole of *The Rape of Lucrece*—it was for nothing. Donleavy
had exposed us.

We were maids and farmers, handymen and washerwomen, and 45
anything higher that we aspired to was farcical and presumptuous.

Then I wished that Gabriel Prosser and Nat Turner had killed all 46
whitefolks in their beds and that Abraham Lincoln had been assassinated before the signing of the Emancipation Proclamation, and that
Harriet Tubman had been killed by that blow on her head and
Christopher Columbus had drowned in the *Santa Maria.*

It was awful to be Negro and have no control over my life. It was 47
brutal to be young and already trained to sit quietly and listen to

charges brought against my color with no chance of defense. We should all be dead. I thought I should like to see us all dead, one on top of the other. A pyramid of flesh with the whitefolks on the bottom, as the broad base, then the Indians with their silly tomahawks and tepees and wigwams and treaties, the Negroes with their mops and recipes and cotton sacks and spirituals sticking out of their mouths. The Dutch children should all stumble in their wooden shoes and break their necks. The French should choke to death on the Louisiana Purchase (1803) while silkworms ate all the Chinese with their stupid pigtails. As a species, we were an abomination. All of us.

Donleavy was running for election, and assured our parents that if 48
he won we could count on having the only colored paved playing field in that part of Arkansas. Also—he never looked up to acknowledge the grunts of acceptance—also, we were bound to get some new equipment for the home economics building and the workshop.

He finished, and since there was no need to give any more than the 49
most perfunctory thank-you's, he nodded to the men on the stage, and the tall white man who was never introduced joined him at the door. They left with the attitude that now they were off to something really important. (The graduation ceremonies at Lafayette County Training School had been a mere preliminary.)

The ugliness they left was palpable. An uninvited guest who 50
wouldn't leave. The choir was summoned and sang a modern arrangement of "Onward, Christian Soldiers," with new words pertaining to graduates seeking their place in the world. But it didn't work. Elouise, the daughter of the Baptist minister, recited "Invictus," and I could have cried at the impertinence of "I am the master of my fate, I am the captain of my soul."

My name had lost its ring of familiarity and I had to be nudged to 51
go and receive my diploma. All my preparations had fled. I neither marched up to the stage like a conquering Amazon, nor did I look in the audience for Bailey's nod of approval. Marguerite Johnson, I heard the name again, my honors were read, there were noises in the audience of appreciation, and I took my place on the stage as rehearsed.

I thought about colors I hated: ecru, puce, lavender, beige and 52
black.

There was shuffling and rustling around me, then Henry Reed 53
was giving his valedictory address, "To Be or Not to Be." Hadn't he heard the whitefolks? We couldn't *be* so the question was a waste of time. Henry's voice came clear and strong. I feared to look at him. Hadn't he got the message? There was no "nobler in the mind" for Negroes because the world didn't think we had minds, and they let us know it. "Outrageous fortune"? Now, that was a joke. When the ceremony was over I had to tell Henry Reed some things. That is, if I still cared. Not "rub," Henry, "erase." "Ah, there's the erase." Us.

Henry had been a good student in elocution. His voice rose on tides 54
of promise and fell on waves of warnings. The English teacher had

helped him to create a sermon winging through Hamlet's soliloquy. To be a man, a doer, a builder, a leader, or to be a tool, an unfunny joke, a crusher of funky toadstools, I marveled that Henry could go through the speech as if we had a choice.

I had been listening and silently rebutting each sentence with my 55
eyes closed; then there was a hush, which in an audience warns that something unplanned is happening. I looked up and saw Henry Reed, the conservative, the proper, the A student, turn his back to the audience and turn to us (the proud graduating class of 1940) and sing, nearly speaking,

> Lift ev'ry voice and sing
> Till earth and heaven ring
> Ring with the harmonies of Liberty. . . .

It was the poem written by James Weldon Johnson. It was the music composed by J. Rosamond Johnson. It was the Negro national anthem. Out of habit we were singing it.

Our mothers and fathers stood in the dark hall and joined the hymn 56
of encouragement. A kindergarten teacher led the small children onto the stage and the buttercups and daisies and bunny rabbits marked time and tried to follow:

> Stony the road we trod
> Bitter the chastening rod
> Felt in the days when hope, unborn, had died.
> Yet with a steady beat
> Have not our weary feet
> Come to the place for which our father sighed?

Every child I knew had learned that song with his ABC's and 57
along with "Jesus Loves Me This I Know." But I personally had never heard it before. Never heard the words, despite the thousands of times I had sung them. Never thought they had anything to do with me.

On the other hand, the words of Patrick Henry had made such an 58
impression on me that I had been able to stretch myself tall and trembling and say, "I know not what course others may take, but as for me, give me liberty or give me death."

And now I heard, really for the first time: 59

> We have come over a way that with tears has been watered,
> We have come, treading our path through the blood of the slaughtered.

While echoes of the song shivered in the air, Henry Reed bowed 60
his head, said "Thank you," and returned to his place in the line. The tears that slipped down many faces were not wiped away in shame.

We were on top again. As always, again. We survived. The 61
depths had been icy and dark, but now a bright sun spoke to our

souls. I was no longer simply a member of the proud graduating class of 1940; I was a proud member of the wonderful beautiful Negro race.

COMPREHENSION

1. Is Angelou a neutral observer or subjective participant in the events of this narrative? How can you tell?
2. How is the author's "presentiment of worse things to come" actually borne out? What is the "ancient tragedy" alluded to? How, specifically, does education relate to this allusion?
3. What do you learn about Marguerite—the young Maya Angelou—from this essay? What are her moods, emotions, thoughts, and attitudes? In what way is she "bound for higher ground"?

RHETORIC

1. Angelou is a highly impressionistic stylist in this essay. Provide examples of details that create vivid descriptive impressions. How do these details control the shifting moods of the selection?
2. Explain Angelou's allusions to *The Rape of Lucrece,* Gabriel Prosser and Nat Turner, Harriet Tubman, and "Invictus." How are these allusions and others related to the thesis? State that thesis in your own words.
3. What is the purpose of the relatively long five-paragraph introduction? What contrasts and latent ironies do you detect?
4. Cite examples of the author's ability to blend description, narration, and exposition. At what points is the expository mode the strongest? What is Angelou's purpose?
5. Why are the descriptions of Henry Reed and Donleavy juxtaposed?
6. Which paragraphs constitute the conclusion? How does Angelou achieve the transition from the body to the end?

WRITING

1. To what extent does American education still try to "track" students? What are the implications of such tracking? Discuss this issue in an essay; be certain to provide appropriate evidence.
2. Reconstruct your own graduation from grade school or high school.
3. Analyze and evaluate the many strategies that Angelou employs to honor and celebrate black culture and black wisdom in this essay.

SANTHA RAMA RAU Santha Rama Rau (1923–) is an Indian novelist and essayist who, throughout her career, has interpreted the Eastern experience for Western audiences. She is a gifted travel writer and memoirist. Her principal works include *Home to India* (1944), *Remember the House* (1955), and *Gifts of Passage* (1961). This narrative essay sensitively portrays the conflict in cultures perceived by the author in her early childhood.

SANTHA RAMA RAU

By Any Other Name

At the Anglo-Indian day school in Zorinabad to which my sister and I 1
were sent when she was eight and I was five and a half, they changed our names. On the first day of school, a hot, windless morning of a north Indian September, we stood in the headmistress's study and she said, "Now you're the *new* girls. What are your names?"

My sister answered for us. "I am Premila, and she"—nodding in my 2
direction—"is Santha."

The headmistress had been in India, I suppose, fifteen years or so, 3
but she still smiled her helpless inability to cope with Indian names. Her rimless half-glasses glittered, and the precarious bun on top of her head trembled as she shook her head. "Oh, my dears, those are much too hard for me. Suppose we give you pretty English names. Wouldn't that be more jolly? Let's see, now—Pamela for you, I think." She shrugged in a baffled way at my sister. "That's as close as I can get. And for *you,*" she said to me, "how about Cynthia? Isn't that nice?"

My sister was always less easily intimidated than I was, and while 4
she kept a stubborn silence, I said, "Thank you," in a very tiny voice.

We had been sent to that school because my father, among his re- 5
sponsibilities as an officer of the civil service, had a tour of duty to perform in the villages around that steamy little provincial town, where he had his headquarters at that time. He used to make his shorter inspection tours on horseback, and a week before, in the stale heat of a typically postmonsoon day, we had waved good-by to him and a little procession—an assistant, a secretary, two bearers, and the man to look after the bedding rolls and luggage. They rode away through our large garden, still bright green from the rains, and we turned back into the twilight of the house and the sound of fans whispering in every room.

Up to then, my mother had refused to send Premila to school in the 6
British-run establishments of that time, because, she used to say, "you can bury a dog's tail for seven years and it still comes out curly, and you can take a Britisher away from his home for a lifetime, and he still

remains insular." The examinations and degrees from entirely Indian schools were not, in those days, considered valid. In my case, the question had never come up, and probably never would have come up if Mother's extraordinary good health had not broken down. For the first time in my life, she was not able to continue the lessons she had been giving us every morning. So our Hindi books were put away, the stories of the Lord Krishna as a little boy were left in midair, and we were sent to the Anglo-Indian school.

That first day at school is still, when I think of it, a remarkable 7
one. At that age, if one's name is changed, one develops a curious form of dual personality. I remember having a certain detached and disbelieving concern in the actions of "Cynthia," but certainly no responsibility. Accordingly, I followed the thin, erect back of the headmistress down the veranda to my classroom feeling, at most, a passing interest in what was going to happen to me in this strange, new atmosphere of School.

The building was Indian in design, with wide verandas opening 8
onto a central courtyard, but Indian verandas are usually whitewashed, with stone floors. These, in the tradition of British schools, were painted dark brown and had matting on the floors. It gave a feeling of extra intensity to the heat.

I suppose there were about a dozen Indian children in the 9
school—which contained perhaps forty children in all—and four of them were in my class. They were all sitting at the back of the room, and I went to join them. I sat next to a small, solemn girl who didn't smile at me. She had long, glossy-black braids and wore a cotton dress, but she still kept on her Indian jewelry—a gold chain around her neck, thin gold bracelets, and tiny ruby studs in her ears. Like most Indian children, she had a rim of black kohl around her eyes. The cotton dress should have looked strange, but all I could think of was that I should ask my mother if I couldn't wear a dress to school, too, instead of my Indian clothes.

I can't remember too much about the proceedings in class that day, 10
except for the beginning. The teacher pointed to me and asked me to stand up. "Now, dear, tell the class your name."

I said nothing. 11

"Come along," she said, frowning slightly. "What's your name, 12
dear?"

"I don't know," I said, finally. 13

The English children in the front of the class—there were about 14
eight or ten of them—giggled and twisted around in their chairs to look at me. I sat down quickly and opened my eyes very wide, hoping in that way to dry them off. The little girl with the braids put out her hand and very lightly touched my arm. She still didn't smile.

Most of that morning I was rather bored. I looked briefly at the chil- 15
dren's drawings pinned to the wall, and then concentrated on a lizard clinging to the ledge of the high, barred window behind the teacher's head. Occasionally it would shoot out its long yellow tongue for a fly, and then it would rest, with its eyes closed and its belly palpitating, as

though it were swallowing several times quickly. The lessons were mostly concerned with reading and writing and simple numbers—things that my mother had already taught me—and I paid very little attention. The teacher wrote on the easel blackboard words like "bat" and "cat," which seemed babyish to me; only "apple" was new and incomprehensible.

When it was time for the lunch recess, I followed the girl with braids 16
out onto the veranda. There the children from the other classes were assembled. I saw Premila at once and ran over to her, as she had charge of our lunchbox. The children were all opening packages and sitting down to eat sandwiches. Premila and I were the only ones who had Indian food—thin wheat chapatties, some vegetable curry, and a bottle of buttermilk. Premila thrust half of it into my hand and whispered fiercely that I should go and sit with my class, because that was what the others seemed to be doing.

The enormous black eyes of the little Indian girl from my class 17
looked at my food longingly, so I offered her some. But she only shook her head and plowed her way solemnly through her sandwiches.

I was very sleepy after lunch, because at home we always took a 18
siesta. It was usually a pleasant time of day, with the bedroom darkened against the harsh afternoon sun, the drifting off into sleep with the sound of Mother's voice reading a story in one's mind, and, finally, the shrill, fussy voice of the ayah waking one for tea.

At school, we rested for a short time on low, folding cots on the ve- 19
randa, and then we were expected to play games. During the hot part of the afternoon we played indoors, and after the shadows had begun to lengthen and the slight breeze of the evening had come up we moved outside to the wide courtyard.

I had never really grasped the system of competitive games. At 20
home, whenever we played tag or guessing games, I was always allowed to "win"—"because," Mother used to tell Premila, "she is the youngest, and we have to allow for that." I had often heard her say it, and it seemed quite reasonable to me, but the result was that I had no clear idea of what "winning" meant.

When we played twos-and-threes that afternoon at school, in accor- 21
dance with my training, I let one of the small English boys catch me, but was naturally rather puzzled when the other children did not return the courtesy. I ran about for what seemed like hours without ever catching anyone, until it was time for school to close. Much later I learned that my attitude was called "not being a good sport," and I stopped allowing myself to be caught, but it was not for years that I really learned the spirit of the thing.

When I saw our car come up to the school gate, I broke away from 22
my classmates and rushed toward it yelling, "Ayah! Ayah!" It seemed like an eternity since I had seen her that morning—a wizened, affectionate figure in her white cotton sari, giving me dozens of urgent and useless instructions on how to be a good girl at school. Premila followed more sedately, and she told me on the way home never to do that again in front of the other children.

When we got home we went straight to Mother's high, white room to have tea with her, and I immediately climbed onto the bed and bounced gently up and down on the springs. Mother asked how we had liked our first day in school. I was so pleased to be home and to have left that peculiar Cynthia behind that I had nothing whatever to say about school, except to ask what "apple" meant. But Premila told Mother about the classes, and added that in her class they had weekly tests to see if they learned their lessons well.

24 I asked, "What's a test?"

25 Premila said, "You're too small to have them. You won't have them in your class for donkey's years." She had learned the expression that day and was using it for the first time. We all laughed enormously at her wit. She also told Mother, in an aside, that we should take sandwiches to school the next day. Not, she said, that *she* minded. But they would be simpler for me to handle.

26 That whole lovely evening I didn't think about school at all. I sprinted barefoot across the lawns with my favorite playmate, the cook's son, to the stream at the end of the garden. We quarreled in our usual way, waded in the tepid water under the lime trees, and waited for the night to bring out the smell of the jasmine. I listened with fascination to his stories of ghosts and demons, until I was too frightened to cross the garden alone in the semidarkness. The ayah found me, shouted at the cook's son, scolded me, hurried me into supper—it was an entirely usual, wonderful evening.

27 It was a week later, the day of Premila's first test, that our lives changed rather abruptly. I was sitting at the back of my class, in my usual inattentive way, only half listening to the teacher. I had started a rather guarded friendship with the girl with the braids, whose name turned out to be Nalini (Nancy, in school). The three other Indian children were already fast friends. Even at that age it was apparent to all of us that friendship with the English or Anglo-Indian children was out of the question. Occasionally, during the class, my new friend and I would draw pictures and show them to each other secretly.

28 The door opened sharply and Premila marched in. At first, the teacher smiled at her in a kindly and encouraging way and said, "Now, you're little Cynthia's sister?"

29 Premila didn't even look at her. She stood with her feet planted firmly apart and her shoulders rigid, and addressed herself directly to me. "Get up," she said. "We're going home."

30 I didn't know what had happened, but I was aware that it was a crisis of some sort. I rose obediently and started to walk toward my sister.

31 "Bring your pencils and your notebook," she said.

32 I went back for them, and together we left the room. The teacher started to say something just as Premila closed the door, but we didn't wait to hear what it was.

33 In complete silence we left the school grounds and started to walk home. Then I asked Premila what the matter was. All she would say was "We're going home for good."

It was a very tiring walk for a child of five and a half, and I dragged 34
along behind Premila with my pencils growing sticky in my hand. I can still remember looking at the dusty hedges, and the tangles of thorns in the ditches by the side of the road, smelling the faint fragrance from the eucalyptus trees and wondering whether we would ever reach home. Occasionally a horse-drawn tonga passed us, and the women, in their pink or green silks, stared at Premila and me trudging along on the side of the road. A few coolies and a line of women carrying baskets of vegetables on their heads smiled at us. But it was nearing the hottest time of day, and the road was almost deserted. I walked more and more slowly, and shouted to Premila, from time to time, "Wait for me!" with increasing peevishness. She spoke to me only once, and that was to tell me to carry my notebook on my head, because of the sun.

When we got to our house the ayah was just taking a tray of lunch 35
into Mother's room. She immediately started a long, worried questioning about what are you children doing back here at this hour of the day.

Mother looked very startled and very concerned, and asked Premila 36
what had happened.

Premila said, "We had our test today, and she made me and the other 37
Indians sit at the back of the room, with a desk between each one."

Mother said, "Why was that, darling?" 38

"She said it was because Indians cheat," Premila added. "So I don't 39
think we should go back to that school."

Mother looked very distant, and was silent a long time. At last she 40
said, "Of course not, darling." She sounded displeased.

We all shared the curry she was having for lunch, and afterward I 41
was sent off to the beautifully familiar bedroom for my siesta. I could hear Mother and Premila talking through the open door.

Mother said, "Do you suppose she understood all that?" 42

Premila said, "I shouldn't think so. She's a baby." 43

Mother said, "Well, I hope it won't bother her." 44

Of course, they were both wrong. I understood it perfectly, and I 45
remember it all very clearly. But I put it happily away, because it had all happened to a girl called Cynthia, and I never was really particularly interested in her.

COMPREHENSION

1. What does the title of this essay mean? State the thesis that emerges from it.
2. Cite five examples the author gives to demonstrate that her attendance at the Anglo-Indian day school was an alien experience for her. How is the author's experience similar to Angelou's in "Graduation"?
3. According to the author's inferences, what was the effect of British rule on Indian society? How does the headmistress embody this impact? Compare and contrast Rau's perception of colonialism and that of Orwell in "Shooting an Elephant."

RHETORIC

1. Define these Indian words, preferably from the contexts in which they are used: *kohl* (paragraph 9); *chapatties* (paragraph 16); *ayah* (paragraph 18); *sari* (paragraph 22); and *tonga* (paragraph 34).
2. Explain the author's use of sensory language in paragraphs 1, 3, 5, 8, 9, 15, 26, and 34.
3. What is the theme of this narrative essay? How does the author state it?
4. Identify the tone and mood of the essay.
5. What is the utility and value of the author's use of dialogue in the essay?
6. How do various causal patterns inform the narrative?

WRITING

1. Although dealing specifically with a colonial situation, the author also illuminates the universal experience of being made to feel different, strange, or alien. Why is this ironic for the author? Why does it remain so vivid in her memory? Do we become more or less conscious of this phenomenon at a later age? Write a narrative essay centering on a time when you were made to feel strange or foreign in an educational situation.
2. Tell of a time when you felt that someone or some group was trying to change your identity or sense of self.
3. Write a comparative essay on this selection and Angelou's "Graduation."

ANNA QUINDLEN Anna Quindlen (1935–), a journalist and editor, began her writing career as a reporter for the *New York Post* and later moved on to the *New York Times,* where she is currently a syndicated columnist. A graduate of Barnard College, Quindlen has written a number of books, including *Living out Loud* (1986) and *Object Lessons* (1991). Quindlen received the Pulitzer Prize for Commentary in 1992. In this essay, she focuses on the problem of teenage pregnancy and suggests children be given more than textbook information to help them cope with their sexuality.

ANNA QUINDLEN

Sex Ed

Several years ago I spent the day at a family planning clinic in one of New York City's poorest neighborhoods. I sat around a Formica table with a half-dozen sixteen-year-old girls and listened with some amazement as they showed off their knowledge of human sexuality. 1

They knew how long sperm lived inside the body, how many women out of a hundred using a diaphragm were statistically likely to 2

get pregnant and the medical term for the mouth of the cervix. One girl pointed out all the parts of the female reproductive system on a placard; another recited the stages of the ovulation cycle from day one to twenty-eight. There was just one problem with this performance: although the results of their laboratory tests would not be available for fifteen more minutes, every last one of them was pregnant.

I always think of that day when someone suggests that sex education at school is a big part of the answer to the problem of teenage pregnancy. I happen to be a proponent of such programs; I think human sexuality is a subject for dispassionate study, like civics and ethics and dozens of other topics that have a moral component. I'd like my sons to know as much as possible about how someone gets pregnant, how pregnancy can be avoided, and what it means when avoidance techniques have failed. 3

I remember adolescence about as vividly as I remember anything, however, and I am not in the least convinced that that information alone will significantly alter the rate of teenage pregnancy. It seemed to me that day in the clinic, and on days I spent at schools and on street corners, that teenage pregnancy has a lot more to do with what it means to be a teenager than with how someone gets pregnant. When I was in high school, at the tail end of the sixties, there was a straightforward line on sex among my friends. Boys could have it; girls couldn't. A girl who was not a virgin pretended she was. A girl who was sleeping with her boyfriend, no matter how long-playing the relationship, pretended she was not. 4

It is the nature of adolescence that there is no past and no future, only the present, burning as fierce, bright, and merciless as a bare light bulb. Girls had sex with boys because nothing seemed to matter except right now, not pregnancy, not parental disapprobation, nothing but those minutes, this dance, that face, those words. Most of them knew that pregnancy could result, but they assured themselves that they would be the lucky ones who would not get caught. Naturally, some of them were wrong, and in my experience they did one of three things: they went to Puerto Rico for a mysterious weekend trip; visited an aunt in some faraway state for three months and came back with empty eyes and a vague reputation, or got married, quickly, in Empire-waist dresses. 5

What seems to have changed most since then is that there is little philosophical counterpoint, hypocritical or not, to the raging hormones of adolescence, and that so many of the once-hidden pregnancies are hidden no more. 6

Not long after the day at the family planning clinic, I went to a public high school in the suburbs. In the girl's room was this graffito: Jennifer Is a Virgin. I asked the kids about it and they said it was shorthand for geek, nerd, weirdo, somebody who was so incredibly out of it that they were in high school and still hadn't had sex. If you were a virgin, they told me, you just lied about it so that no one would think you were that immature. The girls in the family planning clinic told me much the same thing—that everyone did it, that the boys wanted it, that 7 not doing it made them seem out of it. The only difference, really, was that the girls in the clinic were poor and would have their babies, and the girls in the high school were well-to-do and would have abortions. Pleasure didn't seem to have very much to do with sex for either group. After she learned she was pregnant, one of the girls at the clinic said, without a trace of irony, that she hoped childbirth didn't hurt as much as sex had. Birth control was easily disposed of in both cases. The pill, the youngsters said, could give you a stroke; the IUD could make you sterile. A diaphragm was disgusting.

One girl told me the funniest thing her boyfriend—a real original thinker—had told her: they couldn't use condoms because it was like taking a shower with a raincoat on. She was a smart girl, and pretty, and I wanted to tell her that it sounded as if she was sleeping with a jerk who didn't deserve her. But that is the kind of basic fact of life that must be taught not in the classroom, not by a stranger, but at home by the family. It is this that, finally, I will try to teach my sons about sex, after I've explained fertile periods and birth control and all the other mechanics that are important to understand but never really go to the heart of the matter: I believe I will say that when you sleep with someone you take off a lot more than your clothes. 8

COMPREHENSION

1. Does Quindlen approve of sex education? Explain.
2. How does the writer characterize the attitude of adolescents regarding sex and pregnancy?
3. What advice or information about sex will the writer give her sons? Why?

RHETORIC

1. Why did Quindlen choose "Sex Ed" as a title? What is its significance in relation to the thesis?
2. What is Quindlen's thesis? Where is it contained in the essay? Is it directly stated or implied?
3. Is Quindlen's writing an argumentative essay? Support your position with citations from the text.
4. What point is the writer making through use of accumulated details in paragraph 2?
5. What does Quindlen mean by the term "moral component" in paragraph 3? Where else in the essay does she allude to it? How does the author employ definition in this essay?
6. What does Quindlen mean by her final statement that "when you sleep with someone you take off a lot more than your clothes"? How does this ending serve to underscore the thesis of the essay?

WRITING

1. Write a letter to a teenage son or daughter in which you discuss sexuality and pregnancy.

2. Write a research paper describing the most common forms of birth control available and listing the advantages and disadvantages of each.
3. In an essay, consider possible solutions to the problem of teenage pregnancy. What role do you think sex education has in ameliorating the problem? Use support from the Quindlen essay if applicable.

DINESH D'SOUZA Dinesh D'Souza (1961–) was born in Bombay, India. He graduated from Dartmouth College in 1983 and rapidly established himself as a neoconservative spokesperson on education and other public policy issues. He has written a biography of the television evangelist Jerry Falwell (1985) and the controversial *Illiberal Education* (1991), in which he charges that liberals control the nation's universities. In this essay, D'Souza takes issue with the multicultural curriculum.

DINESH D'SOUZA

'Bogus' Multiculturalism

At Stanford University a couple of years ago, Jesse Jackson led protesting students who chanted, "Hey, hey, ho, ho, Western culture has got to go." Ultimately, the university administration acquiesced to the call for the abolition of Stanford's so-called "Great Books" course, which had focused on the classics of Western civilization, and installed a new requirement called "Cultures, Ideas, and Values," which emphasized non-Western and minority cultures. Stanford's example has been inspirational and has been emulated by many other schools and colleges across the country as well. 1

I have spent some time over the last couple of years auditing Stanford's new non-Western curriculum to see what it was that Stanford professors were teaching about the Third World, which is my place of origin and of birth. I realized that Stanford professors were presenting a picture of the Third World that bore no resemblance to what I, as a native of the Third World, knew. Something very funny seemed to be going on. What could this be? What was the shape that multicultural education was taking in practice? 2

I would like to illustrate this problem briefly by talking about one book that I see as a kind of emblem for the new multicultural curriculum at Stanford. The book is called *I, Rigoberta Menchu,* and is subtitled "The Story of a Young Woman in Guatemala." In the introduction, Rigoberta, who is a young woman, says, "I am speaking not for myself, I am speaking for the people, the oppressed people of Latin America." 3

Rigoberta does not claim any individual distinction, but she is speaking on behalf of minority oppression. This is the significance of her book. One might expect that it is a valuable perspective. 4

Rigoberta further says that because she is "in the oral tradition," she 5
has narrated this book to a French feminist writer, Elisabeth Burgos Debray.

One interesting question that occurred to me at the outset was where 6
did young Rigoberta meet Elisabeth Burgos Debray, the French feminist writer? In reading the book's acknowledgments, you realize that they met in Paris, where Rigoberta was apparently attending a socialist conference. Paris, I need not remind you, is not a venue to which many of the Third World's poor routinely travel. Therefore, one might suspect that Rigoberta is not typical of the Latin American or Third World peasantry. As you read the book, this impression is reinforced. You run across a chapter, for example, that is titled "Rigoberta Renounces Marriage and Motherhood." The book describes in some detail Rigoberta's sequential embrace of socialism, of Marxism, of feminism, of gay rights, and so on. This is her story. It dawns on the critical reader that Rigoberta does not, by any stretch of the imagination, represent the poor people or the peasants of Guatemala or of the Third World. This raises the interesting question: Why read this book? Whom does Rigoberta represent? Whom does she speak for?

Perhaps she speaks for the political prejudices of some Stanford 7
professors and Stanford students, who are very interested in her embrace of Marxism, of socialism, of feminism, and so on. The Third World is not like that, but that is the way that some people at Stanford would like to see it. Rigoberta represents, in short, a projection of Western ideological predilections and prejudices onto the Third World.

Multicultural education, in general, is inspired by political activists 8
who are alienated from what they see to be the racism, the sexism, and homophobia of the West. They would like to find in other cultures a better alternative to this terrible Western way of life. But, anybody who looks carefully and critically at non-Western cultures, at Third World cultures, realizes that the Third World cultures are generally quite inhospitable to the basic passions of these multicultural activists. There is not a strong tradition of racial equality in many parts of the Third World. In India, for example, there is the terrible legacy of the caste system. Women are treated very badly in many non-Western cultures. Homosexuality is often a crime, if not a medical ailment, in many Third World countries.

The classics of non-Western cultures have produced important 9
works. But, for example, the *Koran* evinces a notion of male superiority. The great Japanese classic *The Tale of Genji* is a celebration of courtship and of hierarchy. The Indian classics, the *Bhagavad-Gita* and so on, are a rejection of Western materialism and atheism.

The multicultural activists, when they look abroad, don't like what 10
they see and so they engage very routinely in what one may call the *Rigoberta* model: They put aside the reality and great works of non-Western cultures; then they ransack these cultures to find utterly non-representative figures like Rigoberta, figures who reflect not the temper or the accomplishment of their own cultures, but who reflect the politi-

cal prejudices of Western culture. This is what I call a bogus multiculturalism.

There is no reason that we can't have a curriculum that emphasizes what Matthew Arnold once called "the best that has been thought and said." Arnold had in mind Western culture, but there is no reason we can't apply his criterion to non-Western cultures, as well. If we take a critical and honest look at both Western and non-Western cultures, we can then arrive at a sensible basis for the norms according to which we would like to live our lives and shape this multiracial society. Multicultural education is too important, in short, to leave to multicultural ideologues and activists. 11

COMPREHENSION

1. What does D'Souza mean by "bogus" multiculturalism?
2. What are the writer's complaints against books such as *I, Rigoberta Menchu?*
3. What changes would D'Souza like to see at Stanford?

RHETORIC

1. State the thesis of the essay in your own words.
2. What is D'Souza's tone? Cite specific evidence in the essay.
3. Does D'Souza's major example strongly support his thesis? Explain.
4. How does the author structure his argument? Can you find examples of logical fallacies? Explain.
5. Where does D'Souza employ definition in this essay? What is his purpose in using this strategy?
6. What is the purpose of paragraph 9? How does it serve to support the writer's point?

WRITING

1. Write an essay agreeing or disagreeing with D'Souza's statement that multiculturalism "is inspired by political activists who are alienated from what they see to be the racism, the sexism, and homophobia of the West."
2. Pretend you are a college professor teaching an "introduction to civilization" class or any liberal arts course of your choice. What five books would you use in your class, and why? Discuss your choices in the context of a multicultural curriculum.
3. Write a personal essay in which you describe the reading material used in your elementary or high school years. What was the first book in which a different culture was depicted? How was this culture portrayed, and what impressions did you form of it?

RICHARD WRIGHT Richard Wright (1908–1960), an American author, spoke eloquently about the racial experience in America in his novels and essays. Wright was born on a Mississippi plantation. As a young man he moved to Chicago, where he joined the Federal Writers' Project in the 1930s. His experiences in Mississippi and Chicago appear in his early fiction: *Uncle Tom's Children* (1938), about racial oppression in the South, and *Native Son* (1940), about discrimination and exploitation in Chicago during the Depression. Wright became an expatriate after World War II. From Paris, he wrote an autobiography, *Black Boy* (1945), and two novels, *The Outsider* (1953) and *The Long Dream* (1958), among other works. This story, an excerpt from *Black Boy,* describes a turning point in Wright's intellectual development.

RICHARD WRIGHT

The Library Card

One morning I arrived early at work and went into the bank lobby where the Negro porter was mopping. I stood at a counter and picked up the Memphis *Commercial Appeal* and began my free reading of the press. I came finally to the editorial page and saw an article dealing with one H. L. Mencken. I knew by hearsay that he was the editor of the *American Mercury,* but aside from that I knew nothing about him. The article was a furious denunciation of Mencken, concluding with one hot, short sentence: Mencken is a fool. 1

I wondered what on earth this Mencken had done to call down upon him the scorn of the South. The only people I had ever heard denounced in the South were Negroes, and this man was not a Negro. Then what ideas did Mencken hold that made a newspaper like the *Commercial Appeal* castigate him publicly? Undoubtedly he must be advocating ideas that the South did not like. Were there, then, people other than Negroes who criticized the South? I knew that during the Civil War the South had hated northern whites, but I had not encountered such hate during my life. Knowing no more of Mencken than I did at that moment, I felt a vague sympathy for him. Had not the South, which had assigned me the role of a non-man, cast at him its hardest words? 2

Now, how could I find out about this Mencken? There was a huge library near the riverfront, but I knew that Negroes were not allowed to patronize its shelves any more than they were the parks and playgrounds of the city. I had gone into the library several times to get books for the white men on the job. Which of them would now help me to get books? And how could I read them without causing concern to the white men with whom I worked? I had so far been successful in hiding my thoughts and feelings from them, but I knew that I would 3

create hostility if I went about this business of reading in a clumsy way.

I weighed the personalities of the men on the job. There was Don, a 4
Jew; but I distrusted him. His position was not much better than mine and I knew that he was uneasy and insecure; he had always treated me in an offhand, bantering way that barely concealed his contempt. I was afraid to ask him to help me to get books; his frantic desire to demonstrate a racial solidarity with the whites against Negroes might make him betray me.

Then how about the boss? No, he was a Baptist and I had the suspi- 5
cion that he would not be quite able to comprehend why a black boy would want to read Mencken. There were other white men on the job whose attitudes showed clearly that they were Kluxers or sympathizers, and they were out of the question.

There remained only one man whose attitude did not fit into an 6
anti-Negro category, for I had heard the white men refer to him as a "Pope lover." He was an Irish Catholic and was hated by the white Southerners. I knew that he read books, because I had got him volumes from the library several times. Since he, too, was an object of hatred, I felt that he might refuse me but would hardly betray me. I hesitated, weighing and balancing the imponderable realities.

One morning I paused before the Catholic fellow's desk. 7

"I want to ask you a favor," I whispered to him. 8

"What is it?" 9

"I want to read. I can't get books from the library. I wonder if you'd 10
let me use your card?"

He looked at me suspiciously. 11

"My card is full most of the time," he said. 12

"I see," I said and waited, posing my question silently. 13

"You're not trying to get me into trouble, are you, boy?" he asked, 14
staring at me.

"Oh, no, sir." 15

"What book do you want?" 16

"A book by H. L. Mencken." 17

"Which one?" 18

"I don't know. Has he written more than one?" 19

"He has written several." 20

"I didn't know that." 21

"What makes you want to read Mencken?" 22

"Oh, I just saw his name in the newspaper," I said. 23

"It's good of you to want to read," he said. "But you ought to read 24
the right things."

I said nothing. Would he want to supervise my reading? 25

"Let me think," he said. "I'll figure out something." 26

I turned from him and he called me back. He stared at me quizzi- 27
cally.

"Richard, don't mention this to the other white men," he said. 28

"I understand," I said. "I won't say a word." 29

A few days later he called me to him. 30

"I've got a card in my wife's name," he said. "Here's mine."

"Thank you, sir."

"Do you think you can manage it?" 33

"I'll manage fine," I said. 34

"If they suspect you, you'll get in trouble," he said. 35

"I'll write the same kind of notes to the library that you wrote when 36
you sent me for books," I told him. "I'll sign your name."

He laughed.

"Go ahead. Let me see what you get," he said.

That afternoon I addressed myself to forging a note. Now, what were 39
the names of books written by H. L. Mencken? I did not know any of them. I finally wrote what I thought would be a foolproof note: *Dear Madam: Will you please let this nigger boy*—I used the word "nigger" to make the librarian feel that I could not possibly be the author of the note—*have some books by H. L. Mencken?* I forged the white man's name.

I entered the library as I had always done when on errands for 40
whites, but I felt that I would somehow slip up and betray myself. I doffed my hat, stood a respectful distance from the desk, looked as unbookish as possible, and waited for the white patrons to be taken care of. When the desk was clear of people, I still waited. The white librarian looked at me.

"What do you want, boy?" 41

As though I did not possess the power of speech, I stepped forward 42
and simply handed her the forged note, not parting my lips.

"What books by Mencken does he want?" she asked. 43

"I don't know, ma'am," I said, avoiding her eyes. 44

"Who gave you this card?" 45

"Mr. Falk," I said. 46

"Where is he?" 47

"He's at work, at the M—Optical Company," I said. "I've been in 48
here for him before."

"I remember," the woman said. "But he never wrote notes like this." 49

Oh, God, she's suspicious. Perhaps she would not let me have the 50
books? If she had turned her back at that moment, I would have ducked out the door and never gone back. Then I thought of a bold idea.

"You can call him up, ma'am," I said, my heart pounding. 51

"You're not using these books, are you?" she asked pointedly. 52

"Oh, no, ma'am. I can't read." 53

"I don't know what he wants by Mencken," she said under her 54
breath.

I knew now that I had won; she was thinking of other things and the 55
race question had gone out of her mind. She went to the shelves. Once or twice she looked over her shoulder at me, as though she was still doubtful. Finally she came forward with two books in her hand.

"I'm sending him two books," she said. "But tell Mr. Falk to come 56
in next time, or send me the names of the books he wants. I don't know what he wants to read."

I said nothing. She stamped the card and handed me the books. Not daring to glance at them, I went out of the library, fearing that the woman would call me back for further questioning. A block away from the library I opened one of the books and read a title: *A Book of Prefaces.* I was nearing my nineteenth birthday and I did not know how to pronounce the word "preface." I thumbed the pages and saw strange words and strange names. I shook my head, disappointed. I looked at the other book; it was called *Prejudices.* I knew what that word meant; I had heard it all my life. And right off I was on guard against Mencken's books. Why would a man want to call a book *Prejudices?* The word was so stained with all my memories of racial hate that I could not conceive of anybody using it for a title. Perhaps I had made a mistake about Mencken? A man who had prejudices must be wrong. 57

When I showed the books to Mr. Falk, he looked at me and frowned. 58

"That librarian might telephone you," I warned him. 59

"That's all right," he said. "But when you're through reading those books, I want you to tell me what you get out of them." 60

That night in my rented room, while letting the hot water run over my can of pork and beans in the sink, I opened *A Book of Prefaces* and began to read. I was jarred and shocked by the style, the clear, clean, sweeping sentences. Why did he write like that? And how did one write like that? I pictured the man as a raging demon, slashing with his pen, consumed with hate, denouncing everything American, extolling everything European or German, laughing at the weaknesses of people, mocking God, authority. What was this? I stood up, trying to realize what reality lay behind the meaning of the words. . . . Yes, this man was fighting, fighting with words. He was using words as a weapon, using them as one would use a club. Could words be weapons? Well, yes, for here they were. Then, maybe, perhaps, I could use them as a weapon? No. It frightened me. I read on and what amazed me was not what he said, but how on earth anybody had the courage to say it. 61

Occasionally I glanced up to reassure myself that I was alone in the room. Who were these men about whom Mencken was talking so passionately? Who was Anatole France? Joseph Conrad? Sinclair Lewis, Sherwood Anderson, Dostoevski, George Moore, Gustave Flaubert, Maupassant, Tolstoy, Frank Harris, Mark Twain, Thomas Hardy, Arnold Bennett, Stephen Crane, Zola, Norris, Gorky, Bergson, Ibsen, Balzac, Bernard Shaw, Dumas, Poe, Thomas Mann, O. Henry, Dreiser, H. G. Wells, Gogol, T. S. Eliot, Gide, Baudelaire, Edgar Lee Masters, Stendhal, Turgenev, Hunekar, Nietzsche, and scores of others? Were these men real? Did they exist or had they existed? And how did one pronounce their names? 62

I ran across many words whose meanings I did not know, and I either looked them up in a dictionary or, before I had a chance to do that, encountered the word in a context that made its meaning clear. But what strange world was this? I concluded the book with the con- 63 viction that I had somehow overlooked something terribly important in life. I had once tried to write, had once reveled in feeling, had let my crude imagination roam, but the impulse to dream had been slowly beaten out of me by experience. Now it surged up again and I hungered for books, new ways of looking and seeing. It was not a matter of believing or disbelieving what I read, but of feeling something new, of being affected by something that made the look of the world different.

As dawn broke I ate my pork and beans, feeling dopey, sleepy. I 64
went to work, but the mood of the book would not die; it lingered, coloring everything I saw, heard, did. I now felt that I knew what the white men were feeling. Merely because I had read a book that had spoken of how they lived and thought, I identified myself with that book. I felt vaguely guilty. Would I, filled with bookish notions, act in a manner that would make the whites dislike me?

I forged more notes and my trips to the library became frequent. 65
Reading grew into a passion. My first serious novel was Sinclair Lewis's *Main Street.* It made me see my boss, Mr. Gerald, and identify him as an American type. I would smile when I saw him lugging his golf bags into the office. I had always felt a vast distance separating me from the boss, and now I felt closer to him, though still distant. I felt now that I knew him, that I could feel the very limits of his narrow life. And this had happened because I had read a novel about a mythical man called George F. Babbitt.

The plots and stories in the novels did not interest me so much as 66
the point of view revealed. I gave myself over to each novel without reserve, without trying to criticize it; it was enough for me to see and feel something different. And for me, everything was something different. Reading was like a drug, a dope. The novels created moods in which I lived for days. But I could not conquer my sense of guilt, my feeling that the white men around me knew that I was changing, that I had begun to regard them differently.

Whenever I brought a book to the job, I wrapped it in newspaper— 67
a habit that was to persist for years in other cities and under other circumstances. But some of the white men pried into my packages when I was absent and they questioned me.

"Boy, what are you reading those books for?" 68

"Oh, I don't know, sir." 69

"That's deep stuff you're reading, boy." 70

"I'm just killing time, sir." 71

"You'll addle your brains if you don't watch out." 72

I read Dreiser's *Jennie Gerhardt* and *Sister Carrie* and they revived 73
in me a vivid sense of my mother's suffering; I was overwhelmed. I grew silent, wondering about the life around me. It would have been impossible for me to have told anyone what I derived from these novels, for it was nothing less than a sense of life itself. All my life had shaped me for the realism, the naturalism of the modern novel, and I could not read enough of them.

74 Steeped in new moods and ideas, I bought a ream of paper and tried to write; but nothing would come, or what did come was flat beyond telling. I discovered that more than desire and feeling were necessary to write and I dropped the idea. Yet I still wondered how it was possible to know people sufficiently to write about them? Could I ever learn about life and people? To me, with my vast ignorance, my Jim Crow station in life, it seemed a task impossible of achievement. I now knew what being a Negro meant. I could endure the hunger. I had learned to live with hate. But to feel that there were feelings denied me, that the very breath of life itself was beyond my reach, that more than anything else hurt, wounded me. I had a new hunger.

75 In buoying me up, reading also cast me down, made me see what was possible, what I had missed. My tension returned, new, terrible, bitter, surging, almost too great to be contained. I no longer *felt* that the world about me was hostile, killing; I *knew* it. A million times I asked myself what I could do to save myself, and there were no answers. I seemed forever condemned, ringed by walls.

76 I did not discuss my reading with Mr. Falk, who had lent me his library card; it would have meant talking about myself and that would have been too painful. I smiled each day, fighting desperately to maintain my old behavior, to keep my disposition seemingly sunny. But some of the white men discerned that I had begun to brood.

77 "Wake up there, boy!" Mr. Olin said one day.

78 "Sir!" I answered for the lack of a better word.

79 "You act like you've stolen something," he said.

80 I laughed in the way I knew he expected me to laugh, but I resolved to be more conscious of myself, to watch my every act, to guard and hide the new knowledge that was dawning within me.

81 If I went north, would it be possible for me to build a new life then? But how could a man build a life upon vague, unformed yearnings? I wanted to write and I did not even know the English language. I bought English grammars and found them dull. I felt that I was getting a better sense of the language from novels than from grammars. I read hard, discarding a writer as soon as I felt that I had grasped his point of view. At night the printed page stood before my eyes in sleep.

82 Mrs. Moss, my landlady, asked me one Sunday morning: "Son, what is this you keep on reading?"

83 "Oh, nothing. Just novels."

84 "What you get out of 'em?"

85 "I'm just killing time," I said.

86 "I hope you know your own mind," she said in a tone which implied that she doubted if I had a mind.

87 I knew of no Negroes who read the books I liked and I wondered if any Negroes ever thought of them. I knew that there were Negro doctors, lawyers, newspapermen, but I never saw any of them. When I read a Negro newspaper I never caught the faintest echo of my preoccupation in its pages. I felt trapped and occasionally, for a few days,

I would stop reading. But a vague hunger would come over me for books, books that opened up new avenues of feeling and seeing, and again I would forge another note to the white librarian. Again I would read and wonder as only the naïve and unlettered can read and wonder, feeling that I carried a secret, criminal burden about with me each day.

That winter my mother and brother came and we set up housekeeping, buying furniture on the installment plan, being cheated and yet knowing no way to avoid it. I began to eat warm food and to my surprise found that regular meals enabled me to read faster. I may have lived through many illnesses and survived them, never suspecting that I was ill. My brother obtained a job and we began to save toward the trip north, plotting our time, setting tentative dates for departure. I told none of the white men on the job that I was planning to go north; I knew that the moment they felt I was thinking of the North they would change toward me. It would have made them feel that I did not like the life I was living, and because my life was completely conditioned by what they said or did, it would have been tantamount to challenging them. 88

I could calculate my chances for life in the South as a Negro fairly clearly now. 89

I could fight the southern whites by organizing with other Negroes, as my grandfather had done. But I knew that I could never win that way; there were many whites and there were but few blacks. They were strong and we were weak. Outright black rebellion could never win. If I fought openly I would die and I did not want to die. News of lynchings were frequent. 90

I could submit and live the life of a genial slave, but that was impossible. All of my life had shaped me to live by my own feelings and thoughts. I could make up to Bess and marry her and inherit the house. But that, too, would be the life of a slave; if I did that, I would crush to death something within me, and I would hate myself as much as I knew the whites already hated those who had submitted. Neither could I ever willingly present myself to be kicked, as Shorty had done. I would rather have died than do that. 91

I could drain off my restlessness by fighting with Shorty and Harrison. I had seen many Negroes solve the problem of being black by transferring their hatred of themselves to others with a black skin and fighting them. I would have to be cold to do that, and I was not cold and I could never be. 92

I could, of course, forget what I had read, thrust the whites out of my mind, forget them; and find release from anxiety and longing in sex and alcohol. But the memory of how my father had conducted himself made that course repugnant. If I did not want others to violate my life, how could I voluntarily violate it myself? 93

I had no hope whatever of being a professional man. Not only had I been so conditioned that I did not desire it, but the fulfillment of such an ambition was beyond my capabilities. Well-to-do Negroes lived in a world that was almost as alien to me as the world inhabited by whites. 94

What, then, was there? I held my life in my mind, in my consciousness each day, feeling at times that I would stumble and drop it, spill it forever. My reading had created a vast sense of distance between me and the world in which I lived and tried to make a living, and that sense of distance was increasing each day. My days and nights were one long, quiet, continuously contained dream of terror, tension, and anxiety. I wondered how long I could bear it. 95

COMPREHENSION

1. Point out the main episodes in this narrative. What is Wright's purpose in offering readers these episodes?
2. How do books function as the catalyst for the narrator's transformation in this selection? Characterize this transformation. How does the transformation resemble Angelou's in "Graduation"?
3. When does the narrator begin to "hunger for books"? What is the "new hunger" (paragraph 74) that replaces it?

RHETORIC

1. Use an encyclopedia to look up the term "Jim Crow." What does it mean? How does the spirit of Jim Crow infuse the tone of this selection?
2. Define the following words: *castigate* (paragraph 2); *solidarity* (paragraph 4); *doffed* (paragraph 40); and *tantamount* (paragraph 88). Overall, how would you characterize the level of language in this piece?
3. How is the style of paragraphs 1 to 54 different from that of paragraphs 55 to 95? What change in the narrator does this change in style reflect?
4. What impact does the extensive use of dialogue have on the reader?
5. How does Wright break this selection up into specific events? What events are described? What patterns emerge?
6. To what extent is Wright being polemical in this selection? Cite examples to support your response.

WRITING

1. In light of the changes that occur in the main character, was his decision to read entirely positive? In what ways is he worse off? What new burden has he taken on? In an essay, examine the positive and negative results of Wright's experience.
2. Write an essay on the importance of books in a person's education and life.
3. Write an essay in which you compare and contrast the educations of Richard Wright and Maya Angelou.

BERTRAND RUSSELL Bertrand Arthur William Russell (1872–1970), who was born in Monmouthshire, England, was one of the great philosophers, mathematicians, liberal political theorists, and authors of the twentieth century. His works, comprising more than sixty volumes, range from abstract explanations of mathematical theory to fascinating memoirs that record British culture in the early years of the twentieth century. From the early *The Principles of Mathematics* (1903) through *An Inquiry into Meaning and Truth* (1940) to his three-volume *Autobiography* (1967–1969), Russell demonstrated his multivarious talents as a writer, socialist thinker, and activist. He was awarded the Nobel Prize in Literature in 1950. In 1955 he received the Silver Pears Trophy for work on behalf of world peace. In this essay from *Portraits from Memory* (1956), Russell argues that as we advance in knowledge, wisdom becomes an increasingly necessary quality in peoples and cultures.

BERTRAND RUSSELL

Knowledge and Wisdom

Most people would agree that, although our age far surpasses all previous ages in knowledge, there has been no correlative increase in wisdom. But agreement ceases as soon as we attempt to define "wisdom" and consider means of promoting it. I want to ask first what wisdom is, and then what can be done to teach it. 1

There are several factors that contribute to wisdom. Of these I should put first *a sense of proportion:* the capacity to take account of all the important factors in a problem and to attach to each its due weight. This has become more difficult than it used to be owing to the extent and complexity of the specialised knowledge required of various kinds of technicians. Suppose, for example, that you are engaged in research in scientific medicine. The work is difficult and is likely to absorb the whole of your intellectual energy. You have not time to consider the effect which your discoveries or inventions may have outside the field of medicine. You succeed (let us say), as modern medicine has succeeded, in enormously lowering the infant death-rate, not only in Europe and America, but also in Asia and Africa. This has the entirely unintended result of making the food supply inadequate and lowering the standard of life in the most populous parts of the world. To take an even more spectacular example, which is in everybody's mind at the present time: you study the composition of the atom from a disinterested desire for knowledge, and incidentally place in the hands of powerful lunatics the means of destroying the human race. In such ways the pursuit of knowledge may become harmful unless it is combined with wisdom; and wisdom in the sense of comprehensive vision is not necessarily present in specialists in the pursuit of knowledge. 2

3 Comprehensiveness alone, however, is not enough to constitute wisdom. There must be, also, a certain awareness of the ends of human life. This may be illustrated by the study of history. Many eminent historians have done more harm than good because they viewed facts through the distorting medium of their own passions: Hegel had a philosophy of history which did not suffer from any lack of comprehensiveness, since it started from the earliest times and continued into an indefinite future. But the chief lesson of history which he sought to inculcate was that from the year A.D. 400 down to his own time, Germany had been the most important nation and the standard-bearer of progress in the world. Perhaps one could stretch the comprehensiveness that constitutes wisdom to include not only intellect but also feeling. It is by no means uncommon to find men whose knowledge is wide but whose feelings are narrow. Such men lack what I am calling wisdom.

4 It is not only in public ways, but in private life equally, that wisdom is needed. It is needed in the choice of ends to be pursued and in emancipation from personal prejudice. Even an end which it would be noble to pursue if it were attainable may be pursued unwisely if it is inherently impossible of achievement. Many men in past ages devoted their lives to a search for the Philosopher's Stone and the Elixir of Life. No doubt, if they could have found them, they would have conferred great benefits upon mankind, but as it was their lives were wasted. To descend to less heroic matters, consider the case of two men, Mr. A and Mr. B, who hate each other and, through mutual hatred, bring each other to destruction. Suppose you go to Mr. A and say, "Why do you hate Mr. B?" He will no doubt give you an appalling list of Mr. B's vices, partly true, partly false. And now suppose you go to Mr. B. He will give you an exactly similar list of Mr. A's vices with an equal admixture of truth and falsehood. Suppose you now come back to Mr. A and say, "You will be surprised to learn that Mr. B says the same things about you as you say about him," and you go to Mr. B and make a similar speech. The first effect, no doubt, will be to increase their mutual hatred, since each will be so horrified by the other's injustice. But, perhaps, if you have sufficient patience and sufficient persuasiveness, you may succeed in convincing each that the other has only the normal share of human wickedness, and their enmity is harmful to both. If you do this, you will have instilled some fragment of wisdom.

5 The essence of wisdom is emancipation, as far as possible, from the tyranny of the here and the now. We cannot help the egoism of our senses. Sight and sound and touch are bound up with our own bodies and cannot be made impersonal. Our emotions start similarly from ourselves. An infant feels hunger and discomfort, and is unaffected except by his own physical condition. Gradually, with the years, his horizon widens, and, in proportion as his thoughts and feelings become less personal and less concerned with his own physical states, he achieves growing wisdom. This is, of course, a matter

of degree. No one can view the world with complete impartiality; and if anyone could, he would hardly be able to remain alive. But it is possible to make a continual approach towards impartiality: on the one hand, by knowing things somewhat remote in time or space; and, on the other hand, by giving to such things their due weight in our feelings. It is this approach towards impartiality that constitutes growth in wisdom.

Can wisdom in this sense be taught? And, if it can, should the 6
teaching of it be one of the aims of education? I should answer both these questions in the affirmative. We are told on Sundays that we should love our neighbor as ourselves. On the other six days of the week, we are exhorted to hate him. You may say that this is nonsense, since it is not our neighbor whom we are exhorted to hate. But you will remember that the precept was exemplified by saying that the Samaritan was our neighbour. We no longer have any wish to hate Samaritans and so we are apt to miss the point of the parable. If you want to get its point, you should substitute "communist" or "anticommunist," as the case may be, for "Samaritan." It might be objected that it is right to hate those who do harm. I do not think so. If you hate them, it is only too likely that you will become equally harmful; and it is very unlikely you will induce them to abandon their evil ways. Hatred of evil is itself a kind of bondage to evil. The way out is through understanding, not through hate. I am not advocating nonresistance. But I am saying that resistance, if it is to be effective in preventing the spread of evil, should be combined with the greatest degree of understanding and the smallest degree of force that is compatible with the survival of the good things that we wish to preserve.

It is commonly urged that a point of view such as I have been 7
advocating is incompatible with vigour in action. I do not think history bears out this view. Queen Elizabeth I in England and Henry IV in France lived in a world where almost everybody was fanatical, either on the Protestant or on the Catholic side. Both remained free from the errors of their time and both, by remaining free, were beneficent and certainly not ineffective. Abraham Lincoln conducted a great war without ever departing from what I have been calling wisdom.

I have said that in some degree wisdom can be taught. I think that 8
this teaching should have a larger intellectual element than has been customary in what has been thought of as moral instruction. The disastrous results of hatred and narrow-mindedness to those who feel them can be pointed out incidentally in the course of giving knowledge. I do not think that knowledge and morals ought to be too much separated. It is true that the kind of specialised knowledge which is required for various kinds of skill has little to do with wisdom. But it should be supplemented in education by wider surveys calculated to put it in its place in the total of human activities. Even the best technicians should also be good citizens; and when I say "citizens," I mean citizens of the world

and not of this or that sect or nation. With every increase of knowledge and skill, wisdom becomes more necessary, for every such increase augments our capacity for realising our purposes, and therefore augments our capacity for evil, if our purposes are unwise. The world needs wisdom as it has never needed it before; and if knowledge continues to increase, the world will need wisdom in the future even more than it does now.

COMPREHENSION

1. Does Russell's essay give evidence of any purpose other than to inform? Cite examples to support your response.
2. According to Russell, what is the difference between knowledge and wisdom? What constitutes true wisdom? What is the essence of wisdom?
3. How does Russell answer this question: "Can wisdom . . . be taught?"

RHETORIC

1. Explain how the author shades his connotations of the words *knowledge* and *wisdom* so that the audience understands that he thinks the latter more important than the former.
2. Define these words: *correlative* (paragraph 1); *eminent* (paragraph 3); *enmity* (paragraph 4); *exhorted* (paragraph 6); and *advocating* (paragraph 7).
3. What sort of introductory paragraph does the author develop?
4. How does Russell employ a pattern of comparison and contrast to structure his essay?
5. Explain the way that Russell integrates a pattern of exemplification into his comparative essay. How does this strategy help him achieve the definition of *wisdom?*
6. What elements of argumentation and persuasion do you encounter in this essay?

WRITING

1. How successful have your teachers been in imparting wisdom to you? Do you think that a teacher *should* impart wisdom, or is knowledge sufficient?
2. Write your own essay on knowledge and wisdom, using personal examples to highlight differences in the two concepts.
3. Using examples drawn from this chapter and earlier sections, evaluate the ways in which individuals, through a variety of educational processes, can achieve "wisdom."

AUDREY EDWARDS Audrey Edwards (1947–) has coauthored numerous children's books, including *The Picture Life of Muhammed Ali* and *The Picture Life of Stevie Wonder.* Born in Tacoma, Washington, she received her M.A. from Columbia University and was an associate editor at *Redbook* magazine from 1970–1972. Her work has appeared in *Essence* magazine, among other publications. As an African-American writer, Edwards aims for universality in her work and desires to give expression to the African-American experience. Edwards has traveled throughout the United States, as well as Africa, Japan, and the Caribbean. In the following essay, she examines racial conflicts at American colleges and universities and details the attempts being made to achieve harmony.

AUDREY EDWARDS

Fighting Racism on Campus

Despite the progress that the civil rights movement has made in American society over the past 30 years, increasing the level of interaction between whites and minority-group members, this country's diverse races still don't know each other well enough. 1

As a result, whites and minorities often relate to each other on the basis of ignorance, confusion and fear—which sometimes sparks racially motivated slurs or acts of violence. Since college campuses are among the most ethnically diverse communities in this country, they have, in a sense, become a major meeting point for various ethnic groups. College students find themselves living at close quarters with people of widely different backgrounds—often for the very first time in their lives. 2

Some university administrations have reacted—often under pressure from student and minority groups—by aggressively denouncing racist acts and changing curricula to represent disparate views. Minority and white students have also sought to increase mutual understanding. 3

Such dramatic social change is not accomplished without upheaval. Intolerance sparked violence on campuses a few years ago; today bigotry is more likely to be expressed in a war of words or in separatist behavior. So, although awareness has been heightened, racism on campuses is still very real, very disturbing and—because of its subtlety—in some ways even more insidious than it used to be. 4

Underlying Causes

A generation ago, most black students who pursued higher education went to schools that catered primarily to blacks. Today more than 75 per- 5

cent of all black college students attend schools with predominantly white student bodies, yet these students, along with members of other ethnic groups, such as Hispanics and Asians, can feel isolated and suspicious in an environment that seems too large, too white and too impersonal.

White students can also be suspicious. Many of them went to mostly white high schools in the suburbs, and often don't know how to act when first confronted with minority-group members in day-to-day living situations at college. 6

As do other American institutions, college campuses reflect the prevailing sentiments of society at large. Students are products of various socializing forces; they are affected by the feelings and behavior of family members, by the opinions of their professors, by peer pressure, and by the conduct of leaders in such fields as politics and entertainment. 7

"It's a reflection of what's coming from the top down," explains Dr. Marshall Lee, a psychologist at the City University of New York's Baruch College (New York, NY). Lee contends there is a current climate of conservatism that does not "vigorously oppose racial acts. The 1990s are the same as the 1890s, when there was a movement back to conservatism after the liberal period that followed the first great civil rights movement of the 1860s: the Civil War," he notes. 8

But racial "acting out" on the part of college students probably has as much to do with economics and psychology as with history. A highly charged debate is currently being waged over the curriculum changes and quotas that have given many minority students scholarship money and preference in obtaining admission to colleges and universities. 9

"The overall feeling is that minority groups have gotten too much and don't deserve more," says Dr. Niara Sudarkasa, president of historically black Lincoln University in Pennsylvania. "White students feel, 'If you favor equality, why are you doing this for blacks and not for us?' It's a legitimate question. The problem is, we don't talk to students about these issues in terms that make sense to them. The notion of affirmative action rests on the concept of *equity,* not equality. If justice and fairness is the end result we are after, equitable access has to be the principle on which we operate." 10

The confusion and anger surrounding issues of equity and equality may be one part of a larger dynamic. According to Dr. Jean Spaulding, a psychiatrist who specializes in treating children and adolescents, emotional development reaches a critical phase between the ages of 17 and 22. This is when young people leave home for the first time and seek to solidify their identity in terms of career, personal life, and sexuality. 11

Spaulding explains that it is common for college students to be insecure and to project their insecurities onto others. In the case of white students, the objects of their anxiety may be black or other minority students because they are markedly different, and this anxiety might be expressed in racist ways. "Jobs are difficult to come by; the economy is uncertain. It doesn't take much of a leap of logic for some of these students to decide that black and other minorities are to blame," Spaulding explains. 12

The Desire to Change

"I think all of us growing up in America have certain racist ideas," admits Mike Davis, a 21-year-old white junior at the University of Massachusetts at Amherst. Davis grew up in the suburb of Newton, Massachusetts. Most of the minority-group members in his high school were bused in from Boston. Although his primary contact with blacks was through sports, he also noticed that most of his black classmates were not taking college prep courses. "I didn't think it was because of any intellectual inferiority; I understood the sociological implications." Yet, even with such understanding, the different academic choices of members of the two races led Davis to develop a vague, intangible, negative perception of blacks.

Like a lot of white students who are as troubled by racism as minority students are, Davis has struggled to overcome what he terms his own "dogged pattern of racist ideas." He no longer laughs at racist jokes, for instance. "I realize they continue prejudices, so I don't think they're funny." He was also outraged by a white student who one day remarked in class that he felt more "civilized" than people in Africa. "I'm glad it was treated by the rest of the class as the ridiculous statement it was," he says. 14

Perhaps most significantly, Davis is among a growing number of white students who have elected to broaden their horizons by taking the cultural diversity courses now being offered (and increasingly required) by many colleges and universities. 15

On many campuses, students and faculty members debate whether diversity courses should be required and, in fact, whether they make much of a difference in changing racial attitudes. Many people claim these courses are merely an attempt to be "politically correct." This phrase is usually used to describe ideas and activities that appear to be tolerant. Not only do members of some campus factions oppose affirmative action and mandatory diversity courses, they also believe that the fear of being politically incorrect keeps the merits of these programs from being fully discussed. 16

The arguments in the debate over political correctness do not lessen the effects of racism: On the most fundamental level, racism is an insidious assault on one's self-esteem. It also has the potential to bring out the very worst in people. 17

The Impact of Racism

"Devastated" is how student Veronica Chambers felt when a sophomore resident adviser [R.A.] at her school, Simon's Rock College (Great Barrington, MA), told her, "I can say 'nigger, nigger, nigger, nigger' whenever I want, as long as I don't touch you. That's within my free-speech rights." The R.A.'s comment was made last year following an incident in which six black female students walking near campus were called "niggers" by men passing by in a car. What the sophomore 18 resident adviser didn't understand was that her Constitutional rights did not make her words any less reprehensible.

"I was a senior resident adviser at that time," says Chambers, 20, who graduated from Simon's Rock last May with a degree in English. "We were at a meeting with other R.A.s, and I wanted to know whether any of the sophomores had talked to the six girls, who were really shaken. None of the white resident advisers had reached out to them. None of the faculty had. And then this woman makes such an awful comment about her free-speech 'rights'. Saying you have the right to call someone a nigger is like saying you have the right to spit on someone. Because to me that's what being called 'nigger' feels like—like I've been spat on. And as far as I'm concerned, no one has the right to spit on me." 19

What bothered Chambers was not just the racial insensitivity of a fellow student, but the fact that such sentiment was being expressed on the campus of a progressive liberal arts college, home to only three hundred students. 20

She had chosen Simon's Rock because it is an early-admissions college that opened in 1966—the height of the supposedly liberal Sixties. The school allows students to begin college after their sophomore or junior year of high school and, as such, attracts the most academically motivated. "The school sees itself as very tolerant," Chambers says. 21

Despite the good experiences she had with many of her professors, Chambers feels the student body and administration were silent when it came to racial issues. "During my first year, there were no black professors," she notes. When Chambers and other blacks on campus were pushing for the school to hire a black teacher, a white student remarked, "We really need a science professor. Why do we need a black professor?" 22

Chambers notes, "It never occurred to him that we could have a black professor who was also a science professor. To that student, we needed a good professor, not a black professor. The two were mutually exclusive." 23

Administrative Action

The behavior and attitudes of students can often be affected by their university's stance on racism. Schools have a responsibility to provide students with an academic environment that not only is conducive to learning, but also makes students feel comfortable with themselves and with others who are racially and culturally different. 24

For instance, four years ago, when a predominantly white fraternity at the University of Pennsylvania (Philadelphia, PA) gave a stag party that featured two nude dancers—both of them black women—the event prompted a protest from U. Penn's Black Student League. That hiring nude female dancers was probably more sexist than racist didn't diminish the feeling that blacks as well as women had been slighted. Hispanic students at U. Penn were similarly offended when another fraternity advertised a party with a poster showing a sleeping Mexican. 25

U. Penn's administration quickly censured the fraternity that had 26
hired the nude dancers and kicked it out of its campus house for one year. The university also made the other fraternity issue a public apology to Hispanic students for perpetuating the stereotype of the lazy Mexican.

Such swift and public reprimands have created at the school an at- 27
mosphere in which blacks like Rafaa McRae, a 21-year-old senior, can honestly say, "I feel very much at home at U. Penn." McRae adds that university support for such enterprises as the black student newspaper he helped start two years ago is critical to making minority-group members feel there is room and respect for their cultural diversity and political views. Two fraternities—one with black and one with white members—jointly hold an annual program called COLORS (Campus Organized Lectures on Racial Sensitivity), a five-day series of workshops, cultural events and lectures designed to make different racial and cultural groups sensitive to and respectful of each other's differences.

Minorities Reach Out

Members of minority groups say that they have to take responsibili- 28
ty for the quality of their lives on campus. For four years, Patrick Day, a 21-year-old senior at Northwestern University (Evanston, IL) who is majoring in human development and social policy, has been a tireless worker and organizer on behalf of fellow black students. "It's very important for us to be involved," says Day, who has a work-study job as student admissions associate in the school's minority-recruitment office. He has served on the executive board of the Black Student Alliance and on the academic committee of the Associated Student Government, and has participated in required discussions of ethnic diversity for incoming freshmen.

Day believes college is the time when ideas are most likely to be- 29
come internalized, making multicultural courses and special events crucial to helping shape—and sometimes reshape—a student's racial attitudes. "When people go to college they begin to think in a much deeper way about those issues," he says, "and they may try to change some things about their lives that they haven't had the opportunity to alter before. For the first time, you have access to the cultural outlets and mix of people that can lead to the sort of discovery that might not be possible in many high schools."

Changing Curricula

Stanford University (Stanford, CA) reflects the new mix that may 30
mark the campus of the future. Its student body of 13,000 is 28 percent minority-group members. The largest segment of its minority population is Asian-Americans, who make up 14 percent of the enrollment.

"The idea of multiculturalism is very important around here," says Cheo H. Coker, an 18-year-old Stanford sophomore who is majoring in English. "From day one, that's all you hear about." 31

Two years ago, the school gave in to lobbying by students and younger faculty members and initiated a mandatory, year-long sequence of cultural-diversity courses offered in eight tracks. In order to graduate, every Stanford University student must now take three courses chosen from these tracks: history; values, technology, science and society; literature and the arts; Europe and the Americas; philosophy; humanities; structured liberal education; and great works. 32

In the great-works portion of the curriculum, for instance, students read the Koran and the Tao Te Ching, along with the Bible. In the segment on Europe and the Americas, students read not just the works of Marx and Freud, but also those of writers such as Zora Neale Hurston, a black American, Frantz Fanon from the Caribbean, and the South American novelist Gabriel García Márquez. 33

Forging a New Understanding

Change stems not so much from how people think, but how they behave, argues Dr. Fletcher Blanchard, associate professor of social psychology at Smith College (Northampton, MA). The critical factor in curbing racist behavior is having such acts condemned by others, says Blanchard. 34

"Today's increase in racist behavior doesn't reflect broadly negative attitudes and prejudices," he says. "There have been huge favorable changes in whites' attitudes toward minority-group members, and there is increased support for programs that eliminate discrimination. What I think has also happened is that there has been an increase in the public displays by the few who are racist. And there's been a reduction in the constraints against such public displays." 35

Because there is now less speaking out against racist acts by those in the majority than there was 15 years ago, the intolerant feel they have a license to "act out" in racist ways. In a 1991 study Blanchard did examining how prejudices are shaped, he found that when people hear strong antiracist opinions expressed by others of their own race, they are more likely to curb their behavior accordingly. "Each of us can influence the behavior of those around us by the way we react to racism," he says. "And if we modify behavior, attitudes will surely follow." 36

COMPREHENSION

1. According to the article, what is the current racial atmosphere on American college campuses?
2. To what does Edwards attribute the racial unrest?
3. What is being done to defuse the tension and promote racial harmony?

RHETORIC

1. Where in the essay is the thesis stated?
2. Does Edwards present the issues in a subjective or an objective manner? Justify your response.
3. Why does Edwards use subheadings? What does this strategy tell you about her purpose and audience? Choose three adjectives that best describe the writer's style. Use examples from the article as evidence.
4. Consider the use of quotes from other sources and the use of statistics in the article. What effect do they have in advancing Edwards's argument?
5. How does Edwards employ causal analysis in this essay? Cite specific examples of causes and effects. What causal patterns emerge?
6. How is the information organized in this essay?

WRITING

1. Write an essay in which you offer possible solutions to the problem of racial turbulence on college campuses.
2. Argue for or against this proposition: Racial integration at American colleges has failed. It has only served to weaken academic standards and has not helped solve this country's racial problems.
3. Write a research paper tracing the history of school integration in this country.

CLASSIC AND CONTEMPORARY

FREDERICK DOUGLASS Frederick Douglass (1817–1895) was an American abolitionist, orator, and journalist. Born of the union between a slave and a white man, Douglass later escaped to Massachusetts. An impassioned anti-slavery speech brought him recognition as a powerful orator; thereafter he was much in demand for speaking engagements. He described his experience as a black man in America in *Narrative of the Life of Frederick Douglass* (1845). After managing to buy his freedom, Douglass founded the *North Star,* a newspaper he published for the next seventeen years. In the following exerpt from his stirring autobiography, Douglass recounts the tremendous obstacles he overcame in his efforts to become literate.

FREDERICK DOUGLASS

Learning to Read and Write

I lived in Master Hugh's family about seven years. During this time, I succeeded in learning to read and write. In accomplishing this, I was compelled to resort to various stratagems. I had no regular teacher. My mistress, who had kindly commenced to instruct me, had, in compliance with the advice and direction of her husband, not only ceased to instruct, but had set her face against my being instructed by any one else. It is due, however, to my mistress to say of her, that she did not adopt this course of treatment immediately. She at first lacked the depravity indispensable to shutting me up in mental darkness. It was at least necessary for her to have some training in the exercise of irresponsible power, to make her equal to the task of treating me as though I were a brute. 1

My mistress was, as I have said, a kind and tender-hearted woman; and in the simplicity of her soul she commenced, when I first went to live with her, to treat me as she supposed one human being ought to treat another. In entering upon the duties of a slaveholder, she did not seem to perceive that I sustained to her the relation of a mere chattel, and that for her to treat me as a human being was not only wrong, but dangerously so. Slavery proved as injurious to her as it did to me. When I went there, she was a pious, warm, and tender-hearted woman. There was no sorrow or suffering for which she had not a tear. She had bread for the hungry, clothes for the naked, and comfort for every mourner that came within her reach. Slavery soon proved its ability to divest her of these heavenly qualities. Under its influence, the tender heart became stone, and the lamb-like disposition gave way to one of 2

tiger-like fierceness. The first step in her downward course was in her ceasing to instruct me. She now commenced to practise her husband's precepts. She finally became even more violent in her opposition than her husband himself. She was not satisfied with simply doing as well as he had commanded; she seemed anxious to do better. Nothing seemed to make her more angry than to see me with a newspaper. She seemed to think that here lay the danger. I have had her rush at me with a face made all up of fury, and snatch from me a newspaper, in a manner that fully revealed her apprehension. She was an apt woman; and a little experience soon demonstrated, to her satisfaction, that education and slavery were incompatible with each other.

From this time I was most narrowly watched. If I was in a separate 3
room any considerable length of time, I was sure to be suspected of having a book, and was at once called to give an account of myself. All this, however, was too late. The first step had been taken. Mistress, in teaching me the alphabet, had given me the *inch,* and no precaution could prevent me from taking the *ell.*

The plan which I adopted, and the one by which I was most suc- 4
cessful, was that of making friends of all the little white boys whom I met in the street. As many of these as I could, I converted into teachers. With their kindly aid, obtained at different times and in different places, I finally succeeded in learning to read. When I was sent of errands, I always took my book with me, and by going one part of my errand quickly. I found time to get a lesson before my return. I used also to carry bread with me, enough of which was always in the house, and to which I was always welcome; for I was much better off in this regard than many of the poor white children in our neighborhood. This bread I used to bestow upon the hungry little urchins, who, in return, would give me that more valuable bread of knowledge. I am strongly tempted to give the names of two or three of those little boys, as a testimonial of the gratitude and affection I bear them; but prudence forbids;—not that it would injure me, but it might embarrass them; for it is almost an unpardonable offence to teach slaves to read in this Christian country. It is enough to say of the dear little fellows, that they lived on Philpot Street, very near Durgin and Bailey's ship-yard. I used to talk this matter of slavery over with them. I would sometimes say to them, I wished I could be as free as they would be when they got to be men. "You will be free as soon as you are twenty-one, *but I am a slave for life!* Have not I as good a right to be free as you have?" These words used to trouble them; they would express for me the liveliest sympathy, and console me with the hope that something would occur by which I might be free.

I was now about twelve years old, and the thought of being *a slave* 5
for life began to bear heavily upon my heart. Just about this time, I got hold of a book entitled "The Columbian Orator." Every opportunity I got, I used to read this book. Among much of other interesting matter, I found in it a dialogue between a master and his slave. The slave was represented as having run away from his master three times. The dialogue represented the conversation which took place between them,

when the slave was retaken the third time. In this dialogue, the whole argument in behalf of slavery was brought forward by the master, all of which was disposed of by the slave. The slave was made to say some very smart as well as impressive things in reply to his master—things which had the desired though unexpected effect; for the conversation resulted in the voluntary emancipation of the slave on the part of the master.

In the same book, I met with one of Sheridan's mighty speeches 6
on and in behalf of Catholic emancipation. These were choice documents to me. I read them over and over again with unabated interest. They gave tongue to interesting thoughts of my own soul, which had frequently flashed through my mind, and died away for want of utterance. The moral which I gained from the dialogue was the power of truth over the conscience of even a slaveholder. What I got from Sheridan was a bold denunciation of slavery, and a powerful vindication of human rights. The reading of these documents enabled me to utter my thoughts, and to meet the arguments brought forward to sustain slavery; but while they relieved me of one difficulty, they brought on another even more painful than the one of which I was relieved. The more I read, the more I was led to abhor and detest my enslavers. I could regard them in no other light than a band of successful robbers, who had left their homes, and gone to Africa, and stolen us from our homes, and in a strange land reduced us to slavery. I loathed them as being the meanest as well as the most wicked of men. As I read and contemplated the subject, behold! that very discontentment which Master Hugh had predicted would follow my learning to read had already come, to torment and sting my soul to unutterable anguish. As I writhed under it, I would at times feel that learning to read had been a curse rather than a blessing. It had given me a view of my wretched condition, without the remedy. It opened my eyes to the horrible pit, but to no ladder upon which to get out. In moments of agony, I envied my fellow-slaves for their stupidity. I have often wished myself a beast. I preferred the condition of the meanest reptile to my own. Any thing, no matter what, to get rid of thinking! It was this everlasting thinking of my condition that tormented me. There was no getting rid of it. It was pressed upon me by every object within sight or hearing, animate or inanimate. The silver trump of freedom had roused my soul to eternal wakefulness. Freedom now appeared, to disappear no more forever. It was heard in every sound, and seen in every thing. It was ever present to torment me with a sense of my wretched condition. I saw nothing without seeing it, I heard nothing without hearing it, and felt nothing without feeling it. It looked from every star, it smiled in every calm, breathed in every wind, and moved in every storm.

I often found myself regretting my own existence, and wishing 7
myself dead; and but for the hope of being free, I have no doubt but that I should have killed myself, or done something for which I should have been killed. While in this state of mind, I was eager to hear any

one speak of slavery. I was a ready listener. Every little while, I could hear something about the abolitionists. It was some time before I found what the word meant. It was always used in such connections as to make it an interesting word to me. If a slave ran away and succeeded in getting clear, or if a slave killed his master, set fire to a barn, or did any thing very wrong in the mind of a slaveholder, it was spoken of as the fruit of *abolition.* Hearing the word in this connection very often, I set about learning what it meant. The dictionary afforded me little or no help. I found it was "the act of abolishing;" but then I did not know what was to be abolished. Here I was perplexed. I did not dare to ask any one about its meaning, for I was satisfied that it was something they wanted me to know very little about. After a patient waiting, I got one of our city papers, containing an account of the number of petitions from the north, praying for the abolition of slavery in the District of Columbia, and of the slave trade between the States. From this time I understood the words *abolition* and *abolitionist,* and always drew near when that word was spoken, expecting to hear something of importance to myself and fellow-slaves. The light broke in upon me by degrees. I went one day down on the wharf of Mr. Waters; and seeing two Irishmen unloading a scow of stone, I went, unasked, and helped them. When we had finished, one of them came to me and asked me if I were a slave. I told him I was. He asked, "Are ye a slave for life?" I told him that I was. The good Irishman seemed to be deeply affected by the statement. He said to the other that it was a pity so fine a little fellow as myself should be a slave for life. He said it was a shame to hold me. They both advised me to run away to the north; that I should find friends there, and that I should be free. I pretended not to be interested in what they said, and treated them as if I did not understand them; for I feared they might be treacherous. White men have been known to encourage slaves to escape, and then, to get the reward, catch them and return them to their masters. I was afraid that these seemingly good men might use me so; but I nevertheless remembered their advice, and from that time I resolved to run away. I looked forward to a time at which it would be safe for me to escape. I was too young to think of doing so immediately; besides, I wished to learn how to write, as I might have occasion to write my own pass. I consoled myself with the hope that I should one day find a good chance. Meanwhile, I would learn to write.

The idea as to how I might learn to write was suggested to me by 8
being in Durgin and Bailey's ship-yard, and frequently seeing the ship carpenters, after hewing, and getting a piece of timber ready for use, write on the timber the name of that part of the ship for which it was intended. When a piece of timber was intended for the larboard side, it would be marked thus—"L." When a piece was for the starboard side, it would be marked thus—"S." A piece for the larboard side forward, would be marked thus—"L. F." When a piece was for starboard side forward, it would be marked thus—"S. F." For larboard aft, it would be

marked thus—"L. A." For starboard aft, it would be marked thus—"S. A." I soon learned the names of these letters, and for what they were intended when placed upon a piece of timber in the ship-yard. I immediately commenced copying them, and in a short time was able to make the four letters named. After that, when I met with any boy who I knew could write, I would tell him I could write as well as he. The next word would be, "I don't believe you. Let me see you try it." I would then make the letters which I had been so fortunate as to learn, and ask him to beat that. In this way I got a good many lessons in writing, which it is quite possible I should never have gotten in any other way. During this time, my copy-book was the board fence, brick wall, and pavement; my pen and ink was a lump of chalk. With these, I learned mainly how to write. I then commenced and continued copying the Italics in Webster's Spelling Book, until I could make them all without looking on the book. By this time, my little Master Thomas had gone to school, and learned how to write, and had written over a number of copy-books. These had been brought home, and shown to some of our near neighbors, and then laid aside. My mistress used to go to class meeting at the Wilk Street meetinghouse every Monday afternoon, and leave me to take care of the house. When left thus, I used to spend the time in writing in the spaces left in Master Thomas's copy-book, copying what he had written. I continued to do this until I could write a hand very similar to that of Master Thomas. Thus, after a long, tedious effort for years, I finally succeeded in learning how to write.

COMPREHENSION

1. What strategies does Douglass use to continue his education after his mistress's abandonment?
2. Why did the author's mistress find his reading newspapers particularly threatening?
3. Why does Douglass call learning to read "a curse rather than a blessing"?

RHETORIC

1. What is the thesis of Douglass's narration? How well is it supported and developed by the body paragraphs? Explain.
2. The first couple of sentences in the story, though simple, are very powerful. How do they serve to set up the mood of the piece and the reader's expectations?
3. Cite examples of Douglass's use of metaphors, and discuss why they work in those paragraphs.
4. How would you describe Douglass's writing style and level of language? Does it reveal anything about the writer's character? Justify your response.
5. Explain the way in which the author uses comparison and contrast.
6. What is Douglass's definition of *abolition,* and how does Douglass help the reader define it? How does this method contribute to the reader's understanding of the learning process?

WRITING

1. What does Douglass mean when he writes that "education and slavery were incompatible with each other"? Write an essay in which you consider the relationship between the two.
2. Both Douglass and his mistress were in inferior positions to Master Hugh. Write an essay in which you compare and contrast their positions in society at the time.
3. Literacy is still a major problem in the United States. Write an account of what your day-to-day life would be like if you couldn't write or read. What impact would this deficiency have on your life? Use concrete examples to illustrate your narrative.

RICHARD RODRIGUEZ Richard Rodriguez (1944–) was born in San Francisco and received degrees from Stanford University and Columbia University. He also did graduate study at the University of California, Berkeley, and at the Warburg Institute, London. Rodriguez became a nationally known writer with the publication of his autobiography, *Hunger of Memory: The Education of Richard Rodriguez* (1982). In it, he describes the struggles of growing up biculturally—feeling alienated from his Spanish-speaking parents yet not wholly comfortable in the dominant culture of the United States. He opposes bilingualism and affirmative action as they are now practiced in the United States, and his stance has caused much controversy in educational and intellectual circles. Rodriguez continues to write about social issues such as acculturation, education, and language. In the following essay, Rodriguez records his childhood passion for reading.

RICHARD RODRIGUEZ

The Lonely, Good Company of Books

From an early age I knew that my mother and father could read and write both Spanish and English. I had observed my father making his way through what, I now suppose, must have been income tax forms. On other occasions I waited apprehensively while my mother read onion-paper letters air-mailed from Mexico with news of a relative's illness or death. For both my parents, however, reading was something done out of necessity and as quickly as possible. Never did I see either of them read an entire book. Nor did I see them read for pleasure. Their reading consisted of work manuals, prayer books, newspapers, recipes. . . . 1

In our house each school year would begin with my mother's careful instruction: "Don't write in your books so we can sell them at the end of the year." The remark was echoed in public by my teachers, but only in part: "Boys and girls, don't write in your books. You must learn to treat them with great care and respect." 2

OPEN THE DOORS OF YOUR MIND WITH BOOKS, read the red and white poster over the nun's desk in early September. It soon was appar- 3

ent to me that reading was the classroom's central activity. Each course had its own book. And the information gathered from a book was unquestioned. READ TO LEARN, the sign on the wall advised in December. I privately wondered: What was the connection between reading and learning? Did one learn something only by reading it? Was an idea only an idea if it could be written down? In June, CONSIDER BOOKS YOUR BEST FRIENDS. Friends? Reading was, at best, only a chore. I needed to look up whole paragraphs of words in a dictionary. Lines of type were dizzying, the eye having to move slowly across the page, then down, and across. . . . The sentences of the first books I read were coolly impersonal. Toned hard. What most bothered me, however, was the isolation reading required. To console myself for the loneliness I'd feel when I read, I tried reading in a very soft voice. Until: "Who is doing all that talking to his neighbor?" Shortly after, remedial reading classes were arranged for me with a very old nun.

4 At the end of each school day, for nearly six months, I would meet with her in the tiny room that served as the school's library but was actually only a storeroom for used textbooks and a vast collection of *National Geographics*. Everything about our sessions pleased me: the smallness of the room; the noise of the janitor's broom hitting the edge of the long hallway outside the door; the green of the sun, lighting the wall; and the old woman's face blurred white with a beard. Most of the time we took turns. I began with my elementary text. Sentences of astonishing simplicity seemed to me lifeless and drab: "The boys ran from the rain. . . . She wanted to sing. . . . The kite rose in the blue." Then the old nun would read from her favorite books, usually biographies of early American presidents. Playfully she ran through complex sentences, calling the words alive with her voice, making it seem that the author somehow was speaking directly to me. I smiled just to listen to her. I sat there and sensed for the very first time some possibility of fellowship between a reader and a writer, a communication, never *intimate* like that I heard spoken words at home convey, but one nonetheless *personal.*

5 One day the nun concluded a session by asking me why I was so reluctant to read by myself. I tried to explain; said something about the way written words made me feel all alone—almost, I wanted to add but didn't, as when I spoke to myself in a room just emptied of furniture. She studied my face as I spoke; she seemed to be watching more than listening. In an uneventful voice she replied that I had nothing to fear. Didn't I realize that reading would open up whole new worlds? A book could open doors for me. It could introduce me to people and show me places I never imagined existed. She gestured toward the bookshelves. (Bare-breasted African women danced, and the shiny hubcaps of automobiles on the back covers of the *Geographic* gleamed in my mind.) I listened with respect. But her words were not very influential. I was thinking then of another consequence of literacy, one I was too shy to admit but nonetheless trusted. Books were going to make me "educated." *That* confidence enabled me, several months later, to overcome my fear of the silence.

In fourth grade I embarked upon a grandiose reading program. 6
"Give me the names of important books," I would say to startled teachers. They soon found out that I had in mind "adult books." I ignored their suggestion of anything I suspected was written for children. (Not until I was in college, as a result, did I read *Huckleberry Finn* or *Alice's Adventures in Wonderland.*) Instead, I read *The Scarlet Letter* and Franklin's *Autobiography.* And whatever I read I read for extra credit. Each time I finished a book, I reported the achievement to a teacher and basked in the praise my effort earned. Despite my best efforts, however, there seemed to be more and more books I needed to read. At the library I would literally tremble as I came upon whole shelves of books I hadn't read. So I read and I read and I read: *Great Expectations;* all the short stories of Kipling; *The Babe Ruth Story;* the entire first volume of the *Encyclopaedia Britannica* (A-ANSTEY); the *Iliad; Moby Dick; Gone with the Wind; The Good Earth; Ramona; Forever Amber; The Lives of the Saints; Crime and Punishment; The Pearl.* . . . Librarians who initially frowned when I checked out the maximum ten books at a time started saving books they thought I might like. Teachers would say to the rest of the class, "I only wish the rest of you took reading as seriously as Richard obviously does."

But at home I would hear my mother wondering, "What do you see 7
in your books?" (Was reading a hobby like her knitting? Was so much reading even healthy for a boy? Was it the sign of "brains"? Or was it just a convenient excuse for not helping around the house on Saturday mornings?) Always, "What do you see . . . ?"

What *did* I see in my books? I had the idea that they were crucial for 8
my academic success, though I couldn't have said exactly how or why. In the sixth grade I simply concluded that what gave a book its value was some major idea or theme it contained. If that core essence could be mined and memorized, I would become learned like my teachers. I decided to record in a notebook the themes of the books that I read. After reading *Robinson Crusoe,* I wrote that its theme was "the value of learning to live by oneself." When I completed *Wuthering Heights,* I noted the danger of "letting emotions get out of control." Rereading these brief moralistic appraisals usually left me disheartened. I couldn't believe that they were really the source of reading's value. But for many years, they constituted the only means I had of describing to myself the educational value of books.

In spite of my earnestness, I found reading a pleasurable activity. I 9
came to enjoy the lonely good company of books. Early on weekday mornings, I'd read in my bed. I'd feel a mysterious comfort then, reading in the dawn quiet—the blue-gray silence interrupted by the occasional churning of the refrigerator motor a few rooms away or the more distant sounds of a city bus beginning its run. On weekends I'd go to the public library to read, surrounded by old men and women. Or, if the weather was fine, I would take my books to the park and read in the shade of a tree. Neighbors would leave for vacation and I would water their lawns. I would sit through the twilight on the front

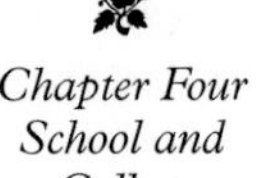

porches or in backyards, reading to the cool, whirling sounds of the sprinklers.

I also had favorite writers. But often those writers I enjoyed most I 10
was least able to value. When I read William Saroyan's *The Human Comedy,* I was immediately pleased by the narrator's warmth and the charm of his story. But as quickly I became suspicious. A book so enjoyable to read couldn't be very "important." Another summer I determined to read all the novels of Dickens. Reading his fat novels, I loved the feeling I got—after the first hundred pages—of being at home in a fictional world where I knew the names of the characters and cared about was going to happen to them. And it bothered me that I was forced away at the conclusion, when the fiction closed tight, like a fortune-teller's fist—the futures of all the major characters neatly resolved. I never knew how to take such feelings seriously, however. Nor did I suspect that these experiences could be part of a novel's meaning. Still, there were pleasures to sustain me after I'd finish my books. Carrying a volume back to the library, I would be pleased by its weight. I'd run my fingers along the edge of the pages and marvel at the breadth of my achievement. Around my room, growing stacks of paperback books reinforced my assurance.

I entered high school having read hundreds of books. My habit of 11
reading made me a confident speaker and writer of English. Reading also enabled me to sense something of the shape, the major concerns, of Western thought. (I was able to say something about Dante and Descartes and Engels and James Baldwin in my high school term papers.) In these various ways, books brought me academic success as I hoped that they would. But I was not a good reader. Merely bookish, I lacked a point of view when I read. Rather, I read in order to acquire a point of view. I vacuumed books for epigrams, scraps of information, ideas, themes—anything to fill the hollow within me and make me feel educated. When one of my teachers suggested to his drowsy tenth-grade English class that a person could not have a "complicated idea" until he had read at least two thousand books, I heard the remark without detecting either its irony or its very complicated truth. I merely determined to compile a list of all the books I had ever read. Harsh with myself, I included only once a title I might have read several times. (How, after all, could one read a book more than once?) And I included only those books over a hundred pages in length. (Could anything shorter be a book?)

There was yet another high school list I compiled. One day I came 12
across a newspaper article about the retirement of an English professor at a nearby state college. The article was accompanied by a list of the "hundred most important books of Western Civilization." "More than anything else in my life," the professor told the reporter with finality, "these books have made me all that I am." That was the kind of remark I couldn't ignore. I clipped out the list and kept it for the several months it took me to read all of the titles. Most books, of course, I barely understood. While reading Plato's *Republic,* for instance, I need-

ed to keep looking at the book jacket comments to remind myself what the text was about. Nevertheless, with the special patience and superstition of a scholarship boy, I looked at every word of the text. And by the time I reached the last word, relieved, I convinced myself that I had read *The Republic*. In a ceremony of great pride, I solemnly crossed Plato off my list.

COMPREHENSION

1. What was Rodriguez's parents' attitude toward reading? Did it influence his attitude? Cite examples from the essay that support your opinion.
2. What does Rodriguez mean by "the fellowship between a reader and a writer"? Why does he differentiate between "intimate" and "personal" forms of communication?
3. Rodriguez hoped that reading would fill "the hollow" inside him. What was the cause of his emptiness? Did he succeed in filling the void? Why did he find reading a lonely experience? Did reading fulfill any of his expectations?

RHETORIC

1. What is the thesis of Rodriguez's essay? Is it stated or implied? Explain.
2. How does the author's use of narrative advance his views on reading and education?
3. What is the writer's tone? How effective is it in conveying his point of view?
4. Rodriguez uses uppercase letters when referring to signs advocating reading. Why does he use this device? How does it support his point of view?
5. The essay ends with an ironic anecdote. Why did Rodriguez choose to conclude this way? Does it satisfactorily illustrate the writer's attitude?
6. What words or phrases imply that there is an ethnic component in Rodriguez's conflict? Is the subtlety effective? Justify your response.

WRITING

1. Rodriguez's parents had a pragmatic attitude toward reading. What was the attitude in your home as you were growing up? Did your parents encourage your interest in reading? Did they read themselves? What is the first book you remember reading by yourself? Write an essay in which you describe your reading history.
2. Rodriguez believed reading would make him "educated." Do you agree or disagree? Is reading vitally important to a person's education? How do you define *education?* Can it only be acquired through reading, or are there other contributing factors? Write an argumentative essay on this topic.
3. Is reading still a significant source of information and entertainment, or has it been usurped by television? Is it important (or necessary) to be a reader today?

CLASSIC AND CONTEMPORARY: QUESTIONS FOR COMPARISON

1. Both Rodriguez and Douglass were motivated to educate themselves in a society inimical to this achievement. Compare and contrast their struggles and attitudes in their quest for knowledge.
2. Pretend you are Richard Rodriguez, and write a letter to Douglass addressing the issues of minorities and education in present-day America. What would Rodriguez say about the progress of minorities in our society?
3. Although Rodriguez and Douglass treat a similar theme, they communicate their messages differently. Which narration do you consider more powerful, and why?
4. Rodriguez explores the theme of isolation in his story. Is there any evidence that this feeling was shared by Douglass in his efforts to learn how to read? Use proof from both narratives to support your view.
5. Slavery was an obvious obstacle to Douglass's attempt to educate himself. What impeded Rodriguez's progress? Were there similar forces at work? Cite examples from Rodriguez's narrative to prove your point.

CONNECTIONS

1. Using the essays of D'Souza and Edwards, write an essay examining the positive and negative consequences of multiculturalism in American schools.
2. Bertrand Russell states: "I do not think that knowledge and morals ought to be too much separated." Compare this view to Quindlen's belief that "there is little philosophical counterpoint" to the issue of teenage sexuality. What is the link between morality and education as seen by these two writers?
3. Write an essay about the special significance of education to African Americans and other minorities in this country. Use quotes from the works of Angelou, Wright, D'Souza, Edwards, Douglass, and Rodriguez.
4. Write a personal narrative recreating an important event connected to your education. Describe the event itself and its impact on your personality. Was it a bittersweet experience like Angelou's, or did it provoke a dawning shift in perspective such as Wright experienced? Use the writers in this section where relevant.
5. Angelou's essay recalls the contribution of African Americans in many other fields besides sports. Research the life and work of someone of your own ethnic or cultural background, and discuss his or her accomplishments.
6. Write an essay in which you favor or oppose affirmative action at work and school. Use the essays of D'Souza, Edwards, and Russell to make your case.
7. In paragraph 25 of her essay, Audrey Edwards makes a connection between racism and sexism. Write an essay in which you probe the similarities and contrasts between the two injustices.
8. Write an essay which argues that sex and morality should be taught at home by parents and not left up to the schools.
9. Compare and contrast the essays by D'Souza and Edwards. How do they deal with the issue of multiculturalism and racism in colleges? Compare the writers' styles, voices, and points of view.

CHAPTER FIVE

Gender and Human Development

There is an essay in this chapter by the anthropologist Mary Leakey. In it, she offers readers one of the most memorable images in this anthology. The image is of two sets of footprints moving toward us out of "the ashes of time." The smaller set of footprints might have been those of a female. These footprints, Leakey speculates, signify our original human prototypes—the first woman and man. These two sets of footprints suggest to Leakey that human development is rooted in gender or "sexual dimorphism."

In many cultures, we still find the smaller set of footprints moving behind the larger because issues of gender stereotyping still dominate many discussions of human development. Today, more than seventy years after they won the right to vote, women in the United States still earn less than men, still hold far fewer high corporate and political positions, and are still expected to be traditional "homemakers." They may be freer than are women in other cultures to determine their own destinies—to walk beside or ahead of men or to dispense with men altogether—but their footprints inevitably cross paths with their male counterparts as American society continues to map out destiny on the basis of gender.

Admittedly, every culture has its own idea of what it means to be a man or a woman; and these ideas affect our major institutions, from the family to school to numerous other social relationships. And although it is difficult to reconcile these various cross-cultural ideas, the writers in this chapter attempt to make sense of sex roles and to liberate themselves from the tyranny of sexual stereotyping. Freud, of course, in his essay "Libidinal Types," asserts that human behavior is rooted in sexuality, that sex is destiny. Whether you agree or disagree with his

premise, it is clear that notions of what it means to be a woman or a man have a definite impact on the way we conduct our lives. For example, when Sandra Cisneros and Adrienne Rich write about the relationship of daughters to their parents, they raise issues concerning the lines of power that operate along sexual lines in many families. Similarly, when Margaret Atwood provides an innovative, multipart catalogue on "the female body," she investigates and critiques lines of sexual power while offering a satire on attitudes that reduce women to sexual objects. Gloria Steinem extends this critique to the realm of literature and art in her evaluation of erotica and pornography and their relationship to human sexual response.

All of the writers above, and others in this chapter, tend to challenge all attitudes that reflect various forms of sexual discrimination and gender stereotyping. They each suggest, in their own ways, that men and women can be better in their relationships than they have been historically. Paul Theroux and Michael Dorris extend this theme in their essays, both of which offer revisionist definitions of what it means to be a man in American culture. The gender issues discussed by writers in this chapter might prove to be controversial. They will force you to confront your own sense of sexual identity. These essays are like a mirror in which you can see and evaluate the ways in which you behave as a man or a woman.

Previewing the Chapter

As you read the essays in this chapter and respond to them in discussion and writing, consider the following questions:

- How does the author define what it means to be a woman or a man?
- What specific gender issues does the author raise?
- Is the author concerned with male behavior, female behavior, or both?
- What perspective does the writer take on the subject of gender stereotyping? Is the writer optimistic, pessimistic, or neutral?
- How does the writer present power relationships between the sexes?
- What social, political, and economic issues are raised by the author?
- Does the author demonstrate a bias for or against men or women? How do you know?
- What changes in human behavior, if any, does the author propose for men and women?
- According to the author, how do women perceive the world? How do men perceive it? How do they judge each other's behavior?

• Do you agree or disagree with the presentation of gender and human development presented by the author?

• Based on your reading of these essays, what overall attitude do you have on gender and human behavior? Have any of the essayists encouraged you to examine your own behavior and beliefs?

SANDRA CISNEROS Sandra Cisneros (1954–) is concerned with the issues of gender, poverty, cultural suppression, and self-identity; and her poems and short stories reflect this interest. Cisneros draws repeatedly from her childhood experiences as the daughter of a Mexican father and Chicana mother. Her novel, *The House on Mango Street* (1983), and *Woman Hollering Creek* (1992), a collection of narratives focusing on a group of Mexican-American characters, have earned her recognition as a powerful storyteller. Although known primarily for her prose, Cisneros is also an accomplished poet. A collection of her poetry, entitled *My Wicked Wicked Ways,* was published in 1987. In the following narrative, Cisneros writes of the pain and frustration she felt trying to make her father take her work and worth seriously.

SANDRA CISNEROS

Only Daughter

Once, several years ago, when I was just starting out my writing career, I was asked to write my own contributor's note for an anthology I was part of. I wrote: "I am the only daughter in a family of six sons. *That* explains everything." 1

Well, I've thought about that ever since, and yes, it explains a lot to me, but for the reader's sake I should have written: "I am the only daughter in a *Mexican* family of six sons." Or even: "I am the only daughter of a Mexican father and a Mexican-American mother." Or: "I am the only daughter of a working-class family of nine." All of these had everything to do with who I am today. 2

I was/am the only daughter and *only* a daughter. Being an only daughter in a family of six sons forced me by circumstance to spend a lot of time by myself because my brothers felt it beneath them to play with a *girl* in public. But that aloneness, that loneliness, was good for a would-be writer—it allowed me time to think and think, to imagine, to read and prepare myself. 3

Being only a daughter for my father meant my destiny would lead me to become someone's wife. That's what he believed. But when I was in the fifth grade and shared my plans for college with him, I was sure he understood. I remember my father saying, "*Que bueno, ni'ja,* that's 4

good." That meant a lot to me, especially since my brothers thought the idea hilarious. What I didn't realize was that my father thought college was good for girls—good for finding a husband. After four years in college and two more in graduate school, and still no husband, my father shakes his head even now and says I wasted all that education.

In retrospect, I'm lucky my father believed daughters were meant 5
for husbands. It meant it didn't matter if I majored in something silly like English. After all, I'd find a nice professional eventually, right? This allowed me the liberty to putter about embroidering my little poems and stories without my father interrupting with so much as a "What's that you're writing?"

But the truth is, I wanted him to interrupt. I wanted my father to 6
understand what it was I was scribbling, to introduce me as "My only daughter, the writer." Not as "This is only my daughter. She teaches." *Es maestra*—teacher. Not even *profesora.*

In a sense, everything I have ever written has been for him, to win 7
his approval even though I know my father can't read English words, even though my father's only reading includes the brown-ink *Esto* sports magazines from Mexico City and the bloody *¡Alarma!* magazines that feature yet another sighting of *La Virgen de Guadalupe* on a tortilla or a wife's revenge on her philandering husband by bashing his skull in with a *molcajete* (a kitchen mortar made of volcanic rock). Or the *fotonovelas,* the little picture paperbacks with tragedy and trauma erupting from the characters' mouths in bubbles.

My father represents, then, the public majority. A public who is un- 8
interested in reading, and yet one whom I am writing about and for, and privately trying to woo.

When we were growing up in Chicago, we moved a lot because of 9
my father. He suffered bouts of nostalgia. Then we'd have to let go our flat, store the furniture with mother's relatives, load the station wagon with baggage and bologna sandwiches and head south. To Mexico City.

We came back, of course. To yet another Chicago flat, another 10
Chicago neighborhood, another Catholic school. Each time, my father would seek out the parish priest in order to get a tuition break, and complain or boast: "I have seven sons."

He meant *siete hijos,* seven children, but he translated it as "sons." "I 11
have seven sons." To anyone who would listen. The Sears Roebuck employee who sold us the washing machine. The short-order cook where my father ate his ham-and-eggs breakfasts. "I have seven sons." As if he deserved a medal from the state.

My papa. He didn't mean anything by that mistranslation, I'm sure. 12
But somehow I could feel myself being erased. I'd tug my father's sleeve and whisper: "Not seven sons. Six! and *one daughter.*"

When my oldest brother graduated from medical school, he ful- 13
filled my father's dream that we study hard and use this—our heads, instead of this—our hands. Even now my father's hands are thick and yellow, stubbed by a history of hammer and nails and twine and coils and springs. "Use this," my father said, tapping his head, "and

not this," showing us those hands. He always looked tired when he said it.

Wasn't college an investment? And hadn't I spent all those years in college? And if I didn't marry, what was it all for? Why would anyone go to college and then choose to be poor? Especially someone who had always been poor.

15 Last year, after ten years of writing professionally, the financial rewards started to trickle in. My second National Endowment for the Arts Fellowship. A guest professorship at the University of California, Berkeley. My book, which sold to a major New York publishing house.

16 At Christmas, I flew home to Chicago. The house was throbbing, same as always; hot *tamales* and sweet *tamales* hissing in my mother's pressure cooker, and everybody—my mother, six brothers, wives, babies, aunts, cousins—talking too loud and at the same time, like in a Fellini film, because that's just how we are.

17 I went upstairs to my father's room. One of my stories had just been translated into Spanish and published in an anthology of Chicano writing, and I wanted to show it to him. Ever since he recovered from a stroke two years ago, my father likes to spend his leisure hours horizontally. And that's how I found him, watching a Pedro Infante movie on Galavisión and eating rice pudding.

18 There was a glass filmed with milk on the bedside table. There were several vials of pills and balled Kleenex. And on the floor, one black sock and a plastic urinal that I didn't want to look at but looked at anyway. Pedro Infante was about to burst into song, and my father was laughing.

19 I'm not sure if it was because my story was translated into Spanish, or because it was published in Mexico, or perhaps because the story dealt with Tepeyac, the *colonia* my father was raised in and the house he grew up in, but at any rate, my father punched the mute button on his remote control and read my story.

20 I sat on the bed next to my father and waited. He read it very slowly. As if he were reading each line over and over. He laughed at all the right places and read lines he liked out loud. He pointed and asked questions: "Is this So-and-so?" "Yes," I said. He kept reading.

21 When he was finally finished, after what seemed like hours, my father looked up and asked: "Where can we get more copies of this for the relatives?"

22 Of all the wonderful things that happened to me last year, that was the most wonderful.

COMPREHENSION

1. Why does the writer feel she should amend her original contributor's note?
2. What does Cisneros mean by the "public majority" in paragraph 8?
3. How does her father react when he finally reads his daughter's work? How does Cisneros feel at the end of the essay? How has her attitude toward being the "only daughter" changed in the course of the essay?

RHETORIC

1. In your own words, state Cisneros's thesis. Where in the essay does it appear?
2. How does Cisneros use details and language in paragraph 7? What effect does the use of Spanish have on the narrative?
3. How does the author combine narration and analysis in this essay? How does she arrange her episodes?
4. What is the purpose behind the writer's use of questions in paragraph 14?
5. What is the purpose of the author's comparative method in paragraphs 9 to 11 and 16 to 18?
6. Cite particularly powerful or effective details in the story, and explain why they made such a strong impression on you.

WRITING

1. Write a letter to Cisneros's father explaining how his daughter feels and what she needs from him. For support, use quotes from the essay as well as your own experiences with parents.
2. Write an essay in which you argue for or against this statement: Children will always be a disappointment to their parents.
3. Write a personal narrative describing the last major conflict you had with your parents. Include what the conflict was and how it was finally resolved.

MARGARET ATWOOD Margaret Atwood (1939–) is a Canadian-born poet, novelist, short-story writer, and critic whose work explores the role of personal consciousness in a troubled world. Her second collection of poems, *The Circle Game* (1966), brought her recognition; she is also well known for her novels, including *Surfacing* (1973), *Life before Man* (1979), *The Handmaid's Tale* (1986), and *Cat's Eye* (1988). Atwood is interested in the complexities of language, and her subjects are wide-ranging, from the personal to the global. In the following essay, Atwood uses a lively, unconventional style to address a serious theme.

MARGARET ATWOOD

The Female Body

. . . entirely devoted to the subject of "The Female Body." Knowing how well you have written on this topic . . . this capacious topic . . .

—Letter from the *Michigan Quarterly Review*

1.
I agree, it's a hot topic. But only one? Look around, there's a wide 1
range. Take my own, for instance.

I get up in the morning. My topic feels like hell. I sprinkle it with water, brush parts of it, rub it with towels, powder it, add lubricant. I dump in the fuel and away goes my topic, my topical topic, my controversial topic, my capacious topic, my limping topic, my nearsighted topic, my topic with back problems, my badly behaved topic, my vulgar topic, my outrageous topic, my aging topic, my topic that is out of the question and anyway still can't spell, in its oversized coat and worn winter boots, scuttling along the sidewalk as if it were flesh and blood, hunting for what's out there, an avocado, an alderman, an adjective, hungry as ever.

2.
The basic Female Body comes with the following accessories: garter 3
belt, panti-girdle, crinoline, camisole, bustle, brassiere, stomacher, chemise, virgin zone, spike heels, nose ring, veil, kid gloves, fishnet stockings, fichu, bandeau, Merry Widow, weepers, chokers, barrettes, bangles, beads, lorgnette, feather boa, basic black, compact, Lycra stretch one-piece with modesty panel, designer peignoir, flannel nightie, lace teddy, bed, head.

3.
The Female Body is made of transparent plastic and lights up when you 4
plug it in. You press a button to illuminate the different systems. The circulatory system is red, for the heart and arteries, purple for the veins; the respiratory system is blue; the lymphatic system is yellow; the digestive system is green, with liver and kidneys in aqua. The nerves are done in orange and the brain is pink. The skeleton, as you might expect, is white.

The reproductive system is optional, and can be removed. It comes 5
with or without a miniature embryo. Parental judgment can thereby be exercised. We do not wish to frighten or offend.

4.
He said, I won't have one of those things in the house. It gives a young 6
girl a false notion of beauty, not to mention anatomy. If a real woman was built like that she'd fall on her face.

She said, If we don't let her have one like all the other girls she'll feel 7
singled out. It'll become an issue. She'll long for one and she'll long to turn into one. Repression breeds sublimation. You know that.

He said, It's not just the pointy plastic tits, it's the wardrobes. The 8
wardrobes and that stupid male doll, what's his name, the one with the underwear glued on.

She said, Better to get it over with when she's young. He said, All right, 9
but don't let me see it.

She came whizzing down the stairs, thrown like a dart. She was stark 10
naked. Her hair had been chopped off, her head was turned back to front, she was missing some toes and she'd been tattooed all over her body with purple ink in a scrollwork design. She hit the potted azalea, trembled there for a moment like a botched angel, and fell.

He said, I guess we're safe. 11

5.

The Female Body has many uses. It's been used as a door knocker, a 12
bottle opener, as a clock with a ticking belly, as something to hold up lampshades, as a nutcracker, just squeeze the brass legs together and out comes your nut. It bears torches, lifts victorious wreaths, grows copper wings and raises aloft a ring of neon stars; whole buildings rest on its marble heads.

It sells cars, beer, shaving lotion, cigarettes, hard liquor; it sells diet 13
plans and diamonds, and desire in tiny crystal bottles. Is this the face that launched a thousand products? You bet it is, but don't get any funny big ideas, honey, that smile is a dime a dozen.

It does not merely sell, it is sold. Money flows into this country or 14
that country, flies in, practically crawls in, suitful after suitful, lured by all those hairless pre-teen legs. Listen, you want to reduce the national debt, don't you? Aren't you patriotic? That's the spirit. That's my girl.

She's a natural resource, a renewable one luckily, because those things 15
wear out so quickly. They don't make 'em like they used to. Shoddy goods.

6.

One and one equals another one. Pleasure in the female is not a re- 16
quirement. Pair-bonding is stronger in geese. We're not talking about love, we're talking about biology. That's how we all got here, daughter.

Snails do it differently. They're hermaphrodites, and work in threes. 17

7.

Each Female Body contains a female brain. Handy. Makes things work. 18
Stick pins in it and you get amazing results. Old popular songs. Short circuits. Bad dreams.

Anyway: each of these brains has two halves. They're joined together 19
by a thick cord; neural pathways flow from one to the other, sparkles of

electric information washing to and fro. Like light on waves. Like a conversation. How does a woman know? She listens. She listens in.

The male brain, now, that's a different matter. Only a thin connection. Space over here, time over there, music and arithmetic in their own sealed compartments. The right brain doesn't know what the left brain is doing. Good for aiming though, for hitting the target when you pull the trigger. What's the target? Who's the target? Who cares? What matters is hitting it. That's the male brain for you. Objective.

This is why men are so sad, why they feel so cut off, why they think of themselves as orphans cast adrift, footloose and stringless in the deep void. What void? she asks. What are you talking about? The void of the universe, he says, and she says Oh and looks out the window and tries to get a handle on it, but it's no use, there's too much going on, too many rustlings in the leaves, too many voices, so she says, Would you like a cheese sandwich, a piece of cake, a cup of tea? And he grinds his teeth because she doesn't understand, and wanders off, not just alone but Alone, lost in the dark, lost in the skull, searching for the other half, the twin who could complete him. 21

Then it comes to him: he's lost the Female Body! Look, it shines in the gloom, far ahead, a vision of wholeness, ripeness, like a giant melon, like an apple, like a metaphor for "breast" in a bad sex novel; it shines like a balloon, like a foggy noon, a watery moon, shimmering in its egg of light. 22

Catch it. Put it in a pumpkin, in a high tower, in a compound, in a chamber, in a house, in a room. Quick, stick a leash on it, a lock, a chain, some pain, settle it down, so it can never get away from you again. 23

COMPREHENSION

1. Why do you think this essay was written? Justify your response.
2. List the different ways in which Atwood views the female body.
3. What distinction does Atwood make between the male and female brains?

RHETORIC

1. What is the tone of Atwood's essay? Supply concrete evidence from her writing.
2. Does the essay contain a thesis? Is it stated or implied?
3. Define the following words in section 2: *fichu, bandeau, Merry Widow, weepers.* Why do the words *bed* and *head* also appear in this list?
4. How does Atwood's use of details and metaphors strengthen her points in the essay? Cite specific examples.

5. What is the object being described in section 4? How does its inclusion help underscore Atwood's point?
6. Why did Atwood choose this particular way to organize her essay? What does it tell the reader about her attitude toward the subject?
7. Is the tone of the final paragraph similar to that of the rest of the essay? Provide evidence from the writing and explain.

WRITING

1. Using a style similar to Atwood's, write a brief essay in which you describe "the female brain," "the male brain," or the Male Body.
2. In an argumentative essay, consider the role played by sex-specific toys in reinforcing sexual stereotyping in children. Use Atwood's essay as well as your personal experience as support.
3. Analyze the ways in which sex and the female body have been used in sales and advertising.

MARY LEAKEY Mary Douglas Leakey (1913–) is the director of the Olduvai Gorge Excavations, one of the most important paleontological sites in the world. Among her publications are *Olduvai Gorge* (1971); *Africa's Vanishing Art* (1983); and *Disclosing the Past* (1984), an autobiography. In addition, Mrs. Leakey has contributed numerous papers to *Nature* and other scientific journals. In this essay, a preliminary report on a remarkable find, Leakey provides insight into the challenging field of paleontology.

MARY LEAKEY

Footprints in the Ashes of Time

It happened some 3,600,000 years ago, at the onset of a rainy season. The East African landscape stretched then, much as it does now, in a series of savannas punctuated by wind-sculptured acacia trees. To the east the volcano now called Sadiman heaved restlessly, spewing ash over the flat expanse known as Laetoli. 1

The creatures that inhabited the region, and they were plentiful, showed no panic. They continued to drift on their random errands. Several times Sadiman blanketed the plain with a thin layer of ash. Tentative showers, precursors of the heavy seasonal rains, moistened the ash. Each layer hardened, preserving in remarkable detail the footprints left by the ancient fauna. The Laetolil Beds, as geologists designate the oldest deposits at Laetoli, captured a frozen moment of time from the remote past—a pageant unique in prehistory. 2

Our serious survey of the beds, which lie in northern Tanzania 30 3
miles by road south of Olduvai Gorge, began in 1975 and gained intensity last summer after the discovery of some startling footprints. This article must stand as a preliminary report; further findings will almost certainly modify early interpretations.

Still, what we have discovered to date at Laetoli will cause yet an- 4
other upheaval in the study of human origins. For in the gray, petrified ash of the beds—among the spoor of the extinct predecessors of today's elephants, hyenas, hares—we have found hominid footprints that are remarkably similar to those of modern man. Prints that, in my opinion, could only have been left by an ancestor of man. Prints that were laid down an incredible 3,600,000 years ago . . . !

In 1976 Peter Jones, my assistant and a specialist in stone tools, and 5
my youngest son, Philip, noticed what they believed to be a trail of hominid footprints. After considerable analysis I agreed and announced the discovery the following year. Of the five prints, three were obscured by overlying sediment impossible to remove. The two clear examples, broad and rather curiously shaped, offered few clues to the primate that had trudged across the plain so long ago.

Nonetheless, the implications of this find were enormous. Dr. 6
Garniss Curtis of the University of California at Berkeley undertook to date the footprint strata. These deposits possess relatively large crystals of biotite, or black mica. Biotite from ash overlying the prints, when subjected to potassium-argon testing, showed an age of about 3.6 million years; that from below tested at about 3.8 million years. The footprints had been preserved sometime within this span. Dr. Richard L. Hay, also of Berkeley, showed that the ash forming the layers fell within a month's time.

The hominid footprints attested, in my considered opinion, to the 7
existence of a direct ancestor of man half a million years before the earliest previous evidence—fossils unearthed by Dr. Donald C. Johanson and his party in the Afar triangle of Ethiopia beginning in 1973.

Faced with this, we largely abandoned our hunt for fossils and fo- 8
cused our three-month campaign of 1978 on the footprints— plotting and photographing them, making plaster and latex casts, and even removing certain specimens. While Dr. Paul Abell of the University of Rhode Island was attempting—delicately and successfully—to quarry out a block of rhinoceros tracks, he noticed a barely exposed, hominid-like heel print.

When we removed the surrounding overburden, we found a trail 9
some 23 meters long; only the end of the excavation season in September prevented our following it still farther. Two individuals, one larger, one smaller, had passed this way 3,600,000 years ago.

The footsteps come from the south, progress northward in a fairly 10
straight line, and end abruptly where seasonal streams have eroded a small, chaotic canyon through the beds. The nature of the terrain leads us to believe that the footprints, though now covered, remain largely intact to the south. And that is where we will continue our effort.

11 The closeness of the two sets of prints indicates that their owners were not walking abreast. Other clues suggest that the hominids may have passed at different times. For example, the imprints of the smaller individual stand out clearly. The crispness of definition and sharp outlines convince me that they were left on a damp surface that retained the form of the foot.

12 On the other hand, the prints of the larger are blurred, as if he had shuffled or dragged his feet. In fact, I think that the surface when he passed was loose and dusty, hence the collapsed appearance of his prints. Nonetheless, luck favored us again; the bigger hominid left one absolutely clear print, probably on a patch of once damp ash.

13 What do these footprints tell us? First, they demonstrate once and for all that at least 3,600,000 years ago, in Pliocene times, what I believe to be man's direct ancestor walked fully upright with a bipedal, free-striding gait. Second, that the form of his foot was exactly the same as ours.

14 One cannot overemphasize the role of bipedalism in hominid development. It stands as perhaps the salient point that differentiated the forebears of man from other primates. This unique ability freed the hands for myriad possibilities—carrying, tool-making, intricate manipulation. From this single development, in fact, stems all modern technology.

15 Somewhat oversimplified, the formula holds that this new freedom of forelimbs posed a challenge. The brain expanded to meet it. And mankind was formed.

16 Even today, millions of years beyond that unchronicled Rubicon, *Homo sapiens* is the only primate to walk upright as a matter of course. And, for better or for worse, *Homo sapiens* dominates the world.

17 But what of those two hominids who crossed the Laetolil Beds so long ago? We have measured their footprints and the length of their stride. Was the larger one a male, the smaller a female? Or was one mature, the other young? It is unlikely that we will ever know with certainty. For convenience, let us postulate a case of sexual dimorphism and consider the smaller one a female.

18 Incidentally, following her path produces, at least for me, a kind of poignant time wrench. At one point, and you need not be an expert tracker to discern this, she stops, pauses, turns to the left to glance at some possible threat or irregularity, and then continues to the north. This motion, so intensely human, transcends time. Three million six hundred thousand years ago, a remote ancestor—just as you or I—experienced a moment of doubt.

19 The French have a proverb: *Plus ça change, plus c'est la même chose*—"The more it changes, the more it is the same." In short, nothing really alters. Least of all, the human condition.

20 Measurements show the length of the smaller prints to be 18.5 centimeters (slightly more than 7 inches) and 21.5 centimeters for the larger. Stride length averages 38.7 centimeters for the smaller hominid,

47.2 centimeters for the larger. Clearly we are dealing with two small creatures.

An anthropological rule of thumb holds that the length of the foot represents about 15 percent of an individual's height. On this basis—and it is far from exact—we can estimate the height of the male as perhaps four feet eight inches (1.4 meters); the female would have stood about four feet.

Leg structure must have been very similar to our own. It seems clear to me that the Laetoli hominid, although much older, relates very closely to the remains found by Dr. Johanson in Ethiopia. Dr. Owen Lovejoy of Kent State University in Ohio studied a knee joint from Ethiopia—the bottom of the femur and the top of the tibia—and concluded that the Afar hominid had walked upright, with a free, bipedal gait. 22

Our footprints confirm this. Furthermore, Dr. Louise Robbins of the University of North Carolina, Greensboro, an anthropologist who specializes in the analysis of footprints, visited Laetoli and concluded: "The movement pattern of the individual is a bipedal walking gait, actually a stride—and quite long relative to the creature's small size. Weight-bearing pressure patterns in the prints resemble human ones. . . ." 23

I can only assume that the prints were left by the hominids whose fossils we also found in the beds. In addition to part of a child's skeleton, we uncovered adult remains—two lower jaws, a section of upper jaw, and a number of teeth. 24

Where can we place the Laetoli hominids and their Afar cousins in the incomplete mosaic of the rise of man? This question, quite honestly, is a subject of some contention among paleontologists. One school, including Dr. Johanson, classifies them as australopithecines. 25

But the two forms of *Australopithecus,* gracile and robust, represent, in my opinion, evolutionary dead ends. These man apes flourished for their season, and perished—unsuccessful twigs on the branch that produced mankind. Of course, the Laetoli hominid resembles the gracile *Australopithecus,* but I believe that, so far back in time, all the hominids shared certain characteristics. However, the simple evidence of the footprints, so very much like our own, indicates to me that the Laetoli hominid stands in the direct line of man's ancestry. 26

We have encountered one anomaly. Despite three years of painstaking search by Peter Jones, no stone tools have been found in the Laetolil Beds. With their hands free, one would have expected this species to have developed tools or weapons of some kind. But, except for the ejecta of erupting volcanoes, we haven't found a single stone introduced into the beds. So we can only conclude, at least for the moment, that the hominids we discovered had not yet attained the toolmaking stage. 27

But in the end one cannot escape the supreme importance of the presence of hominids at Laetoli. Sometimes, during the excavating season, I go out and watch the dusk settle over the gray tuff with its eerie record of time long past. The slanting light of evening throws the ho- 28

minid prints into sharp relief, so sharp that they could have been left this morning.

I cannot help but think about the distant creatures who made them. 29
Where did they come from? Where were they going? We simply do not know. It has been suggested that they were merely crossing this scorched plain toward the greener ridges to the north. Perhaps so.

In any case, those footprints out of the deep past, left by the oldest 30
known hominids, haunt the imagination. Across the gulf of time I can only wish them well on that prehistoric trek. It was, I believe, part of a greater and more perilous journey, one that—through millions of years of evolutionary trial and error, fortune and misfortune—culminated in the emergence of modern man.

COMPREHENSION

1. What is the author's main purpose in this essay? Cite evidence to support your answer.
2. In which paragraph do you discover that Leakey is describing human footprints? What effect is she trying to achieve by delaying this revelation? Does Leakey do an effective job of proving that the footprints "could only have been left by an ancestor of man"? What other interpretation is there? What facts support another interpretation?
3. What is the author's relationship to Donald C. Johanson? How often and where do his theories appear?

RHETORIC

1. Define the following words: *hominid* (paragraph 4); *Pliocene* (paragraph 13); and *dimorphism* (paragraph 17). Is the language in this section specialized? Explain.
2. Use a dictionary or encyclopedia to define *Rubicon* (paragraph 16). In what sense is "that unchronicled Rubicon" a turning point? How does the allusion strengthen the idea?
3. How does the author create her introduction in this essay?
4. What sort of reasoning process does Leakey apply to the development of her essay? Trace this process as carefully as you can.
5. Many of Leakey's paragraphs are relatively short. Cite representative examples, and explain why the overall strategy is successful.
6. Is this report meant to be read by scientists or by lay people? What clues tell you this?

WRITING

1. If Leakey is right, what implications are there to the discovery that humankind is far older than we once believed? In what ways are we like our hominid ancestors? Write an essay explaining the connection between humans and hominids.

2. There is a school of thought that entirely rejects the findings of Leakey and others on the subject of evolution and fossil remains. This school, called "creationism," argues that the biblical account in the Book of Genesis is incompatible with scientific evidence and that where the two disagree, the revealed word of God is a better indicator than is a fossil record. Write an essay explaining which side of this debate you find more compelling. Offer reasons and evidence to support your position.
3. Leakey asserts that "nothing really alters. Least of all the human condition." From your reading of this essay and your perspective, is she right or wrong? Answer this question in an argumentative essay.

PAUL THEROUX Paul Theroux (1941–) has explored the effects of colonialism on Americans and Europeans—effects which he experienced firsthand as a teacher in Malawi, Uganda, and Singapore—in books such as *Saint Jack* (1973) and *The Consul's File* (1977). Theroux's other fictional works include *The Mosquito Coast* (1982), *O-Zone* (1986), and *Chicago Loop* (1990). In addition, he has written a number of travel books, among them *The Great Railway Bazaar* (1975) and *The Old Patagonian Express* (1979). In the following essay, Theroux explores the meaning of masculinity and its relation to writing.

PAUL THEROUX

Being a Man

There is a pathetic sentence in the chapter "Fetishism" in Dr. Norman Cameron's book *Personality Development and Psychopathology*. It goes, "Fetishists are nearly always men; and their commonest fetish is a woman's shoe." I cannot read that sentence without thinking that it is just one more awful thing about being a man—and perhaps it is an important thing to know about us. 1

I have always disliked being a man. The whole idea of manhood in America is pitiful, in my opinion. This version of masculinity is a little like having to wear an ill-fitting coat for one's entire life (by contrast, I imagine femininity to be an oppressive sense of nakedness). Even the expression "Be a man!" strikes me as insulting and abusive. It means: Be stupid, be unfeeling, obedient, soldierly, and stop thinking. Man means "manly"—how can one think about men without considering the terrible ambition of manliness? And yet it is part of every man's life. It is a hideous and crippling lie; it not only insists on difference and connives at superiority, it is also by its very nature destructive—emotionally damaging and socially harmful. 2

The youth who is subverted, as most are, into believing in the masculine ideal is effectively separated from women and he spends the rest 3

of his life finding women a riddle and a nuisance. Of course, there is a female version of this male affliction. It begins with mothers encouraging little girls to say (to other adults) "Do you like my new dress?" In a sense, little girls are traditionally urged to please adults with a kind of coquettishness, while boys are enjoined to behave like monkeys towards each other. The nine-year-old coquette proceeds to become womanish in a subtle power game in which she learns to be sexually indispensable, socially decorative, and always alert to a man's sense of inadequacy.

Femininity—being ladylike—implies needing a man as witness and seducer; but masculinity celebrates the exclusive company of men. That is why it is so grotesque; and that is also why there is no manliness without inadequacy—because it denies men the natural friendship of women. 4

It is very hard to imagine any concept of manliness that does not belittle women, and it begins very early. At an age when I wanted to meet girls—let's say the treacherous years of thirteen to sixteen—I was told to take up a sport, get more fresh air, join the Boy Scouts, and I was urged not to read so much. It was the 1950s and if you asked too many questions about sex you were sent to camp—boy's camp, of course: the nightmare. Nothing is more unnatural or prisonlike than a boy's camp, but if it were not for them we would have no Elks' Lodges, no pool rooms, no boxing matches, no Marines. 5

And perhaps no sports as we know them. Everyone is aware of how few in number are the athletes who behave like gentlemen. Just as high school basketball teaches you how to be a poor loser, the manly attitude towards sports seems to be little more than a recipe for creating bad marriages, social misfits, moral degenerates, sadists, latent rapists, and just plain louts. I regard high school sports as a drug far worse than marijuana, and it is the reason that the average tennis champion, say, is a pathetic oaf. 6

Any objective study would find the quest for manliness essentially right-wing, puritanical, cowardly, neurotic, and fueled largely by a fear of women. It is also certainly philistine. There is no book-hater like a Little League coach. But indeed all the creative arts are obnoxious to the manly ideal, because at their best the arts are pursued by uncompetitive and essentially solitary people. It makes it very hard for a creative youngster, for any boy who expresses the desire to be alone seems to be saying that there is something wrong with him. 7

It ought to be clear by now that I have something of an objection to the way we turn boys into men. It does not surprise me that when the President of the United States has his customary weekend off he dresses like a cowboy—it is both a measure of his insecurity and his willingness to please. In many ways, American culture does little more for a man than prepare him for modeling clothes in the L. L. Bean catalogue. I take this as a personal insult because for many years I found it impossible to admit to myself that I wanted to be a writer. It was my guilty secret, because being a writer was incompatible with being a man. 8

There are people who might deny this, but that is because the 9
American writer, typically, has been so at pains to prove his manliness that we have come to see literariness and manliness as mingled qualities. But first there was a fear that writing was not a manly profession—indeed, not a profession at all. (The paradox in American letters is that it has always been easier for a woman to write and for a man to be published.) Growing up, I had thought of sports as wasteful and humiliating, and the idea of manliness was a bore. My wanting to become a writer was not a flight from that oppressive role-playing, but I quickly saw that it was at odds with it. Everything in stereotyped manliness goes against the life of the mind. The Hemingway personality is too tedious to go into here, and in any case his exertions are well known, but certainly it was not until this aberrant behavior was examined by feminists in the 1960s that any male writer dared question the pugnacity in Hemingway's fiction. All the bullfighting and arm wrestling and elephant shooting diminished Hemingway as a writer, but it is consistent with a prevailing attitude in American writing: one cannot be a male writer without first proving that one is a man.

It is normal in America for a man to be dismissive or even some- 10
what apologetic about being a writer. Various factors make it easier. There is a heartiness about journalism that makes it acceptable—journalism is the manliest form of American writing and, therefore, the profession the most independent-minded women seek (yes, it is an illusion, but that is my point). Fiction-writing is equated with a kind of dispirited failure and is only manly when it produces wealth—money is masculinity. So is drinking. Being a drunkard is another assertion, if misplaced, of manliness. The American male writer is traditionally proud of his heavy drinking. But we are also a very literal-minded people. A man proves his manhood in America in old-fashioned ways. He kills lions, like Hemingway; or he hunts ducks, like Nathanael West, or he makes pronouncements like, "A man should carry enough knife to defend himself with," as James Jones once said to a *Life* interviewer. Or he says he can drink you under the table. But even tiny drunken William Faulkner loved to mount a horse and go fox hunting, and Jack Kerouac roistered up and down Manhattan in a lumberjack shirt (and spent every night of *The Subterraneans* with his mother in Queens). And we are familiar with the lengths to which Norman Mailer is prepared, in his endearing way, to prove that he is just as much a monster as the next man.

When the novelist John Irving was revealed as a wrestler, people 11
took him to be a very serious writer, and even a bubble reputation like Eric *(Love Story)* Segal's was enhanced by the news that he ran the marathon in a respectable time. How surprised we would be if Joyce Carol Oates were revealed as a sumo wrestler or Joan Didion active in pumping iron. "Lives in New York City with her three children" is the typical woman writer's biographical note, for just as the male writer must prove he has achieved a sort of muscular manhood, the woman writer—or rather her publicists—must prove her motherhood.

There would be no point in saying any of this if it were not generally accepted that to be a man is somehow—even now in feminist-influenced America—a privilege. It is on the contrary an unmerciful and punishing burden. Being a man is bad enough; being manly is appalling (in this sense, women's lib has done much more for men than for women). It is the sinister silliness of men's fashions and a clubby attitude in the arts. It is the subversion of good students. It is the so-called Dress Code of the Ritz-Carlton Hotel in Boston, and it is the institutionalized cheating in college sports. It is the most primitive insecurity. 12

And this is also why men often object to feminism, but are afraid to explain why: of course women have a justified grievance, but most men believe—and with reason—that their lives are just as bad. 13

COMPREHENSION

1. What does Theroux hate about being a man?
2. What does the writer mean by "the terrible ambition of manliness"?
3. According to Theroux, why are writing and manliness at odds?

RHETORIC

1. What is Theroux's thesis? Where is it stated?
2. Explain Theroux's choice for an introductory paragraph. How does it help to set up the reader for what follows? What was the writer's intention?
3. Does the writer's example in paragraph 5 help validate the paragraph's topic sentence? Why, or why not?
4. Explain the reference to the L. L. Bean catalogue in paragraph 8. What connection is Theroux making between it and the American concept of masculinity?
5. Trace the sequence of ideas through the paragraphs in the essay. Do they follow a coherent pattern? How does the conclusion help to unify the ideas presented?
6. What argumentative strategies does Theroux employ in this essay?

WRITING

1. Write a definition essay on *manliness,* considering both the denotative and the connotative meanings of the word. Use support from Theroux's work.
2. Theroux states that being a man is "an unmerciful and punishing burden." Write an argumentative essay in which you agree or disagree with this assessment.
3. Write an essay in which you pretend to be a member of the opposite sex for a day. Describe how your conditions, behaviors, and perceptions might be different. Consider how others would respond to you.

GLORIA STEINEM Gloria Steinem (1934–) was born and raised in Toledo, Ohio; she attended Smith College, receiving a B.A. in government in 1956. A noted feminist and political activist, Steinem in 1968 helped to found *New York* magazine; in 1971 she cofounded *Ms.* magazine and has served as its editor since then. Whether campaigning for Robert Kennedy and George McGovern or helping to defend and raise money for Angela Davis and the United Farmworkers, Steinem has been on the cutting edge of American politics for more than two decades. Her books include a collection of essays, *Outrageous Acts and Everyday Rebellions* (1983) and *Revolution from Within: A Book of Self-Esteem* (1992). The essay that follows reflects Steinem's keen ability to relate ideas and issues to the lives of women today.

GLORIA STEINEM

Erotica and Pornography

Human beings are the only animals that experience the same sex drive at times when we can—and cannot—conceive. 1

Just as we developed uniquely human capacities for language, planning, memory, and invention along our evolutionary path, we also developed sexuality as a form of expression; a way of communicating that is separable from our need for sex as a way of perpetuating ourselves. For humans alone, sexuality can be and often is primarily a way of bonding, of giving and receiving pleasure, bridging differentness, discovering sameness, and communicating emotion. 2

We developed this and other human gifts through our ability to change our environment, adapt physically, and in the long run, to affect our own evolution. But as an emotional result of this spiraling path away from other animals, we seem to alternate between periods of exploring our unique abilities to change new boundaries, and feelings of loneliness in the unknown that we ourselves have created; a fear that sometimes sends us back to the comfort of the animal world by encouraging us to exaggerate our sameness. 3

The separation of "play" from "work," for instance, is a problem only in the human world. So is the difference between art and nature, or an intellectual accomplishment and a physical one. As a result, we celebrate play, art, and invention as leaps into the unknown; but any imbalance can send us back to nostalgia for our primate past and the conviction that the basics of work, nature, and physical labor are somehow more worthwhile or even moral. 4

In the same way, we have explored our sexuality as separable from conception: a pleasurable, empathetic bridge to strangers of the same species. We have even invented contraception—a skill that has 5

probably existed in some form since our ancestors figured out the process of birth—in order to extend this uniquely human difference. Yet we also have times of atavistic suspicion that sex is not complete—or even legal or intended-by-god—if it cannot end in conception.

No wonder the concepts of "erotica" and "pornography" can be so 6
crucially different, and yet so confused. Both assume that sexuality can be separated from conception, and therefore can be used to carry a personal message. That's a major reason why, even in our current culture, both may be called equally "shocking" or legally "obscene," a word whose Latin derivative means "dirty, containing filth." This gross condemnation of all sexuality that isn't harnessed to childbirth and marriage has been increased by the current backlash against women's progress. Out of fear that the whole patriarchal structure might be upset if women really had the autonomous power to decide our reproductive futures (that is, if we controlled the most basic means of production), right-wing groups are not only denouncing prochoice abortion literature as "pornographic," but are trying to stop the sending of all contraceptive information through the mails by invoking obscenity laws. In fact, Phyllis Schlafly recently denounced the entire Women's Movement as "obscene."

Not surprisingly, this religious, visceral backlash has a secular, intel- 7
lectual counterpart that relies heavily on applying the "natural" behavior of the animal world to humans. That is questionable in itself, but these Lionel Tiger-ish studies make their political purpose even more clear in the particular animals they select and the habits they choose to emphasize. The message is that females should accept their "destiny" of being sexually dependent and devote themselves to bearing and rearing their young.

Defending against such reaction in turn leads to another tempta- 8
tion: to merely reverse the terms, and declare that *all* nonprocreative sex is good. In fact, however, this human activity can be as constructive or destructive, moral or immoral, as any other. Sex as communication can send messages as different as life and death; even the origins of "erotica" and "pornography" reflect that fact. After all, "erotica" is rooted in *eros* or passionate love, and thus in the idea of positive choice, free will, the yearning for a particular person. (Interestingly, the definition of erotica leaves open the question of gender.) "Pornography" begins with a root meaning "prostitution" or "female captives," thus letting us know that the subject is not mutual love, or love at all, but domination and violence against women. (Though, of course, homosexual pornography may imitate this violence by putting a man in the "feminine" role of victim.) It ends with a root meaning "writing about" or "description of" which puts still more distance between subject and object, and replaces a spontaneous yearning for closeness with objectification and a voyeur.

The difference is clear in the words. It becomes even more so by ex- 9
ample.

10 Look at any photo or film of people making love; really making love. The images may be diverse, but there is usually a sensuality and touch and warmth, an acceptance of bodies and nerve endings. There is always a spontaneous sense of people who are there because they *want* to be, out of shared pleasure.

11 Now look at any depiction of sex in which there is clear force, or an unequal power that spells coercion. It may be very blatant, with weapons or torture or bondage, wounds and bruises, some clear humiliation, or an adult's sexual power being used over a child. It may be much more subtle: a physical attitude of conqueror and victim, the use of race or class difference to imply the same thing, perhaps a very unequal nudity, with one person exposed and vulnerable while the other is clothed. In either case, there is no sense of equal choice or equal power.

12 The first is erotic: a mutually pleasurable, sexual expression between people who have enough power to be there by positive choice. It may or may not strike a sense-memory in the viewer, or be creative enough to make the unknown seem real; but it doesn't require us to identify with a conquerer or a victim. It is truly sensuous, and may give us a contagion of pleasure.

13 The second is pornographic: its message is violence, dominance, and conquest. It is sex being used to reinforce some inequality, or to create one, or to tell us the lie that pain and humiliation (ours or someone else's) are really the same as pleasure. If we are to feel anything, we must identify with conqueror or victim. That means we can only experience pleasure through the adoption of some degree of sadism or masochism. It also means that we may feel diminished by the role of conqueror, or enraged, humiliated, and vengeful by sharing identity with the victim.

14 Perhaps one could simply say that erotica is about sexuality, but pornography is about power and sex-as-weapon—in the same way we have come to understand that rape is about violence, and not really about sexuality at all.

15 Yes, it's true that there are women who have been forced by violent families and dominating men to confuse love with pain; so much so that they have become masochists. (A fact that in no way excuses those who administer such pain.) But the truth is that, for most women—and for men with enough humanity to imagine themselves into the predicament of women—true pornography could serve as aversion therapy for sex.

16 Of course, there will always be personal differences about what is and is not erotic, and there may be cultural differences for a long time to come. Many women feel that sex makes them vulnerable and therefore may continue to need more sense of personal connection and safety before allowing any erotic feelings. We now find competence and expertise erotic in men, but that may pass as we develop those qualities in ourselves. Men, on the other hand, may continue to feel less vulnerable, and therefore more open to such

potential danger as sex with strangers. As some men replace the need for submission from childlike women with the pleasure of co-operation from equals, they may find a partner's competence to be erotic, too.

Such group changes plus individual differences will continue to be reflected in sexual love between people of the same gender, as well as between women and men. The point is not to dictate sameness, but to discover ourselves and each other through sexuality that is an exploring, pleasurable, empathetic part of our lives; a human sexuality that is unchained both from unwanted pregnancies and from violence. 17

But that is a hope, not a reality. At the moment, fear of change is increasing both the indiscriminate repression of all nonprocreative sex in the religious and "conservative" male world, and the pornographic vengeance against women's sexuality in the secular world of "liberal" and "radical" men. It's almost futuristic to debate what is and is not truly erotic, when many women are again being forced into compulsory motherhood, and the number of pornographic murders, tortures, and woman-hating images are on the increase in both popular culture and real life. 18

It's a familiar division: wife or whore, "good" woman who is constantly vulnerable to pregnancy or "bad" woman who is unprotected from violence. *Both* roles would be upset if we were to control our own sexuality. And that's exactly what we must do. 19

In spite of all our atavistic suspicions and training for the "natural" role of motherhood, we took up the complicated battle for reproductive freedom. Our bodies had borne the health burden of endless births and poor abortions, and we had a greater motive for separating sexuality and conception. 20

Now we have to take up the equally complex burden of explaining that all nonprocreative sex is *not* alike. We have a motive: our right to a uniquely human sexuality, and sometimes even to survival. As it is, our bodies have too rarely been enough our own to develop erotica in our own lives, much less in art and literature. And our bodies have too often been the objects of pornography and the woman-hating, violent practice that it preaches. Consider also our spirits that break a little each time we see ourselves in chains or full labial display for the conquering male viewer, bruised or on our knees, screaming a real or pretended pain to delight the sadist, pretending to enjoy what we don't enjoy, to be blind to the images of our sisters that really haunt us—humiliated often enough ourselves by the truly obscene idea that sex and the domination of women must be combined. 21

Sexuality *is* human, free, separate—and so are we. 22

But until we untangle the lethal confusion of sex with violence, there will be more pornography and less erotica. There will be little murders in our beds—and very little love. 23

COMPREHENSION

1. What thesis does the author develop in this essay?
2. How does Steinem define the terms *erotica* and *pornography*? What is the essential distinction that the author draws between these two words?
3. In what ways do the concepts of erotica and pornography affect women's lives?

RHETORIC

1. Look up the words *erotica* and *pornography* in the *Oxford English Dictionary (OED)* or any large dictionary. Trace the etymology of these two words and any shifts in meaning.
2. Use the dictionary as necessary to understand the following biological, psychological, and sociological terms: *evolutionary* (paragraph 2); *environment* (paragraph 3); *primate* (paragraph 4); *atavistic* (paragraph 5); *patriarchal* (paragraph 6); *voyeur* (paragraph 8); *sadism* and *masochism* (paragraph 13); and *aversion therapy* (paragraph 15).
3. Why does the author delay the introduction of her key topic until paragraph 6? What is the relevance of the first five paragraphs? How are these paragraphs developed?
4. What is the relevance of the definition to the essay's development?
5. Explain Steinem's use of comparison and contrast to structure parts of this essay.
6. Examine the author's use of illustration in the essay.

WRITING

1. Do you accept the author's distinction between erotica and pornography? Answer this question in an argumentative essay.
2. Describe and evaluate an erotic scene that you have viewed in a film or read in a book.
3. Should pornography be banned? Answer this question in an essay.

MICHAEL DORRIS Michael Dorris (1945–), a member of the Modoc tribe and a native of Washington, is a professor of anthropology and Native-American studies at Dartmouth College. He has written, among other works, *The Broken Cord: A Family's Ongoing Struggles with Fetal Alcohol Syndrome* (1987). He has also written about the Native-American experience in books such as *Native Americans: Five Hundred Years after Cromwell* (1975). He and his wife, Louise Erdrich, coauthored a novel, *The Crown of Columbus* (1991). In the article below, Dorris shares his feelings about parenting.

MICHAEL DORRIS

What Men Are Missing

I've been changing diapers now for twenty years, half of that time as the single adoptive parent of three young children, and half—with three more daughters, the oldest of whom is now seven—as a partner in a two-career marriage. I started with cloth in 1971, graduated to plastic in 1976, and am ending up, in 1991, with biodegradable. That's progress. By necessity, I've learned to become sanguine about certain inevitable tribulations (chicken pox, science fairs, the escalating price of sneakers) and fairly proficient at handling others (laundry, birthday parties, interviewing baby-sitters). I can tell a snappy version of "Cinderella," make peanut-butter-and-jelly sandwiches in the dark, and qualify for membership in the chauffeur's union. 1

When I was growing up as an only child, I used to envy my friends with younger siblings. I'd listen to their complaints about tagalong brothers and sisters, about the combustion around the breakfast table or the chaos of bedtime, and long for the excitement of a crowded house. My mother, widowed after only four years of marriage, had moved back to Louisville to live with my grandmother and my aunt, and throughout my youth I was doted upon, listened to, encouraged in every project by three smart and independent women. They led me to believe that I could accomplish anything I set my mind to, that nothing was impossible. 2

Perhaps as an adult I was especially impatient to be a father because I missed having one of my own as I grew up, though probably the impulse is not so obscure. Due to the unusual circumstances of my upbringing, I was spared much of the gender typecasting that discourages a good number of men from taking an active role in the primary care of their offspring—because of embarrassment or ignorance of the rewards, or through a basic lack of self-confidence. 3

Women, it should be noted, can be as susceptible to the mythos of the bumbling, inept man-about-the-house as men, though they suffer a different, less abstract consequence when the prophecy is fulfilled. During the tenure of my bachelor fatherhood, the immediate reaction to my situation on the part of certain female acquaintances was to express condolence for my mommy-deprived children and to wonder who, for instance, bathed and dressed the babies—as if the only way our family could function was via Mary Poppins. There's no explaining to people weaned on *The Donna Reed Show* and *Father Knows Best* that the nuclear family is but one style among several or that children tend to accept as "normal" any arrangement that is loving, consistent, and secure. 4

I never theorized about such matters all that much—there was too 5
much else to do in the space of each day—but then again I never quite anticipated that fatherhood would turn out to be my most demanding profession (though teaching at Dartmouth College and writing books paid the bills) and constant occupation: a never-ending round of shopping, cleaning, cajoling, and being late for appointments. I didn't expect to be stigmatized with stereotypes, whether of the patronizing, sexist *3 Men and a Baby* variety or of the unctuous, flat-footed, loser-tinged "house husband" stripe.

In my family, the choice to be a single parent was regarded as a vi- 6
able, normal option, as potentially available (except for the hurdle of biology) to a male who wanted children as it was to a female. After all, gender does not, on a day-to-day basis, make the balancing act of work and responsibility for children easier to manage. When a school or a day-care center closes for "spring vacation" right when a deadline or important meeting is scheduled, you get no extra points for having a Y chromosome.

That's not to say you don't receive a few strange, perhaps even ini- 7
tially sympathetic, glances—the body-language equivalent of "Huh?" or "Ah!"—when you decline an opportunity because you have a prior engagement to read *The Little Engine That Could.* When "real" work is on the table, career men *and* women are expected to be 100 percent on the job.

Last week, for instance, when my wife had to go to Seattle for an 8
important conference, I was unexpectedly summoned to be interviewed the next morning on a national TV news program as a result of my 1989 book on fetal alcohol syndrome, *The Broken Cord.* The good news was that I didn't have time to be nervous, because—the bad news—it meant I had to have our three little girls dressed for school, fed, and in the studio waiting room by 6:30 A.M. I did have the forethought to ask the producer to make sure that the small Vermont affiliate station would provide child care while I was on the air, but somehow that request got lost in the scramble, and no one was free when I arrived. My face and voice may have been beamed to a million viewers by satellite for five minutes, but all the while my mind was on the pointy-edged glass table in the room where my daughters watched cartoons. Don't ask me what I said.

The truth is, though, I wouldn't trade my decades of crayons 9
ground into the carpet and playpens set up in the living room. To experience intimately the freshness of life with a child is to be dazzled all over again by the surprise of snow, the gratification of a wish come true. Fathers who for whatever reason miss these moments are forever cut off from the quintessentially human acts repeated by a new generation. To nurture is, on some basic level, to *be* nurtured—and no matter how old, how successful, we become, we never cease to yearn for that consolation. To divide the labor of parenthood too rigidly along conventional lines—the men on one side, women and children on the other—may satisfy the accepted practice of patriarchal tradition, but it's

not a mode of existence carved in stone. Other societies have always organized family life differently. The goal should be to find an equitable pattern that satisfies all parties rather than one that simply conforms to a generic sitcom plot.

10 When in 1981 I fell in love with Louise Erdrich (and she, miraculously, fell in love back) and we got married, at least one thing soon became clear: parenthood is a new ball game when done in concert. Raising children with a spouse or a partner as opposed to solo is, at best, like the difference between pedaling a bicycle and traveling in a car with alternating drivers: there's a greater chance to occasionally look at a map, to notice where you're headed, and to view the scenery along the way.

11 As the oldest of seven siblings, Louise was practiced, relatively confident, and calmly undaunted as the new mother of my three older children. That doesn't mean that the transition from living in a household headed by a single man to one operated by a husband and a wife was automatic or free of stress. Much of my identity had become anchored in "doing it alone," and at first it wasn't easy to share decision making, responsibility—or credit.

12 Moreover, Louise and I both aspire to careers as writers as well as to warm, rewarding relationships with our children. In delineating our jointly inhabited territory we were determined not to respect artificial or hypothetical boundaries. She no more wanted to completely take over the province of the home than I wanted to totally give it up, but how to carve up the individual precincts? Who cooked, and on what days? Who did the laundry and the shopping? Who went to PTA while who put the children to bed? Who put the kid into the car seat and who took her out? And of course: diapers.

13 With the births—in 1984, 1985, and 1989—of three more daughters, our lives became even more hectic. (The resolution of at least one issue was incontrovertible: Louise gave birth.) From our collective gene pool (Chippewa-Modoc-Irish-German-French) emerged a trio of personalities so disparate as to define the limits of diversity within the species.

14 Persia, now seven, is pure heart. Even as a baby she was empathic, looking up at us in condolence when she needed a midnight change or a feeding. She's an actress, a ballerina, a would-be equestrienne. She weeps freely for either joy or sorrow, and always with great gusto. Her dolls are dressed in the latest styles, told stories, and bathed daily. Persia has the look in her eye that as a child the French Lieutenant's Woman must have sported: romantic, enigmatic, mesmerizing.

15 Pallas, just turned six, is all mind. As a toddler she insisted upon sleeping each night not with a teddy bear but with a red block of wood. Her passion is spiders, and her joy is that one tiny brown arachnid has spun a delicate web in an eave above her bed. When we asked what she wanted for her birthday this year, she said wistfully and despondently, "I have a dream, but I know it can't come true."

"Try us," her mother implored. 16

"Well," she said, "I've decided I want to be a carpenter. Do you think I could have a tool chest?"

Compared with her older sisters, Aza already, at two, is iron will, Gertrude Stein's soul transmigrated. Before the age of one she had taught herself how to instantly dismantle, from within, any crib or other restraint devised by modern science. Her first words were, emphatically, "good girl," and she has seemed ever afterward to be immune to self-doubt. The other day, as I was zipping her jacket, I said, "You're a sweetie pie."

"No," she corrected me. "I'm a woman." 19

It's no accident that whatever Louise and I write, whether fiction or 20
nonfiction, there always seems to be a baby getting born and being cared for. When you're typing with one hand while aiming a bottle of juice at an open mouth with the other, you take your inspiration where you find it. And not just for fiction.

I doubt that we'll ever get all the duties parceled out, or that once 21
distributed they'll stay constant. For now, Louise sorts the laundry. I wash and fold it. We each function periodically as a single parent while the other is immersed in a project or away from home. It's an ongoing trek, with no posted directions, no Michelin guide, no paved surfaces. But we all seem headed in the same direction.

COMPREHENSION

1. Why did Dorris want to become a father?
2. What is the "mythos" Dorris refers to in paragraph 4?
3. Does Dorris see a difference between parenting and "real" work?

RHETORIC

1. What is the purpose of the accumulation of details and examples in the introductory paragraph? What do they help to establish about the essay's thesis or writer?
2. What is the point of Dorris's essay? Where does his main idea become apparent?
3. Who is Dorris's audience? What evidence can you find for this?
4. What tone does Dorris use in his essay? Cite examples to support your response.
5. Define these terms used in the essay: *gender typecasting* (paragraph 3); *nuclear family* (paragraph 4); *stereotypes* (paragraph 5).
6. What is the reason for the extended example used in paragraph 8, and how does it serve the overall thrust of the essay?
7. What forms of comparison appear in this essay? How is the comparative method reflected in the essay's conclusion?

WRITING

1. Dorris's essay argues that children can grow up reasonably well in any loving household regardless of how it deviates from the nuclear-family norm. Do you agree or disagree?
2. Debate this proposition in an essay: If given the choice, most American men would choose *not* to be full-time fathers.
3. Write a definition essay entitled "What Is a Father?"

ADRIENNE RICH Adrienne Rich (1929–) was born in Baltimore and graduated from Radcliffe College. She has taught at many universities, including the City University of New York, Columbia University, and Brandeis University. Presently she is a professor of English and feminist studies at Stanford. Author of over twenty books of poetry and five books of prose, Rich is considered one of America's most important feminist poets, her most recent poems often dealing with women's struggle for identity and power. Her book *Diving into the Wreck: Poems, 1971–1972* received a National Book Award. She has also received a Guggenheim Fellowship, a Bollingen Foundation translation grant, and a grant from the National Endowment for the Arts. Her most recent book is *Collected Early Poems* (1993). In "The Anger of a Child," Rich describes how deeply the dynamics of her family affected her attitude toward herself as a woman and a mother and even her concept of herself as a person.

ADRIENNE RICH

The Anger of a Child

It is hard to write about my mother. Whatever I do write, it is my story I am telling, my version of the past. If she were to tell her own story other landscapes would be revealed. But in my landscape or hers, there would be old, smoldering patches of deep-burning anger. Before her marriage, she had trained seriously for years both as a concert pianist and a composer. Born in a southern town, mothered by a strong, frustrated woman, she had won a scholarship to study with the director at the Peabody Conservatory in Baltimore, and by teaching at girls' schools had earned her way to further study in New York, Paris, and Vienna. From the age of sixteen, she had been a young belle, who could have married at any time, but she also possessed unusual talent, determination, and independence for her time and place. She read—and reads—widely and wrote—as her journals from my childhood and her letters of today reveal—with grace and pungency. 1

She married my father after a ten years' engagement during which he finished his medical training and began to establish himself in acade- 2 mic medicine. Once married, she gave up the possibility of a concert career, though for some years she went on composing, and she is still a skilled and dedicated pianist. My father, brilliant, ambitious, possessed by his own drive, assumed that she would give her life over to the enhancement of his. She would manage his household with the formality and grace becoming to a medical professor's wife, though on a limited budget; she would "keep up" her music, though there was no question of letting her composing and practice conflict with her duties as a wife and mother. She was supposed to bear him two children, a boy and a girl. She had to keep her household books to the last penny—I still can see the big blue-gray ledgers, inscribed in her clear, strong hand; she marketed by streetcar, and later, when they could afford a car, she drove my father to and from his laboratory or lectures, often awaiting him for hours. She raised two children, and taught us all our lessons, including music. (Neither of us was sent to school until the fourth grade.) I am sure that she was made to feel responsible for all our imperfections.

My father, like the transcendentalist Bronson Alcott, believed that 3
he (or rather, his wife) could raise children according to his unique moral and intellectual plan, thus proving to the world the values of enlightened, unorthodox child-rearing. I believe that my mother, like Abigail Alcott, at first genuinely and enthusiastically embraced the experiment, and only later found that in carrying out my father's intense, perfectionist program, she was in conflict with her deep instincts as a mother. Like Abigail Alcott, too, she must have found that while ideas might be unfolded by her husband, their daily, hourly practice was going to be up to her. ("'Mr. A. aids me in general principles, but nobody can aid me in the detail,' she mourned. . . . Moreover her husband's views kept her constantly wondering if she were doing a good job. 'Am I doing what is right? Am I doing enough? Am I doing too much?'" The appearance of "temper" and "will" in Louisa, the second Alcott daughter, was blamed by her father on her inheritance from her mother.) Under the institution of motherhood, the mother is the first to blame if theory proves unworkable in practice, or if anything whatsoever goes wrong. But even earlier, my mother had failed at one part of the plan: she had not produced a son.

For years, I felt my mother had chosen my father over me, had sac- 4
rificed me to his needs and theories. When my first child was born, I was barely in communication with my parents. I had been fighting my father for my right to an emotional life and a selfhood beyond his needs and theories. We were all at a draw. Emerging from the fear, exhaustion, and alienation of my first childbirth, I could not admit even to myself that I wanted my mother, let alone tell her how much I wanted her. When she visited me in the hospital neither of us could uncoil the obscure lashings of feeling that darkened the room, the tangled thread running backward to where she had labored for three days to give birth to me, and I was not a son. Now, twenty-six years later, I lay in a contagious hospital with my allergy, my skin covered with a mysterious rash,

my lips and eyelids swollen, my body bruised and sutured, and, in a cot beside my bed, slept the perfect, golden, male child I had brought forth. How could I have interpreted her feelings when I could not begin to decipher my own? My body had spoken all too eloquently, but it was, medically, just my body. I wanted her to mother me again, to hold my baby in her arms as she had once held me; but that baby was also a gauntlet flung down: *my son.* Part of me longed to offer him for her blessing; part of me wanted to hold him up as a badge of victory in our tragic, unnecessary rivalry as women.

But I was only at the beginning. I know now as I could not possibly 5
know then, that among the tangle of feelings between us, in that crucial yet unreal meeting, was her guilt. Soon I would begin to understand the full weight and burden of maternal guilt, that daily, nightly, hourly, *Am I doing what is right? Am I doing enough? Am I doing too much?* The institution of motherhood finds all mothers more or less guilty of having failed their children; and my mother, in particular, had been expected to help create, according to my father's plan, a perfect daughter. This "perfect" daughter, though gratifyingly precocious, had early been given to tics and tantrums, had become permanently lame from arthritis at twenty-two; she had finally resisted her father's Victorian paternalism, his seductive charm and controlling cruelty, had married a divorced graduate student, had begun to write "modern," "obscure," "pessimistic" poetry, lacking the fluent sweetness of Tennyson, had had the final temerity to get pregnant and bring a living baby into the world. She had ceased to be the demure and precocious child or the poetic, seducible adolescent. Something, in my father's view, had gone terribly wrong. I can imagine that whatever else my mother felt (and I know that part of her *was* mutely on my side) she also was made to feel blame. Beneath the "numbness" that she has since told me she experienced at that time, I can imagine the guilt of Everymother, because I have known it myself.

But I did not know it yet. And it is difficult for me to write of my 6
mother now, because I have known it too well. I struggle to describe what it felt like to be her daughter, but I find myself divided, slipping under her skin; a part of me identified too much with her. I know deep reservoirs of anger toward her still exist: the anger of a four-year-old locked in the closet (my father's orders, but my mother carried them out) for childish misbehavior; the anger of a six-year-old kept too long at piano practice (again, at his insistence, but it was she who gave the lessons) till I developed a series of facial tics. (As a mother I know what a child's facial tic is—a lancet of guilt and pain running through one's own body.) And I still feel the anger of a daughter, pregnant, wanting my mother desperately and feeling she had gone over to the enemy.

And I know there must be deep reservoirs of anger in her; every 7
mother has known overwhelming, unacceptable anger at her children. When I think of the conditions under which my mother became a mother, the impossible expectations, my father's distaste for pregnant women, his hatred of all that he could not control, my anger at her dis-

solves into grief and anger *for* her, and then dissolves back again into anger at her: the ancient, unpurged anger of the child.

My mother lives today as an independent woman, which she was always meant to be. She is a much-loved, much-admired grandmother, an explorer in new realms; she lives in the present and future, not the past. I no longer have fantasies—they are the unhealed child's fantasies, I think—of some infinitely healing conversation with her, in which we could show all our wounds, transcend the pain we have shared as mother and daughter, say everything at last. But in writing these pages, I am admitting, at least, how important her existence is and has been for me.

COMPREHENSION

1. Who is Rich's audience in this essay? Might there be more than one audience? Why, or why not?
2. What is the basis of Rich's anger toward her father? Toward her mother? Does she resolve this anger? Explain.
3. Compare the attitude toward women that existed in Rich's family to that of Kingston's family in "The Woman Warrior."

RHETORIC

1. How do the following examples of figurative language contribute to the tone of the essay: "smoldering patches of deep-burning anger" (paragraph 1); "obscure lashings of feeling" (paragraph 4); "deep reservoirs of anger" (paragraph 6)?
2. Note the length and structure of the following sentence: "This 'perfect' daughter, though gratifyingly precocious, had early been given to tics and tantrums, had become permanently lame from arthritis at twenty-two; she had finally resisted her father's Victorian paternalism, his seductive charm and controlling cruelty, had married a divorced graduate student, had begun to write 'modern,' 'obscure,' 'pessimistic' poetry, lacking the fluent sweetness of Tennyson, had had the final temerity to get pregnant and bring a living baby into the world" (paragraph 5). Why has the author compressed so much information into this sentence? How would the effect on the reader differ if it were broken down into shorter sentences?
3. Why has Rich chosen to include information about Bronson Alcott? Would the essay have been just as effective without it?
4. Why are the questions in paragraph 5 italicized?
5. In paragraph 6, Rich makes extensive use of parentheses. How does this punctuation complement the content of the paragraph?
6. Rich concludes the essay by stating her purpose. Why has she saved it for last?

WRITING

1. Who bears the greatest responsibility for Rich's anger? Her father? Her mother? The society that condoned oppression of women? Rich herself? Analyze these issues in an essay.
2. Write an essay explaining how your father or mother influenced your lifestyle, goals, attitudes, or behavior.
3. Rich's father's view concerning the role of women no longer exists in our society. Agree or disagree with this statement in a brief essay.
4. Compare and contrast the essays by Atwood and Rich.

SIGMUND FREUD Sigmund Freud (1856–1939), founder of psychoanalysis, was an excellent writer. His theories concerning the pleasure principle, repression, and infantile sexuality are still controversial; nevertheless, they have had a profound impact upon culture, education, and art. Some of Freud's psychological works include *The Interpretation of Dreams* (1900), *The Psychopathology of Everyday Life* (1904), and *The Ego and the Id* (1923). He also analyzed the relation of culture and psychology in *Totem and Taboo* (1913) and *Moses and Monotheism* (1939). In the following essay, Freud discusses several character types derived from his theory of the libido.

SIGMUND FREUD

Libidinal Types

Observation teaches us that in individual human beings the general features of humanity are embodied in almost infinite variety. If we follow the promptings of a legitimate desire to distinguish particular types in this multiplicity, we must begin by selecting the characteristics to look for and the points of view to bear in mind in making our differentiation. For this purpose physical qualities will be no less useful than mental; it will be most valuable of all if we can make our classification on the basis of a regularly occurring combination of physical and mental characteristics. 1

It is doubtful whether we are as yet able to discover types of this order, although we shall certainly be able to do so sometime on a basis of which we are still ignorant. If we confine our efforts to defining certain purely psychological types, the libidinal situation will have the first claim to serve as the basis of our classification. It may fairly be demanded that this classification should not merely be deduced from our knowledge or our conjectures about the libido, but that it should be easily verified in actual experience and should help to clarify the mass of our observations and enable us to grasp their meaning. Let it be admit- 2 ted at once that there is no need to suppose that, even in the psychical sphere, these libidinal types are the only possible ones; if we take other characteristics as our basis of classification we might be able to distinguish a whole series of other psychological types. But there is one rule which must apply to all such types: they must not coincide with specific clinical pictures. On the contrary, they should embrace all the variations which according to our practical standards fall within the category of the normal. In their extreme developments, however, they may well approximate to clinical pictures and so help to bridge the gulf which is assumed to exist between the normal and the pathological.

Now we can distinguish three main libidinal types, according as the 3
subject's libido is mainly allocated to one or another region of the mental apparatus. To name these types is not very easy; following the lines of our depth-psychology, I should be inclined to call them the *erotic,* the *narcissistic* and the *obsessional* type.

The *erotic* type is easily characterized. Erotics are persons whose 4
main interest—the relatively largest amount of their libido—is focused on love. Loving, but above all being loved, is for them the most important thing in life. They are governed by the dread of loss of love, and this makes them peculiarly dependent on those who may withhold their love from them. Even in its pure form this type is a very common one. Variations occur according as it is blended with another type and as the element of aggression in it is strong or weak. From the social and cultural standpoint this type represents the elementary instinctual claims of the id, to which the other psychical agencies have become docile.

The second type is that which I have termed the *obsessional*—a 5
name which may at first seem rather strange; its distinctive characteristic is the supremacy exercised by the super-ego, which is segregated from the ego with great accompanying tension. Persons of this type are governed by anxiety of conscience instead of by the dread of losing love; they exhibit, we might say, an inner instead of an outer dependence; they develop a high degree of self-reliance, from the social standpoint they are the true upholders of civilization, for the most part in a conservative spirit.

The characteristics of the third type, justly called the *narcissistic,* are 6
in the main negatively described. There is no tension between ego and super-ego—indeed, starting from this type one would hardly have arrived at the notion of a super-ego; there is no preponderance of erotic needs; the main interest is focused on self-preservation; the type is independent and not easily overawed. The ego has a considerable amount of aggression available, one manifestation of this being a proneness to activity; where love is in question, loving is preferred to being loved. People of this type impress others as being "personalities"; it is on them that their follow-men are specially likely to lean; they readily assume the role of leader, give a fresh stimulus to cultural development or break down existing conditions.

These pure types will hardly escape the suspicion of being deduced 7
from the theory of the libido. But we feel that we are on the firm

ground of experience when we turn to the mixed types which are to be found so much more frequently than the unmixed. These new types: the *erotic-obsessional,* the *erotic-narcissistic* and the *narcissistic-obsessional* do really seem to provide a good grouping of the individual psychical structures revealed in analysis. If we study these mixed types we find in them pictures of characters with which we have long been familiar. In the *erotic-obsessional* type the preponderance of the instincts is restricted by the influence of the super-ego: dependence on persons who are *contemporary* objects and, at the same time, on the residues of *former* objects—parents, educators and ideal figures—is carried by this type to the furthest point. The *erotic-narcissistic* type is perhaps the most common of all. It combines contrasting characteristics which are thus able to moderate one another; studying this type in comparison with the other two erotic types, we can see how aggressiveness and activity go with a predominance of narcissism. Finally, the *narcissistic-obsessional* type represents the variation most valuable from the cultural standpoint, for it combines independence of external factors and regard for the requirements of conscience with the capacity for energetic action, and it reinforces the ego against the super-ego.

8 It might be asked in jest why no mention has been made of another mixed type which is theoretically possible: the *erotic-obsessional-narcissistic.* But the answer to this jest is serious: such a type would no longer be a type at all, but the absolute norm, the ideal harmony. We thereupon realize that the phenomenon of different *types* arises just in so far as one or two of the three main modes of expending the libido in the mental economy have been favoured at the cost of the others.

9 Another question that may be asked is what is the relation of these libidinal types to pathology, whether some of them have a special disposition to pass over into neurosis and, if so, which types lead to which forms of neurosis. The answer is that the hypothesis of these libidinal types throws no fresh light on the genesis of the neuroses. Experience testifies that persons of all these types can live free from neurosis. The pure types marked by the undisputed predominance of a single psychical agency seem to have a better prospect of manifesting themselves as pure character-formations, while we might expect that the mixed types would provide a more fruitful soil for the conditioning factors of neurosis. But I do not think that we should make up our mind on these points until they have been carefully submitted to appropriate tests.

10 It seems easy to infer that when persons of the erotic type fall ill they will develop hysteria, just as those of the obsessional type will develop obsessional neurosis; but even this conclusion partakes of the uncertainty to which I have just alluded. People of the narcissistic type, who, being otherwise independent, are exposed to frustration from the external world, are peculiarly disposed to psychosis; and their mental composition also contains some of the essential conditioning factors which make for criminality.

We know that we have not as yet exact certainty about the aetiological conditions of neurosis. The precipitating occasions are frustrations and inner conflicts: conflicts between the three great psychical agencies, conflicts arising in the libidinal economy by reason of our bisexual disposition, conflicts between the erotic and the aggressive instinctual components. It is the endeavor of the psychology of the neurosis to discover what imparts a pathogenic character to these processes, which are a part of the normal course of mental life. 11

COMPREHENSION

1. State, in your own words, Freud's thesis in this selection.
2. According to Freud, what types of individuals uphold society? What are their psychological characteristics?
3. What relationship does Freud see between mental illness and these character types?

RHETORIC

1. Freud assumes that the reader is familiar with several psychological terms. Make sure you understand the following: *depth-psychology* (paragraph 3); *id* (paragraph 4); *ego* (paragraph 5); *neuroses* (paragraph 9); *psychosis* (paragraph 10); and *aetiological* (paragraph 11).
2. Does Freud use general or specific language in this essay? How does his choice of language relate to the conclusions he draws in paragraphs 9 to 11?
3. Freud's primary rhetorical technique is classification. Identify his categories, and list the distinguishing characteristics of each class.
4. Explain the relations of paragraphs 1 and 2 to the body of the essay.
5. Freud uses definition frequently in this essay. What kinds of definitions does he use? How do they contribute to the structuring of the essay?
6. Explain the importance of paragraph 7 to the essay's structure. What effect does it have on the classification the author has established?

WRITING

1. Judging from your own observations, how valid is Freud's classification of libidinal types? Write an essay defending or attacking Freud's system.
2. There are innumerable ways to classify people. In a classification essay, devise your own method for analyzing a particular group of people.
3. Take one of Freud's terms—for example, *neurosis*—and write an extended definition of it.

CLASSIC AND CONTEMPORARY

D. H. LAWRENCE David Herbert Lawrence (1885–1930), novelist, essayist, and poet, wrote in the great tradition of English romanticism. He chafed under the conventions of his age and zealously extended the content and style of the English novel. His novels, such as *Sons and Lovers* (1913), *The Rainbow* (1915), *Women in Love* (1921), *The Plumed Serpent* (1926) and *Lady Chatterley's Lover* (1928) are famous for their often disquieting depictions of love and ambition in the modern world. Lawrence also wrote criticism: His *Studies in Classic American Literature* (1923) is still a revealing, if idiosyncratic, look at American literature. In the following provocative piece, Lawrence equates beauty with sex appeal.

D. H. LAWRENCE

Sex versus Loveliness

It is a pity that *sex* is such an ugly little word. An ugly little word, and really almost incomprehensible. What *is* sex, after all? The more we think about it the less we know. 1

Science says it is an instinct; but what is an instinct? Apparently an instinct is an old, old habit that has become ingrained. But a habit, however old, has to have a beginning. And there is really no beginning to sex. Where life is, there it is. So sex is no "habit" that has been formed. 2

Again, they talk of sex as an appetite, like hunger. An appetite; but for what? An appetite for propagation? It is rather absurd. They say a peacock puts on all his fine feathers to dazzle the peahen into letting him satisfy his appetite for propagation. But why should the peahen not put on fine feathers, to dazzle the peacock, and satisfy *her* desire for propagation? She has surely quite as great a desire for eggs and chickens as he has. We cannot believe that her sex-urge is so weak that she needs all that blue splendour of feathers to rouse her. Not at all. 3

As for me, I never even saw a peahen so much as look at her lord's bronze and blue glory. I don't believe she ever sees it. I don't believe for a moment that she knows the difference between bronze, blue, brown or green. 4

If I had ever seen a peahen gazing with rapt attention on her lord's flamboyancy, I might believe that he had put on all those feathers just to "attract" her. But she never looks at him. Only she seems to get a lit- 5 tle perky when he shudders all his quills at her, like a storm in the trees. Then she does seem to notice, just casually, his presence.

These theories of sex are amazing. A peacock puts on his glory for the sake of a wall-eyed peahen who never looks at him. Imagine a scientist being so naïve as to credit the peahen with a profound, dynamic appreciation of a peacock's colour and pattern. Oh, highly aesthetic peahen!

And a nightingale sings to attract his female. Which is mighty curi- 7
ous, seeing he sings his best when courtship and honeymoon are over and the female is no longer concerned with him at all, but with the young. Well, then, if he doesn't sing to attract her, he must sing to distract her and amuse her while she's sitting.

How delightful, how naïve theories are! But there is a hidden will 8
behind them all. There is a hidden will behind all theories of sex, implacable. And that is the will to deny, to wipe out the mystery of beauty.

Because beauty is a mystery. You can neither eat it nor make flannel 9
out of it. Well, then, says science, it is just a trick to catch the female and induce her to propagate. How naïve! As if the female needed inducing. She will propagate in the dark, even—so where, then, is the beauty trick?

Science has a mysterious hatred of beauty, because it doesn't fit in 10
the cause-and-effect chain. And society has a mysterious hatred of sex, because it perpetually interferes with the nice money-making schemes of social man. So the two hatreds made a combine, and sex and beauty are mere propagation appetite.

Now sex and beauty are one thing, like flame and fire. If you hate 11
sex you hate beauty. If you love *living* beauty, you have a reverence for sex. Of course you can love old, dead beauty and hate sex. But to love living beauty you must have a reverence for sex.

Sex and beauty are inseparable, like life and consciousness. And the 12
intelligence which goes with sex and beauty, and arises out of sex and beauty, is intuition. The great disaster of our civilization is the morbid hatred of sex. What, for example, could show a more poisoned hatred of sex than Freudian psycho-analysis?—which carries with it a morbid fear of beauty, "alive" beauty, and which causes the atrophy of our intuitive faculty and our intuitive self.

The deep psychic disease of modern men and women is the dis- 13
eased, atrophied condition of the intuitive faculties. There is a whole world of life that we might know and enjoy by intuition, and by intuition alone. This is denied us, because we deny sex and beauty, the source of the intuitive life and of the insouciance which is so lovely in free animals and in plants.

Sex is the root of which intuition is the foliage and beauty the 14
flower. Why is a woman lovely, if ever, in her twenties? It is the time when sex rises softly to her face, as a rose to the top of a rose bush.

And the appeal is the appeal of beauty. We deny it wherever we can. 15
We try to make the beauty as shallow and trashy as possible. But, first and foremost, sex appeal is the appeal of beauty.

Now beauty is a thing about which we are so uneducated we can 16
hardly speak of it. We try to pretend it is a fixed arrangement: straight nose, large eyes, etc. We think a lovely woman must look like Lillian Gish, a handsome man must look like Rudolph Valentino. So we *think.*

In actual life we behave quite differently. We say: "She's quite beau- 17
tiful, but I don't care for her." Which shows we are using the word *beautiful* all wrong. We should say: "She has the stereotyped attributes of beauty, but she is not beautiful to me."

Beauty is an *experience,* nothing else. It is not a fixed pattern or an 18
arrangement of features. It is something *felt,* a glow or a communicated sense of fineness. What ails us is that our sense of beauty is so bruised and blunted, we miss all the best.

But to stick to the films—there is a greater essential beauty in 19
Charlie Chaplin's odd face than ever there was in Valentino's. There is a bit of true beauty in Chaplin's brows and eyes, a gleam of something pure.

But our sense of beauty is so bruised and clumsy, we don't see it, 20
and don't know it when we do see it. We can only see the blatantly obvious, like the so-called beauty of Rudolph Valentino, which only pleases because it satisfies some ready-made notion of handsomeness.

But the plainest person can look beautiful, can *be* beautiful. It only 21
needs the fire of sex to rise delicately to change an ugly face to a lovely one. That is really sex appeal: the communicating of a sense of beauty.

And in the reverse way, no one can be quite so repellent as a re- 22
ally pretty woman. That is, since beauty is a question of experience, not of concrete form, no one can be as acutely ugly as a really pretty woman. When the sex-glow is missing, and she moves in ugly coldness, how hideous she seems, and all the worse for her externals of prettiness.

What sex is, we don't know, but it must be some sort of fire. For it 23
always communicates a sense of warmth, of glow. And when the glow becomes a pure shine, then we feel the sense of beauty.

But the communicating of the warmth, the glow of sex, is true sex 24
appeal. We all have the fire of sex slumbering or burning inside us. If we live to be ninety, it is still there. Or, if it dies, we become one of those ghastly living corpses which are unfortunately becoming more numerous in the world.

Nothing is more ugly than a human being in whom the fire of sex 25
has gone out. You get a nasty clayey creature whom everybody wants to avoid.

But while we are fully alive, the fire of sex smoulders or burns in us. 26
In youth it flickers and shines; in age it glows softer and stiller, but there it is. We have some control over it; but only partial control. That is why society hates it.

While ever it lives, the fire of sex, which is the source of beauty and 27
anger, burns in us beyond our understanding. Like actual fire, while it lives it will burn our fingers if we touch it carelessly. And so social man, who only wants to be "safe," hates the fire of sex.

Luckily, not many men succeed in being merely social men. The 29
fire of the old Adam smoulders. And one of the qualities of fire is that it calls to fire. Sex-fire here kindles sex-fire there. It may only rouse the smoulder into a soft glow. It may call up a sharp flicker. Or rouse a flame; and then flame leans to flame, and starts a blaze.

Whenever the sex-fire glows through, it will kindle an answer some- 29
where or other. It may only kindle a sense of warmth and optimism. Then you say: "I like that girl; she's a real good sort." It may kindle a glow that makes the world look kindlier, and life feel better. Then you say: "She's an attractive woman. I like her."

Or she may rouse a flame that lights up her own face first, before it 30
lights up the universe. Then you say: "She's a lovely woman. She looks lovely to me."

It takes a rare woman to rouse a real sense of loveliness. It is not that 31
a woman is born beautiful. We say that to escape our own poor, bruised, clumsy understanding of beauty. There have been thousands and thousands of women quite as good-looking as Diane de Poitiers, or Mrs. Langtry, or any of the famous ones. There are today thousands and thousands of superbly good-looking women. But oh, how few lovely women!

And why? Because of the failure of their sex appeal. A good-looking 32
woman becomes lovely when the fire of sex rouses pure and fine in her and flickers through her face and touches the fire in me.

Then she becomes a lovely woman to me, then she is in the living 33
flesh a lovely woman: not a mere photograph of one. And how lovely a lovely woman! But, alas! how rare! How bitterly rare in a world full of unusually handsome girls and women!

Handsome, good-looking, but not lovely, not beautiful. Handsome 34
and good-looking women are the women with good features and the right hair. But a lovely woman is an experience. It is a question of communicated fire. It is a question of sex appeal in our poor, dilapidated modern phraseology. Sex appeal applied to Diane de Poitiers, or even, in the lovely hours, to one's wife—why, it is a libel and a slander in itself. Nowadays, however, instead of the fire of loveliness, it is sex appeal. The two are the same thing, I suppose, but on vastly different levels.

The business man's pretty and devoted secretary is still chiefly valu- 35
able because of her sex appeal. Which does not imply "immoral relations" in the slightest.

Even today a girl with a bit of generosity likes to feel she is helping a 36
man if the man will take her help. And this desire that he shall take her help is her sex appeal. It is the genuine fire, if of a very mediocre heat.

Still, it serves to keep the world of "business" alive. Probably, but 37
for the introduction of the lady secretary into the business man's office, the business man would have collapsed entirely by now. She calls up the sacred fire in her and she communicates it to her boss. He feels an added flow of energy and optimism, and—business flourishes.

There is, of course, the other side of sex appeal. It can be the destruction of the one appealed to. When a woman starts using her sex appeal to her own advantage it is usually a bad moment for some poor devil. But this side of sex appeal has been overworked lately, so it is not nearly as dangerous as it was. 38

The sex-appealing courtesans who ruined so many men in Balzac no longer find it smooth running. Men have grown canny. They fight shy even of the emotional vamp. In fact, men are inclined to think they smell a rat the moment they feel the touch of feminine sex appeal today. 39

Which is a pity, for sex appeal is only a dirty name for a bit of life-flame. No man works so well and so successfully as when some woman has kindled a little fire in his veins. No woman does her housework with real joy unless she is in love—and a woman may go on being quietly in love for fifty years almost without knowing it. 40

If only our civilization had taught us how to let sex appeal flow properly and subtly, how to keep the fire of sex clear and alive, flickering or glowing or blazing in all its varying degrees of strength and communication, we might, all of us, have lived all our lives in love, which means we should be kindled and full of zest in all kinds of ways and for all kinds of things. . . . 41

Whereas, what a lot of dead ash there is in life now. 42

COMPREHENSION

1. How does Lawrence define *beauty* in his essay?
2. Which scientific definitions of *sex* does the writer oppose? Why?
3. What does Lawrence mean by "Beauty is an *experience*" (paragraph 18)?

RHETORIC

1. In your own words, what is Lawrence's thesis? Where is it in the essay?
2. How does the writer employ humor in his writing? Does it reflect his attitude? Why, or why not? Provide examples of his use of humor.
3. How does Lawrence use comparison in his essay? Does he use any other rhetorical strategies? Justify your response.
4. Where does Lawrence use repetition and parallel structure in his essay? Why does he use these techniques? How do they contribute to his argument?
5. Examine his use of metaphor and similes in paragraph 14. How do they clarify his point? Where else in the essay does Lawrence use figurative language? Cite especially effective uses in the essay.
6. What is the purpose of paragraphs 35, 36, and 37? How do they serve to expand or support Lawrence's views? Do they add coherence to the essay's structure? Why, or why not?

WRITING

1. In an essay entitled "What Is Beauty?" write a definition of the term *beauty*, using both its denotative and connotative meanings. Use examples from Lawrence's essay if applicable.
2. Write an essay that examines how the media (television, movies, magazines, books) influence our notions of beauty and sex appeal. How do their definitions compare or contrast with your own personal view of these issues? Give concrete examples and details.

SUSAN SONTAG Susan Sontag (1933–) is an intelligent, witty observer of new trends in literature, art, film, photography, and culture. An American essayist, novelist, short-story writer, and filmmaker, Sontag has written *Against Interpretation* (1966), advocating the use of the senses when critiquing art, as well as *On Photography* (1976). While battling cancer, she wrote *Illness as Metaphor* (1978), and in 1989 she wrote *AIDS and Its Metaphors.* Sontag's fictional works include *Death Kit* (1967) and *The Volcano Lover* (1992). In the following essay, written in 1975, she reexamines ancient and modern notions of beauty, especially as they apply to women.

SUSAN SONTAG

Beauty

For the Greeks, beauty was a virtue: a kind of excellence. Persons then were assumed to be what we now have to call—lamely, enviously—*whole* persons. If it did occur to the Greeks to distinguish between a person's "inside" and "outside," they still expected that inner beauty would be matched by beauty of the other kind. The well-born young Athenians who gathered around Socrates found it quite paradoxical that their hero was so intelligent, so brave, so honorable, so seductive—and so ugly. One of Socrates' main pedagogical acts was to be ugly—and teach those innocent, no doubt splendid-looking disciples of his how full of paradoxes life really was. 1

They may have resisted Socrates' lesson. We do not. Several thousand years later, we are more wary of the enchantments of beauty. We not only split off—with the greatest facility—the "inside" (character, intellect) from the "outside" (looks); but we are actually surprised when someone who is beautiful is also intelligent, talented, good. 2

It was principally the influence of Christianity that deprived beauty of the central place it had in classical ideals of human excellence. By limiting excellence (*virtus* in latin) to *moral* virtue only, Christianity set beauty adrift—as an alienated, arbitrary, superficial enchantment. And beauty has continued to lose prestige. For close to two centuries it has 3

beome a convention to attribute beauty to only one of the two sexes: the sex which, however Fair, is always Second. Associating beauty with women has put beauty even further on the defensive, morally.

A beautiful woman, we say in English. But a handsome man. 4
"Handsome" is the masculine equivalent of—and refusal of—a compliment which has accumulated certain demeaning overtones, by being reserved for women only. That one can call a man "beautiful" in French and in Italian suggests that Catholic countries—unlike those countries shaped by the Protestant version of Christianity—still retain some vestiges of the pagan admiration for beauty. But the difference, if one exists, is of degree only. In every modern country that is Christian or post-Christian, women *are* the beautiful sex—to the detriment of the notion of beauty as well as of women.

To be called beautiful is thought to name something essential to 5
women's character and concerns. (In contrast to men—whose essence is to be strong, or effective, or competent.) It does not take someone in the throes of advanced feminist awareness to perceive that the way women are taught to be involved with beauty encourages narcissism, reinforces dependence and immaturity. Everybody (women and men) knows that. For it is "everybody," a whole society, that has identified being feminine with caring about how one *looks.* (In contrast to being masculine—which is identified with caring about what one *is* and *does* and only secondarily, if at all, about how one looks.) Given these stereotypes, it is no wonder that beauty enjoys, at best, a rather mixed reputation.

It is not, of course, the desire to be beautiful that is wrong but the 6
obligation to be—or to try. What is accepted by most women as a flattering idealization of their sex is a way of making women feel inferior to what they actually are—or normally grow to be. For the ideal of beauty is administered as a form of self-oppression. Women are taught to see their bodies in *parts,* and to evaluate each part separately. Breasts, feet, hips, waistline, neck, eyes, nose, complexion, hair, and so on—each in turn is submitted to an anxious, fretful, often despairing scrutiny. Even if some pass muster, some will always be found wanting. Nothing less than perfection will do.

In men, good looks is a whole, something taken in at a glance. It 7
does not need to be confirmed by giving measurements of different regions of the body, nobody encourages a man to dissect his appearance, feature by feature. As for perfection, that is considered trivial—almost unmanly. Indeed, in the ideally good-looking man a small imperfection or blemish is considered positively desirable. According to one movie critic (a woman) who is a declared Robert Redford fan, it is having that cluster of skin-colored moles on one cheek that saves Redford from being merely a "pretty face." Think of the depreciation of women—as well as of beauty—that is implied in that judgment.

"The privileges of beauty are immense," said Cocteau. To be sure, 8
beauty is a form of power. And deservedly so. What is lamentable is

that it is the only form of power that most women are encouraged to seek. This power is always conceived in relation to men; it is not the power to do but the power to attract. It is a power that negates itself. For this power is not one that can be chosen freely—at least, not by women—or renounced without social censure.

To preen, for a woman, can never be just a pleasure. It is also a 9
duty. It is her work. If a woman does real work—and even if she has clambered up to a leading position in politics, law, medicine, business, or whatever—she is always under pressure to confess that she still works at being attractive. But in so far as she is keeping up as one of the Fair Sex, she brings under suspicion her very capacity to be objective, professional, authoritative, thoughtful. Damned if they do—women are. And damned if they don't.

One could hardly ask for more important evidence of the dangers 10
of considering persons as split between what is "inside" and what is "outside" than that interminable half-comic half-tragic tale, the oppression of women. How easy it is to start off by defining women as caretakers of their surfaces, and then to disparage them (or find them adorable) for being "superficial." It is a crude trap, and it has worked for too long. But to get out of the trap requires that women get some critical distance from that excellence and privilege which is beauty, enough distance to see how much beauty itself has been abridged in order to prop up the mythology of the "feminine." There should be a way of saving beauty *from* women—and *for* them.

COMPREHENSION

1. How did the Greeks define *beauty*?
2. To what does Sontag attribute the lowered prestige of beauty in our society?
3. According to the author, what are the consequences of associating beauty exclusively with women?

RHETORIC

1. State Sontag's thesis in your own words. What are her supporting ideas? What transitions does she employ?
2. Describe the level of language used by Sontag. Cite specific examples from the essay. What does the level of language tell us about Sontag's intended audience?
3. Discuss the writer's use of punctuation marks in paragraph 7. Consider the purpose they serve in the paragraph and their effectiveness. Why does Sontag begin with a quotation in paragraph 8? How well is it supported by the subsequent sentences?
4. How does Sontag develop an extended definition in this essay?
5. Where does the comparative method appear in this essay?
6. Examine the essay's conclusion. How well does it help to round out Sontag's ideas? How does it compare to the essay's introduction?

WRITING

1. Write an argumentative essay entitled "Beauty Is Power."
2. Write an essay analyzing the importance of physical appearance in your family. Consider issues such as the amount of time, energy, and money individual family members spend on makeup, hair products, and clothes. Do you feel obligated to look attractive at all times?
3. Compare and contrast Sontag's thoughts on beauty to Atwood's essay on the female body. What ideas do these two writers hold in common? In what areas do they differ? Use quotes from both writers to support your claims.

CLASSIC AND CONTEMPORARY: QUESTIONS FOR COMPARISON

1. Compare Lawrence's and Sontag's definitions of *beauty*. What, if anything, do they have in common, and where do they differ? Use particular examples from the essays to support your opinion.
2. Examine the language, style, and content of both essays. Is there anything in either that is indicative of the time it was written? What use do the writers make of figurative language? How do the essays compare and contrast in tone and organization?
3. Consider the social climates in which these essays were written. Are the writers' views consistent with the beliefs of the society in which they exist? Are Sontag's views acceptable today? How were Lawrence's ideas on beauty and sexuality viewed during his lifetime?

CONNECTIONS

1. Compare the attitudes of Cisneros and Rich toward their fathers. Do you think both women have come to terms with their childhoods? Write an essay exploring this topic.
2. Evaluate the way that Atwood, Leakey, and Steinem view the human body and the way it functions. Where do they differ in their views? What might Leakey tell Atwood and Steinem about the human female body? Do you think Leakey might share their feminist sensibilities? Consider these questions in essay form.
3. Pretend you are Michael Dorris writing a letter to Sandra Cisneros's father. What advice would he give about parenting daughters? What insights do you think he might share?
4. Using the writings of Freud and Lawrence, explore the issues of sex, love, and personality types. What connections can you make between the views of these two men? Use evidence from their work as well as evidence from the work of any other relevant writer in this section.
5. Write a classification essay entitled "Gender Typecasting," using support from any writer in this section.
6. Compare the level of language and writing styles in the scientific essays of Freud and Leakey. What do they have in common, and how do they differ? Use examples from both works.
7. Using the essay of Theroux (as well as any others in this section), write an essay in which you discuss the role of sports in masculine development.
8. Establish your own definition of what it means to be a man or woman. Refer to at least three of the essays in this section to support your definition.

CHAPTER SIX

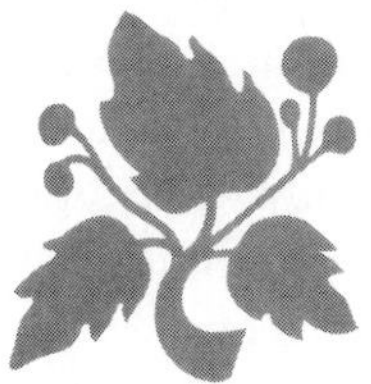

Social Processes and Institutions

Recent studies indicate that American students have a decidedly weak understanding of history and politics. In fact, one-third of all high school juniors cannot identify the main purpose of the Declaration of Independence or say in which fifty-year period it was signed. The Declaration of Independence is one of the selections in this chapter. It appears with other notable essays on history and politics that help us understand our cultural legacies.

Major writers can bring history and politics to life, enabling us to develop a sense of the past and of the various social processes that have influenced the development of cultures over time. By studying the course of history, we develop causal notions of how events are interrelated and how traditions have evolved. Essays, speeches, documents, biographies, narratives, and many other literary forms capture events and illuminate the past while holding up a mirror to the present. History can be brought to life out of the plain but painfully eloquent artifacts of oral culture. On the other hand, Thomas Jefferson employs classical rhetorical structures—notably argumentation—in outlining democratic vistas in the Declaration of Independence. By studying history, we learn to appreciate the texture of past events and their impact on our lives today. This is what the historian Barbara Tuchman terms wisdom, "a decent appreciation of probability."

Even the briefest reflection will remind us of how important social processes and institutions are. But simply, a knowledge of history validates our memory, a remembrance of how important the past is to our current existence. When, for example, Ronald Takaki and Mary Gordon investigate their "roots" in decidedly subjective essays, they tap into a collective memory of the immigrant experience that most

Americans share. Or when Doris Lessing, Martin Luther King Jr., and Vaclav Havel approach the subject of oppression from diverse perspectives, we are reminded of how important the freedom to know our past is to the creation and preservation of democratic societies.

Only through a knowledge of history and politics can we make informed choices. Through a study of history and politics, we learn about challenges and opportunities, conflicts and their resolutions, and the use and abuse of power across time in numerous cultures and civilizations. It is through the study of historical processes and political institutions that we seek to define ourselves and to learn how we have evolved.

Previewing the Chapter

As you read the selections in this chapter and respond to them in discussion and writing, consider the following questions:

- What specific events does the author concentrate on? What is the time frame?
- What larger historical and political issues concern the author?
- From what perspective does the author treat the subject, from that of participant, observer, commentator, or what?
- What is the author's purpose in treating historical events and personalities: to explain, to instruct, to amuse, to criticize, or to celebrate?
- What does the author learn about history and politics from his or her inquiry into events?
- What sorts of conflicts—historical, political, economic, social, religious—emerge in the essay?
- Are there any correspondences among the essays? What analogies do the authors themselves draw?
- What is the relationship of people and personalities to the events under consideration?
- Which biases and ideological positions do you detect in the authors' works?
- How has your understanding of history and politics been challenged by the essays in this section?

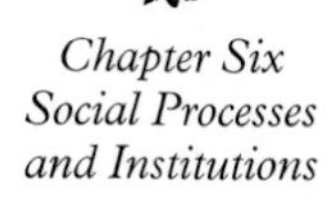

RONALD TAKAKI Ronald Takaki (1939–) was born in Honolulu, Hawaii. He earned his B.A. from the College of Wooster in 1961 and his M.A. and Ph.D. from the University of California, Berkeley, where he is currently a professor of ethnic studies. He also taught American history at the College of San Mateo from 1965–1967. Takaki feels that American history is still viewed from a predominantly white perspective and is devoted to more accurately representing all Americans in our society. He has written several books—*A Pro-Slavery Crusade: The Agitation to Reopen the African Slave Trade* (1971) and the award-winning *Strangers from a Distant Shore: A History of Asian Americans* (1989)—and is a frequent contributor to history journals as well as other publications. In the following essay, he reflects on the internment of Japanese citizens during World War II and describes his attempts to establish a connection with his Japanese relatives.

RONALD TAKAKI

Roots

To confront the current problems of racism, Asian Americans know they must remember the past and break its silence. This need was felt deeply by Japanese Americans during the hearings before the commission reviewing the issue of redress and reparations for Japanese Americans interned during World War II. Memories of the internment nightmare have haunted the older generation like ghosts. But the former prisoners have been unable to exorcise them by speaking out and ventilating their anger. 1

When we were children, 2
you spoke Japanese
in lowered voices
between yourselves.

Once you uttered secrets 3
which we should not know,
were not to be heard by us.
When you spoke
of some dark secret
you would admonish us,
"Don't tell it to anyone else."
It was a suffocated vow of silence.[1]

[1]Richard Oyama, poem published in *Transfer 38* (San Francisco, 1979), p. 43, reprinted in Elaine Kim, *Asian American Literature: An Introduction to the Writings and Their Social Context* (Philadelphia, 1982), pp. 308–309.

"Stigmatized," the ex-internees have been carrying the "burden of 4
shame" for over forty painful years. "They felt like a rape victim," explained Congressman Norman Mineta, a former internee of the Heart Mountain internment camp. "They were accused of being disloyal. They were the victims but they were on trial and they did not want to talk about it." But Sansei, or third-generation Japanese Americans, want their elders to tell their story. Warren Furutani, for example, told the commissioners that young people like himself had been asking their parents to tell them about the concentration camps and to join them in pilgrimages to the internment camp at Manzanar. "Why? Why!" their parents would reply defensively. "Why would you want to know about it? It's not important, we don't need to talk about it." But, Furutani continued, they need to tell the world what happened during those years of infamy.[2]

Suddenly, during the commission hearings, scores of Issei and Nisei 5
came forward and told their stories. "For over thirty-five years I have been the stereotype Japanese American," Alice Tanabe Nehira told the commission. "I've kept quiet, hoping in due time we will be justly compensated and recognized for our years of patient effort. By my passive attitude, I can reflect on my past years to conclude that it doesn't pay to remain silent." The act of speaking out has enabled the Japanese-American community to unburden itself of years of anger and anguish. Sometimes their testimonies before the commission were long and the chair urged them to conclude. But they insisted the time was theirs. "Mr. Commissioner," protested poet Janice Mirikitani,

> So when you tell me my time is
> up I tell you this.
> Pride has kept my lips
> pinned by nails,
> my rage coffined.
> But I exhume my past
> to claim this time.[3]

The former internees finally had spoken, and their voices com- 6
pelled the nation to redress the injustice of internment. In August 1988, Congress passed a bill giving an apology and a payment of $20,000 to each of the survivors of the internment camps. When President Ronald Reagan signed the bill into law, he admitted that the United States had committed "a grave wrong," for during World War II, Japanese Americans had remained "utterly loyal" to this country. "Indeed, scores of Japanese Americans volunteered for our Armed

[2]Congressman Robert Matsui, speech in the House of Representatives on bill 442 for redress and reparations, September 17, 1987, *Congressional Record* (Washington, 1987), p. 7584; Congressman Norman Mineta, interview with author, March 26, 1988; Warren Furutani, testimony, reprinted in *Amerasia*, vol. 8, no. 2 (1981), p. 104.

[3]Alice Tanabe Nehira, testimony, reprinted in *Amerasia*, vol. 8, no. 2 (1981), p. 93; Janice Mirikitani, "Breaking Silences," reprinted ibid., p. 109.

Forces—many stepping forward in the internment camps themselves. The 442nd Regimental Combat Team, made up entirely of Japanese Americans, served with immense distinction to defend this nation, their nation. Yet, back at home, the soldiers' families were being denied the very freedom for which so many of the soldiers themselves were laying down their lives." Then the president recalled an incident that happened forty-three years ago. At a ceremony to award the Distinguished Service Cross to Kazuo Masuda, who had been killed in action and whose family had been interned, a young actor paid tribute to the slain Nisei soldier. "The name of that young actor," remarked the president, who had been having trouble saying the Japanese names, "—I hope I pronounce this right—was Ronald Reagan." The time had come, the president acknowledged, to end "a sad chapter in American history."[4]

Asian Americans have begun to claim their time not only before the 7
commission on redress and reparations but elsewhere as well, in the novels of Maxine Hong Kingston and Milton Murayama, the plays of Frank Chin and Philip Gotanda, the scholarly writings of Sucheng Chan and Elaine Kim, the films of Steve Okazaki and Wa Wang, and the music of Hiroshima and Fred Houn. Others, too, have been breaking silences. Seventy-five-year-old Tomo Shoji, for example, had led a private life, but in 1981 she enrolled in an acting course because she wanted to try something frivolous and to take her mind off her husband's illness. In the beginning, Tomo was hesitant, awkward on the stage. "Be yourself," her teacher urged. Then suddenly she felt something surge through her, springing from deep within, and she began to tell funny and also sad stories about her life. Now Tomo tours the West Coast, a wonderful wordsmith giving one-woman shows to packed audiences of young Asian Americans. "Have we really told our children all we have gone through?" she asks. Telling one of her stories, Tomo recounts: "My parents came from Japan and I was born in a lumber camp. One day, at school, my class was going on a day trip to a show, and I was pulled aside and told I would have to stay behind. All the white kids went." Tomo shares stories about her husband: "When I first met him, I thought, 'wow.' Oh, he was so macho! And he wanted his wife to be a good, submissive wife. But then he married me." Theirs had been at times a stormy marriage. "Culturally we were different because he was Issei and I was American, and we used to argue a lot. Well, one day in 1942 right after World War II had started he came home and told me we had to go to an internment camp. 'I'm not going to one because I'm an American citizen,' I said to him. 'You have to go to camp, but not me.' Well, you know what, that was one time my husband was right!" Tomo remembers the camp: "We were housed in barracks, and we had no privacy. My husband and I had to share a room

[4]"Text of Reagan's Remarks," reprinted in *Pacific Citizen*, August 19–26, 1988, p. 5; *San Francisco Chronicle*, August 5 and 11, 1988.

with another couple. So we hanged a blanket in the middle of the room as a partition. But you could hear everything from the other side. Well, one night, while we were in bed, my husband and I got into an argument, and I dumped him out of the bed. The other couple thought we were making violent love." As she stands on the stage and talks stories excitedly, Tomo cannot be contained: "We got such good, fantastic stories to tell. All our stories are different."[5]

Today, young Asian Americans want to listen to these stories—to 8
shatter images of themselves and their ancestors as "strangers" and to understand who they are as Asian Americans. "What don't you know?" their elders ask. Their question seems to have a peculiar frame: it points to the blank areas of collective memory. And the young people reply that they want "to figure out how the invisible world the emigrants built around [their] childhoods fit in solid America." They want to know more about their "no name" Asian ancestors. They want to decipher the signs of the Asian presence here and there across the landscape of America—railroad tracks over high mountains, fields of cane virtually carpeting entire islands, and verdant agricultural lands.

> Deserts to farmlands 9
> Japanese-American
> Page in history.[6]

They want to know what is their history and "what is the movies." 10
They want to trace the origins of terms applied to them. "Why are we called 'Oriental'?" they question, resenting the appellation that has identified Asians as exotic, mysterious, strange, and foreign. "The word 'orient' simply means 'east.' So why are Europeans 'West' and why are Asians 'East'? Why did empire-minded Englishmen in the sixteenth century determine that Asia was 'east' of London? Who decided what names would be given to the different regions and peoples of the world? Why does 'American' usually mean 'white'?" Weary of Eurocentric history, young Asian Americans want their Asian ancestral lives in America chronicled, "given the name of a place." They have earned the right to belong to specific places like Washington, California, Hawaii, Puunene, Promontory Point, North Adams, Manzanar, Doyers Street. "And today, after 125 years of our life here," one of them insists, "I do not want just a home that time allowed me to have." Seeking to lay claim to America, they realize they can no longer be indifferent to what happened in history no longer embarrassed by the hardships and humiliations experienced by their grandparents and parents.

[5]Tomo Shoji, "Born Too Soon . . . It's Never Too Late: Growing Up Nisei in Early Washington," presentations at the University of California, Berkeley, September 19, 1987, and the Ohana Cultural Center, Oakland, California, March 4, 1988.
[6]Kingston, Maxine Hong, *The Woman Warrior*, p. 6; poem in Kazuo Ito, *Issei: A History of Japanese Immigrants in North America* (Seattle, 1973), p. 493.

My heart, once bent and cracked, once 11
ashamed of your China ways.
Ma, hear me now, tell me your story
again and again.[7]

As they listen to the stories and become members of a "community 12
of memory," they are recovering roots deep within this country and the homelands of their ancestors. Sometimes the journey leads them to discover rich and interesting things about themselves. Alfred Wong, for example, had been told repeatedly for years by his father, "Remember your Chinese name. Remember your village in Toisha. Remember you are Chinese. Remember all this and you will have a home." One reason why it was so important for the Chinese immigrants to remember was that they never felt sure of their status in America. "Unlike German and Scottish immigrants, the Chinese immigrants never felt comfortable here," Wong explained. "So they had a special need to know there was a place, a home for them somewhere."[8]

But Wong had a particular reason to remember. His father had 13
married by mutual agreement two women on the same day in China and had come to America as a merchant in the 1920s. Later he brought over one of his wives. But she had to enter as a "paper wife," for he had given the immigration authorities the name of the wife he had left behind. Born here in 1938, Wong grew up knowing about his father's other wife and the other half of the family in China; his parents constantly talked about them and regularly sent money home to Quangdong. For years the "family plan" had been for him to see China someday. In 1984 he traveled to his father's homeland, and there in the family home—the very house his father had left decades earlier—Alfred Wong was welcomed by his *Chung Gwok Ma* ("China Mama"). "You look just like I had imagined you would look," she remarked. On the walls of the house, he saw hundreds of photographs—of himself as well as sisters, nieces, nephews, and his own daughter—that had been placed there over the years. He suddenly realized how much he had always belonged there, and had a warm connectedness. "It's like you were told there was this box and there was a beautiful diamond in it," Wong said. "But for years and years you couldn't open the box. Then finally you got a chance to open the box and it was as wonderful as you had imagined it would be."[9]

[7]Kingston, *The Woman Warrior,* p. 6; Robert Kwan, "Asian v. Oriental: A difference that Counts," *Pacific Citizen*, April 25, 1980; Sir James Augustus Henry Murry (ed.), *The Oxford English Dictionary* (Oxford, 1933), vol. 7, p. 200; Aminur Rahim, "Is Oriental an Occident?" in *The Asiandian*, vol. 5, no. 1, April 1983, p. 20; Shawn Wong, *Homebase* (New York, 1979), p. 111; Nellie Wong, "From a Heart of Rice Straw," in Nellie Wong, *Dreams in Harrison Railroad Park* (Berkeley, 1977), p. 41.

[8]Robert Bellah et al., *Habits of the Heart: Individualism and Commitment in American Life* (Berkeley, 1985), p. 153; Alfred Wong, interviewed by Carol Takaki, April 6 and 13, 1988.

[9]Ibid.

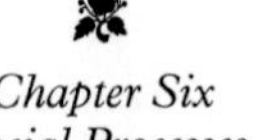

Mine is a different yet similar story. My father, Toshio Takaki, died in 1945, when I was only five years old; my mother married Koon Keu Young about a year later, and I grew up knowing very little about my father. Many years later, in 1968, after my parents had moved to Los Angeles, my mother passed away and I had to clear out her room after the funeral. In one of her dresser drawers, I found an old photograph of my father as a teenager: it was his immigration photograph. I noticed some Japanese writing on the back. Later a friend translated: "This is Toshio Takaki, registered as an emigrant in Mifune, Kumamoto Prefecture, 1918." I wondered how young Toshio managed to come to the United States. Why did he go to Hawaii? Did he go alone? What dreams burned within the young boy? But a huge silence stood before me, and I could only speculate that he must have come alone and entered as a student, since the 1908 Gentlemen's Agreement had prohibited the immigration of Japanese laborers. In Hawaii, he met and married my mother, Catherine Okawa, a Nisei. I had no Takaki relatives in Hawaii, I thought. 14

Ten years later, while on a sabbatical in Hawaii, I was "talking story" with my uncle Richard Okawa. I was telling him about the book I was then writing—*Iron Cages,* a study of race and culture in America. Suddenly his eyes lit up as he exclaimed: "Hey, why you no go write a book about us, huh? About the Japanese in Hawaii. After all, your grandparents came here as plantation workers and your mother and all your aunts and uncles were born on the plantation." Smiling, I replied: "Why not?" I went on to write a history of the plantation laborers. The book was published in 1983, and I was featured on television news and educational programs in Hawaii. One of the programs was aired in January 1985; a plantation laborer on the Puunene Plantation, Maui, was watching the discussion on television when he exclaimed to his wife: "Hey, that's my cousin, Ronald!" "No joke with me," she said, and he replied: "No, for real, for real." 15

A few months later, in July, I happened to visit Maui to give a lecture on the plantation experience. While standing in the auditorium shortly before my presentation, I noticed two Japanese men approaching me. One of them draped a red carnation lei around my shoulders and smiled: "You remember me, don't you?" I had never seen this man before and was confused. Then he said again, "You remember me?" After he asked for the third time, he pulled a family photograph from a plastic shopping bag. I saw among the people in the picture my father as a young man, and burst out excitedly: "Oh, you're a Takaki!" He replied: "I'm your cousin, Minoru. I saw you on television last January and when I found out you were going to come here I wanted to see you again. You were five years old when I last saw you. I was in the army on my way to Japan and I came by your house in Palolo Valley. But I guess you don't remember. I've been wondering what happened to you for forty years." Our families had lost contact with each other because of the war, the isolation of the plantation located on another island, my father's death, and my mother's remarriage. Minoru introduced me to his 16 brother Susumu and his son, Leighton, who works on the Puunene Plantation and represents the fourth generation of Takaki plantation workers. Afterward they took me to the Puunene Plantation, showing me McGerrow Camp, where my branch of the Takaki family had lived, and filling me with stories about the old days. "You also have two cousins, Jeanette and Lillian in Honolulu," Minoru said, "and a big Takaki family in Japan."

A year later I visited my Takaki family in Japan. On the day I arrived, my cousin Nobuo showed me a box of old photographs that had been kept for decades in an upstairs closet. "We don't know who this baby is," he said, pointing to a picture of a baby boy. "That's me!" I exclaimed in disbelief. The box contained many photographs of my father, mother, sister, and me. My father had been sending pictures to the family in Kumamoto. I felt a part of me had been there all along and I had in a sense come home. Nobuo's wife Keiko, told me that I was *Kumamoto kenjin*—"one of the people of Kumamoto." During my visit, I was taken to the farm where my father was born. We drove up a narrow winding road past waterfalls and streams, tea farms, and rice paddies, to a village nestled high in the mountains. The scene reminded me of old Zen paintings of Japanese landscapes and evoked memories of my mother telling me the story of Momotaro. Toshino Watanabe, an old woman in her eighties, gave me a family portrait that her sister had sent in 1915, there they were in fading sepia—my uncle Teizo, grandfather Santaro, aunt Yukino, cousin Tsutako, uncle Nobuyoshi, and father Toshio, just fourteen years old—in McGerrow Camp on the Puunene Plantation. 17

The stories of Alfred Wong and myself branch from the late history of Asian Americans and America itself—from William Hooper and Aaron Palmer, westward expansion, the economic development of California and Hawaii, the Chinese Exclusion Act, the Gentlemen's Agreement. The history of America is essentially the story of immigrants, and many of them, coming from a "different shore" than their European brethren, had sailed east to this new world. After she had traveled across the vast Pacific Ocean and settled here, a woman captured the vision of the immigrants from Asia in haiku's seventeen syllables: 18

> All the dreams of youth
> Shipped in emigration boats
> To reach this far shore.[10]

In America, Asian immigrants and their offspring have been actors in history—the first Chinese working on the plantations of Hawaii and in the gold fields of California, the early Japanese immigrants transforming the brown San Joaquin Valley into verdant farmlands, the Korean immigrants struggling to free their homeland from Japanese colonialism, the Filipino farm workers and busboys seeking the America in their hearts, the Asian-Indian immigrants picking fruit and erecting Sikh temples in

[10]Poem by Shigeko, in Kazuo Ito, *Issei,* p. 40.

the West, the American-born Asians like Jean Park and Jade Snow Wong and Monica Sone trying to find an identity for themselves as Asian Americans, the second-wave Asian immigrants bringing their skills and creating new communities as well as revitalizing old communities with culture and enterprise, and the refugees from the war-torn countries of Southeast Asia trying to put their shattered lives together and becoming our newest Asian Americans. Their dreams and hopes unfurled here before the wind, all of them—from the first Chinese miners sailing through the Golden Gate to the last Vietnamese boat people flying into Los Angeles International Airport—have been making history in America. And they have been telling us about it all along.

COMPREHENSION

1. Why does Takaki think it important for younger Asian Americans to know about their culture?
2. Why were the adults reluctant to talk about their experiences in the internment camps?
3. What does the writer mean when he says, "Asian Americans have begun to claim their time"?

RHETORIC

1. Takaki uses poetry and dialogue in his essay. How do these devices help to advance his point of view?
2. What is the main idea of the essay? Where in the writing does it appear?
3. What use does Takaki make of historical facts and details? Cite some examples of these in the essay, and discuss what effect they have on the theme?
4. How does Takaki organize his essay? Trace his ideas through the first five paragraphs. What transitions does he use to shift focus? What is the reasoning behind this strategy?
5. Much of the information Takaki provides comes from individuals. What makes this a powerful technique? Cite examples from the essay to support your response.
6. Examine the conclusion. Why does Takaki crowd so much information into it? How does it work to reinforce Takaki's thesis?

WRITING

1. Photographs play an important role in Takaki's essay as reminders of the past. Find an old family photograph (preferably one taken before your birth), and describe it in detail, including the people in it, their relation to you, the setting, the year it was taken, and its significance to you and your family. Use details and sensory images.
2. Write a research paper about one of the major historical events mentioned in Takaki's essay (the internment of Asian Americans during WWII or the building of railroads across the United States.)

MARY GORDON Mary Gordon (1949–) was born in Long Island, New York. The daughter of a writer and a legal secretary, she was educated at Barnard College and Syracuse University. Gordon has taught English and is known for both her novels and short stories, which often contain the Catholic themes of devotion, goodness, and redemption. Her major novels are *Final Payments* (1978), *The Company of Women* (1981), and *The Other Side* (1989). Gordon has been a contributor to *Mademoiselle, Harper's,* and *Ms.* In this piece she describes a trip to Ellis Island in which she reestablished bonds with her heritage.

MARY GORDON

More Than Just a Shrine

Paying Homage to the Ghosts of Ellis Island

I once sat in a hotel in Bloomsbury trying to have breakfast alone. A Russian with a habit of compulsively licking his lips asked if he could join me. I was afraid to say no; I thought it might be bad for détente. He explained to me that he was a linguist and that he always liked to talk to Americans to see if he could make any connection between their speech and their ethnic background. When I told him about my mixed ancestry—my mother is Irish and Italian, my father was a Lithuanian Jew—he began jumping up and down in his seat, rubbing his hands together and licking his lips even more frantically. 1

"Ah," he said, "so you are really somebody who comes from what is called the boiling pot of America." Yes, I told him; yes, I was; but I quickly rose to leave. I thought it would be too hard to explain to him the relation of the boiling potters to the main course, and I wanted to get to the British Museum. I told him that the only thing I could think of that united people whose backgrounds, histories, and points of view were utterly diverse was that their people had landed at a place called Ellis Island. 2

I didn't tell him that Ellis Island was the only American landmark I'd ever visited. How could I describe to him the estrangement I'd always felt from the kind of traveler who visits shrines to America's past greatness, those rebuilt forts with muskets behind glass, sabers mounted on the walls and gift shops selling maple syrup candy in the shape of Indian headdresses, those reconstructed villages with tables set for fifty and the Paul Revere silver gleaming. All that Americana—Plymouth Rock, Gettysburg, Mount Vernon, Valley Forge—it all inhabits for me a zone of blurred abstraction with far less hold on my imagination than the Bastille or Hampton Court. I suppose I've always known that my uninterest in it contains a large component of the 3

willed: I am American, and those places purport to be my history. But they are not mine.

Ellis Island is, though; it's the one place I can be sure my people are 4
connected to. And so I made a journey there to find my history like any Rotarian traveling in his Winnebago to Antietam to find his. I had become part of that humbling democracy of people looking in some site for a past that has grown unreal. The monument I traveled to was not, however, a tribute to some old glory. The minute I set foot upon the island I could feel all that it stood for: insecurity, obedience, anxiety, dehumanization, the terrible and careful deference of the displaced. I hadn't traveled to the Battery and boarded a ferry across from the Statue of Liberty to raise flags or breathe a richer, more triumphant air. I wanted to do homage to the ghosts.

I felt them everywhere, from the moment I disembarked I saw the 5
building with its high-minded brick, its hopeful little land, its ornamental cornices. The place was derelict when I arrived; it had not functioned for more than thirty years—almost as long as the time it had operated at full capacity as a major immigration center. I was surprised to learn what a small part of history Ellis Island had occupied. The main building was constructed in 1892, then rebuilt between 1898 and 1900 after a fire. Most of the immigrants who arrived during the latter half of the nineteenth century, mainly northern and western Europeans, landed not at Ellis Island but on the western tip of the Battery, at Castle Garden which had opened as a receiving center for immigrants in 1855.

By the 1880s, the facilities at Castle Garden had grown scandalous- 6
ly inadequate. Officials looked for an island on which to build a new immigration center, because they thought that on an island immigrants could be more easily protected from swindlers and quickly transported to railroad terminals in New Jersey. Bedloe's Island was considered, but New Yorkers were aghast at the idea of a "Babel" ruining their beautiful new treasure, "Liberty Enlightening the World." The statue's sculptor, Frédéric-Auguste Bartholdi, reacted to the prospect of immigrants landing near his masterpiece in horror; he called it a "monstrous plan." So much for Emma Lazarus.

Ellis Island was finally chosen because the citizens of New Jersey 7
petitioned the federal government to remove from the island an old naval powder magazine that they thought dangerously close to the Jersey shore. The explosives were removed; no one wanted the island for anything. It was the perfect place to build an immigration center.

I thought about the island's history as I walked into the building and 8
made my way to the room that was the center in my imagination of the Ellis Island experience: the Great Hall. It had been made real for me in the stark, accusing photographs of Louis Hine and others, who took those pictures to make a point. It was in the Great Hall that everyone had waited—waiting, always, the great vocation of the dispossessed. The room was empty, except for me and a handful of other visitors and

the park ranger who showed us around. I felt myself grow insignificant in that room, with its huge semicircular windows, its air, even in dereliction, of solid and official probity.

I walked in the deathlike expansiveness of the room's disuse and tried to think of what it might have been like, filled and swarming. More than sixteen million immigrants came through that room; approximately 250,000 were rejected. Not really a large proportion, but the implications for the rejected were dreadful. For some, there was nothing to go back to, or there was certain death; for others, who left as adventurers, to return would be to adopt in local memory the fool's role, and the failure's. No wonder that the island's history includes reports of three thousand suicides.

Sometimes immigrants could pass through Ellis Island in mere 10
hours, though for some the process took days. The particulars of the experience in the Great Hall were often influenced by the political events and attitudes on the mainland. In the 1890s and the first years of the new century, when cheap labor was needed, the newly built receiving center took in its immigrants with comparatively little question. But as the century progressed, the economy worsened, eugenics became both scientifically respectable and popular, and World War I made American xenophobia seem rooted in fact.

Immigration acts were passed; newcomers had to prove, besides 11
moral correctness and financial solvency, their ability to read. Quota laws came into effect, limiting the number of immigrants from southern and eastern Europe to less than 14 percent of the total quota. Intelligence tests were biased against all non-English-speaking persons, and medical examinations became increasingly strict, until the machinery of immigration nearly collapsed under its own weight. The Second Quota Law of 1924 provided that all immigrants be inspected and issued visas at American consular offices in Europe, rendering the center almost obsolete.

On the day of my visit, my mind fastened upon the medical inspec- 12
tions, which had always seemed to me most emblematic of the ignominy and terror the immigrants endured. The medical inspectors, sometimes dressed in uniforms like soldiers, were particularly obsessed with a disease of the eyes called trachoma, which they checked for by flipping back the immigrants' top eyelids with a hook used for buttoning gloves—a method that sometimes resulted in the transmission of the disease to healthy people. Mothers feared that if their children cried too much, their red eyes would be mistaken for a symptom of the disease and the whole family would be sent home. Those immigrants suspected of some physical disability had initials chalked on their coats. I remembered the photographs I'd seen of people standing, dumbstruck and innocent as cattle, with their manifest numbers hung around their necks and initials marked in chalk upon their coats: "E" for eye trouble, "K" for hernia, "L" for lameness, "X" for mental defects, "H" for heart disease.

I thought of my grandparents as I stood in the room: my seventeen-year-old grandmother, coming alone from Ireland in 1896, vouched for by a stranger who had found her a place as a domestic servant to some Irish who had done well. I tried to imagine the assault it all must have been for her; I've been to her hometown, a collection of farms with a main street—smaller than the athletic field of my local public school. She must have watched the New York skyline as the first- and second-class passengers were whisked off the gangplank with the most cursory of inspections while she was made to board a ferry to the new immigration center. 13

What could she have made of it—this buff-painted wooden structure with its towers and its blue slate roof, a place *Harper's Weekly* described as "a latter-day watering place hotel"? It would have been the first time she had heard people speaking something other than English. She would have mingled with people carrying baskets on their heads and eating foods unlike any she had ever seen—dark-eyed people, like the Sicilian she would marry ten years later, who came over with his family at thirteen, the man of the family, responsible even then for his mother and sister. I don't know what they thought, my grandparents, for they were not expansive people, nor romantic; they didn't like to think of what they called "the hard times," and their trip across the ocean was the single adventurous act of lives devoted after landing to security, respectability, and fitting in. 14

What is the potency of Ellis Island for someone like me—an American, obviously, but one who has always felt that the country really belonged to the early settlers, that, as J. F. Powers wrote in *Morte D'Urban,* it had been "handed down to them by the Pilgrims, George Washington and others, and that they were taking a risk in letting you live in it." I have never been the victim of overt discrimination; nothing I have wanted has been denied me because of the accidents of blood. But I suppose it is part of being an American to be engaged in a somewhat tiresome but always self-absorbing process of national definition. And in this process, I have found in traveling to Ellis Island an important piece of evidence that could remind me I was right to feel my differentness. Something had happened to my people on that island, a result of the eternal wrongheadedness of American protectionism and the predictabilities of simple greed. I came to the island, too, so I could tell the ghosts that I was one of them, and that I honored them—their stoicism, and their innocence, the fear that turned them inward, and their pride. I wanted to tell them that I liked them better than I did the Americans who made them pass through the Great Hall and stole their names and chalked their weaknesses in public on their clothing. And to tell the ghosts what I have always thought: that American history was a very classy party that was not much fun until they arrived, brought the good food, turned up the music, and taught everyone to dance. 15

COMPREHENSION

1. Why does the writer visit Ellis Island?
2. How were the new arrivals treated on the island?
3. What effect does the visit have on the writer? Does she accomplish her goal?

RHETORIC

1. What purpose is served by the first two paragraphs in the essay? Could the essay have begun with the third paragraph without losing any power? Justify your response.
2. What is Gordon's thesis? Where is it contained?
3. Give a brief sketch of Ellis Island in your own words. Why is this information important to the essay?
4. What is Gordon's tone in paragraph 6? How does it fit in with the rest of the essay?
5. Explain Gordon's choice of title. How appropriate is it?
6. Examine Gordon's use of language in her essay. Are there any particularly strong images or details? Cite them, and explain why they are evocative.

WRITING

1. Write a research paper on the history of Ellis Island. If possible, conduct an interview with an elderly relative or neighbor who came through the island as a child, and relate his or her experiences.
2. Write a narrative essay in which you pretend to be an immigrant newly arrived on Ellis Island. What are your impressions of America and its people? How would you respond to the procedures Gordon depicts in her essay? Use sensory details to evoke a sense of place.
3. Gordon writes: "But I suppose it is part of being an American to be engaged in a somewhat tiresome but always self-absorbing process of national definition." Write an essay in which you analyze the meaning and validity of this statement.

DORIS LESSING Doris Lessing (1919–), a major British novelist, was born in Kermanshah, Iran, of English parents. She moved at an early age with her parents to a large farm in Southern Rhodesia. At the age of 18, she went to Salisbury, entering quickly into the artistic and political life there. Lessing left Africa for London in 1949, and in 1950 she published her first novel, *The Grass Is Singing.* Her later novels include *The Golden Notebook* (1962), *Briefing for a Descent into Hell* (1971), and the four-volume *Canopus in Argos: Archives* (1981). Lessing's short stories, many of the best drawn from her African experience, have been collected in five volumes. In "Being Prohibited," taken from her essay collection *A Small Personal Voice* (1975), Lessing plots over a period of time her several confrontations with apartheid.

DORIS LESSING

Being Prohibited

The border is Mafeking, a little dorp with nothing interesting about it but its name. The train waits (or used to wait) interminably on the empty tracks, while immigration and customs officials made their leisurely way through the coaches, and pale gritty dust settled over everything. Looking out, one saw the long stretch of windows, with the two, three, or four white faces at each; then at the extreme end, the single coach for "natives" packed tight with black humans; and, in between, two or three Indians or Coloured people on sufferance in the European coaches. 1

Outside, on the scintillating dust by the tracks, a crowd of ragged black children begged for *bonsellas.* One threw sandwich crusts or bits of spoiled fruit and watched them dive and fight to retrieve them from the dirt. 2

I was sixteen. I was not, as one says, politically conscious; nor did I know the score. I knew no more, in fact, than on which side my bread was buttered. But I already felt uneasy about being a member of the Herrenvolk. When the immigration official reached me, I had written on the form; *Nationality,* British, *Race,* European; and it was the first time in my life I had had to claim myself as a member of one race and disown the others. I remember distinctly that I had to suppress an impulse opposite *Race:* Human. Of course I *was* very young. 3

The immigration man had the sarcastic surliness which characterises the Afrikaans official, and he looked suspiciously at my form for a long time before saying that I was in the wrong part of the train. I did not understand him. (I forgot to mention that where the form asked, Where were you born?, I had written, Persia.) 4

"Asiatics," said he, "have to go to the back of the train; and anyway you are prohibited from entry unless you have documents proving you conform to the immigration quota for Asians." 5

"But," I said, "I am not an Asiatic." 6

The compartment had five other females in it; skirts were visibly being drawn aside. To prove my bona fides I should, of course, have exclaimed with outraged indignation at any such idea. 7

"You were born in Persia?" 8

"Yes." 9

"Then you are an Asiatic. You know the penalties for filling in the form wrongly?" 10

This particular little imbroglio involved my being taken off the train, escorted to an office, and kept under watch while they telephoned Pretoria for a ruling. 11

When next I entered the Union it was 1939. Sophistication had set in in the interval, and it took me no more than five minutes to persuade the official that one could be born in a country without being its citizen. The next two times there was no trouble at all, although my political views had in the meantime become nothing less than inflammatory: in a word, I had learned to disapprove of the colour bar. 12

This time, two weeks ago, what happened was as follows: one gets off the plane and sits for about fifteen minutes in a waiting room while they check the plane list with a list, or lists, of their own. They called my name first, and took me to an office which had two tables in it. At one sat a young man being pleasant to the genuine South African citizens. At the one where they made me sit was a man I could have sworn I had seen before. He proceeded to go through my form item by item, as follows: "You *say,* Mrs. Lessing, that, etc. . . ." From time to time he let out a disbelieving laugh and exchanged ironical looks with a fellow official who was standing by. Sure enough, when he reached that point on my form when he had to say: "You *claim* that you are British; you *say* you were born in Persia," I merely said *"Yes,"* and sat still while he gave me a long, exasperated stare. Then he let out an angry exclamation in Afrikaans and went next door to telephone Pretoria. Ten minutes later I was informed I must leave at once. A plane was waiting and I must enter it immediately. 13

I did so with dignity. Since then I have been unable to make up my mind whether I should have made a scene or not. I never have believed in the efficacy of dignity. 14

On the plane I wanted to sit near the window but was made to sit by myself and away from the window. I regretted infinitely that I had no accomplices hidden in the long grass by the airstrip, but, alas, I had not thought of it beforehand. 15

It was some time before it came home to me what an honour had been paid me. But now I am uneasy about the whole thing: suppose that I owe these attentions, not to my political views, but to the accident of my birthplace? 16

COMPREHENSION

1. Trace the sequence of conflicts that the author has with South African apartheid. How does her attitude shift with each confrontation? In what way does the conflict come full circle?
2. What do you learn about the author's personality and her beliefs? Cite evidence from the narrative to support your response.

RHETORIC

1. What would you say is the thesis of Lessing's essay? Is it apparent in the narrative?

2. Analyze the imagery in the first paragraph of the essay. What mood or impression is created?
3. Trace Lessing's development of conflict in this narrative. How many episodes are there? How does the author handle the matter of time? Why does she shift tenses from present, to past, to present?
4. Lessing is especially effective in using dialogue to reveal character. Cite examples of this method, and analyze the results.
5. Lessing uses several words drawn from South African dialect: *dorp* (paragraph 1); *Herrenvolk* (paragraph 3); and *Afrikaans* (paragraph 4). Define each word. What do such terms contribute to the tone of the essay?
6. Lessing concludes her narrative with a question. How effective is that device?

WRITING

1. Write a research paper examining the current state of apartheid in South Africa. Use quotes from the Lessing essay for purposes of comparison. What changes, if any, have occurred since the time of her essay?
2. In an analytical essay, compare South Africa's apartheid policies with similar policies in recent U.S. history. Some research may be necessary.
3. Write a personal narrative describing an experience similar to Lessing's where you were "prohibited" because of your nationality, color, sex, or economic situation.

BRUCE CATTON Bruce Catton (1899–1978) was born in Petosky, Michigan. After serving in the Navy during World War I, he attended Oberlin College but left in his junior year to pursue a career in journalism. From 1942 to 1952, Catton served in the government, first on the War Production Board and later in the departments of Commerce and the Interior. He left government to devote himself to literary work as a columnist for the *Nation* and a historian of the Civil War. His many works include *A Stillness at Appomattox* (1953), which won the 1954 Pulitzer Prize; *Mr. Lincoln's Army* (1951); *The Centennial History of the Civil War* (1961–1965); and *Prefaces to History.* In this selection, Catton presents vivid portraits of two well-known but little-understood figures from American history.

BRUCE CATTON

Grant and Lee

A Study in Contrasts

When Ulysses S. Grant and Robert E. Lee met in the parlor of a modest house at Appomattox Court House, Virginia, on April 9, 1865, to 1 work out the terms for the surrender of Lee's Army of Northern Virginia, a great chapter in American life came to a close, and a great new chapter began.

These men were bringing the Civil War to its virtual finish. To be sure, other armies had yet to surrender, and for a few days the fugitive Confederate government would struggle desperately and vainly, trying to find some way to go on living now that its chief support was gone. But in effect it was all over when Grant and Lee signed the papers. And the little room where they wrote out the terms was the scene of one of the poignant, dramatic contrasts in American history.

They were two strong men, these oddly different generals, and they 3
represented the strengths of two conflicting currents that, through them, had come into final collision.

Back of Robert E. Lee was the notion that the old aristocratic con- 4
cept might somehow survive and be dominant in American life.

Lee was tidewater Virginia, and in his background were family, cul- 5
ture, and tradition . . . the age of chivalry transplanted to a New World which was making its own legends and its own myths. He embodied a way of life that had come down through the age of knighthood and the English country squire. America was a land that was beginning all over again, dedicated to nothing much more complicated than the rather hazy belief that all men had equal rights and should have an equal chance in the world. In such a land Lee stood for the feeling that it was somehow of advantage to human society to have a pronounced inequality in the social structure. There should be a leisure class, backed by ownership of land; in turn, society itself should be keyed to the land as the chief source of wealth and influence. It would bring forth (according to this ideal) a class of men with a strong sense of obligation to the community; men who lived not to gain advantage for themselves, but to meet the solemn obligations which had been laid on them by the very fact that they were privileged. From them the country would get its leadership; to them it could look for the higher values—of thought, of conduct, of personal deportment—to give it strength and virtue.

Lee embodied the noblest elements of this aristocratic ideal. 6
Through him, the landed nobility justified itself. For four years, the Southern states had fought a desperate war to uphold the ideals for which Lee stood. In the end, it almost seemed as if the Confederacy fought for Lee; as if he himself was the Confederacy . . . the best thing that the way of life for which the Confederacy stood could ever have to offer. He had passed into legend before Appomattox. Thousands of tired, underfed, poorly clothed Confederate soldiers, long since past the simple enthusiasm of the early days of the struggle, somehow considered Lee the symbol of everything for which they had been willing to die. But they could not quite put this feeling into words. If the Lost Cause, sanctified by so much heroism and so many deaths, had a living justification, its justification was General Lee.

Grant, the son of a tanner on the Western frontier, was everything 7
Lee was not. He had come up the hard way and embodied nothing in

particular except the eternal toughness and sinewy fiber of the men who grew up beyond the mountains. He was one of a body of men who owed reverence and obeisance to no one, who were self-reliant to a fault, who cared hardly anything for the past but who had a sharp eye for the future.

These frontier men were the precise opposites of the tidewater aristocrats. Back of them, in the great surge that had taken people over the Alleghenies and into the opening Western country, there was a deep, implicit dissatisfaction with a past that had settled into grooves. They stood for democracy, not from any reasoned conclusion about the proper ordering of human society, but simply because they had grown up in the middle of democracy and knew how it worked. Their society might have privileges, but they would be privileges each man had won for himself. Forms and patterns meant nothing. No man was born to anything, except perhaps to a chance to show how far he could rise. Life was competition. 8

Yet along with this feeling had come a deep sense of belonging to a national community. The Westerner who developed a farm, opened a shop, or set up in business as a trader, could hope to prosper only as his own community prospered—and his community ran from the Atlantic to the Pacific and from Canada down to Mexico. If the land was settled, with towns and highways and accessible markets, he could better himself. He saw his fate in terms of the nation's own destiny. As its horizons expanded, so did his. He had, in other words, an acute dollars-and-cents stake in the continued growth and development of his country. 9

And that, perhaps, is where the contrast between Grant and Lee becomes most striking. The Virginia aristocrat, inevitably, saw himself in relation to his own region. He lived in a static society which could endure almost anything except change. Instinctively, his first loyalty would go to the locality in which that society existed. He would fight to the limit of endurance to defend it, because in defending it he was defending everything that gave his own life its deepest meaning. 10

The Westerner, on the other hand, would fight with an equal tenacity for the broader concept of society. He fought so because everything he lived by was tied to growth, expansion, and a constantly widening horizon. What he lived by would survive or fall with the nation itself. He could not possibly stand by unmoved in the face of an attempt to destroy the Union. He would combat it with everything he had, because he could only see it as an effort to cut the ground out from under his feet. 11

So Grant and Lee were in complete contrast, representing two diametrically opposed elements in American life. Grant was the modern man emerging; beyond him, ready to come on the stage, was the great age of steel and machinery, of crowded cities and a restless burgeoning vitality. Lee might have ridden down from the old age of chivalry, lance in hand, silken banner fluttering over his head. Each man was the perfect champion of his cause, drawing both his strengths and his weaknesses from the people he led. 12

Yet it was not all contrast, after all. Different as they were—in background, in personality, in underlying aspiration—these two great soldiers had much in common. Under everything else, they were marvelous fighters. Furthermore, their fighting qualities were really very much alike. 13

Each man had, to begin with, the great virtue of utter tenacity and fidelity. Grant fought his way down the Mississippi Valley in spite of acute personal discouragement and profound military handicaps. Lee hung on in the trenches at Petersburg after hope itself had died. In each man there was an indomitable quality . . . the born fighter's refusal to give up as long as he can still remain on his feet and lift his two fists. 14

Daring and resourcefulness they had, too; the ability to think faster and move faster than the enemy. These were the qualities which gave Lee the dazzling campaigns of Second Manassas and Chancellorsville and won Vicksburg for Grant. 15

Lastly, and perhaps greatest of all, there was the ability, at the end, to turn quickly from war to peace once the fighting was over. Out of the way these two men behaved at Appomattox came the possibility of a peace of reconciliation. It was a possibility not wholly realized, in the years to come, but which did, in the end, help the two sections to become one nation again . . . after a war whose bitterness might have seemed to make such a reunion wholly impossible. No part of either man's life became him more than the part he played in their brief meeting in the McLean house at Appomattox. Their behavior there put all succeeding generations of Americans in their debt. Two great Americans, Grant and Lee—very different, yet under everything very much alike. Their encounter at Appomattox was one of the great moments of American history. 16

COMPREHENSION

1. What is the central purpose of Catton's study? Cite evidence to support your view. Who is his audience?
2. What is the primary appeal to readers of describing history through the study of individuals rather than through the recording of events? How does Catton's essay reflect this appeal?
3. According to Catton, what special qualities did Grant and Lee share, and what qualities set them apart?

RHETORIC

1. What role does the opening paragraph have in setting the tone for the essay? Is the tone typical of what you would expect of an essay describing military generals? Explain your view. How does the conclusion echo the introductory paragraph?
2. Note that the sentence, "Two great Americans, Grant and Lee—very different, yet under everything very much alike" (paragraph 16), has no verb.

What does this indicate about Catton's style? What other sentences contain atypical syntax? What is *their* contribution to the unique quality of the writing?

3. While this essay is about a historical era, there is a notable lack of specific facts—for example, dates, statistics, and events. What has Catton focused on instead?
4. What is the function of the one-sentence paragraph 3?
5. Paragraphs 9, 10, 12, and 13 begin with coordinating conjunctions. How do these transitional words give the paragraphs their special coherence? How would more typical introductory expressions, such as "in addition," "furthermore," or "moreover," have altered this coherence?
6. What strategy does Catton use in comparing and contrasting the two generals? Study paragraphs 5 through 16. Which are devoted to describing each man separately, and which include aspects of each man? What is the overall development of the comparisons?

WRITING

1. Does Lee's vision of society exist in the United States today? If not, why not? If so, where do you find this vision? Write a brief essay on this topic.
2. Select two well-known individuals in the same profession—for example, politics, entertainment, or sports. Make a list for each, enumerating the different aspects of their character, behavior, beliefs, and background. Using this list as an outline, devise an essay wherein you compare and contrast the two.
3. Apply, in a comparative essay, Catton's observation about "two diametrically opposed elements in American life" to the current national scene.

VACLAV HAVEL Vaclav Havel (1936–) is an internationally acclaimed Czech dramatist, dissident, and human rights activist. He began writing drama in the 1950s, and his plays are influenced strongly by the absurdist literature of Kafka, Beckett, and Ionesco. Jailed frequently for his activism, Havel was instrumental in the success of the 1989 reform movement in Czechoslovakia, and in 1990 he was elected to his nation's presidency. His major work includes his plays *The Garden Party* (1963) and *The Memorandum* (1965), along with a dazzling collection of prison correspondence to his wife, *Letters to Olga* (1984). In the following selection, delivered in 1990 to a joint meeting of the U.S. Congress, Havel offers his vision of the changing global political structure.

VACLAV HAVEL

The Revolution Has Just Begun

Twice in this century the world has been threatened by a catastrophe. 1

Twice this catastrophe was born in Europe, and twice you Americans, along with others, were called upon to save Europe, the whole world and yourselves. 2

In the meantime, the U.S. became the most powerful nation on earth, and it understood the responsibility that flowed from this. But something else was happening as well. The Soviet Union appeared, grew and transformed the enormous sacrifices of its people suffering under totalitarian rule into a strength that, after World War II, made it the second most powerful nation in the world. 3

Creating the Family of Men

All of this taught us to see the world in bipolar terms as two enormous forces—one a defender of freedom, the other a source of nightmares. Europe became the point of friction between these two powers, and thus it turned into a single enormous arsenal divided into two parts. In this process, one half of the arsenal became part of that nightmarish power, while the other, the free part, bordering on the ocean and having no wish to be driven into it, was compelled, together with you, to build a complicated security system to which we probably owe the fact that we still exist. 4

The totalitarian system in the Soviet Union and in most of its satellites is breaking down, and our nations are looking for a way to democracy and independence. 5

This, I am convinced, is a historically irreversible process and, as a result, Europe will begin again to seek its own identity without being compelled to be a divided armory any longer. Perhaps this will create the hope that sooner or later, your boys will no longer have to stand on guard for freedom in Europe or come to our rescue, because Europe will at last be able to stand guard over itself. 6

But that is still not the most important thing. The main thing is, it seems to me, that these revolutionary changes will enable us to escape from the rather antiquated straitjacket of this bipolar view of the world and to enter at last into an era of multipolarity in which all of us, large and small, former slaves and former masters, will be able to create what your great President Lincoln called "the family of men." 7

The Path of Pluralism

How can the U.S. help us today? My reply is as paradoxical as the whole of my life has been. You can help us most of all if you help the 8

Soviet Union on its irreversible but immensely complicated road to democracy. It is far more complicated than the road open to its former European satellites. You yourselves know best how to support as rapidly as possible the nonviolent evolution of this enormous multinational body politic toward democracy and autonomy for all its people. Therefore, it is not fitting for me to offer you any advice.

I can only say that the sooner, the more quickly and the more peacefully the Soviet Union begins to move along the road toward genuine political pluralism, respect for the rights of the nations to their own integrity and to a working—that is, a market—economy, the better it will be not just for Czechs and Slovaks but for the whole world. 9

And the sooner you yourselves will be able to reduce the burden of the military budget borne by the American people. To put it metaphorically, the millions you give to the East today will soon return to you in the form of billions in savings. American soldiers shouldn't have to be separated from their mothers just because Europe is incapable of being a guarantor of world peace, which it ought to be in order to make some amends, at least, for having given the world two world wars. 10

The Legacy of Oppression

As long as people are people, democracy, in the full sense of the word, will always be no more than an ideal. In this sense, you too are merely approaching democracy. But you have one great advantage: you have been approaching democracy uninterruptedly for more than 200 years, and your journey toward the horizon has never been disrupted by a totalitarian system. 11

The communist type of totalitarian system has left both our nations, Czechs and Slovaks, as it has all the nations of the Soviet Union and the other countries the Soviet Union subjugated in its time, a legacy of countless dead, an infinite spectrum of human suffering, profound economic decline and, above all, enormous human humiliation. It has brought us horrors that fortunately you have not known. 12

It has given us something positive, a special capacity to look from time to time somewhat further than someone who has not undergone this bitter experience. A person who cannot move and lead a somewhat normal life because he is pinned under a boulder has more time to think about his hopes than someone who is not trapped that way. 13

What I'm trying to say is this: we must all learn many things from you, from how to educate our offspring, how to elect our representatives, all the way to how to organize our economic life so that it will lead to prosperity and not to poverty. But it doesn't have to be merely assistance from the well educated, powerful and wealthy to someone who has nothing and therefore has nothing to offer in return. 14

We too can offer something to you: our experience and the knowledge that has come from it. The specific experience I'm talking about has given me one certainty: consciousness precedes being, and not the other way around, as the Marxists claim. For this reason, the salvation 15 of this human world lies nowhere else than in the human heart, in the human power to reflect, in human meekness and in human responsibility.

A New Way of Thinking

Without a global revolution in the sphere of human consciousness, nothing will change for the better in the sphere of our being as humans, and the catastrophe toward which this world is headed—be it ecological, social, demographic or a general breakdown of civilization—will be unavoidable. If we are no longer threatened by world war or by the danger that the absurd mountains of accumulated nuclear weapons might blow up the world, this does not mean that we have definitely won. We are still incapable of understanding that the only genuine backbone of all our actions, if they are to be moral, is responsibility. Responsibility to something higher than my family, my country, my company, my success—responsibility to the order of being where all our actions are indelibly recorded and where and only where they will be properly judged. 16

I think that you Americans should understand this way of thinking. When Thomas Jefferson wrote that "governments are instituted among men, deriving their just powers from the consent of the governed," it was a simple and important act of the human spirit. What gave meaning to that act, however, was the fact that the author backed it up with his life. It was not just his words, it was his deeds as well. 17

COMPREHENSION

1. Havel was directing this speech to a joint meeting of the U.S. Congress. How does he tailor his remarks to his primary audience? Are there other audiences that he seems to be conscious of? Explain.
2. Summarize the main concepts that Havel discusses in this selection. How does he define such ideas as *freedom, bipolarity, totalitarianism, political pluralism,* and *revolution?* What thesis holds these concepts together?
3. What does Havel mean when he writes that "consciousness precedes being" (paragraph 15)?

RHETORIC

1. What is Havel's purpose in quoting from Lincoln in paragraph 7 and Jefferson in paragraph 17? What is the author's stylistic debt to Jefferson? (Reread "The Declaration of Independence" in this section.)
2. How does Havel manipulate the pronouns *you, us,* and *we* to frame his remarks and convey his thesis?
3. Havel sets up several points of comparison and contrast. What are they, and how do these comparative elements help to unify the selection?

4. Does Havel argue from general or specific evidence, or from both? Explain your answer by referring to examples in this selection.
5. How does the author utilize the rhetorical modes of definition and causal analysis to advance his thesis?
6. Analyze the first two paragraphs and the last two paragraphs in this selection. What are the similarities and differences? How do they focus the selection and permit it to cohere?

WRITING

1. Write a brief essay explaining the power or force of Havel's speech. (The members of Congress, after hearing this speech, gave Havel a standing ovation.) What elements give the speech its intellectual and emotional impact?
2. Explain the influence of "The Declaration of Independence" on Havel's remarks. Compare and contrast the social and political visions deriving from these two documents.
3. In their speeches, both Havel and Martin Luther King Jr. have a "dream." In a comparative essay, analyze the nature of their respective dreams.
4. Write your own essay on contemporary world events entitled, "The Revolution Has Just Begun."

J. B. PRIESTLEY John Boynton Priestley (1894–1984), best-selling English novelist and popular dramatist, was also a prolific writer of essays, many of them involving social and political criticism. His work includes *The English Novel* (1927), *The Good Companions* (1929), *Time and the Conways* (1937), *An Inspector Calls* (1946), and *The English* (1973). This selection from *Essays of Five Decades* (1968) offers an astute analysis of contemporary political habits.

J. B. PRIESTLEY

Wrong Ism

There are three isms that we ought to consider very carefully—regionalism, nationalism, internationalism. Of these three the one there is most fuss about, the one that starts men shouting and marching and shooting, the one that seems to have all the depth and thrust and fire, is of course nationalism. Nine people out of ten, I fancy, would say that of this trio it is the one that really counts, the big boss. Regionalism and internationalism, they would add, are comparatively small, shadowy, rather cranky. And I believe all this to be quite wrong. Like many an- 1 other big boss, nationalism is largely bogus. It is like a bunch of flowers made of plastics.

The real flowers belong to regionalism. The mass of people everywhere may never have used the term. They are probably regionalists without knowing it. Because they have been brought up in a certain part of the world, they have formed perhaps quite unconsciously a deep attachment to its landscape and speech, its traditional customs, its food and drink, its songs and jokes. (There are of course always the rebels, often intellectuals and writers, but they are not the mass of people.) They are rooted in their region. Indeed, without this attachment a man can have no roots.

So much of people's lives, from earliest childhood onwards, is 3
deeply intertwined with the common life of the region, they cannot help feeling strongly about it. A threat to it is a knife pointing at the heart. How can life ever be the same if bullying strangers come to change everything? The form and colour, the very taste and smell of dear familiar things will be different, alien, life-destroying. It would be better to die fighting. And it is precisely this, the nourishing life of the region, for which common men have so often fought and died.

This attachment to the region exists on a level far deeper than that 4
of any political hocus-pocus. When a man says "my country" with real feeling, he is thinking about his region, all that has made up his life, and not about that political entity, the nation. There can be some confusion here simply because some countries are so small—and ours is one of them—and so old, again like ours, that much of what is national is also regional. Down the centuries, the nation, itself, so comparatively small, has been able to attach to itself the feeling really created by the region. (Even so there is something left over, as most people in Yorkshire or Devon, for example, would tell you.) This probably explains the fervent patriotism developed early in small countries. The English were announcing that they were English in the Middle Ages, before nationalism had arrived elsewhere.

If we deduct from nationalism all that it has borrowed or stolen 5
from regionalism, what remains is mostly rubbish. The nation, as distinct from the region, is largely the creation of power-men and political manipulators. Almost all nationalist movements are led by ambitious frustrated men determined to hold office. I am not blaming them. I would do the same if I were in their place and wanted power so badly. But nearly always they make use of the rich warm regional feeling, the emotional dynamo of the movement, while being almost untouched by it themselves. This is because they are not as a rule deeply loyal to any region themselves. Ambition and a love of power can eat like acid into the tissues of regional loyalty. It is hard, if not impossible, to retain a natural piety and yet be for ever playing both ends against the middle.

Being itself a power structure, devised by men of power, the nation 6
tends to think and act in terms of power. What would benefit the real life of the region, where men, women and children actually live, is soon sacrificed for the power and prestige of the nation. (And the personal

vanity of presidents and ministers themselves, which historians too often disregard.) Among the new nations of our time innumerable peasants and labourers must have found themselves being cut down from five square meals a week to three in order to provide unnecessary airlines, military forces that can only be used against them and nobody else, great conference halls and official yachts and the rest. The last traces of imperialism and colonialism may have to be removed from Asia and Africa, where men can no longer endure being condemned to a permanent inferiority by the colour of their skins; but even so, the modern world, the real world of our time, does not want and would be far better without more and more nations, busy creating for themselves the very paraphernalia that western Europe is now trying to abolish. You are compelled to answer more questions when trying to spend half a day in Cambodia than you are now travelling from the Hook of Holland to Syracuse.

This brings me to internationalism. I dislike this term, which I used only to complete the isms. It suggests financiers and dubious promoters living nowhere but in luxury hotels; a shallow world of entrepreneurs and impresarios. (Was it Sacha Guitry who said that impresarios were men who spoke many languages but all with a foreign accent?) The internationalism I have in mind here is best described as world civilisation. It is life considered on a global scale. Most of our communications and transport already exist on this high wide level. So do many other things from medicine to meteorology. Our astronomers and physicists (except where they have allowed themselves to be hush-hushed) work here. The UN special agencies, about which we hear far too little, have contributed more and more to this world civilisation. All the arts, when they are arts and not chunks of nationalist propaganda, naturally take their place in it. And it grows, widens, deepens, in spite of the fact that for every dollar, ruble, pound or franc spent in explaining and praising it, a thousand are spent by the nations explaining and praising themselves. 7

This world civilisation and regionalism can get along together, especially if we keep ourselves sharply aware of their quite different but equally important values and rewards. A man can make his contribution to world civilisation and yet remain strongly regional in feeling: I know several men of this sort. There is of course the danger—it is with us now—of the global style flattening out the regional, taking local form, colour, flavour, away for ever, disinheriting future generations, threatening them with sensuous poverty and a huge boredom. But to understand and appreciate regionalism is to be on guard against this danger. And we must therefore make a clear distinction between regionalism and nationalism. 8

It is nationalism that tries to check the growth of world civilisation. And nationalism, when taken on a global scale, is more aggressive and demanding now than it has ever been before. This in the giant powers is largely disguised by the endless fuss in public about rival ideologies, now a largely unreal quarrel. What is intensely real is the glaring na- 9

tionalism. Even the desire to police the world is nationalistic in origin. (Only the world can police the world.) Moreover, the nation-states of today are for the most part far narrower in their outlook, far more inclined to allow prejudice against the foreigner to impoverish their own style of living, than the old imperial states were. It should be part of world civilisation that men with particular skills, perhaps the product of the very regionalism they are rebelling against, should be able to move easily from country to country, to exercise those skills, in anything from teaching the violin to running a new type of factory to managing an old hotel. But nationalism, especially of the newer sort, would rather see everything done badly than allow a few non-nationals to get to work. And people face a barrage of passports, visas, immigration controls, labour permits; and in this respect are worse off than they were in 1900. But even so, in spite of all that nationalism can do—so long as it keeps its nuclear bombs to itself—the internationalism I have in mind, slowly creating a world civilisation, cannot be checked.

10 Nevertheless, we are still backing the wrong ism. Almost all our money goes on the middle one, nationalism, the rotten meat between the two healthy slices of bread. We need regionalism to give us roots and that very depth of feeling which nationalism unjustly and greedily claims for itself. We need internationalism to save the world and to broaden and heighten our civilisation. While regional man enriches the lives that international man is already working to keep secure and healthy, national man, drunk with power, demands our loyalty, money and applause, and poisons the very air with his dangerous nonsense.

COMPREHENSION

1. What thesis does Priestley present? State the thesis in your own words.
2. Define *regionalism, nationalism,* and *internationalism* as Priestley presents these terms.
3. Explain Priestley's objections to nationalism. Where does he state these objections in the essay? What alternative does he propose?

RHETORIC

1. What striking metaphor does the author develop to capture the essence of nationalism? What is its sensory impact? Analyze another example of metaphorical language in the essay.
2. How does the suffix *-ism* function stylistically in the essay?
3. What is Priestley's principle of classification in this essay? How does he maintain proportion in the presentation of categories?
4. Analyze the relationship between definition and classification in the essay.
5. Examine Priestley's use of comparison and contrast.
6. Explain the connection between the introductory and concluding paragraphs.

WRITING

1. Priestley makes many assumptions about regionalism, nationalism, and internationalism. Which assumptions do you accept? Which assumptions do you reject? Explain in an essay.
2. Write a classification essay on at least three related "isms": capitalism, socialism, and communism; Protestantism, Catholicism, and Judaism; or regionalism, nationalism, and internationalism.

BARBARA TUCHMAN Barbara Tuchman (1912–1989), an eminent American historian, twice winner of the Pulitzer Prize, began her career as a research assistant for the Institute of Pacific Relations in 1933. She was a staff writer and correspondent for the *Nation,* covering the Spanish Civil War from 1935 to 1937. Tuchman gained her first significant literary recognition for *The Zimmerman Telegram* (1958); she followed this initial success with *The Guns of August* (1962), *The Proud Tower* (1966), and *Stilwell and the American Experience in China, 1911–1945* (1971). This article offers a wide-ranging historical assessment of the causes of failure, mediocrity, and unwisdom in political life.

BARBARA TUCHMAN

An Inquiry into the Persistence of Unwisdom in Government

A problem that strikes one in the study of history, regardless of period, is why man makes a poorer performance of government than of almost any other human activity. In this sphere, wisdom—meaning judgment acting on experience, common sense, available knowledge, and a decent appreciation of probability—is less operative and more frustrated than it should be. Why do men in high office so often act contrary to the way that reason points and enlightened self-interest suggests? Why does intelligent mental process so often seem to be paralyzed? 1

Why, to begin at the beginning, did the Trojan authorities drag that suspicious-looking wooden horse inside their gates? Why did successive ministries of George III—that "bundle of imbecility," as Dr. Johnson called them collectively—insist on coercing rather than conciliating the Colonies though strongly advised otherwise by many counselors? Why did Napoleon and Hitler invade Russia? Why did the kaiser's government resume unrestricted submarine warfare in 1917 although explicitly warned that this would bring in the United States and that American belligerency would mean Germany's defeat? Why did Chiang Kai-shek 2

refuse to heed any voice of reform or alarm until he woke up to find that his country had slid from under him? Why did Lyndon Johnson, seconded by the best and the brightest, progressively involve this nation in a war both ruinous and halfhearted and from which nothing but bad for our side resulted? Why does the present Administration continue to avoid introducing effective measures to reduce the wasteful consumption of oil while members of OPEC follow a price policy that must bankrupt their customers? How is it possible that the Central Intelligence Agency, whose function it is to provide, at taxpayers' expense, the information necessary to conduct a realistic foreign policy, could remain unaware that discontent in a country crucial to our interests was boiling up to the point of insurrection and overthrow of the ruler upon whom our policy rested? It has been reported that the CIA was ordered *not* to investigate the opposition to the shah of Iran in order to spare him any indication that we took it seriously, but since this sounds more like the theater of the absurd than like responsible government, I cannot bring myself to believe it.

There was a king of Spain once, Philip III, who is said to have died 3
of a fever he contracted from sitting too long near a hot brazier, helplessly overheating himself because the functionary whose duty it was to remove the brazier when summoned could not be found. In the late twentieth century, it begins to appear as if mankind may be approaching a similar stage of suicidal incompetence. The Italians have been sitting in Philip III's hot seat for some time. The British trade unions, in a lunatic spectacle, seem periodically bent on dragging their country toward paralysis, apparently under the impression that they are separate from the whole. Taiwan was thrown into a state of shock by the United States' recognition of the People's Republic of China because, according to one report, in the seven years since the Shanghai Communiqué, the Kuomintang rulers of Taiwan had "refused to accept the new trend as a reality."

Wooden-headedness is a factor that plays a remarkably large role in 4
government. Wooden-headedness consists of assessing a situation in terms of preconceived, fixed notions while ignoring or rejecting any contrary signs. It is acting according to wish while not allowing oneself to be confused by the facts.

A classic case was the French war plan of 1914, which concentrated 5
everything on a French offensive to the Rhine, leaving the French left flank from Belgium to the Channel virtually unguarded. This strategy was based on the belief that the Germans would not use reserves in the front line and, without them, could not deploy enough manpower to extend their invasion through the French left. Reports by intelligence agents in 1913 to the effect that the Germans were indeed preparing their reserves for the front line in case of war were resolutely ignored because the governing spirits in France, dreaming only of their own offensive, did not want to believe in any signals that would require them to strengthen their left at the expense of their march to the Rhine. In the event, the Germans could and did extend themselves around the

French left with results that determined a long war and its fearful consequences for our country.

Wooden-headedness is also the refusal to learn from experience, a form in which fourteenth-century rulers were supreme. No matter how often and obviously devaluation of the currency disrupted the economy and angered the people, French monarchs continued to resort to it whenever they were desperate for cash until they provoked insurrection among the bourgeoisie. No matter how often a campaign that depended on living off a hostile country ran into want and even starvation, campaigns for which this fate was inevitable were regularly undertaken. 6

Still another form is identification of self with the state, as currently exhibited by the ayatollah Khomeini. No wooden-headedness is so impenetrable as that of a religious zealot. Because he is connected with a private wire to the Almighty, no idea coming in on a lesser channel can reach him, which leaves him ill equipped to guide his country in its own best interests. 7

Philosophers of government ever since Plato have devoted their thinking to the major issues of ethics, sovereignty, the social contract, the rights of man, the corruption of power, the balance between freedom and order. Few—except Machiavelli, who was concerned with government as it is, not as it should be—bothered with mere folly, although this has been a chronic and pervasive problem. "Know, my son," said a dying Swedish statesman in the seventeenth century, "with how little wisdom the world is governed." More recently, Woodrow Wilson warned, "In public affairs, stupidity is more dangerous than knavery." 8

Stupidity is not related to type of regime; monarchy, oligarchy, and democracy produce it equally. Nor is it peculiar to nation or class. The working class as represented by the Communist governments functions no more rationally or effectively in power than the aristocracy or the bourgeoisie, as has notably been demonstrated in recent history. Mao Tse-tung may be admired for many things, but the Great Leap Forward, with a steel plant in every backyard, and the Cultural Revolution were exercises in unwisdom that greatly damaged China's progress and stability, not to mention the chairman's reputation. The record of the Russian proletariat in power can hardly be called enlightened, although after sixty years of control it must be accorded a kind of brutal success. If the majority of Russians are better off now than before, the cost in cruelty and tyranny has been no less and probably greater than under the czars. 9

After the French Revolution, the new order was rescued only by Bonaparte's military campaigns, which brought the spoils of foreign wars to fill the treasury, and subsequently by his competence as an executive. He chose officials not on the basis of origin or ideology but on the principle of "la carrière ouverte aux talents"—the said talents being intelligence, energy, industry, and obedience. That worked until the day of his own fatal mistake. 10

I do not wish to give the impression that men in office are incapable of governing wisely and well. Occasionally, the exception appears, ris- 11

ing in heroic size above the rest, a tower visible down the centuries. Greece had her Pericles, who ruled with authority, moderation, sound judgment, and a certain nobility that imposes natural dominion over others. Rome had Caesar, a man of remarkable governing talents, although it must be said that a ruler who arouses opponents to resort to assassination is probably not as smart as he ought to be. Later, under Marcus Aurelius and the other Antonines, Roman citizens enjoyed good government, prosperity, and respect for about a century. Charlemagne was able to impose order upon a mass of contending elements, to foster the arts of civilization no less than those of war, and to earn a prestige supreme in the Middle Ages—probably not equaled in the eyes of contemporaries until the appearance of George Washington.

Possessor of an inner strength and perseverance that enabled him to 12
prevail over a sea of obstacles, Washington was one of those critical figures but for whom history might well have taken a different course. He made possible the physical victory of American independence, while around him, in extraordinary fertility, political talent bloomed as if touched by some tropical sun. For all their flaws and quarrels, the Founding Fathers, who established our form of government, were, in the words of Arthur Schlesinger Sr., "the most remarkable generation of public men in the history of the United States or perhaps of any other nation." It is worth noting the qualities Schlesinger ascribes to them: They were fearless, high-principled, deeply versed in ancient and modern political thought, astute and pragmatic, unafraid of experiment, and—this is significant—"convinced of man's power to improve his condition through the use of intelligence." That was the mark of the Age of Reason that formed them, and though the eighteenth century had a tendency to regard men as more rational than they in fact were, it evoked the best in government from these men.

For our purposes, it would be invaluable if we could know what 13
produced this burst of talent from a base of only two million inhabitants. Schlesinger suggests some contributing factors: wide diffusion of education, challenging economic opportunities, social mobility, training in self-government—all these encouraged citizens to cultivate their political aptitudes to the utmost. Also, he adds, with the Church declining in prestige and with business, science, and art not yet offering competing fields of endeavor, statecraft remained almost the only outlet for men of energy and purpose. Perhaps the need of the moment—the opportunity to create a new political system—is what brought out the best.

Not before or since, I believe, has so much careful and reasonable 14
thinking been invested in the creation of a new political system. In the French, Russian, and Chinese revolutions, too much class hatred and bloodshed were involved to allow for fair results or permanent constitutions. The American experience was unique, and the system so far has always managed to right itself under pressure. In spite of accelerating incompetence, it still works better than most. We haven't had to discard the system and try another after every crisis, as have Italy and

Germany, Spain and France. The founders of the United States are a phenomenon to keep in mind to encourage our estimate of human possibilities, but their example, as a political scientist has pointed out, is "too infrequent to be taken as a basis for normal expectations."

The English are considered to have enjoyed reasonably benign gov- 15
ernment during the eighteenth and nineteenth centuries, except for their Irish subjects, debtors, child laborers, and other unfortunates in various pockets of oppression. The folly that lost the American colonies reappeared now and then, notably in the treatment of the Irish and the Boers, but a social system can survive a good deal of folly when circumstances are historically favorable or when it is cushioned by large resources, as in the heyday of the British Empire, or absorbed by sheer size, as in this country during our period of expansion. Today there are no more cushions, which makes folly less affordable.

Elsewhere than in government, man has accomplished marvels: in- 16
vented the means in our time to leave the world and voyage to the moon; in the past, harnessed wind and electricity, raised earthbound stone into soaring cathedrals, woven silk brocades out of the spinnings of a worm, composed the music of Mozart and the dramas of Shakespeare, classified the forms of nature, penetrated the mysteries of genetics. Why is he so much less accomplished in government? What frustrates, in that sphere, the operation of the intellect? Isaac Bashevis Singer, discoursing as a Nobel laureate on mankind, offers the opinion that God had been frugal in bestowing intellect but lavish with passions and emotions. "He gave us," Singer says, "so many emotions and such strong ones that every human being, even if he is an idiot, is a millionaire in emotions."

I think Singer has made a point that applies to our inquiry. What 17
frustrates the workings of intellect is the passions and the emotions: ambition, greed, fear, facesaving, the instinct to dominate, the needs of the ego, the whole bundle of personal vanities and anxieties.

Reason is crushed by these forces. If the Athenians out of pride and 18
overconfidence had not set out to crush Sparta for good but had been content with moderate victory, their ultimate fall might have been averted. If fourteenth-century knights had not been obsessed by the idea of glory and personal prowess, they might have defeated the Turks at Nicopolis with incalculable consequence for all of Eastern Europe. If the English, 200 years ago, had heeded Chatham's knocking on the door of what he called "this sleeping and confounded Ministry" and his urgent advice to repeal the Coercive Acts and withdraw the troops before the "inexpiable drop of blood is shed in an impious war with a people contending in the great cause of publick liberty," or, given a last chance, if they had heeded Edmund Burke's celebrated plea for conciliation and his warning that it would prove impossible to coerce a "fierce people" of their own pedigree, we might still be a united people bridging the Atlantic, with incalculable consequence for the history of the West. It did not happen that way, because king and Parliament felt it imperative to affirm sovereignty over arrogant colonials. The alternative

choice, as in Athens and medieval Europe, was close to psychologically impossible.

In the case we know best—the American engagement in Vietnam—fixed notions, preconceptions, wooden-headed thinking, and emotions accumulated into a monumental mistake and classic humiliation. The original idea was that the lesson of the failure to halt fascist aggression during the appeasement era dictated the necessity of halting the so-called aggression by North Vietnam, conceived to be the spearhead of international communism. This was applying the wrong model to the wrong facts, which would have been obvious if our policy makers had taken into consideration the history of the people on the spot instead of charging forward wearing the blinders of the cold war.

The reality of Vietnamese nationalism, of which Ho Chi Minh had 20
been the standard-bearer since long before the war, was certainly no secret. Indeed, Franklin Roosevelt had insisted that the French should not be allowed to return after the war, a policy that we instantly abandoned the moment the Japanese were out: Ignoring the Vietnamese demand for self-government, we first assisted the return of the French, and then, when incredibly, they had been put to rout by the native forces, we took their place, as if Dien Bien Phu had no significance whatever. Policy founded upon error multiplies, never retreats. The pretense that North versus South Vietnam represented foreign aggression was intensified. If Asian specialists with knowledge of the situation suggested a reassessment, they were not persuasive. As a Communist aggressor, Hanoi was presumed to be a threat to the United States, yet the vital national interest at stake, which alone may have justified belligerency, was never clear enough to sustain a declaration of war.

A further, more fundamental, error confounded our policy. This 21
was the nature of the client. In war, as any military treatise or any soldier who has seen active service will tell you, it is essential to know the nature—that is, the capabilities *and* intentions—of the enemy and no less so of an ally who is the primary belligerent. We fatally underestimated the one and foolishly overestimated the other. Placing reliance on, or hope in, South Vietnam was an advanced case of wooden-headedness. Improving on the Bourbons, who forgot nothing and learned nothing, our policy makers forgot everything and learned nothing. The oldest lesson in history is the futility and, often, fatality of foreign interference to maintain in power a government unwanted or hated at home. As far back as 500 B.C., Confucius stated, "Without the confidence of the people, no government can stand," and political philosophers have echoed him down through the ages. What else was the lesson of our vain support of Chiang Kai-shek, within such recent experience? A corrupt or oppressive government may be maintained by despotic means but not for long, as the English occupiers of France learned in the fifteenth century. The human spirit protests and generates a Joan of Arc, for people will not passively endure a government that is in fact unendurable.

The deeper we became involved in Vietnam during the Johnson era, 22
the greater grew the self-deception, the lies, the false body counts, the cheating on Tonkin Gulf, the military mess, domestic dissent, and all those defensive emotions in which, as a result, our leaders became fixed. Their concern for personal ego, public image, and government status determined policy. Johnson was not going to be the first President to preside over defeat; generals could not admit failure nor civilian advisers risk their jobs by giving unpalatable advice.

Males, who so far in history have managed government, are obsessed 23
with potency, which is the reason, I suspect, why it is difficult for them to admit error. I have rarely known a man who, with a smile and a shrug, could easily acknowledge being wrong. Why not? *I* can, without any damage to self-respect. I can only suppose the difference is that deep in their psyches, men somehow equate being wrong with being impotent. For a Chief of State, it is almost out of the question, and especially so for Johnson and Nixon, who both seem to me to have had shaky self-images. Johnson's showed in his deliberate coarseness and compulsion to humiliate others in crude physical ways. No self-confident man would have needed to do that. Nixon was a bundle of inferiorities and sense of persecution. I do not pretend to be a psychohistorian, but in pursuit of this inquiry, the psychological factors must be taken into account. Having no special knowledge of Johnson and Nixon, I will not pursue the question other than to say that it was our misfortune during the Vietnam period to have had two Presidents who lacked the self-confidence for a change of course, much less for a grand withdrawal. "Magnanimity in politics," said Edmund Burke, "is not seldom the truest wisdom, and a great Empire and little minds go ill together."

An essential component of that "truest wisdom" is the self-confi- 24
dence to reassess. Congressman Morris Udall made this point in the first few days after the nuclear accident at Three Mile Island. Cautioning against a hasty decision on the future of nuclear power, he said, "We have to go back and reassess. There is nothing wrong about being optimistic or making a mistake. The thing that is wrong, as in Vietnam, is *persisting* in a mistake when you see you are going down the wrong road and are caught in a bad situation."

The test comes in recognizing when persistence has become a fatal 25
error. A prince, says Machiavelli, ought always to be a great asker and a patient hearer of truth about those things of which he has inquired, and he should be angry if he finds that anyone has scruples about telling him the truth. Johnson and Nixon, as far as an outsider can tell, were not great askers; they did not want to hear the truth or to face it. Chiang Kai-shek knew virtually nothing of real conditions in his domain because he lived a headquarters life amid an entourage all of whom were afraid to be messengers of ill report. When, in World War I, a general of the headquarters staff visited for the first time the ghastly landscape of the Somme, he broke into tears, saying, "If I had known we sent men to fight in that, I could not have done it." Evidently he was no great asker either.

Neither, we now know, was the shah of Iran. Like Chiang Kai-shek, 26
he was isolated from actual conditions. He was educated abroad, took his vacations abroad, and toured his country, if at all, by helicopter.

Why is it that the major clients of the United States, a country founded on the principle that government derives its just powers from the consent of the governed, tend to be unpopular autocrats? A certain schizophrenia between our philosophy and our practice afflicts American policy, and this split will always make the policy based on it fall apart. On the day the shah left Iran, an article summarizing his reign said that "except for the generals, he has few friends or allies at home." How useful to us is a ruler without friends or allies at home? He is a kind of luftmensch, no matter how rich or how golden a customer for American business. To attach American foreign policy to a ruler who does not have the acceptance of his countrymen is hardly intelligent. By now, it seems to me, we might have learned that. We must understand conditions—and by conditions, I mean people and history—on the spot. Wise policy can only be made on the basis of *informed,* not automatic, judgments.

When it has become evident to those associated with it that a course 28
of policy is pointed toward disaster, why does no one resign in protest or at least for the peace of his own soul? They never do. In 1917, the German chancellor Bethmann Hollweg pleaded desperately against the proposed resumption of unrestricted submarine warfare, since, by bringing in the United States, it would revive the Allies' resources, their confidence in victory, and their will to endure. When he was overruled by the military, he told a friend who found him sunk in despair that the decision meant "finis Germaniae." When the friend said simply, "You should resign," Bethmann said he could not, for that would sow dissension at home and let the world know he believed Germany would fail.

This is always the refuge. The officeholder tells himself he can do 29
more from within and that he must not reveal division at the top to the public. In fact if there is to be any hope of change in a democratic society, that is exactly what he must do. No one of major influence in Johnson's circle resigned over our Vietnam policy although several, hoping to play it both ways, hinted their disagreement. Humphrey, waiting for the nod, never challenged the President's policy, although he campaigned afterward as an opponent of the war. Since then, I've always thought the adulation given to him misplaced.

Basically, what keeps officeholders attached to a policy they believe 30
to be wrong is nothing more nor less, I believe, than the lure of office, or Potomac fever. It is the same whether the locus is the Thames or the Rhine or, no doubt, the Nile. When Herbert Lehman ran for a second term as senator from New York after previously serving four terms as governor, his brother asked him why on earth he wanted it. "Arthur," replied the senator, "after you have once ridden behind a motorcycle escort, you are never the same again."

Here is a clue to the question of why our performance in govern- 31
ment is worse than in other activities: because government offers

power, excites that lust for power, which is subject to emotional drives—to narcissism, fantasies of omnipotence, and other sources of folly. The lust for power, according to Tacitus, "is the most flagrant of all the passions" and cannot really be satisfied except by power over others. Business offers a kind of power but only to the very successful at the very top, and even they, in our day, have to play it down. Fords and Du Ponts, Hearsts and Pulitzers, nowadays are subdued, and the Rockefeller who most conspicuously wanted power sought it in government. Other activities—in sports, science, the professions, and the creative and performing arts—offer various satisfactions but not the opportunity for power. They may appeal to status seeking and, in the form of celebrity, offer crowd worship and limousines and recognition by headwaiters, but these are the trappings of power, not the essence. Of course, mistakes and stupidities occur in nongovernmental activities too, but since these affect fewer people, they are less noticeable than they are in public affairs. Government remains the paramount field of unwisdom because it is there that men seek power over others—and lose it over themselves.

There are, of course, other factors that lower competence in public 32
affairs, among them the pressure of overwork and overscheduling; bureaucracy, especially big bureaucracy; the contest for votes that gives exaggerated influence to special interests and an absurd tyranny to public opinion polls. Any hope of intelligent government would require that the persons entrusted with high office should formulate and execute policy according to their best judgment and the best knowledge available, not according to every breeze of public opinion. But reelection is on their minds, and that becomes the criterion. Moreover, given schedules broken down into fifteen-minute appointments and staffs numbering in the hundreds and briefing memos of never less than thirty pages, policy makers never have time to think. This leaves a rather important vacuum. Meanwhile, bureaucracy rolls on, impervious to any individual or cry for change, like some vast computer that when once penetrated by error goes on pumping it out forever.

Under the circumstances, what are the chances of improving the 33
conduct of government? The idea of a class of professionals trained for the task has been around ever since Plato's Republic. Something of the sort animates, I imagine, the new Kennedy School of Government at Harvard. According to Plato, the ruling class in a just society should be men apprenticed to the art of ruling, drawn from the rational and the wise. Since he acknowledged that in natural distribution these are few, he believed they would have to be eugenically bred and nurtured. Government, he said, was a special art in which competence, as in any other profession, could be acquired only by study of the discipline and could not be acquired otherwise.

Without reference to Plato, the Mandarins of China were trained, if 34
not bred, for the governing function. They had to pass through years of study and apprenticeship and weeding out by successive examinations, but they do not seem to have developed a form of government much

superior to any other, and in the end, they petered out in decadence and incompetence.

In seventeenth-century Europe, after the devastation of the Thirty Years' War, the electors of Brandenburg, soon to be combined with Prussia, determined to create a strong state by means of a disciplined army and a trained civil service. Applicants for the civil positions, drawn from commoners in order to offset the nobles' control of the military, had to complete a course of study covering political theory, law and legal philosophy, economics, history, penology, and statutes. Only after passing through various stages of examination and probationary terms of office did they receive definitive appointments and tenure and opportunity for advancement. The higher civil service was a separate branch, not open to promotion from the middle and lower levels.

The Prussian system proved so effective that the state was able to 36
survive both military defeat by Napoleon in 1807 and the revolutionary surge of 1848. By then it had begun to congeal, losing many of its most progressive citizens in emigration to America; nevertheless, Prussian energies succeeded in 1871 in uniting the German states in an empire under Prussian hegemony. Its very success contained the seed of ruin, for it nourished the arrogance and power hunger that from 1914 through 1918 was to bring it down.

In England, instead of responding in reactionary panic to the thun- 37
ders from the Continent in 1848, as might have been expected, the authorities, with commendable enterprise, ordered an investigation of their own government practices, which were then the virtually private preserve of the propertied class. The result was a report on the need for a permanent civil service to be based on training and specialized skills and designed to provide continuity and maintenance of the long view as against transient issues and political passions. Though heavily resisted, the system was adopted in 1870. It has produced distinguished civil servants but also Burgess, Maclean, Philby, and the fourth man. The history of British government in the last 100 years suggests that factors other than the quality of its civil service determine a country's fate.

In the United States, civil service was established chiefly as a barrier 38
to patronage and the pork barrel rather than in search of excellence. By 1937, a presidential commission, finding the system inadequate, urged the development of a "real career service . . . requiring personnel of the highest order, competent, highly trained, loyal, skilled in their duties by reason of long experience, and assured of continuity." After much effort and some progress, that goal is still not reached, but even if it were, it would not take care of elected officials and high appointments—that is, of government at the top.

I do not know if the prognosis is hopeful or, given the underlying 39
emotional drives, whether professionalism is the cure. In the Age of Enlightenment, John Locke thought the emotions should be controlled by intellectual judgment and that it was the distinction and glory of man

to be able to control them. As witnesses of the twentieth century's record, comparable to the worst in history, we have less confidence in our species. Although professionalism can help, I tend to think that fitness of character is what government chiefly requires. How that can be discovered, encouraged, and brought into office is the problem that besets us.

No society has yet managed to implement Plato's design. Now, with money and image-making manipulating our elective process, the chances are reduced. We are asked to choose by the packaging, yet the candidate seen in a studio-filmed spot, sincerely voicing lines from the Tele-PrompTer, is not the person who will have to meet the unrelenting problems and crucial decisions of the Oval Office. It might be a good idea if, without violating the First Amendment, we could ban all paid political commercials and require candidates (who accept federal subsidy for their campaigns) to be televised live only. 40

That is only a start. More profound change must come if we are to bring into office the kind of person our form of government needs if it is to survive the challenges of this era. Perhaps rather than educating officials according to Plato's design, we should concentrate on educating the electorate—that is, ourselves—to look for, recognize, and reward character in our representatives and to reject the ersatz. 41

COMPREHENSION

1. Why does Tuchman term her essay an "inquiry"? How does the term govern audience response?
2. According to Tuchman, what are the causes of the persistence of unwisdom in government?
3. What is the author's attitude toward the French, Russian, Chinese, and Iranian revolutions, respectively? Cite evidence to support your response.

RHETORIC

1. How do such phrases as the following contribute to the author's purpose and tone: "theatre of the absurd" (paragraph 2); "lunatic spectacle" (paragraph 3); "the whole bundle of personal vanities and anxieties" (paragraph 17); "charging forward wearing the blinders of the cold war" (paragraph 19); and "schizophrenia between our philosophy and our practice" (paragraph 27)?
2. Analyze the connotations that develop around Tuchman's use of the word *unwisdom.*
3. How does the author's use of rhetorical questions, notably in the introduction, contribute to the thesis? To the causal analysis?
4. How selective are the author's illustrations? What types of illustration does she use in the essay?
5. Analyze the author's transitions for paragraphs 7 to 8, 14 to 15, 23 to 24, 30 to 31, and 39 to 40.
6. What particulars develop Tuchman's generalizations about the emotional and psychological drives of politicians?

WRITING

1. A significant part of Tuchman's critique of unwisdom in government deals specifically with the problems of men as rulers. What is your response to her emotional and psychological profile of men as political leaders? Would women be less susceptible to these emotional and psychological problems? Analyze the issue in an essay.
2. Write your own inquiry into the persistence of unwisdom in government, using a series of relevant examples to support your generalizations.
3. Compare and contrast the principles enunciated in the Declaration of Independence, which follows, and the realities dealt with by Tuchman.

CLASSIC AND CONTEMPORARY

THOMAS JEFFERSON Thomas Jefferson (1743–1826) was Governor of Virginia during the American Revolution, America's first Secretary of State, and the third President of the United States. He had a varied and monumental career as politician, public servant, scientist, architect, educator (he founded the University of Virginia), and man of letters. Jefferson attended the Continental Congress in 1775, where he wrote the rough draft of the Declaration of Independence and revised it; other hands made contributions to the document that was signed on July 4, 1776; but the wording, style, structure, and spirit of the final version are distinctly Jefferson's. Like Thomas Paine, Benjamin Franklin, James Madison, and other major figures of the Revolutionary era, Jefferson was notable for his use of prose as an instrument for social and political change. In the Declaration of Independence, we see the direct, precise, logical, and persuasive statement of revolutionary principles that makes the document one of the best known and best written texts in world history. Jefferson died in his home at Monticello on July 4, fifty years to the day from the signing of the Declaration of Independence.

THOMAS JEFFERSON

The Declaration of Independence

In CONGRESS, JULY 4, 1776

The Unanimous Declaration
of the thirteen united States of America.

When in the Course of human events it becomes necessary for one people to dissolve the political bands which have connected them with another, and to assume among the powers of the earth, the separate and equal station to which the Laws of Nature and of Nature's God entitle them, a decent respect to the opinions of mankind requires that they should declare the causes which impel them to the separation. 1

We hold these truths to be self-evident, that all men are created equal, that they are endowed by their Creator with certain unalienable Rights, that among these are Life, Liberty and the pursuit of Happiness.—That to secure these rights, Governments are instituted among Men, deriving their just powers from the consent of the governed.—That whenever any Form of Government becomes destructive of these ends, it is the Right of the People to alter or to abolish it, and to institute new Government, laying its foundation on such principles and organizing its powers in such form, as to them shall seem most likely to 2 effect their Safety and Happiness. Prudence, indeed, will dictate that Governments long established should not be changed for light and transient causes; and accordingly all experience hath shewn that mankind are more disposed to suffer, while evils are sufferable, than to right themselves by abolishing the forms to which they are accustomed. But when a long train of abuses and usurpations, pursuing invariably the same Object evinces a design to reduce them under absolute Despotism, it is their right, it is their duty, to throw off such Government, and to provide new Guards for their future security.—Such has been the patient sufferance of these Colonies; and such is now the necessity which constrains them to alter their former Systems of Government. The history of the present King of Great Britain is a history of repeated injuries and usurpations, all having in direct object the establishment of an absolute Tyranny over these States. To prove this, let Facts be submitted to a candid world.

He has refused his Assent to Laws, the most wholesome and neces- 3
sary for the public good.

He has forbidden his Governors to pass Laws of immediate and 4
pressing importance, unless suspended in their operation till his Assent should be obtained; and when so suspended, he has utterly neglected to attend to them.

He has refused to pass other Laws for the accommodation of large 5
districts of people, unless those people would relinquish the right of Representation in the Legislature, a right inestimable to them and formidable to tyrants only.

He has called together legislative bodies at places unusual, uncom- 6
fortable, and distant from the depository of their public Records, for the sole purpose of fatiguing them into compliance with his measures.

He has dissolved Representative Houses repeatedly, for opposing 7
with manly firmness his invasions on the rights of the people.

He has refused for a long time, after such dissolutions, to cause oth- 8
ers to be elected; whereby the Legislative powers, incapable of Annihilation, have returned to the People at large for their exercise; the State remaining in the mean time exposed to all the dangers of invasion from without, and convulsions within.

He has endeavoured to prevent the population of these States; for 9
that purpose obstructing the Laws for Naturalization of Foreigners; refusing to pass others to encourage their migrations hither, and raising the conditions of new Appropriations of Lands.

He has obstructed the Administration of Justice, by refusing his 10
Assent to Laws for establishing Judiciary powers.

He was made Judges dependent on his Will alone, for the tenure of 11
their offices, and the amount and payment of their salaries.

He has erected a multitude of New Offices, and sent hither swarms 12
of Officers to harass our people, and eat out their substance.

He has kept among us, in times of peace, Standing Armies without 13
the Consent of our legislatures.

He has affected to render the Military independent of and superior 14
to the Civil power.

He has combined with others to subject us to a jurisdiction foreign 15
to our constitution, and unacknowledged by our laws; giving his Assent to their Acts of pretended Legislation:

For quartering large bodies of armed troops among us:

For protecting them, by a mock Trial, from punishment for any Murders which they should commit on the Inhabitants of these States:

For cutting off our Trade with all parts of the world:

For imposing Taxes on us without our Consent:

For depriving us in many cases, of the benefits of Trial by Jury:

For transporting us beyond Seas to be tried for pretended offences:

For abolishing the free System of English Laws in a neighboring Province, establishing therein an Arbitrary government, and enlarging its Boundaries so as to render it at once an example and fit instrument for introducing the same absolute rule into these Colonies:

For taking away our Charters, abolishing our most valuable Laws and altering fundamentally the Forms of our Governments:

For suspending our own Legislatures, and declaring themselves invested with power to legislate for us in all cases whatsoever.

He has abdicated Government here, by declaring us out of his 16
Protection and waging War against us.

He has plundered our seas, ravaged our Coasts, burnt our towns, 17
and destroyed the lives of our people.

He is at this time transporting large Armies of foreign Mercenaries 18
to complete the works of death, desolation and tyranny, already begun with circumstances of Cruelty & Perfidy scarcely paralleled in the most barbarous ages, and totally unworthy the Head of a civilized nation.

He has constrained our fellow Citizens taken Captive on the high 19
Seas to bear Arms against their Country, to become the executioners of their friends and Brethren, or to fall themselves by their Hands.

He has excited domestic insurrections amongst us, and has endeav- 20
oured to bring on the inhabitants of our frontiers, the merciless Indian Savages, whose known rule of warfare, is an undistinguished destruction of all ages, sexes and conditions.

In every stage of these Oppressions We have Petitioned for Redress in 21
the most humble terms: Our repeated Petitions have been answered only by repeated injury. A Prince, whose character is thus marked by every act which may define a Tyrant, is unfit to be the ruler of a free people.

Nor have We been wanting in attentions to our British brethren. We 22
have warned them from time to time of attempts by their legislature to extend an unwarrantable jurisdiction over us. We have reminded them of the circumstances of our emigration and settlement here. We have appealed to their native justice and magnanimity, and we have conjured them by the ties of our common kindred to disavow these usurpations, which would inevitably interrupt our connections and correspondence. They too have been deaf to the voice of justice and of consanguinity. We must, therefore, acquiesce in the necessity, which denounces our Separation, and hold them, as we hold the rest of mankind, Enemies in War, in Peace Friends.

We, therefore, the Representatives of the United States of America, 23
in General Congress, Assembled, appealing to the Supreme Judge of the world for the rectitude of our intentions, do, in the Name, and by Authority of the good People of these Colonies, solemnly publish and declare, That these United Colonies are, and of Right ought to be Free and Independent States; that they are Absolved from all Allegiance to the British Crown, and that all political connection between them and the State of Great Britain, is and ought to be totally dissolved; and that as Free and Independent States, they have full Power to levy War, conclude Peace, contract Alliances, establish Commerce, and to do all other Acts and Things which Independent States may of right do. And for the support of this Declaration, with a firm reliance on the protection of divine Providence, we mutually pledge to each other our Lives, our Fortunes and our sacred Honor.

COMPREHENSION

1. Explain Jefferson's main and subordinate purposes in this document.
2. What is Jefferson's key assertion, or argument? Mention several reasons that he gives to support his argument.
3. Summarize Jefferson's definition of human nature and of government. Read Forster's "My Wood" in Chapter 7 and consider how Forster might respond to Jefferson's definition.

RHETORIC

1. There are many striking words and phrases in the Declaration of Independence, notably in the beginning. Locate three such examples, and explain their connotative power and effectiveness.
2. Jefferson and his colleagues had to draft a document designed for several audiences. What audiences did they have in mind? How do their language and style reflect their awareness of multiple audiences?
3. The Declaration of Independence is a classic model of syllogistic reasoning and deductive argument (see the Glossary). What is its major premise, and where is this premise stated? The minor premise? The conclusion?
4. What sort of inductive evidence does Jefferson offer?
5. Why is the middle portion, or body, of the Declaration of Independence considerably longer than the introduction or conclusion? What holds the body together?
6. Explain the function and effect of parallel structure in this document.

WRITING

1. Do you believe that "all men are created equal"? Justify your answer.
2. Discuss the relevance of the Declaration of Independence to politics today.
3. Explain why the Declaration of Independence is a model of effective prose.

4. Write your own declaration of independence—from family, employer, required courses, or the like. Develop this declaration as an "op-ed" piece for a newspaper.

MARTIN LUTHER KING, JR. Martin Luther King, Jr. (1929–1968) was born in Atlanta, Georgia, and earned degrees from Morehouse College, Crozer Theological Seminary, Boston University, and Chicago Theological Seminary. As Baptist clergyman, civil rights leader, founder and president of the Southern Christian Leadership Conference, and, in 1964, Nobel Peace Prize winner, King was a celebrated advocate of nonviolent resistance to achieve equality and racial integration in the world. King was a gifted orator and a highly persuasive writer. His books include *Stride toward Freedom* (1958); *Letter from Birmingham City Jail* (1963); *Strength to Love* (1963); *Why We Can't Wait* (1964); and *Where Do We Go from Here: Chaos or Community?* (1967), a book published shortly before Reverend King was assassinated on April 4, 1968, in Memphis, Tennessee. This selection, a milestone of American oratory, was the keynote address at the March on Washington, August 28, 1963.

MARTIN LUTHER KING, JR.

I Have a Dream

I am happy to join with you today in what will go down in history as the greatest demonstration for freedom in the history of our nation. 1

Fivescore years ago, a great American, in whose symbolic shadow we stand today, signed the Emancipation Proclamation. This momentous decree came as a great beacon light of hope to millions of Negro slaves who had been seared in the flames of withering injustice. It came as a joyous daybreak to end the long night of their captivity. 2

But one hundred years later, the Negro still is not free; one hundred years later, the life of the Negro is still sadly crippled by the manacles of segregation and the chains of discrimination; one hundred years later, the Negro lives on a lonely island of poverty in the midst of a vast ocean of material prosperity; one hundred years later, the Negro is still languishing in the corners of American society and finds himself in exile in his own land. 3

So we've come here today to dramatize a shameful condition. In a sense we've come to our nation's capital to cash a check. When the architects of our republic wrote the magnificent words of the Constitution and the Declaration of Independence, they were signing a promissory note to which every American was to fall heir. This note was the promise that all men, yes, black men as well as white men, would be guaranteed the unalienable rights of life, liberty, and the pursuit of happiness. 4

It is obvious today that America has defaulted on this promissory note in so far as her citizens of color are concerned. Instead of honor- 5 ing this sacred obligation, America has given the Negro people a bad check; a check which has come back marked "insufficient funds." We refuse to believe that there are insufficient funds in the great vaults of opportunity of this nation. And so we've come to cash this check, a check that will give us upon demand the riches of freedom and the security of justice.

We have also come to this hallowed spot to remind America of the fierce urgency of now. This is no time to engage in the luxury of cooling off or to take the tranquilizing drug of gradualism. Now is the time to make real the promises of democracy; now is the time to rise from the dark and desolate valley of segregation to the sunlit path of racial justice; now is the time to lift our nation from the quicksands of racial injustice to the solid rock of brotherhood; now is the time to make justice a reality for all God's children. It would be fatal for the nation to overlook the urgency of the moment. This sweltering summer of the Negro's legitimate discontent will not pass until there is an invigorating autumn of freedom and equality. 6

Nineteen sixty-three is not an end, but a beginning. And those who hope that the Negro needed to blow off steam and will now be content, will have a rude awakening if the nation returns to business as usual. 7

There will be neither rest nor tranquility in America until the Negro is granted his citizenship rights. The whirlwinds of revolt will continue to shake the foundations of our nation until the bright day of justice emerges. 8

But there is something that I must say to my people who stand on the warm threshold which leads into the palace of justice. In the process of gaining our rightful place we must not be guilty of wrongful deeds. 9

Let us not seek to satisfy our thirst for freedom by drinking from the cup of bitterness and hatred. We must forever conduct our struggle on the high plane of dignity and discipline. We must not allow our creative protest to degenerate into physical violence. Again and again we must rise to the majestic heights of meeting physical force with soul force. 10

The marvelous new militancy which has engulfed the Negro community must not lead us to a distrust of all white people, for many of our white brothers, as evidenced by their presence here today, have come to realize that their destiny is tied up with our destiny and they have come to realize that their freedom is inextricably bound to our freedom. This offense we share mounted to storm the battlements of injustice must be carried forth by a biracial army. We cannot walk alone. 11

And as we walk, we must make the pledge that we shall always march ahead. We cannot turn back. There are those who are asking the devotees of civil rights, "When will you be satisfied?" We can never be satisfied as long as the Negro is the victim of the unspeakable horrors of police brutality. 12

We can never be satisfied as long as our bodies, heavy with fatigue of travel, cannot gain lodging in the motels of the highways and the ho- 13 tels of the cities. We cannot be satisfied as long as the Negro's basic mobility is from a smaller ghetto to a larger one.

We can never be satisfied as long as our children are stripped of their selfhood and robbed of their dignity by signs stating "for whites only." We cannot be satisfied as long as a Negro in Mississippi cannot vote and a Negro in New York believes he has nothing for which to vote. No, we are not satisfied, and we will not be satisfied until justice rolls down like waters and righteousness like a mighty stream. 14

I am not unmindful that some of you have come here out of excessive trials and tribulation. Some of you have come fresh from narrow jail cells. Some of you have come from areas where your quest for freedom left you battered by the storms of persecution and staggered by the winds of police brutality. You have been the veterans of creative suffering. Continue to work with the faith that unearned suffering is redemptive. 15

Go back to Mississippi; go back to Alabama; go back to South Carolina; go back to Georgia; go back to Louisiana; go back to the slums and ghettos of the northern cities, knowing that somehow this situation can, and will be changed. Let us not wallow in the valley of despair. 16

So I say to you, my friends, that even though we must face the difficulties of today and tomorrow, I still have a dream. It is a dream deeply rooted in the American dream that one day this nation will rise up and live out the true meaning of its creed—we hold these truths to be self-evident, that all men are created equal. 17

I have a dream that one day on the red hills of Georgia, sons of former slaves and sons of former slave-owners will be able to sit down together at the table of brotherhood. 18

I have a dream that one day, even the state of Mississippi, a state sweltering with the heat of injustice, sweltering with the heat of oppression, will be transformed into an oasis of freedom and justice. 19

I have a dream my four little children will one day live in a nation where they will not be judged by the color of their skin but by content of their character. I have a dream today! 20

I have a dream that one day, down in Alabama, with its vicious racists, with its governor having his lips dripping with the words of interposition and nullification, that one day, right there in Alabama, little black boys and black girls will be able to join hands with little white boys and white girls as sisters and brothers. I have a dream today! 21

I have a dream that one day every valley shall be exalted, every hill and mountain shall be made low, the rough places shall be made plain, and the crooked places shall be made straight and the glory of the Lord will be revealed and all flesh shall see it together. 22

This is our hope. This is the faith that I go back to the South with. 23

With this faith we will be able to hear out of the mountain of despair a stone of hope. With this faith we will be able to transform the jangling discords of our nation into a beautiful symphony of brotherhood. 24

With this faith we will be able to work together, to pray together, 25
to struggle together, to go to jail together, to stand up for freedom together, knowing that we will be free one day. This will be the day when all of God's children will be able to sing with new meaning—"my country 'tis of thee; sweet land of liberty; of thee I sing; land where my fathers died, land of the pilgrim's pride; from every mountain side, let freedom ring"—and if America is to be a great nation, this must become true.

So let freedom ring from the prodigious hilltops of New 26
Hampshire.

Let freedom ring from the mighty mountains of New York. 27

Let freedom ring from the heightening Alleghenies of Pennsylvania. 28

Let freedom ring from the snow-capped Rockies of Colorado. 29

Let freedom ring from the curvaceous slopes of California. 30

But not only that. 31

Let freedom ring from Stone Mountain of Georgia. 32

Let freedom ring from Lookout Mountain of Tennessee. 33

Let freedom ring from every hill and molehill of Mississippi, from 34
every mountainside, let freedom ring.

And when we allow freedom to ring, when we let it ring from 35
every village and hamlet, from every state and city, we will be able to speed up that day when all of God's children—black men and white men, Jews and Gentiles, Catholics and Protestants—will be able to join hands and to sing in the words of the old Negro spiritual, "Free at last, free at last; thank God Almighty, we are free at last."

COMPREHENSION

1. What is the main purpose behind this speech? Where does King state this purpose most clearly?
2. Why does King make use of "fivescore years ago" (paragraph 2)? How is this more appropriate than simply saying, "a hundred years ago"?
3. Who is King's audience? Where does he acknowledge the special historic circumstances influencing his speech?

RHETORIC

1. Where else does King adapt phrases from other sources to give his work allusive richness?
2. What do the terms *interposition* and *nullification* (paragraph 21) mean? What is their historical significance?
3. Why does King make use of repetition? Does this technique work well in print? Explain.
4. What is the purpose of the extended metaphor in paragraphs 4 and 5? Which point in paragraph 3 does it refer to?
5. In which paragraphs does King address the problems of African Americans?

6. Why is this selection entitled "I Have a Dream"? How do dreams serve as a motif for this speech?

WRITING

1. "I Have a Dream" is considered by many people to be among the greatest speeches delivered by an American. Do you think that it deserves to be? Explain in an essay.
2. Write a comparative essay analyzing King's assessment of black Americans' condition in 1963 and their condition today. What do you think King would say if he knew of contemporary conditions?
3. Write your own "I Have a Dream" essay, basing it on your vision of America or of a special people.
4. Prepare a newspaper editorial advocating a solution to one aspect of racial, ethnic, or sexual injustice.

CLASSIC AND CONTEMPORARY: QUESTIONS FOR COMPARISON

1. Compare the Declaration of Independence with King's speech in terms of the level of language, style, and content. Are they equally powerful and resonant? Cite specific passages from the essays to illustrate your responses.
2. Rewrite the Declaration of Independence in modern English as you believe Dr. King might, reflecting his concerns about the African American and other minorities in this country. Include a list of grievances similar to the one concerning British rule.
3. Write a research paper about the lives and times of King and Jefferson. Compare and contrast any significant events or pertinent biographical data in their backgrounds.

CONNECTIONS

1. Using the essays of Gordon, Takaki, and others in this chapter, write an essay in which you develop the topic "What Is an American?"
2. Write an essay that links the Declaration of Independence and Havel's essay.
3. Apply Tuchman's argument (that intelligent people often run unwise governments) to one of the issues developed in this section (for example, immigration or apartheid), and argue how wisely or unwisely the governments have dealt with this issue.
4. Compare and contrast the opinions expressed by Tuchman and Priestley about government in their essays.
5. King speaks of the Declaration of Independence as a promissory note to the people of the United States. Using the essays of Takaki, Gordon, and Tuchman, write an essay which considers what the United States may still owe its citizens.
6. Using the essays of Havel and Tuchman as support, write a causal analysis essay on the wisdom or folly of U.S. foreign policy.
7. Both Thomas Jefferson and Martin Luther King Jr. made powerful appeals to the U.S. government on behalf of their people. Write a comparison/contrast essay that examines the language, style, and content of both essays.

CHAPTER SEVEN

Work, Business, and Economics

Work is central to the human experience; in fact, it is work in its economic and social outcomes that provides us with the keys to an understanding of culture and civilization. It tells us much about scarcity and abundance, poverty and affluence, the "haves" and "have-nots" in any society, as well as a nation's economic imperatives. Whether it is the rise and fall of cities, the conduct of businesses and corporations, or the economic policies of government, we see in the culture of work an attempt to impose order on nature. Work is our handprint—much like the handprints discovered in underwater caves in southern France—upon the world.

The work we perform and the careers we pursue also define us in very personal ways. "I'm a professor at Harvard" or "I work for IBM" serve as identity badges, for what we do explains, at least in part, what and who we are. The very act of "looking for work," as Gary Soto tells us in his essay, illuminates one's status in society, one's background, one's aspirations. And as several writers in this chapter argue, notably Jonathan Swift in his classic "A Modest Proposal," labor reveals those configurations of power—both economic and political—that exist in any society or nation.

According to Freud, whom you encountered in a previous chapter, work is the basis of one's social reality. We speak, for example, of "the work ethic" that is ingrained in the American character as if the very reality of labor uniquely defines our culture. You might like your work, or you might loathe it; be employed or unemployed; enjoy the reputation of a workaholic or a person who lives for leisure time; view work as a curse or as a duty. In each instance, it is work that occupies a central position in your relationship to society. Indeed, the complex nature and

economy of work, as Jessica Mitford demonstrates in her savagely satiric essay on American funeral practices, pursues us to the grave.

Regardless of your perspective on the issue, it is important to understand the multiple dimensions of work. In both traditional and modern societies, work prepares us for economic and social roles. It affects families, school curricula, public policy. Ultimately, as many authors here suggest, it determines our self-esteem. Through work we come to terms with ourselves and our environment. The nature and purpose of the work we do provides us with a powerful measure of our worth.

Previewing the Chapter

As you read the essays in this chapter and respond to them in discussion and writing, consider the following questions:

- Does the author have a subjective or an objective view of work? How do you know?
- What assumptions does the author make about the value of work?
- Does the author discuss work in general or focus on one particular aspect of work?
- How does the writer define *work?* In what ways, if any, does the author expand on the simple definition of *work* as "paid employment"?
- What issues of race, class, and gender does the author raise?
- What is the relationship of work to the economic system depicted in the author's essay?
- What tone does the writer take in his or her presentation of the work experience?
- What psychological insights does the author offer into the culture of work?
- What does the writer's style reveal about his or her attitude toward work?
- Considering these essays, identify the needs that people must have met if their labor is to assume significance for them.

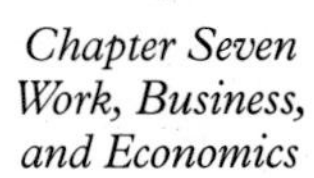

CAROL BLY Carol Bly (1930–) was born in Minnesota and educated at Wellesley College. She has contributed to such publications as the *New Yorker* and *American Review.* Her most recent book is entitled *The Passionate, Accurate Story: Making Your Heart's Truth into Literature* (1990). In an earlier work, *Letters from the Country,* published in 1979, Bly explored the rural consciousness of small-town residents. In the following selection from the latter, she considers the impact of technology on a rural community and gives us a glimpse into its way of life.

CAROL BLY

Getting Tired

The men have left a gigantic 6600 combine a few yards from our grove, at the edge of the stubble. For days it was working around the farm; we heard it on the east, later on the west, and finally we could see it grinding back and forth over the windrows on the south. But now it has been simply squatting at the field's edge, huge, tremendously still, very professional, slightly dangerous. 1

We all have the correct feelings about this new combine: this isn't the good old farming where man and soil are dusted together all day; this isn't farming a poor man can afford, either, and therefore it further threatens his hold on the American "family farm" operation. We have been sneering at this machine for days, as its transistor radio, amplified well over the engine roar, has been grinding up our silence, spreading a kind of shrill ghetto evening all over the farm. 2

But now it is parked, and after a while I walk over to it and climb up its neat little John Deere-green ladder on the left. Entering the big cab up there is like coming up into a large ship's bridge on visitors' day—heady stuff to see the inside workings of a huge operation like the Queen Elizabeth II. On the other hand I feel left out, being only a dumbfounded passenger. The combine cab has huge windows flaring wider at the top; they lean forward over the ground, and the driver sits so high behind the glass in its rubber moldings it is like a movie-set spaceship. He has obviously come to dominate the field, whether he farms it or not. 3

The value of the 66 is that it can do anything, and to change it from a combine into a cornpicker takes one man about half an hour, whereas most machine conversions on farms take several men a half day. It frees its owner from a lot of monkeying. 4

Monkeying, in city life, is what little boys do to clocks so they never run again. In farming it has two quite different meanings. The first is small side projects. You monkey with poultry, unless you're a major egg handler. Or you monkey with ducks or geese. If you have a very small 5

milk herd, and finally decide that prices plus state regulations don't make your few Holsteins worthwhile, you "quit monkeying with them." There is a hidden dignity in this word: it precludes mention of money. It lets the wife of a very marginal farmer have a conversation with a woman who may be helping her husband run fifteen hundred acres. "How you coming with those geese?" "Oh, we've been real disgusted. We're thinking of quitting monkeying with them." It saves her having to say, "We lost our shirts on those darn geese."

The other meaning of monkeying is wrestling with and maintaining 6
machinery, such as changing heads from combining to cornpicking. Farmers who cornpick the old way, in which the corn isn't shelled automatically during picking in the field but must be elevated to the top of a pile by belt and then shelled, put up with some monkeying.

Still, cornpicking and plowing is a marvelous time of the year on 7
farms; one of the best autumns I've had recently had a few days of fieldwork in it. We were outside all day, from six in the morning to eight at night—coming in only for noon dinner. We ate our lunches on a messy truck flatbed. (For city people who don't know it: *lunch* isn't a noon meal; it is what you eat out of a black lunch pail at 9 A.M. and 3 P.M. If you offer a farmer a cup of coffee at 3:30 P.M. he or she is likely to say, "No thanks, I've already had lunch.") There were four of us hired to help—a couple to plow, Celia (a skilled farmhand who worked steady for our boss), and me. Lunch was always two sandwiches of white commercial bread with luncheon meat, and one very generous piece of cake-mix cake carefully wrapped in Saran Wrap. (I never found anyone around here self-conscious about using Saran Wrap when the Dow Chemical Company was also making napalm.)

It was very pleasant on the flatbed, squinting out over the yellow 8
picked cornstalks—each time we stopped for lunch, a larger part of the field had been plowed black. We fell into the easy psychic habit of farmworkers: admiration of the boss. "Ja, I see he's buying one of those big 4010s," someone would say. We always perked up at inside information like that. Or "Ja," as the woman hired steady told us, "he's going to plow the home fields first this time, instead of the other way round." We temporary help were impressed by that, too. Then, with real flair, she brushed a crumb of luncheon meat off her jeans, the way you would make sure to flick a gnat off spotless tennis whites. It is the true feminine touch to brush a crumb off pants that are encrusted with Minnesota Profile A heavy loam, many swipes of SAE 40 oil, and grain dust.

All those days, we never tired of exchanging information on how *he* 9
was making out, what *he* was buying, whom *he* was going to let drive the new tractor, and so on. There is always something to talk about with the other hands, because farming is genuinely absorbing. It has the best quality of work: nothing else seems real. And everyone doing it, even the cheapest helpers like me, can see the layout of the whole—from spring work, to cultivating, to small grain harvest, to cornpicking, to fall plowing.

The second day I was promoted from elevating corncobs at the 10
corn pile to actual plowing. Hour after hour I sat up there on the old Alice, as she was called (an Allis-Chalmers WC that looked rusted from the Flood). You have to sit twisted part way around, checking that the plowshares are scouring clean, turning over and dropping the dead crop and soil, not clogging. For the first two hours I was very political. I thought about what would be good for American farming—stronger marketing organizations, or maybe a law like the Norwegian Odal law, preventing the breaking up of small farms or selling them to business interests. Then the sun got high, and each time I reached the headlands area at the field's end I dumped off something else, now my cap, next my jacket, finally my sweater.

Since the headlands are the last to be plowed, they serve as a field 11
road until the very end. There are usually things parked there—a pickup or a corn trailer—and things dumped—my warmer clothing, our afternoon lunch pails, a broken furrow wheel someone picked up.

By noon I'd dropped all political interest, and was thinking only: 12
how unlike this all is to Keats's picture of autumn, a "season of mists and mellow fruitfulness." This gigantic expanse of horizon, with everywhere the easy growl of tractors, was simply teeming with extrovert energy. It wouldn't calm down for another week, when whoever was lowest on the totem pole would be sent out to check a field for dropped parts or to drive away the last machines left around.

The worst hours for all common labor are the hours after noon 13
dinner. Nothing is inspiring then. That is when people wonder how they ever got stuck in the line of work they've chosen for life. Or they wonder where the cool Indian smoke of secrets and messages began to vanish from their marriage. Instead of plugging along like a cheerful beast working for me, the Allis now smelled particularly gassy. To stay awake I froze my eyes onto an indented circle in the hood around the gas cap. Someone has apparently knocked the screw cap fitting down into the hood, so there was a moat around it. In this moat some overflow gas leapt in tiny waves. Sometimes the gas cap was a castle, this was the moat; sometimes it was a nuclear-fission plant, this was the horrible hot-water waste. Sometimes it was just the gas cap on the old Alice with the split gas bouncing on the hot metal.

Row after row. I was stupefied. But then around 2:30 the shadows 14
appeared again, and the light, which had been dazing and white, grew fragile. The whole prairie began to gather itself for the cool evening. All of a sudden it was wonderful to be plowing again, and when I came to the field end, the filthy jackets and the busted furrow wheel were just benign mistakes: that is, if it chose to, the jacket could be a church robe, and the old wheel could be something with some pride to it, like a helm. And I felt the same about myself: instead of being someone with a half interest in literature and a half interest in farming doing a half-decent job plowing, I could have been someone desperately needed in Washington or Zurich. I drank my three o'clock coffee joyously, and

traded the other plowman a Super-Valu cake-mix lemon cake slice for a Holsum baloney sandwich because it has garlic in it.

By seven at night we had been plowing with headlights for an hour. 15
I tried to make up games to keep going, on my second wind, on my third wind, but labor is labor after the whole day of it; the mind refuses to think of ancestors. It refuses to pretend the stalks marching up to the right wheel in the spooky light are men-at-arms, or to imagine a new generation coming along. It doesn't care. Now the Republicans could have announced a local meeting in which they would propose a new farm program whereby every farmer owning less than five hundred acres must take half price for his crop, and every farmer owning more than a thousand acres shall receive triple price for his crop, and I was so tired I wouldn't have shown up to protest.

A million hours later we sit around in a daze at the dining-room 16
table, and nobody says anything. In low, courteous mutters we ask for the macaroni hotdish down this way, please. Then we get up in ones and twos and go home. Now the farm help are all so tired we *are* a little like the various things left out on the headlands—some tools, a jacket, someone's thermos top—used up for that day. Thoughts won't even stick to us any more.

Such tiredness must be part of farmers' wanting huge machinery 17
like the Deere 6600. That tiredness that feels so good to the occasional laborer and the athlete is disturbing to a man destined to it eight months of every year. But there is a more hidden psychology in the issue of enclosed combines versus open tractors. It is this: one gets too many impressions on the open tractor. A thousand impressions enter as you work up and down the rows: nature's beauty or nature's stubbornness, politics, exhaustion, but mainly the feeling that all this repetition—last year's cornpicking, this year's cornpicking, next year's cornpicking—is taking up your lifetime. The mere repetition reveals your eventual death.

When you sit inside a modern combine, on the other hand, you are 18
so isolated from field, sky, all the real world, that the brain is dulled. You are not sensitized to your own mortality. You aren't sensitive to anything at all.

This must be a common choice of our mechanical era: to hide 19
from life inside our machinery. If we can hide from life in there, some idiotic part of the psyche reasons, we can hide from death in there as well.

COMPREHENSION

1. To what does the title refer? Where is it explained in the essay?
2. Why is Bly ambivalent about the new combine?
3. What is Bly's position in the community? Give proof of this.

RHETORIC

1. What is Bly's thesis? Is it implied or stated directly?
2. Who is Bly's audience? What proof is there for this?
3. At the end of the first paragraph, Bly describes the combine as "huge, tremendously still, very professional, slightly dangerous." How does this description reinforce the author's point?
4. Why does the author choose to define the word *monkeying* so extensively (in paragraphs 5 and 6)? How do these definitions help to support her main idea?
5. How do Bly's use of metaphors contribute to the essay? Cite passages that contain especially evocative language.
6. How does the author use process analysis in her essay? What effect does it have on the narrative?

WRITING

1. At the end of her narrative, Bly draws this conclusion: "This must be a common choice of our mechanical era: to hide from life inside our machinery." Using evidence from her essay, as well as your own observations, write an essay that agrees or disagrees with this opinion.
2. Compare and contrast the farmer's work and lifestyle to those of people doing another type of work (for example: teachers, truck drivers, or factory workers). Which is more exhausting, satisfying, remunerative? Consider these questions in an essay.
3. Write a research paper that responds to these questions: What is the current state of the family farm? Has it lost its place in the American mythos?

GARY SOTO Gary Soto (1958–) is the son of American-born parents and Mexican-born grandparents who worked in the fields and factories of California. Educated at Fresno City College and later California State University at Fresno, Soto has earned recognition for his sensitivity and painstaking attention to craft. His work includes *The Elements of San Joaquin* (1977), *Living up the Street: Narrative Recollections* (1965), *Lesser Evils: Ten Quarters* (1988), and *Home Course in Religion* (1991). As a child, Soto experienced poverty and alienation, at odds with a society that favors assimilation. Soto's writing reflects these issues; and in this selection from *Living up the Street,* he describes a seemingly carefree childhood darkened subtly by unsettling social realities.

GARY SOTO

Looking for Work

One July, while killing ants on the kitchen sink with a rolled newspaper, I had a nine-year-old's vision of wealth that would save us from ourselves. For weeks I had drunk Kool-Aid and watched morning reruns of *Father Knows Best,* whose family was so uncomplicated in its routine that I very much wanted to imitate it. The first step was to get my brother and sister to wear shoes at dinner. 1

"Come on, Rick—come on, Deb," I whined. But Rick mimicked me and the same day that I asked him to wear shoes he came to the dinner table in only his swim trunks. My mother didn't notice, nor did my sister, as we sat to eat our beans and tortillas in the stifling heat of our kitchen. We all gleamed like cellophane, wiping the sweat from our brows with the backs of our hands as we talked about the day: Frankie our neighbor was beat up by Faustino; the swimming pool at the playground would be closed for a day because the pump was broken. 2

Such was our life. So that morning, while doing-in the train of ants which arrived each day, I decided to become wealthy, and right away! After downing a bowl of cereal, I took a rake from the garage and started up the block to look for work. 3

We lived on an ordinary block of mostly working class people: warehousemen, egg candlers, welders, mechanics, and a union plumber. And there were many retired people who kept their lawns green and the gutters uncluttered of the chewing gum wrappers we dropped as we rode by on our bikes. They bent down to gather our litter, muttering at our evilness. 4

At the corner house I rapped the screen door and a very large woman in a muu-muu answered. She sized me up and then asked what I could do. 5

"Rake leaves," I answered, smiling. 6

"It's summer, and there ain't no leaves," she countered. Her face was pinched with lines; fat jiggled under her chin. She pointed to the lawn, then the flower bed, and said: "You see any leaves there—or there?" I followed her pointing arm, stupidly. But she had a job for me and that was to get her a Coke at the liquor store. She gave me twenty cents, and after ditching my rake in a bush, off I ran. I returned with an unbagged Pepsi, for which she thanked me and gave me a nickel from her apron. 7

I skipped off her porch, fetched my rake, and crossed the street to the next block where Mrs. Moore, mother of Earl the retarded man, let me weed a flower bed. She handed me a trowel and for a good part of the morning my fingers dipped into the moist dirt, ripping up runners 8 of Bermuda grass. Worms surfaced in my search for deep roots, and I cut them in halves, tossing them to Mrs. Moore's cat who pawed them playfully as they dried in the sun. I made out Earl whose face was pressed to the back window of the house, and although he was calling to me I couldn't understand what he was trying to say. Embarrassed, I worked without looking up, but I imagined his contorted mouth and the ring of keys attached to his belt—keys that jingled with each palsied step. He scared me and I worked quickly to finish the flower bed. When I did finish Mrs. Moore gave me a quarter and two peaches from her tree, which I washed there but ate in the alley behind my house.

I was sucking on the second one, a bit of juice staining the front of my T-shirt, when Little John, my best friend, came walking down the alley with a baseball bat over his shoulder, knocking over trash cans as he made his way toward me. 9

Little John and I went to St. John's Catholic School, where we sat among the "stupids." Miss Marino, our teacher, alternated the rows of good students with the bad, hoping that by sitting side-by-side with the bright students the stupids might become more intelligent, as though intelligence were contagious. But we didn't progress as she had hoped. She grew frustrated when one day, while dismissing class for recess, Little John couldn't get up because his arms were stuck in the slats of the chair's backrest. She scolded us with a shaking finger when we knocked over the globe, denting the already troubled Africa. She muttered curses when Leroy White, a real stupid but a great softball player with the gift to hit to all fields, openly chewed his host when he made his First Communion; his hands swung at his sides as he returned to the pew looking around with a big smile. 10

Little John asked what I was doing, and I told him that I was taking a break from work, as I sat comfortably among high weeds. He wanted to join me, but I reminded him that the last time he'd gone door-to-door asking for work his mother had whipped him. I was with him when his mother, a New Jersey Italian who could rise up in anger one moment and love the next, told me in a polite but matter-of-fact voice that I had to leave because she was going to beat her son. She gave me a homemade popsicle, ushered me to the door, and said that I could see Little John the next day. But it was sooner than that. I went around to his bedroom window to suck my popsicle and watch Little John dodge his mother's blows, a few hitting their mark but many whirring air. 11

It was midday when Little John and I converged in the alley, the sun blazing in the high nineties, and he suggested that we go to Roosevelt High School to swim. He needed five cents to make fifteen, the cost of admission, and I lent him a nickel. We ran home for my bike and when my sister found out that we were going swimming, she started to cry because she didn't have the fifteen cents but only an empty Coke bottle. I waved for her to come and three of us mounted the bike—Debra on the cross bar, Little John on the handle bars and holding the Coke bottle which we would cash for a nickel and make up the difference that would allow all of us to get in, and me pumping up the crooked streets, 12 dodging cars and pot holes. We spent the day swimming under the afternoon sun, so that when we got home our mom asked us what was darker, the floor or us? She feigned a stern posture, her hands on her hips and her mouth puckered. We played along. Looking down, Debbie and I said in unison, "Us."

That evening at dinner we all sat down in our bathing suits to eat our beans, laughing and chewing loudly. Our mom was in a good mood, so I took a risk and asked her if sometime we could have turtle soup. A few days before I had watched a television program in which a Polynesian tribe killed a large turtle, gutted it, and then stewed it over an open fire. The turtle, basted in a sugary sauce, looked delicious as I ate an afternoon bowl of cereal, but my sister, who was watching the program with a glass of Kool-Aid between her knees, said, "Caca." 13

My mother looked at me in bewilderment. "Boy, are you a crazy Mexican. Where did you get the idea that people eat turtles?" 14

"On television," I said, explaining the program. Then I took it a step further. "Mom, do you think we could get dressed up for dinner one of these days? David King does." 15

"Ay, Dios," my mother laughed. She started collecting the dinner plates, but my brother wouldn't let go of his. He was still drawing a picture in the bean sauce. Giggling, he said it was me, but I didn't want to listen because I wanted an answer from Mom. This was the summer when I spent the mornings in front of the television that showed the comfortable lives of white kids. There were no beatings, no rifts in the family. They wore bright clothes; toys tumbled from their closets. They hopped into bed with kisses and woke to glasses of fresh orange juice, and to a father sitting before his morning coffee while the mother buttered his toast. They hurried through the day making friends and gobs of money, returning home to a warmly lit living room, and then dinner. *Leave It to Beaver* was the program I replayed in my mind: 16

"May I have the mashed potatoes?" asks Beaver with a smile. 17

"Sure, Beav," replies Wally as he taps the corners of his mouth with a starched napkin. 18

The father looks on in his suit. The mother, decked out in earrings and a pearl necklace, cuts into her steak and blushes. Their conversation is politely clipped. 19

"Swell," says Beaver, his cheeks puffed with food. 20

Our own talk at dinner was loud with belly laughs and marked by our pointing forks at one another. The subjects were commonplace. 21

"Gary, let's go to the ditch tomorrow," my brother suggests. He explains that he has made a life preserver out of four empty detergent bottles strung together with twine and that he will make me one if I can find more bottles. "No way are we going to drown." 22

"Yeah, then we could have a dirt clod fight," I reply, so happy to be alive. 23

Whereas the Beaver's family enjoyed dessert in dishes at the table, our mom sent us outside, and more often than not I went into the alley 24 to peek over the neighbor's fences and spy out fruit, apricots and peaches.

I had asked my mom and again she laughed that I was a crazy *chavalo* as she stood in front of the sink, her arms rising and falling with suds, face glistening from the heat. She sent me outside where my brother and sister were sitting in the shade that the fence threw out like a blanket. They were talking about me when I plopped down next to them. They looked at one another and then Debbie, my eight-year-old sister, started in.

"What's this crap about getting dressed up?" 26

She had entered her profanity stage. A year later she would give up 27
such words and slip into her Catholic uniform, and into squealing on my brother and me when we "cussed this" and "cussed that."

I tried to convince them that if we improved the way we looked we 28
might get along better in life. White people would like us more. They might invite us to places, like their homes or front yards. They might not hate us so much.

My sister called me a "craphead," and got up to leave with a stalk of 29
grass dangling from her mouth. "They'll never like us."

My brother's mood lightened as he talked about the ditch—the 30
white water, the broken pieces of glass, and the rusted car fenders that awaited our knees. There would be toads, and rocks to smash them.

David King, the only person we knew who resembled the middle 31
class, called from over the fence. David was Catholic, of Armenian and French descent, and his closet was filled with toys. A bear-shaped cookie jar, like the ones on television, sat on the kitchen counter. His mother was remarkably kind while she put up with the racket we made on the street. Evenings, she often watered the front yard and it must have upset her to see us—my brother and I and others—jump from trees laughing, the unkillable kids of the very poor, who got up unshaken, brushed off, and climbed into another one to try again.

David called again. Rick got up and slapped grass from his pants. 32
When I asked if I could come along he said no. David said no. They were two years older so their affairs were different from mine. They greeted one another with foul names and took off down the alley to look for trouble.

I went inside the house, turned on the television, and was about to 33
sit down with a glass of Kool-Aid when Mom shooed me outside.

"It's still light," she said. "Later you'll bug me to let you stay out 34
longer. So go on."

I downed my Kool-Aid and went outside to the front yard. No one 35
was around. The day had cooled and a breeze rustled the trees. Mr. Jackson, the plumber, was watering his lawn and when he saw me he turned away to wash off his front steps. There was more than an hour of light left, so I took advantage of it and decided to look for work. I felt suddenly alive as I skipped down the block in search of an overgrown flower bed and the dime that would end the day right.

COMPREHENSION

1. What images of family life is the young Soto exposed to on television? How do they contrast with his real family?
2. What kinds of work did Soto have as a boy?
3. Was Soto's childhood a happy one? Justify your answer by specific reference to the essay.

RHETORIC

1. Does the narrative contain a thesis? Where in the essay is it located?
2. What specific descriptive devices does Soto employ to set a mood in his essay? Cite concrete examples of this.
3. Examine the use of dialogue and its effectiveness in the narrative. What does it contribute to the tone of the essay? Where is it used especially well? Provide illustrations from the work.
4. Is there anything in Soto's narrative to emphasize Soto's ethnic background? Why do you think Soto chose not to include Spanish phrases? What impact does this have on his narrative?
5. Notice Soto's use of adjectives and descriptive passages in this essay. Find specific examples of figurative language in the piece, and explain why they're especially evocative.
6. Compare Soto's introductory paragraph and his conclusion. How do they complement each other and provide closure?

WRITING

1. As a child, Soto spent a lot of time envying the family life depicted on television in programs such as *Leave It to Beaver.* Write an essay in which you explore the importance of television on your childhood. Which particular programs did you enjoy, and how did they help form your ideas of family life? How did your family life compare to that seen on television?
2. Write an essay similar to Soto's describing your first work experiences as a child or teenager. What was the job? Did you enjoy it? Did you get paid, and, if so, how did you spend the money?
3. Analyze the vision of family life presented by current television programs. Are today's programs more realistic than those of Soto's childhood? Do they provide positive images and role models?

ELLEN GOODMAN Ellen Holtz Goodman (1941–), is an award-winning journalist who writes a syndicated column for the *Boston Globe.* She is the author of *Close to Home* (1979) and *At Large* (1981) and has been a commentator on television and radio. Goodman is an adept practitioner of the personal essay. In the following selection, her celebrated penchant for irony and satire finds a perfect focus in the working lives of women.

ELLEN GOODMAN

Being a Secretary Can Be Hazardous to Your Health

They used to say it with flowers or celebrate it with a somewhat liquid lunch. National Secretaries Week was always good for at least a token of appreciation. But the way the figures add up now, the best thing a boss can do for a secretary this week is cough up for her cardiogram. 1

"Stress and the Secretary" has become the hottest new syndrome on the heart circuit. 2

It seems that it isn't those Daring Young Women in their Dress-for-Success Suits who are following men down the cardiovascular trail to ruin. Nor is it the female professionals who are winning their equal place in intensive care units. 3

It is powerlessness and not power that corrupts women's hearts. And clerical workers are the number one victims. 4

In the prestigious Framingham study, Dr. Suzanne Haynes, an epidemiologist with the National Heart, Lung and Blood Institute, found that working women as a whole have no higher rate of heart disease than housewives. But women employed in clerical and sales occupations do. Their coronary disease rates are twice that of other women. 5

"This is not something to ignore," says Dr. Haynes, "since such a high percent of women work at clerical jobs." In fact, 35 percent of all working women, or 18 million of us, hold these jobs. 6

When Dr. Haynes looked into their private lives, she found the women at greatest risk—with a one in five chance of heart disease—were clerical workers with blue-collar husbands, and three or more children. When she then looked at their work lives, she discovered that the ones who actually developed heart disease were those with nonsupportive bosses who hadn't changed jobs very often and who had trouble letting their anger out. 7

In short, being frustrated, dead-ended, without a feeling of control over your life is bad for your health. 8

The irony in all the various and sundry heart statistics is that we now have a weird portrait of the Cardiovascular Fun Couple of the Office: The Type A Boss and his secretary. The male heart disease stereotype is, after all, the Type A aggressive man who always needs to be in control, who lives with a great sense of time urgency . . . and is likely to be a white-collar boss. 9

"The Type A man is trying to be in control. But given the way most businesses are organized there are, in fact, few ways for them to be in control of their jobs," says Dr. Haynes. The only thing the Type A boss 10

can be in control of is his secretary who in turn feels . . . well you get the picture. He's not only getting heart disease, he's giving it.

As if all this weren't enough to send you out for the annual three 11
martini lunch, clerical workers are increasingly working for a new Type A boss: the computer.

These days fewer women are sitting in front of bosses with 12
notepads and more are sitting in front of Visual Display Terminals. Word processors, data processors, microprocessors . . . these are the demanding, time-conscious, new automatons of automation.

There is nothing intrinsically evil about computers. I am writing 13
this on a VDT and if you try to take it away from me, I will break your arm. But as Working Women, the national association of office workers, puts it in their release this week, automation is increasingly producing clerical jobs that are de-skilled, down-graded, dead-ended and dissatisfying.

As Karen Nussbaum of the Cleveland office described it, the office 14
of the future may well be the factory of the past. Work on computers is often reduced to simple, repetitive, monotonous tasks. Workers are often expected to produce more for no more pay, and there are also reports of a disturbing trend to processing speed-ups and piece-rate pay, and a feeling among clerical workers that their jobs are computer controlled. 15

"It's not the machine, but the way it's used by employers," says Working Women's research director, Judith Gregory. Too often, automation's most important product is stress. 16

Groups, like Working Women, are trying to get clerical workers to organize in what they call "a race against time" so that computers will become their tools instead of their supervisors. 17

But in the meantime, if you are 1) a female clerical worker, 2) with a blue-collar husband, 3) with three or more children, 4) in a dead-end job, 5) without any way to express anger, 6) with a Type A boss, 7) or a Type A computer controlling your work day . . . *you better start jogging.*

COMPREHENSION

1. What slogan does the author's title play upon? How does it prepare us for Goodman's thesis? What is her thesis?
2. What major problem does Goodman discuss in this essay? What are the causes of the problem?
3. How does the author describe the Type A boss and the Type A female employee?

RHETORIC

1. How does Goodman use colloquial language to help establish the tone of her essay?

2. List examples of comic language. What is Goodman's purpose? Comment on the relationship of Goodman's use of comic language to her thesis.
3. What technique does Goodman use to establish the topic of her essay?
4. What types of examples does Goodman use to reinforce her generalizations? Do any of the examples qualify as expert testimony? Explain.
5. Where does Goodman state her thesis? How does her conclusion reinforce this thesis?
6. What patterns of comparison and contrast do you find? Why does the author employ this technique?

WRITING

1. Does Goodman's range of humor work for or against the seriousness of her topic? Explain your response in an evaluative essay.
2. Analyze the varieties of stress that you have felt while employed at a particular job.
3. Argue for or against the proposition that working women do not experience any more stress than working men.
4. Describe the Type A worker or professional, and propose solutions to his or her problems.

E. M. FORSTER Edward Morgan Forster (1879–1970), English essayist, novelist, biographer, and literary critic, wrote several notable works of fiction dealing with the constricting effects of social and national conventions upon human relationships. These novels include *A Room with a View* (1908), *Howards End* (1910), and *A Passage to India* (1924). In addition, his lectures on fiction, collected as *Aspects of the Novel* (1927), remain graceful elucidations of the genre. In "My Wood," taken from his essay collection *Abinger Harvest* (1936), Forster writes with wit and wisdom about the effect of property upon human behavior—notably his own.

E. M. FORSTER

My Wood

A few years ago I wrote a book which dealt in part with the difficulties of the English in India. Feeling that they would have had no difficulties in India themselves, the Americans read the book freely. The more they read it the better it made them feel, and a cheque to the author was the result. I bought a wood with the cheque. It is not a large wood—it contains scarcely any trees, and it is intersected, blast it, by a public foot- 1 path. Still, it is the first property that I have owned, so it is right that other people should participate in my shame, and should ask themselves, in accents that will vary in horror, this very important question: What is the effect of property upon the character? Don't let's touch economics; the effect of private ownership upon the community as a whole is another question—a more important question, perhaps, but another one. Let's keep to psychology. If you own things, what's their effect on you? What's the effect on me of my wood?

In the first place, it makes me feel heavy. Property does have this effect. Property produces men of weight, and it was a man of weight who failed to get into the Kingdom of Heaven. He was not wicked, that unfortunate millionaire in the parable, he was only stout; he stuck out in front, not to mention behind, and as he wedged himself this way and that in the crystalline entrance and bruised his well-fed flanks, he saw beneath him a comparatively slim camel passing through the eye of a needle and being woven into the robe of God. The Gospels all through couple stoutness and slowness. They point out what is perfectly obvious, yet seldom realized: that if you have a lot of things you cannot move about a lot, that furniture requires dusting, dusters require servants, servants require insurance stamps, and the whole tangle of them makes you think twice before you accept an invitation to dinner or go for a bathe in the Jordan. Sometimes the Gospels proceed further and say with Tolstoy that property is sinful; they approach the difficult ground of asceticism here, where I cannot follow them. But as to the immediate effects of property on people, they just show straightforward logic. It produces men of weight. Men of weight cannot, by definition, move like the lightning from the East unto the West, and the ascent of a fourteen-stone bishop into a pulpit is thus the exact antithesis of the coming of the Son of Man. My wood makes me feel heavy. 2

In the second place, it makes me feel it ought to be larger. 3

The other day I heard a twig snap in it. I was annoyed at first, for I thought that someone was blackberrying, and depreciating the value of the undergrowth. On coming nearer, I saw it was not a man who had trodden on the twig and snapped it, but a bird, and I felt pleased. My bird. The bird was not equally pleased. Ignoring the relation between us, it took fright as soon as it saw the shape of my face, and flew straight over the boundary hedge into a field, the property of Mrs. Henessy, where it sat down with a loud squawk. It had become Mrs. Henessy's bird. Something seemed grossly amiss here, something that would not have occurred had the wood been larger. I could not afford to buy Mrs. Henessy out, I dared not murder her, and limitations of this sort beset me on every side. Ahab did not want that vineyard—he only needed it to round off his property, preparatory to plotting a new curve—and all the land around my wood has become necessary to me in order to round off the wood. A boundary protects. But—poor little thing—the boundary ought in its turn to be protected. Noises on the edge of it. Children throw stones. A little more, and then a little more, until we reach the sea. Happy Canute! Happier Alexander! And after 4 all, why should even the world be the limit of possession? A rocket containing a Union Jack, will, it is hoped, be shortly fired at the moon. Mars. Sirius. Beyond which. . . . But these immensities ended by saddening me. I could not suppose that my wood was the destined nucleus of universal dominion—it is so very small and contains no mineral wealth beyond the blackberries. Nor was I comforted when Mrs. Henessy's bird took alarm for the second time and flew clean away from us all, under the belief that it belonged to itself.

In the third place, property makes its owner feel that he ought to do 5
something to it. Yet he isn't sure what. A restlessness comes over him, a vague sense that he has a personality to express—the same sense which, without any vagueness, leads the artist to an act of creation. Sometimes I think I will cut down such trees as remain in the wood, at other times I want to fill up the gaps between them with new trees. Both impulses are pretentious and empty. They are not honest movements towards money-making or beauty. They spring from a foolish desire to express myself and from an inability to enjoy what I have got. Creation, property, enjoyment form a sinister trinity in the human mind. Creation and enjoyment are both very, very good, yet they are often unattainable without a material basis, and at such moments property pushes itself in as a substitute, saying, "Accept me instead—I'm good enough for all three." It is not enough. It is, as Shakespeare said of lust, "The expense of spirit in a waste of shame": it is "Before, a joy proposed; behind, a dream." Yet we don't know how to shun it. It is forced on us by our economic system as the alternative to starvation. It is also forced on us by an internal defect in the soul, by the feeling that in property may lie the germs of self-development and of exquisite or heroic deeds. Our life on earth is, and ought to be, material and carnal. But we have not yet learned to manage our materialism and carnality properly; they are still entangled with the desire for ownership, where (in the words of Dante) "Possession is one with loss."

And this brings us to our fourth and final point: the blackberries. 6

Blackberries are not plentiful in this meager grove, but they are eas- 7
ily seen from the public footpath which traverses it, and all too easily gathered. Foxgloves, too—people will pull up the foxgloves, and ladies of an educational tendency even grub for toadstools to show them on the Monday in class. Other ladies, less educated, roll down the bracken in the arms of their gentlemen friends. There is paper, there are tins. Pray, does my wood belong to me or doesn't it? And, if it does, should I not own it best by allowing no one else to walk there? There is a wood near Lyme Regis, also cursed by a public footpath, where the owner has not hesitated on this point. He had built high stone walls each side of the path, and has spanned it by bridges, so that the public circulate like termites while he gorges on the blackberries unseen. He really does own his wood, this able chap. Dives in Hell did pretty well, but the gulf dividing him from Lazarus could be traversed by vision, and nothing traverses it here. And perhaps I shall come to this in time. I shall wall in and fence out until I really taste the sweets of property. Enormously

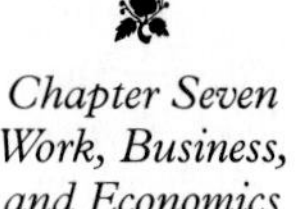

stout, endlessly avaricious, pseudo-creative, intensely selfish, I shall weave upon my forehead the quadruple crown of possession until those nasty Bolshies come and take it off again and thrust me aside into the outer darkness.

COMPREHENSION

1. What sort of essay is Forster writing for his audience? What is his purpose? How do you know?
2. List the four effects that property ownership has upon the author. How serious is he in describing these effects? Explain.
3. Describe the persona that emerges from the essay. What is the relationship of the last sentence to this persona?

RHETORIC

1. What words and phrases does the author use to create a conversational style in the essay?
2. Analyze biblical, historical, and literary allusions in the essay. What is their function?
3. What is the purpose of Forster's reference to Americans at the outset of the essay?
4. How is the thesis reinforced in the first paragraph? How are essay clarity and proper sequence achieved through the placement of topic sentences?
5. Analyze the manner in which Forster integrates the analysis of effects with a personal definition of *property*.
6. Explain the shift in tone, and the movement from concrete to abstract, in paragraph 5.

WRITING

1. Do you agree with Forster that property ownership is as difficult as he declares it to be? Give the basis of your response, and elucidate in an essay.
2. Write an essay of definition in which you explain an abstract term in personal, concrete, and carefully organized terms.
3. Write a comparative essay on the theme of property and nature as developed by Forster in "My Wood" and Thoreau in "Economy," in Chapter 12.

JONATHAN SWIFT Jonathan Swift (1667–1745) is best known as the author of three satires: *A Tale of a Tub* (1704), *Gulliver's Travels* (1726), and *A Modest Proposal* (1729). In these satires, Swift pricks the balloon of many of his contemporaries' and our own most cherished prejudices, pomposities, and delusions. He was also a famous churchman, an eloquent spokesman for Irish rights, and a political journalist. The following selection, perhaps the most famous satiric essay in the English language, offers modest advice to a nation suffering from poverty, overpopulation, and political injustice.

JONATHAN SWIFT

A Modest Proposal

For Preventing the Children of Poor People in Ireland from Being a Burden to Their Parents or Country, and for Making Them Beneficial to the Public

It is a melancholy object to those who walk through this great town or 1
travel in the country, when they see the streets, the roads, and cabin doors, crowded with beggars of the female-sex, followed by three, four, or six children, all in rags and importuning every passenger for an alms. These mothers, instead of being able to work for their honest livelihood, are forced to employ all their time in strolling to beg sustenance for their helpless infants, who, as they grow up, either turn thieves for want of work, or leave their dear native country to fight for the Pretender in Spain, or sell themselves to the Barbadoes.

I think it is agreed by all parties that this prodigious number of chil- 2
dren in the arms, or on the backs, or at the heels of their mothers, and frequently of their fathers, is in the present deplorable state of the kingdom a very great additional grievance; and therefore whoever could find out a fair, cheap, and easy method of making these children sound, useful members of the commonwealth would deserve so well of the public as to have his statue set up for a preserver of the nation.

But my intention is very far from being confined to provide only for 3
the children of professed beggars; it is of a much greater extent, and shall take in the whole number of infants at a certain age who are born of parents in effect as little able to support them as those who demand our charity in the streets.

As to my own part, having turned my thoughts for many years 4
upon this important subject, and maturely weighed the several schemes of other projectors, I have always found them grossly mistaken in their computation. It is true, a child just dropped from its dam may be supported by her milk for a solar year, with little other nourishment; at most not above the value of two shillings, which the mother may certainly get, or the value in scraps, by her lawful occupation of begging; and it is exactly at one year old that I propose to provide for them in such a manner as instead of being a charge upon their parents or the parish, or wanting food and raiment for the rest of their lives, they shall on the contrary contribute to the feeding, and partly to the clothing, of many thousands.

There is likewise another great advantage in my scheme, that it will 5
prevent those voluntary abortions, and that horrid practice of women

murdering their bastard children, alas, too frequent among us, sacrificing the poor innocent babes, I doubt, more to avoid the expense than the shame, which would move tears and pity in the most savage and inhuman breast.

The number of souls in this kingdom being usually reckoned one million and a half, of these I calculate there may be about two hundred thousand couples whose wives are breeders; from which number I subtract thirty thousand couples who are able to maintain their own children, although I apprehend there cannot be so many under the present distresses of the kingdom; but this being granted, there will remain an hundred and seventy thousand breeders. I again subtract fifty thousand for those women who miscarry, or whose children die by accident or disease within the year. There only remain an hundred and twenty thousand children of poor parents annually born. The question therefore is, how this number shall be reared and provided for, which, as I have already said, under the present situation of affairs, is utterly impossible by all the methods hitherto proposed. For we can neither employ them in handicraft or agriculture; we neither build houses (I mean in the country) nor cultivate land. They can very seldom pick up a livelihood by stealing till they arrive at six years old, except where they are of towardly parts; although I confess they learn the rudiments much earlier, during which time they can however be looked upon only as probationers, as I have been informed by a principal gentlemen in the county of Cavan, who protested to me that he never knew above one or two instances under the age of six, even in a part of the kingdom so renowned for the quickest proficiency in that art. 6

I am assured by our merchants that a boy or girl before twelve years old is no salable commodity; and even when they come to this age they will not yield above three pounds, or three pounds and half a crown at most on the Exchange; which cannot turn to account either to the parents or the kingdom, the charge of nutriment and rags having been at least four times that value. 7

I shall now therefore humbly propose my own thoughts, which I hope will not be liable to the least objection. 8

I have been assured by a very knowing American of my acquaintance in London, that a young healthy child well nursed is at a year old a most delicious, nourishing, and wholesome food, whether stewed, roasted, baked or boiled; and I make no doubt that it will equally serve in a fricassee or a ragout. 9

I do therefore humbly offer it to public consideration that of the hundred and twenty thousand children, already computed, twenty thousand may be reserved for breed, whereof only one fourth part to be males, which is more than we allow to sheep, black cattle, or swine; and my reason is that these children are seldom the fruits of marriage, a circumstance not much regarded by our savages, therefore one male will be sufficient to serve four females. That the remaining hundred thousand may at a year old be offered in sale to the persons of quality and fortune through the kingdom, always advising the mother to let 10 them suck plentifully in the last month, so as to render them plump and fat for a good table. A child will make two dishes at an entertainment for friends; and when the family dines alone, the fore or hind quarter will make a reasonable dish, and seasoned with a little pepper or salt will be very good boiled on the fourth day, especially in winter.

I have reckoned upon a medium that a child just born will weigh twelve pounds, and in a solar year if tolerably nursed increaseth to twenty-eight pounds. 11

I grant this food will be somewhat dear, and therefore very proper for landlords, who, as they have already devoured most of the parents, seem to have the best title to the children. 12

Infant's flesh will be in season throughout the year, but more plentiful in March, and a little before and after. For we are told by a grave author, an eminent French physician, that fish being a prolific diet, there are more children born in Roman Catholic countries about nine months after Lent than at any other season: therefore, reckoning a year after Lent, the markets will be more glutted than usual, because the number of popish infants is at least three to one in this kingdom; and therefore it will have one other collateral advantage, by lessening the number of Papists among us. 13

I have already computed the charge of nursing a beggar's child (in which list I reckon all cottagers, laborers, and four fifths of the farmers) to be about two shillings per annum, rags included: and I believe no gentleman would repine to give ten shillings for the carcass of a good fat child, which, as I have said, will make four dishes of excellent nutritive meat, when he hath only some particular friend or his own family to dine with him. Thus the squire will learn to be a good landlord, and grow popular among the tenants; the mother will have eight shillings net profit, and be fit for work till she produces another child. 14

Those who are more thrifty (as I must confess the times require) may flay the carcass; the skin of which artificially dressed will make admirable gloves for ladies, and summer boots for fine gentlemen. 15

As to our city of Dublin, shambles may be appointed for this purpose in the most convenient parts of it, and butchers we may be assured will not be wanting; although I rather recommend buying the children alive, and dressing them hot from the knife as we do roasting pigs. 16

A very worthy person, a true lover of his country, and whose virtues I highly esteem, was lately pleased in discoursing on this matter to offer a refinement upon my scheme. He said that many gentlemen of this kingdom, having of late destroyed their deer, he conceived that the want of venison might be well supplied by the bodies of young lads and maidens, not exceeding fourteen years of age nor under twelve, so great a number of both sexes in every county being now ready to starve for want of work and service; and these to be disposed of by their parents, if alive, or otherwise by their nearest relations. But with due deference to so excellent a friend and so deserving a patriot, I cannot be altogether in his sentiments; for as to the males, my American acquaintance 17 assured me from frequent experience that their flesh was generally tough and lean, like that of our schoolboys, by continual exercise, and their taste disagreeable; and to fatten them would not answer the charge. Then as to the females, it would, I think with humble submission, be a loss to the public, because they soon would become breeders themselves: and besides, it is not improbable that some scrupulous people might be apt to censure such a practice (although indeed very unjustly) as a little bordering upon cruelty; which, I confess, hath always been with me the strongest objection against any project, how well so ever intended.

But in order to justify my friend, he confessed that this expedient was put into his head by the famous Psalmanazar, a native of the island Formosa, who came from thence to London above twenty years ago, and in conversation told my friend that in his country when any young person happened to be put to death, the executioner sold the carcass to persons of quality as a prime dainty; and that in his time the body of a plump girl of fifteen, who was crucified for an attempt to poison the emperor, was sold to his Imperial Majesty's prime minister of state, and other great mandarins of the court, in joints from the gibbet, at four hundred crowns. Neither indeed can I deny that if the same use were made of several plump young girls in this town, who without one single groat to their fortunes cannot stir abroad without a chair, and appear at the playhouse and assemblies in foreign fineries which they never will pay for, the kingdom would not be the worse. 18

Some persons of a desponding spirit are in great concern about that vast number of poor people who are aged, diseased, or maimed, and I have been desired to employ my thoughts what course may be taken to ease the nation of so grievous an encumbrance. But I am not in the least pain upon that matter, because it is very well known that they are every day dying and rotting by cold and famine, and filth and vermin, as fast as can be reasonably expected. And as to the younger laborers, they are now in almost as hopeful a condition. They cannot get work, and consequently pine away for want of nourishment to a degree that if at any time they are accidentally hired to common labor, they have not strength to perform it; and thus the country and themselves are happily delivered from the evils to come. 19

I have too long digressed, and therefore shall return to my subject. I think the advantages by the proposal which I have made are obvious and many, as well as of the highest importance. 20

For first, as I have already observed, it would greatly lessen the number of Papists, with whom we are yearly overrun, being the principal breeders of the nation as well as our most dangerous enemies; and who stay at home on purpose to deliver the kingdom to the Pretender, hoping to take their advantage by the absence of so many good Protestants, who have chosen rather to leave their country than to stay at home and pay tithes against their conscience to an Episcopal curate. 21

Secondly, the poorer tenants will have something valuable of their own, which by law may be made liable to distress, and help to pay their 22 landlord's rent, their corn and cattle being already seized and money a thing unknown.

Thirdly, whereas the maintenance of an hundred thousand children, from two years old and upwards, cannot be computed at less than ten shillings a piece per annum, the nation's stock will be thereby increased fifty thousand pounds per annum, besides the profit of a new dish introduced to the tables of all gentlemen of fortune in the kingdom who have any refinement in taste. And the money will circulate among ourselves, the goods being entirely of our own growth and manufacture.

Fourthly, the constant breeders, besides the gain of eight shillings 24 sterling per annum by the sale of their children, will be rid of the charge of maintaining them after the first year.

Fifthly, this food would likewise bring great custom to taverns, 25 where the vintners will certainly be so prudent as to procure the best receipts for dressing it to perfection, and consequently have their houses frequented by all the fine gentlemen, who justly value themselves upon their knowledge in good eating; and a skillful cook, who understands how to oblige his guests, will contrive to make it as expensive as they please.

Sixthly, this would be a great inducement to marriage, which all 26 wise nations have either encouraged by rewards or enforced by laws and penalties. It would increase the care and tenderness of mothers toward their children, when they were sure of a settlement for life to the poor babes, provided in some sort by the public, to their annual profit instead of expense. We should see an honest emulation among the married women, which of them could bring the fattest child to the market. Men would become as fond of their wives during the time of their pregnancy as they are now of their mares in foal, their cows in calf, or sows when they are ready to farrow; nor offer to beat or kick them (as is too frequent a practice) for fear of a miscarriage.

Many other advantages might be enumerated. For instance, the ad- 27 dition of some thousand carcasses in our exportation of barreled beef, the propagation of swine's flesh, and improvement in the art of making good bacon, so much wanted among us by the great destruction of pigs, too frequent at our tables, which are no way comparable in taste or magnificence to a well-grown, fat yearling child, which roasted whole will make a considerable figure at a lord mayor's feast or any other public entertainment. But this and many others I omit, being studious of brevity.

Supposing that one thousand families in this city would be constant 28 customers for infants' flesh, besides others who might have it at merry meetings, particularly weddings and christenings, I compute that Dublin would take off annually about twenty thousand carcasses, and the rest of the kingdom (where probably they will be sold somewhat cheaper) the remaining eighty thousand.

I can think of no one objection that will possibly be raised against 29 this proposal, unless it should be urged that the number of people will be thereby much lessened in the kingdom. This I freely own, and it was

indeed one principal design in offering it to the world. I desire the reader will observe, that I calculate my remedy for this one individual kingdom of Ireland and for no other that ever was, is, or I think ever can be upon earth. Therefore let no man talk to me of other expedients: of taxing our absentees at five shillings a pound: of using neither clothes nor household furniture except what is of our own growth and manufacture: of utterly rejecting the materials and instruments that promote foreign luxury: of curing the expensiveness of pride, vanity, idleness, and gaming in our women: of introducing a vein of parsimony, prudence, and temperance: of learning to love our country, in the want of which we differ even from Laplanders and the inhabitants of Topinamboo: of quitting our animosities and factions, nor acting any longer like the Jews, who were murdering one another at the very moment their city was taken: of being a little cautious not to sell our country and conscience for nothing: of teaching landlords to have at least one degree of mercy toward their tenants: lastly, of putting a spirit of honesty, industry, and skill into our shopkeepers; who, if a resolution could be now taken to buy only our native goods, would immediately unite to cheat and exact upon us in the price, the measure and the goodness, nor could ever yet be brought to make one fair proposal of just dealing, though often and earnestly invited to it.

30 Therefore I repeat, let no man talk to me of these and the like expedients, till he hath at least some glimpse of hope that there will ever be some hearty and sincere attempt to put them in practice.

31 But as to myself, having been wearied out for many years with offering vain, idle, visonary thoughts, and at length utterly despairing of success, I fortunately fell upon this proposal, which, as it is wholly new, so it hath something solid and real, of no expense and little trouble, full in our own power, and whereby we can incur no danger in disobliging England. For this kind of commodity will not bear exportation, the flesh being of too tender a consistence to admit a long continuance in salt, although perhaps I could name a country which would be glad to eat up our whole nation without it.

32 After all, I am not so violently bent upon my own opinion as to reject any offer proposed by wise men, which shall be found equally innocent, cheap, easy, and effectual. But before something of that kind shall be advanced in contradiction to my scheme, and offering a better, I desire the author or authors will be pleased maturely to consider two points. First, as things now stand, how they will be able to find food and raiment for an hundred thousand useless mouths and backs. And secondly, there being a round million of creatures in human figure throughout this kingdom, whose sole subsistence put into a common stock would leave them in debt two millions of pounds sterling, adding those who are beggars by profession to the bulk of farmers, cottagers, and laborers, with their wives and children who are beggars in effect; I desire those politicians who dislike my overture, and may perhaps be so bold to attempt an answer, that they will first

ask the parents of these mortals whether they would not at this day think it a great happiness to have been sold for food at a year old in the manner I prescribe, and thereby have avoided such a perpetual scene of misfortunes as they have since gone through by the oppression of landlords, the impossibility of paying rent without money or trade, the want of common sustenance, with neither house nor clothes to cover them from the inclemencies of the weather, and the most inevitable prospect of entailing the like or greater miseries upon their breed forever.

I profess, in the sincerity of my heart, that I have not the least per- 33
sonal interest in endeavoring to promote this necessary work, having no other motive than the public good of my country, by advancing our trade, providing for infants, relieving the poor, and giving some pleasure to the rich. I have no children by which I can propose to get a single penny; the youngest being nine years old, and my wife past childbearing.

COMPREHENSION

1. Who is Swift's audience for this essay? Defend your answer.
2. Describe the persona in this essay. How is the unusual narrative personality (as distinguished from Swift's personality) revealed by the author in degrees? How can we tell that the speaker's opinions are not shared by Swift?
3. What are the major propositions behind Swift's modest proposal? What are the minor propositions?

RHETORIC

1. Explain the importance of the word *modest* in the title. What stylistic devices does this "modesty" contrast with?
2. What is the effect of Swift's persistent reference to people as "breeders," "dams," "carcass," and the like? Why does he define *children* in economic terms? Find other words that contribute to this motif.
3. Analyze the purpose of the relatively long introduction, consisting of paragraphs 1 to 7. How does Swift establish his ironic-satiric tone in this initial section?
4. What contrasts and discrepancies are at the heart of Swift's ironic statement in paragraphs 9 and 10? Explain both the subtlety and savagery of the satire in paragraph 12.
5. Paragraphs 13 to 20 develop six advantages of Swift's proposal, while paragraphs 21 to 26 list them in enumerative manner. Analyze the progression of these propositions. What is the effect of the listing? Why is Swift parodying argumentative techniques?
6. How does the author both sustain and suspend the irony in paragraph 29? How is the strategy repeated in paragraph 32? How does the concluding paragraph cap his satiric commentary on human nature?

WRITING

1. Write a modest proposal—on, for example, how to end the drug problem—advancing an absurd proposition through various argumentative techniques.
2. Discuss Swift's social, political, religious, and economic views as they are revealed in the essay.
3. Write a comprehensive critique of America's failure to address the needs of its poor.

JOHN LAME DEER John Lame Deer (1895?–1976), named after his famous grandfather, was a Sioux chief and medicine man, and author of *Lame Deer, Seeker of Vision.* His book was translated into ten languages, and he was recognized as a spiritual leader among Native Americans. In the powerful, mocking essay below, Lame Deer criticizes the white man's greed and his emphasis on money to the detriment of the environment.

JOHN LAME DEER

The Green Frog Skin

The green frog skin—that's what I call a dollar bill. In our attitude to- 1
ward it lies the biggest difference between Indians and whites. My grandparents grew up in an Indian world without money. Just before the Custer battle the white soldiers had received their pay. Their pockets were full of green paper and they had no place to spend it. What were their last thoughts as an Indian bullet or arrow hit them? I guess they were thinking of all that money going to waste, of not having had a chance to enjoy it, of a bunch of dumb savages getting their paws on that hard-earned pay. That must have hurt them more than the arrow between their ribs.

The close hand-to-hand fighting, with a thousand horses gallyhoot- 2
ing all over the place, had covered the battlefield with an enormous cloud of dust, and in it the green frog skins of the soldiers were whirling around like snowflakes in a blizzard. Now, what did the Indians do with all that money? They gave it to their children to play with, to fold those strange bits of colored paper into all kinds of shapes, making them into toy buffalo and horses. Somebody was enjoying that money after all. The books tell of one soldier who survived. He got away, but he went crazy and some women watched him from a distance as he killed himself. The writers always say he must have been afraid of being captured and tortured, but that's all wrong.

Can't you see it? There he is, bellied down in a gully, watching what is going on. He sees the kids playing with the money, tearing it up, the women using it to fire up some dried buffalo chips to cook on, the men lighting their pipes with green frog skins, but mostly all those beautiful dollar bills floating away with the dust and the wind. It's this sight that drove that poor soldier crazy. He's clutching his head, hollering, "Goddam, Jesus Christ Almighty, look at them dumb, stupid, red sons of bitches wasting all that dough!" He watches till he can't stand it any longer, and then he blows his brains out with a six-shooter. It would make a great scene in a movie, but it would take an Indian mind to get the point. 3

The green frog skin—that was what the fight was all about. The gold of the Black Hills, the gold in every clump of grass. Each day you can see ranch hands riding over this land. They have a bagful of grain hanging from their saddle horns, and whenever they see a prairie-dog hole they toss a handful of oats in it, like a kind little old lady feeding the pigeons in one of your city parks. Only the oats for the prairie dogs are poisoned with strychnine. What happens to the prairie dog after he has eaten this grain is not a pleasant thing to watch. The prairie dogs are poisoned, because they eat grass. A thousand of them eat up as much grass in a year as a cow. So if the rancher can kill that many prairie dogs he can run one more head of cattle, make a little more money. When he looks at a prairie dog he sees only a green frog skin getting away from him. 4

For the white man each blade of grass or spring of water has a price tag on it. And that is the trouble, because look at what happens. The bobcats and coyotes which used to feed on prairie dogs now have to go after a stray lamb or a crippled calf. The rancher calls the pest-control officer to kill these animals. This man shoots some rabbits and puts them out as bait with a piece of wood stuck in them. That stick has an explosive charge which shoots some cyanide into the mouth of the coyote who tugs at it. The officer has been trained to be careful. He puts a printed warning on each stick reading, "Danger, Explosive, Poison!" The trouble is that our dogs can't read, and some of our children can't either. 5

And the prairie becomes a thing without life—no more prairie dogs, no more badgers, foxes, coyotes. The big birds of prey used to feed on prairie dogs, too. So you hardly see an eagle these days. The bald eagle is your symbol. You see him on your money, but your money is killing him. When a people start killing off their own symbols they are in a bad way. 6

The Sioux have a name for white men. They call them *wasicun*—fat-takers. It is a good name, because you have taken the fat of the land. But it does not seem to have agreed with you. Right now you don't look so healthy—overweight, yes, but not healthy. Americans are bred like stuffed geese—to be consumers, not human beings. The moment they stop consuming and buying, this frog-skin world has no more use for them. They have become frogs themselves. Some cruel child has 7 stuffed a cigar into their mouths and they have to keep puffing and puffing until they explode. Fat-taking is a bad thing, even for the taker. It is especially bad for Indians who are forced to live in this frog-skin world which they did not make and for which they have no use.

You, Richard, are an artist. That's one reason we get along well. 8
Artists are the Indians of the white world. They are called dreamers who live in the clouds, improvident people who can't hold onto their money, people who don't want to face "reality." They say the same things about Indians. How the hell do these frog-skin people know what reality is? The world in which you paint a picture in your mind, a picture which shows things different from what your eyes sees, that is the world from which I get my visions. I tell you this is the real world, not the Green Frog Skin World. That's only a bad dream, a streamlined, smog-filled nightmare.

Because we refuse to step out of our reality into this frog-skin illu- 9
sion, we are called dumb, lazy, improvident, immature, other-worldly. It makes me happy to be called "other-worldly," and it should make you so. It's a good thing our reality is different from theirs. I remember one white man looking at my grandfather's vest. It was made of black velvet and had ten-dollar gold coins for buttons. The white man had a fit, saying over and over again, "Only a crazy Indian would think of that, using good money for buttons, a man who hasn't got a pot to piss in!" But Grandpa wasn't a bit crazy and he had learned to know the value of money as well as anybody. But money exists to give a man pleasure. Well, it pleasured Grandpa to put a few golden Indian heads on his vest. That made sense.

COMPREHENSION

1. What significance does money have to Lame Deer and to other Native Americans?
2. To what "fight" is Lame Deer alluding in paragraph 4?
3. What connection does Lame Deer make between the whites' attitude toward money and environmental destruction?

RHETORIC

1. What is Lame Deer's thesis? Is it implied or directly stated?
2. Explain the use of the battle scene in paragraphs 2 and 3 in the essay. How does it reinforce Lame Deer's point of view, and does it do so successfully?
3. What is the tone of the essay? Where is this attitude most clearly expressed?
4. Cite examples of Lame Deer's figurative language, and explain how its use supports the author's intent.
5. How does the author use analogy to structure his essay?
6. Examine the conclusion. Does the final anecdote help to establish Lame Deer's point of view?

WRITING

1. Agree or disagree with Lame Deer's indictment of America: "For the white man each blade of grass or spring of water has a price tag on it."
2. In a personal essay, write about your attitude toward money. Examine how you developed this attitude and whether or not it's in conflict with how most Americans feel.

RICHARD RODRIGUEZ Richard Rodriguez (1944–) was born in San Francisco and received degrees from Stanford University and Columbia University. He also did graduate study at the University of California, Berkeley, and at the Warburg Institute, London. Rodriguez became a nationally known writer with the publication of his autobiography, *Hunger of Memory: The Education of Richard Rodriguez* (1982). In it, he describes the struggles of growing up biculturally—feeling alienated from his Spanish-speaking parents yet not wholly comfortable in the dominant culture of the United States. He opposes bilingualism and affirmative action as they are now practiced in the United States, and his stance has caused much controversy in educational and intellectual circles. Rodriguez continues to write about social issues such as acculturation, education, and language. In "Los Pobres," Rodriguez shows us how what starts off as a summer job ends with a personal revelation about social and personal identity.

RICHARD RODRIGUEZ

Los Pobres

It was at Stanford, one day near the end of my senior year, that a friend told me about a summer construction job he knew was available. I was quickly alert. Desire uncoiled within me. My friend said that he knew I had been looking for summer employment. He knew I needed some money. Almost apologetically he explained: It was something I probably wouldn't be interested in, but a friend of his, a contractor, needed someone for the summer to do menial jobs. There would be lots of shoveling and raking and sweeping. Nothing too hard. But nothing more interesting either. Still, the pay would be good. Did I want it? Or did I know someone who did? 1

I did. Yes, I said, surprised to hear myself say it. 2

In the weeks following, friends cautioned that I had no idea how hard physical labor really is. ("You only *think* you know what it is like to shovel for eight hours straight.") Their objections seemed to me challenges. They resolved the issue. I became happy with my plan. I decided, however, not to tell my parents. I wouldn't tell my mother because I 3

could guess her worried reaction. I would tell my father only after the summer was over, when I could announce that, after all, I did know what "real work" is like.

The day I met the contractor (a Princeton graduate, it turned out), he asked me whether I had done any physical labor before. "In high school, during the summer," I lied. And although he seemed to regard me with skepticism, he decided to give me a try. Several days later, expectant, I arrived at my first construction site. I would take off my shirt to the sun. And at last grasp desired sensation. No longer afraid. At last become like a *bracero.* "We need those tree stumps out of here by tomorrow," the contractor said. I started to work. 4

I labored with excitement that first morning—and all the days after. The work was harder than I could have expected. But it was never as tedious as my friends had warned me it would be. There was too much physical pleasure in the labor. Especially early in the day, I would be most alert to the sensations of movement and straining. Beginning around seven each morning (when the air was still damp but the scent of weeds and dry earth anticipated the heat of the sun), I would feel my body resist the first thrusts of the shovel. My arms, tightened by sleep, would gradually loosen; after only several minutes, sweat would gather in beads on my forehead and then—a short while later—I would feel my chest silky with sweat in the breeze. I would return to my work. A nervous spark of pain would fly up my arm and settle to burn like an ember in the thick of my shoulder. An hour, two passed. Three. My whole body would assume regular movements. Even later in the day, my enthusiasm for primitive sensation would survive the heat and the dust and the insects pricking my back. I would strain wildly for sensation as the day came to a close. At three-thirty, quitting time, I would stand upright and slowly let my head fall back, luxuriating in the feeling of tightness relieved. 5

Some of the men working nearby would watch me and laugh. Two or three of the older men took the trouble to teach me the right way to use a pick, the correct way to shovel. "You're doing it wrong, too fucking hard," one man scolded. Then proceeded to show me—what persons who work with their bodies all their lives quickly learn—the most economical way to use one's body in labor. 6

"Don't make your back do so much work," he instructed. I stood impatiently listening, half listening, vaguely watching, then noticed his work-thickened fingers clutching the shovel. I was annoyed. I wanted to tell him that I enjoyed shoveling the wrong way. And I didn't want to learn the right way. I wasn't afraid of back pain. I liked the way my body felt sore at the end of the day. 7

I was about to, but, as it turned out, I didn't say a thing. Rather it was at that moment I realized that I was fooling myself if I expected a few weeks of labor to gain me admission to the world of the laborer. I would not learn in three months what my father had meant by "real work." I was not bound to this job; I could imagine its rapid conclusion. For me the sensations of exertion and fatigue could be savored. 8

For my father or uncle, working at comparable jobs when they were my age, such sensations were to be feared. Fatigue took a different toll on their bodies—and minds.

It was, I know, a simple insight. But it was with this realization that I took my first step that summer toward realizing something even more important about the "worker." In the company of carpenters, electricians, plumbers, and painters at lunch, I would often sit quietly, observant. I was not shy in such company. I felt easy, pleased by the knowledge that I was casually accepted, my presence taken for granted by men (exotics) who worked with their hands. Some days the younger men would talk and talk about sex, and they would howl at women who drove by in cars. Other days the talk at lunchtime was subdued; men gathered in separate groups. It depended on who was around. There were rough, good-natured workers. Others were quiet. The more I remember that summer, the more I realize that there was no single *type* of worker. I am embarrassed to say I had not expected such diversity. I certainly had not expected to meet, for example, a plumber who was an abstract painter in his off hours and admired the work of Mark Rothko. Nor did I expect to meet so many workers with college diplomas. (They were the ones who were not surprised that I intended to enter graduate school in the fall.) I suppose what I really want to say here is painfully obvious, but I must say it nevertheless: The men of that summer were middle-class Americans. They certainly didn't constitute an oppressed society. Carefully completing their work sheets; talking about the fortunes of local football teams; planning Las Vegas vacations; comparing the gas mileage of various makes of campers—they were not *los pobres* my mother had spoken about.

On two occasions, the contractor hired a group of Mexican aliens. 10
They were employed to cut down some trees and haul off debris. In all, there were six men of varying age. The youngest in his late twenties; the oldest (his father?) perhaps sixty years old. They came and they left in a single old truck. Anonymous men. They were never introduced to the other men at the site. Immediately upon their arrival, they would follow the contractor's directions, start working—rarely resting—seemingly driven by a fatalistic sense that work which had to be done was best done as quickly as possible.

I watched them sometimes. Perhaps they watched me. The only 11
time I saw them pay me much notice was one day at lunchtime when I was laughing with the other men. The Mexicans sat apart when they ate, just as they worked by themselves. Quiet. I rarely heard them say much to each other. All I could hear were their voices calling out sharply to one another, giving directions. Otherwise, when they stood briefly resting, they talked among themselves in voices too hard to overhear.

The contractor knew enough Spanish, and the Mexicans—or at 12
least the oldest of them, their spokesman—seemed to know enough English to communicate. But because I was around, the contractor decided one day to make me his translator. (He assumed I could speak

Spanish.) I did what I was told. Shyly I went over to tell the Mexicans that the patrón wanted them to do something else before they left for the day. As I started to speak, I was afraid with my old fear that I would be unable to pronounce the Spanish words. But it was a simple instruction I had to convey. I could say it in phrases.

The dark sweating faces turned toward me as I spoke. They stopped their work to hear me. Each nodded in response. I stood there. I wanted to say something more. But what could I say in Spanish, even if I could have pronounced the words right? Perhaps I just wanted to engage in small talk, to be assured of their confidence, our familiarity. I thought for a moment to ask them where in Mexico they were from. Something like that. And maybe I wanted to tell them (a lie, if need be) that my parents were from the same part of Mexico. 13

I stood there. 14

Their faces watched me. The eyes of the man directly in front of me moved slowly over my shoulder, and I turned to follow his glance toward *el patrón* some distance away. For a moment I felt swept up by that glance into the Mexicans' company. But then I heard one of them returning to work. And then the others went back to work. I left them without saying anything more. 15

When they had finished, the contractor went over to pay them in cash. (He later told me that he paid them collectively—"for the job," though he wouldn't tell me their wages. He said something quickly about the good rate of exchange "in their own country.") I can still hear the loudly confident voice he used with the Mexicans. It was the sound of the *gringo* I had heard as a very young boy. And I can still hear the quiet, indistinct sounds of the Mexican, the oldest who replied. At hearing that voice I was sad for the Mexicans. Depressed by their vulnerability. Angry at myself. The adventure of the summer seemed suddenly ludicrous. I would not shorten the distance I felt from *los pobres* with a few weeks of physical labor. I would not become like them. They were different from me. . . . 16

In the end, my father was right—though perhaps he did not know how right or why—to say that I would never know what real work is. I will never know what he felt at his last factory job. If tomorrow I worked at some kind of factory, it would go differently for me. My long education would favor me. I could act as a public person—able to defend my interests, to unionize, to petition, to speak up—to challenge and demand. (I will never know what real work is.) I will never know what the Mexicans knew, gathering their shovels and ladders and saws. 17

Their silence stays with me now. The wages those Mexicans received for their labor were only a measure of their disadvantaged condition. Their silence is more telling. They lack a public identity. They remain profoundly alien. Persons apart. People lacking a union obviously, people without grounds. They depend upon the relative good will or fairness of their employers each day. For such people, lacking a better alternative, it is not such an unreasonable risk. 18

Their silence stays with me. I have taken these many words to describe its impact. Only: the quiet. Something uncanny about it. Its compliance. Vulnerability. Pathos. As I heard their truck rumbling away, I shuddered, my face mirrored with sweat. I had finally come face to face with *los pobres*. 19

COMPREHENSION

1. How does Rodriguez set the scene for his narrative? What contrasts does he develop in the course of the essay?
2. What are the chief revelations Rodriguez receives from his work experience?
3. Why does Rodriguez focus on the silence of the Mexicans in the final two paragraphs? What is the relationship between this silence and the "real work" his father knows?

RHETORIC

1. In paragraph 9, Rodriguez puts quotes around "worker"; parentheses around "(exotics)"; and italicizes *"type."* What is the purpose of each choice of punctuation?
2. There are several fragments in each of the final two paragraphs. What is the effect of using this sentence structure? Where else are fragments employed in the essay?
3. Why are paragraphs 2 and 14 so short? How does the length of these paragraphs help delineate Rodriguez's mood?
4. What sensations does Rodriguez focus on in paragraph 5? Which words contribute most to evoking them?
5. In what way do the first three paragraphs prepare or fail to prepare you for the narrative that follows?
6. The opening sentence of paragraph 19 repeats that of paragraph 18. What is the purpose of this repetition?

WRITING

1. Imagine yourself in the same situation as Rodriguez. Would your presumptions about "hard work" and your coworkers have been the same? Would you be more or less naive than Rodriguez? Explain in a brief essay.
2. What are the major differences between the Mexican workers and the American workers in the essay? Write an essay focusing on these differences.
3. Write an essay explaining why Rodriguez feels excluded from each of the two groups.

4. Have you ever felt like an outsider in a social situation? Describe a time in your life when you were confronted with the desire to be accepted. How were you different from the others? How did you try to transcend this difference?

JESSICA MITFORD Jessica Mitford (1917–) is an English-born American writer whose lifelong devotion to social justice and civil rights has spurred her into taking on institutions. Most notably, Mitford brought her sharp journalistic skills to bear on the American funeral industry in her scathing, witty, and informative exposé, *The American Way of Death* (1963). In her most recent book, *The American Way of Birth* (1992), Mitford does battle with obstetrical and gynecological care in America. Mitford has also written two autobiographical books, *Daughters and Rebels* (1960) and *A Fine Old Conflict* (1977), in which she gives a lively account of her family, including her sister Nancy, also a respected writer. In this excerpt from *The American Way of Death,* Mitford explains how funeral directors manipulate the American public with sophisticated marketing techniques that play on their vulnerability in their time of grief.

JESSICA MITFORD

The American Way of Death

How long, I would ask, are we to be subjected to the tyranny of custom and undertakers? Truly, it is all vanity and vexation of spirit—a mere mockery of woe, costly to all, far, far beyond its value; and ruinous to many; hateful, and an abomination to all; yet submitted to by all, because none have the moral courage to speak against it and act in defiance of it. —Lord Essex

O death, where is thy sting? O grave, where is thy victory? Where, indeed. Many a badly stung survivor, faced with the aftermath of some relative's funeral, has ruefully concluded that the victory has been won hands down by a funeral establishment—in disastrously unequal battle. 1

Much has been written of late about the affluent society in which we live, and much fun poked at some of the irrational "status symbols" set out like golden snares to trap the unwary consumer at every turn. Until recently, little has been said about the most irrational and weirdest of the lot, lying in ambush for all of us at the end of the road—the modern American funeral. 2

If the Dismal Traders (as an eighteenth-century English writer calls them) have traditionally been cast in a comic role in literature, a universally recognized symbol of humor from Shakespeare to Dickens to Evelyn Waugh, they have successfully turned the tables in recent years to perpetrate a huge, macabre and expensive practical joke on the 3

American public. It is not consciously conceived of as a joke, of course; on the contrary, it is hedged with admirably contrived rationalizations.

Gradually, almost imperceptibly, over the years the funeral men have constructed their own grotesque cloud-cuckoo-land where the trappings of Gracious Living are transformed, as in a nightmare, into the trappings of Gracious Dying. The same familiar Madison Avenue language, with its peculiar adjectival range designed to anesthetize sales resistance to all sorts of products, has seeped into the funeral industry in a new and bizarre guise. The emphasis is on the same desirable qualities that we have all been schooled to look for in our daily search for excellence: comfort, durability, beauty, craftsmanship. The attuned ear will recognize too the convincing quasi-scientific language, so reassuring even if unintelligible.

5 So that this too, too solid flesh might not melt, we are offered "solid copper—a quality casket which offers superb value to the client seeking long-lasting protection," or "the Colonial Classic Beauty—18 gauge lead coated steel, seamless top, lap-jointed welded body construction." Some are equipped with foam rubber, some with innerspring mattresses. Elgin offers "the revolutionary 'Perfect-Posture' bed." Not every casket need have a silver lining, for one may choose between "more than 60 color matched shades, magnificent and unique masterpieces" by the Cheney casket-lining people. Shrouds no longer exist. Instead, you may patronize a grave-wear couturière who promises "handmade original fashions—styles from the best in life for the last memory—dresses, men's suits, negligees, accessories." For the final, perfect grooming: "Nature-Glo—the ultimate in cosmetic embalming." And, where have we heard that phrase "peace of mind protection" before? No matter. In funeral advertising, it is applied to the Wilbert Burial Vault, with its ⅜-inch precast asphalt inner liner plus extra-thick, reinforced concrete—all this "guaranteed by Good Housekeeping." Here again the Cadillac, status symbol par excellence, appears in all its gleaming glory, this time transformed into a pastel-colored funeral hearse.

6 You, the potential customer for all this luxury, are unlikely to read the lyrical descriptions quoted above, for they are culled from *Mortuary Management* and *Casket and Sunnyside,* two of the industry's eleven trade magazines. For you there are ads in your daily newspaper, generally found on the obituary page, stressing dignity, refinement, high-caliber professional service and that intangible quality, *sincerity.* The trade advertisements are, however, instructive, because they furnish an important clue to the frame of mind into which the funeral industry has hypnotized itself.

7 A new mythology, essential to the twentieth-century American funeral rite, has grown up—or rather has been built up step by step—to justify the peculiar customs surrounding the disposal of our dead. And, just as the witch doctor must be convinced of his own infallibility in order to maintain a hold over his clientele, so the funeral industry has had to "sell itself" on its articles of faith in the course of passing them along to the public.

The first of these is the tenet that today's funeral procedures are founded in "American tradition." The story comes to mind of a sign on the freshly sown lawn of a brand-new Midwest college: "There is a tradition on this campus that students never walk on this strip of grass. This tradition goes into effect next Tuesday." The most cursory look at American funerals of past times will establish the parallel. Simplicity to the point of starkness, the plain pine box, the laying out of the dead by friends and family who also bore the coffin to the grave—these were the hallmarks of the traditional funeral until the end of the nineteenth century. 8

Secondly, there is the myth that the American public is only being given what it wants—an opportunity to keep up with the Joneses to the end. "In keeping with our high standard of living, there should be an equally high standard of dying," says the past president of the Funeral Directors of San Francisco. "The cost of a funeral varies according to individual taste and the niceties of living the family has been accustomed to." Actually, choice doesn't enter the picture for the average individual, faced, generally for the first time, with the necessity of buying a product of which he is totally ignorant, at a moment when he is least in a position to quibble. In point of fact the cost of a funeral almost always varies, not "according to individual taste" but according to what the traffic will bear. 9

Thirdly, there is an assortment of myths based on half-digested psychiatric theories. The importance of the "memory picture" is stressed—meaning the last glimpse of the deceased in open casket, done up with the latest in embalming techniques and finished off with a dusting of makeup. A newer one, impressively authentic-sounding, is the need for "grief therapy," which is beginning to go over big in mortuary circles. A historian of American funeral directing hints at the grief-therapist idea when speaking of the new role of the undertaker—"the dramaturgic role, in which the undertaker becomes a stage manager to create an appropriate atmosphere and to move the funeral party through a drama in which social relationships are stressed and an emotional catharsis or release is provided through ceremony." 10

Lastly, a whole new terminology, as ornately shoddy as the satin rayon casket liner, has been invented by the funeral industry to replace the direct and serviceable vocabulary of former times. Undertaker has been supplanted by "funeral director" or "mortician." (Even the classified section of the telephone directory gives recognition of this; in its pages you will find "Undertakers—see Funeral Directors.") Coffins are "caskets"; hearses are "coaches," or "professional cars"; flowers are "floral tributes"; corpses generally are "loved ones," but mortuary etiquette dictates that a specific corpse be referred to by name only—as, "Mr. Jones"; cremated ashes are "cremains." Euphemisms such as "slumber room," "reposing room," and "calcination—the *kindlier* heat" abound in the funeral business. 11

If the undertaker is the stage manager of the fabulous production that is the modern American funeral, the stellar role is reserved for the 12

occupant of the open casket. The decor, the stagehands, the supporting cast are all arranged for the most advantageous display of the deceased, without which the rest of the paraphernalia would lose its point—*Hamlet* without the Prince of Denmark. It is to this end that a fantastic array of costly merchandise and services is pyramided to dazzle the mourners and facilitate the plunder of the next of kin.

Grief therapy, anyone? But it's going to come high. According to the funeral industry's own figures, the *average* undertaker's bill in 1961 was $708 for casket and "services," to which must be added the cost of a burial vault, flowers, clothing, clergy and musician's honorarium, and cemetery charges. When these costs are added to the undertaker's bill, the total average cost for an adult's funeral is, as we shall see, closer to $1,450. 13

The question naturally arises, *is* this what most people want for themselves and their families? For several reasons, this has been a hard one to answer until recently. It is a subject seldom discussed. Those who have never had to arrange for a funeral frequently shy away from its implications, preferring to take comfort in the thought that sufficient unto the day is the evil thereof. Those who have acquired personal and painful knowledge of the subject would often rather forget about it. Pioneering "Funeral Societies" or "Memorial Associations," dedicated to the principle of dignified funerals at reasonable cost, have existed in a number of communities throughout the country, but their membership has been limited for the most part to the more sophisticated element in the population—university people, liberal intellectuals—and those who, like doctors and lawyers, come up against problems in arranging funerals for their clients. 14

Some indication of the pent-up resentment felt by vast numbers of people against the funeral interests was furnished by the astonishing response to an article by Roul Tunley, titled "Can You Afford to Die?" in *The Saturday Evening Post* of June 17, 1961. As though a dike had burst, letters poured in from every part of the country to the *Post,* to the funeral societies, to local newspapers. They came from clergymen, professional people, old-age pensioners, trade unionists. Three months after the article appeared, an estimated six thousand had taken pen in hand to comment on some phase of the high cost of dying. Many recounted their own bitter experiences at the hands of funeral directors; hundreds asked for advice on how to establish a consumer organization in communities where none exists; others sought information about pre-need plans. The membership of the funeral societies skyrocketed. The funeral industry, finding itself in the glare of public spotlight, has begun to engage in serious debate about its own future course—as well it might. 15

Is the funeral inflation bubble ripe for bursting? A few years ago, the United States public suddenly rebelled against the trend in the auto industry towards ever more showy cars, with their ostentatious and nonfunctional fins, and a demand was created for compact cars patterned after European models. The all-powerful auto industry, accustomed to *telling* the customer what sort of car he wanted, was suddenly 16 forced to *listen* for a change. Overnight, the little cars became for millions a new kind of status symbol. Could it be that the same cycle is working itself out in the attitude towards the final return of dust to dust, that the American public is becoming sickened by ever more ornate and costly funerals, and that a status symbol of the future may indeed be the simplest kind of "funeral without fins"?

COMPREHENSION

1. According to the essay, what role does consumerism play in the funeral industry?
2. What image does the funeral industry want to advance?
3. What does Mitford mean by "a new mythology" in paragraph 7?

RHETORIC

1. To what end does Mitford use the Lord Essex quote at the beginning of her essay?
2. What is Mitford's thesis? What is her tone? Cite evidence from the essay to support your view.
3. Mitford quotes Shakespeare in a few places. Locate one of these instances, and explain why it's an effective device.
4. Which paragraphs rely on classification and division? What is the purpose of this rhetorical strategy?
5. Find some examples of what Mitford calls "Madison Avenue language," and explain how they work to strengthen her thesis.
6. Assess Mitford's use of illustrations and evidence. How effective do you find it?

WRITING

1. In an analytical essay, examine the attitudes of Americans toward death and burial. How do their attitudes make them more susceptible to the practices cited in Mitford's essay?
2. In an essay, describe in detail how you would like your own funeral to be arranged and by whom. Be specific: Include instructions regarding guests, flowers, music, and the eulogy.

CLASSIC AND CONTEMPORARY

VIRGINIA WOOLF Virginia Woolf (1882–1941), novelist and essayist, was the daughter of Sir Leslie Stephen, a famous critic and writer on economics. An experimental novelist, Woolf attempted to portray consciousness through a poetic, symbolic, and concrete style. Her novels include *Jacob's Room* (1922), *Mrs. Dalloway* (1925), *To the Lighthouse* (1927), and *The Waves* (1931). She was also a perceptive reader and critic; her criticism appears in *The Common Reader* (1925) and *The Second Common Reader* (1933). In the following essay, which was delivered originally as a speech to The Women's Service League in 1931, Woolf argues that women must overcome several "angels," or phantoms, in order to succeed in professional careers.

VIRGINIA WOOLF

Professions for Women

When your secretary invited me to come here, she told me that your Society is concerned with the employment of women and she suggested that I might tell you something about my own professional experiences. It is true I am a woman; it is true I am employed; but what professional experiences have I had? It is difficult to say. My profession is literature; and in that profession there are fewer experiences for women than in any other, with the exception of the stage—fewer, I mean, that are peculiar to women. For the road was cut many years ago—by Fanny Burney, by Aphra Behn, by Harriet Martineau, by Jane Austen, by George Eliot—many famous women, and many more unknown and forgotten, have been before me, making the path smooth, and regulating my steps. Thus, when I came to write, there were very few material obstacles in my way. Writing was a reputable and harmless occupation. The family peace was not broken by the scratching of a pen. No demand was made upon the family purse. For ten and sixpence one can buy paper enough to write all the plays of Shakespeare—if one has a mind that way. Pianos and models, Paris, Vienna and Berlin, masters and mistresses, are not needed by a writer. The cheapness of writing paper is, of course, the reason why women have succeeded as writers before they have succeeded in the other professions. 1

But to tell you my story—it is a simple one. You have only got to figure to yourselves a girl in a bedroom with a pen in her hand. She had only to move that pen from left to right—from ten o'clock to one. Then it occurred to her to do what is simple and cheap enough after all—to slip a few of those pages into an envelope, fix a penny stamp in the cor- 2

ner, and drop the envelope into the red box at the corner. It was thus that I became a journalist; and my effort was rewarded on the first day of the following month—a very glorious day it was for me—by a letter from an editor containing a cheque for one pound ten shillings and six-pence. But to show you how little I deserve to be called a professional woman, how little I know of the struggles and difficulties of such lives, I have to admit that instead of spending that sum upon bread and butter, rent, shoes and stockings, or butcher's bills, I went out and bought a cat—a beautiful cat, a Persian cat, which very soon involved me in bitter disputes with my neighbors.

3 What could be easier than to write articles and to buy Persian cats with the profits? But wait a moment. Articles have to be about something. Mine, I seem to remember, was about a novel by a famous man. And while I was writing this review, I discovered that if I were going to review books I should need to do battle with a certain phantom. And the phantom was a woman, and when I came to know her better I called her after the heroine of a famous poem, The Angel in the House. It was she who used to come between me and my paper when I was writing reviews. It was she who bothered me and wasted my time and so tormented me that at last I killed her. You who come of a younger and happier generation may not have heard of her—you may not know what I mean by the Angel in the House. I will describe her as shortly as I can. She was intensely sympathetic. She was immensely charming. She was utterly unselfish. She excelled in the difficult arts of family life. She sacrificed herself daily. If there was chicken, she took the leg; if there was a draught she sat in it—in short she was so constituted that she never had a mind or a wish of her own, but preferred to sympathize always with the minds and wishes of others. Above all—I need not say it—she was pure. Her purity was supposed to be her chief beauty—her blushes, her great grace. In those days—the last of Queen Victoria—every house had its Angel. And when I came to write I encountered her with the very first words. The shadow of her wings fell on my page; I heard the rustling of her skirts in the room. Directly, that is to say, I took my pen in hand to review that novel by a famous man, she slipped behind me and whispered: "My dear, you are a young woman. You are writing about a book that has been written by a man. Be sympathetic; be tender; flatter; deceive; use all the arts and wiles of our sex. Never let anybody guess that you have a mind of your own. Above all, be pure." And she made as if to guide my pen. I now record the one act for which I take some credit to myself, though the credit rightly belongs to some excellent ancestors of mine who left me a certain sum of money—shall we say five hundred pounds a year?—so that it was not necessary for me to depend solely on charm for my living. I turned upon her and caught her by the throat. I did my best to kill her. My excuse, if I were to be had up in a court of law, would be that I acted in self-defense. Had I not killed her she would have killed me. She would have plucked the heart out of my writing. For, as I found, directly I put pen to paper, you cannot review even a novel without having a mind of

your own, without expressing what you think to be the truth about human relations, morality, sex. And all these questions, according to the Angel in the House, cannot be dealt with freely and openly by women; they must charm, they must conciliate, they must—to put it bluntly—tell lies if they are to succeed. Thus, whenever I felt the shadow of her wing or the radiance of her halo upon my page, I took up the inkpot and flung it at her. She died hard. Her fictitious nature was of great assistance to her. It is far harder to kill a phantom than a reality. She was always creeping back when I thought I had dispatched her. Though I flatter myself that I killed her in the end, the struggle was severe; it took much time that had better have been spent upon learning Greek grammar; or in roaming the world in search of adventures. But it was a real experience; it was an experience that was bound to befall all women writers at that time. Killing the Angel in the House was part of the occupation of a woman writer.

But to continue my story. The Angel was dead; what then re- 4
mained? You may say that what remained was a simple and common object—a young woman in a bedroom with an inkpot. In other words, now that she had rid herself of falsehood, that young woman had only to be herself. Ah, but what is "herself"? I mean, what is a woman? I assure you, I do not know. I do not believe that you know. I do not believe that anybody can know until she has expressed herself in all the arts and professions open to human skill. That indeed is one of the reasons why I have come here—out of respect for you, who are in process of showing us by your experiments what a woman is, who are in process of providing us, by your failures and successes, with that extremely important piece of information.

But to continue the story of my professional experiences. I made 5
one pound ten and six by my first review; and I bought a Persian cat with the proceeds. Then I grew ambitious. A Persian cat is all very well, I said; but a Persian cat is not enough. I must have a motor car. And it was thus that I became a novelist—for it is a very strange thing that people will give you a motor car if you will tell them a story. It is a still stranger thing that there is nothing so delightful in the world as telling stories. It is far pleasanter than writing reviews of famous novels. And yet, if I am to obey your secretary and tell you my professional experiences as a novelist, I must tell you about a very strange experience that befell me as a novelist. And to understand it you must try first to imagine a novelist's state of mind. I hope I am not giving away professional secrets if I say that a novelist's chief desire is to be as unconscious as possible. He has to induce in himself a state of perpetual lethargy. He wants life to proceed with the utmost quiet and regularity. He wants to see the same faces, to read the same books, to do the same things day after day, month after month, while he is writing, so that nothing may break the illusion in which he is living—so that nothing may disturb or disquiet the mysterious nosings about, feelings round, darts, dashes and sudden discoveries of that very shy and illusive spirit, the imagination. I suspect that this state is the same both for men and women. Be

that as it may, I want you to imagine me writing a novel in a state of trance. I want you to figure to yourselves a girl sitting with a pen in her hand, which for minutes, and indeed for hours, she never dips into the inkpot. The image that comes to my mind when I think of this girl is the image of a fisherman lying sunk in dreams on the verge of a deep lake with a rod held out over the water. She was letting her imagination sweep unchecked round every rock and cranny of the world that lies submerged in the depths of our unconscious being. Now came the experience, the experience that I believe to be far commoner with women writers than with men. The line raced through the girl's fingers. Her imagination had rushed away. It had sought the pools, the depths, the dark places where the largest fish slumber. And then there was a smash. There was an explosion. There was foam and confusion. The imagination had dashed itself against something hard. The girl was roused from her dream. She was indeed in a state of the most acute and difficult distress. To speak without figure she had thought of something, something about the body, about the passions which it was unfitting for her as a woman to say. Men, her reason told her, would be shocked. The consciousness of what men will say of a woman who speaks the truth about her passions had roused her from her artist's state of unconsciousness. She could write no more. The trance was over. Her imagination could work no longer. This I believe to be a very common experience with women writers—they are impeded by the extreme conventionality of the other sex. For though men sensibly allow themselves great freedom in these respects, I doubt that they realize or can control the extreme severity with which they condemn such freedom in women.

These then were two very genuine experiences of my own. These 6
were two of the adventures of my professional life. The first—killing the Angel in the House—I think I solved. She died. But the second, telling the truth about my own experiences as a body, I do not think I solved. I doubt that any woman has solved it yet. The obstacles against her are still immensely powerful—and yet they are very difficult to define. Outwardly, what is simpler than to write books? Outwardly, what obstacles are there for a woman rather than for a man? Inwardly, I think, the case is very different; she has still many ghosts to fight, many prejudices to overcome. Indeed it will be a long time still, I think, before a woman can sit down to write a book without finding a phantom to be slain, a rock to be dashed against. And if this is so in literature, the freest of all professions for women, how is it in the new professions which you are now for the first time entering?

Those are the questions that I should like, had I time, to ask you. 7
And indeed, if I have laid stress upon these professional experiences of mine, it is because I believe that they are, though in different forms, yours also. Even when the path is nominally open—when there is nothing to prevent a woman from being a doctor, a lawyer, a civil servant—there are many phantoms and obstacles, as I believe, looming in her way. To discuss and define them is I think of great value and impor-

tance; for thus only can the labour be shared, the difficulties be solved. But besides this, it is necessary also to discuss the ends and the aims for which we are fighting, for which we are doing battle with these formidable obstacles. Those aims cannot be taken for granted; they must be perpetually questioned and examined. The whole position, as I see it—here in this hall surrounded by women practising for the first time in history I know not how many different professions—is one of extraordinary interest and importance. You have won rooms of your own in the house hitherto exclusively owned by men. You are able, though not without great labour and effort, to pay the rent. You are earning your five hundred pounds a year. But this freedom is only a beginning; the room is your own, but it is still bare. It has to be furnished; it has to be decorated; it has to be shared. How are you going to furnish it, how are you going to decorate it? With whom are you going to share it, and upon what terms? These, I think, are questions of the utmost importance and interest. For the first time in history you are able to ask for them; for the first time you are able to decide for yourselves what the answers should be. Willingly would I stay and discuss those questions and answers—but not tonight. My time is up; and I must cease.

COMPREHENSION

1. This essay was presented originally as a speech. What internal evidence indicates that it was intended as a talk? How do you respond to it today as a reader?
2. Who or what is the "angel" that Woolf describes in this essay? Why must she kill it? What other obstacles does a professional woman encounter?
3. Paraphrase the last two paragraphs of this essay. What is the essence of Woolf's argument?

RHETORIC

1. There is a significant amount of figurative language in the essay. Locate and explain examples. What does the figurative language contribute to the tone of the essay? Compare and contrast the figurative language in this essay and in Woolf's "The Death of the Moth" in Chapter 10.
2. How do we know that Woolf is addressing an audience of women? Why does she pose so many questions, and what does this strategy contribute to the rapport that she wants to establish? Explain the effect of the last two sentences.
3. How does Woolf use analogy to structure part of her argument?
4. Why does Woolf rely on personal narration? How does it affect the logic of her argument?
5. Evaluate Woolf's use of contrast to advance her argument.
6. Where does Woolf place her main proposition? How emphatic is it, and why?

WRITING

1. How effectively does Woolf use her own example as a professional writer to advance a broader proposition concerning all women entering professional life? Answer this question in a brief essay.
2. Explain the value of Woolf's essay for women today.
3. Discuss the problems and obstacles that you anticipate when you enter your chosen career.
4. Compare and contrast the essays by Goodman and Woolf.

HENRY LOUIS GATES JR. Henry Louis Gates (1950–) is an educator, writer, and editor. He was born in West Virginia and educated at Yale and at Clare College in Cambridge. Gates has had a varied career, working as a general anesthetist in Tanzania and as a staff correspondent for *Time* magazine in London. His essays have appeared in such diverse publications as *Black American Literature Forum, Yale Review, The New York Times Book Review,* and *Sports Illustrated.* He is also the author of *Figures in Black: Words, Signs, and the Racial Self* (1987) and *The Signifying Monkey: A Theory of Afro-American Literary Criticism* (1988). In this article from *Sports Illustrated,* Gates turns his attention to the limited career choices presented as viable to African-American youth and to public misconceptions about blacks in sports.

HENRY LOUIS GATES JR.

Delusions of Grandeur

Standing at the bar of an all-black VFW post in my hometown of Piedmont, W.Va., I offered five dollars to anyone who could tell me how many African-American professional athletes were at work today. There are 35 million African-Americans, I said. 1

"Ten million!" yelled one intrepid soul, too far into his cups. 2

"No way . . . more like 500,000," said another. 3

"You mean *all* professional sports," someone interjected, "including golf and tennis, but not counting the brothers from Puerto Rico?" Everyone laughed. 4

"Fifty thousand, minimum," was another guess. 5

Here are the facts: 6

There are 1,200 black professional athletes in the U.S.

There are 12 times more black lawyers than black athletes.

There are 2½ times more black dentists than black athletes.

There are 15 times more black doctors than black athletes.

Nobody in my local VFW believed these statistics; in fact, few people would believe them if they weren't reading them in the pages of *Sports Illustrated.* In spite of these statistics, too many African-American youngsters still believe that they have a much better chance 7 of becoming another Magic Johnson or Michael Jordan than they do of matching the achievements of Baltimore Mayor Kurt Schmoke or neurosurgeon Dr. Benjamin Carson, both of whom, like Johnson and Jordan, are black.

In reality, an African-American youngster has about as much chance of becoming a professional athlete as he or she does of winning the lottery. The tragedy for our people, however, is that few of us accept that truth.

9 Let me confess that I love sports. Like most black people of my generation—I'm 40—I was raised to revere the great black athletic heroes, and I never tired of listening to the stories of triumph and defeat that, for blacks, amount to a collective epic much like those of the ancient Greeks: Joe Louis's demolition of Max Schmeling; Satchel Paige's dazzling repertoire of pitches; Jesse Owens's in-your-face performance in Hitler's 1936 Olympics; Willie Mays's over-the-shoulder basket catch; Jackie Robinson's quiet strength when assaulted by racist taunts; and a thousand other grand tales.

10 Nevertheless, the blind pursuit of attainment in sports is having a devastating effect on our people. Imbued with a belief that our principal avenue to fame and profit is through sport, and seduced by a win-at-any-cost system that corrupts even elementary school students, far too many black kids treat basketball courts and football fields as if they were classrooms in an alternative school system. "O.K., I flunked English," a young athlete will say. "But I got an A plus in slam-dunking."

11 The failure of our public schools to educate athletes is part and parcel of the schools' failure to educate almost everyone. A recent survey of the Philadelphia school system, for example, stated that "more than half of all students in the third, fifth and eighth grades cannot perform minimum math and language tasks." One in four middle school students in that city fails to pass to the next grade each year. It is a sad truth that such statistics are repeated in cities throughout the nation. Young athletes—particularly young black athletes—are especially ill-served. Many of them are functionally illiterate, yet they are passed along from year to year for the greater glory of good old Hometown High. We should not be surprised to learn, then, that only 26.6% of black athletes at the collegiate level earn their degrees. For every successful educated black professional athlete, there are thousands of dead and wounded. Yet young blacks continue to aspire to careers as athletes, and it's no wonder why; when the University of North Carolina recently commissioned a sculptor to create archetypes of its student body, guess which ethnic group was selected to represent athletes?

12 Those relatively few black athletes who do make it in the professional ranks must be prevailed upon to play a significant role in the education of all of our young people, athlete and nonathlete alike. While some have done so, many others have shirked their social obligations: to earmark small percentages of their incomes for the United Negro

College Fund; to appear on television for educational purposes rather than merely to sell sneakers; to let children know the message that becoming a lawyer, a teacher or a doctor does more good for our people than winning the Super Bowl; and to form productive liaisons with educators to help forge solutions to the many ills that beset the black community. These are merely a few modest proposals.

A similar burden falls upon successful blacks in all walks of life. 13
Each of us must strive to make our young people understand the realities. Tell them to cheer Bo Jackson but to emulate novelist Toni Morrison or businessman Reginald Lewis or historian John Hope Franklin or Spelman College president Johnetta Cole—the list is long.

Of course, society as a whole bears responsibility as well. Until col- 14
leges stop using young blacks as cannon fodder in the big-business wars of so-called nonprofessional sports, until training a young black's mind becomes as important as training his or her body, we will continue to perpetuate a system akin to that of the Roman gladiators, sacrificing a class of people for the entertainment of the mob.

COMPREHENSION

1. What is the general assumption made about African Americans in sports?
2. Why do American schools continue to perpetuate this myth?
3. According to Gates, what should successful African-American athletes do to help guide the career choices of young black males?

RHETORIC

1. What is Gates's thesis? Where does it appear?
2. How does the introductory paragraph work to set up the writer's focus?
3. State Gates's purpose in using statistics in his essay.
4. What is the tone of Gates's essay? Cite specific sections where this tone seems strongest.
5. Examine the accumulation of facts in paragraph 11. How does this technique underscore Gates's point?
6. Explain Gates's allusion to Roman gladiators in his conclusion. How does it aid in emphasizing his main point?

WRITING

1. Write a brief essay in which you analyze your personal reaction to Gates's statistics. Were you surprised by them? What assumptions did you have about the number of black athletes? Why do you think most Americans share these assumptions?
2. Pretend you are addressing a group of young African Americans at an elementary school. What will you tell them about sports, their career choices, and education?

3. Write a biographical research paper on the life and career of an African-American athlete.

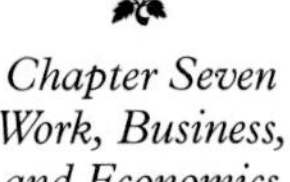

CLASSIC AND CONTEMPORARY: QUESTIONS FOR COMPARISON

1. Examine the argumentative styles of Woolf and Gates. What is their main proposition? What are their minor propositions? What evidence do they provide?
2. Woolf first presented her paper as a speech before an audience of women. Gates wrote his essay as an opinion piece for *Sports Illustrated.* Write a comparative audience analysis of the two selections. Analyze purpose, tone, style, and any other relevant aspects of the two essays.
3. Argue for or against the proposition that white women and African-American men face the same barriers to employment in today's professions. Refer to the essays by Woolf and Gates to support your position.

CONNECTIONS

1. Using the essays of Bly and Rodriguez, compare the effects of physical labor on the human body and mind.
2. Using the essays of Bly and Goodman, consider the impact that technological progress has had on the American work landscape.
3. Compare and contrast the opinions of Lame Deer and Forster regarding ownership and land.
4. Write an essay about "real" work (as defined by Rodriguez) versus "unreal" work (for example, Woolf's writing). Use any relevant writer in this section to explore this issue.
5. Using the works of any of the writers in this section for support, write an essay that equates money and power.
6. Compare the writings of Swift, Rodriguez, and Gates in terms of the work options of the poor in Western society.
7. Using the writings of Bly, Woolf, and Goodman, consider the role of women in the job market.
8. Write a definition essay entitled "What Is Work?" Refer to any of the selections in this section to substantiate your opinions.
9. Write an essay that establishes a link between money and environmental exploitation using the works of Lame Deer, Forster, and any other writer whose writing supports your views.
10. Compare the work experiences of Soto and Rodriguez as Hispanics living in American society.
11. Compare the essays of Mitford and Swift in the writer's use of humor and satire to convey their points. How does the period in which each essay was written affect the type of humor used? Cite specific examples of satire and humor in both essays and compare them as to effectiveness and audience response.

CHAPTER EIGHT

Language and Communication

At the outset of his classic essay "Politics and the English Language," George Orwell asserts that English "is in a bad way." Yet Orwell's essay and the others in this chapter suggest that the English language is in a good way when we are alert and responsive to its many dimensions, careful and precise in our usage of it. As you know from political campaigns, advertising, and ordinary conversations, language is a powerful weapon. It can be used creatively or destructively. Through the power of language, we make sense of our culture, our values, and ourselves.

We all know that language—spoken, written, and nonverbal—is the vehicle whereby we communicate with each other, but language is also the means whereby we communicate our understanding of culture—both our own and the culture of others. English is spoken and written as a primary language by almost 400 million people in five nations; another 700 million nonnative speakers employ the language worldwide. With more than a billion people professing knowledge of English, we might be tempted to call it our "universal" language. However, as several writers in this chapter attest—among them Amy Tan, Rosario Ferré and Bharati Mukherjee—ethnic diversity and the global movement of populations highlight language differences. These cross-cultural influences alert us to the ways in which language informs our economic and social condition, empowering certain groups and blocking others from full participation in society.

Language molds our social, ethnic, racial, and cultural identity. It can liberate or enslave us, place us at an advantage or at a disadvantage. If we can communicate in more than one language, for example, we probably have an advantage over those who command only one lan-

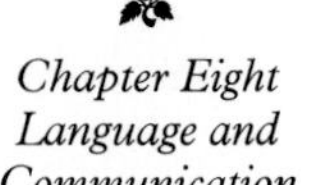

guage. From the name we are given (as Mary McCarthy reminds us), to our most powerful convictions, language is primordial and powerful. Through language we constantly create and return to a sense of ourselves.

Previewing the Chapter

As you read the essays in this chapter and respond to them in discussion and writing, consider the following questions:

- Does the author deal with spoken language, written language, or both?
- What is the author's attitude toward language? Is it positive or negative? Why?
- What are some of the misunderstandings about language that are raised by the writer?
- How does language reveal the writer's sense of herself or himself?
- In what way does language reveal certain cultural conflicts?
- According to the author, how does language relate to one's ethnic, racial, and cultural identity?
- What political dimensions to language do the writers explore?
- How can language be used to enforce the codes and values of a majority culture?
- Do you agree or disagree with the assumptions that the author makes about language and communication?
- What cross-cultural problems with language do you encounter in these essays?

JOAN DIDION Joan Didion (1934–) grew up in California and graduated from the University of California at Berkeley in 1956. She began her career writing for national magazines such as *Mademoiselle, Saturday Evening Post,* and *Life.* Didion published her first novel, *Run River,* in 1963. Although she has continued to write novels and has written several screenplays, her most acclaimed work is in nonfiction. This work includes *Slouching Towards Bethlehem* (1968), *The White Album* (1979), *Salvador* (1983), *Democracy* (1984), *Miami* (1987), and her latest collection, *After Henry* (1992). Didion, an intensely introspective writer, attempts, in her essays, to draw significance from the particulars of her own life. In this essay, she describes one of the sources of her work—her own notebooks.

JOAN DIDION

On Keeping a Notebook

1 " 'That woman Estelle,' " the note reads, " 'is partly the reason why George Sharp and I are separated today.' *Dirty crepe-de-Chine wrapper, hotel bar, Wilmington RR, 9:45 a.m. August Monday morning.*"

2 Since the note is in my notebook, it presumably has some meaning to me. I study it for a long while. At first I have only the most general notion of what I was doing on an August Monday morning in the bar of the hotel across from the Pennsylvania Railroad station in Wilmington, Delaware (waiting for a train? missing one? 1960? 1961? why Wilmington?), but I do remember being there. The woman in the dirty crepe-de-Chine wrapper had come down from her room for a beer, and the bartender had heard before the reason why George Sharp and she were separated today. "Sure," he said, and went on mopping the floor. "You told me." At the other end of the bar is a girl. She is talking, pointedly, not to the man beside her but to a cat lying in the triangle of sunlight cast through the open door. She is wearing a plaid silk dress from Peck & Peck, and the hem is coming down.

3 Here is what it is: the girl has been on the Eastern Shore, and now she is going back to the city, leaving the man beside her, and all she can see ahead are the viscous summer sidewalks and the 3 a.m. long-distance calls that will make her lie awake and then sleep drugged through all the steaming mornings left in August (1960? 1961?). Because she must go directly from the train to lunch in New York, she wishes that she had a safety pin for the hem of the plaid silk dress, and she also wishes that she could forget about the hem and the lunch and stay in the cool bar that smells of disinfectant and malt and make friends with the woman in the crepe-de-Chine wrapper. She is afflicted by a little

self-pity, and she wants to compare Estelles. That is what that was all about.

Why did I write it down? In order to remember, of course, but ex- 4
actly what was it I wanted to remember? How much of it actually happened? Did any of it? Why do I keep a notebook at all? It is easy to deceive oneself on all those scores. The impulse to write things down is a peculiarly compulsive one, inexplicable to those who do not share it, useful only accidentally, only secondarily, in the way that any compulsion tries to justify itself. I suppose that it begins or does not begin in the cradle. Although I have felt compelled to write things down since I was five years old, I doubt that my daughter ever will, for she is a singularly blessed and accepting child, delighted with life exactly as life presents itself to her, unafraid to go to sleep and unafraid to wake up. Keepers of private notebooks are a different breed altogether, lonely and resistant rearrangers of things, anxious malcontents, children afflicted apparently at birth with some presentiment of loss.

My first notebook was a Big Five tablet, given to me by my mother 5
with the sensible suggestion that I stop whining and learn to amuse myself by writing down my thoughts. She returned the tablet to me a few years ago; the first entry is an account of a woman who believed herself to be freezing to death in the Arctic night, only to find, when day broke, that she had stumbled onto the Sahara Desert, where she would die of the heat before lunch. I have no idea what turn of a five-year-old's mind could have prompted so insistently "ironic" and exotic a story, but it does reveal a certain predilection for the extreme which has dogged me into adult life; perhaps if I were analytically inclined I would find it a truer story than any I might have told about Donald Johnson's birthday party or the day my cousin Brenda put Kitty Litter in the aquarium.

So the point of my keeping a notebook has never been, nor is it 6
now, to have an accurate factual record of what I have been doing or thinking. That would be a different impulse entirely, an instinct for reality which I sometimes envy but do not possess. At no point have I ever been able successfully to keep a diary; my approach to daily life ranges from the grossly negligent to the merely absent, and on those few occasions when I have tried dutifully to record a day's events, boredom has so overcome me that the results are mysterious at best. What is this business about "shopping, typing piece, dinner with E, depressed"? Shopping for what? Typing what piece? Who is E? Was this "E" depressed, or was I depressed? Who cares?

In fact I have abandoned altogether that kind of pointless entry; in- 7
stead I tell what some would call lies. "That's simply not true," the members of my family frequently tell me when they come up against my memory of a shared event. "The party was *not* for you, the spider was *not* a black widow, *it wasn't that way at all.*" Very likely they are right, for not only have I always had trouble distinguishing between what happened and what merely might have happened, but I remain unconvinced that the distinction, for my purposes, matters. The

cracked crab that I recall having for lunch the day my father came home from Detroit in 1945 must certainly be embroidery, worked into the day's pattern to lend verisimilitude; I was ten years old and would not now remember the cracked crab. The day's events did not turn on cracked crab. And yet it is precisely that fictitious crab that makes me see the afternoon all over again, a home movie run all too often, the father bearing gifts, the child weeping, an exercise in family love and guilt. Or that is what it was to me. Similarly, perhaps it never did snow that August in Vermont; perhaps there never were flurries in the night wind, and maybe no one else felt the ground hardening and summer already dead even as we pretended to bask in it, but that was how it felt to me, and it might as well have snowed, could have snowed, did snow.

How it felt to me: that is getting closer to the truth about a notebook. 8
I sometimes delude myself about why I keep a notebook, imagine that some thrifty virtue derives from preserving everything observed. See enough and write it down, I tell myself, and then some morning when the world seems drained of wonder, some day when I am only going through the motions of doing what I am supposed to do, which is write—on that bankrupt morning I will simply open my notebook and there it will all be, a forgotten account with accumulated interest, paid passage back to the world out there: dialogue overheard in hotels and elevators and at the hatcheck counter in Pavillon (one middle-aged man shows his hatcheck to another and says, "That's my old football number"); impressions of Bettina Aptheker and Benjamin Sonnenberg and Teddy ("Mr. Acapulco") Stauffer; careful *apercus* about tennis bums and failed fashion models and Greek shipping heiresses, one of whom taught me a significant lesson (a lesson I could have learned from F. Scott Fitzgerald, but perhaps we all must meet the very rich for ourselves) by asking, when I arrived to interview her in her orchid-filled sitting room on the second day of a paralyzing New York blizzard, whether it was snowing outside.

I imagine, in other words, that the notebook is about other people. 9
But of course it is not. I have no real business with what one stranger said to another at the hatcheck counter in Pavillon; in fact I suspect that the line "That's my old football number" touched not my own imagination at all, but merely some memory of something once read, probably "The Eighty-Yard Run." Nor is my concern with a woman in a dirty crepe-de-Chine wrapper in a Wilmington bar. My stake is always, of course, in the unmentioned girl in the plaid silk dress. *Remember what it was to be me:* that is always the point.

It is a difficult point to admit. We are brought up in the ethic that 10
others, any others, all others, are by definition more interesting than ourselves; taught to be diffident, just this side of self-effacing. ("You're the least important person in the room and don't forget it," Jessica Mitford's governess would hiss in her ear on the advent of any social occasion; I copied that into my notebook because it is only recently that I have been able to enter a room without hearing some such phrase in my inner ear.) Only the very young and the very old may recount their

dreams at breakfast, dwell upon self, interrupt with memories of beach picnics and favorite Liberty lawn dresses and the rainbow trout in a creek near Colorado Springs. The rest of us are expected, rightly, to affect absorption in other people's favorite dresses, other people's trout.

And so we do. But our notebooks give us away, for however dutifully we record what we see around us, the common denominator of all we see is always, transparently, shamelessly, the implacable "I." We are not talking here about the kind of notebook that is patently for public consumption, a structural conceit for binding together a series of graceful *pensées;* we are talking about something private, about bits of the mind's string too short to use, an indiscriminate and erratic assemblage with meaning only for its maker. 11

And sometimes even the maker has difficulty with the meaning. There does not seem to be, for example, any point in my knowing for the rest of my life that, during 1964, 720 tons of soot fell on every square mile of New York City, yet there it is in my notebook, labeled "FACT." Nor do I really need to remember that Ambrose Bierce liked to spell Leland Stanford's name "£eland $tanford" or that "smart women almost always wear black in Cuba," a fashion hint without much potential for practical application. And does not the relevance of these notes seem marginal at best? 12

> In the basement museum of the Inyo County Courthouse in Independence, California, sign pinned to a mandarin coat: "This MANDARIN COAT was often worn by Mrs. Minnie S. Brooks when giving lectures on her TEAPOT COLLECTION." Redhead getting out of car in front of Beverly Wilshire Hotel, chinchilla stole, Vuitton bags with tags reading:
>
> MRS. LOU FOX
> HOTEL SAHARA
> VEGAS

Well, perhaps not entirely marginal. As a matter of fact, Mrs. Minnie S. Brooks and her MANDARIN COAT pull me back into my own childhood, for although I never knew Mrs. Brooks and did not visit Inyo County until I was thirty, I grew up in just such a world, in houses cluttered with Indian relics and bits of gold ore and ambergris and the souvenirs my Aunt Mercy Farnsworth brought back from the Orient. It is a long way from that world to Mrs. Lou Fox's world, where we all live now, and is it not just as well to remember that? Might not Mrs. Minnie S. Brooks help me to remember what I am? Might not Mrs. Lou Fox help me to remember what I am not? 13

But sometimes the point is harder to discern. What exactly did I have in mind when I noted down that it cost the father of someone I know $650 a month to light the place on the Hudson in which he lived before the Crash? What use was I planning to make of this line by Jimmy Hoffa: "I may have my faults, but being wrong ain't one of them"? And although I think it interesting to know where the girls who travel with the Syndicate have their hair done when they find them- 14 selves on the West Coast, will I ever make suitable use of it? Might I not be better off just passing it on to John O'Hara? What is a recipe for sauerkraut doing in my notebook? What kind of magpie keeps this notebook? *"He was born the night the Titanic went down."* That seems a nice enough line, and I even recall who said it, but is it not really a better line in life than it could ever be in fiction?

But of course that is exactly it: not that I should ever use the line, 15
but that I should remember the woman who said it and the afternoon I heard it. We were on her terrace by the sea, and we were finishing the wine left from lunch, trying to get what sun there was, a California winter sun. The woman whose husband was born the night the *Titanic* went down wanted to rent her house, wanted to go back to her children in Paris. I remember wishing that I could afford the house, which cost $1,000 a month. "Someday you will," she said lazily. "Someday it all comes." There in the sun on her terrace it seemed easy to believe in someday, but later I had a low-grade afternoon hangover and ran over a black snake on the way to the supermarket and was flooded with inexplicable fear when I heard the checkout clerk explaining to the man ahead of me why she was finally divorcing her husband. "He left me no choice," she said over and over as she punched the register. "He has a little seven-month-old baby by her, he left me no choice." I would like to believe that my dread then was for the human condition, but of course it was for me, because I wanted a baby and did not then have one and because I wanted to own the house that cost $1,000 a month to rent and because I had a hangover.

It all comes back. Perhaps it is difficult to see the value in having 16
one's self back in that kind of mood, but I do see it; I think we are well advised to keep on nodding terms with the people we used to be whether we find them attractive company or not. Otherwise they turn up unannounced and surprise us, come hammering on the mind's door at 4 a.m. of a bad night and demand to know who deserted them, who betrayed them, who is going to make amends. We forget all too soon the things we thought we could never forget. We forget the loves and the betrayals alike, forget what we whispered and what we screamed, forget who we were. I have already lost touch with a couple of people I used to be; one of them, a seventeen-year-old, presents little threat, although it would be of some interest to me to know again what it feels like to sit on a river levee drinking vodka-and-orange-juice and listening to Les Paul and Mary Ford and their echoes sing "How High the Moon" on the car radio. (You see I still have the scenes, but I no longer perceive myself among those present, no longer could even improvise the dialogue.) The other one, a twenty-three-year-old, bothers me more. She was always a good deal of trouble, and I suspect she will reappear when I least want to see her, skirts too long, shy to the point of aggravation, always the injured party, full of recriminations and little hurts and stories I do not want to hear again, at once saddening me and angering me with her vulnerability and ignorance, an apparition all the more insistent for being so long banished.

It is a good idea, then, to keep in touch, and I suppose that keeping in touch is what notebooks are all about. And we are all on our own when it comes to keeping those lines open to ourselves: your notebook will never help me, nor mine you. *"So what's new in the whiskey business?"* What could that possibly mean to you? To me it means a blonde in a Pucci bathing suit sitting with a couple of fat men by the pool at the Beverly Hills Hotel. Another man approaches, and they all regard one another in silence for a while. "So what's new in the whiskey business?" one of the fat men finally says by way of welcome, and the blonde stands up, arches one foot and dips it in the pool, looking all the while at the cabana where Baby Pignatari is talking on the telephone. That is all there is to that, except that several years later I saw the blonde coming out of Saks Fifth Avenue in New York with her California complexion and a voluminous mink coat. In the harsh wind that day she looked old and irrevocably tired to me, and even the skins in the mink coat were not worked the way they were doing them that year, not the way she would have wanted them done, and there is the point of the story. For a while after that I did not like to look in the mirror, and my eyes would skim the newspapers and pick out only the deaths, the cancer victims, the premature coronaries, the suicides, and I stopped riding the Lexington Avenue IRT because I noticed for the first time that all the strangers I had seen for years—the man with the seeing-eye dog, the spinster who read the classified pages every day, the fat girl who always got off with me at Grand Central—looked older than they once had. 17

It all comes back. Even that recipe for sauerkraut: even that brings it back. I was on Fire Island when I first made that sauerkraut, and it was raining, and we drank a lot of bourbon and ate the sauerkraut and went to bed at ten, and I listened to the rain and the Atlantic and felt safe. I made the sauerkraut again last night and it did not make me feel any safer, but that is, as they say, another story. 18

COMPREHENSION

1. Why does Didion mention "keeping" a notebook in her title? How is her essay about keeping rather than writing a notebook?
2. What sort of entries does Didion make in her notebooks? How and why does Didion alter the reality of the events she described in her notebooks?
3. What are the various reasons Didion explores for keeping a notebook? What is her purpose in examining so many possible reasons?

RHETORIC

1. What is the function of the numerous rhetorical questions in the essay?
2. How does the style of Didion's notebooks differ from her regular writing style?

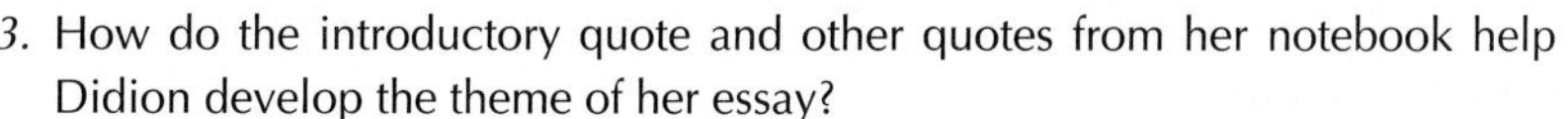

3. How do the introductory quote and other quotes from her notebook help Didion develop the theme of her essay?
4. Repetition is a key device used to unify the essay. Identify examples of important repetitions.
5. Identify topic sentences in the essay. How does Didion prepare us for the thesis through her topic sentences?
6. Analyze causal patterns of development that appear in the essay.

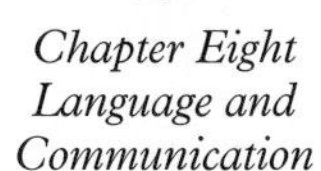

WRITING

1. If you were to keep a notebook, what would you record in it? Why would you keep it? Write a brief essay on this topic.
2. Write an essay about some events that have occurred in your own past that you feel were significant to your growth.
3. Didion speaks of "lying" or "embroidery" in recounting events. Write an essay about an episode in your life that you like to embellish.

AMY TAN Amy Tan (1952–) is the daughter of a minister/electrical engineer and a vocational nurse. She was born in California and educated at San Jose State and the University of California, Berkeley. Tan has worked as a reporter and as a technical writer; her fiction focuses on the lives of Chinese-American women seeking to reconcile their traditional Chinese heritage with modern American culture. Her novels are *The Joy Luck Club* (1989), *The Kitchen God's Wife* (1991), and a children's book, *The Moon Lady* (1992). In this narrative essay, from *The State of the Language,* Tan writes with both emotion and clarity about growing up with two languages, and attacks some linguists who make hasty assumptions.

AMY TAN

The Language of Discretion

1 At a recent family dinner in San Francisco, my mother whispered to me: "Sau-sau [Brother's Wife] pretends too hard to be polite! Why bother? In the end, she always takes everything."

2 My mother thinks like a *waixiao,* an expatriate, temporarily away from China since 1949, no longer patient with ritual courtesies. As if to prove her point, she reached across the table to offer my elderly aunt from Beijing the last scallop from the Happy Family seafood dish.

3 Sau-sau scowled. *"B'yao, zhen b'yao!"* (I don't want it, really I don't!) she cried, patting her plump stomach.

4 "Take it! Take it!" scolded my mother in Chinese.

5 “Full, I’m already full,” Sau-sau protested weakly, eyeing the beloved scallop.

6 “Ai!” exclaimed my mother, completely exasperated. “Nobody else wants it. If you don’t take it, it will only rot!”

7 At this point, Sau-sau sighed, acting as if she were doing my mother a big favor by taking the wretched scrap off her hands.

8 My mother turned to her brother, a high-ranking communist official who was visiting her in California for the first time: “In America a Chinese person could starve to death. If you say you don’t want it, they won’t ask you again forever.”

9 My uncle nodded and said he understood fully: Americans take things quickly because they have no time to be polite.

10 I thought about this misunderstanding again—of social contexts failing in translation—when a friend sent me an article from the *New York Times Magazine* (24 April 1988). The article, on changes in New York’s Chinatown, made passing reference to the inherent ambivalence of the Chinese language.

11 Chinese people are so “discreet and modest,” the article stated, there aren’t even words for “yes” and “no.”

12 That’s not true, I thought, although I can see why an outsider might think that. I continued reading.

13 If one is Chinese, the article went on to say, “One compromises, one doesn’t hazard a loss of face by an overemphatic response.”

14 My throat seized. Why do people keep saying these things? As if we truly were those little dolls sold in Chinatown tourist shops, heads bobbing up and down in complacent agreement to anything said!

15 I worry about the effect of one-dimensional statements on the unwary and guileless. When they read about this so-called vocabulary deficit, do they also conclude that Chinese people evolved into a mild-mannered lot because the language only allowed them to hobble forth with minced words?

16 Something enormous is always lost in translation. Something insidious seeps into the gaps, especially when amateur linguists continue to compare, one-for-one, language differences and then put forth notions wide open to misinterpretation: that Chinese people have no direct linguistic means to make decisions, assert or deny, affirm or negate, just say no to drug dealers, or behave properly on the witness stand when told, “Please answer yes or no.”

17 Yet one can argue, with the help of renowned linguists, that the Chinese are indeed up a creek without “yes” and “no.” Take any number of variations on the old language-and-reality theory stated years ago by Edward Sapir: “Human beings . . . are very much at the mercy of the particular language which has become the medium for their society. . . . The fact of the matter is that the ‘real world’ is to a large extent built up on the language habits of the group.”[1]

[1]Edward Sapir, *Selected Writings,* ed. D. G. Mandelbaum (Berkeley and Los Angeles, 1949).

This notion was further bolstered by the famous Sapir-Whorf hy- 18
pothesis, which roughly states that one's perception of the world and how one functions in it depends a great deal on the language used. As Sapir, Whorf, and new carriers of the banner would have us believe, language shapes our thinking, channels us along certain patterns embedded in words, syntactic structures, and intonation patterns. Language has become the peg and the shelf that enables us to sort out and categorize the world. In English, we see "cats" and "dogs"; what if the language had also specified *glatz,* meaning "animals that leave fur on the sofa," and *glotz,* meaning "animals that leave fur and drool on the sofa"? How would language, the enabler, have changed our perceptions with slight vocabulary variations?

And if this were the case—of language being the master of destined 19
thought—think of the opportunities lost from failure to evolve two little words, *yes* and *no,* the simplest of opposites! Ghenghis Khan could have been sent back to Mongolia. Opium wars might have been averted. The Cultural Revolution could have been sidestepped.

There are still many, from serious linguists to pop psychology 20
cultists, who view language and reality as inextricably tied, one being the consequence of the other. We have traversed the range from the Sapir-Whorf hypothesis to est and neurolinguistic programming, which tell us "you are what you say."

I too have been intrigued by the theories. I can summarize, albeit 21
badly, ages-old empirical evidence: of Eskimos and their infinite ways to say "snow," their ability to *see* the differences in snowflake configurations, thanks to the richness of their vocabulary, while non-Eskimo speakers like myself founder in "snow," "more snow," and "lots more where that came from."

I too have experienced dramatic cognitive awakenings via the word. 22
Once I added "mauve" to my vocabulary I began to see it everywhere. When I learned how to pronounce *prix fixe,* I ate French food at prices better than the easier-to-say *à la carte* choices.

But just how seriously are we supposed to take this? 23

Sapir said something else about language and reality. It is the part 24
that often gets left behind in the dot-dot-dots of quotes: ". . . No two languages are ever sufficiently similar to be considered as representing the same social reality. The worlds in which different societies live are distinct worlds, not merely the same world with different labels attached."

When I first read this, I thought, Here at last is validity for the 25
dilemmas I felt growing up in a bicultural, bilingual family! As any child of immigrant parents knows, there's a special kind of double bind attached to knowing two languages. My parents, for example, spoke to me in both Chinese and English; I spoke back to them in English.

"Amy-ah!" they'd call to me. 26

"What?" I'd mumble back. 27

"Do not question us when we call," they scolded me in Chinese. "It 28
is not respectful."

"What do you mean?" 29

"Ai! Didn't we just tell you not to question?" 30

To this day, I wonder which parts of my behavior were shaped by 31
Chinese, which by English. I am tempted to think, for example, that if I am of two minds on some matter it is due to the richness of my linguistic experiences, not to any personal tendencies toward wishy-washiness. But which mind says what?

Was it perhaps patience—developed through years of deciphering 32
my mother's fractured English—that had me listening politely while a woman announced over the phone that I had won one of five valuable prizes? Was it respect—pounded in by the Chinese imperative to accept convoluted explanations—that had me agreeing that I might find it worthwhile to drive seventy-five miles to view a time-share resort? Could I have been at a loss for words when asked, "Wouldn't you like to win a Hawaiian cruise or perhaps a fabulous Star of India designed exclusively by Carter and Van Arpels?"

And when this same woman called back a week later, this time com- 33
plaining that I had missed my appointment, obviously it was my type A language that kicked into gear and interrupted her. Certainly, my blunt denial—"Frankly I'm not interested"—was as American as apple pie. And when she said, "But it's in Morgan Hill," and I shouted, "Read my lips. I don't care if it's Timbuktu," you can be sure I said it with the precise intonation expressing both cynicism and disgust.

It's dangerous business, this sorting out of language and behavior. 34
Which one is English? Which is Chinese? The categories manifest themselves: passive and aggressive, tentative and assertive, indirect and direct. And I realize they are just variations of the same theme: that Chinese people are discreet and modest.

Reject them all! 35

If my reaction is overly strident, it is because I cannot come across 36
as too emphatic. I grew up listening to the same lines over and over again, like so many rote expressions repeated in an English phrasebook. And I too almost came to believe them.

Yet if I consider my upbringing more carefully, I find there was 37
nothing discreet about the Chinese language I grew up with. My parents made everything abundantly clear. Nothing wishy-washy in their demands, no compromises accepted: "Of course you will become a famous neurosurgeon," they told me. "And yes, a concert pianist on the side."

In fact, now that I remember, it seems that the more emphatic out- 38
bursts always spilled over into Chinese: "Not that way! You must wash rice so not a single grain spills out."

I do not believe that my parents—both immigrants from mainland 39
China—are an exception to the modest-and-discreet rule. I have only to look at the number of Chinese engineering students skewing minority ratios at Berkeley, MIT, and Yale. Certainly they were not raised by passive mothers and fathers who said, "It is up to you, my daughter. Writer, welfare recipient, masseuse, or molecular engineer—you decide."

And my American mind says, See, those engineering students 40
weren't able to say no to their parents' demands. But then my Chinese mind remembers: Ah, but those parents all wanted their sons and daughters to be *pre-med.*

Having listened to both Chinese and English, I also tend to be sus- 41
picious of any comparisons between the two languages. Typically, one language—that of the person doing the comparing—is often used as the standard, the benchmark for a logical form of expression. And so the language being compared is always in danger of being judged deficient or superfluous, simplistic or unnecessarily complex, melodious or cacophonous. English speakers point out that Chinese is extremely difficult because it relies on variations in tone barely discernible to the human ear. By the same token, Chinese speakers tell me English is extremely difficult because it is inconsistent, a language of too many broken rules, of Mickey Mice and Donald Ducks.

Even more dangerous to my mind is the temptation to compare 42
both language and behavior *in translation.* To listen to my mother speak English, one might think she has no concept of past or future tense, that she doesn't see the difference between singular and plural, that she is gender blind because she calls my husband "she." If one were not careful, one might also generalize that, based on the way my mother talks, all Chinese people take a circumlocutory route to get to the point. It is, in fact, my mother's idiosyncratic behavior to ramble a bit.

Sapir was right about differences between two languages and their real- 43
ities. I can illustrate why word-for-word translation is not enough to translate meaning and intent. I once received a letter from China which I read to non-Chinese speaking friends. The letter, originally written in Chinese, had been translated by my brother-in-law in Beijing. One portion described the time when my uncle at age ten discovered his widowed mother (my grandmother) had remarried—as a number three concubine, the ultimate disgrace for an honorable family. The translated version of my uncle's letter read in part:

> In 1925, I met my mother in Shanghai. When she came to me, I didn't have greeting to her as if seeing nothing. She pull me to a corner secretly and asked me why didn't have greeting to her. I couldn't control myself and cried, "Ma! Why did you leave us? People told me: one day you ate a beancake yourself. Your sister-in-law found it and sweared at you, called your names. So . . . is it true?" She clasped my hand and answered immediately, "It's not true, don't say what like this." After this time, there was a few chance to meet her.

"What!" cried my friends. "Was eating a beancake so terrible?" 44

Of course not. The beancake was simply a euphemism; a ten-year- 45
old boy did not dare question his mother on something as shocking as concubinage. Eating a beancake was his equivalent for committing this selfish act, something inconsiderate of all family members, hence, my grandmother's despairing response to what seemed like a ludicrous

charge of gluttony. And sure enough, she was banished from the family, and my uncle saw her only a few times before her death.

46 While the above may fuel people's argument that Chinese is indeed a language of extreme discretion, it does not mean that Chinese people speak in secrets and riddles. The contexts are fully understood. It is only to those on the *outside* that the language seems cryptic, the behavior inscrutable.

47 I am, evidently, one of the outsiders. My nephew in Shanghai, who recently started taking English lessons, has been writing me letters in English. I had told him I was a fiction writer, and so in one letter he wrote, "Congratulate to you on your writing. Perhaps one day I should like to read it." I took it in the same vein as "Perhaps one day we can get together for lunch." I sent back a cheery note. A month went by and another letter arrived from Shanghai. "Last one perhaps I hadn't writing distinctly," he said. "In the future, you'll send a copy of your works for me."

48 I try to explain to my English-speaking friends that Chinese language use is more *strategic* in manner, whereas English tends to be more direct; an American business executive may say, "Let's make a deal," and the Chinese manager may reply, "Is your son interested in learning about your widget business?" Each to his or her own purpose, each with his or her own linguistic path. But I hesitate to add more to the pile of generalizations, because no matter how many examples I provide and explain, I fear that it appears defensive and only reinforces the image: that Chinese people are "discreet and modest"—and it takes an American to explain what they really mean.

49 Why am I complaining? The description seems harmless enough (after all, the *New York Times Magazine* writer did not say "slippery and evasive"). It is precisely the bland, easy acceptability of the phrase that worries me.

50 I worry that the dominant society may see Chinese people from a limited—and limiting—perspective. I worry that seemingly benign stereotypes may be part of the reason there are few Chinese in top management positions, in mainstream political roles. I worry about the power of language: that if one says anything enough times—in *any* language—it might become true.

51 Could this be why Chinese friends of my parents' generation are willing to accept the generalization?

52 "Why are you complaining?" one of them said to me. "If people think we are modest and polite, let them think that. Wouldn't Americans be pleased to admit they are thought of as polite?"

53 And I do believe anyone would take the description as a compliment—at first. But after a while, it annoys, as if the only things that people heard one say were phatic remarks: "I'm so pleased to meet you. I've heard many wonderful things about you. For me? You shouldn't have!"

54 These remarks are not representative of new ideas, honest emotions, or considered thought. They are what is said from the polite dis-

tance of social contexts: of greetings, farewells, wedding thank-you notes, convenient excuses, and the like.

It makes me wonder though. How many anthropologists, how many sociologists, how many travel journalists have documented so-called "natural interactions" in foreign lands, all observed with spiral notebook in hand? How many other cases are there of the long-lost primitive tribe, people who turned out to be sophisticated enough to put on the stone-age show that ethnologists had come to see?

And how many tourists fresh off the bus have wandered into 56
Chinatown expecting the self-effacing shopkeeper to admit under duress that the goods are not worth the price asked? I have witnessed it.

"I don't know," the tourist said to the shopkeeper, a Cantonese 57
woman in her fifties. "It doesn't look genuine to me. I'll give you three dollars."

"You don't like my price, go somewhere else," said the shopkeeper. 58

"You are not a nice person," cried the shocked tourist, "not a nice 59
person at all!"

"Who say I have to be nice," snapped the shopkeeper. 60

"So how does one say 'yes' and 'no' in Chinese?" ask my friends a bit 61
warily.

And here I do agree in part with the *New York Times Magazine* arti- 62
cle. There is no one word for "yes" or "no"—but not out of necessity to be discreet. If anything, I would say the Chinese equivalent of answering "yes" or "no" is dis*crete,* that is, specific to what is asked.

Ask a Chinese person if he or she has eaten, and he or she might 63
say *chrle* (eaten already) or perhaps *meiyou* (have not).

Ask, "So you had insurance at the time of the accident?" and the 64
response would be *dwei* (correct) or *meiyou* (did not have).

Ask, "Have you stopped beating your wife?" and the answer refers 65
directly to the proposition being asserted or denied: stopped already, still have not, never beat, have no wife.

What could be clearer? 66

As for those who are still wondering how to translate the language of 67
discretion, I offer this personal example.

My aunt and uncle were about to return to Beijing after a three- 68
month visit to the United States. On their last night I announced I wanted to take them out to dinner.

"Are you hungry?" I asked in Chinese. 69

"Not hungry," said my uncle promptly, the same response he once 70
gave me ten minutes before he suffered a low-blood-sugar attack.

"Not too hungry," said my aunt. "Perhaps you're hungry?" 71

"A little," I admitted. 72

"We can eat, we can eat," they both consented. 73

"What kind of food?" I asked. 74

"Oh, doesn't matter. Anything will do. Nothing fancy, just some 75
simple food is fine."

"Do you like Japanese food? We haven't had that yet," I suggested. 76

They looked at each other. 77

"We can eat it," said my uncle bravely, this survivor of the Long 78
March.

"We have eaten it before," added my aunt. "Raw fish." 79

"Oh, you don't like it?" I said. "Don't be polite. We can go some- 80
where else."

"We are not being polite. We can eat it," my aunt insisted. 81

So I drove them to Japantown and we walked past several restau- 82
rants featuring colorful plastic displays of sushi.

"Not this one, not this one either," I continued to say, as if search- 83
ing for a Japanese restaurant similar to the last. "Here it is," I finally said, turning into a restaurant famous for its Chinese fish dishes from Shandong.

"Oh, Chinese food!" cried my aunt, obviously relieved. 84

My uncle patted my arm. "You think Chinese." 85

"It's your last night here in America," I said. "So don't be polite. 86
Act like an American."

And that night we ate a banquet. 87

COMPREHENSION

1. Why is the writer suspicious of any comparisons made between Chinese and English? What dangerous generalizations may be drawn?
2. What is meant by "the double-bind attached to knowing two languages"?
3. In your own words, define Sapir's language theory.

RHETORIC

1. What tone does Tan use in her essay? Is her approach objective or subjective? Justify your response.
2. What is Tan's thesis? Is it implied or stated explicitly?
3. How do the anecdotes at the beginning and conclusion of the essay help frame what happens in between? How well do they illustrate or support the essay's body?
4. Cite specific examples of irony or humor in the essay. Is it used consistently throughout the piece? How does its use advance Tan's main ideas?
5. How does Tan employ comparison and contrast to structure this essay?
6. How many sections are there in this essay? What principles of writing and coherence govern each section?

WRITING

1. Tan writes about the generalizations made by "outsiders" about Chinese culture based on the language. Write an essay in which you explore this topic by focusing on misconceptions others may have about you or you may have about others based on language.

2. Linguistic theories are presented by both Tan and Marshall ("Poets in the Kitchen") in their essays. Using support from either or both writers, consider the dangers of linking behavior to language. Can these theories be used to further racist notions? Are they valid, scientific attempts to study human behavior?

SAMUEL ICHIZE HAYAKAWA Samuel Ichize Hayakawa (1906–1992) began his career as a professor of linguistics and was the author of numerous books on languages, such as *Language in Thought and Action* (1941), *Our Language and Our World* (1959), and *Symbol, Status, and Personality* (1963). When Hayakawa became president of San Francisco State College, student unrest was at its height. By defending traditional values and, indeed, authority itself, Hayakawa became a national and controversial figure. His notoriety propelled him into the U.S. Senate. The present essay reflects his original career as a semanticist.

S. I. HAYAKAWA

Words and Children

Those who still believe, after all the writing that semanticists have done, that semantics is a science of words, may be surprised to learn that semantics has the effect—at least, it has had on me and on many others—of reducing rather than increasing one's preoccupation with words. First of all, there is that vast area of nonverbal communication with children that we accomplish through holding, touching, rocking, caressing our children, putting food in their mouths, and all of the little attentions that we give them. These are all communication, and we communicate in this way for a long time before the children even start to talk. 1

Then, after they start to talk, there is always the problem of interpretation. There is a sense in which small children are recent immigrants in our midst. They have trouble both in understanding and in using the language, and they often make errors. Many people (you can notice this in the supermarkets, especially with parents of two- and three-year-old children) get angry at their children when they don't seem to mind. Anyone standing within earshot of one of these episodes can tell that the child just hasn't understood what the mother said. But the mother feels, "Well, I said it, didn't I? What's wrong with the child that he doesn't understand? It's English, isn't it?" But, as I say, the child is a recent immigrant in our midst and there are things that the child doesn't understand. 2

There are curious instances. Once, when our daughter was three years old, she found the bath too hot and she said, "Make it warmer." 3

It took me a moment to figure out that she meant, "Bring the water more nearly to the condition we call warm." It makes perfectly good sense looked at that way. Confronted with unusual formulations such as these which children constantly make, many of us react with incredible lack of imagination. Sometimes children are laughed at for making "silly statements," when it only requires understanding their way of abstracting and their way of formulating their abstractions to see that they are not silly at all.

Children are newcomers to the language. Learning a language isn't 4
just learning words; rules of the language are learned at the same time. Prove this? Very simple. Little children use a past tense like "I runned all the way to the park and I swimmed in the pool." "Runned" and "swimmed" are words they did not hear. They made them up by analogy from other past tenses they had heard. This means that they learned not only the vocabulary, they learned the rule for making the past tense—except that the English language doesn't follow its own rules. And when the child proves himself to be more logical than the English language, we take it out on the child—which is nonsense. Children's language should be listened to with great attentiveness and respect.

Again, when our daughter was three years old, I was pounding away 5
at my typewriter in my study and she was drawing pictures on the floor when she suddenly said, "I want to go see the popentole."

I kept typing. 6

Then I stopped and said, "What?!" 7

She said, "I want to see the popentole." 8

"Did you say *popentole?*" 9

I just stopped. It was a puzzle to figure out, but I did. In a few sec- 10
onds I said, "You mean like last Saturday, you want to go to Lincoln Park and see the totem pole?"

She said, "Yes." 11

And what was so warm about this, so wonderful about it, was that 12
having got her point across she played for another twenty minutes singing to herself, happy that she had communicated. I didn't say to her, "Okay, I'll take you next Sunday to see the popentole." The mere fact that she'd made her point and got it registered was a source of satisfaction to her. And I felt very proud of myself at the time for having understood.

One of the things we tend to overlook in our culture is the tremen- 13
dous value of the acknowledgment of message. Not, "I agree with you" or "I disagree with you" or "That's a wonderful idea" or "That's a silly idea," but just the acknowledgment, "I know exactly what you've said. It goes on the record. You said that." She said, "I want to go see the totem pole." I said, "Okay, you want to go see the totem pole." The acknowledgment of message says in effect, "I know you're around. I know what you're thinking. I acknowledge your presence."

There is also a sense in which a child understands far more than we 14
suspect. Because a child doesn't understand words too well (and also because his nervous system is not yet deadened by years spent as a

lawyer, accountant, advertising executive, or professor of philosophy), a child attends not only to what we say but to everything about us as we say it—tone of voice, gesture, facial expression, bodily tensions, and so on. A child attends to a conversation between grown-ups with the same amazing absorption. Indeed, a child listening is, I hope, like a good psychiatrist listening—or like a good semanticist listening—because she watches not only the words but also the nonverbal events to which words bear, in all too many cases, so uncertain a relationship. Therefore a child is in some matters quite difficult to fool, especially on the subject of one's true attitude toward her. For this reason many parents, without knowing it, are to a greater or lesser degree in the situation of the worried mother who said to the psychiatrist to whom she brought her child, "I tell her a dozen times a day that I love her, but the brat still hates me. Why, doctor?"

"Life in a big city is dangerous," a mother once said to me. "You 15
hear so often of children running thoughtlessly out in the street and being struck by passing cars. They will never learn unless you keep telling them and telling them." This is the communication theory that makes otherwise pleasant men and women into nagging parents: You've got to keep telling them; then you've got to remind them; then tell 'em again. Are there no better ways to teach children not to run out into the street? Of course there are. I think it was done in our family without words.

Whenever my wife crossed the street with our boy Alan—he was then 16
about three—she would come to a stop at the curb whether there was any traffic in sight or not, and look up and down the boulevard before crossing. It soon became a habit. One day I absentmindedly started crossing the street without looking up and down—the street was empty. Alan grabbed my coat and pulled me back on the curb to look up and down before we started out again. Children love to know the right way to do things. They learn by imitation far more than by precept.

The uncritical confidence that many people place in words is a mat- 17
ter of constant amazement to me. When we were living in Chicago there was a concrete courtyard behind our apartment house. I heard a great deal of noise and shouting out there one day, and I looked out and saw a father teaching his boy to ride a bicycle. The father was shouting instructions: "Keep your head up. Now push down with your left foot. Now look out, you're running into the wall. Steer away from it. *Steer away from it!* Now push down with your right foot. Don't fall down!" and so on and so on. The poor boy was trying to keep his balance, manage the bicycle, obey his father's instructions all at the same time, and he looked about as totally confused as it is possible for a little boy to get. One thing we learn from general semantics, if we haven't learned it some other way already, is that there are limits to what can be accomplished in words. Learning to ride a bicycle is beyond those limits. Having sensed those limits, we become content to let many things take care of themselves without words. All this makes for a quieter household.

18 The anthropologist Ray Birdwhistell has undertaken a study that he calls "kinesics"* which is the systematic examination of gesture and body motion in communication; this is a rich area of concern about which many students of human behavior have been much excited. But there is a danger in going too far in this direction—in going overboard to the extent of saying that words are of *no* importance. There are thousands of things children must know and enjoy that it is not possible for them to get *without* words.

19 The sense of what one misses through the lack of words has been brought home to us by the fact that our second boy, Mark, now twenty-nine, is seriously mentally retarded. At the age of six he was hardly able to talk at all. Now he talks quite a bit, but his speech is very difficult to understand; members of the family can understand it about half the time. He was always able to understand words with direct physical referents—watch, glass of water, orange juice, record player, television, and so on. But there are certain things that exist only in words, like the concept of the future. I remember the following incident when he was six years old. He came across a candy bar at ten minutes to twelve when lunch was just about to be served. I tried to take it away from him and said, "Look, Mark, you can have it right after lunch. Don't eat it now. You can have it right after lunch." Well, when he was six all he could understand was that it was being taken away from him *now,* and the idea that there was a future in which he'd have it back was something he just couldn't get at the time. Of course, the concept of futurity developed later, but it took him much longer to develop it than it took the other children.

20 For human beings, the future, which exists *only in language,* is a wonderful dimension in which to live. That is, human beings can readily endure and even enjoy postponement; the anticipation of future pleasures is itself a pleasure. But futurity is something that has no physical referent like "a glass of water." It exists only in language. Mark's frequent frustrations and rage when he was younger were a constant reminder to us that all the warmth and richness of nonverbal communication, all that we could communicate by holding him and feeding him and patting his head and playing on the floor with him, were not enough for the purpose of human interaction. Organized games of any kind all have linguistically formulated rules. Take an organized game like baseball. Can there be a baseball without language? No, there can't. What's the difference between a ball and a strike? There are linguistically formulated rules by which we define the difference. All systematic games, even much simpler games that children play, have to have a language to formulate the rules. An enormous amount of human life is possible only with language, and without it one is very much impoverished.

*Ray Birdwhistell, *Kinesics and Context.* Philadelphia: University of Pennsylvania Press, 1970.

COMPREHENSION

1. How does the author encourage readers to understand what *semantics* means? Cite examples.
2. Hayakawa says that as a semanticist he has learned that we don't communicate only through words. What other ways of communication does he mention?
3. Hayakawa also points out some of the advantages of language as a communicative skill. What are they?

RHETORIC

1. Hayakawa uses two metaphors to explain a child's relation to language. What are they?
2. Cite examples of Hayakawa's use of scientific jargon. What does this suggest about the audience for which he is writing?
3. Explain how Hayakawa uses process to develop his essay.
4. Hayakawa makes several statements about communication. What are they? How does he use examples to illustrate these points?
5. Where does Hayakawa use personal examples? How do they contribute to the development of the essay?
6. Explain the importance of paragraphs 3, 14, and 18 to the development of the essay.

WRITING

1. Write an essay describing how we use nonverbal forms of communication, such as signals in sports or streetlights. Consider how we communicate through arts such as music, ballet, and painting.
2. Write an essay about the language of children based on your personal experience.
3. Imagine yourself an immigrant or a newcomer to a language. In what ways would you be like a child? Describe the situation in an essay.

ROSARIO FERRÉ Rosario Ferré (1942–) is a poet as well as the founder and director of *Zona de cargo y descargos,* a Latin-American journal devoted to Puerto-Rican writers. Ferré was born in Ponce, Puerto Rico, and received her Ph.D. from the University of Maryland in 1986. Her poetry collections include *Arbor y sombras* (1989) and *Sonatinas* (1989); Ferré's verse also appears in various anthologies, including *Contemporary Latin American Literature: 1960–1984.* In the essay below, Ferré describes the process of freeing herself from ghostly mentors in order to develop as a woman writer.

ROSARIO FERRÉ

The Writer's Kitchen

Throughout time, women narrators have written for many reasons: Emily Brontë wrote to prove the revolutionary nature of passion; Virginia Woolf wrote to exorcise her terror of madness and death; Joan Didion writes to discover what and how she thinks; Clarice Lispector discovered in her writing a reason to love and be loved. In my case, writing is simultaneously a constructive and a destructive urge, a possibility for growth and change. I write to build myself word by word, to banish my terror of silence; I write as a speaking, human mask. With respect to words, I have much for which to be grateful. Words have allowed me to forge for myself a unique identity, one that owes its existence only to my efforts. For this reason, I place more trust in the words I use than perhaps I ever did in my natural mother. When all else fails, when life becomes an absurd theater, I know words are there, ready to return my confidence to me. This need to reconstruct which moves me to write is closely tied to my need for love: I write so as to reinvent myself, to convince myself that what I love will endure. 1

But my urge to write is also destructive, an attempt to annihilate myself and the world. Words are infinitely wise and, like all mothers, they know when to destroy what is worn out or corrupt so that life may be rebuilt on new foundations. To the degree that I take part in the corruption of the world, I turn my instrument against myself. I write because I am poorly adjusted to reality; because the deep disillusionment within me has given rise to a need to re-create life, to replace it with a more compassionate, tolerable reality. I carry within me a utopian person, a utopian world. 2

This destructive urge that moves me to write is tied to my need for hate, my need for vengeance. I write so as to avenge myself against reality and against myself; I write to give permanence to what hurts me and to what tempts me. I believe that deep wounds and harsh insults might someday release within me all the creative forces available to human expression, a belief that implies, after all, that I love the word passionately. 3

Now I would like to address these constructive and destructive forces with relation to my work. The day I finally sat down at my typewriter to write my first story. I knew from experience how hard it was for a woman to obtain her own room with a lock on the door, as well as those metaphorical five hundred pounds a year that assure her independence. I had gotten divorced and had suffered many changes because of love, or because of what I had then thought was love: the re- 4

nouncing of my own intellectual and spiritual space for the sake of the relationship with the one I loved. What made me turn against myself was the determination to become the perfect wife. I wanted to be as they were telling me I should be, so I had ceased to exist; I had renounced my soul's private obligations. It has always seemed to me that living intensely was the most important of these obligations. I did not like the protected existence I had led until then in the sanctuary of my home, free from all danger but also from any responsibilities. I wanted to live, to enjoy firsthand knowledge, art, adventure, danger, without waiting for someone else to tell me about them. In fact, what I wanted was to dispel my fear of death. We all fear death, but I had a special terror of it, the terror of those who have not lived. Life tears us apart, making us become partners to its pleasures and terrors, yet in the end it consoles us; it teaches us to accept death as a necessary and natural end. But to see myself forced to face death without having known life—without passing through its apprenticeship—seemed to me unforgivable cruelty. I would tell myself that that was why children who die without having lived, without having to account for their own acts, all went to Limbo. I was convinced that Heaven was for the good, and Hell for the evil, for those men who had arduously earned either salvation or damnation. But in Limbo there were only women and children, unaware of how we had gotten there.

The day of my debut as a writer, I sat at my typewriter for a long 5
time, mulling over these thoughts. Inevitably, writing my first story meant taking my first step toward Heaven or Hell, and that made me vacillate between a state of euphoria and a state of depression. It was as if I were about to be born, peering timidly through the doors of Limbo. If my voice rings false or my will fails me, I said to myself, all my sacrifices will have been in vain. I will have foolishly given up the protection that despite its disadvantages, at least allowed me to be a good wife and mother, and I will have justly fallen from the frying pan into the fire.

In those days, Virginia Woolf and Simone de Beauvoir were my 6
mentors; I wanted them to show me how to write well, or at least how not to write poorly. I would read everything they had written like a person who takes several spoonfuls of a health potion nightly before retiring. The potion would prevent death from a host of plagues and ills that had killed off the majority of women writers before them, as well as some of their contemporaries. I must admit that those readings didn't do much to strengthen my as yet newborn and fragile identity as a writer. My hand's instinctive reflex was still to hold the frying pan patiently over the fire—not to brandish my pen aggressively through the flames—and Simone and Virginia, while recognizing the achievements that women writers had attained up to that time, criticized them quite severely. Simone was of the opinion that women too frequently insisted on themes traditionally considered feminine, the preoccupation with love, for example, or the denunciation of training and customs that had irreparably limited their existence. Justifiable though these themes were, to reduce oneself to them meant that the capacity for freedom had not

been adequately internalized. "Art, literature, and philosophy," Simone would say to me, "are attempts to base the world on a new human freedom, the freedom of the individual creator, and to achieve this goal a woman must, above all, assume the status of a being who already has freedom."

In her opinion, a woman should be constructive in her literature, not of interior realities, but of exterior realities, principally of those of a historical and social nature. For Simone, the intuitive capacity, the contact with irrational forces, the capacity for emotion, were all important talents, but they were also of secondary importance. "The functioning of the world, the order of political and social events which determine the course of our lives, are in the hands of those who make their decisions in the light of knowledge and reason," Simone would say to me, "and not in the light of intuition and emotion," and it was with those themes that women should henceforth occupy themselves in their literature. 7

Virginia Woolf, for her part, was obsessed with the need for an objectivity and distance which, she thought, had seldom been found in the writings of women. Of the writers of the past, Virginia excluded only Jane Austen and Emily Brontë, because only they had managed to write, like Shakespeare, "with a mind incandescent, unimpeded." "It is deadly for a writer to think about his or her gender," Virginia would say to me, and "it is deadly for a woman to register a complaint, however mild, to advocate a cause, however justifiably—deadly, then, to speak consciously as a woman. In Virginia's opinion, the books of a woman writer who doesn't free herself from rage will contain distortions, deviations. She will write with anger instead of with sensitivity. She will speak of herself, instead of about her characters. At war with her fate, how can she avoid dying young, frustrated, always at odds with the world? Clearly, for Virginia, women's literature should never be destructive or irate, but rather harmonious and translucid as was her own. 8

I had, then, chosen my subject—nothing less than the world—as well as my style—nothing less than an absolutely neutral and serene language, which could let the truth of the material emerge, exactly as Simone and Virginia had advised. Now I had only to find my starting point, that most personal window, from among the thousands that Henry James says fiction possesses, through which I would gain access to my theme, the window to my story. I thought it best to select a historical anecdote, perhaps something related to how our Puerto Rican bourgeois culture changed from an agrarian one based on sugar cane and ruled by a rural oligarchy to an urban or industrial one ruled by a new professional class, an anecdote that would convey how this change brought about a shift in values at the turn of the century—the abandonment of the land and the replacement of a patriarchal code of behavior, based on exploitation but also on certain ethical principles and on Christian charity, with a new utilitarian code that came to us from the United States. 9

A story centered on this series of events seemed excellent to me in 10
every way. There was no possibility whatever that I might be accused of useless constructions or destructions; there was nothing further from the boring feminine conflicts than that kind of plot. With the context of my plot finally chosen, I raised my hands to the typewriter, ready to begin writing. Under my fingers, ready to leap to the fore, trembled the twenty-six letters of the Latin alphabet, like the chords of a powerful instrument. An hour passed, two, then three, without a single idea crossing the frighteningly limpid horizon of my mind. There was so much information, so many writable events in that moment of our historical becoming, that I had not the faintest idea where to begin. Everything seemed worthy, not just of the clumsy and amateurish story I might write, but of a dozen novels yet to be written.

I decided to be patient and not to despair, to spend the whole night 11
keeping vigil if necessary. Maturity is everything, I told myself, and this was, after all, my first story. If I concentrated hard enough, I would at last find the starting point of my story. It was dawn and a purple light washed over my study windows. Surrounded by full ashtrays and abandoned cups of cold coffee, I fell into a deep sleep, draped over my typewriter's silent keyboard.

Fortunately, I have since learned that the setbacks we must face 12
don't matter, for life keeps right on living us. That night's defeat, after all, had nothing to do with my love for short stories. If I couldn't write stories I could at least listen to them, and in daily life I have always been an avid listener of stories. Verbal tales, the ones people tell me in the street, are the ones that always interest me the most, and I marvel at the fact that those who tell them tend to be unaware that what they are telling me is a story. Something like this took place a few days later, when I was invited to lunch at my aunt's house.

Sitting at the head of the table, dropping a slow spoonful of honey 13
into her tea, my aunt began to tell a story while I listened. It had taken place at a sugarcane plantation some distance away, at the beginning of the century, she said, and its heroine was a distant cousin of hers who made dolls filled with honey. The strange woman had been the victim of her husband, a ne'er-do-well and a drunkard who had wasted away her fortune, kicked her out of the house, and taken up with another woman. My aunt's family, out of respect for the customs of the time, had offered her room and board, despite the fact that by the time the cane plantation on which they lived was on the verge of ruin. To reciprocate for their generosity she had dedicated herself to making honey-filled dolls for the girls in the family.

Soon after her arrival at the plantation, my aunt's cousin, who was 14
still young and beautiful, had developed a strange ailment: her right leg began to swell with no apparent cause, and her relatives sent for the doctor from the nearby town so he could examine her. The doctor, an unscrupulous young man recently graduated from a university in the United States, made the young woman fall in love with him, then falsely diagnosed her ailment as being incurable. Applying plasters like a

quack, he condemned her to live like an invalid in an armchair while he dispassionately relieved her of the little money the unfortunate woman had managed to save from her marriage. The doctor's behavior seemed reprehensible to me, of course, but what moved me most about the story were not his despicable acts but the absolute resignation with which, in the name of love, that woman had let herself be exploited for twenty years.

15 I am not going to repeat here the rest of the story my aunt told me that afternoon because it appears in "La muñeca menor," my first story. True, I didn't tell it with the words my aunt used, nor did I repeat her naive praises to a world fortunately gone by, a world in which day-laborers in the cane fields died of malnutrition while the daughters of plantation owners played with honey-filled dolls. But the story I listened to, in its broad outlines, fulfilled the requirements I had imposed on myself: it dealt with the ruin of one social class and its replacement by another, with the metamorphosis of a value system based on the concept of family into one based on profit and personal gain, a value system implanted among us by strangers from the United States.

16 The flame was lit. That very afternoon I locked myself in my study and didn't stop until the spark that danced before my eyes stopped right at the heart of what I wanted to say. With my story finished, I leaned back in my chair to read the whole thing, sure of having written a story with an objective theme, a story absolutely free of feminine conflicts, a story with transcendence. Then I realized that all my care had been in vain. That strange relative, victim of a love that subjected her twice to exploitation by her loved one, had appropriated my story; she reigned over it like a tragic, implacable vestal. My theme, while framed in the historical and sociopolitical context I had outlined, was still love, complaint, and—oh! I had to admit it—even vengeance. The image of that woman, hovering for years on end at the edge of the cane field with her broken heart, had touched me deeply. It was she who had finally opened the window for me, the window that had been so hermetically sealed, the window to my story.

17 I had betrayed Simone, writing once again about the interior reality of women; and I had betrayed Virginia, letting myself get carried away by my anger, by the fury the story produced in me. I confess that I was on the verge of throwing my story into the trash so as to rid myself of the evidence that, in the opinion of my mentors, identified me with all the women writers past and present who had tragically wasted themselves. Luckily I didn't do it; I kept it in a desk drawer to await better times, to await a day when I would perhaps arrive at a better understanding of myself.

18 Ten years have passed since I wrote, "La muñeca menor," and I have written many stories since then; I think now I can objectively analyze the lessons I learned that day with more maturity. I feel less guilt toward Simone and Virginia because I have discovered that, when one tries to write a story (or a poem or novel), stopping to listen to advice, even from those masters whom one most admires, almost always has

negative consequences. Today I know from experience that it is no use to write by setting out beforehand to construct exterior realities or to deal with universal and objective themes if one doesn't first create one's own interior reality. It is no use to try to write in a neutral, harmonious, distant way if one doesn't first have the courage to destroy one's own interior reality. When writing about her characters, a writer is always writing about herself, or about possible versions of herself because, as with all human beings, no virtue or vice is alien to her.

By identifying with the strange relative from "La muñeca menor" I 19
had made possible both processes. On the one hand I had reconstructed, in her misfortune, my own amorous misfortune; and on the other hand, by realizing where her weaknesses and failings were—her passivity, her acceptance, her terrifying resignation—I had destroyed her in my name. Although I may also have saved her. In subsequent stories, my heroines have managed to be braver, freer, more energetic and positive, perhaps because they were born from the ashes of "La muñeca menor." Her betrayal was, in any case, what brought about my fall from the frying pan into the fire of literature.

COMPREHENSION

1. In your own words, explain why Ferré writes. What forces govern her writing?
2. What advice about writing and women did Ferré receive from her literary mentors? Why did she finally discard this advice?
3. Why is Ferré unsuccessful in her initial attempt to write about "external realities"?

RHETORIC

1. What is Ferré's point in writing this essay? Justify your response.
2. Find examples of figurative language in Ferré's essay. How do they enrich the author's thesis?
3. Comment on Ferré's use of extended metaphor in paragraphs 5 and 6 and at the end of paragraph 9. Does it resonate anywhere else in the essay?
4. How is Ferré's concept about the destructive and constructive forces in her writing carried through in the body of the essay?
5. Examine the vocabulary Ferré uses in paragraph 9. How do words like "oligarchy," "exploitation," and "utilitarian code" illustrate the point of that paragraph?
6. What is the point of the narrative in paragraphs 13 and 14? Why does the writer choose not to finish it?

WRITING

1. Write an essay that considers these questions: Is there any connection between gender and writing? What assumptions are made about feminine ver-

sus masculine writers (external versus internal)? Which is considered more legitimate?

2. Ferré uses the word *kitchen* in her title. Write an essay exploring the way in which the writer uses the word and the connections she makes between the word and her life as a woman and a writer.
3. Agree or disagree with Ferré's contention that "a writer is always writing about herself." Is this true of all writers, male and female? In what situations might this *not* be true, or at least not obvious?

BHARATI MUKHERJEE Bharati Mukherjee (1940–), whose writing largely reflects her personal experiences, was born in India and came to the Untied States for study in 1961. She and her husband later returned to her birthplace, a trip about which they wrote in a book entitled *Days and Nights in Calcutta* (1977). Dismayed by the social conditions in India and its oppression of women, Mukherjee became a Canadian citizen in 1972. Her books include *The Middleman and Other Stories,* for which she won a National Book Critics Circle Award in 1989; and *Jasmine,* a novel published in 1989. In the piece below, Mukherjee explains her desire not to be limited as a writer by her ethnicity, preferring to broaden her literary scope.

BHARATI MUKHERJEE

A Four-Hundred-Year-Old Woman

I was born into a class that did not live in its native language. I was born into a city that feared its future, and trained me for emigration. I attended a school run by Irish nuns, who regarded our walled-off school compound in Calcutta as a corner (forever green and tropical) of England. My "country"—called in Bengali *desh,* and suggesting more a homeland than a nation of which one is a citizen—I have never seen. It is the ancestral home of my father and is now in Bangladesh. Nevertheless, I speak his dialect of Bengali, and think of myself as "belonging" to Faridpur, the tiny green-gold village that was his birthplace. I was born into a religion that placed me, a Brahmin, at the top of its hierarchy while condemning me, as a woman, to a role of subservience. The larger political entity to which I gave my first allegiance—India—was not even a sovereign nation when I was born. 1

My horoscope, cast by a neighborhood astrologer when I was a week-old infant, predicted that I would be a writer, that I would win some prizes, that I would cross "the black waters" of oceans and make my home among aliens. Brought up in a culture that places its faith in horoscopes, it never occurred to me to doubt it. The astrologer meant to offer me a melancholy future; to be destined to leave India was to be 2 banished from the sources of true culture. The nuns at school, on the other hand, insinuated that India had long outlived its glories, and that if we wanted to be educated, modern women and make something of our lives, we'd better hit the trail westward. All my girlhood, I straddled the seesaw of contradictions. *Bilayat,* meaning the scary, unknown "abroad," was both boom time and desperate loss.

I have found my way to the United States after many transit stops. 3
The unglimpsed phantom Faridpur and the all too real Manhattan have merged as "desh." I am an American. I am an American writer, in the American mainstream, trying to extend it. This is a vitally important statement for me—I am not an Indian writer, not an exile, not an expatriate. I am an immigrant; my investment is in the American reality, not the Indian. I look on ghettoization—whether as a Bengali in India or as a hyphenated Indo-American in North America—as a temptation to be surmounted.

It took me ten painful years, from the early seventies to the early 4
eighties, to overthrow the mothering tyranny of nostalgia. The remaining struggle for me is to make the American readership, meaning the editorial and publishing industries as well, acknowledge the same fact. (As the reception of such films as *Gandhi* and *A Passage to India* as well as *The Far Pavilions* and *The Jewel in the Crown* shows, nostalgia is a two-way street. Americans can feel nostalgic for a world they never knew.) The foreign-born, the exotically raised Third World immigrant with a non-Western religion and non-European language and appearance, can be as American as any steerage passenger from Ireland, Italy, or the Russian Pale. As I have written in another context (a review article in *The Nation* on books by Studs Terkel and Al Santoli), we are probably only a few years away from a Korean *What Makes Choon-li Run?* or a Hmong *Call It Sleep.* In other words, my literary agenda begins by acknowledging that America has transformed *me.* It does not end until I show how I (and the hundreds of thousands like me) have transformed America.

The agenda is simply stated, but in the long run revolutionary. 5
Make the familiar exotic, the exotic familiar.

I have had to create an audience. I cannot rely on shorthand refer- 6
ences to my community, my religion, my class, my region, or my old school tie. I've had to sensitize editors as well as readers to the richness of the lives I'm writing about. The most moving form of praise I receive from readers can be summed up in three words: *I never knew.* Meaning, I see these people (call them Indian, Filipino, Korean, Chinese) around me all the time and I never knew they had an inner life. I never knew they schemed and cheated, suffered, felt so strongly, cared so passionately. When even the forms of praise are so rudimentary, the writer knows she has an inexhaustible fictional population to enumerate. Perhaps even a mission, to appropriate a good colonial word.

I have been blessed with an enormity of material. I can be 7
Chekhovian and Tolstoyan—with melancholic and philosophical perspectives on the breaking of hearts as well as the fall of civilizations—

and I can be a brash and raucous homesteader, Huck Finn and Woman Warrior, on the unclaimed plains of American literature. My material, reduced to jacket-flap copy, is the rapid and dramatic transformation of the United States since the early 1970s. Within that perceived perimeter, however, I hope to wring surprises.

Yet (I am a writer much given to "yet") my imaginative home is 8
also in the tales told by my mother and grandmother, the world of the Hindu epics. For all the hope and energy I have placed in the process of immigration and accommodation—I'm a person who couldn't ride a public bus when she first arrived, and now I'm someone who watches tractor pulls on obscure cable channels—there are parts of me that remain Indian, parts that slide against the masks of newer selves. The form that my stories and novels take inevitably reflects the resources of Indian mythology—shape-changing, miracles, godly perspectives. My characters can, I hope, transcend the straitjacket of simple psychologizing. The people I write about are culturally and politically several hundred years old: consider the history they have witnessed (colonialism, technology, education, liberation, civil war, uprooting). They have shed old identities, taken on new ones, and learned to hide the scars. They may sell you newspapers, or clean your offices at night.

Writers (especially American writers, weaned on the luxury of af- 9
fluence and freedom) often disavow the notion of a "literary duty" or "political consciousness," citing the all-too-frequent examples of writers ruined by their shrill commitments. Glibness abounds on both sides of the argument, but finally I have to side with my "Third World" compatriots: I do have a duty, beyond telling a good story or drawing a convincing character. My duty is to give voice to continents, but also to redefine the nature of *American* and what makes an American. In the process, work like this by myself and others will open up the canon of American literature.

It has not been an easy transition, from graduate student to citizen, 10
from natural-born expatriate to the hurly-burly of immigration. My husband Clark Blaise and I spent fifteen years in his *desh* of Canada, and Canada was a country that discouraged the very process of assimilation. Eventually, it also discouraged the very presence of "Pakis" in its midst, and in 1980, a low point in our lives, we left, gave up our tenured, full-professor lives for the free-lancing life in the United States.

We were living in Iowa City in 1983 when Emory University called 11
me to be writer-in-residence for the winter semester. My name, apparently, had been suggested to them by an old friend. I hadn't published a book in six years (two earlier novels, *The Tiger's Daughter* and *Wife,* as well as our joint nonfiction study, *Days and Nights in Calcutta,* were out of print), but somehow Emory didn't hold that against me.

Atlanta turned out to be the luckiest writing break of my life. For 12
one of those mysterious reasons, stories that had been gathering in me suddenly exploded. I wrote nearly all the stories in *Darkness* (1985) in those three months. I finally had a glimpse of my true material, and that is immigration. In other words, transformation—not preservation. I saw

myself and my own experience refracted through a dozen separate lives. Clark, who remained in Iowa City until our younger son finished high school, sent me newspaper accounts, and I turned them into stories. Indian friends in Atlanta took me to dinners, and table gossip became stories. Suddenly, I had begun appropriating the American language. My stories were about the hurly-burly of the unsettled magma between two worlds.

Eventually—inevitably—we made our way to New York. My next batch of stories (*The Middleman and Other Stories,* 1988) appropriates the American language in ways that are personally most satisfying to me (one Chicago reviewer likened it to Nabokov's *Lolita*), and my characters are now as likely to be American as immigrant, and Chinese, Filipino, or Middle Eastern as much as Indian. That book has enjoyed widespread support both critically and commercially, and empowered me to write a new novel, *Jasmine,* and to contract for a major work, historical in nature, that nevertheless incorporates a much earlier version of my basic theme, due for completion in the next three years. *Days and Nights in Calcutta* is being made into a feature film. 13

My theme is the making of new Americans. Wherever I travel in the (very) Old World, I find "Americans" in the making, whether or not they ever make it to these shores. I see them as dreamers and conquerors, not afraid of transforming themselves, not afraid of abandoning some of their principles along the way. In *Jasmine,* my "American" is born in a Punjabi village, marries at fourteen, and is widowed at sixteen. Nevertheless, she is an American and will enter the book as an Iowa banker's wife. 14

Ancestral habits of mind can be constricting; they also confer one's individuality. I know I can appropriate the American language, but I can never be a minimalist. I have too many stories to tell. I am aware of myself as a four-hundred-year-old woman, born in the captivity of a colonial, preindustrial, oral culture and living now as a contemporary New Yorker. 15

My image of artistic structure and artistic excellence is Moghul miniature painting, with its crazy foreshortening of vanishing point, its insistence that everything happens simultaneously, bound only by shape and color. In the miniature paintings of India, there are a dozen separate foci, the most complicated stories can be rendered on a grain of rice, the corners are as elaborated as the centers. There is a sense of the interpenetration of all things. In the Moghul miniature of my life, there would be women investigating their bodies with mirrors, but they would be doing it on a distant balcony under fans wielded by bored serving girls; there would be a small girl listening to a bent old woman; there would be a white man eating popcorn and watching a baseball game; there would be cocktail parties and cornfields and a village set among rice paddies and skyscrapers. In a sense, I wrote that story, "Courtly Vision," at the end of *Darkness.* And in a dozen other ways I'm writing it today, and I will be writing, in the Moghul style, till I get it right. 16

COMPREHENSION

1. Why does the writer refuse to be limited by her ethnic origins? What does she see as her duty as a writer?
2. Explain what Mukherjee means by the term *ghettoization* in paragraph 3.
3. Explain the writer's statement that she "straddled the seesaw of contradiction."

RHETORIC

1. What is Mukherjee's essay about? Give a specific response.
2. How does the first sentence capture the reader's interest? How does the rest of the introductory paragraph explain or expand on the topic sentence?
3. Explain the use of parenthetical references in paragraph 4. Is Mukherjee making an assumption about her readers? Justify your answer.
4. How does the writer use biographical, historical, and literary allusions? Point to concrete examples, and explain how they help clarify or support her thesis.
5. Examine and find examples of parallel structure in Mukherjee's writing. To what end is it used?
6. How does the writer's conclusion serve to emphasize the main idea of the essay? What device does she employ to achieve this?

WRITING

1. Write an essay exploring the ways in which immigrants are transforming America or how this country transforms new arrivals. Consider the effects on those being transformed, what is lost and what is gained in the experience. Use support from Mukherjee's essay as well as your own experiences and observations.
2. In a short essay, elaborate on the image Mukherjee uses in her conclusion (miniaturist painting) as it applies to her goals as a writer. What connections exist between writing and painting? What does the final sentence imply about the creative process?

MARY McCARTHY Mary McCarthy (1912–1989) was born in Seattle, Washington, and attended Vassar College; among her friends at Vassar were future poets Elizabeth Bishop and Muriel Rukeyser. Her second husband, Edmund Wilson, was the first to encourage her to write fiction. A novelist, journalist, essayist, and literary critic, McCarthy is the author of *The Company She Keeps* (1942), *The Groves of Academe* (1952), *Memories of a Catholic Girlhood* (1946), *The Group* (1963), and *Vietnam* (1967), among numerous works. Known for her elegant style and sharp comic wit, McCarthy was a foremost—and controversial—literary figure for more than three decades. In the following essay, she reflects with witty and penetrating vigor on the importance of names at Forest Ridge Convent in Seattle, which she attended as a child.

MARY McCARTHY

Names

Anna Lyons, Mary Louise Lyons, Mary von Phul, Emilie von Phul, Eugenia McLellan, Majorie McPhail, Marie-Louise L'Abbé, Mary Danz, Julia Dodge, Mary Fordyce Blake, Janet Preston—these were the names (I can still tell them over like a rosary) of some of the older girls in the convent: the Virtues and Graces. The virtuous ones wore wide blue or green moire good-conduct ribbons, bandoleer-style, across their blue serge uniforms; the beautiful ones wore rouge and powder or at least were reputed to do so. Our class, the eighth grade, wore pink ribbons (I never got one myself) and had names like Patricia ("Pat") Sullivan, Eileen Donohoe, and Joan Kane. We were inelegant even in this respect; the best name we could show, among us, was Phyllis ("Phil") Chatham, who boasted that her father's name, Ralph, was pronounced "Rafe" as in England. 1

Names had a great importance for us in the convent, and foreign names, French, German, or plain English (which, to us, were foreign, because of their Protestant sound), bloomed like prize roses among a collection of spuds. Irish names were too common in the school to have any prestige either as surnames (Gallagher, Sheehan, Finn, Sullivan, McCarthy) or as Christian names (Kathleen, Eileen). Anything exotic had value: an "olive" complexion, for example. The pet girl of the convent was a fragile Jewish girl named Susie Lowenstein, who had pale red-gold hair and an exquisite retroussé nose, which, if we had had it, might have been called "pug." We liked her name too and the name of a child in the primary grades: Abbie Stuart Baillargeon. My favorite name, on the whole, though, was Emilie von Phul (pronounced "Pool"); her oldest sister, recently graduated, was called Celeste. Another name that appealed to me was Genevieve Albers, Saint Genevieve being the patron saint of Paris who turned back Attila from the gates of the city. 2

All these names reflected the still-pioneer character of the Pacific Northwest. I had never heard their like in the parochial school in Minneapolis, where "foreign" extraction, in any case, was something to be ashamed of, the whole drive being toward Americanization of first name and surname alike. The exceptions to this were the Irish, who could vaunt such names as Catherine O'Dea and the name of my second cousin, Mary Catherine Anne Rose Violet McCarthy, while an unfortunate German boy named Manfred was made to suffer for his. But that was Minneapolis. In Seattle, and especially in the convent of the Ladies of the Sacred Heart, foreign names suggested not immigration but emigration—distinguished exile. Minneapolis was a granary; Seattle 3

was a port, which had attracted a veritable Foreign Legion of adventurers—soldiers of fortune, younger sons, gamblers, traders, drawn by the fortunes to be made in virgin timber and shipping and by the Alaska Gold Rush. Wars and revolutions had sent the defeated out to Puget Sound, to start a new life; the latest had been the Russian Revolution, which had shipped us, via Harbin, a Russian colony, complete with restaurant, on Queen Anne Hill. The English names in the convent, when they did not testify to direct English origin, as in the case of "Rafe" Chatham, had come to us from the South and represented a kind of internal exile; such girls as Mary Fordyce Blake and Mary McQueen Street (a class ahead of me; her sister was named Francesca) bore their double-barreled first names like titles of aristocracy from the ante-bellum South. Not all our girls, by any means, were Catholic; some of the very prettiest ones—Julia Dodge and Janet Preston, if I remember rightly—were Protestants. The nuns had taught us to behave with special courtesy to these strangers in our midst; and the whole effect was of some superior hostel for refugees of all the lost causes of the past hundred years. Money could not count for much in such an atmosphere; the fathers and grandfathers of many of our "best" girls were ruined men.

Names, often, were freakish in the Pacific Northwest, particularly 4
girls' names. In the Episcopal boarding school I went to later, in Tacoma, there was a girl called De Vere Utter, and there was a girl called Rocena and another called Hermoine. Was Rocena a mistake for Rowena and Hermoire for Hermoine? And was Vere, as we called her, Lady Clara Vere de Vere? Probably. You do not hear names like those often, in any case, east of the Cascade Mountains; they belong to the frontier, where books and libraries were few and memory seems to have been oral, as in the time of Homer.

Names have more significance for Catholics than they do for other 5
people; Christian names are chosen for the spiritual qualities of the saints they are taken from; Protestants used to name their children out of the Old Testament and now they name them out of novels and plays, whose heroes and heroines are perhaps the new patron saints of a secular age. But with Catholics it is different. The saint a child is named for is supposed to serve, literally, as a model or pattern to imitate; your name is your fortune and it tells you what you are or must be. Catholic children ponder their names for a mystic meaning, like birthstones; my own, I learned, besides belonging to the Virgin and Saint Mary of Egypt, originally meant "bitter" or "star of the sea." My second name, Therese, could dedicate me either to Saint Theresa or to the saint called the Little Flower, Soeur Thérèse of Lisieux, on whom God was supposed to have descended in the form of a shower of roses. At Confirmation, I had added a third name (for Catholics then rename themselves, as most nuns do, yet another time, when they take orders); on the advice of a nun, I had taken "Clementina," after Saint Clement, an early pope—a step I soon regretted on account of "My Darling Clementine" and her number nine shoes. By the time I was in the con-

vent, I would no longer tell anyone what my Confirmation name was. The name I had nearly picked was "Agnes," after a little Roman virgin martyr, always shown with a lamb, because of her purity. But Agnes would have been just as bad, I recognized in Forest Ridge Convent—not only because of the possibility of "Aggie," but because it was subtly, indefinably *wrong* in itself. Agnes would have made me look like an ass.

The fear of appearing ridiculous first entered my life, as a governing motive, during my second year in the convent. Up to then, a desire for prominence had decided many of my actions and, in fact, still persisted. But in the eighth grade, I became aware of mockery and perceived that I could not seek prominence without attracting laughter. Other people could, but I couldn't. This laughter was proceeding, not from my classmates, but from the girls of the class just above me, in particular from two boon companions, Elinor Heffernan and Mary Harty, a clownish pair—oddly assorted in size and shape, as teams of clowns generally are, one short, plump, and baby-faced, the other tall, lean, and owlish—who entertained the high-school department by calling attention to the oddities of the younger girls. Nearly every school has such a pair of satirists, whose marks are generally low and who are tolerated just because of their laziness and nonconformity; one of them (in this case, Mary Harty, the plump one) usually appears to be half asleep. Because of their low standing, their indifference to appearances, the sad state of their uniforms, their clowning is taken to be harmless, which, on the whole, it is, their object being not to wound but to divert; such girls are bored in school. We in the eighth grade sat directly in front of the two wits in study hall, so that they had us under close observation; yet at first I was not afraid of them, wanting, if anything, to identify myself with their laughter, to be initiated into the joke. One of their specialties was giving people nicknames, and it was considered an honor to be the first in the eighth grade to be let in by Elinor and Mary on their latest invention. This often happened to me; they would tell me, on the playground, and I would tell the others. As their intermediary, I felt myself almost their friend and it did not occur to me that I might be next on their list. 6

I had achieved prominence not long before by publicly losing my faith and regaining it at the end of a retreat. I believe Elinor and Mary questioned me about this on the playground, during recess, and listened with serious, respectful faces while I told them about my conversations with the Jesuits. Those serious faces ought to have been an omen, but if the two girls used what I had revealed to make fun of me, it must have been behind my back. I never heard any more of it, and yet just at this time I began to feel something, like a cold breath on the nape of my neck, that made me wonder whether the new position I had won for myself in the convent was as secure as I imagined. I would turn around in study hall and find the two girls looking at me with speculation in their eyes. 7

It was just at this time, too, that I found myself in a perfectly absurd situation, a very private one, which made me live, from month to 8

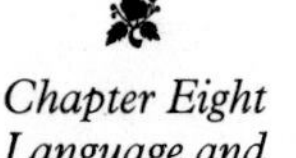

month, in horror of discovery. I had waked up one morning, in my convent room, to find a few small spots of blood on my sheet; I had somehow scratched a trifling cut on one of my legs and opened it during the night. I wondered what to do about this, for the nuns were fussy about bedmaking, as they were about our white collars and cuffs, and if we had an inspection these spots might count against me. It was best, I decided, to ask the nun on dormitory duty, tall, stout Mother Slattery, for a clean bottom sheet, even though she might scold me for having scratched my leg in my sleep and order me to cut my toenails. You never know what you might be blamed for. But Mother Slattery, when she bustled in to look at the sheet, did not scold me at all; indeed, she hardly seemed to be listening, as I explained to her about the cut. She told me to sit down: she would be back in a minute. "You can be excused from athletics today," she added, closing the door. As I waited, I considered this remark, which seemed to me strangely munificent, in view of the unimportance of the cut. In a moment, she returned, but without the sheet. Instead, she produced out of her big pocket a sort of cloth girdle and a peculiar flannel object which I first took to be a bandage, and I began to protest that I did not need or want a bandage; all I needed was a bottom sheet. "The sheet can wait," said Mother Slattery, succinctly, handing me two large safety pins. It was the pins that abruptly enlightened me; I saw Mother Slattery's mistake, even as she was instructing me as to how this flannel article, which I now understood to be a sanitary napkin, was to be put on.

"Oh, no, Mother," I said, feeling somewhat embarrassed. "You 9
don't understand. It's just a little cut, on my leg." But Mother, again, was not listening; she appeared to have grown deaf, as the nuns had a habit of doing when what you were saying did not fit in with their ideas. And now that I knew what was in her mind, I was conscious of a funny constraint; I did not feel it proper to name a natural process, in so many words, to a nun. It was like trying not to think of their going to the bathroom or trying not to see the straggling iron-gray hair coming out of their coifs (the common notion that they shaved their heads was false). On the whole, it seemed better just to show her my cut. But when I offered to do so and unfastened my black stocking, she only glanced at my leg, cursorily. "That's only a scratch, dear," she said. "Now hurry up and put this on or you'll be late for chapel. Have you any pain?" "No, no, Mother!" I cried. "You don't understand!" "Yes, yes, I understand," she replied soothingly, "and you will too, a little later. Mother Superior will tell you about it some time during the morning. There's nothing to be afraid of. You have become a woman."

"I know all about that," I persisted. "Mother, please listen. I just cut 10
my leg. On the athletic field. Yesterday afternoon." But the more excited I grew, the more soothing, and yet firm, Mother Slattery became. There seemed to be nothing for it but to give up and do as I was bid. I was in the grip of a higher authority, which almost had the power to persuade me that it was right and I was wrong. But of course I was not wrong; that would have been too good to be true. While Mother

Slattery waited, just outside my door, I miserably donned the equipment she had given me, for there was no place to hide it, on account of drawer inspection. She led me down the hall to where there was a chute and explained how I was to dispose of the flannel thing, by dropping it down the chute into the laundry. (The convent arrangements were very old-fashioned, dating back, no doubt, to the days of Louis Philippe.)

The Mother Superior, Madame MacIllvra, was a sensible woman, and all through my early morning classes, I was on pins and needles, chafing for the promised interview with her which I trusted would clear things up. *"Ma Mére,"* I would begin, "Mother Slattery thinks. . . ." Then I would tell her about the cut and the athletic field. But precisely the same impasse confronted me when I was summoned to her office at recess-time. *I* talked about my cut, and *she* talked about becoming a woman. It was rather like a round, in which she was singing "Scotland's burning, Scotland's burning," and I was singing "Pour on water, pour on water." Neither of us could hear the other, or, rather, I could hear her, but she could not hear me. Owing to our different positions in the convent she was free to interrupt me, whereas I was expected to remain silent until she had finished speaking. When I kept breaking in, she hushed me, gently, and took me on her lap. Exactly like Mother Slattery, she attributed all my references to the cut to a blind fear of this new, unexpected reality that had supposedly entered my life. Many young girls, she reassured me, were frightened if they had not been prepared. "And you, Mary, have lost your dear mother, who could have made this easier for you." Rocked on Madame MacIllvra's lap, I felt paralysis overtake me and I lay, mutely listening, against her bosom, my face being tickled by her white, starched, fluted wimple, while she explained to me how babies were born, all of which I had heard before. 11

There was no use fighting the convent. I had to pretend to have become a woman, just as, not long before, I had had to pretend to get my faith back—for the sake of peace. This pretense was decidedly awkward. For fear of being found out by the lay sisters downstairs in the laundry (no doubt an imaginary contingency, but the convent was so very thorough), I reopened the cut on my leg, so as to draw a little blood to stain the napkins, which were issued me regularly, not only on this occasion, but every twenty-eight days thereafter. Eventually, I abandoned this bloodletting, for fear of lockjaw, and trusted to fate. Yet I was in awful dread of detection; my only hope, as I saw it, was either to be released from the convent or to become a woman in reality, which might take a year at least, since I was only twelve. Getting out of athletics once a month was not sufficient compensation for the farce I was going through. It was not my fault; they had forced me into it; nevertheless, it was I who would look silly—worse than silly; half mad—if the truth ever came to light. 12

I was burdened with this guilt and shame when the nickname finally found me out. "Found me out," in a general sense, for no one ever did learn the particular secret I bore about with me, pinned to the linen band. "We've got a name for you," Elinor and Mary called out to me, 13 one day on the playground. "What is it?" I asked half hoping, half fearing, since not all their sobriquets were unfavorable. "Cye," they answered, looking at each other and laughing. "Si?" I repeated, supposing that it was based on Simple Simon. Did they regard me as a hick? "C.Y.E.," they elucidated, spelling it out in chorus. "The letters stand for something. Can you guess?" I could not and I cannot now. The closest I could come to it in the convent was "Clean Your Ears." Perhaps that was it, though in later life I have wondered whether it did not stand, simply, for "Clever Young Egg" or "Champion Young Eccentric." But in the convent I was certain that it stood for something horrible, something even worse than dirty ears (as far as I knew, my ears were clean), something I could never guess because it represented some aspect of myself that the world could see and I couldn't, like a sign pinned on my back. Everyone in the convent must have known what the letters stood for, but no one would tell me. Elinor and Mary had made them promise. It was like halitosis; not even my best friend, my deskmate, Louise, would tell me, no matter how much I pleaded. Yet everyone assured me that it was "very good," that is, very apt. And it made everyone laugh.

This name reduced all my pretensions and solidified my sense of *wrongness*. Just as I felt I was beginning to belong to the convent, it turned me into an outsider, since I was the only pupil who was not in the know. I liked the convent, but it did not like me, as people say of certain foods that disagree with them. By this, I do not mean that I was actively unpopular, either with the pupils or with the nuns. The Mother Superior cried when I left and predicted that I would be a novelist, which surprised me. And I had finally made friends; even Emilie von Phul smiled upon me softly out of her bright blue eyes from the far end of the study hall. It was just that I did not fit into the convent pattern; the simplest thing I did, like asking for a clean sheet, entrapped me in consequences that I never could have predicted. I was not bad; I did not consciously break the rules; and yet I could never, not even for a week, get a pink ribbon, and this was something I could not understand, because I was trying as hard as I could. It was the same case as with the hated name; the nuns, evidently, saw something about me that was invisible to me. 14

The oddest part was all that pretending. There I was, a walking mass of lies, pretending to be a Catholic and going to confession while really I had lost my faith, and pretending to have monthly periods by cutting myself with nail scissors; yet all this had come about without my volition and even contrary to it. But the basest pretense I was driven to was the acceptance of the nickname. Yet what else could I do? In the convent, I could not live it down. To all those girls, I had become "Cye McCarthy." That was who I was. That was how I had to identify myself when telephoning my friends during vacations to ask them to the movies: "Hello, this is Cye." I loathed myself when I said it, and yet I succumbed to the name totally, making myself over into a sort of hearty to go with it—the kind of girl I hated. "Cye" was my new patron saint. 15

This false personality stuck to me, like the name, when I entered public high school, the next fall, as a freshman, having finally persuaded my grandparents to take me out of the convent, although they could never get to the bottom of my reasons, since, as I admitted, the nuns were kind, and I had made many nice new friends. What I wanted was a fresh start, a chance to begin life over again, but the first thing I heard in the corridors of the public high school was that name called out to me, like the warmest of welcomes: "Hi, there, Si!" That was the way they thought it was spelled. But this time I was resolute. After the first weeks, I dropped the hearties who called me "Si" and I never heard it again. I got my own name back and sloughed off Clementina and even Therese—the names that did not seem to me any more to be mine but to have been imposed on me by others. And I preferred to think that Mary meant "bitter" rather than "star of the sea."

COMPREHENSION

1. According to McCarthy, what was the significance of names in her Catholic convent? What is the relationship of names to culture?
2. Describe the author's life in the convent school. How does she respond to her nickname? Why does she leave the convent school?
3. Explain McCarthy's idea of *wrongness* (see paragraph 14).

RHETORIC

1. Locate names in the essay that have unusually vivid connotations for the author. What is the cumulative effect of the listing of so many names on the tone of the essay?
2. Why does the author use the word *names* at the beginning of paragraphs 1, 2, 3, 4, and 5? How does this one word contribute to the unity of the essay?
3. Does McCarthy use examples objectively or subjectively in this essay? Explain. Select one paragraph, and show how the examples contribute to an understanding of McCarthy's view of the importance of names and naming things properly.
4. How does the author use personal experience as an example? What other types of example does she use?
5. Where do the patterns of explanation and description blend in this essay?
6. In what sense is this a definition essay? What is the thesis? What does the last paragraph contribute to the thesis?

WRITING

1. Why do personal names actually mean certain things? What does your name mean? What does it reveal to you? Prepare an essay on these questions.
2. Write about your nickname or the nicknames of some of your friends.

3. Prepare a list of the most popular names for boys and girls in American culture today. Evaluate the importance of names and naming as symbolic acts that tell us about ourselves and our culture.

LEWIS THOMAS Lewis Thomas (1913–), physician, educator, and author, was born in New York City. He received a B.S. from Princeton in 1933, an M.D. from Harvard in 1937, and an M.A. from Yale in 1969. In addition to a monthly column in *Nature,* Thomas is the author of *Lives of a Cell* (1974), which won the National Book Award; *Medusa and the Snail* (1979); *The Youngest Science* (1983); and *The Fragile Species* (1992). Dr. Thomas has also published extensively in scientific and medical journals. Although best known for his ability to explain the life sciences to lay persons, in this essay he takes up the subject of punctuation in a unique and amusing way.

LEWIS THOMAS

Notes on Punctuation

1 There are no precise rules about punctuation (Fowler lays out some general advice (as best as he can under the complex circumstances of English prose (he points out, for example, that we possess only four stops (the comma, the semicolon, the colon and the period (the question mark and exclamation point are not, strictly speaking, stops; they are indicators of tone (oddly enough, the Greeks employed the semicolon for their question mark (it produces a strange sensation to read a Greek sentence which is a straightforward question: Why weepest thou; (instead of Why weepest thou? (and, of course, there are parentheses (which are surely a kind of punctuation making this whole matter much more complicated by having to count up the left-handed parentheses in order to be sure of closing with the right number (but if the parentheses were left out, with nothing to work with but the stops, we would have considerably more flexibility in the deploying of layers of meaning than if we tried to separate all the clauses by physical barriers (and in the latter case, while we might have more precision and exactitude for our meaning, we would lose the essential flavor of language, which is its wonderful ambiguity))))))))))).

2 The commas are the most useful and usable of all the stops. It is highly important to put them in place as you go along. If you try to come back after doing a paragraph and stick them in the various spots that tempt you you will discover that they tend to swarm like minnows into all sorts of crevices whose existence you hadn't realized and before you know it the whole long sentence becomes immobilized and lashed up squirming in commas. Better to use them sparingly, and

with affection, precisely when the need for each one arises, nicely, by itself.

I have grown fond of semicolons in recent years. The semicolon tells you that there is still some question about the preceding full sentence; something needs to be added; it reminds you sometimes of the Greek usage. It is almost always a greater pleasure to come across a semicolon than a period. The period tells you that that is that; if you didn't get all the meaning you wanted or expected, anyway you got all the writer intended to parcel out and now you have to move along. But with a semicolon there you get a pleasant little feeling of expectancy; there is more to come; read on; it will get clearer.

Colons are a lot less attractive, for several reasons: firstly, they give 4
you the feeling of being rather ordered around, or at least having your nose pointed in a direction you might not be inclined to take if left to yourself, and, secondly, you suspect you're in for one of those sentences that will be labeling the points to be made: firstly, secondly and so forth, with the implication that you haven't sense enough to keep track of a sequence of notions without having them numbered. Also, many writers use this system loosely and incompletely, starting out with number one and number two as though counting off on their fingers but then going on and on without the succession of labels you've been led to expect, leaving you floundering about searching for the ninethly or seventeenthly that ought to be there but isn't.

Exclamation points are the most irritating of all. Look! they say, 5
look at what I just said! How amazing is my thought! It is like being forced to watch someone else's small child jumping up and down crazily in the center of the living room shouting to attract attention. If a sentence really has something of importance to say, something quite remarkable, it doesn't need a mark to point it out. And if it is really, after all, a banal sentence needing more zing, the exclamation point simply emphasizes its banality!

Quotation marks should be used honestly and sparingly, when there 6
is a genuine quotation at hand, and it is necessary to be very rigorous about the words enclosed by the marks. If something is to be quoted, the *exact* words must be used. If part of it must be left out because of space limitations, it is good manners to insert three dots to indicate the omission, but it is unethical to do this if it means connecting two thoughts which the original author did not intend to have tied together. Above all, quotation marks should not be used for ideas that you'd like to disown, things in the air so to speak. Nor should they be put in place around clichés; if you want to use a cliché you must take full responsibility for it yourself and not try to fob it off on anon., or on society. The most objectionable misuse of quotation marks, but one which illustrates the dangers of misuse in ordinary prose, is seen in advertising, especially in advertisements for small restaurants, for example "just around the corner," or "a good place to eat." No single, identifiable, citable person ever really said, for the record, "just around the corner," much less "a good place to eat," least likely of all for restaurants of the type that use this type of prose.

The dash is a handy device, informal and essentially playful, telling you that you're about to take off on a different tack but still in some way connected with the present course—only you have to remember that the dash is there, and either put a second dash at the end of the notion to let the reader know that he's back on course, or else end the sentence, as here, with a period.

The greatest danger in punctuation is for poetry. Here it is neces- 8
sary to be as economical and parsimonious with commas and periods as with the words themselves, and any marks that seem to carry their own subtle meanings, like dashes and little rows of periods, even semicolons and question marks, should be left out altogether rather than inserted to clog up the thing with ambiguity. A single exclamation point in a poem, no matter what else the poem has to say, is enough to destroy the whole work.

The things I like best in T. S. Eliot's poetry, especially in the *Four* 9
Quartets, are the semicolons. You cannot hear them, but they are there, laying out the connections between the images and the ideas. Sometimes you get a glimpse of a semicolon coming, a few lines farther on, and it is like climbing a steep path through woods and seeing a wooden bench just at a bend in the road ahead, a place where you can expect to sit for a moment, catching your breath.

Commas can't do this sort of thing; they can only tell you how the 10
different parts of a complicated thought are to be fitted together, but you can't sit, not even take a breath, just because of a comma,

COMPREHENSION

1. Does a formal definition of *punctuation* appear in the essay? Why, or why not?
2. What is Thomas's purpose in writing "Notes on Punctuation"? What is his thesis?
3. What is Thomas's favorite form of punctuation? What about it does he like? What about it does he find irritating?

RHETORIC

1. What stylistic technique does Thomas use to illustrate punctuation? What is his purpose in doing it this way?
2. Is Thomas's style subjective or objective? Why?
3. Carefully analyze the author's introductory paragraph. How does it set up the rest of the essay?
4. How does Thomas use classification to develop the essay? What is the basis of his classification scheme?
5. In which paragraphs is illustration used? What is its purpose?
6. What use of transitional devices does Thomas make? Why does he organize his paragraphs in this way?

WRITING

1. Write a brief, amusing essay on your favorite form of punctuation.
2. Analyze and evaluate the approach to language taken by Thomas in his essay.
3. In an essay entitled "Language and Evolution," Thomas marvels over the common root for the words *human, humane,* and *humble.* Develop a paper on these related words or any other set of related words that interests you.

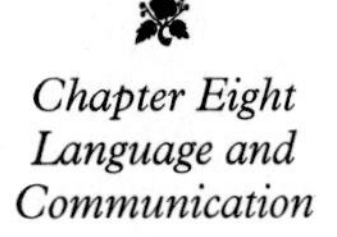

CLASSIC AND CONTEMPORARY

GEORGE ORWELL George Orwell (1903–1950) was the pseudonym of Eric Blair, an English novelist, essayist, and journalist. Orwell served with the Indian Imperial Police from 1922 to 1927 in Burma, fought in the Spanish Civil War, and acquired from his experience a disdain of totalitarian and imperialistic systems. This attitude is reflected in the satiric fable *Animal Farm* (1945) and in the bleak, futuristic novel *1984* (1949). This essay, one of the more famous of the twentieth century, relates sloppy thinking and writing with political oppression.

GEORGE ORWELL

Politics and the English Language

Most people who bother with the matter at all would admit that the English language is in a bad way, but it is generally assumed that we cannot by conscious action do anything about it. Our civilisation is decadent, and our language—so the argument runs—must inevitably share in the general collapse. It follows that any struggle against the abuse of language is a sentimental archaism, like preferring candles to electric light or hansom cabs to aeroplanes. Underneath this lies the half-conscious belief that language is a natural growth and not an instrument which we shape for our own purposes. 1

Now, it is clear that the decline of a language must ultimately have political and economic causes: it is not due simply to the bad influence of this or that individual writer. But an effect can become a cause, reinforcing the original cause and producing the same effect in an intensified form, and so on indefinitely. A man may take to drink because he feels himself to be a failure, and then fail all the more completely because he drinks. It is rather the same thing that is happening to the English language. It becomes ugly and inaccurate because our thoughts are foolish, but the slovenliness of our language makes it easier for us to have foolish thoughts. The point is that the process is reversible. Modern English, especially written English, is full of bad habits which spread by imitation and which can be avoided if one is willing to take the necessary trouble. If one gets rid of these habits one can think more clearly, and to think clearly is a necessary first step towards political regeneration: so that the fight against bad English is not frivolous and is not the exclusive concern of professional writers. I will come back to this presently, and I hope 2 that by that time the meaning of what I have said here will have become clearer. Meanwhile, here are five specimens of the English language as it is now habitually written.

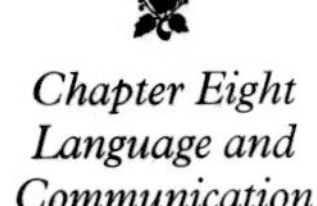

These five passages have not been picked out because they are especially bad—I could have quoted far worse if I had chosen—but because they illustrate various of the mental vices from which we now suffer. They are a little below the average, but are fairly representative samples. I number them so that I can refer back to them when necessary:

> *1.* I am not, indeed, sure whether it is not true to say the Milton who once seemed not unlike a seventeenth-century Shelley had not become, out of an experience even more bitter in each year, more alien (sic) to the founder of that Jesuit sect which nothing could induce him to tolerate.
>
> —Professor Harold Laski (essay in *Freedom of Expression*)
>
> *2.* Above all, we cannot play ducks and drakes with a native battery of idioms which prescribes such egregious collocations of vocables as the Basic *put up with* for *tolerate* or *put at a loss* for *bewilder.*
>
> —Professor Lancelot Hogben (*Interglossa*)
>
> *3.* On the one side we have the free personality: by definition it is not neurotic, for it has neither conflict nor dream. Its desires, such as they are, are transparent, for they are just what institutional approval keeps in the forefront of consciousness; another institutional pattern would alter their number and intensity; there is little in them that is natural, irreducible, or culturally dangerous. But *on the other side,* the social bond itself is nothing but the mutual reflection of these self-secure integrities. Recall the definition of love. Is not this the very picture of a small academic? Where is there a place in this hall of mirrors for either personality or fraternity?
>
> —Essay on psychology in *Politics* (New York)
>
> *4.* All the "best people" from the gentlemen's clubs, and all the frantic Fascist captains, united in common hatred of Socialism and bestial horror of the rising tide of the mass revolutionary movement, have turned to acts of provocation, to foul incendiarism, to medieval legends of poisoned wells, to legalise their own destruction to proletarian organisations, and rouse the agitated petty-bourgeoisie to chauvinistic fervour on behalf of the fight against the revolutionary way out of the crisis.
>
> —Communist pamphlet
>
> *5.* If a new spirit *is* to be infused into this old country, there is one thorny and contentious reform which must be tackled, and that is the humanisation and galvanisation of the BBC. Timidity here will bespeak canker and atrophy for the soul. The heart of Britain may be sound and of strong beat, for instance, but the British lion's roar at present is like that of Bottom in Shakespeare's *Midsummer Night's Dream*—as gentle as any sucking dove. A virile new Britain cannot continue indefinitely to

> be traduced in the eyes, or rather ears, of the world by the effete languors of Langham Place, brazenly masquerading as "standard English." When the Voice of Britain is heard at nine o'clock, better far and infinitely less ludicrous to hear aitches honestly dropped than the present priggish, inflated, inhibited, school-ma'amish braying of blameless bashful mewing maidens!
>
> —Letter in *Tribune*

4 Each of these passages has faults of its own, but, quite apart from avoidable ugliness, two qualities are common to all of them. The first is staleness of imagery: the other is lack of precision. The writer either has a meaning and cannot express it, or he inadvertently says something else, or he is almost indifferent as to whether his words mean anything or not. This mixture of vagueness and sheer incompetence is the most marked characteristic of modern English prose, and especially of any kind of political writing. As soon as certain topics are raised, the concrete melts into the abstract and no one seems able to think of turns of speech that are not hackneyed: prose consists less and less of *words* chosen for the sake of their meaning, and more of *phrases* tacked together like the sections of a prefabricated henhouse. I list below, with notes and examples, various of the tricks by means of which the work of prose construction is habitually dodged:

Dying Metaphors

5 A newly invented metaphor assists thought by evoking a visual image, while on the other hand a metaphor which is technically "dead" (e.g., *iron resolution*) has in effect reverted to being an ordinary word and can generally be used without loss of vividness. But in between these two classes there is a huge dump of worn-out metaphors which have lost all evocative power and are merely used because they save people the trouble of inventing phrases for themselves. Examples are: *Ring the changes on, take up the cudgels for, toe the line, ride roughshod over, stand shoulder to shoulder with, play into the hands of, no axe to grind, grist to the mill, fishing in troubled waters, rift within the lute, on the order of the day, Achilles' heel, swan song, hotbed.* Many of these are used without knowledge of their meaning (what is a "rift," for instance?), and incompatible metaphors are frequently mixed, a sure sign that the writer is not interested in what he is saying. Some metaphors now current have been twisted out of their original meaning without those who use them even being aware of the fact. For example, *toe the line* is sometimes written *tow the line*. Another example is *the hammer and the anvil,* now always used with the implication that the anvil gets the worst of it. In real life it is always the anvil that breaks the hammer, never the other way about: a writer who stopped to think what he was saying would be aware of this, and would avoid perverting the original phrase.

Operators, or Verbal False Limbs

These save the trouble of picking out appropriate verbs and nouns, and at the same time pad each sentence with extra syllables which give it an appearance of symmetry. Characteristic phrases are: *render inoperative, militate against, prove unacceptable, make contact with, be subjected to, give rise to, give grounds for, have the effect of, play a leading part (rôle) in, make itself felt, take effect, exhibit a tendency to, serve the purpose of,* etc. etc. The keynote is the elimination of simple verbs. Instead of being a single word, such as *break, stop, spoil, mend, kill,* a verb becomes a *phrase,* made up of a noun or adjective tacked on to some general-purposes verb such as *prove, serve, form, play, render.* In addition, the passive voice is wherever possible used in preference to the active, and noun constructions are used instead of gerunds (*by examination of* instead of *by examining*). The range of verbs is further cut down by means of the *-ise* and *de-* formations, and banal statements are given an appearance of profundity by means of the *not un-* formation. Simple conjunctions and prepositions are replaced by such phrases as *with respect to, having regard to, the fact that, by dint of, in view of, in the interests of, on the hypothesis that;* and the ends of sentences are saved from anticlimax by such resounding commonplaces as *greatly to be desired, cannot be left out of account, a development to be expected in the near future, deserving of serious consideration, brought to a satisfactory conclusion,* and so on and so forth.

Pretentious Diction

Words like *phenomenon, element, individual* (as noun), *objective, cate-* 7
gorical, effective, virtual, basic, primary, promote, constitute, exhibit, exploit, utilise, eliminate, liquidate, are used to dress up simple statements and give an air of scientific impartiality to biassed judgements. Adjectives like *epoch-making, epic, historic, unforgettable, triumphant, age-old, inevitable, inexorable, veritable,* are used to dignify the sordid processes of international politics, while writing that aims at glorifying war usually takes on an archaic colour, its characteristic words being: *realm, throne, chariot, mailed fist, trident, sword, shield, buckler, banner, jackboot, clarion.* Foreign words and expressions such as *cul de sac, ancien régime, deus ex machina, mutatis mutandis, status quo, Gleichschaltung, Weltanschauung,* are used to give an air of culture and elegance. Except for the useful abbreviations *i.e., e.g.,* and *etc.,* there is no real need for any of the hundreds of foreign phrases now current in English. Bad writers, and especially scientific, political and sociological writers, are nearly always haunted by the notion that Latin or Greek words are grander than Saxon ones, and unnecessary words like *expedite, ameliorate, predict, extraneous, deracinated, clandestine, subaqueous* and hundreds of others constantly gain ground from their Anglo-Saxon

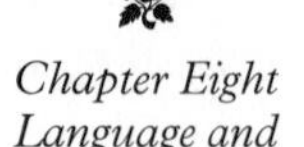

opposite numbers.[1] The jargon peculiar to Marxist writing (*hyena, hangman, cannibal, petty bourgeois, these gentry, lacquey, flunkey, mad dog, White Guard,* etc.) consists largely of words and phrases translated from Russian, German or French; but the normal way of coining a new word is to use a Latin or Greek root with the appropriate affix and, where necessary, the *-ise* formation. It is often easier to make up words of this kind (*deregionalise, impermissible, extramarital, non-fragmentatory* and so forth) than to think up the English words that will cover one's meaning. The result, in general, is an increase in slovenliness and vagueness.

Meaningless Words

In certain kinds of writing, particularly in art criticism and literary 8
criticism, it is normal to come across long passages which are almost completely lacking in meaning.[2] Words like *romantic, plastic, values, human, dead, sentimental, natural, vitality,* as used in art criticism, are strictly meaningless, in the sense that they not only do not point to any discoverable object, but are hardly even expected to do so by the reader. When one critic writes, "The outstanding features of Mr X's work is its living quality," while another writes, "The immediately striking thing about Mr X's work is its peculiar deadness," the reader accepts this as a simple difference of opinion. If words like *black* and *white* were involved, instead of the jargon words *dead* and *living,* he would see at once that language was being used in an improper way. Many political words are similarly abused. The word *Fascism* has now no meaning except in so far as it signifies "something not desirable." The words *democracy, socialism, freedom, patriotic, realistic, justice,* have each of them several different meanings which cannot be reconciled with one another. In the case of a word like *democracy,* not only is there no agreed definition, but the attempt to make one is resisted from all sides. It is almost universally felt that when we call a country democratic we are praising it: consequently the defenders of every kind of régime claim that it is a democracy, and fear that they might have to stop using the word if it were tied down to any one meaning. Words of this kind are often used in a consciously dishonest way. That is, the person who

[1]An interesting illustration of this is the way in which the English flower names which were in use till very recently are being ousted by Greek ones, *snapdragon* becoming *antirrhinum, forget-me-not* becoming *myosotis,* etc. It is hard to see any practical reason for this change of fashion: it is probably due to an instinctive turning-away from the more homely word and a vague feeling that the Greek word is scientific.

[2]Example: "Comfort's catholicity of perception and image, strangely Whitmanesque in range, almost the exact opposite in aesthetic compulsion, continues to evoke that trembling atmospheric accumulative hinting at a cruel, an inexorably serene timelessness. . . . Wrey Gardiner scores by aiming at simple bullseyes with precision. Only they are not so simple, and through this contented sadness runs more than the surface bitter-sweet of resignation." (*Poetry Quarterly*).

uses them has his own private definition, but allows his hearer to think he means something quite different. Statements like *Marshal Pétain was a true patriot, The Soviet press is the freest in the world, The Catholic Church is opposed to persecution,* are almost always made with intent to deceive. Other words used in variable meanings, in most cases more or less dishonestly, are: *class, totalitarian, science, progressive, reactionary, bourgeois, equality.*

Now that I have made this catalogue of swindles and perversions, 9
let me give another example of the kind of writing that they lead to. This time it must of its nature be an imaginary one. I am going to translate a passage of good English into modern English of the worst sort. Here is a well-known verse from *Ecclesiastes:*

> I returned, and saw under the sun, that the race is not to the swift, nor the battle to the strong, neither yet bread to the wise, nor yet riches to men of understanding, not yet favour to men of skill; but time and chance happeneth to them all.

Here it is in modern English: 10

> Objective consideration of contemporary phenomena compels the conclusion that success or failure in competitive activities exhibits no tendency to be commensurate with innate capacity, but that a considerable element of the unpredictable must invariably be taken into account.

This is a parody, but not a very gross one. Exhibit 3, above, for 11
instance, contains several patches of the same kind of English. It will be seen that I have not made a full translation. The beginning and ending of the sentence follow the original meaning fairly closely, but in the middle the concrete illustrations—race, battle, bread—dissolve into the vague phrase "success or failure in competitive activities." This had to be so, because no modern writer of the kind I am discussing—no one capable of using phrases like "objective consideration of contemporary phenomena"—would ever tabulate his thoughts in that precise and detailed way. The whole tendency of modern prose is away from concreteness. Now analyse these two sentences a little more closely. The first contains 49 words but only 60 syllables, and all its words are those of everyday life. The second contains 38 words of 90 syllables: 18 of its words are from Latin roots, and one from Greek. The first sentence contains six vivid images, and only one phrase ("time and chance") that could be called vague. The second contains not a single fresh, arresting phrase, and in spite of its 90 syllables it gives only a shortened version of the meaning contained in the first. Yet without a doubt it is the second kind of sentence that is gaining ground in modern English. I do not want to exaggerate. This kind of writing is not yet universal, and outcrops of simplicity will occur here and there in the worst-written page. Still, if you or I were told to write a few lines on the uncertainty of human fortunes, we should probably come much nearer to my imaginary sentence than to the one from *Ecclesiastes.*

As I have tried to show, modern writing at its worst does not consist 12
in picking out words for the sake of their meaning and inventing images in order to make the meaning clearer. It consists in gumming together long strips of words which have already been set in order by someone else, and making the results presentable by sheer humbug. The attraction of this way of writing is that it is easy. It is easier—even quicker, once you have the habit—to say *In my opinion it is a not unjustifiable assumption that* than to say *I think.* If you use ready-made phrases, you not only don't have to hunt about for words; you also don't have to bother with the rhythms of your sentences, since these phrases are generally so arranged as to be more or less euphonious. When you are composing in a hurry—when you are dictating to a stenographer, for instance, or making a public speech—it is natural to fall into a pretentious, latinised style. Tags like *a consideration which we should do well to bear in mind* or *a conclusion to which all of us would readily assent* will save many a sentence from coming down with a bump. By using stale metaphors, similes and idioms, you save much mental effort, at the cost of leaving your meaning vague, not only for your reader but for yourself. This is the significance of mixed metaphors. The sole aim of a metaphor is to call up a visual image. When these images clash—as in *The Fascist octopus has sung its swan song, the jackboot is thrown into the melting-pot*—it can be taken as certain that the writer is not seeing a mental image of the objects he is naming; in other words he is not really thinking. Look again at the examples I gave at the beginning of this essay. Professor Laski (1) uses five negatives in 53 words. One of these is superfluous, making nonsense of the whole passage, and in addition there is the slip *alien* for akin, making further nonsense, and several avoidable pieces of clumsiness which increase the general vagueness. Professor Hogben (2) plays ducks and drakes with a battery which is able to write prescriptions, and, while disapproving of the everyday phrase *put up with,* is unwilling to look *egregious* up in the dictionary and see what it means. (3), if one takes an uncharitable attitude towards it, is simply meaningless: probably one could work out its intended meaning by reading the whole of the article in which it occurs. In (4) the writer knows more or less what he wants to say, but an accumulation of stale phrases chokes him like tea-leaves blocking a sink. In (5) words and meaning have almost parted company. People who write in this manner usually have a general emotional meaning—they dislike one thing and want to express solidarity with another—but they are not interested in the detail of what they are saying. A scrupulous writer, in every sentence that he writes, will ask himself at least four questions, thus: What am I trying to say? What words will express it? What image or idiom will make it clearer? Is this image fresh enough to have an effect? And he will probably ask himself two more: Could I put it more shortly? Have I said anything that is avoidably ugly? But you are not obliged to go to all this trouble. You can shirk it by simply throwing your mind open and letting the ready-made phrases come crowding in. They will construct your sentences for you—even think your thoughts

for you, to a certain extent—and at need they will perform the important service of partially concealing your meaning even from yourself. It is at this point that the special connection between politics and the debasement of language becomes clear.

14 In our time it is broadly true that political writing is bad writing. Where it is not true, it will generally be found that the writer is some kind of rebel, expressing his private opinions, and not a "party line." Orthodoxy, of whatever colour, seems to demand a lifeless, imitative style. The political dialects to be found in pamphlets, leading articles, manifestos, White Papers and the speeches of Under-Secretaries do, of course, vary from party to party, but they are all alike in that one almost never finds in them a fresh, vivid, home-made turn of speech. When one watches some tired hack on the platform mechanically repeating the familiar phrases—*bestial atrocities, iron heel, blood-stained tyranny, free peoples of the world, stand shoulder to shoulder*—one often has a curious feeling that one is not watching a live human being but some kind of dummy: a feeling which suddenly becomes stronger at moments when the light catches the speaker's spectacles and turns them into blank discs which seem to have no eyes behind them. And this is not altogether fanciful. A speaker who uses that kind of phraseology has gone some distance towards turning himself into a machine. The appropriate noises are coming out of his larynx, but his brain is not involved as it would be if he were choosing his words for himself. If the speech he is making is one that he is accustomed to make over and over again, he may be almost unconscious of what he is saying, as one is when one utters the responses in church. And this reduced state of consciousness, if not indispensable, is at any rate favourable to political conformity.

15 In our time, political speech and writing are largely the defence of the indefensible. Things like the continuance of British rule in India, the Russian purges and deportations, the dropping of the atom bombs on Japan, can indeed be defended, but only by arguments which are too brutal for most people to face, and which do not square with the professed aims of political parties. Thus political language has to consist largely of euphemism, question-begging and sheer cloudy vagueness. Defenceless villages are bombarded from the air, the inhabitants driven out into the countryside, the cattle machine-gunned, the huts set on fire with incendiary bullets: this is called *pacification*. Millions of peasants are robbed of their farms and sent trudging along the roads with no more than they can carry: this is called *transfer of population* or *rectification of frontiers*. People are imprisoned for years without trial, or shot in the back of the neck or sent to die of scurvy in Arctic lumber camps: this is called *elimination of unreliable elements*. Such phraseology is needed if one wants to name things without calling up mental pictures of them. Consider for instance some comfortable English professor defending Russian totalitarianism. He cannot say outright, "I believe in killing off your opponents when you can get good results by doing so." Probably, therefore, he will say something like this:

> While freely conceding that the Soviet régime exhibits certain features which the humanitarian may be inclined to deplore, we must, I think, agree that a certain curtailment of the right to political opposition is an unavoidable concomitant of transitional periods, and that the rigours which the Russian people have been called upon to undergo have been amply justified in the sphere of concrete achievement.

The inflated style is itself a kind of euphemism. A mass of Latin 15
words falls upon the facts like soft snow, blurring the outlines and covering up all the details. The great enemy of clear language is insincerity. When there is a gap between one's real and one's declared aims, one turns as it were instinctively to long words and exhausted idioms, like a cuttlefish squirting out ink. In our age there is no such thing as "keeping out of politics." All issues are political issues, and politics itself is a mass of lies, evasions, folly, hatred and schizophrenia. When the general atmosphere is bad, language must suffer. I should expect to find—this is a guess which I have not sufficient knowledge to verify—that the German, Russian and Italian languages have all deteriorated in the last ten or fifteen years, as a result of dictatorship.

But if thought corrupts language, language can also corrupt 16
thought. A bad usage can spread by tradition and imitation, even among people who should and do know better. The debased language that I have been discussing is in some ways very convenient. Phrases like *a not unjustifiable assumption, leaves much to be desired, would serve no good purpose, a consideration which we should do well to bear in mind,* are a continuous temptation, a packet of aspirins always at one's elbow. Look back through this essay, and for certain you will find that I have again and again committed the very faults I am protesting against. By this morning's post I have received a pamphlet dealing with conditions in Germany. The author tells me that he "felt impelled" to write it. I open it at random, and here is almost the first sentence that I see: "(The Allies) have an opportunity not only of achieving a radical transformation of Germany's social and political structure in such a way as to avoid a nationalistic reaction in Germany itself, but at the same time of laying the foundations of a co-operative and unified Europe." You see, he "feels impelled" to write—feels, presumably, that he has something new to say—and yet his words, like cavalry horses answering the bugle, group themselves automatically into the familiar dreary pattern. This invasion of one's mind by ready-made phrases *(lay the foundations, achieve a radical transformation)* can only be prevented if one is constantly on guard against them, and every such phrase anaesthetises a portion of one's brain.

I said earlier that the decadence of our language is probably curable. 17
Those who deny this would argue, if they produced an argument at all, that language merely reflects existing social conditions, and that we cannot influence its development by any direct tinkering with words and constructions. So far as the general tone or spirit of a language

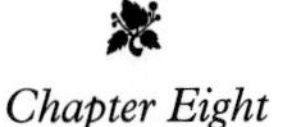

goes, this may be true, but it is not true in detail. Silly words and expressions have often disappeared, not through any evolutionary process but owing to the conscious action of a minority. Two recent examples were *explore every avenue* and *leave no stone unturned,* which were killed by the jeers of a few journalists. There is a long list of fly-blown metaphors which could similarly be got rid of if enough people would interest themselves in the job; and it should also be possible to laugh the *not un-* formation out of existence,[3] to reduce the amount of Latin and Greek in the average sentence, to drive out foreign phrases and strayed scientific words, and, in general, to make pretentiousness unfashionable. But all these are minor points. The defence of the English language implies more than this, and perhaps it is best to start by saying what it does *not* imply.

To begin with, it has nothing to do with archaism, with the sal- 18
vaging of obsolete words and turns of speech, or with the setting up of a "standard English" which must never be departed from. On the contrary, it is especially concerned with the scrapping of every word or idiom which has outworn its usefulness. It has nothing to do with correct grammar and syntax, which are of no importance so long as one makes one's meaning clear, or with the avoidance of Americanisms, or with having what is called a "good prose style." On the other hand it is not concerned with fake simplicity and the attempt to make written English colloquial. Nor does it even imply in every case preferring the Saxon word to the Latin one, though it does imply using the fewest and shortest words that will cover one's meaning. What is above all needed is to let the meaning choose the word, and not the other way about. In prose, the worst thing one can do with words is to surrender to them. When you think of a concrete object, you think wordlessly, and then, if you want to describe the thing you have been visualising, you probably hunt about till you find the exact words that seem to fit it. When you think of something abstract you are more inclined to use words from the start, and unless you make a conscious effort to prevent it, the existing dialect will come rushing in and do the job for you, at the expense of blurring or even changing your meaning. Probably it is better to put off using words as long as possible and get one's meaning as clear as one can through pictures or sensations. Afterwards one can choose—not simply *accept*—the phrases that will best cover the meaning, and then switch around and decide what impression one's words are likely to make on another person. This last effort of the mind cuts out all stale or mixed images, all prefabricated phrases, needless repetitions, and humbug and vagueness generally. But one can often be in doubt about the effect of a word or a phrase, and one needs rules that one can rely on when instinct fails. I think the following rules will cover most cases:

[3]One can cure oneself of the *not un-* formation by memorising this sentence: *A not unblack dog was chasing a not unsmall rabbit across a not ungreen field.*

i. Never use a metaphor, simile or other figure of speech which you are used to seeing in print.

ii. Never use a long word where a short one will do.

iii. If it is possible to cut a word out, always cut it out.

iv. Never use the passive where you can use the active.

v. Never use a foreign phrase, a scientific word or a jargon word if you can think of an everyday English equivalent.

vi. Break any of these rules sooner than say anything outright barbarous.

These rules sound elementary, and so they are, but they demand a deep change of attitude in anyone who has grown used to writing in the style now fashionable. One could keep all of them and still write bad English, but one could not write the kind of stuff that I quoted in those five specimens at the beginning of this article.

I have not here been considering the literary use of language, but 19
merely language as an instrument for expressing and not for concealing or preventing thought. Stuart Chase and others have come near to claiming that all abstract words are meaningless, and have used this as a pretext for advocating a kind of political quietism. Since you don't know what Fascism is, how can you struggle against Fascism? One need not swallow such absurdities as this, but one ought to recognise that the present political chaos is connected with the decay of language, and that one can probably bring about some improvement by starting at the verbal end. If you simplify your English, you are freed from the worst follies of orthodoxy. You cannot speak any of the necessary dialects, and when you make a stupid remark its stupidity will be obvious, even to yourself. Political language—and with variations this is true of all political parties, from Conservatives to Anarchists—is designed to make lies sound truthful and murder respectable, and to give an appearance of solidity to pure wind. One cannot change this all in a moment, but one can at least change one's own habits, and from time to time one can even, if one jeers loudly enough, send some worn-out and useless phrase—some *jackboot, Achilles' heel, hotbed, melting pot, acid test, veritable inferno* or other lump of verbal refuse—into the dustbin where it belongs.

COMPREHENSION

1. What is Orwell's purpose? For what type of audience is he writing? Where does he summarize his concerns for readers?
2. According to Orwell, "thought corrupts language" and "language can also corrupt thought." Give examples of these assertions in the essay.
3. In what ways does Orwell believe that politics and language are related?

RHETORIC

1. Orwell himself uses similes and metaphors. Locate five of them, and explain their relationship to the author's analysis.
2. Orwell claims that concrete language is superior to abstract language. Give examples of Orwell's attempt to write concretely.
3. One of the most crucial rhetorical devices in this essay is definition. What important concepts does Orwell define? What methods of definition does he tend to use?
4. Identify an example of hypothetical reasoning in the essay. How does it contribute to the thesis of the essay?
5. After having given five examples of bad English, why does Orwell, in paragraph 9, give another example? How does this example differ from the others? What does it add to the essay?
6. Explain the use of extended analogy in paragraph 13.

WRITING

1. In an analytical essay, assess the state of language in politics today. Cite examples from newspapers and television reports.
2. Apply Orwell's advice on language to "Shooting an Elephant" in Chapter 2.
3. Prepare an essay analyzing the use and abuse of any word that sparks controversy today—for example, *abortion, AIDS,* or *greed.*

MICHELLE CLIFF Michelle Cliff (1946–) is concerned with social issues and political realities as well as ethnic identity and gender, themes she explores in her writing. Born in Kingston, Jamaica, she is now an American citizen. Cliff was once a researcher and reporter in New York City and now teaches creative writing and history. Her books include *Claiming an Identity They Taught Me to Despise* (poetry) and *The Land of Look Behind* (poetry and prose). She has also contributed articles and reviews to numerous publications, including *Feminist Review.* In the following essay, she relates her attempts to find an authentic voice as a black female writer raised under British colonialism.

MICHELLE CLIFF

A Journey into Speech

The first piece of writing I produced, beyond a dissertation on intellectual game-playing in the Italian Renaissance, was entitled "Notes on Speechlessness," published in *Sinister Wisdom,* no. 5. In it I talked about my identification with Victor, the wild boy of Aveyron, who, after his rescue from the forest and wildness by a well-meaning doctor of Enlightenment Europe, became "civilized," but never came to speech. I felt, with Victor, that my wildness had been tamed—that which I had been taught was my wildness. 1

2 My dissertation was produced at the Warburg Institute, University of London, and was responsible for giving me an intellectual belief in myself that I had not had before, while at the same time distancing me from who I am, almost rendering me speechless about who I am. At least I believed in the young woman who wrote the dissertation—still, I wondered who she was and where she had come from.

3 I could speak fluently, but I could not reveal. I immersed myself in the social circles and academies of Siena, Florence, Urbino, as well as Venice, creating a place for myself there, and describing this ideal world in eloquent linear prose.

4 When I began, finally, partly through participation in the feminist movement, to approach myself as a subject, my writing was jagged, nonlinear, almost shorthand. The "Notes on Speechlessness" were indeed notes, written in snatches on a nine-to-five job. I did not choose the note form consciously; a combination of things drew me to it. An urgency for one thing. I also felt incompetent to construct an essay in which I would describe the intimacies, fears, and lies I wrote of in "Speechlessness." I felt my thoughts, things I had held within for a lifetime, traversed so wide a terrain, had so many stops and starts, apparent non sequiturs, that an essay—with its cold-blooded dependence on logical construction, which I had mastered practically against my will—could not work. My subject could not respond to that form, which would have contradicted the idea of speechlessness. This tender approach to myself within the confines and interruptions of a forty-hour-a-week job and against a history of forced fluency was the beginning of a journey into speech.

5 To describe this journey further, I must begin at the very beginning, with origins, and the significance of these origins. How they have made me the writer I am.

6 I originate in the Caribbean, specifically on the island of Jamaica, and although I have lived in the United States and in England, I travel as a Jamaican. It is Jamaica that forms my writing for the most part, and which has formed for the most part, myself. Even though I often feel what Derek Walcott expresses in his poem "The Schooner *Flight*": "I had no nation now but the imagination." It is a complicated business.

7 Jamaica is a place halfway between Africa and England, to put it simply, although historically one culture (guess which one) has been esteemed and the other denigrated (both are understatements)—at least among those who control the culture and politics of the island—the Afro-Saxons. As a child among these people, indeed of these people, as one of them, I received the message of anglocentrism, of white supremacy, and I internalized it. As a writer, as a human being, I have had to accept that reality and deal with its effect on me, as well as finding what has been lost to me from the darker side, and what may be hidden, to be dredged from memory and dream. And it *is* there to be dredged. As my writing delved longer and deeper into this part of myself, I began to dream and imagine. I was able to clearly envision

Nanny, the leader of a group of guerilla fighters known as the Windward Maroons, as she is described: an old Black woman naked except for a necklace made from the teeth of white men. I began to love her.

It is a long way from the court of Urbino to Nanny the Coromantyn warrier. (Coromantyn, or Coromantee, was used by the British in Jamaica to describe slaves from the Gold Coast of Africa, especially slaves who spoke Akan.) 8

One of the effects of assimilation, indoctrination, passing into the anglocentrism of British West Indian culture is that you believe absolutely in the hegemony of the King's English and in the form in which it is meant to be expressed. Or else your writing is not literature; it is folklore, and folklore can never be art. Read some poetry by West Indian writers—some, not all—and you will see what I mean. You have to dissect stanza after extraordinarily anglican stanza for Afro-Caribbean truth; you may never find the latter. But this has been our education. The anglican ideal—Milton, Wordsworth, Keats—was held before us with an assurance that we were unable, and would never be enabled, to compose a work of similar correctness. No reggae spoken here. 9

To write as a complete Caribbean woman, or man for that matter, demands of us retracing the African part of ourselves, reclaiming as our own, and as our subject, a history sunk under the sea, or scattered as potash in the canefields, or gone to bush, or trapped in a class system notable for its rigidity and absolute dependence on color stratification. On a past bleached from our minds. It means finding the art forms of these of our ancestors and speaking in the *patois* forbidden us. It means realizing our knowledge will always be wanting. It means also, I think, mixing in the forms taught us by the oppressor, undermining his language and co-opting his style, and turning it to our purpose. In my current work-in-progress, a novel, I alternate the King's English with *patois,* not only to show the class background of characters, but to show how Jamaicans operate within a split consciousness. It would be as dishonest to write the novel entirely in *patois* as to write entirely in the King's English. Neither is the novel a linear construction; its subject is the political upheavals of the past twenty years. Therefore, I have mixed time and incident and space and character and also form to try to mirror the historical turbulence. 10

For another example, I wrote a long poem, actually half-poem, half-prose, in which I imagine the visit of Botha of South Africa to the heads of western Europe in the summer of 1984. I wrote this as a parody of Gilbert and Sullivan because their work epitomizes salient aspects of the British Empire which remain vibrant. And because as a child I was sick to death of hearing "I am the very model of a modern major general." I enjoyed writing this, playing with rhyme and language—it was like spitting into their cultural soup. 11

We are a fragmented people. My experience as a writer coming from a culture of colonialism, a culture of Black people riven from each 12

other, my struggle to get wholeness from fragmentation while working within fragmentation, producing work which may find its strength in its depiction of fragmentation, through form as well as content, is similar to the experience of other writers whose origins are in countries defined by colonialism.

Ama Ata Aidoo, the Ghanaian writer, in her extraordinary book, 13
Our Sister Killjoy or Reflections from a Black-Eyed Squint (NOK Publishers, Lagos and New York, 1979), plots this fragmentation, and shows how both the demand and solace of the so-called mother country can claim us, while we long for our homeland and are shamed for it and ourselves at the same time. The form Aidoo uses to depict this dilemma of colonial peoples—part prose, fictional and epistolary, part poetry—illustrates the fragmentation of the heroine and grasps the fury of the heroine, living in Europe but drawn back to Ghana, knowing she can never be European. She will only be a been-to; that is, one who has been to the mother country. *Our Sister Killjoy* affected me directly, not just because like Aidoo's heroine I was a been-to. I was especially drawn by the way in which Aidoo expresses rage against colonialism—crystallized for her by the white man she calls the "Christian Doctor" throughout, excising Black African hearts to salvage white South African lives. In her expression of the rage she feels her prose breaks apart sharply into a staccato poetry—direct, short, brilliantly bitter—as if measured prose would disintegrate under her fury.

I wanted that kind of directness in my writing, as I came into closer 14
contact with my rage, and a realization that rage could fuel and shape my work. As a light-skinned colonial girlchild, both in Jamaica and in the Jamaican milieu of my family abroad, rage was the last thing expected of me.

After reading Aidoo I knew I wanted to tell exactly how things were, 15
what had been done, to us and by us, without muddying the issue with conventional beauty, avoiding becoming trapped in the grace of language for its own sake, which is always seductive.

In *Claiming an Identity They Taught Me to Despise,* a piece published 16
before I read Aidoo, halfway between poetry and prose, as I am halfway between Africa and England, patriot and expatriate, white and Black, I felt my use of language and imagery had sometimes masked what I wanted to convey. It seemed sometimes that the reader was able to ignore what I was saying while admiring the way in which it was said.

And yet, *Claiming* is an honest self-portrait of who I was at the 17
time. Someone who was unable, for the most part, to recapture the native language of Jamaica, and who relied on the King's English and European allusions, but who wrote from a feminist consciousness and a rapidly evolving consciousness of colonialism, and a knowledge of self-hatred. Someone who also dreamed in Latin—as I did and as I recorded in the title section, included here. *Claiming*'s strengths, I think, are in the more intimate, private places of the piece, which I constructed much as the "Notes on Speechlessness" are constructed. Shorthand—

almost—as memory and dream emerge; fast, at once keen, at once incomplete. I was also, in those sections, laboring under the ancient taboos of the assimilated: don't tell outsiders anything real about yourself. Don't reveal *our* secrets to *them*. Don't make us seem foolish, or oppressed. Write it quickly before someone catches you. Before you catch yourself.

After reading *Our Sister Killjoy,* something was set loose in me, I directed rage outward rather than inward, and I was able to write a piece called "If I Could Write This in Fire I Would Write This in Fire." In it I let myself go, any thought of approval for my words vanished; I strung together myth, dream, historical detail, observation, as I had done before, but I added native language, tore into the indoctrination of the colonizer, surprised myself with the violence of my words. 18

That piece of writing led to other pieces in which I try to depict personal fragmentation and describe political reality, according to the peculiar lens of the colonized. 19

COMPREHENSION

1. Why did the author feel that the conventional essay structure was unsuited to her purposes? What is the conventional structure of an expository essay?
2. What effect did the supremacy of the Anglo-Saxon culture and language have on Cliff's development as a writer?
3. What does Cliff mean by *speechlessness?* Consider the impact of the word as it relates to Cliff's situation.

RHETORIC

1. What specific passages in Cliff's essay analyze the writing process? How does this information contribute to her thesis? In your own words, state what Cliff's thesis is.
2. Cliff describes the essay's "cold-blooded dependence on logical construction." Does Cliff's essay conform to this convention? Why, or why not? Give specific evidence to support your views.
3. Examine the writer's use of literary and historical allusions in the essay and the purpose they serve.
4. What rhetorical modes does Cliff use in her essay?
5. In paragraph 5, Cliff shifts focus. What transitions does she employ? What has she accomplished in paragraphs 1 to 4?
6. Critique Cliff's conclusion. How successfully does it reinforce her thesis?

WRITING

1. In a brief essay, elaborate on the sense of fragmentation felt by writers whose origins are rooted in colonialism.
2. Cliff mentions finding ways to sabotage the King's English through her writing. Write an essay analyzing how and why a writer would attempt this.

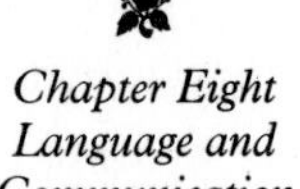

CLASSIC AND CONTEMPORARY: QUESTIONS FOR COMPARISON

1. Compare the rhetorical strategies and levels of language used by Cliff and Orwell in their essays, as well as the main points each is making. Pay special attention to the vocabulary and diction used by the writers.
2. Using Orwell's guidelines for good writing, consider how he would evaluate Cliff's use of language in her essay. How would he judge her use of evocative metaphors and concrete language, as well as the clarity of her ideas? Provide examples from both writers in your essay.
3. As an Anglo-Saxon, Orwell is using the language of the oppressor, while Cliff is attempting to free herself from its domination and find her own au- 16
thentic voice. Is there a common ground on which the two writers can meet? Would Orwell sympathize with Cliff's struggles, or would he accuse her of manipulating the language for her own ends? Would Cliff agree with Orwell's ideas about effective, responsible writing or see his advice as another example of domination? Consider these questions in essay form, using support from Orwell's and Cliff's essays.
4. Write another version of "Politics and the English Language" as you imagine Cliff would write it, using her essay as a base. Would she concentrate on the use of correct, clear prose as Orwell does, or would she have different advice for writers, perhaps focusing on the issue of "speechlessness" and other concerns of minority writers?

17

CONNECTIONS

1. Compare the attitudes of Tan, Mukherjee, and Cliff regarding the connection between language and cultural or ethnic identity.
2. Write an essay exploring Mukherjee's description of immigrants: "They 18
have shed old identities, taken on new ones and learned to hide the scars." How would Cliff and Tan respond to that statement? Would they agree or disagree? Use evidence from their writing to support your opinions.
3. Some of the writers in this section mention specific literary influences on their writing. What have these writers learned from their mentors? Use examples from their essays.
4. Compare the views of Hayakawa and Tan regarding the value of linguistic theories and their possible effect on developing the identities of immigrant children.
5. Expand on Cliff's theme of "myself as subject," using Ferré's struggles with gender as a writer. Use any other writers whose work may apply.
6. Write an essay on the effects of a dominant culture and language on the creative development of a writer. How does an artist escape "speechlessness" in a racist society? Support your opinion with quotes from any writer in this section.
7. Explore the theme of "language as refuge," using the work of Tan and Cliff.

CHAPTER NINE

Literature, Media, and the Arts

Imagine a world without fiction, poetry, or drama; music, art, or dance; radio, television, or film. We are so accustomed to taking "the arts" in their totality for granted that it is hard for us to conceive of contemporary culture without them. Our fondness for stories or paintings or any other creative form might help us to understand our culture or might even move us to action. Yet the value of various artistic forms doesn't derive exclusively from their ability to tell us something about life. The arts can also take us into an imaginative realm offering perhaps more intense experiences than anything we encounter in the "ordinary" world.

Think of literature and the arts as an exercise in imaginative freedom. You are free to select the books you read, the movies you see, the exhibitions and concerts you attend. Some of your decisions—for example, to look more deeply into the work of Sylvia Plath or Chinua Achebe after reading their essays in this chapter—might be serious and consequential to your education. Other decisions, perhaps to watch a few soaps on a rainy afternoon or to buy something you see in a commercial, are less important. The way you view the arts—whether as a temporary escape from conventional reality or as a way to learn something about the temper of civilization—is entirely a matter of taste. Regardless of your purpose or intent, you approach the arts initially for the sheer exhilaration and pleasure they provide. Art, as Plato observed, is a dream for awakened minds.

The arts awaken you to the power and intensity of the creative spirit. At the same time, you make judgments and evaluations of the nature of your creative encounter. When you assert that you "like" this painting or "dislike" that movie, you are assessing the worth or value of the artistic experience. As Marya Mannes states in her essay "How Do You Know It's Good?" it is clear that "the more you read and see and hear, the more equipped you'll be to practice that art of association which is at the basis of all understanding and judgment."

Perhaps you prefer to keep your experience of literature and the arts a pleasurable pastime or escape from reality. Or you may wish to participate in them as a creative writer, musician, painter, or dancer. Ultimately, you may come to view the arts as a transformational experience, a voyage of discovery in which you encounter diverse peoples and cultures, learn to see the world in creative terms, and begin to perceive your own creative potential in a new light.

Previewing the Chapter

As you read the essays in this chapter and respond to them in discussion and writing, consider the following questions:

- According to the author, what is the value of the art or literary form under discussion?
- What function does literature or art serve?
- Is the writer's perspective subjective or objective, and why?
- How does the author define his or her subject—whether it is poetry, fiction, art, or advertising?
- Is the writer's experience of literature or art similar to or different from your own?
- In what ways do gender and race influence the writer's perspective on the subject?
- What is the nature of the creative process under discussion?
- In what specific cultural context does the writer place his or her subject?
- What is the main idea that the author wants to present about literature, advertising, or the arts? Do you agree or disagree with this key concept?
- What have you learned about the importance of literature, media, and the arts from reading these essays?

SYLVIA PLATH Sylvia Plath (1932–1963), American poet and novelist, graduated from Smith College and took a master's at Cambridge University. She married the English poet Ted Hughes in 1956. Plath committed suicide at the age of 30. Her best known work is *The Bell-Jar* (1962), a highly autobiographical novel about a young woman overwhelmed by crises and suicidal tendencies. Plath's poetry, often reflecting a fascination with suffering, pain, and death, is collected in *The Colossus* (1960), *Ariel* (1968), *Crossing the Water* (1971), and *Winter Trees* (1972). This essay, written in 1962, is an energetic and highly poetic celebration of the artist's craft.

SYLVIA PLATH

A Comparison

How I envy the novelist! 1

I imagine him—better say her, for it is the women I look to for . . . a parallel—I imagine her, then, pruning a rosebush with a large pair of shears, adjusting her spectacles, shuffling about among the teacups, humming, arranging ashtrays or babies, absorbing a slant of light, a fresh edge to the weather, and piercing, with a kind of modest, beautiful X-ray vision, the psychic interiors of her neighbors—her neighbors on trains, in the dentist's waiting room, in the corner teashop. To her, this fortunate one, what is there that *isn't* relevant! Old shoes can be used, doorknobs, air letters, flannel nightgowns, cathedrals, nail varnish, jet planes, rose arbors and budgerigars; little mannerisms—the sucking at a tooth, the tugging at a hemline—any weird or warty or fine or despicable thing. Not to mention emotions, motivations—those rumbling, thunderous shapes. Her business is Time, the way it shoots forward, shunts back, blooms, decays and double-exposes itself. Her business is people in Time. And she, it seems to me, has all the time in the world. She can take a century if she likes, a generation, a whole summer. 2

I can take about a minute. 3

I'm not talking about epic poems. We all know how long *they* can take. I'm talking about the smallish, unofficial garden-variety poem. How shall I describe it?—a door opens, a door shuts. In between you have had a glimpse: a garden, a person, a rainstorm, a dragonfly, a heart, a city. I think of those round glass Victorian paperweights which I remember, yet can never find—a far cry from the plastic mass-productions which stud the toy counters in Woolworth's. This sort of paperweight is a clear globe, self-complete, very pure, with a forest or village or family group within it. You turn it upside down, then back. It snows. Everything is changed in a minute. It will never be the same in there—not the fir trees, nor the gables, nor the faces. 4

So a poem takes place. 5

And there is really so little room! So little time! The poet becomes 6
an expert packer of suitcases:

> The apparition of these faces in the crowd;
> Petals on a wet black bough.

There it is: the beginning and the end in one breath. How would the 7
novelist manage that? In a paragraph? In a page? Mixing it, perhaps, like paint, with a little water, thinning it, spreading it out.

Now I am being smug, I am finding advantages. 8

If a poem is concentrated, a closed fist, then a novel is relaxed and 9
expansive, an open hand: it has roads, detours, destinations; a heart line, a head line; morals and money come into it. Where the fist excludes and stuns, the open hand can touch and encompass a great deal in its travels.

I have never put a toothbrush in a poem. 10

I do not like to think of all the things, familiar, useful and worthy 11
things, I have never put into a poem. I did, once, put a yew tree in. And that yew tree began, with astounding egotism, to manage and order the whole affair. It was not a yew tree by a church on a road past a house in a town where a certain woman lived . . . and so on, as it might have been in a novel. Oh, no. It stood squarely in the middle of my poem, manipulating its dark shades, the voices in the churchyard, the clouds, the birds, the tender melancholy with which I contemplated it—everything! I couldn't subdue it. And, in the end, my poem was a poem about a yew tree. That yew tree was just too proud to be a passing black mark in a novel.

Perhaps I shall anger some poets by implying that the *poem* is 12
proud. The poem, too, can include everything, they will tell me. And with far more precision and power than those baggy, disheveled and undiscriminate creatures we call novels. Well, I concede these poets their steamshovels and old trousers. I really *don't* think poems should be all that chaste. I would, I think, even concede a toothbrush, if the poem was a real one. But these apparitions, these poetical toothbrushes, are rare. And when they do arrive, they are inclined, like my obstreperous yew tree, to think themselves singled out and rather special.

Not so in novels. 13

There the toothbrush returns to its rack with beautiful promptitude 14
and is forgot. Time flows, eddies, meanders, and people have leisure to grow and alter before our eyes. The rich junk of life bobs all about us: bureaus, thimbles, cats, the whole much-loved, well-thumbed catalog of the miscellaneous which the novelist wishes us to share. I do not mean that there is no pattern, no discernment, no rigorous ordering here.

I am only suggesting that perhaps the pattern does not insist so 15
much.

The door of the novel, like the door of the poem, also shuts. 16

But not so fast, nor with such manic, unanswerable finality. 17

COMPREHENSION

1. Does this essay have a thesis? Explain.
2. What distinctions does the author draw between the poem and the novel? Why does she envy the novelist? What stated and implied preferences does she have for the poem rather than the novel?
3. Explain the relevance of rosebushes, toothbrushes, and yew trees to Plath's discussion. What is her purpose in incorporating these details into her essay?

RHETORIC

1. The author employs a remarkable variety of poetic techniques in this essay, including metaphors, symbols, allusions, imagery, personification, onomatopoeia, alliteration, consonance, and assonance. Locate and analyze examples of these techniques.
2. Analyze Plath's use of parallelism in paragraphs 2, 4, and 14.
3. Plath uses a series of figurative comparisons to structure the entire essay. Trace and examine the main figurative comparisons that serve to organize the selection.
4. Examine the spatial and rhetorical effects of the numerous one-sentence paragraphs in the essay.
5. How does Plath's method serve to identify and define the novelist and poet?
6. Analyze the cumulative use of illustration to achieve emphasis in this essay.

WRITING

1. Comment in a brief essay on Plath's view that the poem, unlike the novel, closes with "manic, unanswerable finality."
2. Write an essay that compares and contrasts—either figuratively or literally—two forms of literature, art, music, or film.
3. Select a poem that you like, and assess it, using Plath's observations on poetry as a guideline.

DAVID HERBERT LAWRENCE David Herbert Lawrence (1885–1930), novelist, essayist, and poet, wrote in the great tradition of English romanticism. He chafed under the conventions of his age and zealously extended the content and style of the English novel. His novels, such as *Sons and Lovers* (1913), *The Rainbow* (1915), *Women in Love* (1921), *The Plumed Serpent* (1926), and *Lady Chatterley's Lover* (1928), are famous for their often disquieting depictions of love and ambition in the modern world. Lawrence also wrote criticism: His *Studies in Classic American Literature* (1923) is still a revealing, if idiosyncratic, look at American literature. In the following essay, what matters for Lawrence is not simply the novel, which he treats with energy and enthusiasm, but life itself.

D. H. LAWRENCE

Why the Novel Matters

We have curious ideas of ourselves. We think of ourselves as a body with a spirit in it, or a body with a soul in it, or a body with a mind in it. *Mens sana in corpore sano.* The years drink up the wine, and at last throw the bottle away, the body, of course, being the bottle. 1

It is a funny sort of superstition. Why should I look at my hand, as it so cleverly writes these words, and decide that it is a mere nothing compared to the mind that directs it? Is there really any huge difference between my hand and my brain? Or my mind? My hand is alive, it flickers with a life of its own. It meets all the strange universe in touch, and learns a vast number of things, and knows a vast number of things. My hand, as it writes these words, slips gaily along, jumps like a grasshopper to dot an *i,* feels the table rather cold, gets a little bored if I write too long, has its own rudiments of thought, and is just as much *me* as is my brain, my mind, or my soul. Why should I imagine that there is a *me* which is more *me* than my hand is? Since my hand is absolutely alive, me alive. 2

Whereas, of course, as far as I am concerned, my pen isn't alive at all. My pen *isn't me* alive. Me alive ends at my finger-tips. 3

Whatever is me alive is me. Every tiny bit of my hands is alive, every little freckle and hair and fold of skin. And whatever is me alive is me. Only my finger-nails, those ten little weapons between me and an inanimate universe, they cross the mysterious Rubicon between me alive and things like my pen, which are not alive, in my own sense. 4

So, seeing my hand is all alive, and me alive, wherein is it just a bottle, or a jug, or a tin can, or a vessel of clay, or any of the rest of that nonsense? True, if I cut it it will bleed, like a can of cherries. But then the skin that is cut, and the veins that bleed, and the bones that should never be seen, they are all just as alive as the blood that flows. So the tin can business, or vessel of clay, is just bunk. 5

And that's what you learn, when you're a novelist. And that's what you are very liable *not* to know, if you're a parson, or a philosopher, or a scientist, or a stupid person. If you're a parson, you talk about souls in heaven. If you're a novelist, you know that paradise is in the palm of your hand, and on the end of your nose, because both are alive; and alive, and man alive, which is more than you can say, for certain, of paradise. Paradise is after life, and I for one am not keen on anything that is *after* life. If you are a philosopher, you talk about infinity, and the pure spirit which knows all things. But if you pick up a novel, you realize immediately that infinity is just a handle to this self-same jug of a body of mine; while as for knowing, if I find my finger in fire, I know 6 that fire burns, with a knowledge so emphatic and vital, it leaves Nirvana merely a conjecture. Oh, yes, my body, me alive, *knows,* and knows intensely. And as for the sum of all knowledge, it can't be anything more than an accumulation of all the things I know in the body, and you, dear reader, know in the body.

These damned philosophers, they talk as if they suddenly went off in steam, and were then much more important than they are when they're in their shirts. It is nonsense. Every man, philosopher included, ends in his own finger-tips. That's the end of his man alive. As for the words and thoughts and sighs and aspirations that fly from him, they are so many tremulations in the ether, and not alive at all. But if the tremulations reach another man alive, he may receive them into his life, and his life may take on a new colour, like a chameleon creeping from a brown rock on to a green leaf. All very well and good. It still doesn't alter the fact that the so-called spirit, the message or teaching of the philosopher or the saint, isn't alive at all, but just a tremulation upon the ether, like a radio message. All this spirit stuff is just tremulations upon the ether into new life, that is because you are man alive, and you take sustenance and stimulation into your alive man in a myriad ways. But to say that the message, or the spirit which is communicated to you, is more important than your living body, is nonsense. You might as well say that the potato at dinner was more important. 7

Nothing is important but life. And for myself, I can absolutely see life nowhere but in the living. Life with a capital L is only man alive. Even a cabbage in the rain is cabbage alive. All things that are alive are amazing. And all things that are dead are subsidiary to the living. Better a live dog than a dead lion. But better a live lion than a live dog. *C'est la vie!* 8

It seems impossible to get a saint, or a philosopher, or a scientist, to stick to this simple truth. They are all, in a sense, renegades. The saint wishes to offer himself up as spiritual food for the multitude. Even Francis of Assisi turns himself into a sort of angel-cake, of which anyone may take a slice. But an angel-cake is rather less than man alive. And poor St. Francis might well apologize to his body, when he is dying: "Oh, pardon me, my body, the wrong I did you through the years!" It was no wafer, for others to eat. 9

The philosopher, on the other hand, because he can think, decides that nothing but thoughts matter. It is as if a rabbit, because he can make little pills, should decide that nothing but little pills matter. As for the scientist, he has absolutely no use for me so long as I am man alive. To the scientist, I am dead. He puts under the microscope a bit of dead me, and calls it me. He takes me to pieces, and says first one piece, and then another piece, is me. My heart, my liver, my stomach have all been scientifically me, according to the scientist; and nowadays I am either a brain, or nerves, or glands, or something more up-to-date in the tissue line. 10

Now I absolutely flatly deny that I am a soul, or a body, or a mind, or an intelligence, or a brain, or a nervous system, or a bunch of glands, or any of the rest of these bits of me. The whole is greater than the 11

part. And therefore, I, who am man alive, am greater than my soul, or spirit, or body, or mind, or consciousness, or anything else that is merely a part of me. I am man, and alive. I am man alive, and as long as I can, I intend to go on being man alive.

For this reason I am a novelist. And being a novelist, I consider my- 12
self superior to the saint, the scientist, the philosopher, and the poet, who are all great masters of different bits of man alive, but never get the whole hog. 13

The novel is the one bright book of life. Books are not life. They are only tremulations on the ether. But the novel as a tremulation can make the whole man alive tremble. Which is more than poetry, philosophy, science, or any other book-tremulation can do.

The novel is the book of life. In this sense, the Bible is a great con- 14
fused novel. You may say, it is about God. But it is really about man alive. Adam, Eve, Sarai, Abraham, Isaac, Jacob, Samuel, David, Bath-Sheba, Ruth, Esther, Solomon, Job, Isaiah, Jesus, Mark, Judas, Paul, Peter: what is it but man alive, from start to finish? Man alive, not mere bits. Even the Lord is another man alive, in a burning bush, throwing the tablets of stone at Moses's head.

I do hope you begin to get my idea, why the novel is supremely im- 15
portant, as a tremulation on the ether. Plato makes the perfect ideal being tremble in me. But that's only a bit of me. Perfection is only a bit, in the strange make-up of man alive. The Sermon on the Mount makes the selfless spirit of me quiver. But that, too, is only a bit of me. The Ten Commandments set the old Adam shivering in me, warning me that I am a thief and a murderer, unless I watch it. But even the old Adam is only a bit of me.

I very much like all these bits of me to be set trembling with life and 16
the wisdom of life. But I do ask that the whole of me shall tremble in its wholeness, some time or other.

And this, of course, must happen in me, living. 17

But as far as it can happen from a communication, it can only hap- 18
pen when a whole novel communicates itself to me. The Bible—but *all* the Bible—and Homer, and Shakespeare: these are the supreme old novels. These are all things to all men. Which means that in their wholeness they affect the whole man alive, which is the man himself, beyond any part of him. They set the whole tree trembling with a new access of life, they do not just stimulate growth in one direction.

I don't want to grow in any one direction any more. And, if I can 19
help it, I don't want to stimulate anybody else into some particular direction. A particular direction ends in a *cul-de-sac*. We're in a *cul-de-sac* at present.

I don't believe in any dazzling revelation, or in any supreme Word. 20
"The grass withereth, the flower fadeth, but the Word of the Lord shall stand for ever." That's the kind of stuff we've drugged ourselves with. As a matter of fact, the grass withereth, but comes up all the greener for that reason, after the rains. The flower fadeth, and therefore the bud opens. But the Word of the Lord, being man-uttered and a mere vibration on

the ether, becomes staler and staler, more and more boring, till at last we turn a deaf ear and it ceases to exist, far more finally than any withered grass. It is grass that renews its youth like the eagle, not any Word.

We should ask for no absolutes, or absolute. Once and for all and for ever, let us have done with the ugly imperialism of any absolute. There is no absolute good, there is nothing absolutely right. All things flow and change, and even change is not absolute. The whole is a strange assembly of apparently incongruous parts, slipping past one another.

Me, man alive, I am a very curious assembly of incongruous parts. 22
My yea! of today is oddly different from my yea! of yesterday. My tears of tomorrow will have nothing to do with my tears of a year ago. If the one I love remains unchanged and unchanging, I shall cease to love her. It is only because she changes and startles me into change and defies my inertia, and is herself staggered in her inertia by my changing, that I can continue to love her. If she stayed put, I might as well love the pepper-pot.

In all this change, I maintain a certain integrity. But woe betide me 23
if I try to put my finger on it. If I say of myself, I am this, I am that!—then, if I stick to it, I turn into a stupid fixed thing like a lamp-post. I shall never know wherein lies my integrity, my individuality, my me. I *can* never know it. It is useless to talk about my ego. That only means that I have made up an *idea* of myself, and that I am trying to cut myself out to pattern. Which is no good. You can cut your cloth to fit your coat, but you can't clip bits off your living body, to trim it down to your idea. True, you can put yourself into ideal corsets. But even in ideal corsets, fashions change.

Let us learn from the novel. In the novel, the characters can do 24
nothing but *live*. If they keep on being good, according to pattern, or bad, according to pattern, or even volatile, according to pattern, they cease to live, and the novel falls dead. A character in a novel has got to live, or it is nothing.

We, likewise, in life have got to live, or we are nothing. 25

What we mean by living is, of course, just as indescribable as what 26
we mean by *being*. Men get ideas into their heads, of what they mean by Life, and they proceed to cut life out to pattern. Sometimes they go into the desert to seek God, sometimes they go into the desert to seek cash, sometimes it is wine, woman, and song, and again it is water, political reform, and votes. You never know what it will be next: from killing your neighbour with hideous bombs and gas that tears the lungs, to supporting a Foundlings Home and preaching infinite Love, and being co-respondent in a divorce.

In all this wild welter, we need some sort of guide. It's no good in- 27
venting Thou Shalt Nots!

What then? Turn truly, honourably to the novel, and see wherein 28
you are man alive, and wherein you are dead man in life. You may love a woman as man alive, and you may be making love to a woman as sheer dead man in life. You may eat your dinner as man alive, or as a

mere masticating corpse. As man alive you may have a shot at your enemy. But as a ghastly simulacrum of life you may be firing bombs into men who are neither your enemies nor your friends, but just things you are dead to. Which is criminal, when the things happen to be alive.

To be alive, to be man alive, to be whole man alive: that is the point. 29
And at its best, the novel, and the novel supremely, can help you. It can help you not to be dead man in life. So much of man walks about dead and a carcass in the street and house, today: so much of woman is merely dead. Like a pianoforte with half the notes mute.

But in the novel you can see, plainly, when the man goes dead, the 30
woman goes inert. You can develop an instinct for life, if you will, instead of a theory of right and wrong, good and bad.

In life, there is right and wrong, good and bad, all the time. But 31
what is right in one case is wrong in another. And in the novel you see one man becoming a corpse, because of his so-called goodness, another going dead because of his so-called wickedness. Right and wrong is an instinct: but an instinct of the whole consciousness in a man, bodily, mental, spiritual at once. And only in the novel are *all* things given full play, or at least, they may be given full play, when we realize that life itself, and not inert safety, is the reason for living. For out of the full play of all things emerges the only thing that is anything, the wholeness of a man, the wholeness of a woman, man alive, and live woman.

COMPREHENSION

1. State Lawrence's thesis in your own words.
2. According to Lawrence, what is the relationship between life and the novel? Why does the novel matter? Why is the novel "the one bright book of life"?
3. What contrasts does Lawrence establish between the novelist and the parson, philosopher, and scientist?

RHETORIC

1. Analyze the levels of diction, the very "sound" of Lawrence's prose. Examine the admixture of declarative, interrogative, and exclamatory sentences in the essay. Explain the author's use of fragments, his application of figurative language, and his use of italics for typographical emphasis. Examine Lawrence's persistent devices of repetition and overstatement in the essay. Evaluate the effect of these numerous strategies on the tone of the essay.
2. What patterns of imagery do you detect in the essay? How do they relate to the thesis?
3. How do the terms "tremulation on the ether" and "bright book of life" serve as structuring principles in the essay?
4. Trace the association of ideas advancing Lawrence's thesis. In the absence of strictly logical development, how unified and coherent is the essay?

5. Analyze patterns of comparison and contrast in the essay. Compare them to the pattern employed by Plath in "A Comparison."
6. Examine the relation of point of view to theme and tone in the essay.

WRITING

1. Do you agree with Lawrence's assertion that the novelist is better equipped than the scientist, philosopher, or theologian to capture the wholeness of life? Explain in an essay.
2. Write a personalized essay on why music, film, drama, or a similar subject matters.
3. Lawrence asserts that the "Bible—and Homer, and Shakespeare" are "supreme old novels." Do you agree or disagree with his position? Answer this question in a brief essay.

OCTAVIO PAZ Octavio Paz (1914–) is a Mexican poet, philosopher, and critic distinguished for his insight and the elegance of his writing. Paz published his first book of poetry at the age of 19, and his work continues to reflect an interest in the Mexican past and the richness of its landscape. His collections of poetry include *Configurations* (tr. 1971) and *A Drift of Shadows* (1979); his erudite nonfiction includes *Children of the Mire: Modern Poetry from Romanticism to the Avant-Garde* (1974) and *The Monkey Grammarian* (1981). His topics range from sex and religion to modern history. In the essay that follows, written in 1956, Paz examines how the poet Walt Whitman is symbolic of and indistinguishable from the American spirit of re-creation.

OCTAVIO PAZ

Walt Whitman

Walt Whitman is the only great modern poet who does not seem to experience discord when he faces his world. Not even solitude; his monologue is a universal chorus. No doubt there are at least two people in him: the public poet and the private person who conceals his true erotic inclinations. But the mask—that of the poet of democracy—is rather more than a mask; it is his true face. Despite certain recent interpretations, in Whitman the poetic and the historical dream come together. There is no gap between his beliefs and social reality. And this fact is more important—I mean, more widely pertinent and significant—than any psychological consideration. The uniqueness of Whitman's poetry in the modern world cannot be explained except as a function of another, even greater, uniqueness which includes it: that of America. 1

In a book[*] which is a model of its genre, Edmundo O'Gorman has 2
shown that our continent was never discovered. In effect, it is impossible to discover something which does not exist, and America, before its so-called discovery, did not exist. One ought rather to speak of the *invention* of America than of its discovery. If America is a creation of the European spirit, it begins to emerge from the sea-mists centuries before the expeditions of Columbus. And what the Europeans discover when they reach these lands is their own historic dream. Reyes has devoted some lucid pages to this subject: America is a sudden embodiment of a European utopia. The dream becomes a reality, a present; America is a present: a gift, a given of history. But it is an open present, a today that is tinged with tomorrow. The presence and the present of America are a future; our continent is, by its nature, the land which does not exist on its own, but as something which is created and invented. Its being, its reality or substance, consists of being always future, history which is justified not by the past but by what is to come. Our foundation is not what America was but what it will be. America never was; and *it is, only if it is utopia,* history on its way to a golden age.

This may not be entirely true if one considers the colonial period of 3
Spanish and Portuguese America. But it is revealing how, just as soon as the Latin Americans acquire self-consciousness and oppose the Spaniards, they rediscover the utopian nature of America and make the French utopias their own. All of them see in wars of independence a return to first principles, a reversion to what America really is. The War of Independence is a correction of American history and, as such, a restoration of the original reality. The exceptional and genuinely paradoxical nature of this restoration becomes clear if one notes that it consists of a restoration of the future. Thanks to French revolutionary principles, Latin America becomes again what it was at its birth: not a past, but a future, a dream. The dream of Europe, the place of choice, spatial and temporal, of all that the European reality could not be except by denying itself and its past. America is the dream of Europe, now free of European history, free of the burden of tradition. Once the problem of independence is resolved, the abstract and utopian nature of liberal America begins to show again in episodes such as the French intervention in Mexico. Neither Juarez nor his soldiers ever believed—according to Cosío Villegas—that they fought against France, but against a French usurpation. The true France was ideal and universal and more than just a nation, it was an idea, a philosophy. Cuesta says, with some justice, that the war with the French should be seen as a "civil war." It needed the Mexican Revolution to wake the country from this philosophical dream—which, in another way, concealed an historical reality hardly touched upon by the Independence, the Reform, and the Dictatorship—and discover itself, no longer as an abstract future but as an origin in which the three times needed to be

[*] *La idea del descubrimiento de America* (1951).

sought: our past, our present, our future. The historical emphasis changed tense, and in this consists the true spiritual significance of the Mexican Revolution.

The utopian character of America is even purer in the Saxon portion of the continent. There were no complex Indian cultures there, nor did Roman Catholicism erect its vast nontemporal structures: America was—if it was anything—geography, pure space, open to human action. Lacking historical substance—old class divisions, ancient institutions, inherited beliefs and laws—reality presented only natural obstacles. Men fought, not against history, but against nature. And where there was an historical obstacle—as in the Indian societies—it was erased from history and, reduced to a mere act of nature, action followed as if this were so. The North American attitude can be condemned in these terms: all that does not have a part in the utopian nature of America does not properly belong to history; it is a natural event and, thus, it doesn't exist, or it exists only as an inert obstacle, not as an alien conscience. Evil is outside, part of the natural world—like Indians, rivers, mountains, and other obstacles which must be domesticated or destroyed; or it is an intrusive reality (the English past, Spanish Catholicism, monarchy, etc.). The American War of Independence is the expulsion of the intrusive elements, alien to the American essence. If American reality is the reinvention of itself, whatever is found in any way irreducible or unassimilable is not American. In other places the future is a human attribute: because we are men, we have a future; in the Anglo-Saxon America of the last century, the process is inverted and the future determines man: we are men because we have a future. And whatever has no future is not man. Thus, reality leaves no gap at all for contradiction, ambiguity, or conflict to appear.

Whitman can sing confidently and in blithe innocence about 5
democracy militant because the American utopia is confused with and indistinguishable from American reality. Whitman's poetry is a great prophetic dream, but it is a dream within another even greater one that feeds it. America is dreamed in Whitman's poetry because it is a dream itself. And it is dreamed as a concrete reality, almost a *physical* reality, with its men, its rivers, its cities and mountains. All that huge mass of reality moves lightly, as if it were weightless; and in fact, it is without historic weight: it is the future incarnate. The reality Whitman sings is utopian. By this I do not mean that it is unreal or exists only as idea, but that its essence, what enlivens it, justifies and makes sense of its progress and gives weight to its movements, is the future. Dream within a dream, Whitman's poetry is realistic only on this count: his dream is the dream of the reality itself, which has no other substance but to invent itself and dream itself. "When we dream that we dream," Novalis says, "waking is near at hand." Whitman was never aware that he dreamed and always thought himself a poetic realist. And he was, but only insofar as the reality he celebrated was not something given, but a substance crossed and recrossed by the future.

America dreams itself in Whitman because it was itself a dream, pure creation. Before and since Whitman we have had other poetic dreams. All of them—whether the dreamer's name is Poe or Dario, Melville or Dickinson—are more like attempts to escape from the American nightmare. 6

COMPREHENSION

1. What does Paz mean by "the *invention* of America" (paragraph 2)?
2. According to Paz, why are Whitman and America synonymous?
3. What makes Whitman's poetry particularly American?

RHETORIC

1. State Paz's thesis in your own words.
2. What is the tone of the piece? Where do you find specific proof of Paz's attitude toward his subject?
3. Who is Paz's intended audience? What indicates this in the writing?
4. Find examples of Paz's use of abstract language in the essay. What effect does it have on the work?
5. Examine the points made in paragraph 3. How does this historical data help advance Paz's main idea?
6. How does Paz conclude his essay? What effect does the word *nightmare* have on the reader? What was Paz's intention in using it? Are there any earlier indications of discordance in the essay?

WRITING

1. Choose a famous person whom you feel embodies the ideals and spirit of a particular country. Write an essay examining this connection. Some research may be necessary if biographical data is essential to your essay.
2. In a brief essay, explain what Paz means by "America is the future incarnate."
3. Paz's essay contains very little factual information about Whitman. In a biographical research paper, compare the poet's life and beliefs to the points Paz makes in his essay.

CHINUA ACHEBE Chinua Achebe (1930–) is one of Africa's leading contemporary writers. Born in Nigeria, he has written novels, poems, short stories, and essays—many of them exploring the effects of Western concepts of African traditionalism. Achebe's first novel, a depiction of Igbo (a variation of Ibo) culture, was *Things Fall Apart* (1958). Its local imagery and folk legends gained him an international audience. Achebe was once a broadcaster and diplomat for Biafra and has written a collection of essays entitled *The Trouble with Nigeria* (1983). In the following piece, originally written for a museum exhibition, Achebe describes how life and art blend in Igbo culture.

CHINUA ACHEBE

The Igbo World and Its Art

The Igbo world is an arena for the interplay of forces. It is a dynamic world of movement and of flux. Igbo art, reflecting this world-view, is never tranquil but mobile and active, even aggressive. 1

Ike, energy, is the essence of all things human, spiritual, animate and inanimate. Everything has its own unique energy which must be acknowledged and given its due. *Ike di na awaja na awaja* is a common formulation of this idea: "Power runs in many channels." Sometimes the saying is extended by an exemplifying coda about a mild and gentle bird, *obu,* which nonetheless possesses the power to destroy a snake. *Onye na nkie, onye na nkie*—literally, "everyone and his own"—is a social expression of the same notion often employed as a convenient formula for saluting *en masse* an assembly too large for individual greetings. 2

In some cultures a person may worship one of the gods or goddesses in the pantheon and pay scant attention to the rest. In Igbo religion such selectiveness is unthinkable. All the people must placate all the gods all the time! For there is a cautionary proverb which states that even when a person has satisfied the deity Udo completely he may yet be killed by Ogwugwu. The degree of peril propounded by this proverb is only dimly apprehended until one realizes that Ogwugwu is not a stranger to Udo but his very consort! 3

It is the striving to come to terms with a multitude of forces and demands which gives Igbo life its tense and restless dynamism and its art an outward, social and kinetic quality. But it would be a mistake to take the extreme view that Igbo art has no room for contemplative privacy. In the first place, all extremism is abhorrent to the Igbo sensibility; but specifically, the Igbo word which is closest to the English word "art" is *nka,* and Igbo people do say: *Onye nakwa nka na-eme ka ona-adu iru,* which means that an artist at work is apt to wear an unfriendly face. In other words, he is excused from the normal demands of sociability! If further proof is required of this need for privacy in the creative process, it is provided clearly and definitively in the ritual seclusion of the makers of *mbari,* to which we shall return shortly. 4

But once made, art emerges from privacy into the public domain. There are no private collections among the Igbo beyond personal ritual objects like the *ikenga.* Indeed, the very concept of collections would be antithetical to the Igbo artistic intention. Collections by their very nature will impose rigid, artistic attitudes and conventions on creativity which the Igbo sensibility goes out of its way to avoid. The purposeful neglect of the painstakingly and devoutly accomplished *mbari* houses 5 with all the art objects in them, as soon as the primary mandate of their creation has been served, provides a significant insight into the Igbo aesthetic value as process rather than product. Process is motion while product is rest. When the product is preserved or venerated, the impulse to repeat the process is compromised. Therefore the Igbo choose to eliminate the product and retain the process so that every occasion and every generation will receive its own impulse and kinesis of creation. Interestingly, this aesthetic disposition receives powerful endorsement from the tropical climate which provides an abundance of materials for making art, such as wood, as well as formidable enemies of stasis, such as humidity and the termite. Visitors to Igboland are often shocked to see that artefacts are rarely accorded any particular value on account of age alone.

In popular contemporary usage the Igbo formulate their view of the 6
world as: "No condition is permanent." In Igbo cosmology even gods could fall out of use; and new forces are liable to appear without warning in the temporal and metaphysical firmament. The practical purpose of art is to channel a spiritual force into an aesthetically satisfying physical form that captures the presumed attributes of that force. It stands to reason, therefore, that new forms must stand ready to be called into being as often as new (threatening) forces appear on the scene. It is like "earthing" an electrical charge to ensure communal safety.

The frequent representation of the alien district officer among tradi- 7
tional *mbari* figures is an excellent example of the mediating role of art between old and new, between accepted norms and extravagant aberrations. Art must interpret all human experience, for anything against which the door is barred can cause trouble. Even if harmony is not achievable in the heterogeneity of human experience, the dangers of an open rupture are greatly lessened by giving to everyone his due in the same forum of social and cultural surveillance. The alien district officer may not, after all, be a greater oddity than a local woman depicted in the act of copulating with a dog, and such powerful aberrations must be accorded tactful artistic welcome-cum-invigilation.

Of all the art forms, the dance and the masquerade would appear to 8
have satisfied the Igbo artistic appetite most completely. If the masquerade were not limited to the male sex alone, one might indeed call it the art form *par excellence* for it subsumes not only the dance but all other forms—sculpture, music, painting, drama, costumery, even architecture, for the Ijele masquerade is indeed a most fabulously extravagant construction.

What makes the dance and the masquerade so satisfying to the Igbo 9
disposition is, I think, their artistic deployment of motion, of agility, which informs the Igbo concept of existence. The masquerade (which is really an elaborated dance) not only moves spectacularly but those who want to enjoy its motion fully must follow its progress up and down the arena. This seemingly minor observation was nonetheless esteemed important enough by the Igbo to be elevated into a proverb of

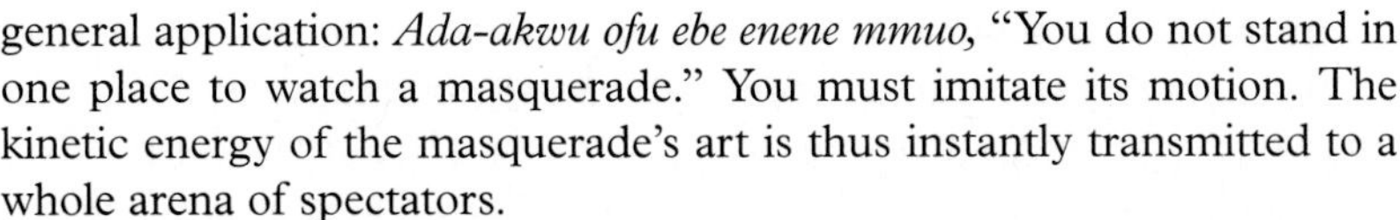

general application: *Ada-akwu ofu ebe enene mmuo,* "You do not stand in one place to watch a masquerade." You must imitate its motion. The kinetic energy of the masquerade's art is thus instantly transmitted to a whole arena of spectators.

So potent is motion stylized into dance that the Igbo have sought to defeat with its power even the final immobility of death by contriving a funeral rite in which the bearers of the corpse perform the *abia* dance with their burden, transforming by their motion the body's imminent commitment to earth into an active rite of passage.

This body, appropriately transfigured, will return on festival or ritu- 11
al occasions or during serious social crises as a masquerade to participate with an enhanced presence and authority in the affairs of the community, speaking an esoteric dialect in which people are referred to as bodies: "The body of so-and-so, I salute you!"

Masquerades are of many kinds, representing the range of human 12
experience—from youth to age; from playfulness to terror; from the delicate beauty of the maiden spirit, *agbogho mmuo,* to the candid ugliness of *njo ka-oya,* "ugliness greater than disease"; from the athleticism of *ogolo* to the legless and armless inertia of *ebu-ebu,* a loquacious masquerade that has to be carried from place to place on the head of its attendant from which position it is wont to shout: Off we go! (*Ije abulu ufia!*); from masquerades that appear at every festival to the awesome ancestors that are enticed to the world by rare crises such as the desecration of a masked spirit; from the vast majority that appear in daytime to the dreaded invisible chorus, *ayaka,* and the night-runner, *ogbazulobodo.*

I hasten to add that the examples given above are merely localized 13
impressionistic illustrations taken from my own experience of growing up in Ogidi in the 1930s and 1940s. There are variations from one village community to the next and certainly from one region of Igboland to another. Nothing here can do justice, for instance, to the extraordinary twin traditions of Odo and Omabe of the Nsukka region. To encounter an Omabe masquerade just descended from the hills for a brief sojourn in the world after an absence of three years, its body of tiny metal discs throwing back the dying lights of dusk, can be a truly breathtaking experience!

The awesomeness of masquerades has suffered in modern times. 14
This is not due, as some imagine, to the explosion of the secret concerning what lies behind the mask. Even in the past the women merely pretended not to know! I remember as a child a masquerade whose name was *Omanu kwue*—meaning, "If you know, speak." This was a dare, of course, and nobody was about to take up the challenge. But this masquerade was of such towering height that there was only one man in the whole of Ogidi, perhaps even in the whole world, who could carry it; the same man, incidentally, whose brief career as a policeman at the beginning of the century had left a powerful enough legend for him to be represented in his uniform in an *mbari* house in faraway Owerri and simply called Ogidi.

In the past, knowing who walked within the mask did not detract 15
from the numinous, dramatic presence of a representative of the ancestors on a brief mission to the living. Disbelief was easily suspended! The decline today is merely a symptom of the collapse of a whole eschatology. But at least in my dreams masquerades have not ceased to bring forth the panic terror of childhood.

COMPREHENSION

1. According to Achebe, the Igbo world and its art are interconnected. What traits do they share? Give examples.
2. In your own words, describe the Igbo religion.
3. Describe what takes place during a masquerade.

RHETORIC

1. What is the main idea of this essay? What strategy does Achebe use to get this idea across?
2. Is Achebe's description of Igbo art concrete or abstract? Does he employ any descriptive language in his essay? Why, or why not?
3. For whom was this essay written? Does Achebe make any assumptions about his reader? Justify your answer with evidence from the essay.
4. In paragraph 11, how does Achebe organize his details?
5. There is a shift in point of view in paragraph 13. How does this shift affect the tone of the essay and its structure?
6. The concepts of change and movement are central to the Igbo world. How does Achebe's use of language and images reflect this? Cite specific vocabulary and images that are especially powerful in conveying the essence of Igbo art.

WRITING

1. Write an essay comparing the Igbo attitude toward art to attitudes in Europe and America. Is the Igbo belief that the process is paramount to the product in accord with American values?
2. Pick an art form of interest to you (painting, music, photography, dance), and describe it in detail, emphasizing how it is representative of a particular culture or lifestyle.
3. White a brief essay imaging what the Igbo people are like, based on the information Achebe offers about their philosophy, religion, and art forms.

JOAN DIDION Joan Didion (1934–) grew up in California and graduated from the University of California at Berkeley in 1956. She began by writing for national magazines such as *Mademoiselle, Saturday Evening Post,* and *Life* and published her first novel, *Run River,* in 1963. Although she has continued to write novels and has written several screenplays, her most acclaimed work is in nonfiction. This work includes *Slouching Towards Bethlehem* (1968), *The White Album* (1979), *Salvador* (1983), *Democracy* (1984), Miami (1987), and *After Henry* (1992). "Georgia O'Keeffe" paints a portrait of a highly irreverent and independent woman who challenged the status quo at a time when "the men" were supposed to dictate artistic style.

JOAN DIDION

Georgia O'Keeffe

"Where I was born and where and how I have lived is unimportant," Georgia O'Keeffe told us in the book of paintings and words published in her ninetieth year on earth. She seemed to be advising us to forget the beautiful face in the Stieglitz photographs. She appeared to be dismissing the rather condescending romance that had attached to her by then, the romance of extreme good looks and advanced age and deliberate isolation. "It is what I have done with where I have been that should be of interest." I recall an August afternoon in Chicago in 1973 when I took my daughter, then seven, to see what Georgia O'Keeffe had done with where she had been. One of the vast O'Keeffe "Sky Above Clouds" canvases floated over the back stairs in the Chicago Art Institute that day, dominating what seemed to be several stories of empty light, and my daughter looked at it once, ran to the landing, and kept on looking. "Who drew it," she whispered after a while. I told her. "I need to talk to her," she said finally. 1

My daughter was making, that day in Chicago, an entirely unconscious but quite basic assumption about people and the work they do. She was assuming that the glory she saw in the work reflected a glory in its maker, that the painting was the painter as the poem is the poet, that every choice one made alone—every word chosen or rejected, every brush stroke laid or not laid down—betrayed one's character. *Style is character.* It seemed to me that afternoon that I had rarely seen so instinctive an application of this familiar principle, and I recall being pleased not only that my daughter responded to style as character but that it was Georgia O'Keeffe's particular style to which she responded: this was a hard woman who had imposed her 192 square feet of clouds on Chicago. 2

"Hardness" has not been in our century a quality much admired in women, nor in the past twenty years has it even been in official favor for men. When hardness surfaces in the very old we tend to transform it into "crustiness" or eccentricity, some tonic pepperiness to be indulged at a distance. On the evidence of her work and what she has said about it, Georgia O'Keeffe is neither "crusty" nor eccentric. She is simply hard, a straight shooter, a woman clean of received wisdom and open to what she sees. This is a woman who could early on dismiss 3 most of her contemporaries as "dreamy," and would later single out one she liked as "a very poor painter." (And then add, apparently by way of softening the judgment: "I guess he wasn't a painter at all. He had no courage and I believe that to create one's own world in any of the arts takes courage.") This is a woman who in 1939 could advise her admirers that they were missing her point, that their appreciation of her famous flowers was merely sentimental. "When I paint a red hill," she observed coolly in the catalogue for an exhibition that year, "you say it is too bad that I don't always paint flowers. A flower touches almost everyone's heart. A red hill doesn't touch everyone's heart." This is a woman who could describe the genesis of one of her most well-known paintings—the "Cow's Skull: Red, White and Blue" owned by the Metropolitan—as an act of quite deliberate and derisive orneriness. "I thought of the city men I had been seeing in the East," she wrote. "They talked so often of writing the Great American Novel—the Great American Play—the Great American Poetry. . . . So as I was painting my cow's head on blue I thought to myself, 'I'll make it an American painting. They will not think it great with the red stripes down the sides—Red, White and Blue—but they will notice it.'"

The city men. The men. They. The words crop up again and again 4
as this astonishingly aggressive woman tells us what was on her mind when she was making her astonishingly aggressive paintings. It was those city men who stood accused of sentimentalizing her flowers: "I made you take time to look at what I saw and when you took time to really notice my flower you hung all your associations with flowers on my flower and you write about my flower as if I think and see what you think and see—and I don't." *And I don't.* Imagine those words spoken, and the sound you hear is *don't tread on me.* "The men" believed it impossible to paint New York, so Georgia O'Keeffe painted New York. "The men" didn't think much of her bright color, so she made it brighter. The men yearned toward Europe so she went to Texas, and then New Mexico. The men talked about Cézanne, "long involved remarks about the 'plastic quality' of his form and color," and took one another's long involved remarks, in the view of this angelic rattlesnake in their midst, altogether too seriously. "I can paint one of those dismal-colored paintings like the men," the woman who regarded herself always as an outsider remembers thinking one day in 1922, and she did: a painting of a shed "all low-toned and dreary with the tree beside the door." She called this act of rancor "The Shanty" and hung it in her next show. "The men seemed to approve of it," she reported fifty-four years later, her contempt undimmed. "They seemed to think that maybe I was beginning to paint. That was my only low-toned dismal-colored painting."

Some women fight and others do not. Like so many successful 5
guerrillas in the war between the sexes, Georgia O'Keeffe seems to have been equipped early with an immutable sense of who she was and a fairly clear understanding that she would be required to prove it. On the surface her upbringing was conventional. She was a child on the

Wisconsin prairie who played with china dolls and painted watercolors with cloudy skies because sunlight was too hard to paint and, with her brother and sisters, listened every night to her mother read stories of the Wild West, of Texas, of Kit Carson and Billy the Kid. She told adults that she wanted to be an artist and was embarrassed when they asked what kind of artist she wanted to be: she had no idea "what kind." She had no idea what artists did. She had never seen a picture that interested her, other than a pen-and-ink Maid of Athens in one of her mother's books, some Mother Goose illustrations printed on cloth, a tablet cover that showed a little girl with pink roses, and the painting of Arabs on horseback that hung in her grandmother's parlor. At thirteen, in a Dominican convent, she was mortified when the sister corrected her drawing. At Chatham Episcopal Institute in Virginia she painted lilacs and sneaked time alone to walk out to where she could see the line of the Blue Ridge Mountains on the horizon. At the Art Institute in Chicago she was shocked by the presence of live models and wanted to abandon anatomy lessons. At the Art Students League in New York one of her fellow students advised her that, since he would be a great painter and she would end up teaching painting in a girls' school, any work of hers was less important than modeling for him. Another painted over her work to show her how the Impressionists did trees. She had not before heard how the Impressionists did trees and she did not much care.

At twenty-four she left all those opinions behind and went for the first time to live in Texas, where there were no trees to paint and no one to tell her how not to paint them. In Texas there was only the horizon she craved. In Texas she had her sister Claudia with her for a while, and in the late afternoons they would walk away from town and toward the horizon and watch the evening star come out. "That evening star fascinated me," she wrote. "It was in some way very exciting to me. My sister had a gun, and as we walked she would throw bottles into the air and shoot as many as she could before they hit the ground. I had nothing but to walk into nowhere and the wide sunset space with the star. Ten watercolors were made from that star." In a way one's interest is compelled as much by the sister Claudia with the gun as by the painter Georgia with the star, but only the painter left us this shining record. Ten watercolors were made from that star. 6

COMPREHENSION

1. Does this essay have an explicit or implied thesis? Explain.
2. What does Didion suggest is O'Keeffe's greatest attribute as an artist? Compare her approach to O'Keeffe to Walker's approach to the artists in her life in the next reading.
3. Didion refers to specific paintings, museums, and artists in the essay. List them. What assumptions is she making about the cultural and educational background of her reading audience?

RHETORIC

1. What is the purpose of the repetition of the word *men* in paragraph 4? Why is the word italicized and quoted?
2. What do Didion's phrases "ninetieth year on earth" (paragraph 1) and "imposed her 192 square feet of clouds" (paragraph 2) suggest about her attitude toward her subject?
3. Didion begins the essay with a quote from the artist. How does this strategy help set the tone of the essay?
4. In paragraph 3, Didion begins three sentences with the words, "This is a woman . . ."; how do they contribute to the unity and rhetorical effect of the paragraph?
5. Why has Didion included detailed biographical material in paragraph 5? Why has she included this information *after* she discusses O'Keeffe's life as a painter? Which of the facts help us understand O'Keeffe's development as "a woman clean of received wisdom and open to what she sees" (paragraph 3)?
6. Why does Didion's conclusion include a commentary about O'Keeffe's sister? Where and for what purpose does Didion make an implied comparison between O'Keeffe's personality and her sister's habit of firing a gun?

WRITING

1. In what way can O'Keeffe's outlook and behavior be considered existential? Write a brief essay on the topic.
2. Select a woman whom you admire, and write an essay describing how her professional life reflects her values, attitude, and character.
3. Consider one of your own pursuits, for example, a hobby, sport, pastime, or interest. Write an essay in which you explain how this activity reflects an aspect of your personality.
4. Examine the theme of "influence" in the essays by Paz, Walker, and Didion.

ALICE WALKER Alice Walker (1944–) was born in Eatonton, Georgia, and now lives in San Francisco and Mendocino County, California. A celebrated poet, short-story writer, and novelist, she is the author of *Revolutionary Petunias and Other Poems, In Love and Trouble: Stories of Black Women,* and *Meridian,* among other works. Her 1983 novel, *The Color Purple,* won the American Book Award and the Pulitzer Prize. The following essay, from *In Search of Our Mothers' Gardens* (1983), offers a highly personalized and perceptive analysis of the importance of influence in both art and life.

ALICE WALKER

Saving the Life That Is Your Own

The Importance of Models in the Artist's Life

There is a letter Vincent Van Gogh wrote to Emile Bernard that is very meaningful to me. A year before he wrote the letter, Van Gogh had had a fight with his domineering friend Gauguin, left his company, and cut off, in desperation and anguish, his own ear. The letter was written in Saint-Remy, in the South of France, from a mental institution to which Van Gogh had voluntarily committed himself. 1

I imagine Van Gogh sitting at a rough desk too small for him, looking out at the lovely Southern light, and occasionally glancing critically next to him at his own paintings of the landscape he loved so much. The date of the letter is December 1889. Van Gogh wrote: 2

> However hateful painting may be, and however cumbersome in the times we are living in, if anyone who has chosen this handicraft pursues it zealously, he is a man of duty, sound and faithful.
>
> Society makes our existence wretchedly difficult at times, hence our impotence and the imperfection of our work.
>
> . . . I myself am suffering under an absolute lack of models.
>
> But on the other hand, there are beautiful spots here. I have just done five size 30 canvasses, olive trees. And the reason I am staying on here is that my health is improving a great deal.
>
> What I am doing is hard, dry, but that is because I am trying to gather new strength by doing some rough work, and I'm afraid abstractions would make me soft.

Six months later, Van Gogh—whose health was "improving a great deal"—committed suicide. He had sold one painting during his lifetime. Three times was his work noticed in the press. But these are just details. 3

The real Vincent Van Gogh is the man who has "just done five size 30 canvasses, olive trees." To me, in context, one of the most moving and revealing descriptions of how a real artist thinks. And the knowledge that when he spoke of "suffering under an absolute lack of models" he spoke of that lack in terms of both the intensity of his commitment and the quality and singularity of his work, which was frequently ridiculed in his day. 4

The absence of models, in literature as in life, to say nothing of painting, is an occupational hazard for the artist, simply because models in 5 art, in behavior, in growth of spirit and intellect—even if rejected—enrich and enlarge one's view of existence. Deadlier still, to the artist who lacks models, is the curse of ridicule, the bringing to bear on an artist's best work, especially his or her most original, most strikingly deviant, only a fund of ignorance and the presumption that, as an artist's critic, one's judgment is free of the restrictions imposed by prejudice, and is well informed, indeed, about all the art in the world that really matters.

What is always needed in the appreciation of art, or life, is the larger perspective. Connections made, or at least attempted, where none existed before, the straining to encompass in one's glance at the varied world the common thread, the unifying theme through immense diversity, a fearlessness of growth, of search, of looking, that enlarges the private and the public world. And yet, in our particular society, it is the narrowed and narrowing view of life that often wins. 6

Recently, I read at a college and was asked by one of the audience what I considered the major difference between the literature written by black and by white Americans. I had not spent a lot of time considering this question, since it is not the difference between them that interests me, but, rather, the way black writers and white writers seem to me to be writing one immense story—the same story, for the most part—with different parts of this immense story coming from a multitude of different perspectives. Until this is generally recognized, literature will always be broken into bits, black and white, and there will always be questions, wanting neat answers, such as this. 7

Still, I answered that I thought, for the most part, white American writers tended to end their books and their characters' lives as if there were no better existence for which to struggle. The gloom of defeat is thick. 8

By comparison, black writers seem always involved in a moral and/or physical struggle, the result of which is expected to be some kind of larger freedom. Perhaps this is because our literary tradition is based on the slave narratives, where escape for the body and freedom for the soul went together, or perhaps this is because black people have never felt themselves guilty of global, cosmic sins. 9

This comparison does not hold up in every case, of course, and perhaps does not really hold up at all. I am not a gatherer of statistics, only a curious reader, and this has been my impression from reading many books by black and white writers. 10

There are, however, two books by American women that illustrate what I am talking about: *The Awakening,* by Kate Chopin, and *Their Eyes Were Watching God,* by Zora Neale Hurston. 11

The plight of Mme Pontellier is quite similar to that of Janie Crawford. Each woman is married to a dull, society-conscious husband and living in a dull, propriety-conscious community. Each woman desires a life of her own and a man who loves her and makes her feel alive. Each woman finds such a man. 12

Mme Pontellier, overcome by the strictures of society and the existence of her children (along with the cowardice of her lover), kills her- 13 self rather than defy the one and abandon the other. Janie Crawford, on the other hand, refuses to allow society to dictate behavior to her, enjoys the love of a much younger, freedom-loving man, and lives to tell others of her experience.

When I mentioned these two books to my audience, I was not surprised to learn that only one person, a young black poet in the first row, had ever heard of *Their Eyes Were Watching God (The Awakening* they had fortunately read in their "Women in Literature" class), primarily because it was written by a black woman, whose experience—in love and life—was apparently assumed to be unimportant to the students (and the teachers) of a predominantly white school.

Certainly, as a student, I was not directed toward this book, which 15
would have urged me more toward freedom and experience than toward comfort and security, but was directed instead toward a plethora of books by mainly white male writers who thought most women worthless if they didn't enjoy bullfighting or hadn't volunteered for the trenches in World War I.

Loving both these books, knowing each to be indispensable to my 16
own growth, my own life, I choose the model, the example, of Janie Crawford. And yet this book, as necessary to me and to other women as air and water, is again out of print.* But I have distilled as much as I could of its wisdom in this poem about its heroine, Janie Crawford:

> I love the way Janie Crawford
> left her husbands
> the one who wanted to change her
> into a mule
> and the other who tried to interest her
> in being a queen.
> A woman, unless she submits,
> is neither a mule
> nor a queen
> though like a mule she may suffer
> and like a queen pace the floor.

It has been said that someone asked Toni Morrison why she writes 17
the kind of books she writes, and that she replied: Because they are the kind of books I want to read.

This remains my favorite reply to that kind of question. As if any- 18
one reading the magnificent, mysterious *Sula* or the grim, poetic *The Bluest Eye* would require more of a reason for their existence than for the brooding, haunting *Wuthering Heights,* for example, or the melancholy, triumphant *Jane Eyre.* (I am not speaking here of the most famous short line of that book, "Reader, I married him," as the triumph, but, rather, of the triumph of Jane Eyre's control over her own sense of morality and her own stout will, which are but reflections of her cre-

*Reissued by the University of Illinois Press, 1979.

ator's, Charlotte Brontë, who no doubt wished to write the sort of books *she* wished to read.)

Flannery O'Connor has written that more and more the serious novelist will write, not what other people want, and certainly not what other people expect, but whatever interests her or him. And that the direction taken, therefore, will be away from sociology, away from the "writing of explanation," of statistics, and further into mystery, into poetry, and into prophecy. I believe this is true, *fortunately true;* especially for "Third World Writers"; Morrison, Marquez, Ahmadi, Camara Laye make good examples. And not only do I believe it is true for serious writers in general, but I believe, as firmly as did O'Connor, that this is our only hope—in a culture so in love with flash, with trendiness, with superficiality, as ours—of acquiring a sense of essence, of timelessness, and of vision. Therefore, to write the books one wants to read is both to point in the direction of vision and, at the same time, to follow it. 19

When Toni Morrison said she writes the kind of books she wants to read, she was acknowledging the fact that in a society in which "accepted literature" is so often sexist and racist and otherwise irrelevant or offensive to so many lives, she must do the work of two. She must be her own model as well as the artist attending, creating, learning from, realizing the model, which is to say, herself. 20

(It should be remembered that, as a black person, one cannot completely identify with a Jane Eyre, or with her creator, no matter how much one admires them. And certainly, if one allows history to impinge on one's reading pleasure, one must cringe at the thought of how Heathcliff, in the New World far from Wuthering Heights, amassed his Cathy-dazzling fortune.) I have often been asked why, in my own life and work, I have felt such a desperate need to know and assimilate the experiences of earlier black women writers, most of them unheard of by you and by me, until quite recently; why I felt a need to study them and to teach them. 21

I don't recall the exact moment I set out to explore the works of black women, mainly those in the past, and certainly, in the beginning, I had no desire to teach them. Teaching being for me, at that time, less rewarding than star-gazing on a frigid night. My discovery of them—most of them out of print, abandoned, discredited, maligned, nearly lost—came about, as many things of value do, almost by accident. As it turned out—and this should not have surprised me—I found I was in need of something that only one of them could provide. 22

Mindful that throughout my four years at a prestigious black and then a prestigious white college I had heard not one word about early black women writers, one of my first tasks was simply to determine whether they had existed. After this, I could breathe easier, with more assurance about the profession I myself had chosen. 23

But the incident that started my search began several years ago: I sat down at my desk one day, in a room of my own, with key and lock, 24 and began preparations for a story about voodoo, a subject that had always fascinated me. Many of the elements of this story I had gathered from a story my mother several times told me. She had gone, during the Depression, into town to apply for some government surplus food at the local commissary, and had been turned down, in a particularly humiliating way, by the white woman in charge.

My mother always told this story with a most curious expression on 25
her face. She automatically raised her head higher than ever—it was always high—and there was a look of righteousness, a kind of holy *heat* coming from her eyes. She said she had lived to see this same white woman grow old and senile and so badly crippled she had to get about on *two* sticks.

To her, this was clearly the working of God, who, as in the old spiri- 26
tual, ". . . may not come when you want him, but he's right on time!" To me, hearing the story for about the fiftieth time, something else was discernible: the possibilities of the story, for fiction.

What, I asked myself, would have happened if, after the crippled 27
old lady died, it was discovered that someone, my mother perhaps (who would have been mortified at the thought, Christian that she is), had voodooed her?

Then, my thoughts sweeping me away into the world of hexes and 28
conjurings of centuries past, I wondered how a larger story could be created out of my mother's story; one that would be true to the magnitude of her humiliation and grief, and to the white woman's lack of sensitivity and compassion.

My third quandary was: How could I find out all I needed to know 29
in order to write a story that used *authentic* black witchcraft?

Which brings me back, almost, to the day I became really interested 30
in black women writers. I say "almost" because one other thing, from my childhood, made the choice of black magic a logical and irresistible one for my story. Aside from my mother's several stories about root doctors she had heard of or known, there was the story I had often heard about my "crazy" Walker aunt.

Many years ago, when my aunt was a meek and obedient girl 31
growing up in a strict, conventionally religious house in the rural South, she had suddenly thrown off her meekness and had run away from home, escorted by a rogue of a man permanently attached elsewhere.

When she was returned home by her father, she was declared 32
quite mad. In the backwoods South at the turn of the century, "madness" of this sort was cured not by psychiatry but by powders and by spells. (One can see Scott Joplin's *Treemonisha* to understand the role voodoo played among black people of that period.) My aunt's madness was treated by the community conjurer, who promised, and delivered, the desired results. His treatment was a bag of white powder, bought for fifty cents, and sprinkled on the ground around her house, with some of it sewed, I believe, into the bodice of her nightgown.

So when I sat down to write my story about voodoo, my crazy Walker aunt was definitely on my mind. 33

But she had experienced her temporary craziness so long ago that her story had all the excitement of a might-have-been. I needed, instead of family memories, some hard facts about the *craft* of voodoo, as practiced by Southern blacks in the nineteenth century. (It never once, fortunately, occurred to me that voodoo was not worthy of the interest I had in it, or was too ridiculous to study seriously.) 34

I began reading all I could find on the subject of "The Negro and His Folkways and Superstitions." There were Botkin and Puckett and others, all white, most racist. How was I to believe anything they wrote, since at least one of them, Puckett, was capable of wondering, in his book, if "The Negro" had a large enough brain? 35

Well, I thought, where are the *black* collectors of folklore? Where is the *black* anthropologist? Where is the *black* person who took the time to travel the back roads of the South and collect the information I need: how to cure heat trouble, treat dropsy, hex somebody to death, lock bowels, cause joints to swell, eyes to fall out, and so on. Where was this black person? 36

And that is when I first saw, in a *footnote* to the white voices of authority, the name Zora Neale Hurston. 37

Folklorist, novelist, anthropologist, serious student of voodoo, also all-around black woman, with guts enough to take a slide rule and measure random black heads in Harlem; not to prove their inferiority, but to prove that whatever their size, shape, or present condition of servitude, those heads contained all the intelligence anyone could use to get through this world. 38

Zora Hurston, who went to Barnard to learn how to study what she really wanted to learn: the ways of her own people, and what ancient rituals, customs, and beliefs had made them unique. 39

Zora, of the sandy-colored hair and the daredevil eyes, a girl who escaped poverty and parental neglect by hard work and a sharp eye for the main chance. 40

Zora, who left the South only to return to look at it again. Who went to root doctors from Florida to Louisiana and said, "Here I am. I want to learn your trade." 41

Zora, who had collected all the black folklore I could ever use. 42

That Zora. 43

And having found *that Zora* (like a golden key to a storehouse of varied treasure), I was hooked. 44

What I had discovered, of course, was a model. A model, who, as it happened, provided more than voodoo for my story, more than one of the greatest novels America had produced—though, being America, it did not realize this. She had provided, as if she knew someday I would come along wandering in the wilderness, a nearly complete record of her life. And though her life sprouted an occasional wart, I am eternally grateful for that life, warts and all. 45

It is not irrelevant, nor is it bragging (except perhaps to gloat a little on the happy relatedness of Zora, my mother and me), to mention here 46

that the story I wrote, called "the Revenge of Hannah Kemhuff," based on my mother's experiences during the Depression, and on Zora Hurston's folklore collection of the 1920s, and on my own response to both out of a contemporary existence, was immediately published and was later selected, by a reputable collector of short stories, as one of the *Best Short Stories of 1974*.

I mention it because this story might never have been written, because the very bases of its structure, authentic black folklore, viewed from a black perspective, might have been lost. 47

Had it been lost, my mother's story would have had no historical underpinning, none I could trust, anyway. I would not have written the story, which I enjoyed writing as much as I've enjoyed writing anything in my life, had I not known that Zora had already done a thorough job of preparing the ground over which I was then moving. 48

In that story I gathered up the historical and psychological threads of the life my ancestors lived, and in the writing of it I felt joy and strength and my own continuity. I had that wonderful feeling writers get sometimes, not very often, of being *with* a great many people, ancient spirits, all very happy to see me consulting and acknowledging them, and eager to let me know, through the joy of their presence, that, indeed, I am not alone. 49

To take Toni Morrison's statement further, if that is possible, in my own work I write not only what I want to read—understanding fully and indelibly that if I don't do it no one else is so vitally interested, or capable of doing it to my satisfaction—I write all the things *I should have been able to read.* Consulting, as belatedly discovered models, those writers—most of whom, not surprisingly, are women—who understood that their experience as ordinary human beings was also valuable, and in danger of being misrepresented, distorted, or lost: 50

Zora Hurston—novelist, essayist, anthropologist, autobiographer;

Jean Toomer—novelist, poet, philosopher, visionary, a man who cared what women felt;

Colette—whose crinkly hair enhances her French, part-black face; novelist, playwright, dancer, essayist, newspaperwoman, lover of women, men, small dogs; fortunate not to have been born in America;

Anaïs Nin—recorder of everything, no matter how minute;

Tillie Olson—a writer of such generosity and honesty, she literally saves lives;

Virginia Woolf—who has saved so many of us.

It is, in the end, the saving of lives that we writers are about. Whether we are "minority" writers or "majority." It is simply in our power to do this. 51

We do it because we care. We care that Vincent Van Gogh mutilated his ear. We care that behind a pile of manure in the yard he destroyed his life. We care that Scott Joplin's music *lives!* We care because we know this: *the life we save is our own.* 52

COMPREHENSION

1. Explain the significance of Walker's title. How does it serve her purpose and guide readers to her thesis? What is her thesis?
2. According to the author, what is the importance of models in art? What is the relationship of models to life? List the models in Walker's life. Which of them stand out?
3. Paraphrase Walker's remarks on the relationship between black American and white American writing.

RHETORIC

1. Walker uses many allusions in this essay. Identify as many as you can. What is the allusion in the title? Comment on the general effectiveness of her allusions.
2. Is the author's style and choice of diction suitable to her subject matter and to her audience? Why, or why not?
3. Why does the author personalize her treatment of the topic? What does she gain? Is there anything lost?
4. Walker employs several unique structuring devices in this essay. Cite at least three, and analyze their utility.
5. Explain Walker's use of examples to reinforce her generalizations and to organize the essay.
6. Which paragraphs constitute Walker's conclusion? What is their effect?

WRITING

1. Discuss the meaning of Walker's remark, "What is always needed in the appreciation of art, or life, is the larger perspective."
2. If you were planning on a career as a writer, artist, actor, or musician, who would your models be, and why?

MARYA MANNES Marya Mannes (1904–1990), wrote several novels and some light verse, but she is best known for her essays, which appeared in *Vogue, McCall's, Harper's,* and *The New Republic.* She collected her essays in *More in Anger* (1958) and in *The New York I Know* (1961). Mannes also wrote on such subjects as suicide and euthanasia in *Last Rights* (1974) and television in *Who Owns the Air?* (1960). In this essay from *But Will It Sell?* (1964), she establishes standards for judging excellence in the arts.

MARYA MANNES

How Do You Know It's Good?

Suppose there were no critics to tell us how to react to a picture, a play, or a new composition of music. Suppose we wandered innocent as the dawn into an art exhibition of unsigned paintings. By what standards, by what values would we decide whether they were good or bad, talented or untalented, successes or failures? How can we ever know that what we think is right? 1

For the last fifteen or twenty years the fashion in criticism or appreciation of the arts has been to deny the existence of any valid criteria and to make the words "good" or "bad" irrelevant, immaterial, and inapplicable. There is no such thing, we are told, as a set of standards, first acquired through experience and knowledge and later imposed on the subject under discussion. This has been a popular approach, for it relieves the critic of the responsibility of judgment and the public of the necessity of knowledge. It pleases those resentful of disciplines, it flatters the empty-minded by calling them open-minded, it comforts the confused. Under the banner of democracy and the kind of equality which our forefathers did *not* mean, it says, in effect, "Who are you to tell us what *is* good or bad?" This is the same cry used so long and so effectively by the producers of mass media who insist that it is the public, not they, who decides what it wants to hear and see, and that for a critic to say that *this* program is bad and *this* program is good is purely a reflection of personal taste. Nobody recently has expressed this philosophy more succinctly than Dr. Frank Stanton, the highly intelligent president of CBS television. At a hearing before the Federal Communications Commission, this phrase escaped him under questioning: "One man's mediocrity is another man's good program." 2

There is no better way of saying "No values are absolute." There is another important aspect to this philosophy of *laissez faire:* It is the fear, in all observers of all forms of art, of guessing wrong. This fear is well come by, for who has not heard of the contemporary outcries against artists who later were called great? Every age has its arbiters who do not grow with their times, who cannot tell evolution from revolution or the difference between frivolous faddism, amateurish experimentation, and profound and necessary change. Who wants to be caught *flagrante delicto* with an error of judgment as serious as this? It is far safer, and certainly easier, to look at a picture or a play or a poem and to say "This is hard to understand, but it may be good," or simply to welcome it as a new form. The word "new"—in our country especially—has magical connotations. What is new must be good; what is old is proba- 3

bly bad. And if a critic can describe the new in language that nobody can understand, he's safer still. If he has mastered the art of saying nothing with exquisite complexity, nobody can quote him later as saying anything.

4 But all these, I maintain, are forms of abdication from the responsibility of judgment. In creating, the artist commits himself; in appreciating, you have a commitment of your own. For after all, it is the audience which makes the arts. A climate of appreciation is essential to its flowering, and the higher the expectations of the public, the better the performance of the artist. Conversely, only a public ill-served by its critics could have accepted as art and as literature so much in these last years that has been neither. If anything goes, everything goes; and at the bottom of the junkpile lie the discarded standards too.

5 But what are these standards? How do you get them? How do you know they're the right ones? How can you make a clear pattern out of so many intangibles, including that greatest one, the very private I?

6 Well for one thing, it's fairly obvious that the more you read and see and hear, the more equipped you'll be to practice that art of association which is at the basis of all understanding and judgment. The more you live and the more you look, the more aware you are of a consistent pattern—as universal as the stars, as the tides, as breathing, as night and day—underlying everything. I would call this pattern and this rhythm an order. Not order—*an* order. Within it exists an incredible diversity of forms. Without it lies chaos—the wild cells of destruction—sickness. It is in the end up to you to distinguish between the diversity that is health and the chaos that is sickness, and you can't do this without a process of association that can link a bar of Mozart with the corner of a Vermeer painting, or a Stravinsky score with a Picasso abstraction; or that can relate an aggressive act with a Franz Kline painting and a fit of coughing with a John Cage composition.

7 There is no accident in the fact that certain expressions of art live for all time and that others die with the moment, and although you may not always define the reasons, you can ask the questions. What does an artist say that is timeless; how does he say it? How much is fashion, how much is merely reflection? Why is Sir Walter Scott so hard to read now, and Jane Austen not? Why is baroque right for one age and too effulgent for another?

8 Can a standard of craftsmanship apply to art of all ages, or does each have its own, and different, definitions? You may have been aware, inadvertently, that craftsmanship has become a dirty word these years because, again, it implies standards—something done well or done badly. The result of this convenient avoidance is a plentitude of actors who can't project their voices, singers who can't phrase their songs, poets who can't communicate emotion, and writers who have no vocabulary—not to speak of painters who can't draw. The dogma now is that craftsmanship gets in the way of expression. You can do better if you don't know *how* you do it, let alone *what* you're doing.

9 I think it is time you helped reverse this trend by trying to rediscov-

er craft: the command of the chosen instrument, whether it is a brush, a word, or a voice. When you begin to detect the difference between freedom and sloppiness, between serious experimentation and egotherapy, between skill and slickness, between strength and violence, you are on your way to separating the sheep from the goats, a form of segregation denied us for quite a while. All you need to restore it is a small bundle of standards and a Geiger counter that detects fraud, and we might begin our tour of the arts in an area where both are urgently needed: contemporary painting.

I don't know what's worse: to have to look at acres of bad art to find 10
the little good, or to read what the critics say about it all. In no other field of expression has so much double-talk flourished, so much confusion prevailed, and so much nonsense been circulated: further evidence of the close interdependence between the arts and the critical climate they inhabit. It will be my pleasure to share with you some of this double-talk so typical of our times.

Item one: preface for a catalogue of an abstract painter: 11

"Time-bound meditation experiencing a life; sincere with plastic 12
piety at the threshold of hallowed arcana; a striving for pure ideation giving shape to inner drive; formalized patterns where neural balances reach a fiction." End of quote. Know what this artist paints like now?

Item two: a review in the *Art News:* 13

". . . a weird and disparate assortment of material, but the mon- 14
strosity which bloomed into his most recent cancer of aggregations is present in some form everywhere. . . ." Then, later, "A gluttony of things and processes terminated by a glorious constipation."

Item three, same magazine, review of an artist who welds automo- 15
bile fragments into abstract shapes:

"Each fragment . . . is made an extreme of human exasperation, 16
torn at and fought all the way, and has its rightness of form as if by accident. *Any technique that requires order or discipline would just be the human ego.* No, these must be egoless, uncontrolled, undesigned and different enough to give you a bang—fifty miles an hour around a telephone pole. . . ."

"Any technique that requires order or discipline would just be the 17
human ego." What does he mean—"just be"? What are they really talking about? Is this journalism? Is it criticism? Or is it that other convenient abdication from standards of performance and judgment practiced by so many artists and critics that they, like certain writers who deal only in sickness and depravity, "reflect the chaos about them"? Again, whose chaos? Whose depravity?

I had always thought that the prime function of art was to create 18
order *out* of chaos—again, not the order of neatness or rigidity or convention or artifice, but the order of clarity by which one will and one vision could draw the essential truth out of apparent confusion. I still do. It is not enough to use parts of a car to convey the brutality of the machine. This is as slavishly representative, and just as easy, as arranging dried flowers under glass to convey nature.

Speaking of which, i.e., the use of real materials (burlap, old gloves, bottletops) in lieu of pigment, this is what one critic had to say about an exhibition of Assemblage at the Museum of Modern Art last year: 19

> Spotted throughout the show are indisputable works of art, accounting for a quarter or even a half of the total display. But the remainder are works of non-art, anti-art, and art substitutes that are the aesthetic counterparts of the social deficiencies that land people in the clink on charges of vagrancy. These aesthetic bankrupts . . . have no legitimate ideological roof over their heads and not the price of a square intellectual meal, much less a spiritual sandwich, in their pockets.

I quote these words of John Canaday of *The New York Times* as an example of the kind of criticism which puts responsibility to an intelligent public above popularity with an intellectual coterie. Canaday has the courage to say what he thinks and the capacity to say it clearly: two qualities notably absent from his profession. 20

Next to art, I would say that appreciation and evaluation in the field of music is the most difficult. For it is rarely possible to judge a new composition at one hearing only. What seems confusing or fragmented at first might well become clear and organic a third time. Or it might not. The only salvation here for the listener is, again, an instinct born of experience and association which allows him to separate intent from accident, design from experimentation, and pretense from conviction. Much of contemporary music is, like its sister art, merely a reflection of the composer's own fragmentation: an absorption in self and symbols at the expense of communication with others. The artist, in short, says to the public: If you don't understand this, it's because you're dumb. I maintain that you are not. You may have to go part way or even halfway to meet the artist, but if you must go the whole way, it's his fault, not yours. Hold fast to that. And remember it too when you read new poetry, that estranged sister of music. 21

> A multitude of causes, unknown to former times, are now acting with a combined force to blunt the discriminating powers of the mind, and, unfitting it for all voluntary exertion, to reduce it to a state of almost savage torpor. The most effective of these causes are the great national events which are daily taking place and the increasing accumulation of men in cities, where the uniformity of their occupations produces a craving for extraordinary incident, which the rapid communication of intelligence hourly gratifies. To this tendency of life and manners, the literature and theatrical exhibitions of the country have conformed themselves. 22

This startlingly applicable comment was written in the year 1800 by William Wordsworth in the preface to his "Lyrical Ballads"; and it has been cited by Edwin Muir in his recently published book "The Estate of Poetry." Muir states that poetry's effective range and influence have diminished alarmingly in the modern world. He believes in the inherent 23 and indestructible qualities of the human mind and the great and permanent objects that act upon it, and suggests that the audience will increase when "poetry loses what obscurity is left in it by attempting greater themes, for great themes have to be stated clearly." If you keep that firmly in mind and resist, in Muir's words, "the vast dissemination of secondary objects that isolate us from the natural world," you have gone a long way toward equipping yourself for the examination of any work of art.

When you come to theatre, in this extremely hasty tour of the arts, you can approach it on two different levels. You can bring to it anticipation and innocence, giving yourself up, as it were, to the life on the stage and reacting to it emotionally, if the play is good, or listlessly, if the play is boring; a part of the audience organism that expresses its favor by silence or laughter and its disfavor by coughing and rustling. Or you can bring to it certain critical faculties that may heighten, rather than diminish, your enjoyment. 24

You can ask yourselves whether the actors are truly in their parts or merely projecting themselves; whether the scenery helps or hurts the mood; whether the playwright is honest with himself, his characters, and you. Somewhere along the line you can learn to distinguish between the true creative art and the false arbitrary gesture; between fresh observation and stale cliché; between the avant-garde play that is pretentious drivel and the avant-garde play that finds new ways to say old truths. 25

Purpose and craftsmanship—end and means—these are the keys to your judgment in all the arts. What is this painter trying to say when he slashes a broad band of black across a white canvas and lets the edges dribble down? Is it a statement of violence? Is it a self-portrait? If it is *one* of these, has he made you believe it? Or is this a gesture of the ego or a form of therapy? If it shocks you, what does it shock you into? 26

And what of this tight little painting of bright flowers in a vase? Is the painter saying anything new about flowers? Is it different from a million other canvases of flowers? Has it any life, any meaning, beyond its statement? Is there any pleasure in its forms or texture? The question is not whether a thing is abstract or representational, whether it is "modern" or conventional. The question, inexorably, is whether it is good. And this is a decision which only you, on the basis of instinct, experience, and association, can make for yourself. It takes independence and courage. It involves, moreover, the risk of wrong decision and the humility, after the passage of time, of recognizing it as such. As we grow and change and learn, our attitudes can change too, and what we once thought obscure or "difficult" can later emerge as coherent and illuminating. Entrenched prejudices, obdurate opinions are as sterile as no opinions at all. 27

Yet standards there are, timeless as the universe itself. And when you have committed yourself to them, you have acquired a passport to that elusive but immutable realm of truth. Keep it with you in the forests of bewilderment. And never be afraid to speak up. 28

COMPREHENSION

1. What is the author's thesis? Where does she state it most emphatically?
2. What examples does Mannes provide of the "abdication from the responsibility of judgment" (paragraph 4)?
3. Explain Mannes's criteria, or standards, for judging excellence in the arts.

RHETORIC

1. Account for the author's use of the pronoun *you* in addressing her audience. How does it affect tone, notably at the end of the essay?
2. Explain Mannes's strategy of formulating questions, starting with the title and moving consistently through the essay to the conclusion.
3. Where does the author's introduction end? Analyze the material presented in the introduction and the rhetorical strategies involved. What paragraphs constitute the conclusion of the essay? Describe the nature of the conclusion.
4. Explain the function of paragraphs 5 to 9.
5. How does Mannes employ illustration to structure paragraphs 10 to 25? Analyze the main stages in the organization of this section.
6. Explain the author's use of process and causal analysis in the essay.

WRITING

1. Mannes maintains that standards are absolutely necessary in distinguishing good from bad work in the arts. Do you agree or disagree with her premise? Why? What standards do you employ in determining whether an artistic product is good or bad?
2. Write your own essay entitled "How Do You Know It's Good?" Focus on some aspect of music, art, literature, or film that you know well.
3. Evaluate one literary, artistic, or media work, making clear the standards you are applying.
4. Analyze the various models—personal, cultural, and artistic—in your own life.
5. Explore the types of literature, art, film, and music that you like. How do these varieties of art influence your life?

CLASSIC AND CONTEMPORARY

SAMUEL JOHNSON Dr. Samuel Johnson (1709–1784) was born in England, the early victim of illness and poverty. He entered Oxford University in 1728 but was forced to withdraw for lack of funds. In 1737, he came to London and began writing essays, poems, and biographies for *Gentleman's Magazine*. He achieved increasing fame through his writings, in particular with the publication of his *Dictionary of the English Language* in 1755. For this work he received the honorary degree from Oxford that became part of his name. Johnson continued to write, publishing *Rasselas* (1759)—a moral romance—and a collection of essays called *The Idler* (1761). He befriended the Scottish lawyer James Boswell, who eventually wrote and published a famous biography of Johnson. Johnson's last work was *Lives of the Poets* (1783), a criticism of British authors of the preceding 200 years. Although the following essay from a 1759 issue of *The Idler* is over 230 years old, Johnson's insights and observations apply as well to the world of advertising today.

DR. SAMUEL JOHNSON

On the Art of Advertising

The practice of appending to the narratives of public transactions more minute and domestic intelligence, and filling the newspapers with advertisements, has grown up by slow degrees to its present state. 1

Genius is shown only by invention. The man who first took advantage of the general curiosity that was excited by a siege or battle, to betray the readers of news into the knowledge of the shop where the best puffs and powder were to be sold, was undoubtedly a man of great sagacity and profound skill in the nature of man. But when he had once shown the way, it was easy to follow him; and every man now knows a ready method of informing the public of all that he desires to buy or sell, whether his wares be material or intellectual; whether he makes clothes, or teaches the mathematics; whether he be a tutor that wants a pupil, or a pupil that wants a tutor. 2

Whatever is common is despised. Advertisements are now so numerous that they are very negligently perused, and it is therefore become necessary to gain attention by magnificence of promises, and by eloquence sometimes sublime and sometimes pathetic. 3

Promise, large promise, is the soul of an advertisement. I remember a *wash-ball* that had a quality truly wonderful—it gave *an exquisite edge to the razor.* And there are now to be sold, *for ready money only,* some *duvets for bed-coverings of down, beyond comparison, superior to what is* 4

called otter-down, and indeed such, that its *many excellences cannot be here set forth.* With one excellence we are made acquainted—*it is warmer than four or five blankets, and lighter than one.*

There are some, however, that know the prejudice of mankind 5
in favour of modest sincerity. The vender of the *beautifying fluid* sells a lotion that repels pimples, washes away freckles, smooths the skin, and plumps the flesh, and yet, with a generous abhorrence of ostentation, confesses that it will not *restore the bloom of fifteen to a lady of fifty.*

The true pathos of advertisements must have sunk deep into the 6
heart of every man that remembers the zeal shown by the seller of the *anodyne necklace,* for the ease and safety of *poor teething infants,* and the affection with which he warned every mother that *she would never forgive herself* if her infant should perish without a necklace.

I cannot but remark to the celebrated author who gave, in his notifi- 7
cations of the camel and dromedary, so many specimens of the genuine sublime, that there is now arrived another subject yet more worthy of his pen. *A famous Mohawk Indian warrior, who took Dieskaw, the French General prisoner, dressed in the same manner with the native Indians when they go to war, with his face and body painted, with his scalping-knife, tom-axe, and all other implements of war! a sight worthy the curiosity of every true Briton!* This is a very powerful description; but a critic of great refinement would say that it conveys rather *horror* than *terror.* An Indian, dressed as he goes to war, may bring company together; but if he carries the scalping-knife and tom-axe, there are many true Britons that will never be persuaded to see him but through a grate.

It has been remarked by the severer judges that the salutary sorrow 8
of tragic scenes is too soon effaced by the merriment of the epilogue; the same inconvenience arises from the improper disposition of advertisements. The noblest objects may be so associated as to be made ridiculous. The camel and dromedary themselves might have lost much of their dignity between *the true flour of mustard* and the *original Daffy's elixir;* and I could not but feel some indignation when I found this illustrious Indian warrior immediately succeeded by a *fresh parcel of Dublin butter.*

The trade of advertising is now so near to perfection, that it is not 9
easy to propose any improvement. But as every art ought to be exercised in due subordination to the public good, I cannot but propose it as a moral question to these masters of the public ear, whether they do not sometimes play too wantonly with our passions, as when the registrar of lottery tickets invites us to his shop by an account of the prizes which he sold last year; and whether the advertising controvertists do not indulge asperity of language without any adequate provocation; as in the dispute about *straps for razors,* now happily subsided, and in the altercation which at present subsists concerning *eau de luce?*

In an advertisement it is allowed to every man to speak well of him- 10
self, but I know not why he should assume the privilege of censuring his neighbour. He may proclaim his own virtue or skill, but ought not to exclude others from the same pretensions.

Every man that advertises his own excellence should write with some consciousness of a character which dares to call the attention of the public. He should remember that his name is to stand in the same paper with those of the King of Prussia and the Emperor of Germany, and endeavour to make himself worthy of such association. 11

Some regard is likewise to be paid to posterity. There are men of diligence and curiosity who treasure up the papers of the day merely because others neglect them, and in time they will be scarce. When these collections shall be read in another century, how will numberless contradictions be reconciled; and how shall fame be possibly distributed among the tailors and bodice-makers of the present age? 12

Surely these things deserve consideration. It is enough for me to have hinted my desire that these abuses may be rectified; but such is the state of nature, that what all have the right of doing, many will attempt without sufficient care or due qualifications. 13

COMPREHENSION

1. Is Johnson using irony in his title by calling advertising an "art"? What does he mean by this? What other examples of irony occur in the essay?
2. What is Johnson's main concern about the influence of advertising? Where in the essay does he enunciate this concern?
3. What is the author's main purpose? Where does he state it?

RHETORIC

1. Study the following sentence from paragraph 2. What aspects of its vocabulary, syntax, or tone "date" the writing style? "But when he had once shown the way, it was easy to follow him; and every man now knows a ready method of informing the public of all that he desires to buy or sell, whether his wares be material or intellectual; whether he makes clothes, or teaches the mathematics; whether he be a tutor that wants a pupil, or a pupil that wants a tutor."
2. How do the following words contribute to the diction of the essay: *sagacity, magnificence, pathos, sublime,* and *altercation.*
3. What seems to be Johnson's tone? What is his particular attitude toward the "art of advertising"? Cite examples to support your view.
4. How does Johnson's introduction prepare you for his essay? Why does it conceal his point of view on the subject?
5. In paragraph 13, Johnson refers to the "abuses" of advertising. What are these abuses? Where in the essay does he begin to enumerate them?
6. What is the function of using italics for many of the words and phrases?

WRITING

1. How apt are Johnson's criticisms of advertising today? Are they any less or more valid than they were in Johnson's time?

2. Select several print advertisements from newspapers and magazines. Write an essay discussing the various techniques the advertiser uses in his or her attempt to persuade the reader.

DAVE BARRY Dave Barry (1947–) was born in Armonk, New York. He graduated from Haverford College in 1969 and was a reporter and editor at the *Daily Local News* from 1971 to 1975. Since 1983, he has been a columnist for *The Miami Herald.* Besides writing his columns, Barry has written numerous books, all with his unique, amusing point of view. His books include *Stay Fit and Healthy until You're Dead* (1985), *Dave Barry's Greatest Hits* (1988), *Dave Barry Turns 40* (1990), and *Dave Barry's Only Travel Guide You'll Ever Need* (1991). Barry won the 1988 Pulitzer Prize for commentary. In the piece below, he comments on the relation between television commercials and patriotism.

DAVE BARRY

Red, White, and Beer

Lately I've been feeling very patriotic, especially during commercials. 1
Like, when I see those strongly pro-American Chrysler commercials, the ones where the winner of the Bruce Springsteen Sound-Alike Contest sings about how The Pride Is Back, the ones where Lee Iacocca himself comes striding out and practically challenges the president of Toyota to a knife fight, I get this warm, proud feeling inside, the same kind of feeling I get whenever we hold routine naval maneuvers off the coast of Libya.

But if you want to talk about *real* patriotism, of course, you have to 2
talk about beer commercials. I would have to say that Miller is the most patriotic brand of beer. I grant you it tastes like rat saliva, but we are not talking about taste here. What we are talking about, according to the commercials, is that Miller is by God an *American* beer, "born and brewed in the U.S.A.," and the men who drink it are American men, the kind of men who aren't afraid to perspire freely and shake a man's hand. That's mainly what happens in Miller commercials: Burly American men go around, drenched in perspiration, shaking each other's hands in a violent and patriotic fashion.

You never find out exactly why these men spend so much time 3
shaking hands. Maybe shaking hands is just their simple straightforward burly masculine American patriotic way of saying to each other: "Floyd, I am truly sorry I drank all that Miller beer last night and went to the bathroom in your glove compartment." Another possible explanation is that, since there are never any women in the part of America where beer commercials are made, the burly men have become lonesome and desperate for any form of physical contact. I have noticed that sometimes, in addition to shaking hands, they hug each other.

Maybe very late at night, after the David Letterman show, there are Miller commercials in which the burly men engage in slow dancing. I don't know.

4 I do know that in one beer commercial, I think this is for Miller—although it could be for Budweiser, which is also a very patriotic beer—the burly men build a house. You see them all getting together and pushing up a brand-new wall. Me, I worry some about a house built by men drinking beer. In my experience, you run into trouble when you ask a group of beer-drinking men to perform any task more complex than remembering not to light the filter ends of cigarettes.

5 For example, in my younger days, whenever anybody in my circle of friends wanted to move, he'd get the rest of us to help, and, as an inducement, he'd buy a couple of cases of beer. This almost always produced unfortunate results, such as the time we were trying to move Dick "The Wretch" Curry from a horrible fourth-floor walk-up apartment in Manhattan's Lower East Side to another horrible fourth-floor walk-up apartment in Manhattan's Lower East Side, and we hit upon the labor-saving concept of, instead of carrying The Wretch's possessions manually down the stairs, simply dropping them out the window, down onto the street, where The Wretch was racing around, gathering up the broken pieces of his life and shrieking at us to stop helping him move, his emotions reaching a fever pitch when his bed, which had been swinging wildly from a rope, entered the apartment two floors below his through what had until seconds earlier been a window.

6 This is the kind of thinking you get, with beer. So I figure what happens, in the beer commercial where the burly men are building the house, is they push the wall up so it's vertical, and then, after the camera stops filming them, they just keep pushing, and the wall crashes down on the other side, possibly onto somebody's pickup truck. And then they all shake hands.

7 But other than that, I'm in favor of the upsurge in retail patriotism, which is lucky for me because the airwaves are saturated with pro-American commercials. Especially popular are commercials in which the newly restored Statue of Liberty—and by the way, I say Lee Iacocca should get some kind of medal for that, or at least be elected president—appears to be endorsing various products, as if she were Mary Lou Retton or somebody. I saw one commercial strongly suggesting that the Statue of Liberty uses Sure brand underarm deodorant.

8 I have yet to see a patriotic laxative commercial, but I imagine it's only a matter of time. They'll show some actors dressed up as hard-working country folk, maybe at a church picnic, smiling at each other and eating pieces of pie. At least one of them will be a black person. The Statue of Liberty will appear in the background. Then you'll hear a country-style singer singing:

> Folks 'round here they love this land;
> They stand by their beliefs;
> An' when they git themselves stopped up;
> They want some quick relief.

Well, what do you think? Pretty good commercial concept, huh? 9

Nah, you're right. They'd never try to pull something like that. 10
They'd put the statue in the *foreground.*

COMPREHENSION

1. What does Barry mean by "retail patriotism"? How does the essay's title illustrate this concept?
2. According to Barry, what makes beer commercials, especially those for Miller, patriotic?
3. In Barry's opinion, what do sexism, patriotism, and beer have in common?

RHETORIC

1. Barry doesn't explicitly state his thesis anywhere in the essay. In your own words, what is his implied thesis? Use evidence from the essay to support your view.
2. Barry uses irony and humor very effectively in this piece. Cite some examples of his humor, and analyze how he achieves the desired effect.
3. The writer uses specific brand names in his essay. How does this device help to strengthen his argument? Would eliminating them make the essay less persuasive? Why, or why not?
4. Barry seems to digress from his point in paragraphs 4, 5, and 6. Why does he do this? How does this digression serve the purpose of the piece?
5. Does the anecdote Barry uses in paragraph 5 ring true? Why, or why not? What purpose does it serve in the essay? Does its plausibleness affect the strength of Barry's argument?
6. How does paragraph 10 function as a conclusion? Is it in keeping with the essay's tone and style? Is it an effective device? Justify your response.

WRITING

1. Barry's essay examines how television sells patriotism. Write an essay analyzing how television sells other abstract ideas, such as success, love, freedom, democracy. Pattern your essay after Barry's, using humor. Also, use specific television commercials you have seen as examples.
2. Write an essay entitled "Patriotism," using both denotative and connotative definitions of the word.
3. In an essay, examine the impact that television advertising has had on American consumers and its repercussions.

CLASSIC AND CONTEMPORARY: QUESTIONS FOR COMPARISON

1. Explain how Barry and Johnson use humor and irony in their essays to express their opinions. Use concrete examples from their writing, and discuss why humor is particularly effective for the particular topic.
2. According to Johnson, "Promise, large promise, is the soul of an advertisement." In an essay, discuss why this statement is valid, using evidence from the work of Johnson and Barry. Do the printed ads of Johnson's day promise the same things as beer commercials today? What are these promises? Are they ever kept? Use support from your own observations.
3. Compare the language used in both essays. How do they reflect the times in which the essays were written as well as the kind of audience the writers are addressing? Has the language of advertising changed much since Johnson's day? Which essay do you find more effective? Is there any correlation between the medium being discussed and the language used in the essay? Consider these questions in an essay, and use support from both writers.

CONNECTIONS

1. Write an essay comparing and contrasting poetry and novel writing. What merits does each form have? Are there any limitations in either form? Which do you find more satisfying to read? Which form is more accessible? Use the essays of Lawrence and Plath to illustrate or support your thesis.
2. According to Achebe's essay, Igbo art represents "a dynamic world of movement and of flux." How would Lawrence respond to this energetic art form and the Igbo philosophy of life in general? Use quotes from both writers to explore this question.
3. In their essays, Paz and Didion draw sketches of other artists. How do they approach their subjects? What strategies do they use? Are their goals similar?
4. Write an essay exploring the importance of role models in art and literature, especially for women and minorities. Use the writing of Didion and Walker to address this issue.
5. Compare Paz's essay on Whitman to Didion's essay on O'Keeffe in terms of their subjects' connection to America. In what ways is O'Keefe as representative of America as Whitman? Use support from the writers.
6. Use any writer in this section to address Mannes's question, "How do you know it's good?" For example, judging from her essay, how do you think Didion knows O'Keeffe's work is good?
7. Examine the role of the artist in society and the artist's purpose or duty to humanity or to himself or herself. How would any of the writers in this section address this issue?

CHAPTER TEN

Philosophy and Ethics

You do not have to be an academician in an ivory tower to think about values and the destiny of humankind or about questions of right and wrong. All of us possess beliefs about human nature and conduct, about standards of behavior and moral duty. In fact, as Robert Coles argues in an essay appearing in this chapter, even children make ethical choices every day and are attuned to the "moral currents and issues in the larger society."

Most of us have a system of ethical beliefs, a philosophy of sorts, although it may not be a fully logical and systematic philosophy. This system of beliefs and values is transmitted to us by family members, friends, educators, religious figures, and representatives of social groups. Such a philosophical system is not unyielding or unchanging because our typical conflicts and the choices that we make often force us to test our ethical assumptions and our values. For example, you may believe in nonviolence, but what would you do if someone threatened physical harm to you or a loved one? Or you may support the death penalty but encounter an essay—perhaps Coretta Scott King's—that causes you to reassess your position. Our beliefs about nonviolence, capital punishment, abortion, cheating, equality, and so on are often paradoxical and place us in a universe of ethical dilemmas.

Your ability to resolve such dilemmas and make complex ethical decisions depends on your storehouse of knowledge and experience and on how well formulated your philosophy or system of belief is. When you know what is truly important in your life, you can make choices and decisions carefully and responsibly. Yet as Plato observes in his classic "The Allegory of the Cave," the idea of what is truly good and correct never appears without wisdom and effort.

At the end of this section, Virginia Woolf and Annie Dillard contemplate a seemingly insignificant creature—a moth—that tells them (and us) a great deal about life and death. They seek the "essence" of existence in the moth's struggle. We, too, engage in a life struggle; and the values and ideas that we develop during our brief moment on this planet are what lend meaning and vitality to our lives.

Previewing the Chapter

As you read the essays in this chapter and respond to them in discussion and writing, consider the following questions:

- On what ethical problem or conflict does the author focus?
- Is the author's view of life optimistic or pessimistic? Why?
- Do you agree or disagree with the philosophical perspective that the author adopts?
- Is there a clear solution to the issue the author investigates?
- Does the author present rational arguments or engage in emotional appeals and weak reasoning?
- Does the author approach ethical and philosophical issues in an objective or in a subjective way?
- How significant is the ethical or philosophical subject addressed by the author?
- What social, political, or racial issues are raised by the author?
- Are there religious dimensions to the essay? If so, how does religion reinforce the author's philosophical inquiry?
- How do these essays encourage you to examine your own attitudes and values? In reading them, what do you discover about your own system of beliefs and the beliefs of society at large?

CORETTA SCOTT KING Coretta Scott King (1927–) is a civil-rights activist, free-lance journalist, and, since 1980, writer and commentator for CNN. Born in Alabama, she graduated from Antioch College and the New England Conservatory of Music. She first gained international prominence as the wife of Martin Luther King Jr., whom she married in 1953. She wrote about her experiences with the revered civil-rights leader and orator in a book entitled *My Life with Martin Luther King, Jr.* (1969). The following essay states in clear, thoughtful prose her feelings about the death penalty, which she considers both racist and immoral.

CORETTA SCOTT KING

The Death Penalty Is a Step Back

When Steven Judy was executed in Indiana [in 1981] America took another step backwards towards legitimizing murder as a way of dealing with evil in our society. 1

Although Judy was convicted of four of the most horrible and brutal murders imaginable, and his case is probably the worst in recent memory for opponents of the death penalty, we still have to face the real issue squarely: Can we expect a decent society if the state is allowed to kill its own people? 2

In recent years, an increase of violence in America, both individual and political, has prompted a backlash of public opinion on capital punishment. But however much we abhor violence, legally sanctioned executions are no deterrent and are, in fact, immoral and unconstitutional. 3

Although I have suffered the loss of two family members by assassination, I remain firmly and unequivocally opposed to the death penalty for those convicted of capital offenses. 4

An evil deed is not redeemed by an evil deed of retaliation. Justice is never advanced in the taking of a human life. 5

Morality is never upheld by legalized murder. Morality apart, there are a number of practical reasons which form a powerful argument against capital punishment. 6

First, capital punishment makes irrevocable any possible miscarriage of justice. Time and again we have witnessed the specter of mistakenly convicted people being put to death in the name of American criminal justice. To those who say that, after all, this doesn't occur too often, I can only reply that if it happens just once, that is too often. And it has occurred many times. 7

Second, the death penalty reflects an unwarranted assumption that the wrongdoer is beyond rehabilitation. Perhaps some individuals can- 8

not be rehabilitated; but who shall make that determination? Is any amount of academic training sufficient to entitle one person to judge another incapable of rehabilitation?

Third, the death penalty is inequitable. Approximately half of the 711 persons now on death row are black. From 1930 through 1968, 53.5% of those executed were black Americans, all too many of whom were represented by court-appointed attorneys and convicted after hasty trials. 9

The argument that this may be an accurate reflection of guilt, and homicide trends, instead of a racist application of laws lacks credibility in light of a recent Florida survey which showed that persons convicted of killing whites were four times more likely to receive a death sentence than those convicted of killing blacks. 10

Proponents of capital punishment often cite a "deterrent effect" as the main benefit of the death penalty. Not only is there no hard evidence that murdering murderers will deter other potential killers, but even the "logic" of this argument defies comprehension. 11

Numerous studies show that the majority of homicides committed in this country are the acts of the victim's relatives, friends and acquaintances in the "heat of passion." 12

What this strongly suggests is that rational consideration of future consequences are seldom a part of the killer's attitude at the time he commits a crime. 13

The only way to break the chain of violent reaction is to practice nonviolence as individuals and collectively through our laws and institutions. 14

COMPREHENSION

1. On what grounds does King oppose capital punishment?
2. King calls the death penalty "immoral" and "unconstitutional." What does she mean by this?
3. Does King offer any solutions to the problem of crime and violence? What are they?

RHETORIC

1. Where in the essay does King place her thesis statement? In your own words, what is this thesis?
2. What function do paragraphs 1 to 5 have in the essay?
3. What impact do the words *practical* and *powerful* (in paragraph 6) have on the reader? Who is King's intended audience?
4. Comment on the use of language in King's essay. Is it concrete or abstract? How would you characterize her writing style?
5. Trace King's use of transitions in paragraphs 7, 8, and 9.
6. Where does the writer use refutation in her essay? How does she use it to strengthen her argument? How effective are her responses?
7. Is King's ordering of ideas inductive or deductive? Justify your answer.

WRITING

1. Write an essay for or against capital punishment, using quotes from King's essay either as support or as refutation. Provide examples and your own observations as proof.
2. If capital punishment doesn't deter crime, what will? Write an essay in which you offer detailed solutions to the problem of crime and violence. How can society take a step forward in its treatment of criminals?
3. King's essay makes a connection between the death penalty and racism. Develop this theme in an essay. Consider the issues of class, race, legal representation, and political empowerment in determining who goes to prison and who gets executed.

ROBERT COLES Robert Coles (1929–), author and psychologist, won the Pulitzer Prize in general nonfiction for volumes 1 and 2 of *Children of Crisis,* in which he examines with compassion and intelligence the effects of the controversy over integration on children in the South. Walker Percy has praised Coles because he "spends his time listening to people and trying to understand them." In its final form, *Children of Crisis* has five volumes, and Coles has widened its focus to include the children of the wealthy and the poor, the exploited and the exploiters. In collaboration with Jane Coles, he completed *Women of Crisis II* (1980). Below, Coles demonstrates his capacity to listen to and to understand children.

ROBERT COLES

I Listen to My Parents and I Wonder What They Believe

Not so long ago children were looked upon in a sentimental fashion as "angels," or as "innocents." Today, thanks to Freud and his followers, boys and girls are understood to have complicated inner lives; to feel love, hate, envy and rivalry in various and subtle mixtures; to be eager participants in the sexual and emotional politics of the home, neighborhood and school. Yet some of us parents still cling to the notion of childhood innocence in another way. We do not see that our children also make ethical decisions every day in their own lives, or realize how attuned they may be to moral currents and issues in the larger society. 1

In Appalachia I heard a girl of eight whose father owns coal fields (and gas stations, a department store and much timberland) wonder about "life" one day: "I'll be walking to the school bus, and I'll ask myself why there's some who are poor and their daddies can't find a job, and there's some who are lucky like me. Last month there was an ex- 2 plosion in a mine my daddy owns, and everyone became upset. Two miners got killed. My daddy said it was their own fault, because they'll be working and they get careless. When my mother asked if there was anything wrong with the safety down in the mine, he told her no and she shouldn't ask questions like that. Then the Government people came and they said it was the owner's fault—Daddy's. But he has a lawyer and the lawyer is fighting the Government and the union. In school, kids ask me what I think, and I sure do feel sorry for the two miners and so does my mother—I know that. She told me it's just not a fair world and you have to remember that. Of course, there's no one who can be sure there won't be trouble; like my daddy says, the rain falls on the just and the unjust. My brother is only six and he asked Daddy awhile back who are the 'just' and the 'unjust,' and Daddy said there are people who work hard and they live good lives, and there are lazy people and they're always trying to sponge off others. But I guess you have to feel sorry for anyone who has a lot of trouble, because it's poured-down, heavy rain."

Listening, one begins to realize that an elementary-school child is no stranger to moral reflection—and to ethical conflict. This girl was torn between her loyalty to her particular background, its values and assumptions, and to a larger affiliation—her membership in the nation, the world. As a human being whose parents were kind and decent to her, she was inclined to be thoughtful and sensitive with respect to others, no matter what their work or position in society. But her father was among other things a mineowner, and she had already learned to shape her concerns to suit that fact of life. The result: a moral oscillation of sorts, first toward nameless others all over the world and then toward her own family. As the girl put it later, when she was a year older: "You should try to have 'good thoughts' about everyone, the minister says, and our teacher says that too. But you should honor your father and mother most of all; that's why you should find out what they think and then sort of copy them. But sometimes you're not sure if you're on the right track." 3

Sort of copy them. There could be worse descriptions of how children acquire moral values. In fact, the girl understood how girls and boys all over the world "sort of" develop attitudes of what is right and wrong, ideas of who the just and the unjust are. And they also struggle hard and long, and not always with success, to find out where the "right track" starts and ends. Children need encouragement or assistance as they wage that struggle. 4

In home after home that I have visited, and in many classrooms, I have met children who not only are growing emotionally and intellectually but also are trying to make sense of the world morally. That is to say, they are asking themselves and others about issues of fair play, justice, liberty, equality. Those last words are abstractions, of course—the stuff of college term papers. And there are, one has to repeat, those in psychology and psychiatry who would deny elementary-school children access to that "higher level" of moral reflection. But any parent who 5 has listened closely to his or her child knows that girls and boys are capable of wondering about matters of morality, and knows too that often it is their grown-up protectors (parents, relatives, teachers, neighbors) who are made uncomfortable by the so-called "innocent" nature of the questions children may ask or the statements they may make. Often enough the issue is not the moral capacity of children but the default of us parents who fail to respond to inquiries put to us by our daughters and sons—and fail to set moral standards for both ourselves and our children.

Do's and don't's are, of course, pressed upon many of our girls and boys. But a moral education is something more than a series of rules handed down, and in our time one cannot assume that every parent feels able—sure enough of her own or his own actual beliefs and values—to make even an initial explanatory and disciplinary effect toward a moral education. Furthermore, for many of us parents these days it is a child's emotional life that preoccupies us. 6

In 1963, when I was studying school desegregation in the South, I had extended conversations with Black and white elementary-school children caught up in a dramatic moment of historical change. For longer than I care to remember, I concentrated on possible psychiatric troubles, on how a given child was managing under circumstances of extreme stress, on how I could be of help—with "support," with reassurance, with a helpful psychological observation or interpretation. In many instances I was off the mark. These children weren't "patients"; they weren't even complaining. They were worried, all right, and often enough they had things to say that were substantive—that had to do not so much with troubled emotions as with questions of right and wrong in the real-life dramas taking place in their worlds. 7

Here is a nine-year-old white boy, the son of ardent segregationists, telling me about his sense of what desegregation meant to Louisiana in the 1960s: "They told us it wouldn't happen—never. My daddy said none of us white people would go into schools with the colored. But then it did happen, and when I went to school the first day I didn't know what would go on. Would the school stay open or would it close up? We didn't know what to do; the teacher kept telling us that we should be good and obey the law, but my daddy said the law was wrong. Then my mother said she wanted me in school even if there were some colored kids there. She said if we all stayed home she'd be a 'nervous wreck.' So I went. 8

"After a while I saw that the colored weren't so bad. I saw that there are different kinds of colored people, just like with us whites. There was one of the colored who was nice, a boy who smiled, and he played real good. There was another one, a boy, who wouldn't talk with anyone. I don't know if it's right that we all be in the same school. Maybe it isn't right. My sister is starting school next year, and she says she doesn't care if there's 'mixing of the races.' She says they told her in Sunday school that everyone is a child of God, and then a kid asked if that goes for the colored too and the teacher said yes, she thought so. My daddy 9 said that it's true, God made everyone—but that doesn't mean we all have to be living together under the same roof in the home or the school. But my mother said we'll never know what God wants of us but we have to try to read His mind, and that's why we pray. So when I say my prayers I ask God to tell me what's the right thing to do. In school I try to say hello to the colored, because they're kids, and you can't be mean or you'll be 'doing wrong,' like my grandmother says."

Children aren't usually long-winded in the moral discussions they 10
have with one another or with adults, and in quoting this boy I have pulled together comments he made to me in the course of several days. But everything he said was of interest to me. I was interested in the boy's changing racial attitudes. It was clear he was trying to find a coherent, sensible moral position too. It was also borne in on me that if one spends days, weeks in a given home, it is hard to escape a particular moral climate just as significant as the psychological one.

In many homes parents establish moral assumptions, mandates, pri- 11
orities. They teach children what to believe in, what not to believe in. They teach children what is permissible or not permissible—and why. They may summon up the Bible, the flag, history, novels, aphorisms, philosophical or political sayings, personal memories—all in an effort to teach children how to behave, what and whom to respect and for which reasons. Or they may neglect to do so, and in so doing teach their children *that*—a moral abdication, of sorts—and in this way fail their children. Children need and long for words of moral advice, instruction, warning, as much as they need words of affirmation or criticism from their parents about other matters. They must learn how to dress and what to wear, how to eat and what to eat; and they must also learn how to behave under X or Y or Z conditions, and why.

All the time, in 20 years of working with poor children and rich 12
children, Black children and white children, children from rural areas and urban areas and in every region of this country, I have heard questions—thoroughly intelligent and discerning questions—about social and historical matters, about personal behavior, and so on. But most striking is the fact that almost all those questions, in one way or another, are moral in nature: Why did the Pilgrims leave England? Why didn't they just stay and agree to do what the king wanted them to do? . . . Should you try to share all you've got or should you save a lot for yourself? . . . What do you do when you see others fighting—do you try to break up the fight, do you stand by and watch or do you leave as fast as you can? . . . Is it right that some people haven't got enough to eat? . . . I see other kids cheating and I wish I could copy the answers too; but I won't cheat, though sometimes I feel I'd like to and I get all mixed up. I go home and talk with my parents, and I ask them what should you do if you see kids cheating—pay no attention, or report the kids or do the same thing they are doing?

Those are examples of children's concerns—and surely millions of 13
American parents have heard versions of them. Have the various "experts" on childhood stressed strongly enough the importance of such

questions—and the importance of the hunger we all have, no matter what our age or background, to examine what we believe in, are willing to stand up for, and what we are determined to ask, likewise, of our children?

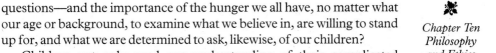

Children not only need our understanding of their complicated emotional lives; they also need a constant regard for the moral issues that come their way as soon as they are old enough to play with others and take part in the politics of the nursery, the back yard and the schoolroom. They need to be told what they must do and what they must not do. They need control over themselves and a sense of what others are entitled to from them—cooperation, thoughtfulness, an attentive ear and eye. They need discipline not only to tame their excesses of emotion but discipline also connected to stated and clarified moral values. They need, in other words, something to believe in that is larger than their own appetites and urges and, yes, bigger than their "psychological drives." They need a larger view of the world, a moral context, as it were—a faith that addresses itself to the meaning of this life we all live and, soon enough, let go of.

15 Yes, it is time for us parents to begin to look more closely at what ideas our children have about the world; and it would be well to do so before they become teenagers and young adults and begin to remind us, as often happens, of how little attention we did pay to their moral development. Perhaps a nine-year-old girl from a well-off suburban home in Texas put it better than anyone else I've met:

> I listen to my parents, and I wonder what they believe in more than anything else. I asked my mom and my daddy once: What's the thing that means most to you? They said they didn't know but I shouldn't worry my head too hard with questions like that. So I asked my best friend, and she said she wonders if there's a God and how do you know Him and what does He want you to do—I mean, when you're in school or out playing with your friends. They talk about God in church, but is it only in church that He's there and keeping an eye on you? I saw a kid steal in a store, and I know her father has a lot of money—because I hear my daddy talk. But stealing's wrong. My mother said she's a 'sick girl,' but it's still wrong what she did. Don't you think?

16 There was more—much more—in the course of the months I came to know that child and her parents and their neighbors. But those observations and questions—a "mere child's"—reminded me unforgettably of the aching hunger for firm ethical principles that so many of us feel. Ought we not begin thinking about this need? Ought we not all be asking ourselves more intently what standards we live by—and how we can satisfy our children's hunger for moral values?

COMPREHENSION

1. How does the author's title capture the substance of his essay? What is his thesis?

2. According to Coles, why do parents have difficulty explaining ethics to their children? On what aspects of their children's development do they tend to concentrate? Why?
3. There is an implied contrast between mothers' and fathers' attitudes toward morality in Coles's essay. Explain this contrast, and cite examples for your explanation.

RHETORIC

1. What point of view does Coles use here? How does that viewpoint affect the tone of the essay?
2. Compare Coles's sentence structure with the sentence structure of the children he quotes. How do they differ?
3. Does this essay present an inductive or a deductive argument? Give evidence for your answer.
4. How does paragraph 13 differ from paragraphs 3, 10, and 17? How do all four paragraphs contribute to the development of the essay?
5. Explain the line of reasoning in the first paragraph. Why does Coles allude to Freud? How is that allusion related to the final sentence of the paragraph?
6. What paragraphs constitute the conclusion of the essay? Why? How do they summarize Coles's argument?

WRITING

1. Coles asserts the need for clear ethical values. How have your parents provided such values? What kind of values will you give your children?
2. Write an essay describing conflict between your parents' ethical views and your own.
3. Gather evidence, from conversations with your friends and relatives about an ethical issue such as poverty, world starvation, abortion, or capital punishment. Incorporate their opinions in your essay through direct and indirect quotation.
4. Compare Coles's observations in this essay with those of Hayakawa in "Words and Children" (Chapter 8).

PLATO Plato (427?–347 B.C.), pupil and friend of Socrates, was one of the greatest philosophers of the ancient world. Plato's surviving works are all dialogues and epistles, many of the dialogues purporting to be conversations of Socrates and his disciples. Two key aspects of his philosophy are the dialectical method—represented by the questioning and probing of the particular event to reveal the general truth—and the existence of Forms. Plato's best-known works include the *Phaedo, Symposium, Phaedrus,* and *Timaeus.* The following selection, from the *Republic,* is an early description of the nature of Forms.

PLATO

The Allegory of the Cave

1 And now, I said, let me show in a figure how far our nature is enlightened or unenlightened: Behold! human beings living in an underground den, which has a mouth open towards the light and reaching all along the den; here they have been from their childhood, and have their legs and necks chained so that they cannot move, and can only see before them, being prevented by the chains from turning round their heads. Above and behind them a fire is blazing at a distance, and between the fire and the prisoners there is a raised way; and you will see, if you look, a low wall built along the way, like the screen which marionette players have in front of them, over which they show the puppets.

2 I see.

3 And do you see, I said, men passing along the wall carrying all sorts of vessels, and statues and figures of animals made of wood and stone and various materials, which appear over the wall? Some of them are talking, others silent.

4 You have shown me a strange image, and they are strange prisoners.

5 Like ourselves, I replied; and they see only their own shadows, or the shadows of one another, which the fire throws on the opposite wall of the cave?

6 True, he said; how could they see anything but the shadows if they were never allowed to move their heads?

7 And of the objects which are being carried in like manner they would only see the shadows?

8 Yes, he said.

9 And if they were able to converse with one another, would they not suppose that they were naming what was actually before them?

10 Very true.

11 And suppose further that the prison had an echo which came from the other side, would they not be sure to fancy when one of the passers-by spoke that the voice which they heard came from the passing shadow?

12 No question, he replied.

13 To them, I said, the truth would be literally nothing but the shadows of the images.

14 That is certain.

15 And now look again, and see what will naturally follow if the prisoners are released and disabused of their error. At first, when any of them is liberated and compelled suddenly to stand up and turn his neck round and walk and look towards the light, he will suffer sharp pains; the glare will distress him and he will be unable to see the realities of

which in his former state he had seen the shadows; and then conceive
some one saying to him, that what he saw before was an illusion, but
that now, when he is approaching nearer to being and his eye is turned
towards more real existence, he has a clearer vision—what will be his
reply? And you may further imagine that his instructor is pointing to
the objects as they pass and requiring him to name them—will he not
be perplexed? Will he not fancy that the shadows which he formerly
saw are truer than the objects which are now shown to him?

Far truer. 16

And if he is compelled to look straight at the light, will he not have a 17
pain in his eyes which will make him turn away to take refuge in the objects of vision which he can see, and which he will conceive to be in reality clearer than the things which are now being shown to him?

True, he said. 18

And suppose once more, that he is reluctantly dragged up a steep 19
and rugged ascent, and held fast until he is forced into the presence of
the sun himself, is he not likely to be pained and irritated? When he approaches the light his eyes will be dazzled and he will not be able to see
anything at all of what are now called realities.

Not all in a moment, he said. 20

He will require to grow accustomed to the sight of the upper world. 21
And first he will see the shadows best, next the reflections of men and
other objects in the water, and then the objects themselves; then he will
gaze upon the light of the moon and the stars and the spangled heaven;
and he will see the sky and the stars by night better than the sun or the
light of the sun by day?

Certainly. 22

Last of all he will be able to see the sun, and not mere reflections of 23
him in the water, but he will see him in his own proper place, and not
in another; and he will contemplate him as he is.

Certainly. 24

He will then proceed to argue that this is he who gives the season 25
and the years, and is the guardian of all that is in the visible world, and
in a certain way the cause of all things which he and his fellows have
been accustomed to behold?

Clearly, he said, he would first see the sun and then reason about 26
him.

And when he remembered his old habitation, and the wisdom of the 27
den and his fellow-prisoners, do you not suppose that he would felici-
tate himself on the change, and pity them?

Certainly, he would. 28

And if they were in the habit of conferring honors among them- 29
selves on those who were quickest to observe the passing shadows
and to remark which of them went before, and which followed after,
and which were together; and who were therefore best able to draw
conclusions as to the future, do you think that he would care for
such honors and glories, or envy the possesors of them? Would he
not say with Homer, Better to be the poor servant of a poor master,

and to endure anything, rather than think as they do and live after their manner?

Yes, he said, I think that he would rather suffer anything than entertain these false notions and live in this miserable manner.

Imagine once more, I said, such as one coming suddenly out of the sun to be replaced in his old situation; would he not be certain to have his eyes full of darkness? 31

To be sure, he said. 32

And if there were a contest, and he had to compete in measuring the shadows with the prisoners who had never moved out of the den, while his sight was still weak, and before his eyes had become steady (and the time which would be needed to acquire this new habit of sight might be very considerable) would he not be ridiculous? Men would say of him that up he went and down he came without his eyes; and that it was better not even to think of ascending; and if any one tried to loose another and lead him up to the light, let them only catch the offender, and they would put him to death. 33

No question, he said. 34

This entire allegory, I said, you may now append, dear Glaucon, to the previous argument; the prison-house is the world of sight, the light of fire is the sun, and you will not misapprehend me if you interpret the journey upwards to be the ascent of the soul into the intellectual world according to my poor belief, which, at your desire, I have expressed—whether rightly or wrongly God knows. But, whether true or false, my opinion is that in the world of knowledge the idea of good appears last of all, and is seen only with an effort; and, when seen, is also inferred to be the universal author of all things beautiful and right, parent of light and of the lord of light in this visible world, and the immediate source of reason and truth in the intellectual; and that this is the power upon which he who would act rationally either in public or private life must have his eye fixed. 35

I agree, he said, as far as I am able to understand you. 36

Moreover, I said, you must not wonder that those who attain to this beautiful vision are unwilling to descend to human affairs; for their souls are ever hastening into the upper world where they desire to dwell; which desire of their is very natural, if our allegory may be trusted. 37

Yes, very natural. 38

And is there anything surprising in one who passes from divine contemplations to the evil state of man, misbehaving himself in a ridiculous manner; if, while his eyes are blinking and before he has become accustomed to the surrounding darkness, he is compelled to fight in courts of law, or in other places, about the images or the shadows of images of justice, and is endeavouring to meet the conceptions of those who have never yet seen absolute justice? 39

Anything but surprising, he replied. 40

Any one who has common sense will remember that the bewilderments of the eyes are of two kinds, and arise from two causes, either 41

from coming out of the light or from going into the light, which is true of the mind's eye, quite as much as of the bodily eye; and he who remembers this when he sees any one whose vision is perplexed and weak, will not be too ready to laugh; he will first ask whether that soul of man has come out of the brighter life, and is unable to see because unaccustomed to the dark, or having turned from darkness to the day is dazzled by excess of light. And he will count the one happy in his condition and state of being, and he will pity the other; or, if he have a mind to laugh at the soul which comes from below into the light, there will be more reason in this than in the laugh which greets him who returns from above out of the light into the den.

That, he said, is a very just distinction. 42

COMPREHENSION

1. What does Plato hope to convey to readers of his allegory?
2. According to Plato, do human beings typically perceive reality? To what does he compare the world?
3. According to Plato, what often happens to people who develop a true idea of reality? How well do they compete with others? Who is usually considered superior? Why?

RHETORIC

1. Is the conversation portrayed here realistic? How effective is this conversational style at conveying information?
2. How do you interpret such details of this allegory as the chains, the cave, and the fire? What connotations do such symbols have?
3. How does Plato use conversation to develop his argument? What is Glaucon's role in the conversation?
4. Note examples of transition words that mark contrasts between the real and the shadow world. How does Plato use contrast to develop his idea of the true real world?
5. Plato uses syllogistic reasoning to derive human behavior from his allegory. Trace his line of reasoning, noting transitional devices and the development of ideas in paragraphs 5 to 14. Find and describe a similar line of reasoning.
6. In what paragraph does Plato explain his allegory? Why do you think he locates his explanation where he does?

WRITING

1. Are Plato's ideas still influencing contemporary society? How do his ideas affect our evaluation of materialism, sensuality, sex, and love?
2. Write an allegory based upon a sport, business, or space flight to explain how we act in the world.
3. Imagine an encounter with Plato. Report briefly on your conversation.

JOSEPH WOOD KRUTCH Joseph Wood Krutch (1893–1970), American journalist, naturalist, and literary critic, is best known for *The Desert Year* (1952) and *The Modern Temper* (1929). The following essay, first published in 1960, reflects Krutch's concern for the contemporary condition. In it, he argues against an immoral society and criticizes what he terms "the paradox of our age."

JOSEPH WOOD KRUTCH

The New Immorality

The provost of one of our largest and most honored institutions told me not long ago that a questionnaire was distributed to his undergraduates and that 40 percent refused to acknowledge that they believed cheating on examinations to be reprehensible. 1

Recently a report for a New York newspaper stopped six people on the street and asked them if they would consent to take part in a rigged television quiz for money. He reported that five of the six said yes. Yet most of these five, like most of the college cheaters, would probably profess a strong social consciousness. They may cheat, but they vote for foreign aid and for enlightened social measures. 2

These two examples exhibit a paradox of our age. It is often said, and my observation leads me to believe it true, that our seemingly great growth in social morality has oddly enough taken place in a world where private morality—a sense of the supreme importance of purely personal honor, honesty, and integrity—seems to be declining. Beneficent and benevolent social institutions are administered by men who all too frequently turn out to be accepting "gifts." The world of popular entertainment is rocked by scandals. College students, put on their honor, cheat on examinations. Candidates for the Ph.D. hire ghost writers to prepare their theses. 3

But, one may object, haven't all these things always been true? Is there really any evidence that personal dishonesty is more prevalent than it always was? 4

I have no way of making a historical measurement. Perhaps these things are not actually more prevalent. What I do know is that there is an increasing tendency to accept and take for granted such personal dishonesty. The bureaucrat and disk jockey say, "Well, yes, I took presents, but I assure you that I made just decisions anyway." The college student caught cheating does not even blush. He shrugs his shoulders and comments: "Everybody does it, and besides, I can't see that it really hurts anybody." 5

Jonathan Swift once said: "I have never been surprised to find men wicked, but I have often been surprised to find them not ashamed." It 6 is my conviction that though men may be no more wicked than they always have been, they seem less likely to be ashamed. If anybody does it, it must be right. Honest, moral, decent mean only what is usual. This is not really a wicked world, because morality means mores or manners and usual conduct is the only standard.

The second part of the defense, "it really doesn't hurt anybody," is equally revealing. "It doesn't hurt anybody" means it doesn't do that abstraction called society any harm. The harm it did the bribe-taker and the cheater isn't important; it is purely personal. And personal as opposed to social decency doesn't count for much. Sometimes I am inclined to blame sociology for part of this paradox. Sociology has tended to lay exclusive stress upon social morality, and tended too often to define good and evil as merely the "socially useful" or its reverse. 7

What social morality and social conscience leave out is the narrower but very significant concept of honor—as opposed to what is sometimes called merely "socially desirable conduct." The man of honor is not content to ask merely whether this or that will hurt society, or whether it is what most people would permit themselves to do. He asks, and he asks first of all, would it hurt him and his self-respect? Would it dishonor him personally? 8

It was a favorite and no doubt sound argument among early twentieth-century reformers that "playing the game" as the gentleman was supposed to play it was not enough to make a decent society. They were right: it is not enough. But the time has come to add that it is indeed inevitable that the so-called social conscience unsupported by the concept of personal honor will create a corrupt society. But suppose that it doesn't? Suppose that no one except the individual suffers from the fact that he sees nothing wrong in doing what everybody else does? Even so, I still insist that for the individual himself nothing is more important than this personal, interior sense of right and wrong and his determination to follow that rather than to be guided by what everybody does or merely the criterion of "social usefulness." It is impossible for me to imagine a good society composed of men without honor. 9

We hear it said frequently that what present-day men most desire is security. If that is so, then they have a wrong notion of what the real, the ultimate, security is. No one who is dependent on anything outside himself, upon money, power, fame, or whatnot, is or ever can be secure. Only he who possesses himself and is content with himself is actually secure. Too much is being said about the importance of adjustment and "participation in the group." Even cooperation, to give this thing its most favorable designation, is no more important than the ability to stand alone when the choice must be made between the sacrifice of one's own integrity and adjustment to or participation in group activity. 10

No matter how bad the world may become, no matter how much the mass man of the future may lose such of the virtues as he still has, one fact remains. If one person alone refuses to go along with him, if one person alone asserts his individual and inner right to believe in 11 and be loyal to what his fellow men seem to have given up, then at least he will still remain what is perhaps the most important part of humanity.

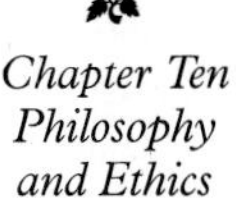

COMPREHENSION

1. How do you know that Krutch is writing for a general audience rather than a specialized one?
2. According to Krutch, what is the paradox of our age? What is unique about this paradox in terms of history?
3. What are the standard defenses and assumptions concerning the new immorality? How does Krutch respond to them?

RHETORIC

1. Krutch employs highly connotative language in this essay. What are some of these words? How does the author both control and exploit connotative language in advancing his analysis and argument?
2. Why is the allusion to Jonathan Swift especially appropriate?
3. Explain the patterns of development in paragraphs 1 to 4, 5 to 7, and 8 to 11.
4. Does Krutch present an inductive or a deductive argument in this essay? Explain your answer by reference to the text.
5. In what ways do causal analysis and extended definition enter into the development of the essay?
6. Analyze the last paragraph of the essay and evaluate its effectiveness.

WRITING

1. Do you accept Krutch's premise that a good society depends on people of honor? Why, or why not? Cite examples to support your contention.
2. Write an analytical essay on cheating on your campus. Is it a problem or not?
3. Argue for or against the proposition that personal morality in the United States is declining.

THOMAS SOWELL Thomas Sowell (1930–) is an economist, teacher, and father involved in issues of civil liberties, human rights, culture, and ethnicity. Born in North Carolina, he was educated at Harvard, Columbia, and the University of Chicago. He has contributed to many publications, including *Administrative Science Quarterly, Journal of Economic Issues,* and *Western Review.* He also published *Preferential Politics: An International Perspective* (1990). In the following thought-provoking piece, from *Newsweek,* September 7, 1981, he reexamines the definition of *equality* and its bearing on American justice.

THOMAS SOWELL

We're Not Really Equal

As a teacher I have learned from sad experience that nothing so bores students as being asked to define their terms systematically before discussing some exciting issue. They want to get on with it, without wasting time on petty verbal distinctions. 1

Much of our politics is conducted in the same spirit. We are for "equality" or "the environment," or against an "arms race," and there is no time to waste on definitions and other Mickey Mouse stuff. This attitude may be all right for those for whom political crusades are a matter of personal excitement, like rooting for your favorite team and jeering the opposition. But for those who are serious about the consequences of public policy, nothing can be built without a solid foundation. 2

"Equality" is one of the great undefined terms underlying much current controversy and antagonism. This one confused word might even become the rock on which our civilization is wrecked. It should be worth defining. 3

Equality is such an easily understood concept in mathematics that we may not realize it is a bottomless pit of complexities anywhere else. That is because in mathematics we have eliminated the concreteness and complexities of real things. When we say that two plus two equals four, we either don't say two *what* or we say the same what after each number. But if we said that two apples plus two apples equals four oranges, we would be in trouble. 4

Sense

Yet that is what we are saying in our political reasoning. And we are in trouble. Nothing is more concrete or complex than a human being. Beethoven could not play center field like Willie Mays, and Willie never tried to write a symphony. In what sense are they equal—or unequal? The common mathematical symbol for inequality points to the smaller quantity. But which is the smaller quantity—and in whose eyes—when such completely different things are involved? 5

When women have children and men don't, how can they be either equal or unequal? Our passionate desire to reduce things to the simplicity of abstract concepts does not mean that it can be done. Those who want to cheer their team and boo the visitors may like to think that the issue is equality versus inequality. But the real issue is whether or not we are going to talk sense. Those who believe in inequality have the 6 same confusion as those who believe in equality. The French make better champagne than the Japanese, but the Japanese make better cameras than the French. What sense does it make to add champagne to cameras to a thousand other things and come up with a grand total showing who is "superior"?

When we speak of "equal justice under law," we simply mean applying the same rules to everybody. That has nothing whatsoever to do with whether everyone performs equally. A good umpire calls balls and strikes by the same rules for everyone, but one batter may get twice as many hits as another. 7

In recent years we have increasingly heard it argued that if outcomes are unequal, then the rules must have been applied unequally. It would destroy my last illusion to discover that Willie Mays didn't really play baseball any better than anybody else, but that the umpires and sportswriters just conspired to make it look that way. Pending the uncovering of intricate plots of this magnitude, we must accept the fact that performances are very unequal in different aspects of life. And there is no way to add up these apples, oranges, and grapes to get one sum total of fruit. 8

Anyone with the slightest familiarity with history knows that rules have often been applied very unequally to different groups. (A few are ignorant or misguided enough to think that this is a peculiarity of American society.) The problem is not in seeing that unequal rules can lead to unequal outcomes. The problem is in trying to reason backward from unequal outcomes to unequal rules as the sole or main cause. 9

There are innumerable places around the world where those who have been the victims of unequal rules have nevertheless vastly outperformed those who are favored. Almost nowhere in Southeast Asia have the Chinese minority had equal rights with the native peoples, but the average Chinese income in these countries has almost invariably been much higher than that of the general population. A very similar story could be told from the history of the Jews in many countries of Europe, North Africa, and the Middle East. To a greater or lesser extent, this has also been the history of the Ibos in Nigeria, the Italians in Argentina, the Armenians in Turkey, the Japanese in the United States—and on and on. 10

Confused Terms

It would be very convenient if we could infer discriminatory rules whenever we found unequal outcomes. But life does not always accommodate itself to our convenience. 11

Those who are determined to find villains but cannot find evidence often resort to "society" as the cause of all our troubles. What do they mean by "society" or "environment"? They act as if these terms were self-evident. But environment and society are just new confused terms introduced to save the old confused term, equality. 12

The American environment or society cannot explain historical behavior patterns found among German-Americans if these same patterns can be found among Germans in Brazil, Australia, Ireland, and elsewhere around the world. These patterns may be explained by the history of German society. But if the words "environment" or "society" refer to things that may go back a thousand years, we are no longer talking about either the causal or the moral responsibility of American society. If historic causes include such things as the peculiar geography of Africa or of southern Italy, then we are no longer talking about human responsibility at all. 13

This does not mean that there are no problems. There are very serious social problems. But that means that serious attention will be required to solve them—beginning with defining our terms. 14

COMPREHENSION

1. In Sowell's opinion, what is problematic about defining *equality*?
2. What does Sowell mean by "historic behavior patterns"?
3. Discuss the role of performance in Sowell's definition of *equality*.

RHETORIC

1. How does the introductory paragraph help establish Sowell's tone and point of view? How does it prepare the reader for the argument that follows?
2. Sowell uses examples liberally throughout his piece. Where are they most effective? How do they clarify the writer's points?
3. Comment on the logic of Sowell's reasoning in paragraph 9. What device does he employ to support his argument?
4. Examine the accumulation of examples in paragraph 10. How do they serve to support Sowell's topic sentence? What is the point of the paragraph?
5. What rhetorical strategies does Sowell employ? In what way is it a definition essay? Does Sowell actually define his terms?
6. How effective is Sowell's conclusion? Does it give the essay closure? Why, or why not?

WRITING

1. In an essay, argue that in order for humanity to survive, certain terms must be defined and these definitions accepted however faulty they may be. Is it ever possible to achieve total agreement on language and meaning? Argue that the common interpretation of the word *equality* is sufficient.
2. Using Sowell's essay as a guide, write an essay defining *justice, honesty, morality, evil,* or some other abstract term. Consider the connotation of the term you're using and Sowell's possible responses to your definition.

3. In paragraph 9, Sowell seems to dismiss the fact that "rules have often been applied very unequally to different groups." Explore this issue in an essay focusing on a specific group thus affected. What impact does defining terms accurately or inaccurately have on this group in terms of the "equality" meted out in it?

JOAN DIDION Joan Didion (1934–) grew up in California and graduated from the University of California at Berkeley in 1956. She began writing for national magazines such as *Mademoiselle,* the *Saturday Evening Post,* and *Life* and published her first novel, *Run River,* in 1963. Although she has continued to write novels and has written several screenplays, her most acclaimed work is in nonfiction. This work includes *Slouching Towards Bethlehem* (1968), *The White Album* (1979), *Salvador* (1983), *Democracy* (1984), *Miami* (1987), and *After Henry* (1992). In "On Morality," (1965), Didion finds the issue of morality arising in strange circumstances, and she comes to a personal conclusion on the topic that is at odds with conventional wisdom.

JOAN DIDION

On Morality

As it happens I am in Death Valley, in a room at the Enterprise Motel and Trailer Park, and it is July, and it is hot. In fact it is 119°. I cannot seem to make the air conditioner work, but there is a small refrigerator, and I can wrap ice cubes in a towel and hold them against the small of my back. With the help of the ice cubes I have been trying to think, because *The American Scholar* asked me to, in some abstract way about "morality," a word I distrust more every day, but my mind veers inflexibly toward the particular. 1

Here are some particulars. At midnight last night, on the road in from Las Vegas to Death Valley Junction, a car hit a shoulder and turned over. The driver, very young and apparently drunk, was killed instantly. His girl was found alive but bleeding internally, deep in shock. I talked this afternoon to the nurse who had driven the girl to the nearest doctor, 185 miles across the floor of the Valley and three ranges of lethal mountain road. The nurse explained that her husband, a talc miner, had stayed on the highway with the boy's body until the coroner could get over the mountains from Bishop, at dawn today. "You can't just leave a body on the highway," she said. "It's immoral." 2

It was one instance in which I did not distrust the word, because she meant something quite specific. She meant that if a body is left alone for even a few minutes on the desert, the coyotes close in and eat the flesh. Whether or not a corpse is torn apart by coyotes may seem only a 3 sentimental consideration, but of course it is more: one of the promises we make to one another is that we will try to retrieve our casualties, try not to abandon our dead to the coyotes. If we have been taught to keep our promises—if, in the simplest terms, our upbringing is good enough—we stay with the body, or have bad dreams.

4 I am talking, of course, about the kind of social code that is sometimes called, usually pejoratively, "wagon-train morality." In fact that is precisely what it is. For better or worse, we are what we learned as children: my own childhood was illuminated by graphic litanies of the grief awaiting those who failed in their loyalties to each other. The Donner-Reed Party, starving in the Sierra snows, all the ephemera of civilization gone save that one vestigial taboo, the provision that no one should eat his own blood kin. The Jayhawkers, who quarreled and separated not far from where I am tonight. Some of them died in the Funerals and some of them died down near Badwater and most of the rest of them died in the Panamints. A woman who got through gave the Valley its name. Some might say that the Jayhawkers were killed by the desert summer, and the Donner Party by the mountain winter, by circumstances beyond control; we were taught instead that they had somewhere abdicated their responsibilities, somehow breached their primary loyalties, or they would not have found themselves helpless in the mountain winter or the desert summer, would not have given way to acrimony, would not have deserted one another, would not have *failed.* In brief, we heard such stories as cautionary tales, and they still suggest the only kind of "morality" that seems to me to have any but the most potentially mendacious meaning.

5 You are quite possibly impatient with me by now; I am talking, you want to say, about a "morality" so primitive that it scarcely deserves the name, a code that has as its point only survival, not the attainment of the ideal good. Exactly. Particularly out here tonight, in this country so ominous and terrible that to live in it is to live with antimatter, it is difficult to believe that "the good" is a knowable quantity. Let me tell you what it is like out here tonight. Stories travel at night on the desert. Someone gets in his pickup and drives a couple of hundred miles for a beer, and he carries news of what is happening, back wherever he came from. Then he drives another hundred miles for another beer, and passes along stories from the last place as well as from the one before; it is a network kept alive by people whose instincts tell them that if they do not keep moving at night in the desert they will lose all reason. Here is a story that is going around the desert tonight: over across the Nevada line, sheriff's deputies are diving in some underground pools, trying to retrieve a couple of bodies known to be in the hole. The widow of one of the drowned boys is over there; she is eighteen, and pregnant, and is said not to leave the hole. The divers go down and come up, and she just stands there and stares into the water. They have been diving for ten days but have found no bottom to the caves, no bodies and no trace of them, only the black 90° water going down and

down and down, and a single translucent fish, not classified. The story tonight is that one of the divers has been hauled up incoherent, out of his head, shouting—until they got him out of there so that the widow could not hear—about water that got hotter instead of cooler as he went down, about light flickering through the water, about magma, about underground nuclear testing.

That is the tone stories take out here, and there are quite a few of them. And it is more than the stories alone. Across the road at the Faith Community Church a couple of dozen old people, come here to live in trailers and die in the sun, are holding a prayer sing. I cannot hear them and do not want to. What I can hear are occasional coyotes and a constant chorus of "Baby the Rain Must Fall" from the jukebox in the Snake Room next door, and if I were also to hear those dying voices, those Midwestern voices drawn to this lunar country for some unimaginable atavistic rites, *rock of ages cleft for me,* I think I would lose my own reason. Every now and then I imagine I hear a rattlesnake, but my husband says that it is a faucet, a paper rustling, the wind. Then he stands by a window, and plays a flashlight over the dry wash outside. 6

What does it mean? It means nothing manageable. There is some sinister hysteria in the air out here tonight, some hint of the monstrous perversion to which any human idea can come. "I followed my own conscience." "I did what I thought was right." How many madmen have said it and meant it? How many murderers? Klaus Fuchs said it, and the men who committed the Mountain Meadows Massacre said it, and Alfred Rosenberg said it. And, as we are rotely and rather presumptuously reminded by those who would say it now, Jesus said it. Maybe we have all said it, and maybe we have been wrong. Except on that most primitive level—our loyalties to those we love—what could be more arrogant than to claim the primacy of personal conscience? ("Tell me," a rabbi asked Daniel Bell when he said, as a child, that he did not believe in God. "Do you think God cares?") At least some of the time, the world appears to me as a painting by Hieronymous Bosch; were I to follow my conscience then, it would lead me out onto the desert with Marion Faye, out to where he stood in *The Deer Park* looking east to Los Alamos and praying, as if for rain, that it would happen: " . . . *let it come and clear the rot and the stench and the stink, let it come for all of everywhere, just so it comes and the world stands clear in the white dead dawn.*" 7

Of course you will say that I do not have the right, even if I had the power, to inflict that unreasonable conscience upon you; nor do I want you to inflict your conscience, however reasonable, however enlightened, upon me. ("We must be aware of the dangers which lie in our most generous wishes," Lionel Trilling once wrote. "Some paradox of our nature leads us, when once we have made our fellow men the objects of our enlightened interest, to go on to make them the objects of our pity, then of our wisdom, ultimately of our coercion.") That the ethic of conscience is intrinsically insidious seems scarcely a revelatory 8

point, but it is one raised with increasing infrequency; even those who do raise it tend to *segue* with troubling readiness into the quite contradictory position that the ethic of conscience is dangerous when it is "wrong," and admirable when it is "right."

You see I want to be quite obstinate about insisting that we have no way of knowing—beyond that fundamental loyalty to the social code—what is "right" and what is "wrong," what is "good" and what "evil." I dwell so upon this because the most disturbing aspect of "morality" seems to me to be the frequency with which the word now appears; in the press, on television, in the most perfunctory kinds of conversation. Questions of straightforward power (or survival) politics, questions of quite indifferent public policy, questions of almost anything: they are all assigned these factitious moral burdens. There is something facile going on, some self-indulgence at work. Of course we would all like to "believe" in something, like to assuage our private guilts in public causes, like to lose our tiresome selves; like, perhaps, to transform the white flag of defeat at home into the brave white banner of battle away from home. And of course it is all right to do that; that is how, immemorially, things have gotten done. But I think it is all right only so long as we do not delude ourselves about what we are doing, and why. It is all right only so long as we remember that all the *ad hoc* committees, all the picket lines, all the brave signatures in *The New York Times,* all the tools of agitprop straight across the spectrum, do not confer upon anyone any *ipso facto* virtue. It is all right only so long as we recognize that the end may or may not be expedient, may or may not be a good idea, but in any case has nothing to do with "morality." Because when we start deceiving ourselves into thinking not that we want something or need something, not that it is a pragmatic necessity for us to have it, but that it is a *moral imperative* that we have it, then is when we join the fashionable madmen, and then is when the thin whine of hysteria is heard in the land, and then is when we are in bad trouble. And I suspect we are already there. 9

COMPREHENSION

1. Who is the implied audience of this essay? Where does Didion offer a clue to the nature of this audience?
2. Why is Didion suspicious of the word *morality?* What examples does she provide of this mistrust?
3. Explain Didion's emphasis on the importance of "specificity" in morality.

RHETORIC

1. Apropos of question 1 in "Comprehension," what specific references does Didion make that indicate her intended audience? How necessary is familiarity with these references to an understanding of her theme?

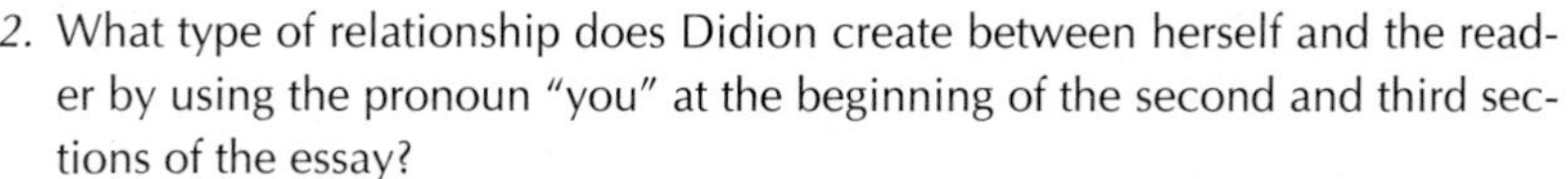

2. What type of relationship does Didion create between herself and the reader by using the pronoun "you" at the beginning of the second and third sections of the essay?
3. Why does Didion begin her essay with a description of her physical surroundings? How does this strategy complement her general view of the nature of morality?
4. Paragraph 7 begins with "What does it mean? It means nothing manageable." How does Didion use example, illustration, and anecdote in the rest of the paragraph to support this "unmanageability"?
5. How does Didion's repetition of the words *what, questions,* and *like* contribute to the coherence of paragraph 9?
6. Study the final two sentences of the essay. One is quite long, the other short. What is the effect of this juxtaposition in length? Find other examples of this technique. What similar effects do they create?

WRITING

1. Why does Didion say that "the ethic of conscience is intrinsically insidious" (paragraph 8)? What are your reasons for either agreeing or disagreeing with her?
2. How is morality shaped by the group that adheres to it? Select a group—for example, athletes, criminals, model students—and write an essay describing its particular morality. What are the group's values? How do its members exhibit these values?
3. Do you have a personal morality? Write an essay describing it, and explain how it helps you to shape your behavior.
4. Examine the ways in which Didion's essay illuminates Coles's "I Listen to My Parents and I Wonder What They Believe."

CHARLES SIMIC Charles Simic (1938–) is an American poet and translator born in what was then Yugoslavia. His poetry has been influenced by surrealism, with a focus on dreams and the human psyche. His poetry collection *Dismantling the Silence* (1971) won him critical acclaim. Among his other volumes of poetry are *Austerities* (1982), *Weather Forecast for Utopia and Vicinity: Poems 1967–1982* (1983), and his most recent, *Hotel Insomnia* (1992). In the following essay, Simic delights in contemplations about life and philosophy interspersed with eerily disturbing childhood memories.

Chapter Ten Philosophy and Ethics

CHARLES SIMIC

Reading Philosophy at Night

It is night again around me; I feel as though there had been lightning—for a brief span of time I was entirely *in my element and in my light.*

—Nietzsche

The mind loves the unknown. It loves images whose meaning is unknown, since the meaning of the mind itself is unknown. —Magritte

I wore Buster Keaton's expression of exaggerated calm. I could have been sitting on the edge of a cliff with my back to the abyss trying to look normal. 1

Now I read philosophy in the morning. When I was younger and lived in the city it was always at night. "That's how you ruined your eyes," my mother keeps saying. I sat and read late into the night. The quieter it got, the more clearheaded I became—or so it seemed to me. In the sparsely furnished room above the Italian grocery, I would be struggling with some intricate epistemological argument which promised a magnificent insight at its conclusion. I could smell it, so to speak. I couldn't put the book away, and it was getting very late. I had to be at work in the morning. Even had I tried to sleep my head would have been full of Immanuel Kant. So, I wouldn't sleep. I remember well such moments of decision: the great city that had suddenly turned quiet, the open book, and my face reflected dimly in the darkened windowpane. 2

At such hours I thought I understood everything. The first time it happened I was twenty. It was six o'clock in the morning. It was winter. It was dark and very cold. I was in Chicago riding the El to work seated between two heavily bundled-up old women. The train was overheated, but each time the door opened at one of the elevated platforms, a blast of cold air would send shivers through us. The lights, too, kept flickering. As the train changed tracks, the lights would go out and I would stop reading the history of philosophy I had borrowed the previous day from the library. "Why is there something rather than nothing?" the book asked, quoting Parmenides. It was as if my eyes were opened. I could not stop looking at my fellow passengers. How incredible, I thought, being here, existing. 3

I have a recurring dream about the street where I was born. It is always night. I'm walking past vaguely familiar buildings trying to find our house, but somehow it is not there. I retrace my steps on that short 4 block of only a few buildings, all of which are there except the one I want. The effort leaves me exhausted and saddened.

In another version of this same dream, I catch a glimpse of our house. There it is, at last, but for some reason I'm unable to get any closer to it. No lights are on. I look for our window, but it is even darker there on the third floor. The whole building seems abandoned. "It's not possible," I tell myself.

Once in one of these dreams, many years ago, I saw someone at my window, hunched over, watching the street intently. That's how my grandmother would wait late into the night for us to come home, except this was a stranger. Even without being able to make out his face, I was sure of that. 6

Most of the time, however, there's no one in sight during the dream. The façades of buildings still retain the pockmarks and other signs of the war. The streetlights are out and there's no moon in the sky so it's not clear to me how I am able to see all that in complete darkness. 7

Whoever reads philosophy reads himself as much as he reads the philosopher. I am in a dialogue with certain decisive events in my life as much as I am with the ideas on the page. Meaning is the matter of my existence. My effort to understand is a perpetual circling around a few obsessive images. 8

Like everyone else, I have my hunches. All my experiences make a kind of untaught ontology which precedes all my readings. What I am trying to conceptualize with the help of the philosopher is that which I have already intuited. 9

That's one way of looking at it. 10

> The Meditation of yesterday filled my mind with so many doubts that it is no longer in my power to forget them. And yet, I do not see in what manner I can resolve them; and, just as if I had all of a sudden fallen into very deep water, I am so disconcerted that I can neither make certain of setting my feet on the bottom, nor can I swim and so support myself on the surface. I shall nevertheless make an effort and follow anew the same path as that on which I yesterday entered, i.e., I shall proceed by setting aside all that in which the least doubt could be supposed to exist, just as if I had discovered that it was absolutely false; and I shall ever follow in this road until I have met with something which is certain, or at least, if I can do nothing else, until I have learned for certain that there's nothing in the world that is certain. Archimedes, in order that he might draw the terrestrial globe out of its place, and transport it elsewhere, demanded only that one point should be fixed and immovable; in the same way I shall have the right to conceive high hopes if I am happy enough to discover one thing only which is certain and indubitable. 11

I love this passage of Descartes; his beginning again, his not wanting to be fooled. It describes the ambition of philosophy in all its nobility and desperation. I prefer this doubting Descartes to his famous later conclusions. Here everything is still unsettled. The poetry of the mo- 12

ment still casts its spell. Of course, he's greedy for the absolute, but so is his reader.

There's an Eastern European folk song which tells of a girl who tossed 13
an apple higher and higher in the air until she tossed it as high as the clouds. To her surprise the apple didn't come down. The cloud got it. She waited with arms outstretched, but the apple stayed up there. All she could do is plead with the cloud to return her apple, but that's another story. I like the first part when the impossible happens.

I remember lying in a ditch and looking at some pebbles while 14
German bombers were flying over our heads. That was long ago. I don't remember the face of my mother nor the faces of the people who were there with us, but I still see those perfectly ordinary pebbles.

"It is not *how* things are in the world that is mystical, but that it ex- 15
ists," says Wittgenstein. I had a feeling of great clarity. Time had stopped. I was watching myself watching the pebbles and trembling with fear. Then time moved on.

The pebbles stayed in their otherness, stayed forever as far as I am 16
concerned. I'm talking about the experience of heightened consciousness. Can language do it justice? Speech is always less. When it comes to consciousness, one approximates, one speaks poorly. Competing phenomenologies are impoverishments, splendid poverties.

Wittgenstein puts it this way: "What finds its reflection in language, 17
language cannot represent. What expresses *itself* in language, we cannot express by means of language." We are not, most certainly, thinking about the same thing, nor were he and his followers subsequently very happy with this early statement of his, but this has been my experience on a number of occasions.

I knew someone who once tried to persuade me otherwise. He consid- 18
ered himself a logical positivist. There are people who tell you, for example, that you can speak of a pencil's dimension, location, appearance, state of motion or rest but not of its intelligence and love of music. The moment I hear that the poet in me rebels and I want to write a poem about an intelligent pencil in love with music. In other words, what they regard as nonsense, I suspect to be full of unknown imaginative possibilities.

There's a wonderful story told about Wittgenstein and his 19
Cambridge colleague, the Italian economist Piero Sraffa. Apparently they often discussed philosophy. "One day," as Justus Hartnack has it, "when Wittgenstein was defending his view that a proposition has the same logical form as the fact it depicts, Sraffa made a gesture used by Neapolitans to express contempt and asked Wittgenstein what the logical form of that was. According to Wittgenstein's own recollection, it was this question which made him realize that his belief that a fact could have a logical form was untenable."

As for my logical friend, we argued all night. "What cannot be said, 20
cannot be thought." And then again, after I blurted out something

about silence being the language of consciousness, "you're silent because you have nothing to say." It got to the point where we were calling each other "you dumb shit." We were drinking large quantities of red wine, misunderstanding each other liberally, and only stopped bickering when his disheveled wife came to the bedroom door and told us to shut up.

Then I told him a story. 21

One day in Yugoslavia, just after the war, we made a class trip to the town War Museum. At the entrance we found a battered German tank which delighted us. Inside the museum one could look at a few rifles, hand grenades and uniforms, but not much else. Most of the space was taken up by photographs. These we were urged to examine. One saw people hanged and people about to be hanged; people on tips of their toes. The executioners stood around smoking. There were piles of corpses everywhere. Some were naked. Men and women with their genitals showing. That made some kid laugh.

Then we saw a man having his throat cut. The killer sat on the man's chest with a knife in his hand. He seemed pleased to be photographed. The victim's eyes I don't remember. A few men stood around gawking. There were clouds in the sky.

There were always clouds, as well as blades of grass, tree stumps, bushes and rocks no one was paying any attention to. At times the earth was covered with snow. A miserable, teeth-chattering January morning and someone making someone's life even more miserable. Or the rain would be falling. A small hard rain that would wash the blood off the hands immediately, that would make one of the killers catch a bad cold. I imagined him sitting that same night with his feet in a bucket of hot water and sipping tea.

That occurred to me much later. Now that we had seen all there was to see, we were made to sit on the lawn outside the museum and eat our lunch. It was poor fare. Most of us had plum jam spread on slices of bread. A few had lard sprinkled with paprika. One kid had nothing but bread and scallions. Everybody thought that was funny. Someone threw his thick slice of black bread in the air and got it caught in a tree. The poor fellow tried to get it down by throwing pebbles at it. He kept missing. Then, he wanted to climb the tree. He kept sliding back. Even our teacher who came over to look thought it was hilarious.

As for the grass, there was plenty of it, each blade distinct and carefully sharpened, as it were. There were also clouds in the sky and many large flies of the kind one encounters at slaughterhouses that kept interrupting our thoughts and our laughter.

And here's what went through my head just the other night as I lay 22
awake in the dark:

The story had nothing to do with what you were talking about.

The story had everything to do with what we were talking about.

I can think of a hundred objections. 23

Only idiots want something neat, something categorical . . . and I 24
never talk unless I know!

Aha! You're mixing poetry and philosophy. Bertrand Russell 25
wouldn't give you the time of day. . . .

"Everything looks very busy to me," says Jasper Johns, and that's 26
the problem. I remember a strange cat, exceedingly emaciated, that scratched on my door the day I was scratching my head over Hegel's phenomenology.

Who said, "Whatever can be thought must be fictitious"? 27

You got me there! Error is my first love. I'm shouting her name 28
from the rooftops.

Still and all! And nevertheless! And above all! Let's not forget 29
"above all."

"The Only Humane Way to Catch a Metaphysical Mouse" is the 30
name of the book I work on between three and four in the morning.

Here's what Nietzsche said to the ceiling: "The rank of the philoso- 31
pher is determined by the rank of his laughter." But he couldn't really laugh. No matter how hard he tried he couldn't laugh.

I know because I'm a connoisseur of chaos. All the good-looking 32
oxymorons come to visit me in my bed. . . .

Wallace Stevens has several beautiful poems about solitary readers. 33
"The House Was Quiet and the World Was Calm" is one. It speaks of a "truth in a calm world." It happens! The world and the mind being so calm that truth becomes visible.

It must be late night—"where shines the light that lets be the things 34
that are"—which might be a good description of insomnia. The solitude of the reader and the solitude of the philosopher drawing together. The impression that one is on the verge of anticipating another man's next turn of thought. My own solitude doubled, tripled, as if I were the only one awake on the earth.

Understanding depends upon the relation of what I am to what I 35
have been. The being of the moment, in other words. Consciousness waking up conscience—waking up history. Consciousness as clarity and history as the dark night of the soul.

The pleasures of philosophy are the pleasures of reduction—the 36
epiphanies of saying in a few words what seems to be the gist of the matter. It pleases me, for instance, to think of both philosophy and poetry as concerned with Being. What is a lyric poem, one might say, but an acknowledgment of the Being of beings. The philosopher thinks Being; the poet in the lyric poem re-creates the experience of Being.

History, on the other hand, is antireductive. Nothing tidy about it. 37
Chaos! Bedlam! Hopeless tangle! My history and the History of this century like a child and his blind mother on the street—and the blind mother leading the way! You'd think the sole purpose of history is to stand truth happily upon its head.

Poor poetry! For some reason I can't get Buster Keaton out of my 38
mind. Poetry as imperturbable Keaton alone with the woman he loves

on an ocean liner set adrift on the stormy sea. Or, poetry as that kid throwing stones at a tree to bring down his lunch. Wise enough to play the fool, perhaps?

And always the dialectic: I have Don Quixote and his windmills in my head and Sancho Panza and his mule in my heart.

That's a figure of speech—one figure among many other figures of speech. Who could live without them? Do they tell the truth? Do they conceal it? I don't know. That's why I keep going back to philosophy. 40

It is morning. It is night. The book is open. The text is difficult, the text is momentarily opaque. My mind is wandering. My mind is struggling to grasp the always elusive . . . the always hinting. . . . What do you call it? 41

It, it, I keep calling it. An infinity of *it* without a single antecedent—like a hum in my ear. 42

Just then, about to give up, I find the following on a page of Heidegger: 43

> No thinker has ever entered into another thinker's solitude. Yet it is only from its solitude that all thinking, in a hidden mode, speaks to the thinking that comes after or that went before.

And it all comes together: poetry, philosophy, history. I see—in the sense of being able to picture and feel the human weight of another's solitude. So many of them. Seated with a book. Day breaking. Thought becoming image. Image becoming thought. 44

COMPREHENSION

1. Why does Simic read philosophy? Would you label Simic a philosopher? Why, or why not?
2. Simic provides biographical details in his essay. In your opinion, how has history helped shape Simic's views?
3. "Whoever reads philosophy reads himself as much as he reads the philosopher." What does Simic mean by this statement? Is it true of Simic's readers as well?

RHETORIC

1. Does Simic's essay have a thesis? How does the reader glean Simic's main idea from the piece? Is it mentioned directly?
2. How does the image of Buster Keaton (in the first paragraph and in the conclusion) serve Simic's purposes? Is it important for the reader to be familiar with Keaton? Why, or why not?
3. Is the writer's level of language intended for a specialized audience? Do words such as *ontology* (paragraph 9) and *epistemological* (paragraph 2) impede the general reader's understanding of the essay?
4. How does Simic use metaphors and similes in his writing? Cite specific examples of figurative language in his essay.

5. How do the narrative portions of Simic's essay enrich his reflections on philosophy? Cite particular examples of their effectiveness.
6. Discuss Simic's use of sentence fragments, especially in his conclusion. Why are they more effective than conventional sentences? To what end are they used?

WRITING

1. Argue Simic's contention that "Speech is always less." Does that apply only to the study of philosophy? What are the limitations of language when expressing emotions or concepts? Develop this theme in a short essay.
2. Simic is obsessed with pursuing *it.* What is *it?* Do you spend any of your time philosophizing, delving into the nature of reality and being? Do you think it is a valid pursuit? Does humanity spend time reflecting? Why, or why not? Consider these questions in essay form, using exposition and narration.
3. Simic refers to "Thought becoming image. Image becoming thought." How does his essay reflect that process? Give specific examples from the piece, and discuss them in a brief essay.

CLASSIC AND CONTEMPORARY

VIRGINIA WOOLF Virginia Woolf (1882–1941), English novelist and essayist, was the daughter of Sir Leslie Stephen, a famous critic and writer on economics. An experimental novelist, Woolf attempted to portray consciousness through a poetic, symbolic, and concrete style. Her novels include *Jacob's Room* (1922), *Mrs. Dalloway* (1925), *To the Lighthouse* (1927), and *The Waves* (1931). She was also a perceptive reader and critic, and her criticism appears in *The Common Reader* (1925) and *The Second Common Reader* (1933). The following essay, which demonstrates Woolf's capacity to find profound meaning even in commonplace events, appeared in *The Death of a Moth and Other Essays* (1948).

VIRGINIA WOOLF

The Death of the Moth

1 Moths that fly by day are not properly to be called moths; they do not excite that pleasant sense of dark autumn nights and ivy-blossom which the commonest yellow-underwing asleep in the shadow of the curtain never fails to rouse in us. They are hybrid creatures, neither gay like butterflies nor sombre like their own species. Nevertheless the present specimen, with his narrow hay-coloured wings, fringed with a tassel of the same colour, seemed to be content with life. It was a pleasant morning, mid-September, mild, benignant, yet with a keener breath than that of the summer months. The plough was already scoring the field opposite the window, and where the share had been, the earth was pressed flat and gleamed with moisture. Such vigour came rolling in from the fields and the down beyond that it was difficult to keep the eyes strictly turned upon the book. The rooks too were keeping one of their annual festivities; soaring round the tree tops until it looked as if a vast net with thousands of black knots in it had been cast up into the air; which, after a few moments sank slowly down upon the trees until every twig seemed to have a knot at the end of it. Then, suddenly, the net would be thrown into the air again in a wider circle this time, with the utmost clamour and vociferation, as though to be thrown into the air and settle down upon the tree tops were a tremendously exciting experience.

2 The same energy which inspired the rooks, the ploughmen, the horses, and even, it seemed, the lean bare-backed downs, sent the moth fluttering from side to side of his square of the windowpane. One could

not help watching him. One was, indeed, conscious of a queer feeling of pity for him. The possibilities of pleasure seemed that morning so enormous and so various that to have only a moth's part in life, and a day moth's at that, appeared a hard fate, and his zest in enjoying his meagre opportunities to the full, pathetic. He flew vigorously to one corner of his compartment, and, after waiting there a second, flew across to the other. What remained for him but to fly to a third corner and then to a fourth? That was all he could do, in spite of the size of the downs, the width of the sky, the far-off smoke of houses, and the romantic voice, now and then, of a steamer out at sea. What he could do he did. Watching him, it seemed as if a fibre, very thin but pure, of the enormous energy of the world had been thrust into his frail and diminutive body. As often as he crossed the pane, I could fancy that a thread of vital light became visible. He was little or nothing but life.

Yet, because he was so small, and so simple a form of the energy 3
that was rolling in at the open window and driving its way through so many narrow and intricate corridors in my own brain and in those of other human beings, there was something marvellous as well as pathetic about him. It was as if someone had taken a tiny bead of pure life and decking it as lightly as possible with down and feathers, had set it dancing and zigzagging to show us the true nature of life. Thus displayed one could not get over the strangeness of it. One is apt to forget all about life, seeing it humped and bossed and garnished and cumbered so that it has to move with the greatest circumspection and dignity. Again, the thought of all that life might have been had he been born in any other shape caused one to view his simple activities with a kind of pity.

After a time, tired by his dancing apparently, he settled on the win- 4
dow ledge in the sun, and, the queer spectacle being at an end, I forgot about him. Then, looking up, my eye was caught by him. He was trying to resume his dancing, but seemed either so stiff or so awkward that he could only flutter to the bottom of the windowpane; and when he tried to fly across it he failed. Being intent on other matters I watched these futile attempts for a time without thinking, unconsciously waiting for him to resume his flight, as one waits for a machine, that has stopped momentarily, to start again without considering the reason of its failure. After perhaps a seventh attempt he slipped from the wooden ledge and fell, fluttering his wings, on to his back on the window sill. The helplessness of his attitude roused me. It flashed upon me that he was in difficulties; he could no longer raise himself; his legs struggled vainly. But, as I stretched out a pencil, meaning to help him to right himself, it came over me that the failure and awkwardness were the approach of death. I laid the pencil down again.

The legs agitated themselves once more. I looked as if for the 5
enemy against which he struggled. I looked out of doors. What had happened there? Presumably it was midday, and work in the fields had stopped. Stillness and quiet had replaced the previous animation. The birds had taken themselves off to feed in the brooks. The horses stood

still. Yet the power was there all the same, massed outside, indifferent, impersonal, not attending to anything in particular. Somehow it was opposed to the little hay-coloured moth. It was useless to try to do anything. One could only watch the extraordinary efforts made by those tiny legs against an oncoming doom which could, had it chosen, have submerged an entire city, not merely a city, but masses of human beings; nothing, I knew, had any chance against death. Nevertheless after a pause of exhaustion the legs fluttered again. It was superb this last protest, and so frantic that he succeeded at last in righting himself. One's sympathies, of course, were all on the side of life. Also, when there was nobody to care or to know, this gigantic effort on the part of an insignificant little moth, against a power of such magnitude, to retain what no one else valued or desired to keep, moved one strangely. Again, somehow, one saw life, a pure bead. I lifted the pencil again, useless though I knew it to be. But even as I did so, the unmistakable tokens of death showed themselves. The body relaxed, and instantly grew stiff. The struggle was over. The insignificant little creature now knew death. As I looked at the dead moth, this minute wayside triumph of so great a force over so mean an antagonist filled me with wonder. Just as life had been strange a few minutes before, so death was now as strange. The moth having righted himself now lay most decently and uncomplainingly composed. O yes, he seemed to say, death is stronger than I am.

COMPREHENSION

1. Why is Woolf so moved by the moth's death? Why does she call the moth's protest (paragraph 5) "superb"?
2. What, according to Woolf, is the "true nature of life"?
3. What paradox is inherent in the death of the moth?

RHETORIC

1. Examine Woolf's use of similes in paragraph 1. Where else does she use similes? Are any of them similar to the similes used in paragraph 1?
2. Why does the author personify the moth?
3. What sentences constitute the introduction of this essay? What rhetorical device do they use?
4. Divide the essay into two parts. Why did you divide the essay where you did? How are the two parts different? How are they similar?
5. Explain the importance of description in this essay. Where, particularly, does Woolf describe the setting of her scene? How does that description contribute to the development of her essay? How does she describe the moth, and how does this description affect tone?
6. How is narration used to structure the essay?

WRITING

1. Woolf implicitly connects insect and human life. What else can we learn about human development by looking at other forms of life? Analyze this connection in an essay.
2. Write a detailed description of a small animal. Try to invest it with the importance that Woolf gives her moth.
3. Analyze Woolf's use of figurative language in "The Death of the Moth."

ANNIE DILLARD Annie Dillard (1945–), whose writings include poems, autobiographies, and novels, was born in Pennsylvania. Her books include *Pilgrim at Tinker Creek* (1974), for which she won the 1975 Pulitzer Prize in general nonfiction, *Teaching a Stone to Talk* (1982), and *The Living* (1992), a novel that celebrates the spirit of pioneer women. Dillard's work has been published in *Harper's, Atlantic Monthly, Cosmopolitan,* and *Sports Illustrated.* In the essay below, Dillard uses evocative sensory images to examine the process of creating and the nature of solitude.

ANNIE DILLARD

Death of a Moth

I live alone with two cats, who sleep on my legs. There is a yellow one, and a black one whose name is Small. In the morning I joke to the black one, Do you remember last night? Do you remember? I throw them both out before breakfast, so I can eat. 1

There is a spider, too, in the bathroom, of uncertain lineage, bulbous at the abdomen and drab, whose six-inch mess of web works, works somehow, works miraculously, to keep her alive and me amazed. The web is in a corner behind the toilet, connecting tile wall to tile wall. The house is new, the bathroom immaculate, save for the spider, her web, and the sixteen or so corpses she's tossed to the floor. 2

The corpses appear to be mostly sow bugs, those little armadillo creatures who live to travel flat out in houses, and die round. In addition to sow-bug husks, hollow and sipped empty of color, there are what seem to be two or three wingless moth bodies, one new flake of earwig, and three spider carcasses crinkled and clenched. 3

I wonder on what fool's errand an earwig, or a moth, or a sow bug, would visit that clean corner of the house behind the toilet; I have not noticed any blind parades of sow bugs blundering into corners. Yet they do hazard there, at a rate of more than one a week, and the spider thrives. Yesterday she was working on the earwig, mouth on gut; today he's on the floor. It must take a certain genius to throw things away from there, to find a straight line through that sticky tangle to the floor. 4

Today the earwig shines darkly, and gleams, what there is of him: a dorsal curve of thorax and abdomen, and a smooth pair of pincers by which I knew his name. Next week, if the other bodies are any indica- 5 tion, he'll be shrunk and gray, webbed to the floor with dust. The sow bugs beside him are curled and empty, fragile, a breath away from brittle fluff. The spiders lie on their sides, translucent and ragged, their legs drying in knots. The moths stagger against each other, headless, in a confusion of arcing strips of chitin like peeling varnish, like a jumble of buttresses for cathedral vaults, like nothing resembling moths, so that I would hesitate to call them moths, except that I have had some experience with the figure Moth reduced to a nub.

Two summers ago I was camped alone in the Blue Ridge 6
Mountains of Virginia. I had hauled myself and gear up there to read, among other things, *The Day on Fire,* by James Ullman, a novel about Rimbaud that had made me want to be a writer when I was sixteen; I was hoping it would do it again. So I read every day sitting under a tree by my tent, while warblers sang in the leaves overhead and bristle worms trailed their inches over the twiggy dirt at my feet; and I read every night by candlelight, while barred owls called in the forest and pale moths seeking mates massed round my head in the clearing, where my light made a ring.

Moths kept flying into the candle. They would hiss and recoil, reel- 7
ing upside down in the shadows among my cooking pans. Or they would singe their wings and fall, and their hot wings, as if melted, would stick to the first thing they touched—a pan, a lid, a spoon—so that the snagged moths could struggle only in tiny arcs, unable to flutter free. These I could release by a quick flip with a stick; in the morning I would find my cooking stuff decorated with torn flecks of moth wings, ghostly triangles of shiny dust here and there on the aluminum. So I read, and boiled water, and replenished candles, and read on.

One night a moth flew into the candle, was caught, burnt dry, and 8
held. I must have been staring at the candle, or maybe I looked up when a shadow crossed my page; at any rate, I saw it all. A golden female moth, a biggish one with a two-inch wingspread, flapped into the fire, drooped abdomen into the wet wax, stuck, flamed, and frazzled in a second. Her moving wings ignited like tissue paper, like angels' wings, enlarging the circle of light in the clearing and creating out of the darkness the sudden blue sleeves of my sweater, the green leaves of jewelweed by my side, the ragged red trunk of a pine; at once the light contracted again and the moth's wings vanished in a fine, foul smoke. At the same time, her six legs clawed, curled, blackened, and ceased, disappearing utterly. And her head jerked in spasms, making a spattering noise; her antennae crisped and burnt away and her heaving mouthparts cracked like pistol fire. When it was all over, her head was, so far as I could determine, gone, gone the long way of her wings and legs. Her head was a hole lost to time. All that was left was the glowing horn shell of her abdomen and thorax—a fraying, partially collapsed gold tube jammed upright in the candle's round pool.

And then this moth-essence, this spectacular skeleton, began to act 9
as a wick. She kept burning. The wax rose in the moth's body from her

soaking abdomen to her thorax to the shattered hole where her head should have been, and widened into flame, a saffron-yellow flame that robed her to the ground like an immolating monk. That candle had two wicks, two winding flames of identical light, side by side. The moth's head was fire. She burned for two hours, until I blew her out.

She burned for two hours without changing, without swaying or 10
kneeling—only glowing within, like a building fire glimpsed through silhouetted walls, like a hollow saint, like a flame-faced virgin gone to God, while I read by her light, kindled, while Rimbaud in Paris burnt out his brain in a thousand poems, while night pooled wetly at my feet.

So. That is why I think those hollow shreds on the bathroom floor 11
are moths. I believe I know what moths look like, in any state.

I have three candles here on the table which I disentangle from the 12
plants and light when visitors come. The cats avoid them, although Small's tail caught fire once; I rubbed it out before she noticed. I don't mind living alone. I like eating alone and reading. I don't mind sleeping alone. The only time I mind being alone is when something is funny; then, when I am laughing at something funny, I wish someone were around. Sometimes I think it is pretty funny that I sleep alone.

COMPREHENSION

1. What is the link between the moth, its death, and Dillard's writing?
2. What is the significance of Dillard's reading material (paragraph 6) to the moth? What associations does it have?
3. Do we learn anything of Dillard's emotional response to the death of the moth? Why, or why not?

RHETORIC

1. Why do you think Dillard has written this essay?
2. How do images like "moth-essence" and "immolating monk" (in paragraph 9) help to enrich the meaning of the paragraph? What are other examples of Dillard's figurative language?
3. Comment on the use of transitions in paragraph 10 and the beginning of paragraph 11. How is repetition used effectively here? What impact does it have on the tone?
4. Note Dillard's use of similes in paragraph 10. What mood is the writer trying to evoke? How does the rest of the paragraph set off these images?
5. Dillard organizes this essay in three sections. What is the relationship of these sections to each other?
6. How well does Dillard's conclusion work? Does it serve to frame the essay? How does it relate to the paragraphs preceding it?

WRITING

1. In a brief essay, explore what the moth represents to Dillard. Use support or examples from her piece to develop your theme.
2. Both Dillard and Simic (in "Reading Philosophy at Night") explore the nature of solitude and introspection. In an essay, consider how the former can facilitate the latter. How do you feel about solitude? What do you think about when you're alone? Are your powers of observation and perception heightened by solitude? Is solitude at night different?
3. Have you ever witnessed the death of an insect or small animal? How did you respond physically, emotionally? In a descriptive narrative, relate the experience and its effect on you.

CLASSIC AND CONTEMPORARY: QUESTIONS FOR COMPARISON

1. Why is the moth so central to the essays of Dillard and Woolf? Do the two writers use a moth to symbolize the same thing? How does the article in Dillard's title affect her focus? Why does Woolf use the definite article? Do the two writers respond similarly to the event?
2. How do the writers use setting and mood in their essays? How do these enrich the essays? What role does solitude play in establishing the writer's theme?
3. Analyze the levels of language used by Woolf and Dillard. Cite examples of their use of figurative language to enhance their narratives. How do they use language to set the tone of the essays? Who is the intended audience, and how does their language reflect this?
4. In a brief essay, compare the writers' attitudes toward the event. Does the fact that Woolf personifies the moth in her essay and attempts to rescue it reveal anything about her sensibilities? Does Dillard's reactions to the moth show a lack of compassion? Respond to these questions, using the writers' work as a foundation for your responses.

CONNECTIONS

1. How do you think Coretta Scott King would respond to Sowell's essay on defining terms? Do you believe she defines her terms adequately in her argument? Do you think she has problems with the language of morality?
2. Simic links history, philosophy, and poetry in his essay. How would writers like King, Plato, or Sowell respond to this connection? Use support from the above-mentioned authors to form your answer.
3. Are people "wicked," as Krutch infers in his essay? Left to their own devices, without the regulations of church and state, would most people behave morally? Use the ideas of Coles, Didion, or King to develop your theme.
4. Explore the connection between Plato, the philosopher, and Simic, the reader of philosophy. How do their essays complement each other? How does Simic's attitude toward thinking and being reflect Plato's philosophy of the cave?
5. Coles argues that the moral education of children is essential to a well-functioning society. How would Krutch respond to Coles's argument? What might Krutch advise parents to teach their children?
6. What is *morality?* What is its origin? Use the work of King, Didion, or Sowell to respond to this question. How would these writers define the word?
7. Consider the differences between *public morality* and *private morality* as expressed in Krutch's essay. How would Sowell argue for or against Krutch's definition of these terms?
8. How would Krutch, Didion, and Coles respond to the issue of "the ideal good"? How would each define the concept? Use their essays as a foundation for your opinion.
9. Write an essay entitled "The Purpose of Life." Using examples and evidence from their works, choose three writers in this section to develop this theme.

CHAPTER ELEVEN

Religious Thought and Experience

Religion is central to our understanding of culture. As an example, Shusha Guppy demonstrates, in her essay "Ramadan," how religious practice, in this case Islam, informs family life. Similarly, Martin Buber, in "The Third Leg of the Table," shows how Judaism determines the texture and the lives of the community. Whether you are Muslim, Christian, Jewish, or a member of any other religion, your beliefs, rituals, and religious practices root you to a cultural past, inform your present, and shape your future.

Although the nature and intensity of one's religious beliefs is a personal matter, it is important to acknowledge religion as a major feature of cultural life. It is equally important, especially at a time when religion has become a highly charged instrument of social and political conflict around the world, to develop an understanding of and tolerance for the role of diverse religions as a conserving force for values. When the anthropologist Ruth Benedict explains the rituals and myths of the Zuñis and N. Scott Momaday seeks his origins by journeying to "sacred and ancestral ground," we are reminded that religious thought and experience takes many forms and that we can learn from other cultures the value of religious difference. Indeed, the toleration of differences, religious and otherwise, is the hallmark of an educated person.

Religion is also intrinsically connected to our sense of morality and ethics. Our personal code of ethics often has a religious grounding. Our religion often determines the way in which we apply our ethics—for instance, it may determine our attitude toward contraception, equality of the races or the sexes, and evolution. In all instances, competing religious and secular values may force us to make hard decisions about our positions on significant cultural issues.

Not all religious decisions are difficult to make. Whether or not to observe a particular religious holiday is generally an easy decision. Other decisions, however, go to the complex heart of our value system. As you read the essays in this chapter, ask yourself which religious attitudes you share with the writers, how your values and traditions differ from theirs, and what influence the authors may have on your thinking and future behavior.

Previewing the Chapter

As you read the essays in this chapter and respond to them in discussion and writing, consider the following questions:

- What specific religion does the author deal with?
- What is the author's attitude toward religion and religious experience?
- What is the thesis or central point that the author makes in his or her essay?
- According to the author, what is the function of religion?
- Is the author objective or subjective in the essay? Do you detect any biases. Why?
- Which religious problems or conflicts does the author treat? How are they resolved?
- How do cross-cultural issues involving gender, race, ethnicity, and class influence your understanding of the essay?
- What ethical and moral issues grow out of the essay?
- Which additional disciplinary areas—for example, history or anthropology—does the author bring to bear on the subject?
- What religious themes do the essays have in common?
- How has your understanding of religion been enhanced by these essays?

SHUSHA GUPPY (1938–) was born in Iran and attended the Sorbonne and the University of Paris. She worked as a professional singer for many years and has been a free-lance journalist since 1969. Besides contributing to periodicals in England and the United States, Guppy serves as the London editor of *Paris Review*. Her books include *Blindfold Horse: Memories of a Persian Childhood* (1988). In the following essay from that book, Guppy recalls the innocent pleasures of celebrating a religious holiday, but the recollection is marred by the current political and religious unrest in her place of birth.

SHUSHA GUPPY

Ramadan

Ramadan is the seventh month of the lunar calendar and the Muslim equivalent of Lent. For thirty days, Muslims must fast from sunrise to sunset, which means total abstinence not only from food and drink but also from smoking and sexual intercourse. As the lunar calendar, based on the rotation of the moon round the earth, is ten days or so shorter than the solar year, the date of Ramadan varies accordingly. When it occurs in winter, when the days are short, fasting is fairly easy, but in summer when a long fifteen-hour day stretches between the "dawn-meal" and the "break-fast" dinner at sunset, hunger and thirst—particularly the latter—are very hard to bear. Yet fasting, like the daily prayers, is one of the major duties of a Muslim. Only on health grounds can it be abandoned, as the care and preservation of the body are paramount duties too. Women must stop fasting during menstruation and childbirth, which gives them a few days of respite in the month. But, for whatever reason the Ramadan has been interrupted, the number of lost fasting days have to be compensated for sometime in the course of the year, otherwise "fasting debts" accumulate and will be counted against one on Judgement Day. My mother often fasted in winter: "I have a lot of debts," she would say, making up for the days she had been ill or "indisposed." 1

Rich men who died without having performed all the fasting days of their lives allocated a portion of their estate to the "purchase of prayers and fasts," usually performed by impoverished theology students in *madrasahs* who supplemented their inadequate grants by fasting all winter and praying all day. 2

In those days of religious tolerance and social ferment, not everyone observed Ramadan: agnostics, the weak-willed, the underaged and religious minorities disregarded it, but no Muslim adult would flaunt his fast-breaking. Public places, cafés and restaurants, were less crowded during the day, while the mosques were fuller at noon for the midday 3

prayer and the sermon that followed, Ramadan being the month of abstinence and prayer, of meditation and repentance. People who were lax in their duties all year round tried to make up for it during this period.

4 In our house, the daily routine changed completely during Ramadan. A few hours before dawn, Nanny and Ali would wake up and start preparing the "dawn-meal," which had to be substantial enough to sustain us through the day: rice and stew, salad, cheese, yoghurt, cold soft drinks and plenty of tea. When the meal was ready, an hour or so before dawn, Ali went round the house and woke up everybody else. Oh, the agony of being dragged out of a deep sleep! Eyes refused to open, feet were numb and hands hardly capable of grasping the spoon. . . .

5 In winter, the tablecloth was spread over my mother's large *korsi* and the aromatic food displayed upon it. But we were so sleepy that we would have gladly relinquished caviar and champagne for permission to go back to bed. To be fair, we were never coerced into keeping religious observances; rather we were prompted by our own faith, and by the sense of participation in the collective life with its special ritual and social activities. So Ramadan had an element of fun in it. When, in later years, some of us wavered and gave up the more exacting religious duties such as fasting, my mother's anguish was painful to watch. She was certain we would go straight to Hell and, worse still, be separated from her! She did not try to force or admonish us, but she pleaded. When it proved ineffective, she turned to my father:

6 "Won't *you* tell them something?" But he knew it would be no use, that preaching and bullying would be counter-productive and only fuel the adolescent rebelliousness. You could only set an example with your own conduct and hope for the best. Faith had to come from within, and if we had lost it, for the time being, there was nothing anyone could do. And, of course, he was right: one by one, and by different paths, we returned to some form of spiritual discipline later in life, though they were no longer alive to witness and rejoice.

7 In the summer, the table was set in the garden. Father presided over the meal which was swallowed reluctantly in silence. Only the purring of the samovar and the click of the ice-cubes in the water jug provided a soft accompaniment to the nocturnal rites. Over the walls, we could see lights in the neighbouring houses, and occasionally hear the faint clutter of crockery and glass as other families consumed their meal as silently and sleepily as we. All the garden insects gathered around the table, attracted by the pool of light. One night, we saw a large, yellow scorpion fixed on the wall behind my mother. Aunt Ashraf took off her slipper and banged it hard against the wall, without saying anything so as not to cause panic. The frightful creature fell on the ground and was killed. "Those little yellow ones are deadly," she said.

8 The next day she told us how, in Kashan, a town famous for its fine rugs and lethal scorpions, people placed the feet of their beds in bowls of water to stop them climbing into their beds; nonetheless casualties were reported every year.

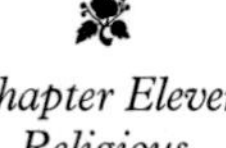

The sting of a scorpion does not come from malice 9
But from its nature.

She quoted the poet, and told us the following story: A frog was passing a river when he saw a scorpion struggling in the water and shouting for help: "I can't swim, save me!" it begged. The good-natured frog offered to carry it to the other side on its back. When they reached the middle of the stream the scorpion stang its benefactor. "What did you do that for?" asked the frog. "Now we will both die!" "I can't help it—it's my nature," answered the scorpion, apologetically.

"The moral of the story is that you must not offer lifts to scorpi- 10
ons!" we ventured.

"No, the moral is that you must try and save the scorpion, but *ex-* 11
pect it to sting you for your pain and take precautions!"

Sometimes we would hear the voice of a cantor chanting 12
Monajat—a special Ramadan prayer compounded of poetry and improvisation, a kind of supplication addressed to God, which sounds more like a lyrical outpouring of a lover to the object of his affection. In summer, those who had beautiful voices climbed on to their roofs and sang to their hearts' content. When there was more than one in the neighbourhood, a chorus of vocal arabesques and modulations wafted through the night air and imbued the atmosphere with a wistful, spiritual harmony.

Presently the black sky turned pigeon-breast, the stars faded, and 13
the call of the muezzin was heard. We rushed to do our dawn prayers before the sun rose on the horizon, then went back to bed. Everyone slept late, even such early risers as Nanny and Zahra, as there was to be no preparation of lunch. Too small to fast, I was given a midday meal from the night's leftovers. Even in later years, I never managed more than a few days fasting in the middle of the month—it interfered with school work, and I was not strong enough to sustain the physical strain.

At noon, Nanny sometimes went to the local mosque to pray and 14
hear the sermon. She would come back relaxed and smiling.

"Ah, the mullah talked so well today, it gladdened my heart!" 15

"What did he say, Nanny?" we would ask. 16

"I haven't got a clue, but it was very good!" 17

"How do you know it was good, if you didn't know what he said?" 18

"I haven't been to school like you! Don't ask me clever questions! 19
All I can tell you is that he spoke well and made sense!"

There was a famous preacher on the radio too, and occasionally we 20
listened to him, but *he* didn't say anything in particular either, although he sounded eloquent. He had a mellifluous voice which he used like a musical instrument to convey all the crescendos and diminuendos of his rhetoric. I had made up a comedy number about a very eloquent-sounding sermon which was complete gibberish and regaled our friends with it.

"A bunch of narrow-minded parasitic charlatans all these mullahs!," 21
we all thought, "but quite harmless." Would that it had been true!

The hardest time of the day was the last couple of hours before sunset. My father would walk round and round the garden murmuring prayers as the last rays of the sun left the top of the trees and shadows lengthened on the lawn. Ali laid the table and brought out the samovar. The smell of Nanny's cooking floated through the kitchen windows and made us dizzy. As a child, I used to sit on a stool and watch while she cooked in front of an open fire, frying cutlets and aubergines and courgettes, sweat pouring down her face. "It's not hunger that's killing me, it's thirst!" she would say. 22

I felt sorry for her and guilty that I could drink as much as I wanted. Worse still was the plight of workers on building sites and on the roads. You could see them struggling, weakened by hunger and parched with thirst to finish the day's work. "My tongue is like a stick rattling against my palate," Ali once remarked, which summed up the state of all those who worked in the torrid sun of the summer midday, when temperatures reached a hundred in the shade. Yet they carried on, upheld by a faith that was stronger than the dictates of their bodies. It gave them satisfaction and informed their lives with meaning. That such sincerity and trust could be ruthlessly exploited by power-maniacs and demagogues has become evident now. 23

At last, the cry of the muezzin would announce the breaking of the fast and we would all sit round the table to eat. The impulse was to go for the glass of iced water, but it was unhealthy and spoiled the appetite, so we were urged to refrain until some food had been consumed first. Unlike the dawn meal, the "break-fast" was a cheerful affair. We always had guests—cousins and aunts and uncles and friends. Others would often join us after dinner and we would spend the evening having a party, consuming quantities of nuts and seeds and fruit, until late into the night. 24

There was an extra dimension to the month of fasting for the Shiites: the anniversary of the martyrdom, on the twenty-first day of the month, of Imam Ali, son-in-law of the Prophet and the first of the twelve Imams of the Shia sect. The account of his martyrdom at the hands of a terrorist, one of his disaffected political disciples, can be read in history books; suffice it to say that it gave rise later to the first schism in Islam. Since then, the majority of Muslims throughout the world belong to the Sunni (Orthodox) sect, except in Persia where an overwhelming majority is Shiite, and Shiism has been the state religion of the country since the end of the sixteenth century. 25

Imam Ali is the patron saint of the Sufis and dervishes. One Sufi sect even believes in his divinity, and all others, even Sunni mystics, regard him as the greatest saint and statesman in all Islamic history. He represents the Perfect Man, of which the first example is the Prophet himself, an embodiment of all virtues—valour, fortitude, justice, tolerance, wisdom, etc. 26

The date of Imam Ali's martyrdom coincides with the Night of Atonement—evidently a variation on the Jewish Day of Atonement— 27 during which everyone's fate for the coming year is decided by Providence and written in his/her ledger by the angels.

For three days and nights there were lamentations and prayers of propitiation, all-night vigils and sermons at the mosques. We never went to the night sessions, ever-wary of mixing with crowds, but prayed at home. Once my sister and I begged to be allowed to go with some friends and Nanny, and were granted permission.

The local mosque was packed to the rafters and the crowd over- 29
flowed into the street. Loudspeakers relayed the mullah's sermon, which was based on the goodness and greatness of the First Imam, who was bound to be interceding on this Night of Atonement for his followers. At the end of his speech, he burst into chant, lamenting the Imam's martyrdom, to which the crowd responded with cries of supplication and invocations. When it was all over, the congregation dispersed. Only with hindsight can one see how dangerous such manipulation of popular emotions can be. Would that we had perceived it at the time, and taken the necessary measures to avert the catastrophe which hit the country several decades later!

After the three days of mourning for the Imam, the back of 30
Ramadan was broken. There was only a week or so left before the new moon would mark the end of the month.

The last days of Ramadan were the hardest. After close to thirty days 31
of fasting, bodies were weakened, nerves stretched, will-power overtaxed. But there was also a feeling of exhilaration and achievement for carrying through an act of will and an exercise in self-discipline.

No one was sure when exactly Ramadan ended, as it depended on 32
the sighting of the new moon and could be a day sooner or later than the date indicated by the calendar. Never was "the bride of the sky" more closely and longingly observed as it changed its shape from a luminous crescent to a golden disc and back to a thin pale thread through the month! On the last evening, people climbed on to their roofs at sunset to find the new moon before it disappeared. It was not easy, as it rose early and vanished soon after in the milky light diffused by the setting sun.

"I see it! I see it!" 33

"Where? Where? I can't see. . . ." 34

"Over there, to the left, above the poplars. . . ." 35

Everybody was cheering and pointing to a spot on the eastern hori- 36
zon. Then a cannon ball was heard, announcing the sighting of the new moon and the end of Ramadan.

In later years, this pattern broke up in our house. My eldest brother left 37
for Europe on his first diplomatic posting. We younger children had lost faith and were much more interested in new ideologies. We thought religion was obsolete, a leftover from the dark, superstitious past, and that it would disappear completely when everyone received the education we were privileged to have. Ali had moved out, so had Nanny, and the new Ali was not given to rigid observance of Ramadan. Something

was lost, to which we already looked back with nostalgia. But from the 19th to the 23rd day of the month my mother would still hold ceremonies of commemoration for the Imam's martyrdom. Many friends came and took part, and when the cathartic lamentation was over, the gathering would naturally develop into a party. Once in later years, I was in Persia with my small sons. They were astonished at the whole ceremony and its development from mourning to feast in the space of a couple of hours! On our return, I heard them relate the experience to their father:

"You know Persians are funny people! They get together and sit 38
around while a mullah comes and sings something sad and makes them all cry. Then they have a party and eat lots of cakes and fruit!"

In the end, hardly anyone fasted. "The world is changing," Mother 39
once said. "People are becoming Godless. What will happen to the world when no one prays and god forgets humanity?" To which father answered: "Don't worry, there will always be some beacon of faith burning in the depth of darkness. God will never abandon humanity completely."

I wonder! 40

The end of Ramadan is marked by a holiday—the most popular in the 41
Islamic calendar all over the world. But in Persia in those days it was just one closing day among others, without special ceremonies. For Persians have preserved their ancient, Zoroastrian customs of seasonal feasts and celebrations, often adapting them to Islamic landmarks, which they observe more fully. The greatest of these is the New Year, *Norooz* (New Day), which occurs at the spring equinox on 21 March. It goes back to the rites of the spring in Zoroastrian times, and corresponds to Easter in Christianity and the Passover in Judaism. But that is another story.

COMPREHENSION

1. Describe Ramadan in your own words. What other important religious duties does a Muslim have?
2. What was the atmosphere in Guppy's house during Ramadan while the writer was growing up? How important are religious observances to Guppy as an adult?
3. To what political and religious unrest does the adult writer refer in the midst of her innocent childhood memories?

RHETORIC

1. What major rhetorical strategies does Guppy combine in her essay, and how do they complement each other?

2. What is the overall tone of the essay? Does the tone change at any point? What purpose does the writer have for doing this, and how does it affect the reader's response?
3. Why does Guppy include the story of the scorpion in paragraph 7? What relevance does it have to the rest of the story?
4. Define the words *mosques* (paragraph 3); *muezzin* (paragraph 13); *mullah* (paragraph 15); and *Imam* (paragraph 25).
5. How does Guppy use sensory details in her writing? Find specific examples in the essay, and discuss how they enrich her narration.
6. Consider the accumulation of information in Guppy's conclusion. What is the point of this technique? What is the point of the final sentence in the paragraph? What effect does it have on the reader?

WRITING

1. Write an essay narrating a significant religious holiday celebrated in your home as a child. Use sensory details in describing the event. Also discuss your feelings, both as a child and now as an adult, about these observances.
2. In her essay, Guppy states that religious devotion has been "ruthlessly exploited by power maniacs and demagogues." Write an essay exploring the validity of this opinion. Use support from the essay itself as well as from your own experiences and observances.
3. Research the Islamic religion and write an essay explaining its principal tenets and listing its major religious holidays. Use quotes from the Guppy essay where applicable.

GEORGE ELIOT Mary Ann (or Marian) Evans (1819–1880) is better known by her pen name, George Eliot. Born in Victorian England, Evans broke away from her father's evangelical beliefs. She later became an assistant editor for the *Westminster Review.* In her work, Evans examined Victorian society's attitudes and morals in novels such as *Adam Bede* (1859), *The Mill on the Floss* (1860), *Silas Marner* (1861), *Daniel Deronda* (1876), and what is considered to be her masterpiece, *Middlemarch* (1871–1872). Evans was interested in people's moral choices. She herself lived a rather unconventional life with George Henry Lewes, a married man. In the selection below, from the prelude to *Middlemarch,* Evans ponders the role of women in the spiritual quest and the arena of public good.

GEORGE ELIOT

Saint Theresa

Who that cares much to know the history of man, and how the mysterious mixture behaves under the varying experiments of Time, has not dwelt, at least briefly, on the life of Saint Theresa, has not smiled with some gentleness at the thought of the little girl walking forth one morning hand-in-hand with her still smaller brother, to go and seek martyrdom in the country of the Moors? Out they toddled from rugged Avila, wide-eyed and helpless-looking as two fawns, but with human hearts, already beating to a national idea; until domestic reality met them in the shape of uncles, and turned them back from their great resolve. That child-pilgrimage was a fit beginning. Theresa's passionate, ideal nature demanded an epic life: what were many-volumed romances of chivalry and the social conquests of a brilliant girl to her? Her flame quickly burned up that light fuel; and, fed from within, soared after some illimitable satisfaction, some object which would never justify weariness, which would reconcile self-despair with the rapturous consciousness of life beyond self. She found her epos in the reform of a religious order. 1

That Spanish woman who lived three hundred years ago was certainly not the last of her kind. Many Theresas have been born who found for themselves no epic life wherein there was a constant unfolding of far-resonant action; perhaps only a life of mistakes, the offspring of a certain spiritual grandeur ill-matched with the meanness of opportunity; perhaps a tragic failure which found no sacred poet and sank unwept into oblivion. With dim lights and tangled circumstance they tried to shape their thought and deed in noble agreement; but after all, to common eyes their struggles seemed mere inconsistency and formlessness; for these later-born Theresas were helped by no coherent social faith and order which could perform the function of knowledge for the ardently willing soul. Their ardour alternated between a vague ideal and the common yearning of womanhood; so that the one was disapproved as extravagance, and the other condemned as a lapse. 2

Some have felt that these blundering lives are due to the inconvenient indefiniteness with which the Supreme Power has fashioned the natures of women: if there were one level of feminine incompetence as strict as the ability to count three and no more, the social lot of women might be treated with scientific certitude. Meanwhile the indefiniteness remains, and the limits of variation are really much wider than any one would imagine from the sameness of women's coiffure and the favourite love-stories in prose and verse. Here and there a cygnet is reared uneasily among the ducklings in the brown pond, and never finds the living stream in fellowship with its own oary-footed kind. 3

Here and there is born a Saint Theresa, foundress of nothing, whose loving heart-beats and sobs after an unattained goodness tremble off and are dispersed among hindrances, instead of centering in some long-recognizable deed.

COMPREHENSION

1. Is Eliot's essay actually about Saint Theresa? What was Eliot's purpose in writing this piece?
2. Define what Eliot means by an "epic life" (in paragraph 2).
3. What does the author mean by the "indefiniteness" of the natures of women (paragraph 3)?

RHETORIC

1. What is Eliot's purpose in the introductory section? How does this approach help to set up her argument?
2. Trace the development of ideas in paragraph 2. How is the topic sentence supported by what follows? Is the support strong? Why, or why not?
3. What is the tone of Eliot's essay? Justify your response.
4. What is Eliot's level of language? Who is her intended audience? How do her syntax, vocabulary, and style reflect this?
5. How does Eliot use figurative language in her piece? Is it effective in clarifying her point? Cite specific examples of the language.
6. Examine Eliot's final paragraph. How does it function as a conclusion? How does her metaphor work to reinforce her thesis?

WRITING

1. Write an essay in which you interpret Eliot's concepts of an "epic life" and "life beyond self." What do these concepts mean to you? Can you think of a modern person whose life and work embody those ideas?
2. Research the life of George Eliot. Consider her efforts as a woman and an artist in terms of the possibilities and limitations of women's lives in her time. Is Eliot's argument limited to the spiritual realm?

MARTIN BUBER Martin Buber (1878–1965) was born in Vienna. He taught philosophy and religion at the University of Frankfurt-am-Main until 1933, when he fled the Nazis; from 1938 to 1951, he taught at the Hebrew University in Jerusalem. Greatly influenced by the mystical Jewish tradition of Hasidism, as well as existentialism, Buber's work is important to both secular and religious readers. Among his works are *I and Thou* (1923; 2d ed., 1958), *Jewish Mysticism and the Legends of Baalshem* (1931), *Moses* (1946), and *A Believing Humanism: My Testament 1902–1965* (tr. 1967). In this selection, Buber relates a religious teaching story reflecting his concern about both the community and the soul.

MARTIN BUBER

The Third Leg of the Table

When Rabbi Yeheskel Landau came to Prague, he spoke to his congregation Sabbath after Sabbath of nothing else except the bitter need of the destitute in the city. One had expected to hear from his mouth profound meanings of interpretations and subtle meanings of disputations, but he only thought of reminding them of the wretched who spread out unrelieved, unnoticed, in this lane and its surroundings. "Help! Go there even today in the evening and help!" thus he called ever again. But the people took it for a sermon and were vexed that it was so insipid and flat. 1

Then on a busy market day something wonderful took place. Right through the middle of the tumult came the rabbi and remained standing in the center of the thickest swarm as though he had wares to offer for sale and only waited for a favorable moment to commend them to the crowd. Those who recognized him passed the incomprehensible fact on to others; from everywhere traders and buyers crowded to that place; they stared at him, but no one dared to question him. Finally there broke from the lips of one who imagined himself intimate with him, "What is our rabbi doing here?" 2

At once Rabbi Yeheskel began: 3

"If a table has three legs and a piece is broken off of one of the three legs, what does one do? One supports the leg as well as one can, and the table stands. But now if still another of the three legs breaks in two, there is no longer a support. What does one do then? One shortens the third leg too, and the table stands again.

"Our sages say: 'The world stands on three things: on the teaching, on the service, and on the deeds of love.' When the holiness is destroyed, then the leg of the service breaks. Then our sages support it by saying: 'Service with the heart, that is what is meant by prayer.' But now when the acts of love disappear and the second leg suffers injury, how shall the world still endure? Therefore, I have left the house of teaching and have come to the market place. We must shorten the leg of the teaching in order that the table of the world may again stand firm." 4

COMPREHENSION

1. What is Buber's purpose in telling this story? What does Rabbi Landau represent to Buber?

2. When does this story take place? What clues are there that locate it in time?
3. Compare Buber's understanding of "holiness" and Dillard's (Chapter 10).

RHETORIC

1. Define the following: *vexed* (paragraph 1); *tumult* (paragraph 2); and *incomprehensible* (paragraph 2).
2. Is there any figurative language in this essay? Explain.
3. Is Buber relating a story from his own experience or from tradition? How many levels of narrative are there here?
4. What is the purpose of the example of the table?
5. What strategy does Buber use to describe Landau?
6. How does point of view reinforce the tone of this piece?

WRITING

1. What responsibility do religious leaders and their congregations have to do service in the community? To what extent have organized religions fulfilled this duty? Answer in a brief essay.
2. What responsibility do you feel toward the homeless and destitute of our society? How do you meet this responsibility? Is such a duty religious or merely ethical? Write an explanatory essay dealing with these questions.
3. Is there a necessary conflict between teaching and service? What is your position?

WOLE SOYINKA Wole Soyinka (1934–) was born Akinwande Oluwole Soyinka in Nigeria and educated at universities in England. Soyinka is a poet, playwright, and essayist; his work focuses on the freedom of the individual. He became interested in drama while in England, and later he helped establish an indigenous theater in Nigeria. He has written numerous plays—including *Madmen and Specialists* (1972), *Death of the King's Horseman* (1975), and *A Play of Giants* (1984)—that use Nigerian folk motifs. In 1986, Soyinka received the Nobel Prize in Literature. In the following excerpt from his autobiography, *Aké: The Years of Childhood,* published in 1981, he describes in humorous, lyrical language the uneasy coexistence of Nigerian folklore and Christianity as viewed through the eyes of a child—himself.

WOLE SOYINKA

Aké: The Years of Childhood

The sprawling, undulating terrain is all of Aké. More than mere loyalty 1
to the parsonage gave birth to a puzzle, and a resentment, that God should choose to look down on his own pious station, the parsonage compound, from the profane heights of Itókò. There was of course the mystery of the Chief's stable with live horses near the crest of the hill, but beyond that, this dizzying road only sheered upwards from one noisy market to the other, looking down across Ibàràpa and Ita Aké into the most secret recesses of the parsonage itself.

On a misty day, the steep rise towards Itókò would join the sky. If 2
God did not actually live there, there was little doubt that he descended first on its crest, then took his one gigantic stride over those babbling markets—which dared to sell on Sundays—into St. Peter's Church, afterwards visiting the parsonage for tea with the Canon. There was the small consolation that, in spite of the temptation to arrive on horseback, he never stopped first at the Chief's, who was known to be a pagan; certainly the Chief was never seen at a church service except at the anniversaries of the Alake's coronation. Instead God strode straight into St. Peter's for morning service, paused briefly at the afternoon service, but reserved his most formal, exotic presence for the evening service which, in his honour, was always held in the English tongue. The organ took on a dark, smoky sonority at evening service, and there was no doubt that the organ was adapting its normal sounds to accompany God's own sepulchral responses, with its timbre of the *egúngún,*[1] to those prayers that were offered to him.

Only the Canon's residence could have housed the weekly Guest. 3
For one thing, it was the only storey-building in the parsonage, square and stolid as the Canon himself, riddled with black wooden-framed windows. BishopsCourt was also a storey-building but only pupils lived in it, so it was not a house. From the upper floor of the Canon's home one *almost* looked the top of Itókò straight in its pagan eye. It stood at the highest lived-in point of the parsonage, just missing overlooking the gate. Its back was turned to the world of spirits and ghommids who inhabited the thick woods and chased home children who had wandered too deeply in them for firewood, mushrooms and snails. The Canon's square, white building was a bulwark against the menace and the siege of the wood spirits. Its rear wall demarcated their territory, stopped them from taking liberties with the world of humans.

[1]Ancestral masquerade.

4 Only the school-rooms of the primary school shared this closeness to the woods, and they were empty at night. Fenced by rough plastered walls, by the windowless rear walls of its houses, by tumuli of rocks which the giant trees tried vainly to obscure, Aké parsonage with its corrugated roofs gave off an air of fortifications. Secure within it, we descended or climbed at will into overlapping, interleaved planes, sheer rock-face drops, undergrowths and sudden hideouts of cultivated fruit groves. The hibiscus was rampant. The air hung heavy with the perfumes of lemon leaves, guavas, mangoes, sticky with the sap of *boum-boum* and the secretions of the rain-tree. The school-compounds were lined with these rain-trees with widespread shade-filled branches. Needle-pines rose above the acacia and forests of bamboos kept us permanently nervous; if monster snakes had a choice, the bamboo clumps would be their ideal habitation.

5 Between the left flank of the Canon's house and the school playing-fields was—the Orchard. It was too varied, much too profuse to be called a garden, even a fruit-garden. And there were plants and fruits in it which made the orchard an extension of scripture classes, church lessons or sermons. A leaf-plant, mottled white-and-red, was called the Cana lily. As Christ was nailed to the Cross and his wounds spurted blood, a few drops stuck to the leaves of the lily, stigmatizing it for ever. No one bothered to explain the cause of the abundant white spots which also appeared on every leaf. Perhaps it had to do with the washing of sins in the blood of Christ, leaving even the most mottled spots in a person's soul snow-white. There was the Passion fruit also, born of another part of that same history, not however a favourite of any of us children. Its lush green skin was pleasant to fondle in one's palm, but it ripened into a dessicated yellow, collapsing like the faces of the old men and women we knew. And it barely managed to be sweet, thus failing the infallible test of a real fruit. But the queen of the orchard was the pomegranate which grew, not so much from a seed of the stone church as of the lyrical Sunday School. For it was at the Sunday School that the real stories were told, stories that lived in the events themselves, crossed the time-border of Sundays or leaves of the Bible and entered the world of fabled lands, men and women. The pomegranate was most niggardly in producing. It yielded its outwardly hardy fruit only once in a while, tended with patience by the thick-veined hands and face which belonged to someone we only knew as Gardener. Only Gardener could be trusted to share the occasional fruit among the small, dedicated band of pomegranate watchers, yet even the tiniest wedge transported us to the illustrated world of the Biblical Tales Retold. The pomegranate was the Queen of Sheba, rebellions and wars, the passion of Salome, the siege of Troy, the Praise of beauty in the Song of Solomon. This fruit, with its stone-hearted look and feel unlocked the cellars of Ali Baba, extracted the genie from Aladdin's lamp, plucked the strings of the harp that restored David to sanity, parted the waters of the Nile and filled our parsonage with incense from the dim temple of Jerusalem.

It grew only in the Orchard, Gardener said. The pomegranate was 6
foreign to the black man's soil, but some previous bishop, a white man, had brought the seeds and planted them in the Orchard. We asked if it was *the* apple but Gardener only laughed and said No. Nor, he added, would that apple be found on the black man's soil. Gardener was adjudged ignorant. It was clear that only the pomegranate could be the apple that lost Adam and Eve the joys of paradise. There existed yet another fruit that was locally called apple, soft yet crisp, a soft pink skin and reasonably juicy. Before the advent of the pomegranate it had assumed the identity of the apple that undid the naked pair. The first taste of the pomegranate unmasked that impostor and took its place.

Swarms of bats inhabited the fig tree; their seed-pocked droppings 7
would cake the stones, lawns, paths and bushes before dawn. An evergreen tree, soft and rampant, bordered the playing-field on the side of the bookseller's compound, defying the Harmattan; it filled the parsonage with a tireless concert of weaver-birds.

An evil thing has happened to Aké parsonage. The land is eroded, the 8
lawns are bared and mystery driven from its once secretive combs. Once, each new day opened up an unseen closure, a pocket of rocks, a clump of bush and a colony of snails. The motor-hulk has not moved from its staging-point where children clambered into it for journeys to fabled places; now it is only a derelict, its eyes rusted sockets, its dragon face collapsed with a progressive loss of teeth. The abandoned incinerator with its lush weeds and glistening snakes is marked by a mound of mud. The surviving houses, houses which formed the battlements of Aké parsonage, are now packing cases on a depleted landscape, full of creaks, exposed and nerveless.

And the moods are gone. Even the open lawns and broad paths, 9
bordered with whitewashed stones, lilies and lemon grass clumps, changed nature from season to season, from weekday to Sunday and between noon and nightfall. And the echoes off the walls in Lower Parsonage acquired new tonalities with the seasons, changed with the emptying of the lawns as the schools dispersed for holidays.

If I lay across the lawn before our house, face upwards to the sky, 10
my head towards BishopsCourt, each spread-out leg would point to the inner compounds of Lower Parsonage. Half of the Anglican Girls' School occupied one of these lower spaces, the other half had taken over BishopsCourt. The lower area contained the school's junior classrooms, a dormitory, a small fruit-garden of pawpaws, guava, some bamboo and wild undergrowth. There were always snails to be found in the rainy season. In the other lower compound was the mission bookseller, a shrivelled man with a serene wife on whose ample back we all, at one time or the other, slept or reviewed the world. His compound became a short cut to the road that led to Ibarà. Lafenwá or Igbèin and its Grammar School, over which Ransome-Kuti presided and lived with his family. The bookseller's compound contained the only well in

the parsonage; in the dry season, his place was never empty. And his soil appeared to produce the only coconut trees.

BishopsCourt, of Upper Parsonage, is no more. Bishop Ajayi Crowther would sometimes emerge from the cluster of hydrangea and bougainvillea, a gnomic face with popping eyes whose formal photograph had first stared at us from the frontispiece of his life history. He had lived, the teacher said, in BishopsCourt, and from that moment, he peered out from among the creeping plants whenever I passed by the house on an errand to our Great Aunt, Mrs. Lijadu. BishopsCourt had become a boarding house for the girls' school and an extra playground for us during the holidays. The Bishop sat, silently, on the bench beneath the wooden porch over the entrance, his robes twined through and through with the lengthening tendrils of the bougainvillea. I moved closer when his eyes turned to sockets. My mind wandered then to another photograph in which he wore a clerical suit with waistcoat and I wondered what he really kept at the end of the silver chain that vanished into the pocket. He grinned and said, Come nearer, I'll show you. As I moved towards the porch he drew on the chain until he had lifted out a wholly round pocket-watch that gleamed of solid silver. He pressed a button and the lid opened, revealing, not the glass and the face-dial but a deep cloud-filled space. Then he winked one eye, and it fell from his face into the bowl of the watch. He winked the other and this joined its partner in the watch. He snapped back the lid, nodded again and his head went bald, his teeth disappeared and the skin pulled backward till the whitened cheekbones were exposed. Then he stood up and, tucking the watch back into the waistcoat pocket, moved a step towards me. I fled homewards.

BishopsCourt appeared sometimes to want to rival the Canon's 12
house. It looked a house-boat despite its guard of whitewashed stones and luxuriant flowers, its wooden fretwork frontage almost wholly immersed in bougainvillea. And it was shadowed also by those omnipresent rocks from whose clefts tall, stout-boled trees miraculously grew. Clouds gathered and the rocks merged into their accustomed grey turbulence, then the trees were carried to and fro until they stayed suspended over BishopsCourt. This happened only in heavy storms. BishopsCourt, unlike the Canon's house, did not actually border the rocks or the woods. The girls' playing fields separated them and we knew that this buffer had always been there. Obviously bishops were not inclined to challenge the spirits. Only the vicars could. That Bishop Ajayi Crowther frightened me out of that compound by his strange transformations only confirmed that the bishops, once they were dead, joined the world of spirits and ghosts. I could not see the Canon decaying like that in front of my eyes, nor the Rev J. J. who had once occupied that house, many years before, when my mother was still like us. J. J. Ransome-Kuti had actually ordered back several ghommids in his life-time; my mother confirmed it. She was his grand niece and, before she came to live at our house, she had lived in the Rev J. J.'s household. Her brother Sanya also lived there and he was

acknowledged by all to be an *òrò,* which made him at home in the woods, even at night. On one occasion, however, he must have gone too far.

"They had visited us before," she said, "to complain. Mind you, 13
they wouldn't actually come into the compound, they stood far off at the edge, where the woods ended. Their leader, the one who spoke, emitted wild sparks from a head that seemed to be an entire ball of embers—no, I'm mixing up two occasions—that was the second time when he chased us home. The first time, they had merely sent an emissary. He was quite dark, short and swarthy. He came right to the backyard and stood there while he ordered us to call the Reverend.

"It was as if Uncle had been expecting the visit. He came out of the 14
house and asked him what he wanted. We all huddled in the kitchen, peeping out."

"What was his voice like? Did he speak like an *egúngún?*" 15

"I'm coming to it. This man, well, I suppose one should call him a 16
man. He wasn't quite human, we could see that. Much too large a head, and he kept his eyes on the ground. So, he said he had come to report us. They didn't mind our coming to the woods, even at night, but we were to stay off any area beyond the rocks and that clump of bamboo by the stream."

"Well, what did Uncle say? And you haven't said what his voice was 17
like."

Tinu turned her elder sister's eye on me. "Let Mama finish the 18
story."

"You want to know everything. All right, he spoke just like your fa- 19
ther. Are you satisfied?"

I did not believe that but I let it pass. "Go on. What did Grand 20
Uncle do?"

"He called everyone together and warned us to keep away from the 21
place."

"And yet you went back!" 22

"Well, you know your Uncle Sanya. He was angry. For one thing 23
the best snails are on the other side of that stream. So he continued to complain that those *òrò* were just being selfish, and he was going to show them who he was. Well, he did. About a week later he led us back. And he was right you know. We gathered a full basket and a half of the biggest snails you ever saw. Well, by this time we had all forgotten about the warning, there was plenty of moonlight and anyway, I've told you Sanya is an *òrò* himself. . . ."

"But why? He looks normal like you and us." 24

"You won't understand yet. Anyway, he is *òrò*. So with him we 25
felt quite safe. Until suddenly this sort of light, like a ball of fire, began to glow in the distance. Even while it was still far we kept hearing voices, as if a lot of people around us were grumbling the same words together. They were saying something like, 'You stubborn, stiff-necked children, we've warned you and warned you but you just won't listen. . . .'"

Wild Christian looked above our heads, frowning to recollect the 26
better. "One can't even say, 'they.' It was only this figure of fire that I saw and he was still very distant. Yet I heard him distinctly, as if he had many mouths which were pressed against my ears. Every moment, the fireball loomed larger and larger."

"What did Uncle Sanya do? Did he fight him?" 27

"Sanya wo ni yen? He was the first to break and run. *Bo o ló o yǎ* 28
mi, o di kítìpà kítìpà![2] No one remembered all those fat snails. That *iwin*[3] followed us all the way to the house. Our screams had arrived long before us and the whole household was—well, you can imagine the turmoil. Uncle had already dashed down the stairs and was in the backyard. We ran past him while he went out to meet the creature. This time that *iwin* actually passed the line of the woods, he continued as if he meant to chase us right into the house, you know, he wasn't running, just pursuing us steadily." We waited. This was it! Wild Christian mused while we remained in suspense. Then she breathed deeply and shook her head with a strange sadness.

"The period of faith is gone. There was faith among our early 29
christians, real faith, not just church-going and hymn-singing. Faith. *Igbàgbó*. And it is out of that faith that real power comes. Uncle stood there like a rock, he held out his Bible and ordered, 'Go back! Go back to that forest which is your home. Back I said, in the name of God.' Hm. And that was it. The creature simply turned and fled, those sparks falling off faster and faster until there was just a faint glow receding into the woods." She sighed. "Of course, after prayers that evening, there was the price to be paid. Six of the best on every one's back. Sanya got twelve. And we all cut grass every day for the next week."

I could not help feeling that the fright should have sufficed as pun- 30
ishment. Her eyes gazing in the direction of the square house, Wild Christian nonetheless appeared to sense what was going on in my mind. She added, "Faith and—Discipline. That is what made those early believers. Psheeaw! God doesn't make them like that any more. When I think of that one who now occupies that house. . . ."

Then she appeared to recall herself to our presence. "What are you 31
both still sitting here for? Isn't it time for your evening bath? Lawanle!" Auntie Lawanle replied "Ma" from a distant part of the house. Before she appeared I reminded Wild Christian, "But you haven't told us why Uncle Sanya is *òrò*."

She shrugged, "He is. I saw it with my own eyes." 32

We both clamoured. "When? When?" 33

She smiled. "You won't understand. But I'll tell you about it some 34
other time. Or let him tell you himself next time he is here."

"You mean you saw him turn into an *òrò?*" 35

Lawanle came in just then and she prepared to hand us over, "Isn't 36
it time for these children's bath?"

[2]If you aren't moving, get out of my way!

[3]A "ghommid" a wood sprite which is also believed to live in the ground.

I pleaded, "No, wait Auntie Lawanle," knowing it was a waste of time. She had already gripped us both, one arm each. I shouted back, "Was Bishop Crowther an *òrò?*" 37

Wild Christian laughed. "What next are you going to ask? Oh I see. They have taught you about him in Sunday school have they?" 38

"I saw him." I pulled back at the door, forcing Lawanle to stop. "I see him all the time. He comes and sits under the porch of the Girls School. I've seen him when crossing the compound to Auntie Mrs. Lijadu." 39

"All right," sighed Wild Christian. "Go and have your bath." 40

"He hides among the bougainvillea. . . ." Lawanle dragged me out of hearing. 41

Later that evening, she told us the rest of the story. On that occasion, Rev J. J. was away on one of his many mission tours. He travelled a lot, on foot and on bicycle, keeping in touch with all the branches of his diocese and spreading the Word of God. There was frequent opposition but nothing deterred him. One frightening experience occurred in one of the villages in Ijebu. He had been warned not to preach on a particular day, which was the day for an *egúngún* outing, but he persisted and held a service. The *egúngún* procession passed while the service was in progress and, using his ancestral voice, called on the preacher to stop at once, disperse his people and come out to pay obeisance. Rev J. J. ignored him. The *egúngún* then left, taking his followers with him but, on passing the main door, he tapped on it with his wand, three times. Hardly had the last member of his procession left the church premises than the building collapsed. The walls simply fell down and the roof disintegrated. Miraculously, however, the walls fell outwards while the roof supports fell among the aisles or flew outwards—anywhere but on the congregation itself. Rev J. J. calmed the worshippers, paused in his preaching to render a thanksgiving prayer, then continued his sermon. 42

Perhaps this was what Wild Christian meant by Faith. And this tended to confuse things because, after all, the *egúngún* did make the church building collapse. Wild Christian made no attempt to explain how that happened, so that feat tended to be of the same order of Faith which moved mountains or enabled Wild Christian to pour ground-nut oil from a broad-rimmed bowl into an empty bottle without spilling a drop. She had the strange habit of sighing with a kind of rapture, crediting her steadiness of hand to Faith and thanking God. If however the basin slipped and she lost a drop or two, she murmured that her sins had become heavy and that she needed to pray more. 43

If Rev J. J. had Faith, however, he also appeared to have Stubborness in common with our Uncle Sanya. Stubborness was one of the earliest sins we easily recognized, and no matter how much Wild Christian tried to explain the Rev J. J. preaching on the *egúngún's* outing day, despite warnings, it sounded much like stubborness. As for Uncle Sanya there was no doubt about his own case; hardly did the Rev J. J. pedal out of sight on his pastoral duties than he was off into the woods on one pretext or the other, and making for the very areas which the 44 *òrò* had declared out of bounds. Mushrooms and snails were the real goals, with the gathering of firewood used as the dutiful excuse.

Even Sanya had however stopped venturing into the woods at night, accepting the fact that it was far too risky; daytime and early dusk carried little danger as most wood spirits only came out at night. Mother told us that on this occasion she and Sanya had been picking mushrooms, separated by only a few clumps of bushes. She could hear his movements quite clearly, indeed, they took the precaution of staying very close together.

Suddenly, she said, she heard Sanya's voice talking animatedly with 46
someone. After listening for some time she called out his name but he did not respond. There was no voice apart from his, yet he appeared to be chatting in friendly, excited tones with some other person. So she peeped through the bushes and there was Uncle Sanya seated on the ground chattering away to no one that she could see. She tried to penetrate the surrounding bushes with her gaze but the woods remained empty except for the two of them. And then her eyes came to rest on his basket.

It was something she had observed before, she said. It was the 47
same, no matter how many of the children in the household went to gather snails, berries or whatever, Sanya would spend most of the time playing and climbing rocks and trees. He would wander off by himself, leaving his basket anywhere. And yet, whenever they prepared to return home, his basket was always fuller than the others'. This time was no different. She came closer, startling our Uncle who snapped off his chatter and pretended to be hunting snails in the undergrowth.

Mother said that she was frightened. The basket was filled to the 48
brim, impossibly bursting. She was also discouraged, so she picked up her near empty basket and insisted that they return home at once. She led the way but after some distance, when she looked back, Sanya appeared to be trying to follow her but was being prevented, as if he was being pulled back by invisible hands. From time to time he would snatch forward his arm and snap,

"Leave me alone. Can't you see I have to go home? I said I have 49
to go."

She broke into a run and Sanya did the same. They ran all the way 50
home.

That evening, Sanya took ill. He broke into a sweat, tossed on his 51
mat all night and muttered to himself. By the following day the household was thoroughly frightened. His forehead was burning to the touch and no one could get a coherent word out of him. Finally, an elderly woman, one of J. J.'s converts, turned up at the house on a routine visit. When she learnt of Sanya's condition, she nodded wisely and acted like one who knew exactly what to do. Having first found out what things he last did before his illness, she summoned my mother and questioned her. She told her everything while the old woman kept on nodding with understanding. Then she gave instructions:

52 "I want a basket of *àgìdi,* containing 50 wraps. Then prepare some *èkuru* in a large bowl. Make sure the *èkuru* stew is prepared with plenty of locust bean and crayfish. It must smell as appetizing as possible."

53 The children were dispersed in various directions, some to the market to obtain the *àgìdi,* others to begin grinding the beans for the amount of *èkuru* which was needed to accompany 50 wraps of *àgìdi.* The children's mouths watered, assuming at once that this was to be an appeasement feast, a *sàarà*[4] for some offended spirits.

54 When all was prepared, however, the old woman took everything to Sanya's sick-room, plus a pot of cold water and cups, locked the door on him and ordered everybody away.

55 "Just go about your normal business and don't go anywhere near the room. If you want your brother to recover, do as I say. Don't attempt to speak to him and don't peep through the keyhole."

56 She locked the windows too and went herself to a distant end of the courtyard where she could monitor the movements of the children. She dozed off soon after, however, so that mother and the other children were able to glue their ears to the door and windows, even if they could not see the invalid himself. Uncle Sanya sounded as if he was no longer alone. They heard him saying things like:

57 "Behave yourself, there is enough for everybody. All right you take this, have an extra wrap. . . . Open your mouth. . . . here . . . you don't have to fight over that bit, here's another piece of crayfish . . . behave, I said. . . ."

58 And they would hear what sounded like the slapping of wrists, a scrape of dishes on the ground or water slopping into a cup.

59 When the woman judged it was time, which was well after dusk, nearly six hours after Sanya was first locked up, she went and opened the door. There was Sanya fast asleep but, this time, very peacefully. She touched his forehead and appeared to be satisfied by the change. The household who had crowded in with her had no interest in Sanya however. All they could see, with astonished faces, were the scattered leaves of 50 wraps of *àgìdi,* with the contents gone, a large empty dish which was earlier filled with *èkuru,* and a water-pot nearly empty.

60 No, there was no question about it, our Uncle Sanya was an *òrò;* Wild Christian had seen and heard proofs of it many times over. His companions were obviously the more benevolent type or he would have come to serious harm on more than one occasion, J. J.'s protecting Faith notwithstanding. Uncle Sanya was very rarely with us at this time, so we could not ask him any of the questions which Wild Christian refused to answer. When he next visited us at the parsonage, I noticed his strange eyes which hardly ever seemed to blink but looked straight over our heads even when he talked to us. But he seemed far too active to be an *òrò;* indeed for a long time I confused him with a local scoutmaster who was nicknamed Activity. So I began to watch the Wolf Cubs who seemed nearest to the kind of secret company which our Uncle Sanya

[4]An offering, food shared out as offering.

may have kept as a child. As their tight little faces formed circles on the lawns of Aké, building little fires, exchanging secret signs with hands and twigs, with stones specially placed against one another during their jamboree, I felt I had detected the hidden companions who crept in unseen through chinks in the door and even from the ground, right under the aggrieved noses of Wild Christian and the other children in J. J.'s household, and feasted on 50 wraps of *àgìdi* and a huge bowl of *èkuru*.

COMPREHENSION

1. As a child, what significant link does Soyinka make between Christianity and nature?
2. How does Christian dogma coexist with Soyinka's world of tree demons and ghosts?
3. What is the attitude of Soyinka, the adult, toward Christianity's dominance over native beliefs?

RHETORIC

1. What is the writer's attitude toward his subject? Where is the writer's tone evident in the essay? Pick specific examples.
2. What narrative strategies does Soyinka employ in his essay?
3. Does the essay have a thesis? If not, where in the essay does Soyinka's purpose for writing it become clear?
4. Provide examples of Soyinka's use of descriptive language. How does it contribute to the force of his narrative?
5. Comment on Soyinka's use of dialogue in the essay. To what end is it employed? Is it successful?
6. Cite biblical references in the essay, and discuss how their inclusion strengthens or clarifies Soyinka's thesis.

WRITING

1. In a brief essay, examine how the people in Soyinka's essay bridged the gap between Christianity and their own beliefs.
2. Write an essay arguing that Christianity's conversion of other religions has usually done more harm than good, both to those being converted and to humanity as a whole. Some research may be necessary.

C. S. LEWIS Clive Staples Lewis (1898–1963) was born in Belfast, Ireland, but spent the most important years of his life as a lecturer in English at Oxford. His first book, *Dymer*, was published in 1926, but it was not until the publication of *The Pilgrim's Regress* in 1933 that he addressed the central work of his life: a passionate defense of the Christian faith. Lewis's immense output embraced science fiction, fantasy, children's books, theology, and literary criticism. Among his best-known works are *The Screwtape Letters* (1942); *The*

Lion, the Witch, and the Wardrobe (1950); and *"The Narnia Chronicle"* (1956). In this essay, Lewis describes the reasoning that led to his conversion.

C. S. LEWIS

The Rival Conceptions of God

I have been asked to tell you what Christians believe, and I am going to begin by telling you one thing that Christians do not need to believe. If you are a Christian you do not have to believe that all the other religions are simply wrong all through. If you are an atheist you do have to believe that the main point in all the religions of the whole world is simply one huge mistake. If you are a Christian, you are free to think that all these religions, even the queerest ones, contain at least some hint of the truth. When I was an atheist I had to try to persuade myself that most of the human race have always been wrong about the question that mattered to them most; when I became a Christian I was able to take a more liberal view. But, of course, being a Christian does mean thinking that where Christianity differs from other religions, Christianity is right and they are wrong. As in arithmetic—there is only one right answer to a sum, and all other answers are wrong: but some of the wrong answers are much nearer being right than others. 1

The first big division of humanity is into the majority, who believe in some kind of God or gods, and the minority who do not. On this point, Christianity lines up with the majority—lines up with ancient Greeks and Romans, modern savages, Stoics, Platonists, Hindus, Mohammedans, etc., against the modern Western European materialist. 2

Now I go on to the next big division. People who all believe in God can be divided according to the sort of God they believe in. There are two very different ideas on this subject. One of them is the idea that He is beyond good and evil. We humans call one thing good and another thing bad. But according to some people that is merely our human point of view. These people would say that the wiser you become the less you would want to call anything good or bad, and the more clearly you would see that everything is good in one way and bad in another, and that nothing could have been different. Consequently, these people think that long before you got anywhere near the divine point of view the distinction would have disappeared altogether. We call a cancer bad, they would say, because it kills a man; but you might just as well call a successful surgeon bad because he kills a cancer. It all depends on the point of view. The other and opposite idea is that God is quite definitely "good" or "righteous," a God who takes sides, who loves love 3

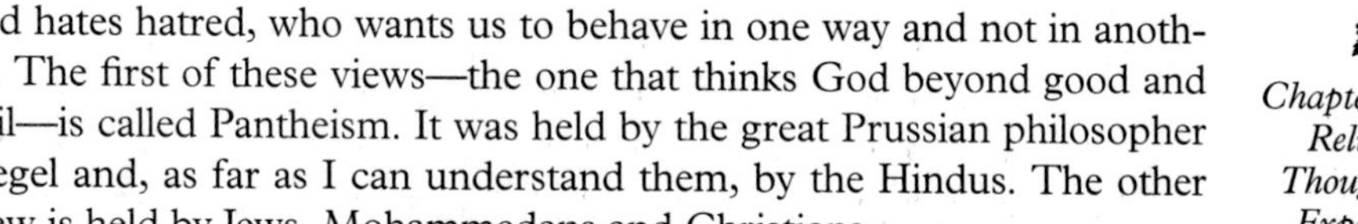

and hates hatred, who wants us to behave in one way and not in another. The first of these views—the one that thinks God beyond good and evil—is called Pantheism. It was held by the great Prussian philosopher Hegel and, as far as I can understand them, by the Hindus. The other view is held by Jews, Mohammedans and Christians.

And with this big difference between Pantheism and the Christian 4
idea of God, there usually goes another. Pantheists usually believe that God, so to speak, animates the universe as you animate your body: that the universe almost *is* God, so that if it did not exist He would not exist either, and anything you find in the universe is a part of God. The Christian idea is quite different. They think God invented and made the universe—like a man making a picture or composing a tune. A painter is not a picture, and he does not die if his picture is destroyed. You may say, "He's put a lot of himself into it," but you only mean that all its beauty and interest has come out of his head. His skill is not in the picture in the same way that it is in his head, or even in his hands. I expect you see how this difference between Pantheists and Christians hangs together with the other one. If you do not take the distinction between good and bad very seriously, then it is easy to say that anything you find in this world is a part of God. But, of course, if you think some things really bad, and God really good, then you cannot talk like that. You must believe that God is separate from the world and that some of the things we see in it are contrary to His will. Confronted with a cancer or a slum the Pantheist can say, "If you could only see it from the divine point of view, you would realize that this also is God." The Christian replies, "Don't talk damned nonsense."* For Christianity is a fighting religion. It thinks God made the world—that space and time, heat and cold, and all the colours and tastes, and all the animals and vegetables, are things that God "made up out of His head" as a man makes up a story. But it also thinks that a great many things have gone wrong with the world that God made and that God insists, and insists very loudly, on our putting them right again.

And, of course, that raises a very big question. If a good God made 5
the world why has it gone wrong? And for many years I simply refused to listen to the Christian answers to this question, because I kept on feeling "whatever you say, and however clever your arguments are, isn't it much simpler and easier to say that the world was not made by any intelligent power? Aren't all your arguments simply a complicated attempt to avoid the obvious?" But then that threw me back into another difficulty.

My argument against God was that the universe seemed so cruel and 6
unjust. But how had I got this idea of *just* and *unjust?* A man does not call a line crooked unless he has some idea of a straight line. What was I comparing this universe with when I called it unjust? If the whole show was

*One listener complained of the word *damned* as frivolous swearing. But I mean exactly what I say—nonsense that is *damned* is under God's curse, and will (apart from God's grace) lead those who believe it to eternal death.

bad and senseless from A to Z, so to speak, why did I, who was supposed to be part of the show, find myself in such violent reaction against it? A man feels wet when he falls into water, because man is not a water animal: a fish would not feel wet. Of course I could have given up my idea of justice by saying it was nothing but a private idea of my own. But if I did that, then my argument against God collapsed too—for the argument depended on saying that the world was really unjust, not simply that it did not happen to please my private fancies. Thus in the very act of trying to prove that God did not exist—in other words, that the whole of reality was senseless—I found I was forced to assume that one part of reality—namely my idea of justice—was full of sense. Consequently atheism turns out to be too simple. If the whole universe has no meaning, we should never have found out that it has no meaning: just as, if there were no light in the universe and therefore no creature with eyes, we should never know it was dark. *Dark* would be without meaning.

COMPREHENSION

1. Who is Lewis's audience? What is his purpose? How do you know?
2. Lewis divides humanity into a number of distinct categories. Name them, and discuss his purpose in establishing these categories.
3. What is Lewis's purpose in likening Christianity to arithmetic? In what sense is this apt? Where does he use a similar image?

RHETORIC

1. Look up the following words in paragraph 2 in a dictionary or encyclopedia: *Stoics, Platonists, Hindus,* and *Mohammedans.* What are the major tenets of their beliefs?
2. Explain Lewis's use of the word *damned* (paragraph 4). What is specific about his use of this word? Is it appropriate?
3. How does Lewis develop his argument? What line of reasoning does he follow? What transition markers does Lewis use?
4. How does Lewis use definition to structure certain parts of his argument?
5. In which paragraph is Lewis making what he considers the one irrefutable argument in favor of the existence of God? Is this paragraph coherently reasoned in terms of the whole essay? Explain.
6. Why is Lewis's idea of justice critical to the evaluation of his thought? Is his use of the word *justice* idiosyncratic or objective? How does accepting his definition make an important difference to the response that a reader would give to this piece?

WRITING

1. The Western tradition is based, in large part, on the belief that "Christianity is right" and other religions are wrong. Is this belief as strong today as it was in the past? Does it still cohere as an argument?

2. Write an essay describing your religious beliefs and how they originated.
3. Argue for or against atheism.

MARGARET MEAD Margaret Mead (1901–1979), famed American anthropologist, was curator of ethnology at the American Museum of Natural History, New York City, and a professor at Columbia University. Her field expeditions to Samoa, New Guinea, and Bali in the 1920s and 1930s produced several major studies, notably *Coming of Age in Samoa* (1928), *Growing Up in New Guinea* (1930), and *Sex and Temperament in Three Primitive Societies* (1935). In this essay, Mead discusses the role that superstition plays in our daily life.

MARGARET MEAD

New Superstitions for Old

Once in a while there is a day when everything seems to run smoothly and even the riskiest venture comes out exactly right. You exclaim, "This is my lucky day!" Then as an afterthought you say, "Knock on wood!" Of course, you do not really believe that knocking on wood will ward off danger. Still, boasting about your own good luck gives you a slightly uneasy feeling—and you carry out the little protective ritual. If someone challenged you at that moment, you would probably say, "Oh, that's nothing. Just an old superstition." 1

But when you come to think about it, what is superstition? 2

In the contemporary world most people treat old folk beliefs as superstitions—the belief, for instance, that there are lucky and unlucky days or numbers, that future events can be read from omens, that there are protective charms or that what happens can be influenced by casting spells. We have excluded magic from our current world view, for we know that natural events have natural causes. 3

In a religious context, where truths cannot be demonstrated, we accept them as a matter of faith. Superstitions, however, belong to the category of beliefs, practices and ways of thinking that have been discarded because they are inconsistent with scientific knowledge. It is easy to say that other people are superstitious because they believe what we regard to be untrue. "Superstition" used in that sense is a derogatory term for the beliefs of other people that we do not share. But there is more to it than that. For superstitions lead a kind of half life in a twilight world where, sometimes, we partly suspend our disbelief and act as if magic worked. 4

Actually, almost every day, even in the most sophisticated home, something is likely to happen that evokes the memory of some old folk belief. The salt spills. A knife falls to the floor. Your nose tickles. Then 5

perhaps, with a slightly embarrassed smile, the person who spilled the salt tosses a pinch over his left shoulder. Or someone recites the old rhyme, "Knife falls, gentleman calls." Or as you rub your nose you think, That means a letter. I wonder who's writing? No one takes these small responses very seriously or gives them more than a passing thought. Sometimes people will preface one of these ritual acts—walking around instead of under a ladder or hastily closing an umbrella that has been opened inside a house—with such remarks as "I remember my great-aunt used to . . ." or "Germans used to say you ought not. . . ." And then, having placed the belief at some distance away in time or space, they carry out the ritual.

Everyone also remembers a few of the observances of childhood— 6
wishing on the first star; looking at the new moon over the right shoulder; avoiding the cracks in the sidewalk on the way to school while chanting, "Step on a crack, break your mother's back"; wishing on white horses, on loads of hay, on covered bridges, on red cars; saying quickly, "Bread-and-butter" when a post or a tree separated you from the friend you were walking with. The adult may not actually recite the formula "Star light, star bright . . ." and may not quite turn to look at the new moon, but his mood is tempered by a little of the old thrill that came when the observance was still freighted with magic.

Superstition can also be used with another meaning. When I dis- 7
cuss the religious beliefs of other peoples, especially primitive peoples, I am often asked, "Do they really have a religion, or is it all just superstition?" The point of contrast here is not between a scientific and a magical view of the world but between the clear, theologically defensible religious beliefs of members of civilized societies and what we regard as the false and childish views of the heathen who "bow down to wood and stone." Within the civilized religions, however, where membership includes believers who are educated and urbane and others who are ignorant and simple, one always finds traditions and practices that the more sophisticated will dismiss offhand as "just superstition" but that guide the steps of those who live by older ways. Mostly these are very ancient beliefs, some handed on from one religion to another and carried from country to country around the world.

Very commonly, people associate superstition with the past, with 8
very old ways of thinking that have been supplanted by modern knowledge. But new superstitions are continually coming into being and flourishing in our society. Listening to mothers in the park in the 1930s, one heard them say, "Now, don't you run out into the sun, or Polio will get you." In the 1940's elderly people explained to one another in tones of resignation, "It was the Virus that got him down." And every year the cosmetics industry offers us new magic—cures for baldness, lotions that will give every woman radiant skin, hair coloring that will restore to the middle-aged the charm and romance of youth—results that are promised if we will just follow the simple directions. Families and individuals also have their cherished, private superstitions. You must leave by the back door when you are going

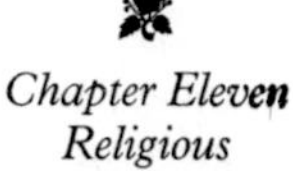

on a journey, or you must wear a green dress when you are taking an examination. It is a kind of joke, of course, but it makes you feel safe.

These old half-beliefs and new half-beliefs reflect the keenness of our wish to have something come true or to prevent something bad from happening. We do not always recognize new superstitions for what they are, and we still follow the old ones because someone's faith long ago matches our contemporary hopes and fears. In the past people "knew" that a black cat crossing one's path was a bad omen, and they turned back home. Today we are fearful of taking a journey and would give anything to turn back—and then we notice a black cat running across the road in front of us.

Child psychologists recognize the value of the toy a child holds in 10
his hand at bedtime. It is different from his thumb, with which he can close himself in from the rest of the world, and it is different from the real world, to which he is learning to relate himself. Psychologists call these toys—these furry animals and old, cozy baby blankets—"transitional objects"; that is, objects that help the child move back and forth between the exactions of everyday life and the world of wish and dream.

Superstitions have some of the qualities of these transitional objects. 11
They help people pass between the areas of life where what happens has to be accepted without proof and the areas where sequences of events are explicable in terms of cause and effect, based on knowledge. Bacteria and viruses that cause sickness have been identified; the cause of symptoms can be diagnosed and a rational course of treatment prescribed. Magical charms no longer are needed to treat the sick; modern medicine has brought the whole sequence of events into the secular world. But people often act as if this change had not taken place. Laymen still treat germs as if they were invisible, malign spirits, and physicians sometimes prescribe antibiotics as if they were magic substances.

Over time, more and more of life has become subject to the con- 12
trols of knowledge. However, this is never a one-way process. Scientific investigation is continually increasing our knowledge. But if we are to make good use of this knowledge, we must not only rid our minds of old, superseded beliefs and fragments of magical practice, but also recognize new superstitions for what they are. Both are generated by our wishes, our fears and our feeling of helplessness in difficult situations.

Civilized people are not alone in having grasped the idea of super- 13
stitions—beliefs and practices that are superseded but that still may evoke the different worlds in which we live—the sacred, the secular and the scientific. They allow us to keep a private world also, where, smiling a little, we can banish danger with a gesture and summon luck with a rhyme, make the sun shine in spite of storm clouds, force the stranger to do our bidding, keep an enemy at bay and straighten the paths of those we love.

COMPREHENSION

1. Explain in your own words the religious context for this essay.
2. What point is Mead making about superstition in modern life? Where does she state her main idea?
3. Where does Mead define *superstition?* How does it differ from folk beliefs?

RHETORIC

1. Explain what Mead means by "transitional objects." Why does she mention them?
2. Discuss the author's use of the pronouns *we* and *us* in the conclusion. Why does she state the conclusion in personal terms?
3. How does Mead use definition to differentiate *superstition* from *faith?* Explain the logic behind her distinction.
4. How does Mead use classification to describe the "worlds in which we live"? What are these worlds? What examples does she give of superstition in each of these worlds?
5. Look at paragraph 10. What is the purpose of this example? How does it figure in the context of Mead's essay?
6. Discuss the term "theologically defensible" as used in paragraph 7. Does Mead support this concept by example or evidence? Why?

WRITING

1. This article was published in 1966. Have we made any progress toward banishing superstition since then? Will we ever live in a culture free of superstition? Do we want to?
2. Write an essay about beliefs you once held that you have since abandoned. Why did you abandon them? What was the practical result?
3. Select a saying or phrase based in superstition or folk belief that you or a friend is fond of. Analyze its appeal.

FRANCINE DU PLESSIX GRAY Francine du Plessix Gray (1930–) is the daughter of a diplomat and a painter. Born in France, she came to the United States in 1941. Du Plessix Gray worked as a United Press International reporter in New York in the 1950s and, later, as a free-lance writer and editor. Her works include both fiction such as *October Blood* (1985) and *Adam and Eve and the City* (1987), and nonfiction, including *Hawaii: The Sugar-Coated Fortress* (1972) and *Soviet Women: Walking the Tightrope* (1990). She has also contributed extensively to publications such as the *New York Review of Books* and *Vogue.* In this clever, lyrical essay from *Harper's,* du Plessix Gray looks at work, leisure, and the wonder of language from a theological perspective.

FRANCINE DU PLESSIX GRAY

In Praise of Idleness

Hold aloof from every Christian brother who falls into idle habits.
—From the second letter of Paul to the Thessalonians

I plan this morning to challenge St. Paul to a public debate: I shall counter the apostle's attack against idleness by exalting, in the broadest possible way, the indispensable riches and rewards of leisure. 1

To begin with, let us recall that in Aristotle's *Ethics,* leisure is a far more noble, spiritual goal than work. Unlike work, which is pursued for our financial advancement or for our egos, leisure is pursued solely for its own sake. The Greek word for leisure is telling: It is *skole,* the pursuit of true learning, our absorption in activities desirable for their own sake—highest of these being the pleasures of music and poetry, the exchange of conversation with friends, and the joy of gratuitous, playful speculation. The same esteem of leisure prevailed among the Romans: The Latin words for leisure and work are also notable—leisure, the ultimate good, is *otium;* and the verbal opposite, formed by a negative prefix, is *negotium,* or gainful work. 2

Which leads me to think that St. Paul might well have freaked out at those symposia or banquets described by Plato that were the highest educational forums of ancient times, those indolent round-the-clock dinner parties at which—over the passing of the libation cup—some of our earliest definitions of freedom, liberty, and love were born. And how would he have reacted to Matthew's adage: "They sow not, neither do they reap, nor gather into barns; yet your Heavenly Father feedeth them"? 3

And so I ask you to consider the possibility that we have sought too much counsel in the proto-Calvinist work ethic preached by St. Paul and that many of us constantly run the risk of losing our compassion, if not our souls and our very selves, by channeling our energies too exclusively into useful, gainful toil. 4

For it is only during the cessation of work that we nurture our family bonds, educate our children, nourish our friendships; it is in "recreation" that we literally re-create, renew, restore ourselves after the wear of labor. And those of us who are painters, writers, and musicians know that it is in a particular form of idleness, in the suspension of everyday, routine work, in loafing and inviting our souls, that most of our innovations and breakthroughs, our best inspiration, come; only then can we enjoy what the Hindu philosopher Krishnamurti called a Blessed Freedom from the Known. It is in the essential lazing offered by the Sabbath ritual that prayer and recollection proceed; it is only in 5

our ungainful unemployed time that we can tune in to God's Word by dimming out the static created by our egos and our drive to excel. And it is only in our moments of deepest repose and just plain loafing that we are offered those miraculous peak moments in which we're suddenly startled to realize that we exist, that anything exists in which the gift of existence suddenly shines out at us, like chalk on a blackboard, against the possibility of not existing at all.

Finally, one might also say that it is only in a certain kind of idling that true compassion begins. For compassion is the art of acute selfless listening, of becoming alert and mindful to the needs of others by listening to them unconditionally with what St. Benedict called the "ear of our hearts." Compassion is an acuteness of attention difficult indeed to cultivate at the workplace and most readily reached over leisurely talk or a shared walk or cup, or during visits to jails, shelters, hospitals, wherever our social concerns draw us during our time off. So I would argue against Paul that the routine of our daily work has too often served as deep, dumb, deaf sleep, a refuge from two of life's most crucial states of being—keen awakedness to the needs of others and equal awakedness to the transcendent, which only comes in some state of loitering, dallying, tarrying, goofing off. 6

I'd like to move on to the literary implications of good idleness. For beyond the human community, if there is one thing on our planet most oppressed by soul-killing labor, by a dearth of recreation, it is the medium of my craft and of all human communication—language—which has been subjected to a round-the-clock shift as a drudge of media hype and of mass communication. 7

For here I must comment on a dilemma central and unique to that terrifyingly versatile symbolic system we call language: Compared to the mediums of music and painting, language has precious little Sabbath time in which to renew and re-create itself. Unlike the serenely abstract, leisured notations of music, or those means as free from daily labor as the visual artist's paint, canvas, and clay, our poor medium of language works like a slave in a salt mine. Look how vast a spectrum is covered by that one entity "word": From denoting the Word of God, "word" descends to those menial symbolic signs with which we holler and whimper our most primitive needs and fears, with which we execute our crassest commercial transactions. Compare the tranquility of the musician's or painter's means to the incessant laboring of that verbal idiom we might use, within the span of a few hours, to say such diverse things as I love you unto death: please pass the horseradish; the Dow Jones went up seventeen points at closing; Winston tastes good like a cigarette should. This is the exhausted, plodding dray horse—language—we prose writers are stuck with, and our central task is to air it and freshen it and reinfuse it with playfulness and honor and integrity in order to spiritualize it into art. In sum, our vocation, as writers, is the vacation of language; our task is to liberate words from their mercantile, pragmatic, everyday labor and usher them into the frolicking idleness of a perpetual Sunday; and, 8 hopefully, to craft them into units of sound and meaning as free from everyday toil as James Agee's phrase "His eyes had the opal lightings of dark oil," or Vladimir Nabokov's "I stared at the window whence the wounded music came," or Joyce's "riverrun, past Eve and Adam's, from bend of bay to swerve of shore. . . ."

How to resuscitate the exhausted word after relieving it of the 9
drudgery of full-time employment? Few writers have answered that question more eloquently than St. Augustine, whose entire process of conversion to Christianity was marked by his rebellion against the mass media of his time. For St. Augustine spent his early adulthood—when he was still a pagan—as a rhetorician, as a salesman of gross commercial language. And in late antiquity rhetoricians were the PR magnates and advertising tycoons and TV anchors of their society. Employed by politicians to write their speeches, using the techniques of eloquence to win friends and influence people, they were very dangerous precisely because they were so powerful.

So a fair part of Augustine's conversion to Christianity is based on 10
his realization that the art of rhetoric has turned his colleagues into a society of corrupt hot-air artists, on his disillusionment with what he calls "the peddling of tongue science." And a crucial step in his spiritual progress was to drop out of the work force, to abandon his lucrative peddling job, to liberate himself and his language into the gratuitous idleness of reading and talking about philosophy. Eventually, during that famous conversion scene in the garden, St. Augustine picks up the book nearest at hand and happens upon the chapter from St. Paul's Corinthians telling him to put on the *word* of Christ. That is the moment when Augustine, former taskmaster of enslaved words, is reborn into the truth and freedom of the absolute Word, thereby liberating his own verbal idiom and crafting the "language of the soul" that he will use to write his great *Confessions.*

The implications of St. Augustine's conversion to the higher Word 11
are as deeply literary as they are religious: Once he's given up the practice of commercial writing, he begins to see his former sin, in part, as an addition to debased and fettered language, to any discourse in which sheer technique prevails over ethics or genuine emotion.

Those passages of St. Augustine's *Confessions* that deal with his 12
conversion to a purified language intimate, as few moments in literature have, that there is a particular form of grace to be sought by all writers; that, as we parole words from their perennial salt mines, it is our spiritual duty to follow an ethic of the written sign—or, to use the phrasing of the Commandments, "Honor thy medium as thyself." St. Augustine suggests that all those devices that he and his predecessors in the art of rhetoric pioneered—simile, irony, metaphor—must be used with care and precision and never with excess or with undue striving for a flamboyant effect.

Which is why I turn to another writer who saw the perils of any lan- 13
guage engaged in daily gainful employment—our beloved contemporary Flannery O'Connor. In her book *Mystery and Manners,* O'Connor

left us a small treasure house of literary ethics. And although her thoughts were often couched in theological terms, they have been decoded by even the most hard-headed agnostics as some of the most precious literary advice of our time.

For instance, O'Connor believed that the highest purpose of literature is "the accurate naming of the things of God"—as good a metaphor as any for a fastidiously responsible, selfless, nonexploitative attitude toward language. She often turns to another injunction she has learned from St. Thomas Aquinas: The artist, she tells us, must solely be concerned with the good of that which he makes, not with the good that it can bring into his life, for only thus can his work enlarge the glory of God's creation. 14

O'Connor went on to remind us that whatever talent we have comes from the Holy Spirit. This gift is given to us to plumb the mystery of evil, the mystery of personality, the mystery of our incompleteness. It is a considerable responsibility, a mystery in itself, something gratuitous and totally undeserved whose real uses will probably always be hidden from us. 15

To which I would add: Like the spirituality of our Sabbath, our fragile, beleaguered, exhausted language—the preserver of our civilization and the vehicle for most of our gifts—thrives on attitudes of release, of labor suspended. It will best endure not on the work ethic preached by St. Paul but rather on that message expressed by Thomas Merton in the following words: "The Lord plays and diverts Himself in the garden of His creation, and if we could let go of our own obsessions with what we think is the meaning of it all, we might be able to hear His call and follow Him in His mysterious, cosmic dance. . . . For the world and time are the dance of the Lord in emptiness. The silence of the spheres is the music of a wedding feast." 16

COMPREHENSION

1. According to the author, why is idleness held in disrepute? What are its merits?
2. How does the writer adapt her argument to language?
3. What connection does du Plessix Gray make between language and religion?

RHETORIC

1. Consider the connotations of the words *idleness* and *leisure* as they apply to the essay. Which do you think the author is referring to?
2. How does the quote from St. Paul before the introduction and other biblical and religious references work to advance the writer's ideas? What is the main idea of the essay?
3. How does paragraph 2 help to pave the way for du Plessix Gray's argument? Justify your response.

4. Du Plessix Gray's argument is twofold. What transitions or other methods does she employ to switch focus in her essay?
5. Examine, in paragraph 8, the writer's examples of "drudge" language and language on "vacation." How well do they clarify the writer's definitions?
6. What purpose do paragraphs 9, 10, 11, and 12 have? How do they help the focus of the essay?

WRITING

1. Write your own essay on idleness, discussing how you feel about leisure time and what you do when you have free time. Use support from du Plessix Gray's essay where appropriate.
2. In a brief essay, critique the level of language the writer uses in her essay. Does it employ language on "vacation" or "pragmatic" prose? Give concrete support from her work to illustrate your opinion.
3. Write an argumentation essay supporting the work ethic du Plessix Gray seems to be criticizing. Some research may be necessary to supply background information.

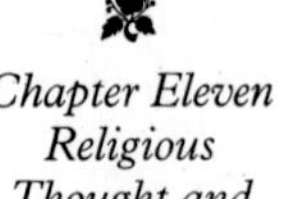

CLASSIC AND CONTEMPORARY

RUTH BENEDICT Ruth Benedict (1887–1948), an anthropologist and educator, began her career as a poet. Later, she studied anthropology under Franz Boas and succeeded him as chairman of the department of anthropology at Columbia University (1936–1939). In 1934, she wrote *Patterns of Culture;* in 1940, *Race: Science and Politics.* In her work, Benedict attempted to study anthropology through sociology, psychology, and philosophy, of which this examination of Zuñi life and worship is an excellent example.

RUTH BENEDICT

Periodic Worship of the Zuñis

The Zuñis are a ceremonious people, a people who value sobriety and inoffensiveness above all other virtues. Their interest is centered upon their rich and complex ceremonial life. Their cults of the masked gods, of healing, of the sun, of the sacred fetishes, of war, of the dead, are formal and established bodies of ritual with priestly officials and calendric observances. No field of activity competes with ritual for foremost place in their attention. Probably most grown men among the western Pueblos give to it the greater part of their waking life. It requires the memorizing of an amount of word-perfect ritual that our less trained minds find staggering, and the performance of neatly dovetailed ceremonies that are charted by the calendar and complexly interlock all the different cults and the governing body in endless formal procedure. 1

The ceremonial life not only demands their time; it preoccupies their attention. Not only those who are responsible for the ritual and those who take part in it, but all the people of the pueblo, women and families who "have nothing," that is, that have no ritual possessions, centre their daily conversation about it. While it is in progress, they stand all day as spectators. If a priest is ill, or if no rain comes during his retreat, village gossip runs over and over his ceremonial missteps and the implications of his failure. Did the priest of the masked gods give offence to some supernatural being? Did he break his retreat by going home to his wife before the days were up? These are the subjects of talk in the village for a fortnight. If an impersonator wears a new feather on his mask, it eclipses all talk of sheep or gardens or marriage or divorce. 2

This preoccupation with detail is logical enough. Zuñi religious practices are believed to be supernaturally powerful in their own right. At every step of the way, if the procedure is correct, the costume of the 3 masked god traditional to the last detail, the offerings unimpeachable, the words of the hours-long prayers letter-perfect, the effect will follow according to man's desires. One has only, in the phrase they have always on their tongues, to "know how." According to all the tenets of their religion, it is a major matter if one of the eagle feathers of a mask has been taken from the shoulder of the bird instead of from the breast. Every detail has magical efficacy.

Zuñis place great reliance upon imitative magic. In the priests' re- 4
treats for rain they roll round stones across the floor to produce thunder, water is sprinkled to cause the rain, a bowl of water is placed upon the altar that the springs may be full, suds are beaten up from a native plant that clouds may pile in the heavens, tobacco smoke is blown out that the gods "may not withhold their misty breath." In the masked-god dances mortals clothe themselves with the "flesh" of the supernaturals, that is, their paint and their masks, and by this means gods are constrained to grant their blessings. Even the observances that are less obviously in the realm of magic partake in Zuñi thought of the same mechanistic efficacy. One of the obligations that rest upon every priest or official during the time when he is actively participating in religious observances is that of feeling no anger. But anger is not tabu in order to facilitate communication with a righteous god who can only be approached by those with a clean heart. Its absence is a sign of concentration upon supernatural affairs, a state of mind that constrains the supernaturals and makes it impossible for them to withhold their share of the bargain. It has magical efficacy.

Their prayers also are formulas, the effectiveness of which comes 5
from their faithful rendition. The amount of traditional prayer forms of this sort in Zuñi can hardly be exaggerated. Typically they describe in ritualistic language the whole course of the reciter's ceremonial obligations leading up to the present culmination of the ceremony. They itemize the appointment of the impersonator, the gathering of willow shoots for prayer-sticks, the binding of the bird feathers to them with cotton string, the painting of the sticks, the offering to the gods of the finished plume wands, the visits to sacred springs, the periods of retreat. No less than the original religious act, the recital must be meticulously correct.

> Seeking yonder along the river courses 6
> The ones who are our fathers,
> Male willow,
> Female willow,
> Four times cutting the straight young shoots,
> To my house
> I brought my road.
> This day
> With my warm human hands
> I took hold of them.
> I gave my prayer-sticks human form.

With the striped cloud tail
Of the one who is my grandfather,
With eagle's thin cloud tail,
With the striped cloud wings
And massed cloud tails
Of all the birds of summer,
With these four times I gave my prayer-sticks human form.
With the flesh of the one who is my mother,
Cotton woman,
Even a poorly made cotton thread,
Four times encircling them and tying it about their bodies.
I gave my prayer-sticks human form.
With the flesh of the one who is our mother,
Black paint woman,
Four times covering them with flesh,
I gave my prayer-sticks human form.

Prayer in Zuñi is never an outpouring of the human heart. There 7
are some ordinary prayers that can be slightly varied, but this means little more than that they can be made longer or shorter. And the prayers are never remarkable for their intensity. They are always mild and ceremonious in form, asking for orderly life, pleasant days, shelter from violence. Even war priests conclude their prayer:

I have sent forth my prayers.
Our children,
Even those who have erected their shelters
At the edge of the wilderness,
May their roads come in safely,
May the forests
And the brush
Stretch out their water-filled arms
To shield their hearts;
May their roads come in safely;
May their roads all be fulfilled,
May it not somehow become difficult for them
When they have gone but a little way.
May all the little boys,
All the little girls,
And those whose roads are ahead,
May they have powerful hearts,
Strong spirits;
On roads reaching to Dawn Lake
May you grow old;
May your roads be fulfilled;
May you be blessed with life.
Where the life-giving road of your sun father comes out,
May your roads reach;
May your roads be fulfilled.

If they are asked the purpose of any religious observance, they have 8
a ready answer. It is for rain. This is of course a more or less conventional answer. But it reflects a deep-seated Zuñi attitude. Fertility is above all else the blessing within the bestowal of the gods and in the desert country of the Zuñi plateau, rain is the prime requisite for the growth of crops. The retreats of the priests, the dances of the masked gods, even many of the activities of the medicine societies are judged by whether or not there has been rain. To "bless with water" is the synonym of all blessing. Thus, in the prayers, the fixed epithet the gods apply in blessing to the rooms in Zuñi to which they come, is "water-filled," their ladders are "water ladders," and the scalp taken in warfare is "the water-filled covering." The dead, too, come back in the rain clouds, bringing the universal blessing. People say to the children when the summer afternoon rain clouds come up the sky, "Your grandfathers are coming," and the reference is not to individual dead relatives, but applies impersonally to all forbears. The masked gods also are the rain and when they dance they constrain their own being—rain—to descend upon the people. The priests, again, in their retreat before their altars sit motionless and withdrawn for eight days, summoning the rain.

> From wherever you abide permanently 9
> You will make your roads come forth.
> Your little wind blown clouds,
> Your thin wisp of clouds
> Replete with living waters,
> You will send forth to stay with us.
> Your fine rain caressing the earth,
> Here at Itiwana,[1]
> The abiding place of our fathers,
> Our mothers,
> The ones who first had being,
> With your great pile of waters
> You will come together.

Rain, however, is only one of the aspects of fertility for which 10
prayers are constantly made in Zuñi. Increase in the gardens and increase in the tribe are thought of together. They desire to be blessed with happy women:

> Even those who are with child,
> Carrying one child on the back,
> Holding another on a cradle board,
> Leading one by the hand,
> With yet another going before.

Their means of promoting human fertility are strongly symbolic and impersonal, as we shall see, but fertility is one of the recognized objects of religious observances.

[1] "The Middle," the ceremonial name of Zuñi, the center of the world.

This ceremonial life that preoccupies Zuñi attention is organized 11
like a series of interlocking wheels. The priesthoods have their sacred objects, their retreats, their dances, their prayers, and their year-long programme is annually initiated by the great winter solstice ceremony that makes use of all the different groups and sacred things and focuses all their functions. The tribal masked-god society has similar possessions and calendric observances, and these culminate in the great winter tribal masked-god ceremony, the Shalako. In like fashion the medicine societies, with their special relation to curing, function throughout the year, and have their annual culminating ceremony for tribal health. These three major cults of Zuñi ceremonial life are not mutually exclusive. A man may be, and often is, for the greater part of his life, a member of all three. They each give him sacred possessions "to live by" and demand of him exacting ceremonial knowledge.

The priesthoods stand on the highest level of sanctity. There are 12
four major and eight minor priesthoods. They "hold their children[2] fast." They are holy men. Their sacred medicine bundles, in which their power resides, are, as Dr. Bunzel says, of "indescribable sanctity." They are kept in great covered jars, in bare, inner rooms of the priests' houses, and they consist of pairs of stoppered reeds, one filled with water, in which there are miniature frogs, and the other with corn. The two are wrapped together with yards and yards of unspun native cotton. No one ever enters the holy room of the priests' medicine bundle except the priests when they go in for their rituals, and an elder woman of the household or the youngest girl child, who go in before every meal to feed the bundle. Anyone entering, for either purpose, removes his moccasins.

The priests, as such, do not hold public ceremonies, though in great 13
numbers of the rites their presence is necessary or they initiate essential first steps in the undertaking. Their retreats before their sacred bundle are secret and sacrosanct. In June, when rain is needed for the corn, at that time about a foot above the ground, the series of retreats begins. In order, each new priesthood going "in" as the preceding one comes out, they "make their days." The heads of the sun cult and of the war cult are included also in this series of the priests' retreats. They must sit motionless, with their thoughts fixed upon ceremonial things. Eight days for the major priesthoods, four for the lesser. All Zuñis await the granting of rain during these days, and priests blessed with rain are greeted and thanked by everyone upon the street after their retreat is ended. They have blessed their people with more than rain. They have upheld them in all their ways of life. Their position as guardians of their people has been vindicated. The prayers they have prayed during their retreat have been answered:

> All my ladder-descending children,
> All of them I hold in my hands,

[2]That is, the people of Zuñi.

May no one fall from my grasp
After going but a little way.
Even every little beetle,
Even every dirty little beetle
Let me hold them all fast in my hands,
Let none of them fall from my grasp.
May my children's roads all be fulfilled;
May they grow old;
May their roads reach all the way to Dawn Lake;
May their roads be fulfilled;
In order that your thoughts may bend to this
Your days are made.

The heads of the major priesthoods, with the chief priest of the sun cult and the two chief priests of the war cult, constitute the ruling body, the council, of Zuñi. Zuñi is a theocracy to the last implication. Since priests are holy men and must never during the prosecution of their duties feel anger, nothing is brought before them about which there will not be unanimous agreement. They initiate the great ceremonial events of the Zuñi calendar, they make ritual appointments, and they give judgment in cases of witchcraft. To our sense of what a governing body should be, they are without jurisdiction and without authority. 14

If the priesthoods stand on the level of greatest sanctity, the cult of the masked gods is most popular. It has first claim in Zuñi affection, and it flourishes today like the green bay tree. 15

There are two kinds of masked gods: the masked gods proper, the kachinas; and the kachina priests. These kachina priests are the chiefs of the supernatural world and are themselves impersonated with masks by Zuñi dancers. Their sanctity in Zuñi eyes makes it necessary that their cult should be quite separate from that of the dancing gods proper. The dancing gods are happy and comradely supernaturals who live at the bottom of a lake far off in the empty desert south of Zuñi. There they are always dancing. But they like best to return to Zuñi to dance. To impersonate them, therefore, is to give them the pleasure they most desire. A man, when he puts on the mask of the gods, becomes for the time being the supernatural himself. He has no longer human speech, but only the cry which is peculiar to that god. He is tabu, and must assume all the obligations of anyone who is for the time being sacred. He not only dances, but he observes an esoteric retreat before the dance, and plants prayer-sticks and observes continence. 16

There are more than a hundred different masked gods of the Zuñi pantheon, and many of these are dance groups that come in sets, thirty or forty of a kind. Others come in sets of six, coloured for the six directions—for Zuñi counts up and down as cardinal points. Each of these gods has individual details of costuming, an individual mask, an individual place in the hierarchy of the gods, myths that recount his doings, and ceremonies during which he is expected. 17

The dances of the masked gods are administered and carried out by a tribal society of all adult males. Women too may be initiated "to save 18 their lives," but it is not customary. They are not excluded because of any tabu, but membership for a woman is not customary, and there are today only three women members. As far back as tradition reaches there seem not to have been many more at any one time. The men's tribal society is organized in six groups, each with its kiva or ceremonial chamber. Each kiva has its officials, its dances that belong to it, and its own roll of members.

Membership in one or the other of these kivas follows from the
choice of a boy's ceremonial father at birth, but there is no initiation till 19
the child is between five and nine years old. It is his first attainment of ceremonial status. This initiation, as Dr. Bunzel points out, does not teach him esoteric mysteries; it establishes a bond with supernatural forces. It makes him strong, and, as they say, valuable. The "scare kachinas," the punitive masked gods, come for the initiation, and they whip the children with their yucca whips. It is a rite of exorcism, "to take off the bad happenings," and to make future events propitious. In Zuñi whipping is never used as a corrective of children. The fact that white parents use it in punishment is a matter for unending amazement. In the initiation children are supposed to be very frightened, and they are not shamed if they cry aloud. It makes the rite the more valuable.

COMPREHENSION

1. What is the importance of ritual and ceremony to the Zuñi people?
2. What are the major levels of the Zuñi religion?
3. What role does rain play in the beliefs and rituals of the Zuñi religion?

RHETORIC

1. Explain the purpose of definition in the introduction. Cite other paragraphs where definition is used as an expository technique.
2. Does Benedict approach the subject as a scientist or as a practitioner? What about the tone or language in the essay supports your opinion?
3. What function does the prayer in paragraph 6 serve? How is it reflective of the Zuñi religion? Would the essay be just as effective without it? Justify your response.
4. Does Benedict use abstract or concrete language in her essay? Cite examples from the writing.
5. Where does the writer use classification in her essay? How does it serve the purpose of the writing?
6. Why does Benedict choose not to elaborate on the role of the "medicine societies" mentioned in paragraph 11? Does this detract from her exposition?

WRITING

1. Research in more detail a particular area of Zuñi religious practices—for example, the role of women in rituals, the function of medicine societies, or children's rite-of-passage ceremonies.
2. Benedict mentions that the Zuñis are baffled by the practice of using physical punishment on children. Write a brief essay using information given in the essay, about other customs in the Judeo-Christian world that they might find confusing.
3. Write an essay arguing that non-Native Americans could learn a great deal from the Zuñis. What do you find especially interesting or reasonable about them? How could their beliefs or practices be used in other contexts to enrich humanity?

N. SCOTT MOMADAY N. Scott Momaday (1934–), Pulitzer Prize-winning poet, critic, and academician, is the author of *House Made of Dawn* (1968), *The Way to Rainy Mountain* (1969), *The Names* (1976), and other works. "I am an American Indian (Kiowa), and am vitally interested in American Indian art, history and culture," Momaday has written. In the following essay, he writes about an important journey back to his ancestral roots and the significance of sacred ground to the American Indian.

N. SCOTT MOMADAY

Sacred and Ancestral Ground

There is great good in returning to a landscape that has had extraordinary meaning in one's life. It happens that we return to such places in our minds irresistibly. There are certain villages and towns, mountains and plains that, having seen them, walked in them, lived in them, even for a day, we keep forever in the mind's eye. They become indispensable to our well-being; they define us, and we say: I am who I am because I have been there, or there. There is good, too, in actual, physical return. 1

Some years ago I made a pilgrimage into the heart of North America. I began the journey proper in western Montana. From there I traveled across the high plains of Wyoming into the Black Hills, then southward to the southern plains, to a cemetery at Rainy Mountain, in Oklahoma. It was a journey made by my Kiowa ancestors long before. In the course of their migration they became a people of the Great Plains, and theirs was the last culture to evolve in North America. They had been for untold generations a mountain tribe of hunters. Their ancient nomadism, which had determined their way of life even before they set foot on this continent, perhaps 30,000 years ago, was raised to its highest level of expression when they entered upon the Great Plains and acquired horses. Their migration brought them to a Golden Age. 2

At the beginning of their journey they were a people of hard circumstances, often hungry and cold, fighting always for sheer survival. At its end, and for a hundred years, they were the lords of the land, a daring race of centaurs and buffalo hunters whose love of freedom and space was profound.

Recently I returned to the old migration route of the Kiowas. I had 3
in me a need to behold again some of the principal landmarks of that long, prehistoric quest, to descend again from the mountain to the plain.

With my close friend Charles, a professor of American literature at 4
a South Dakota university, I headed north to the Montana-Wyoming border. I wanted to intersect the Kiowa migration route at the Bighorn Medicine Wheel, high in the Bighorn Mountains. We ascended to 8,000 feet gradually, on a well-maintained but winding highway. Then we climbed sharply, bearing upon the timberline. Although the plain below had been comfortable, even warm at midday, the mountain air was cold, and much of the ground was covered with snow. We turned off the pavement, on a dirt road that led three miles to the Medicine Wheel. The road was forbidding; it was narrow and winding, and the grades were steep and slippery, here and there the shoulders fell away into deep ravines. But at the same time something wonderful happened: we crossed the line between civilization and wilderness. Suddenly the earth persisted in its original being. Directly in front of us a huge white-tailed buck crossed our path, ambling without haste into a thicket of pines. As we drove over his tracks we saw four does above on the opposite bank, looking down at us, their great black eyes bright and benign, curious. There seemed no wariness, nothing of fear or alienation. Their presence was a good omen, we thought; somehow in their attitude they bade us welcome to their sphere of wilderness.

There was a fork in the road, and we took the wrong branch. At a 5
steep, hairpin curve we got out of the car and climbed to the top of a peak. An icy wind whipped at us; we were among the bald summits of the Bighorns. Great flumes of sunlit snow erupted on the ridges and dissolved in spangles on the sky. Across a deep saddle we caught sight of the Medicine Wheel. It was perhaps two miles away.

When we returned to the car we saw another vehicle approaching. It 6
was a very old Volkswagen bus, in much need of repair, cosmetic repair, at least. Out stepped a thin, bearded young man in thick glasses. He wore a wool cap, a down parka, jeans and well-worn hiking boots. "I am looking for Medicine Wheel," he said, having nodded to us. He spoke softly, with a pronounced accent. His name was Jürg, and he was from Switzerland; he had been traveling for some months in Canada and the United States. Chuck and I shook his hand and told him to follow us, and we drove down into the saddle. From there we climbed on foot to the Medicine Wheel.

The Medicine Wheel is a ring of stones, some 80 feet in diameter. 7
Stone spokes radiate from the center to the circumference. Cairns are placed at certain points on the circumference, one in the center and

one just outside the ring to the southwest. We do not know as a matter of fact who made this wheel or to what purpose. It has been proposed that it was an astronomical observatory, a solar calendar and the ground design of a Kiowa sun dance lodge. What we know without doubt is that it is a sacred expression, an equation of man's relation to the cosmos.

There was a great calm upon that place. The hard, snow-bearing wind that had burned our eyes and skin only minutes before had died away altogether. The sun was warm and bright, and there was a profound silence. On the wire fence that had been erected to enclose and protect the wheel were fixed offerings, small prayer bundles. Chuck and Jürg and I walked about slowly, standing for long moments here and there, looking into the wheel or out across the great distances. We did not say much; there was little to be said. But we were deeply moved by the spirit of that place. The silence was such that it must be observed. To the north we could see down to the timberline, to the snowfields and draws that marked the black planes of forest among the peaks of the Bighorns. To the south and west the mountains fell abruptly to the plains. We could see thousands of feet down and a hundred miles across the dim expanse. 8

When we were about to leave, I took from my pocket an eagle-bone whistle that my father had given me, and I blew it in the four directions. The sound was very high and shrill, and it did not break the essential silence. As we were walking down we saw far below, crossing our path, a coyote sauntering across the snow into a wall of trees. It was just there, a wild being to catch sight of, and then it was gone. The wilderness, which had admitted us with benediction, with benediction let us go. 9

When we came within a stone's throw of the highway, Chuck and I said goodbye to Jürg, but not before Jürg had got out his camp stove and boiled water for tea. There in the dusk we enjoyed a small ceremonial feast of tea and crackers. The three of us had become friends. Only later did I begin to understand the extraordinary character of that friendship. It was the friendship of those who come together in recognition of the sacred. If we never meet again, I thought, we shall not forget this day. 10

On the plains the fences and roads and windmills and houses seemed almost negligible, all but overwhelmed by the earth and sky. It is a landscape of great clarity; its vastness is that of the ocean. It is the near revelation of infinity. Antelope were everywhere in the grassy folds, grazing side by side with horses and cattle. Hawks sailed above, and crows scattered before us. The place names were American—Tensleep, Buffalo, Dull Knife, Crazy Woman, Spotted Horse. 11

The Black Hills are an isolated and ancient group of mountains in South Dakota and Wyoming. They lie very close to both the geographic center of the United States (including Alaska and Hawaii) and the geographic center of the North American continent. They form an is- 12

land, an elliptical area of nearly 6,000 square miles, in the vast sea of grasses that is the northern Great Plains. The Black Hills form a calendar of geologic time that is truly remarkable. The foundation rocks of these mountains are older than much of the sedimentary layer of which the Americas are primarily composed. An analysis of this foundation, made in 1975, indicates an age of between two billion and three billion years.

A documented record of exploration in this region is found in the Lewis and Clark journals, 1804–6. The first white party known definitely to have entered the Black Hills proper was led by Jedediah Smith in 1823. The diary of this expedition, kept by one James Clyman, is notable. Clyman reports a confrontation between Jedediah Smith and a grizzly bear, in which Smith lost one of his ears. There is also reported the discovery of a petrified ("putrified," as Clyman has it) forest, where petrified birds sing petrified songs. 13

Toward the end of the century, after rumors of gold had made the Black Hills a name known throughout the country, Gen. (then Lieut. Col.) George Armstrong Custer led an expedition from Fort Abraham Lincoln into the Black Hills in July and August, 1874. The Custer expedition traveled 600 miles in 60 days. Custer reported proof of gold, but he had an eye to other things as well: 14

> Every step of our march that day was amid flowers of the most exquisite colors and perfume. So luxuriant in growth were they that men plucked them without dismounting from the saddle. . . . It was a strange sight to glance back at the advancing columns of cavalry and behold the men with beautiful bouquets in their hands, while the headgear of the horses was decorated with wreaths of flowers fit to crown a queen of May. Deeming it a most fitting appellation, I named this Floral Valley.

In the evening of that same day, sitting at mess in a meadow, the officers competed to see how many different flowers could be picked by each man, without leaving his seat. Seven varieties were gathered so. Some 50 different flowers were blooming then in Floral Valley. 15

The Lakota, or Teton Sioux, called these mountains Paha Sapa, "Hills That Are Black." Other tribes, besides the Kiowa and the Sioux, thought of the Black Hills as sacred ground, a place crucial in their past. The Arapaho lived here. So did the Cheyenne Bear Butte, near Sturgis, S.D. On the northeast edge of the Black Hills, is the Cheyenne's sacred mountain. It remains, like the Medicine Wheel, a place of the greatest spiritual intensity. So great was thought to be the power inherent in the Black Hills that the Indians did not camp there. It was a place of rendezvous, a hunting ground, but above all inviolate, a place of thunder and lightning, a dwelling place of the gods. 16

On the edge of the Black Hills nearest the Bighorn Mountains is Devils Tower, the first of our National Monuments. The Lakotas called it Mateo Tepee, "Grizzly Bear Lodge." The Kiowas called it Tsoai, "Rock Tree." Devils Tower is a great monolith that rises high above the 17 timber of the Black Hills. In conformation it closely resembles the stump of a tree. It is a cluster of rock columns (phonolite porphyry) 1,000 feet across at the base and 275 feet across at the top. It rises 865 feet above the high ground on which it stands and 1,280 feet above the Belle Fourche River, in the valley below.

It has to be seen to be believed. "There are things in nature that engender an awful quiet in the heart of man; Devils Tower is one of them." I wrote these words almost 20 years ago. They remain true to my experience. Each time I behold this Tsoai, I am more than ever in awe of it. 18

Two hundred years ago, more or less, the Kiowas came upon this place. They were moved to tell a story about it: 19

> Eight children were there at play, seven sisters and their brother. Suddenly the boy was struck dumb; he trembled and began to run upon his hands and feet. His fingers became claws, and his body was covered with fur. Directly there was a bear where the boy had been. The sisters were terrified; they ran, and the bear ran after them. They came to the stump of a great tree, and the tree spoke to them. It bade them climb upon it, and as they did so it began to rise into the air. The bear came to kill them, but they were just beyond its reach. It reared against the tree and scored the bark all around with its claws. The seven sisters were borne into the sky, and they became the stars of the Big Dipper.

This story, which I have known from the time I could first understand language, exemplifies the sacred for me. The storyteller, that anonymous, illiterate man who told the story for the first time, succeeded in raising the human condition to the level of universal significance. Not only did he account for the existence of the rock tree, but in the process he related his human race to the stars. 20

When Chuck and I had journeyed over this ground together, when we were about to go our separate ways, I reminded him of our friend Jürg, knowing well enough that I needn't have: Jürg was on our minds. He had touched us deeply with his trust, not unlike that of the wild animals we had seen. I can't account for it. Jürg had touched us deeply with his generosity of spirit, his concern to see beneath the surface of things, his attitude of free, direct, disinterested kindness. 21

"Did he tell us what he does?" I asked. "Does he have a profession?" 22

"I don't think he said," Chuck replied. "I think he's a pilgrim." 23

"Yes." 24

"Yes." 25

COMPREHENSION

1. Why does the author return to his ancestral ground?
2. Explain the significance of Jürg, the Swiss traveler.

3. What happens at the Medicine Wheel? Why is this a meaningful part of the journey?

RHETORIC

1. Examine Momaday's use of pronouns in the first paragraph. What point of view does he have? What response does this elicit from the reader?
2. Define the words *pilgrim* and *pilgrimage* in the essay. How does the use of these words contribute to the religious theme of the essay?
3. How does the writer's use of descriptive detail enhance his essay? Provide examples of descriptive language in the essay.
4. Why does Momaday include an excerpt from Custer's journal in his essay? What effect does its inclusion have on the mood set up in the essay to that point?
5. Why does the writer blend historical fact and Native-American religious beliefs in his essay?
6. How does the essay's conclusion serve to reinforce the writer's original focus? What device does Momaday use to achieve a sense of unity?

WRITING

1. Write a descriptive essay about a trip to a place that has (or had) special spiritual or emotional significance for you. Describe the trip there, how long it has been since you last saw the place, and what it means to you. Use sensory details in your essay.
2. Compare and contrast the importance of ancestral grounds to Native Americans to anything comparable in Judeo-Christian beliefs.

CLASSIC AND CONTEMPORARY: QUESTIONS FOR COMPARISON

1. Both Momaday and Benedict write about the religions of Native Americans, but they approach the subject quite differently. In an essay, discuss those differences. Consider the writers' priorities, the content of their essays, and the language and style of their writing.
2. Write a research paper comparing the religious practices of Momaday's Kiowa ancestors to the practices of the Zuñis described in Benedict's essay. What beliefs do the two tribes hold in common? Where do they differ?
3. In a casual-analysis essay, explore the effects of Christian encroachment on Native-American religious practices in this country. Have attempts at conversion done more harm than good? Is conversion a thing of the past? Concentrate on the Zuñi and Kiowa people. Some research will be necessary.

CONNECTIONS

1. What is the difference between superstition and religion? Is it merely a matter of belief? Address this question in an essay, using support from Mead, Soyinka, Benedict, or others in this section.
2. C. S. Lewis writes: "If you are a Christian you do not have to believe that all the other religions are simply wrong all through." Do you feel most Christians adhere to this opinion? Answer his essay, and use support from relevant sources in this section.
3. Both Mead and Benedict take a scientific approach to their subjects. Compare their work in respect to their attitudes, language, and tone.
4. Explore du Plessix Gray's opinion of idleness in a non-Christian context. How do you feel Benedict's Zuñis or Guppy's Muslims might approach the concept of idleness versus work? Use any applicable writers in this section to support your opinions.
5. Explain what George Eliot meant by "life beyond self," and consider whether any of the people mentioned by the writers in this section would be illustrative of that definition. Some research may be necessary.
6. Examine the negative use of religion (for example, to oppress a people) in a causal-analysis essay that uses the work of Guppy, Buber, Momaday, or other writers in this section.
7. Choose one or two writers in this section whose use of language represents du Plessix Gray's idea of "language on vacation." Analyze the writers' sentence structure, vocabulary, and style in terms of its freshness and inventiveness.

CHAPTER TWELVE

Nature and the Environment

We are at a point in the history of civilization where consciousness of our fragile relationship to nature and the environment is high. Even as you spend an hour reading a few of the essays in this chapter, it is estimated that we are losing 3,000 acres of rain forest around the world and four species of plants or animals. From pollution to the population explosion to the depletion of the ozone layer, we seem to be confronted with ecological catastrophe. Nevertheless, as Rachel Carson reminds us, we have "an obligation to endure," to survive potential natural catastrophe by understanding and managing our relationship with the natural world.

Ecology, or the study of nature and the environment, as many of the essayists in this chapter attest, involves us in the conservation of the earth. It moves us to suppress our suicidally rapacious destruction of the planet. Clearly, the biological stability of the planet is increasingly precarious. More plants, insects, birds, and animals are becoming extinct in the twentieth century than in any era since the Cretaceous catastrophe more than 65 million years ago that led to the extinction of the dinosaurs. Within this ecological context, writers like Thoreau and Carson become our literary conscience, reminding us of how easily natural processes can break down unless we insist on a degree of ecological "economy."

Of course, any modification of human behavior in an effort to conserve nature is a complex matter. To save the spotted owl in the Pacific Northwest, we must sacrifice the jobs of people in the timber industry. To reduce pollution, we must forsake gas and oil for alternate energy sources that are costly to develop. To reduce the waste stream, we must shift from a consumption to a conservation society. The ecological debate is complicated, but it is clear that the preservation of the myriad life cycles on earth is crucial, for we, too, could become an endangered species.

The language of nature is as enigmatic as the sounds of dolphins and whales communicating with their respective species. Writers like John McPhee, Alice Walker, and John Steinbeck, who appear in this chapter, help us to decipher the language of our environment. They encourage us to converse with nature, learn from it, and even revere it. All of us are guests on this planet; the natural world is our host. If we do not protect the earth, how can we guarantee the survival of global civilization?

Previewing the Chapter

As you read the essays in this chapter and respond to them in discussion and writing, consider the following questions:

- According to the author, what should our relationship to the natural world be?
- What claims or arguments does the author make about the importance of nature? Do you agree or disagree with these claims and arguments?
- What specific ecological problem does the author investigate?
- How does the author think that nature influences human behavior?
- What cultural factors are involved in our approach to the environment?
- Is the writer optimistic, pessimistic, or neutral in the assessment of our ability to conserve nature?
- Do you find that the author is too idealistic or sentimental in the depiction of nature? Why?
- Based on the author's essay, how does he or she qualify as a "nature writer"?
- How have you been challenged or changed by the essays in this section?

RACHEL CARSON Rachel Carson (1907–1964) was a seminal figure in the environmental movement. Born in Pennsylvania, she awakened public consciousness to environmental issues through her writing. Her style was both literary and scientific as she described nature's riches in such books as *The Sea Around Us* (1951) and *The Edge of the Sea* (1954). Her last book, *Silent Spring* (1962), aroused controversy and concern with its indictment of insecticides. In the following excerpt from that important book, Carson provides compelling evidence of the damage caused by indiscriminate use of insecticides and the danger of disturbing the earth's delicate balance.

RACHEL CARSON

The Obligation to Endure

The history of life on earth has been a history of interaction between living things and their surroundings. To a large extent, the physical form and the habits of the earth's vegetation and its animal life have been molded by the environment. Considering the whole span of earthly time, the opposite effect, in which life actually modifies its surroundings, has been relatively slight. Only within the moment of time represented by the present century has one species—man—acquired significant power to alter the nature of his world. 1

During the past quarter century this power has not only increased to one of disturbing magnitude but it has changed in character. The most alarming of all man's assaults upon the environment is the contamination of air, earth, rivers, and sea with dangerous and even lethal materials. This pollution is for the most part irrecoverable; the chain of evil it initiates not only in the world that must support life but in living tissues is for the most part irreversible. In this now universal contamination of the environment, chemicals are the sinister and little-recognized partners of radiation in changing the very nature of the world—the very nature of its life. Strontium 90, released through nuclear explosions into the air, comes to earth in rain or drifts down as fallout, lodges in soil, enters into the grass or corn or wheat grown there, and in time takes up its abode in the bones of a human being, there to remain until his death. Similarly, chemicals sprayed on croplands or forests or gardens lie long in soil, entering into living organisms, passing from one to another in a chain of poisoning and death. Or they pass mysteriously by underground streams until they emerge and, through the alchemy of air and sunlight, combine into new forms that kill vegetation, sicken cattle, and work unknown harm on those who drink from once pure wells. As Albert Schweitzer has said, "Man can hardly even recognize the devils of his own creation." 2

Chapter Twelve Nature and the Environment

It took hundreds of millions of years to produce the life that now inhabits the earth—eons of time in which that developing and evolving and diversifying life reached a state of adjustment and balance with its surroundings. The environment, rigorously shaping and directing the life it supported, contained elements that were hostile as well as supporting. Certain rocks gave out dangerous radiation; even within the light of the sun, from which all life draws its energy, there were shortwave radiations with power to injure. Given time—time not in years but in millennia—life adjusts, and a balance has been reached. For time is the essential ingredient; but in the modern world there is no time. 3

The rapidity of change and the speed with which new situations are created follow the impetuous and heedless pace of man rather than the deliberate pace of nature. Radiation is no longer merely the background radiation of rocks, the bombardment of cosmic rays, the ultraviolet of the sun that have existed before there was any life on earth; radiation is now the unnatural creation of man's tampering with the atom. The chemicals to which life is asked to make its adjustment are no longer merely the calcium and silica and copper and all the rest of the minerals washed out of the rocks and carried in rivers to the sea; they are the synthetic creations of man's inventive mind, brewed in his laboratories, and having no counterparts in nature. 4

To adjust to these chemicals would require time on the scale that is nature's; it would require not merely the years of a man's life but the life of generations. And even this, were it by some miracle possible, would be futile, for the new chemicals come from our laboratories in an endless stream; almost five hundred annually find their way into actual use in the United States alone. The figure is staggering and its implications are not easily grasped—500 new chemicals to which the bodies of men and animals are required somehow to adapt each year, chemicals totally outside the limits of biologic experience. 5

Among them are many that are used in man's war against nature. Since the mid-1940's over 200 basic chemicals have been created for use in killing insects, weeds, rodents, and other organisms described in the modern vernacular as "pests"; and they are sold under several thousand different brand names. 6

These sprays, dusts, and aerosols are now applied almost universally to farms, gardens, forests, and homes—nonselective chemicals that have the power to kill every insect, the "good" and the "bad," to still the song of birds and the leaping of fish in the streams, to coat the leaves with a deadly film, and to linger on in soil—all this though the intended target may be only a few weeds or insects. Can anyone believe it is possible to lay down such a barrage of poisons on the surface of the earth without making it unfit for all life? They should not be called "insecticides," but "biocides." 7

The whole process of spraying seems caught up in an endless spiral. Since DDT was released for civilian use, a process of escalation has been going on in which ever more toxic materials must be found. This has happened because insects, in a triumphant vindication of Darwin's 8

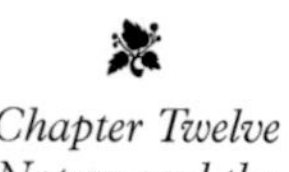

principle of the survival of the fittest, have evolved super races immune to the particular insecticide used, hence a deadlier one has always to be developed—and then a deadlier one than that. It has happened also because, for reasons to be described later, destructive insects often undergo a "flareback," or resurgence, after spraying in numbers greater than before. Thus the chemical war is never won, and all life is caught in its violent crossfire.

Along with the possibility of the extinction of mankind by nuclear war, the central problem of our age has therefore become the contamination of man's total environment with such substances of incredible potential for harm—substances that accumulate in the tissues of plants and animals and even penetrate the germ cells to shatter or alter the very material of heredity upon which the shape of the future depends. 9

Some would-be architects of our future look toward a time when it will be possible to alter the human germ plasm by design. But we may easily be doing so now by inadvertence, for many chemicals, like radiation, bring about gene mutations. It is ironic to think that man might determine his own future by something so seemingly trivial as the choice of an insect spray. 10

All this has been risked—for what? Future historians may well be amazed by our distorted sense of proportion. How could intelligent beings seek to control a few unwanted species by a method that contaminated the entire environment and brought the threat of disease and death even to their own kind? Yet this is precisely what we have done. We have done it, moreover, for reasons that collapse the moment we examine them. We are told that the enormous and expanding use of pesticides is necessary to maintain farm production. Yet is our real problem not one of *overproduction?* Our farms, despite measures to remove acreages from production and to pay farmers *not* to produce, have yielded such a staggering excess of crops that the American taxpayer in 1962 is paying out more than one billion dollars a year as the total carrying cost of the surplus-food storage program. And is the situation helped when one branch of the Agriculture Department tries to reduce production while another states, as it did in 1958, "It is believed generally that reduction of crop acreages under provisions of the Soil Bank will stimulate interest in use of chemicals to obtain maximum production on the land retained in crops." 11

All this is not to say there is no insect problem and no need of control. I am saying, rather, that control must be geared to realities, not to mythical situations, and that the methods employed must be such that they do not destroy us along with the insects. 12

The problem whose attempted solution has brought such a train of disaster in its wake is an accompaniment of our modern way of life. Long before the age of man, insects inhabited the earth—a group of extraordinarily varied and adaptable beings. Over the course of time since man's advent, a small percentage of the more than half a million species of insects have come into conflict with human welfare in two principal ways: as competitors for the food supply and as carriers of human disease. 13

Disease-carrying insects become important where human beings are crowded together, especially under conditions where sanitation is poor, as in time of natural disaster or war or in situations of extreme poverty and deprivation. Then control of some sort becomes necessary. It is a sobering fact, however, as we shall presently see, that the method of massive chemical control has had only limited success, and also threatens to worsen the very conditions it is intended to curb. 14

Under primitive agricultural conditions the farmer had few insect problems. These arose with the intensification of agriculture—the devotion of immense acreages to a single crop. Such a system set the stage for explosive increases in specific insect populations. Single-crop farming does not take advantage of the principles by which nature works; it is agriculture as an engineer might conceive it to be. Nature has introduced great variety into the landscape, but man has displayed a passion for simplifying it. Thus he undoes the built-in checks and balances by which nature holds the species within bounds. One important natural check is a limit on the amount of suitable habitat for each species. Obviously then, an insect that lives on wheat can build up its population to much higher levels on a farm devoted to wheat than on one in which wheat is intermingled with other crops to which the insect is not adapted. 15

The same thing happens in other situations. A generation or more ago, the towns of large areas of the United States lined their streets with the noble elm tree. Now the beauty they hopefully created is threatened with complete destruction as disease sweeps through the elms, carried by a beetle that would have only limited chance to build up large populations and to spread from tree to tree if the elms were only occasional trees in a richly diversified planting. 16

Another factor in the modern insect problem is one that must be viewed against a background of geologic and human history: the spreading of thousands of different kinds of organisms from their native homes to invade new territories. This worldwide migration has been studied and graphically described by the British ecologist Charles Elton in his recent book *The Ecology of Invasions.* During the Cretaceous Period, some hundred million years ago, flooding seas cut many land bridges between continents and living things found themselves confined in what Elton calls "colossal separate nature reserves." There, isolated from others of their kind, they developed many new species. When some of the land masses were joined again, about 15 million years ago, these species began to move out into new territories—a movement that is not only still in progress but is now receiving considerable assistance from man. 17

The importation of plants is the primary agent in the modern spread of species, for animals have almost invariably gone along with the plants, quarantine being a comparatively recent and not completely effective innovation. The United States Office of Plant Introduction alone has introduced almost 200,000 species and varieties of plants from all over the world. Nearly half of the 180 or so major insect ene- 18 mies of plants in the United States are accidental imports from abroad, and most of them have come as hitchhikers on plants.

In new territory, out of reach of the restraining hand of the natural enemies that kept down its numbers in its native land, an invading plant or animal is able to become enormously abundant. Thus it is no accident that our most troublesome insects are introduced species.

These invasions, both the naturally occurring and those dependent 20
on human assistance, are likely to continue indefinitely. Quarantine and massive chemical campaigns are only extremely expensive ways of buying time. We are faced, according to Dr. Elton, "with a life-and-death need not just to find new technological means of suppressing this plant or that animal"; instead we need the basic knowledge of animal populations and their relations to their surroundings that will "promote an even balance and damp down the explosive power of outbreaks and new invasions."

Much of the necessary knowledge is now available but we do not 21
use it. We train ecologists in our universities and even employ them in our governmental agencies but we seldom take their advice. We allow the chemical death rain to fall as though there were no alternative, whereas in fact there are many, and our ingenuity could soon discover many more if given opportunity.

Have we fallen into a mesmerized state that makes us accept as in- 22
evitable that which is inferior or detrimental, as though having lost the will or the vision to demand that which is good? Such thinking, in the words of the ecologist Paul Shepard, "idealizes life with only its head out of water, inches above the limits of toleration of the corruption of its own environment. . . . Why should we tolerate a diet of weak poisons, a home in insipid surroundings, a circle of acquaintances who are not quite our enemies, the noise of motors with just enough relief to prevent insanity? Who would want to live in a world which is just not quite fatal?"

Yet such a world is pressed upon us. The crusade to create a chemi- 23
cally sterile, insect-free world seems to have engendered a fanatic zeal on the part of many specialists and most of the so-called control agencies. On every hand there is evidence that those engaged in spraying operations exercise a ruthless power. "The regulatory entomologists . . . function as prosecutor, judge and jury, tax assessor and collector and sheriff to enforce their own orders," said Connecticut entomologist Neely Turner. The most flagrant abuses go unchecked in both state and federal agencies.

It is not my contention that chemical insecticides must never be 24
used. I do contend that we have put poisonous and biologically potent chemicals indiscriminately into the hands of persons largely or wholly ignorant of their potentials for harm. We have subjected enormous numbers of people to contact with these poisons, without their consent and often without their knowledge. If the Bill of Rights contains no guarantee that a citizen shall be secure against lethal poisons distributed either by private individuals or by public officials, it is surely only be-

cause our forefathers, despite their considerable wisdom and foresight, could conceive of no such problem.

25 I contend, furthermore, that we have allowed these chemicals to be used with little or no advance investigation of their effect on soil, water, wildlife, and man himself. Future generations are unlikely to condone our lack of prudent concern for the integrity of the natural world that supports all life.

26 There is still very limited awareness of the nature of the threat. This is an era of specialists, each of whom sees his own problem and is unaware of or intolerant of the larger frame into which it fits. It is also an era dominated by industry, in which the right to make a dollar at whatever cost is seldom challenged. When the public protests, confronted with some obvious evidence of damaging results of pesticide applications, it is fed little tranquilizing pills of half truth. We urgently need an end to these false assurances, to the sugar coating of unpalatable facts. It is the public that is being asked to assume the risks that the insect controllers calculate. The public must decide whether it wishes to continue on the present road, and it can do so only when in full possession of the facts. In the words of Jean Rostand, "The obligation to endure gives us the right to know."

COMPREHENSION

1. What does Carson mean by "the obligation to endure"?
2. What reasons does the author cite for the overpopulation of insects?
3. What remedies does Carson propose?

RHETORIC

1. What tone does Carson use in her essay? Does she seem to be a subjective or an objective speaker? Give specific support for your response.
2. How does the use of words such as *dangerous, evil, irrevocable,* and *sinister* help to shape the reader's reaction to the piece?
3. Examine the ordering of ideas in paragraph 4, and consider how such an order serves to reinforce Carson's argument.
4. Paragraph 9 consists of only one sentence. What is its function in the essay's scheme?
5. Examine Carson's use of expert testimony. How does it help to strengthen her thesis?
6. How effectively does the essay's conclusion help to tie up Carson's points? What is the writer's intent in this final paragraph? How does she accomplish this aim?

WRITING

1. Write an essay in which you suggest solutions to the problems brought up in Carson's piece. You may want to suggest measures that the average citizen can take to eliminate the casual use of insecticides to control the insect population.

2. Write an essay entitled "Insects Are Not the Problem; Humanity Is." In this essay, argue that it is humanity's greed that has caused such an imbalance in nature as to threaten the planet's survival.
3. Write a biographical research paper on Rachel Carson that focuses on her involvement with nature and environmental issues.

LOREN EISELEY Loren Eiseley (1907–1977) was an educator, anthropologist, poet, and author. He is best known for his books *The Immense Journey* (1957), *Darwin's Century* (1958), *The Firmament of Time* (rev. ed., 1960), and The *Night Country* (1971). His books wonderfully combine poetic imagination with scientific objectivity. In the following essay, Eiseley shows his capacity for seeing profoundly into the most common scenes.

LOREN EISELEY

How Natural Is Natural?

In the more obscure scientific circles which I frequent there is a legend circulating about a late distinguished scientist who, in his declining years, persisted in wearing enormous padded boots much too large for him. He had developed, it seems, what to his fellows was a wholly irrational fear of falling through the interstices of that largely empty molecular space which common men in their folly speak of as the world. A stroll across his living-room floor had become, for him, something as dizzily horrendous as the activities of a window washer on the Empire State Building. Indeed, with equal reason he could have passed a ghostly hand through his own ribs. 1

The quivering network of his nerves, the awe-inspiring movement of his thought had become a vague cloud of electrons interspersed with the light-year distances that obtain between us and the farther galaxies. This was the natural world which he had helped to create, and in which, at last, he had found himself a lonely and imprisoned occupant. All around him the ignorant rushed on their way over the illusion of substantial floors, leaping, though they did not see it, from particle to particle, over a bottomless abyss. There was even a question as to the reality of the particles which bore them up. It did not, however, keep insubstantial newspapers from being sold, or insubstantial love from being made. 2

Not long ago I became aware of another world perhaps equally natural and real, which man is beginning to forget. My thinking began in New England under a boat dock. The lake I speak of has been preempted and civilized by man. All day long in the vacation season high- 3

speed motorboats, driven with the reckless abandon common to the young Apollos of our society, speed back and forth, carrying loads of equally attractive girls. The shores echo to the roar of powerful motors and the delighted screams of young Americans with uncounted horsepower surging under their hands. In truth, as I sat there under the boat dock, I had some desire to swim or to canoe in the older ways of the great forest which once lay about this region. Either notion would have been folly. I would have been gaily chopped to ribbons by teen-age youngsters whose eyes were always immutably fixed on the far horizons of space, or upon the dials which indicated the speed of their passing. There was another world, I was to discover, along the lake shallows and under the boat dock, where the motors could not come.

4 As I sat there one sunny morning when the water was peculiarly translucent, I saw a dark shadow moving swiftly over the bottom. It was the first sign of life I had seen in this lake, whose shores seemed to yield little but washed-in beer cans. By and by the gliding shadow ceased to scurry from stone to stone over the bottom. Unexpectedly, it headed almost directly for me. A furry nose with gray whiskers broke the surface. Below the whiskers green water foliage trailed out in an inverted V as long as his body. A muskrat still lived in the lake. He was bringing in his breakfast.

5 I sat very still in the strips of sunlight under the pier. To my surprise the muskrat came almost to my feet with his little breakfast of greens. He was young, and it rapidly became obvious to me that he was laboring under an illusion of his own, and that he thought animals and men were still living in the Garden of Eden. He gave me a friendly glance from time to time as he nibbled his greens. Once, even, he went out into the lake again and returned to my feet with more greens. He had not, it seemed, heard very much about men. I shuddered. Only the evening before I had heard a man describe with triumphant enthusiasm how he had killed a rat in the garden because the creature had dared to nibble his petunias. He had even showed me the murder weapon, a sharp-edged brick.

6 On this pleasant shore a war existed and would go on until nothing remained but man. Yet this creature with the gray, appealing face wanted very little: a strip of shore to coast up and down, sunlight and moonlight, some weeds from the deep water. He was an edge-of-the-world dweller, caught between a vanishing forest and a deep lake preempted by unpredictable machines full of chopping blades. He eyed me nearsightedly, a green leaf posed in his mouth. Plainly he had come with some poorly instructed memory about the lion and the lamb.

7 "You had better run away now," I said softly, making no movement in the shafts of light. "You are in the wrong universe and must not make this mistake again. I am really a very terrible and cunning beast. I can throw stones." With this I dropped a little pebble at his feet.

8 He looked at me half blindly, with eyes much better adjusted to the wavering shadows of his lake bottom than to sight in the open air. He made almost as if to take the pebble up into his forepaws. Then a

thought seemed to cross his mind—a thought perhaps telepathically received, as Freud once hinted, in the dark world below and before man, a whisper of ancient disaster heard in the depths of a burrow. Perhaps after all this was not Eden. His nose twitched carefully; he edged toward the water.

As he vanished in an oncoming wave, there went with him a natural world, distinct from the world of girls and motorboats, distinct from the world of the professor holding to reality by some great snowshoe effort in his study. My muskrat's shore-line universe was edged with the dark wall of hills on one side and the waspish drone of motors farther out, but it was a world of sunlight he had taken down into the water weeds. It hovered there, waiting for my disappearance. I walked away, obscurely pleased that darkness had not gained on life by any act of mine. In so many worlds, I thought, how natural is "natural"—and is there anything we can call a natural world at all? 9

COMPREHENSION

1. State in your own words the thesis of this essay.
2. Describe the three "worlds" mentioned in this essay by Eiseley.
3. Why is Eiseley surprised that a muskrat still lives in the lake? Cite specific details that might threaten a muskrat in the lake's world.

RHETORIC

1. The phrases "world of sunlight" and "darkness" (paragraph 9) are meant to be taken figuratively. What do they mean?
2. Explain the allusions to "Apollos" (paragraph 3); "the Garden of Eden" (paragraph 5); and Freud (paragraph 8).
3. Explain the relation between paragraphs 1 to 2 and 3 to 9. What rhetorical technique do both groups use?
4. How does Eiseley use narration and description in his essay? Cite examples of both.
5. What details does Eiseley use in contrasting the muskrat's world to the typical American's world?
6. Analyze the way Eiseley develops his concluding paragraph.

WRITING

1. Why does Eiseley despair at the disappearance of the other world? Why should we protect wildlife and wilderness if it means limiting our own growth?
2. Write an essay in which you contrast aspects of the natural world with the artificial world. Use details to support your contrast. For example, you can describe the life of a bird in the city, of a raccoon in the suburbs, or a deer or bear in a state park.

3. Both Eiseley and E. B. White (in "Once More to the Lake," Chapter 1) focus on specific bodies of water in order to develop insights into human nature and the natural world. In a comparative essay, explain their purpose and how they develop it.
4. Analyze the writing styles of Eiseley and Carson. Examine sentence structure, descriptive techniques, use of evidence, and figurative language.

GRETEL EHRLICH Gretel Ehrlich (1949–) was born in California and educated at Bennington College, UCLA, and The New School for Social Research. She currently lives on a ranch in Shell, Wyoming. She has worked as a professional documentary filmmaker. Her essays have appeared in the *New York Times, The Atlantic, Harper's,* and the *New Age Journal.* She has also published two books of poetry and a story collection, *City Tales, Wyoming Stories.* Ehrlich has received awards from the National Endowment for the Arts and the Wyoming Council for the Arts. In the following selection, with the eyes and ears of an anthropologist and the knowledge of a historian, Ehrlich provides us with a comprehensive view of a life most Americans are no longer familiar with.

GRETEL EHRLICH

Wyoming: The Solace of Open Spaces

It's May, and I've just awakened from a nap, curled against sagebrush the way my dog taught me to sleep—sheltered from wind. A weather front is pulling the huge sky over me, and from the dark a hailstone has hit me on the head. 1

I'm trailing a band of 2000 sheep across a stretch of Wyoming badland, a 50-mile trip that takes five days because sheep shade up in the hot sun and won't budge until it cools. Bunched together now, and excited into a run by the storm, they drift across dry land, tumbling into draws like water and surging out again onto the rugged, choppy plateaus that are the building blocks of this state. 2

The name "Wyoming" comes from an Indian word meaning "at the great plains," but the plains are really valleys, great arid valleys, 1600 square miles' worth of them, with the horizon bending up on all sides into mountain ranges. This gives the vastness a sheltering look. 3

Winter lasts six months here. Prevailing winds spill snowdrifts to the east, and new storms from the northwest replenish them. This white bulk is sometimes dizzying, even nauseating, to look at. At 20, 30, 40 degrees below zero, it is not only your car that doesn't work but also your mind and body. 4

The landscape hardens into a dungeon of space. During the winter, while I was riding to find a new calf, my legs half froze to the saddle, and in the silence that such cold creates, I felt like the first person on earth, or the last.

Today the sun is out—only a few clouds billowing. In the east, where the sheep have started off without me, the benchland tilts up in a series of red-earthed, eroded mesas, planed flat on top by a million years of water. Behind them, a bold line of muscular scraps rears up 10,000 feet to become the Big Horn Mountains. A tidal pattern is engraved into the ground, as if left by the sea that once covered this state. Canyons curve down like galaxies to meet the oncoming rush of flat land. 6

To live and work in this kind of open country, with its 100-mile views, is to lose the distinction between background and foreground. When I asked an older ranch hand to describe Wyoming's openness, he said, "It's all a bunch of nothing—wind and rattlesnakes—and so much of it you can't tell where you're going or where you've been and it don't make much difference." 7

John, a sheepman I know, is tall and handsome and has an explosive temperament. He has a perfect intuition about people and sheep. They call him "Highpockets" because he's so long-legged; his graceful stride matches the distances he has to cover. 8

"Open space hasn't affected me at all. It's all the people moving in on it," he said. The huge ranch he was born on takes up much of one county and spreads into another state. For him to put 100,000 miles on his pickup in three years and never leave home is not unusual. 9

Most of Wyoming has a "lean-to" look. Instead of big, roomy barns and Victorian houses, there are dugouts, low sheds, log cabins, sheep camps and fence lines that look like driftwood blown haphazardly into place. People in Wyoming still feel pride because they live in such a harsh place, part of the glamorous cowboy past, and they are determined not to be the victims of a mining-dominated future. 10

Most characteristic of the state's landscape is what a developer euphemistically describes as "indigenous growth right up to your front door"—a reference to waterless stands of salt sage, snakes, jack-rabbits, deerflies, red dust, a brief respite of wildflowers, dry washes and no trees. 11

Sagebrush covers 58,000 square miles of Wyoming. The biggest city has a population of 50,000, and there are only five settlements that could be called cities in the whole state. The rest are towns, scattered across the expanse with as much as 60 miles between them, their populations 2000, 50 or 10. They are fugitive-looking, perched on a barren, windblown bench, or tagged onto a river or a railroad, or laid out straight in a farming valley with implement stores and a block-long Mormon church. 12

In the eastern part of the state, which slides down into the Great Plains, the new mining settlements are boomtowns, trailer cities, metal knots on flat land. 13

14 Despite the desolate look, there's a coziness to living in this state.

15 There are so few people (only 470,000) that ranchers who buy and sell cattle know each other statewide. The kids who choose to go to college usually go to the state's one university, in Laramie. Hired hands work their way around Wyoming in a lifetime of hirings and firings. And, despite the physical separation, people stay in touch, often driving two or three hours to another ranch for dinner.

16 Seventy-five years ago, when travel was by buckboard or horseback, cowboys who were temporarily out of work rode the grub line—drifting from ranch to ranch, mending fences or milking cows, and receiving in exchange a bed and meals. Gossip and messages traveled this slow circuit with them, creating an intimacy among ranchers who were three and four weeks' ride apart.

17 One old-time couple I know, whose turn-of-the-century homestead was used by an outlaw gang as a relay station for stolen horses, recall that if you were traveling, desperado or not, any lighted ranch house was a welcome sign.

18 Even now, for someone who lives in a remote spot, arriving at a ranch or coming to town for supplies is cause for celebration. To emerge from isolation can be disorienting. Everything looks bright, new, vivid. After I had been herding sheep for only three days, the sound of the camp-tender's pickup flustered me. Longing for human company, I felt a foolish grin take over my face, yet I had to resist an urgent temptation to run and hide.

19 Things happen suddenly in Wyoming: the change of seasons and weather; for people, the violent swings into and out of isolation. But goodnaturedness goes hand in hand with severity. Friendliness is a tradition. Strangers passing on the road wave hello.

20 A common sight is two pickups stopped side by side far out on a range, on a dirt track winding through the sage. The drivers will share a cigarette, uncap their Thermos bottles, and pass a battered cup, steaming with coffee, between windows. These meetings summon up the details of several generations, because in Wyoming private histories are largely public knowledge.

21 In most parts of Wyoming, the human population is visibly outnumbered by the animal. Not far from my town of 50, I rode into a narrow valley and startled a herd of 200 elk. Eagles look like small people as they eat car-killed deer by the road. Antelope, moving in small, graceful bands, travel at 60 m.p.h., their mouths open as if drinking in the space.

22 The solitude in which Westerners live makes them quiet. They telegraph thoughts and feelings by the way they tilt their heads and listen; pulling their Stetsons into a steep dive over their eyes or pigeon-toeing one boot over the other, they lean against a fence and take the whole scene in. These detached looks of quiet amusement are sometimes cynical, but they can also come from a dry-eyed humility as lucid as the air is clear.

23 Conversation goes on in what sounds like a private code. A few phrases imply a complex of meanings. Asking directions you get a curi-

ous list of details. While trailing sheep, I was told to "ride up to that kinda upturned rock, follow the pin wash, turn left at the dump, and then you'll see the waterhole."

I've spent hours riding to sheep camp at dawn in a pickup when 24
nothing was said and eaten meals in the cookhouse when the only words spoken were a mumbled "Thank you, ma'am" at the end of dinner. The silence is profound. Instead of talking, we seem to share one eye. The landscape is engorged with detail, every movement on it chillingly sharp. The air between people is charged.

Spring weather is capricious and mean. It snows, then blisters with 25
heat. There have been tornadoes. They lay their elephant trunks out in the sage until they find houses, then slurp everything up and leave. I've noticed that melting snowbanks hiss and rot, viperous, then drip into calm pools where ducklings hatch and livestock, being trailed to summer range, drink.

With the ice cover gone, rivers churn a milkshake brown, taking 26
culverts and small bridges with them. Water in such an arid place (the average annual rainfall where I live is less than eight inches) is like blood. It festoons drab land with green veins: a line of cottonwoods following a stream; a strip of alfalfa, and on ditchbanks, wild asparagus growing.

I try to imagine a world of uncharted land, in which one could look 27
over an uncompleted map and ride a horse past where all the lines have stopped. There is no real wilderness left; wilderness, yes, but true wilderness has been gone on this continent since the time of Lewis and Clark's overland journey.

Two hundred years ago, the Crow, Shoshone, Arapaho, Cheyenne, 28
and Sioux roamed the intermountain West, orchestrating their movements according to hunger, season, and warfare. Once they acquired horses, they traversed the spines of all the big Wyoming ranges—the Absarokas, the Wind Rivers, the Tetons, the Big Horns—and wintered on the unprotected plains that fan out from them. Space was life. The word was their home.

What was life-giving to native Americans was often nightmarish to 29
sod-busters who arrived encumbered with families and ethnic pasts to be transplanted in nearly uninhabitable land. The great distances, the shortage of water and trees, and the loneliness created unexpected hardships for them.

In her book *O Pioneers!* Willa Cather gives a settler's version of the 30
bleak landscape: "The little town behind them had vanished as if it had never been, had fallen behind the swell of the prairie, and the stern frozen country received them into its bosom. The homesteads were few and far apart; here and there a windmill gaunt against the sky, a sod house crouching in a hollow."

The emptiness of the West was for others a geography of possibility. 31
Men and women who amassed great chunks of land and struggled to preserve unfenced empires were, despite their self-serving motives, unwitting geographers. They understood the lay of the land.

But by the 1850s, the Oregon and Mormon trails sported bumper- 32
to-bumper traffic. Wealthy landowners, many of them aristocratic absentee landlords, known as remittance men because they were paid to come West and get out of their families' hair, overstocked the range with more than a million head of cattle. By 1885, the feed and water were desperately short, and the winter of 1886 laid out the gaunt bodies of dead animals so closely together that when the thaw came, one rancher from Kaycee claimed to have walked on cowhide all the way to Crazy Woman Creek, 20 miles away.

Territorial Wyoming was a boy's world. The land was generous with 33
everything but water. At first there was room enough and food enough for everyone. And, as with all beginnings, an expansive mood set in. The young cowboys, drifters, shopkeepers, and schoolteachers were heroic, lawless, generous, rowdy, and tenacious. The individualism and optimism generated during those times have endured.

Cattle barons tried to control all the public grazing land by restrict- 34
ing membership in the Wyoming Stock Growers Association, as if it were a country club. They ostracized from roundups and brandings cowboys and ranchers who were not members, then denounced them as rustlers.

One cold-blooded murder of a small-time stockman kicked off the 35
Johnson County cattle war, which was no simple good guy–bad guy shootout but a complicated class struggle between landed gentry and less affluent settlers—a shocking reminder that the West was not an egalitarian sanctuary after all.

Fencing ultimately enforced boundaries, but barbed wire abolished 36
space. It was stretched across the beautiful valleys, into mountains, over desert badlands, through buffalo grass.

The "anything is possible" fever—the lure of any place—was con- 37
stricted. The integrity of the land as a geographical body, and the freedom to ride anywhere on it, was lost.

I punched cows with a young man named Martin, who is the great- 38
grandson of John Tisdale. His inheritance is not the open land that Tisdale knew and prematurely lost but a rage against restraint.

In all this open space, values crystalize quickly. People are strong on 39
scruples but tenderhearted about quirky behavior. A friend and I found one ranch hand, who's "not right in the head," sitting in front of the badly decayed carcass of a cow, shaking his finger and saying, "Now, I don't want you to do this ever again!"

When I asked what was wrong with him, I was told, "He's goofier 40
than hell, just like the rest of us."

Perhaps because the West is historically new, conventional morality 41
is still felt to be less important than rock-bottom truths. Though there's always a lot of teasing and sparring around, people are blunt with each other, sometimes even cruel, believing honesty is stronger medicine than sympathy, which may console but often conceals.

The formality that goes hand in hand with the rowdiness is known 42
as "the Western Code." It's a list of practical do's and don'ts, faithfully

observed. A friend, Cliff, who runs a trapline in the winter, cut off half his foot while axing a hole in the ice. Alone, he dragged himself to his pickup and headed for town, stopping to open the ranch gate as he left, and getting out to close it again, thus losing, in his observance of rules, precious time and blood.

Later, he commented, "How would it look, them having to come to the hospital to tell me their cows had gotten out?" 43

The roominess of the state has affected political attitudes. Ranchers keep up with world politics and the convulsions of the economy but are basically isolationists. Used to running their own small empires of land and livestock, they're suspicious of big government. 44

It's a "don't fence me in" holdover from a century ago. They still want the elbow room their grandfathers had, so they're strongly conservative, but with a populist twist. 45

Summer is the season when we get our "cowboy tans"—on the lower parts of our faces and on three fourths of our arms. Excessive heat, in the 90s and higher, sends us outside with the mosquitoes. 46

After the brief lushness of summer, the sun moves south. The range grass is brown. Livestock has been trailed back down from the mountains. Waterholes begin to frost over at night. Last fall Martin asked me to accompany him on a pack trip. With five horses, we followed a river into the mountains behind the tiny Wyoming town of Meeteetse. Groves of aspen, red and orange, gave off a light that made us look toasted. 47

One of our evening entertainments was to watch the night sky. My dog, who also came on the trip, a dingo bred to herd sheep, is so used to the silence and empty skies that when an airplane flies over he always looks up and eyes the distant intruder quizzically. 48

The sky, lately, seems to be much more crowded than it used to be. Satellites make their silent passes in the dark with great regularity. We counted 18 in one hour's viewing. How odd to think that while they circumnavigated the planet, Martin and I had moved only six miles into our local wilderness, and had seen no other human for the two weeks we stayed there. 49

At night, by moonlight, the land is whittled to slivers—a ridge, a river, a strip of grassland stretching to the mountains, then the huge sky. One morning a full moon was setting in the west just as the sun was rising. I felt precariously balanced between the two as I loped across a meadow. For a moment, I could believe that the stars, which were still visible, work like cooper's bands, holding everything above Wyoming together. 50

Space has a spiritual equivalent, and can heal what is divided and burdensome in us. My grandchildren will probably use space shuttles for a honeymoon trip or to recover from heart attacks, but closer to home we might also learn how to carry space inside ourselves in the effortless way we carry our skins. Space represents sanity, not a life purified, dull, or "spaced out" but one that might accommodate intelligently any idea or situation. 51

COMPREHENSION

1. What is Wyoming's predominant appeal to the author? Why has she chosen to live in its rather inhospitable climate?
2. Explain the ways in which Wyoming, for Ehrlich, symbolizes the American West.
3. In the concluding paragraph, Ehrlich says, "Space has a spiritual equivalent." What does she mean by this? How do the Wyoming natives display this spirituality? How has it affected the author?

RHETORIC

1. How do the following descriptions help create the nature of Wyoming space: "This gives the vastness a sheltering look" (paragraph 3); "The landscape hardens into a dungeon of space" (paragraph 5); and "Canyons curve down like galaxies" (paragraph 6)?
2. None of the direct speech in this essay is in the form of dialogue. How is this indicative of the Westerner's attitude toward speech? How does it support the idea that "A few phrases imply a complex of meanings" (paragraph 23)?
3. How does Ehrlich's introductory comment that "my dog taught me to sleep" (paragraph 1) set the general tone for the bond between humans and nature in Wyoming? What other evidence is there in the essay of this special relationship?
4. Paragraphs 28 through 37 describe Wyoming's history. What function does this serve in the essay? How does it explain life in present-day Wyoming?
5. In the conclusion, Ehrlich suggests that the relationship of humans to space as it exists in Wyoming may be dying out. What references are there in the essay that seem to move toward this conclusion?
6. Compare the use of direct speech in this essay to its use in McPhee's "Travels in Georgia." In what way does the dialogue suggest that the residents depicted in the two essays are similar in their outlook and attitudes?

WRITING

1. How can one's environment affect the nature of one's relationship with others? How can it affect one's "communicative style"? For example, do city dwellers speak differently from rural ones? Do people from one region—for example, the South—relate differently toward one another than do people from another region? Explore these issues in an essay, focusing on a locale you are familiar with. Your topics don't have to be limited to speech but may include body language, dress, jewelry, and so forth.
2. Compare and contrast the sense of space in this essay with that in Orwell's "Shooting an Elephant" in Chapter 2.
3. Think about some quality that is important to you—for example, solitude or brightness—and then write an essay about a place or environment that captures this quality.

JOHN McPHEE John McPhee (1931–) began his career writing for television and was an associate editor of *Time* magazine and a staff writer for *The New Yorker.* He received an A.B. from Princeton and did graduate work at Cambridge University in England. He is known for his offbeat subjects—often agriculture and geography—and detailed, lucid prose. McPhee often focuses on little-known aspects of his subject matter, which results in making the commonplace interesting. Among the best known of his over twenty nonfiction books are *Oranges* (which describes the history and growth cycle of the fruit and the manufacture of its by-products), published in 1967; *The Survival of the Bark Canoe* (1975); *Coming into the Country* (1977); and, most recently, *Assembling California* (1993). His awards include four honorary doctorates from various universities and the Woodrow Wilson Award from Princeton. In this selection from *Pieces of the Frame* (1975), a seemingly insignificant incident reveals a lot about character, place, and attitude.

JOHN McPHEE

Travels in Georgia

I asked for the gorp. Carol passed it to me. Breakfast had been heavy with cathead biscuits, sausage, boiled eggs, Familia, and chicory coffee, but that was an hour ago and I was again hungry. Sam said, "The little Yankee bastard wants the gorp, Carol. Shall we give him some?" Sam's voice was as soft as sphagnum, with inflections of piedmont Georgia. 1

"The little Yankee bastard can have all he wants this morning," Carol said. "It's such a beautiful day." 2

Although Sam was working for the state, he was driving his own Chevrolet. He was doing seventy. In a reverberation of rubber, he crossed Hunger and Hardship Creek and headed into the sun on the Swainsboro Road. I took a ration of gorp—soybeans, sunflower seeds, oats, pretzels, Wheat Chex, raisins, and kelp—and poured another ration into Carol's hand. At just about that moment, a snapping turtle was hit on the road a couple of miles ahead of us, who knows by what sort of vehicle, a car, a pickup; run over like a manhole cover, probably with much the same sound, and not crushed, but gravely wounded. It remained still. It appeared to be dead on the road. 3

Sam, as we approached, was the first to see it. "D.O.R.," he said. "Man, that is a big snapper." Carol and I both sat forward. Sam pressed hard on the brakes. Even so, he was going fifty when he passed the turtle. 4

Carol said, "He's not dead. He didn't look dead." 5

Sam reversed. He drove backward rapidly, fast as the car would go. He stopped on the shoulder, and we all got out. There was a pond be- 6

yond the turtle. The big, broad head was shining with blood, but there was, as yet, very little blood on the road. The big jaws struck as we came near, opened and closed bloodily—not the kind of strike that, minutes ago, could have cut off a finger, but still a strike with power. The turtle was about fourteen inches long and a shining horn-brown. The bright spots on its marginal scutes were like light bulbs around a mirror. The neck lunged out. Carol urged the turtle, with her foot, toward the side of the road. "I know, big man," she said to it. "I know it's bad. We're not tormenting you. Honest we're not." Sam asked her if she thought it had a chance to live and she said she was sure it had no chance at all. A car, coming west, braked down and stopped. The driver got out, with some effort and a big paunch. He looked at the turtle and said, "Fifty years old if he's a day." That was the whole of what the man had to say. He got into his car and drove on. Carol nudged the snapper, but it was too hurt to move. It could only strike the air. Now, in a screech of brakes, another car came onto the scene. It went by us, then spun around with squealing tires and pulled up on the far shoulder. It was a two-tone, high-speed, dome-lighted Ford, and in it was the sheriff of Laurens County. He got out and walked toward us, all Technicolor in his uniform, legs striped like a pine-barrens tree frog's, plastic plate on his chest, name of Wade.

"Good morning," Sam said to him. 7

"How y'all?" said Sheriff Wade. 8

Carol said, "Would you mind shooting this turtle for us, please?" 9

"Surely, Ma'am," said the sheriff, and he drew his .38. He extended 10
his arm and took aim.

"Uh, Sheriff," I said. "If you don't mind. . . ." And I asked him if 11
he would kindly shoot the turtle over soil and not over concrete. The sheriff paused and looked slowly, with new interest, from one of us to another: a woman in her twenties, good-looking, with long tawny hair, no accent (that he could hear), barefoot, and wearing a gray sweatshirt and brown dungarees with a hunting knife in the belt; a man (Sam) around forty, in weathered khaki, also without an accent, and with a full black beard divided by a short white patch at the chin—an authentic, natural split beard; and then this incongruous little Yankee bastard telling him not to shoot the road. Carol picked up the turtle by its long, serrated tail and carried it, underside toward her leg, beyond the shoulder of the highway, where she set it down on a patch of grass. The sheriff followed with his .38. He again took aim. He steadied the muzzle of the pistol twelve inches from the turtle. He fired, and missed. The gun made an absurdly light sound, like a screen door shutting. He fired again. The third shot killed the turtle. The pistol smoked. The sheriff blew the smoke away, and smiled, apparently at himself. He shook his head a little. "He should be good," he said, with a nod at the turtle. The sheriff crossed the road and got into his car. "Y'all be careful," he said. With a great screech of tires, he wheeled around and headed on west.

Carol guessed that the turtle was about ten years old. By the tail, 12
she carried it down to the edge of the pond, like a heavy suitcase with

a broken strap. Sam fetched plastic bags from the car. I found a long two-by-ten plank and carried it to the edge of the water. Carol placed the snapper upside down on the plank. Kneeling, she unsheathed her hunting knife and began, in a practiced and professional way, to slice around the crescents in the plastron, until the flesh of the legs—in thick steaks of red meat—came free. Her knife was very sharp. She put the steaks into a plastic bag. All the while, she talked to the dead turtle, soothingly, reassuringly, nurse to patient, doctor to child, and when she reached in under the plastron and found an ovary, she shifted genders with a grunt of surprise. She pulled out some globate yellow fat and tossed it into the pond. Hundreds of mosquito fish came darting through the water, sank their teeth, shook their heads, worried the fat. Carol began to remove eggs from the turtle's body. The eggs were like ping-pong balls in size, shape, and color, and how they all fitted into the turtle was more than I could comprehend, for there were fifty-six of them in there, fully finished, and a number that had not quite taken their ultimate form. "Look at those eggs. Aren't they beautiful?" Carol said. "Oh, that's sad. You were just about to do your thing, weren't you, girl?" That was why the snapper had gone out of the pond and up onto the road. She was going to bury her eggs in some place she knew, perhaps drawn by an atavistic attachment to the place where she herself had hatched out and where many generations of her forebears had been born when there was no road at all. The turtle twitched. Its neck moved. Its nerves were still working, though its life was gone. The nails on the ends of the claws were each an inch long. The turtle draped one of these talons over one of Carol's fingers. Carol withdrew more fat and threw a huge hunk into the pond. "Wouldn't it be fun to analyze *that* for pesticides?" she said. "You're fat as a pig, Mama. You sure lived high off the hog." Finishing the job—it took forty minutes—Carol found frog bones in the turtle. She put more red meat into plastic sacks and divided the eggs. She kept half for us to eat. With her knife she carefully buried the remaining eggs, twenty-eight or so, in a sandbank, much as the mother turtle might have been doing at just that time. Carol picked away some leeches from between her fingers. The leeches had come off the turtle's shell. She tied the sacks and said, "All right. That's all we can say grace over. Let's send her back whence she came." Picking up the inedible parts—plastron, carapace, neck, claws—she heaved them into the pond. They hit with a slap and sank without bubbles.

COMPREHENSION

1. What is the narrator's role during the sequence of events that occur in the essay?

2. Why is the turtle so important to Carol and Sam? At what point do you understand its significance to them?

3. What was your emotional response to this essay? Why did the essay affect you as it did?

RHETORIC

1. McPhee explains, in detail, his breakfast, the composition of gorp, and the innards of the turtle. What function does this straightforward reporting serve? How does the diction mirror the attitudes and behavior of the characters?
2. In addition to reportage, McPhee uses a considerable amount of figurative language in his descriptions. Locate examples of this language in the essay. How do they enrich the effect of the writing?
3. How effective is the opening sentence of the essay in attracting your attention? Why is it effective?
4. How does the dialogue between the sheriff and Carol contribute to the overall tone and mood of the essay? How does it strengthen the portrait of the locale and its people?
5. Why does McPhee devote so much attention to describing the turtle in paragraph 12? What do Carol's behavior and comments reveal about her personality and profession?
6. How do Carol's and Sam's initial comments about the narrator set up his role in the story? How is this role maintained throughout the action?

WRITING

1. Had the story been told through the point of view of Carol or Sam, how would it have differed from McPhee's version? How does McPhee's perspective determine which elements are focused on? Write a brief analysis of this rhetorical issue.
2. Have you ever visited a place where you were an "outsider"? Write an essay about this visit, and explain how others responded to you and how you responded to them. Title your essay, "Travels in ———."
3. Narrate an event in which you witnessed the killing or death of an animal. Capture your emotional response to the event as well as the response of any others who might have witnessed it.

ALICE WALKER Alice Walker (1944–) was born in Eatonton, Georgia, and now lives in San Francisco and Mendecino County, California. A celebrated poet, short-story writer, and novelist, she is the author of *Revolutionary Petunias and Other Poems* (1973), *In Love and Trouble: Stories of Black Women* (1973), and *Meridian* (1976), among other works. Her 1982 novel, *The Color Purple,* won the American Book Award and the 1983 Pulitzer Prize for Fiction. Her latest book, *Possessing the Secret of Joy,* was published in 1992 and continues the story of the characters introduced in *The Color Purple.* With her usual sensitivity and insight, Walker reminisces in this essay about a horse and what it taught her about communication and social injustice.

ALICE WALKER

Am I Blue?

*Ain't these tears in these eyes tellin' you?**

1 For about three years my companion and I rented a small house in the country that stood on the edge of a large meadow that appeared to run from the end of our deck straight into the mountains. The mountains, however, were quite far away, and between us and them there was, in fact, a town. It was one of the many pleasant aspects of the house that you never really were aware of this.

2 It was a house of many windows, low, wide, nearly floor to ceiling in the living room, which faced the meadow, and it was from one of these that I first saw our closest neighbor, a large white horse, cropping grass, flipping its mane, and ambling about—not over the entire meadow, which stretched well out of sight of the house, but over the five or so fenced-in acres that were next to the twenty-odd that we had rented. I soon learned that the horse, whose name was Blue, belonged to a man who lived in another town, but was boarded by our neighbors next door. Occasionally, one of the children, usually a stock teenager, but sometimes a much younger girl or boy, could be seen riding Blue. They would appear in the meadow, climb up on his back, ride furiously for ten or fifteen minutes, then get off, slap Blue on the flanks, and not be seen again for a month or more.

3 There were many apple trees in our yard, and one by the fence that Blue could almost reach. We were soon in the habit of feeding him apples, which he relished, especially because by the middle of summer the meadow grasses—so green and succulent since January—had dried out from lack of rain, and Blue stumbled about munching the dried stalks half-heartedly. Sometimes he would stand very still just by the apple tree, and when one of us came out he would whinny, snort loudly, or stamp the ground. This meant, of course: I want an apple.

4 It was quite wonderful to pick a few apples, or collect those that had fallen to the ground overnight, and patiently hold them, one by one, up to his large, toothy mouth. I remained as thrilled as a child by his flexible dark lips; huge, cubelike teeth that crunched the apples, core and all, with such finality; and high, broad-breasted *enormity* beside which I felt small indeed. When I was a child, I used to ride horses, and was especially friendly with one named Nan until the day I was riding and my brother deliberately spooked her and I was thrown, head first, against

the trunk of a tree. When I came to, I was in bed and my mother was bending worriedly over me; we silently agreed that perhaps horseback riding was not the safest sport for me. Since then I have walked, and prefer walking to horseback riding—but I had forgotten the depth of feeling one could see in horses' eyes.

5 I was therefore unprepared for the expression in Blue's. Blue was lonely. Blue was horribly lonely and bored. I was not shocked that this should be the case; five acres to tramp by yourself, endlessly, even in the most beautiful of meadows—and his was—cannot provide many interesting events, and once rainy season turned to dry that was about it. No, I was shocked that I had forgotten that human animals and nonhuman animals can communicate quite well; if we are brought up around animals as children we take this for granted. By the time we are adults we no longer remember. However, the animals have not changed. They are in fact *completed* creations (at least they seem to be, so much more than we) who are not likely *to* change; it is their nature to express themselves. What else are they going to express? And they do. And, generally speaking, they are ignored.

6 After giving Blue the apples, I would wander back to the house, aware that he was observing me. Were more apples not forthcoming then? Was that to be his sole entertainment for the day? My partner's small son had decided he wanted to learn how to piece a quilt; we worked in silence on our respective squares as I thought. . . .

7 Well, about slavery: about white children, who were raised by black people, who knew their first all-accepting love from black women, and then, when they were twelve or so, were told they must "forget" the deep levels of communication between themselves and the "mammy" that they knew. Later they would be able to relate quite calmly. "My old mammy was sold to another good family." "My old mammy was ——— ——." Fill in the blank. Many more years later a white woman would say: "I can't understand these Negroes, these blacks. What do they want? They're so different from us."

8 And about the Indians, considered to be "like animals" by the "settlers" (a very benign euphemism for what they actually were), who did not understand their description as a compliment.

9 And about the thousands of American men who marry Japanese, Korean, Filipino, and other non-English-speaking women and of how happy they report they are, *"blissfully,"* until their brides learn to speak English, at which point the marriages tend to fall apart. What then did the men see, when they looked into the eyes of the women they married, before they could speak English? Apparently only their own reflections.

10 I thought of society's impatience with the young. "Why are they playing the music so loud?" Perhaps the children have listened to much of the music of oppressed people their parents danced to before they were born, with its passionate but soft cries for acceptance and love, and they have wondered why their parents failed to hear.

11 I do not know how long Blue had inhabited his five beautiful, boring acres before we moved into our house; a year after we had ar-

rived—and had also traveled to other valleys, other cities, other worlds—he was still there.

But then, in our second year at the house, something happened in Blue's life. One morning, looking out the window at the fog that lay like a ribbon over the meadow, I saw another horse, a brown one, at the other end of Blue's field. Blue appeared to be afraid of it, and for several days made no attempt to go near. We went away for a week. When we returned, Blue had decided to make friends and the two horses ambled or galloped along together, and Blue did not come nearly as often to the fence underneath the apple tree.

When he did, bringing his new friend with him, there was a differ- 13
ent look in his eyes. A look of independence, of self-possession, of inalienable *horse*ness. His friend eventually became pregnant. For months and months there was, it seemed to me, a mutual feeling between me and the horses of justice, of peace. I fed apples to them both. The look in Blue's eyes was one of unabashed "this is *it*ness."

It did not, however, last forever. One day, after a visit to the city, I 14
went out to give Blue some apples. He stood waiting, or so I thought, though not beneath the tree. When I shook the tree and jumped back from the shower of apples, he made no move. I carried some over to him. He managed to half-crunch one. The rest he let fall to the ground. I dreaded looking into his eyes—because I had of course noticed that Brown, his partner, had gone—but I did look. If I had been born into slavery, and my partner had been sold or killed, my eyes would have looked like that. The children next door explained that Blue's partner had been "put with him" (the same expression that old people used, I had noticed, when speaking of an ancestor during slavery who had been impregnated by her owner) so that they could mate and she conceive. Since that was accomplished, she had been taken back by her owner, who lived somewhere else.

Will she be back? I asked. 15

They didn't know. 16

Blue was like a crazed person. Blue *was,* to me, a crazed person. He 17
galloped furiously, as if he were being ridden, around and around his five beautiful acres. He whinnied until he couldn't. He tore at the ground with his hooves. He butted himself against his single shade tree. He looked always and always toward the road down which his partner had gone. And then, occasionally, when he came up for apples, or I took apples to him, he looked at me. It was a look so piercing, so full of grief, a look so *human,* I almost laughed (I felt too sad to cry) to think there are people who do not know that animals suffer. People like me who have forgotten, and daily forget, all that animals try to tell us. "Everything you do to us will happen to you; we are your teachers, as you are ours. We are one lesson" is essentially it, I think. There are those who never once have even considered animals' rights: those who have been taught that animals actually want to be used and abused by us, as small children "love" to be frightened, or women "love" to be mutilated and raped. . . . They are the great-grandchildren of those

who honestly thought, because someone taught them this: "Women can't think," and "niggers can't faint." But most disturbing of all, in Blue's large brown eyes was a new look, more painful than the look of despair: the look of disgust with human beings, with life; the look of hatred. And it was odd what the look of hatred did. It gave him, for the first time, the look of a beast. And what that meant was that he had put up a barrier within to protect himself from further violence; all the apples in the world wouldn't change that fact.

And so Blue remained, a beautiful part of our landscape, very peaceful to look at from the window, white against the grass. Once a friend came to visit and said, looking out on the soothing view: "And it *would* have to be a *white* horse; the very image of freedom." And I thought, yes, the animals are forced to become for us merely "images" of what they once so beautifully expressed. And we are used to drinking milk from containers showing "contented" cows, whose real lives we want to hear nothing about, eating eggs and drumsticks from "happy" hens, and munching hamburgers advertised by bulls of integrity who seem to command their fate. 18

As we talked of freedom and justice one day for all, we sat down to steaks. I am eating misery, I thought, as I took the first bite. And spit it out. 19

COMPREHENSION

1. What correlation does Walker make between the treatment of animals in our society and that of African Americans and women?
2. What point does the writer make about communication? How does the essay's opening quote help to support this?
3. What assumptions might you make about Alice Walker as a human being from what she recounts in her essay?

RHETORIC

1. What is the origin of the essay's title? What levels of meaning resonate in it, and how does it relate to Walker's thesis?
2. To what extent does Walker use personification in her essay? Find evidence of this in the writing.
3. Would you say Walker's approach to her subject is objective or subjective? What about her strategies and her language indicate that her approach is personal? Why does she begin with description before shifting to analysis and commentary in paragraph 5?
4. Consider Walker's use of similes in the essay. Cite specific examples of their use. How important are similes to the narrative?
5. Examine how language is used and how points are expressed in paragraphs 7 to 10. Why does this device work? How does dialogue function in this section? How do these different elements serve to enrich the overall essay?

6. What is the tone of Walker's conclusion? Explain the switch to the present tense in the final phrase.

WRITING

1. Write an essay expanding on the connection between the way society treats animals and the way it treats women, minorities, and the homeless. Is reverence for *some* forms of life enough?
2. Write a narrative about your own relationships with animals (as pets, on a farm, in a zoo). How do you communicate with them? How do they respond to you? How do your feelings about them translate into everyday behavior? Are humans responsible for animals?
3. Pretend to be an animal (in a home, on a farm, in a science lab, in a zoo), and write a letter to a specific group of humans or humanity at large describing your situation, your needs, any complaints you have against humankind. Be as detailed and specific as possible in your letter.

JOYCE CAROL OATES Joyce Carol Oates (1938–) is a poet, novelist, short-story writer, and essayist. She received her B.A. in 1960 from Syracuse University, where she was class valedictorian; and her M.A. in 1961 from the University of Wisconsin. Her first book, *By the North Gate* (1963), is a collection of short stories. Since then, Oates's life has been "more or less dedicated to promoting and exploring literature," both as a university professor and as the author of many works, including *Wonderland* (1971), *Do With Me What You Will* (1973), *Solstice* (1985), and *Because It Is Bitter, and It Is My Heart* (1990). In this piece, written in 1986, Oates finds discrepancies between the bucolic images presented by some nature writers and the often unpleasant realities.

JOYCE CAROL OATES

Against Nature

We soon get through with Nature. She excites an expectation which she cannot satisfy.
—Thoreau, *Journal,* 1854

Sir, if a man has experienced the inexpressible, he is under no obligation to attempt to express it.
—Samuel Johnson

The writer's resistance to Nature. 1

It has no sense of humor: In its beauty, as in its ugliness, or its neutrality, there is no laughter.

It lacks a moral purpose.

It lacks a satiric dimension, registers no irony.

Its pleasures lack resonance, being accidental; its horrors, even when premeditated, are equally perfunctory, "red in tooth and claw" et cetera.

It lacks a symbolic subtext—excepting that provided by man.

It has no (verbal) language.

It has no interest in ours.

It inspires a painfully limited set of responses in "nature-writers"—REVERENCE, AWE, PIETY, MYSTICAL ONENESS.

It eludes us even as it prepares to swallow us up, books and all.

I was lying on my back in the dirt-gravel of the towpath beside the Delaware-Raritan Canal, Titusville, New Jersey, staring up at the sky and trying, with no success, to overcome a sudden attack of tachycardia that had come upon me out of nowhere—such attacks are always "out of nowhere," that's their charm—and all around me Nature thrummed with life, the air smelling of moisture and sunlight, the canal reflecting the sky, red-winged blackbirds testing their spring calls—the usual. I'd become the jar in Tennessee, a fictitious center, or parenthesis, aware beyond my erratic heartbeat of the numberless heartbeats of the earth, its pulsing pumping life, sheer life, incalculable. Struck down in the midst of motion—I'd been jogging a minute before—I was "out of time" like a fallen, stunned boxer, privileged (in an abstract manner of speaking) to be an involuntary witness to the random, wayward, nameless motion on all sides of me. 2

Paroxysmal tachycardia is rarely fatal, but if the heartbeat accelerates to 250–270 beats a minute you're in trouble. The average attack is about 100–150 beats and mine seemed so far to be about average; the trick now was to prevent it from getting worse. Brainy people try brainy strategies, such as thinking calming thoughts, pseudo-mystic thoughts, *If I die now it's a good death,* that sort of thing, *if I die this is a good place and a good time,* the idea is to deceive the frenzied heartbeat that, really, you don't care: You hadn't any other plans for the afternoon. The important thing with tachycardia is to prevent panic! you must prevent panic! otherwise you'll have to be taken by ambulance to the closest emergency room, which is not so very nice a way to spend the afternoon, really. So I contemplated the blue sky overhead. The earth beneath my head. Nature surrounding me on all sides, I couldn't quite see it but I could hear it, smell it, sense it—there is something *there,* no mistake about it. Completely oblivious to the predicament of the individual but that's only "natural" after all, one hardly expects otherwise. 3

When you discover yourself lying on the ground, limp and unresisting, head in the dirt, and helpless, the earth seems to shift forward as a presence; hard, emphatic, not mere surface but a genuine force—there is no other word for it but *presence.* To keep in motion is to keep in time and to be stopped, stilled, is to be abruptly out of time, in another time-dimension perhaps, an alien one, where human language has no resonance. Nothing to be said about it expresses it, nothing touches it, it's 4 an absolute against which nothing human can be measured. . . . Moving through space and time by way of your own volition you inhabit an interior consciousness, a hallucinatory consciousness, it might be said, so long as breath, heartbeat, the body's autonomy hold; when motion is stopped you are jarred out of it. The interior is invaded by the exterior. The outside wants to come in, and only the self's fragile membrane prevents it.

The fly buzzing at Emily's death. 5

Still, the earth *is* your place. A tidy grave-site measured to your size. 6
Or, from another angle of vision, one vast democratic grave.

Let's contemplate the sky. Forget the crazy hammering heartbeat, 7
don't listen to it, don't start counting, remember that there is a clever way of breathing that conserves oxygen as if you're lying below the surface of a body of water breathing through a very thin straw but you *can* breathe through it if you're careful, if you don't panic, one breath and then another and then another, isn't that the story of all lives? careers? Just a matter of breathing. Of course it is. But contemplate the sky, it's there to be contemplated. A mild shock to see it so blank, blue, a thin airy ghostly blue, no clouds to disguise its emptiness. You are beginning to feel not only weightless but near-bodiless, lying on the earth like a scrap of paper about to be blown off. Two dimensions and you'd imagined you were there! And there's the sky rolling away forever, into infinity—if "infinity" can be "rolled into"—and the forlorn truth is, that's where you're going too. And the lovely blue isn't even blue, is it? isn't even there, is it? a mere optical illusion, isn't it? no matter what art has urged you to believe.

Early Nature memories. Which it's best not to suppress. 8

. . . Wading, as a small child, in Tonawanda Creek near our house, and afterward trying to tear off, in a frenzy of terror and revulsion, the sticky fat black bloodsuckers that had attached themselves to my feet, particularly between my toes.

. . . Coming upon a friend's dog in a drainage ditch, dead for several days, evidently the poor creature had been shot by a hunter and left to die, bleeding to death, and we're stupefied with grief and horror but can't resist sliding down to where he's lying on his belly, and we can't resist squatting over him, turning the body over. . . .

. . . The raccoon, mad with rabies, frothing at the mouth and tearing at his own belly with his teeth, so that his intestines spilled out onto the ground . . . a sight I seem to remember though in fact I did not see. I've been told I did not see.

Consequently, my chronic uneasiness with Nature-mysticism; Nature- 9
adoration; Nature-as-(moral)-instruction-for-mankind. My doubt that one can, with philosophical validity, address "Nature" as a single coherent noun, anything other than a Platonic, hence discredited, isness. My resistance to "Nature-writing" as a genre, except when it is brilliantly fictionalized in the service of a writer's individual vision—Thoreau's books and *Journal,* of course—but also, less known in this

country, the miniaturist prose-poems of Colette (*Flowers and Fruit*) and Ponge (*Taking the Side of Things*)—in which case it becomes yet another, and ingenious, form of storytelling. The subject is *there* only by the grace of the author's language.

Nature has no instructions for mankind except that our poor belea- 10
guered humanist-democratic way of life, our fantasies of the individual's high worth, our sense that the weak, no less than strong, have a right to survive, are absurd.

In any case, where *is* Nature? one might (skeptically) inquire. Who 11
has looked upon her/its face and survived?

But isn't this all exaggeration, in the spirit of rhetorical contentious- 12
ness? Surely Nature is, for you, as for most reasonably intelligent people, a "perennial" source of beauty, comfort, peace, escape from the delirium of civilized life; a respite from the ego's ever-frantic strategies of self-promotion, as a way of insuring (at least in fantasy) some small measure of immortality? Surely Nature, as it is understood in the usual slapdash way, as human, if not dilettante, *experience* (hiking in a national park, jogging on the beach at dawn, even tending, with the usual comical frustrations, a suburban garden), is wonderfully consoling; a place where, when you go there, it has to take you in?—a palimpsest of sorts you choose to read, layer by layer, always with care, always cautiously, in proportion to your psychological strength?

Nature: as in Thoreau's upbeat Transcendentalist mode ("The in- 13
describable innocence and beneficence of Nature,—such health, such cheer, they afford forever! and such sympathy have they ever with our race, that all Nature would be affected . . . if any man should ever for a just cause grieve"), and not in Thoreau's grim mode ("Nature is hard to be overcome but she must be overcome").

Another way of saying, not *Nature-in-itself* but *Nature-as-experience.* 14

The former, Nature-in-itself, is, to allude slantwise to Melville, a 15
blankness ten times blank; the latter is what we commonly, or perhaps always, mean when we speak of Nature as a noun, a single entity—something of ours. Most of the time it's just an activity, a sort of hobby, a weekend, a few days, perhaps a few hours, staring out of the window at the mind-dazzling autumn foliage of, say, Northern Michigan, being rendered speechless—temporarily—at the sight of Mt. Shasta, the Grand Canyon, Ansel Adams's West. Or Nature writ small, contained in the back yard. Nature filtered through our optical nerves, our "sense," our fiercely romantic expectations. Nature that pleases us because it mirrors our souls, or gives the comforting illusion of doing so. As in our first mother's awakening to the self's fatal beauty—

> I thither went
> With unexperienc't thought, and laid me down
> On the green bank, to look into the clear
> Smooth Lake, that to me seem'd another Sky.
> As I bent down to look, just opposite,

A Shape within the watr'y gleam appear'd
Bending to look on me, I started back,
It started back, but pleas'd I soon return'd,
Pleas'd it return'd as soon with answering looks
Of sympathy and love; there I had fixt
Mine eyes till now, and pin'd with vain desire.

—in these surpassingly beautiful lines from Book IV of Milton's *Paradise Lost.*

Nature as the self's (flattering) mirror, but not ever, no never, Nature-in-itself. 16

Nature is mouths, or maybe a single mouth. Why glamorize it, romanticize it, well yes but we must, we're writers, poets, mystics (of a sort) aren't we, precisely what else are we to do but glamorize and romanticize and generally exaggerate the significance of anything we focus the white heat of our "creativity" upon . . . ? And why not Nature, since it's there, common property, mute, can't talk back, allows us the possibility of transcending the human condition for a while, writing prettily of mountain ranges, white-tailed deer, the purple crocuses outside this very window, the thrumming dazzling "life-force" we imagine we all support. Why not. 17

Nature *is* more than a mouth—it's a dazzling variety of mouths. And it pleases the senses, in any case, as the physicists' chill universe of numbers certainly does not. 18

Oscar Wilde, on our subject: 19

> Nature is no great mother who has borne us. She is our creation. It is in our brain that she quickens to life. Things are because we see them, and what we see, and how we see it, depends on the Arts that have influenced us. To look at a thing is very different from seeing a thing. . . . At present, people see fogs, not because there are fogs, but because poets and painters have taught them the mysterious loveliness of such effects. There may have been fogs for centuries in London. I dare say there were. But no one saw them. They did not exist until Art had invented them. . . . Yesterday evening Mrs. Arundel insisted on my going to the window and looking at the glorious sky, as she called it. And so I had to look at it. . . . And what was it? It was simply a very second-rate Turner, a Turner of a bad period, with all the painter's worst faults exaggerated and over-emphasized.

(If we were to put it to Oscar Wilde that he exaggerates, his reply might well be: "Exaggeration? I don't know the meaning of the word.") 20

Walden, that most artfully composed of prose fictions, concludes, in the rhapsodic chapter "Spring," with Henry David Thoreau's contemplation of death, decay, and regeneration as it is suggested to him, or to his protagonist, by the spectacle of vultures feeding off carrion. There is a 21

dead horse close by his cabin and the stench of its decomposition, in certain winds, is daunting. Yet:

> . . . the assurance it gave me of the strong appetite and inviolable health of Nature was my compensation. I love to see that Nature is so rife with life that myriads can be afforded to be sacrificed and suffered to prey upon one another; that tender organizations can be so serenely squashed out of existence like pulp,—tadpoles which herons gobble up, and tortoises and toads run over in the road; and that sometimes it has rained flesh and blood! . . . The impression made on a wise man is that of universal innocence.

Come off it, Henry David. You've grieved these many years for 22
your elder brother John, who dies a ghastly death of lockjaw, you've never wholly recovered from the experience of watching him die. And you know, or must know, that you're fated too to die young of consumption. . . . But this doctrinaire Transcendentalist passage ends *Walden* on just the right note. It's as impersonal, as coolly detached, as the Oversoul itself: A "wise man" filters his emotions through his brain.

Or through his prose. 23

Nietzsche: "We all pretend to ourselves that we are more simple-mind- 24
ed than we are: That is how we get a rest from our fellow men."

> Once out of nature I shall never take 25
> My bodily form from any natural thing,
> But such a form as Grecian goldsmiths make
> Of hammered gold and gold enamelling
> To keep a drowsy Emperor awake;
> Or set upon a golden bough to sing
> To lords and ladies of Byzantium
> Of what is past, or passing, or to come.
> —William Butler Yeats, "Sailing to Byzantium"

Yet even the golden bird is a "bodily form taken from [a] natural thing." No, it's impossible to escape!

The writer's resistance to Nature. 26

Wallace Stevens: "In the presence of extraordinary actuality, con- 27
sciousness takes the place of imagination."

Once, years ago, in 1972 to be precise, when I seemed to have been an- 28
other person, related to the person I am now as one is related, tangentially, sometimes embarrassingly, to cousins not seen for decades,—once, when we were living in London, and I was very sick, I had a mystical vision. That is, I "had" a "mystical vision"—the heart sinks: such pretension—or something resembling one. A fever-dream, let's call it. It impressed me enormously and impresses me still, though I've long since lost the capacity to see it with my mind's eye, or even, I sup-

pose, to believe in it. There is a statute of limitations on "mystical visions" as on romantic love.

I was very sick, and I imagined my life as a thread, a thread of breath, or heartbeat, or pulse, or light, yes it was light, radiant light, I was burning with fever and I ascended to that plane of serenity that might be mistaken for (or *is,* in fact) Nirvana, where I had a waking dream of uncanny lucidity—

My body is a tall column of light and heat.

My body is not "I" but "it."

My body is not one but many.

My body, which "I" inhabit, is inhabited as well by other creatures, 30
unknown to me, imperceptible—the smallest of them mere sparks of light.

My body, which I perceive as substance, is in fact an organization of 31
infinitely complex, overlapping, imbricated structures, radiant light their manifestation, the "body" a tall column of light and blood-heat, a temporary agreement among atoms, like a high-rise building with numberless rooms, corridors, corners, elevator shafts, windows. . . . In this fantastical structure the "I" is deluded as to its sovereignty, let alone its autonomy in the (outside) world; the most astonishing secret is that the "I" doesn't exist!—but it behaves as if it does, as if it were one and not many.

In any case, without the "I" the tall column of light and heat would 32
die, and the microscopic life-particles would die with it . . . will die with it. The "I," which doesn't exist, is everything.

But Dr. Johnson is right, the inexpressible need not be expressed. 33
And what resistance, finally? There is none.

This morning, an invasion of tiny black ants. One by one they appear, 34
out of nowhere—that's their charm too!—moving single file across the white Parsons table where I am sitting, trying without much success to write a poem. A poem of only three or four lines is what I want, something short, tight, mean. I want it to hurt like a white-hot wire up the nostrils, small and compact and turned in upon itself with the density of a hunk of rock from the planet Jupiter. . . .

But here come the black ants: harbingers, you might say, of spring. 35
One by one they appear on the dazzling white table and one by one I kill them with a forefinger, my deft right forefinger, mashing each against the surface of the table and then dropping it into a wastebasket at my side. Idle labor, mesmerizing, effortless, and I'm curious as to how long I can do it, sit here in the brilliant March sunshine killing ants with my right forefinger, how long I, and the ants, can keep it up.

After a while I realize that I can do it a long time. And that I've writ- 36
ten my poem.

COMPREHENSION

1. What event precipitates the writer's contemplation of nature?
2. According to Oates, what is the artist's relationship to nature? Why does she object to nature writers?
3. What associations or memories does Oates have while lying on the grass? How may they have influenced her opinion of nature?

RHETORIC

1. What is the purpose of the introductory section? How does it aid in setting up Oates's argument? Why does she capitalize the words *reverence, awe, pity,* and *mystical oneness*?
2. How does the narrative part of the essay contribute to the development of Oates's argument? Could the essay have succeeded without it? Why, or why not?
3. To what end does Oates use quotes from other writers? What does she assume about her readers? Do the quotes help to illustrate her points?
4. What is the significance of paragraph 5? To what does it refer, and how does its use help advance the ideas of the writer?
5. Closely examine the language and punctuation used in paragraph 7. How do these elements strengthen the argument?
6. Why does Oates refute her own observations in paragraph 12? What is her aim? Does this help or hurt her argument?

WRITING

1. Write an essay about your own response to nature. What formed this relationship? When was the last time you felt close to nature? How does nature affect your everyday life and actions?
2. In a brief essay, define Oates's concept of "Nature-in-itself" versus "Nature-as-experience." Use your own observations and examples.
3. Write a definition essay on *nature* that explores the connotations and denotations of the word.

JOHN STEINBECK John Steinbeck (1902–1968) was born in California, the setting for some of his best fiction. Steinbeck's fiction of the 1930s, including *The Pastures of Heaven* (1932), *Tortilla Flat* (1935), *In Dubious Battle* (1936), *Of Mice and Men* (1937), and the Pulitzer Prize-winning epic *The Grapes of Wrath* (1939), offers one of the best imaginative presentations of the American Depression. Steinbeck won the Nobel Prize in Literature in 1962 for "realistic and imaginative writings, distinguished as they are by a sympathetic humor and a social perception." In this section from *America and Americans* (1966), Steinbeck offers a probing, critical appraisal of American social development.

JOHN STEINBECK

Americans and the Land

I have often wondered at the savagery and thoughtlessness with which our early settlers approached this rich continent. They came at it as though it were an enemy, which of course it was. They burned the forests and changed the rainfall; they swept the buffalo from the plains, blasted the streams, set fire to the grass, and ran a reckless scythe through the virgin and noble timber. Perhaps they felt that it was limitless and could never be exhausted and that a man could move on to new wonders endlessly. Certainly there are many examples to the contrary, but to a large extent the early people pillaged the country as though they hated it, as though they held it temporarily and might be driven off at any time. 1

This tendency toward irresponsibility persists in very many of us today; our rivers are poisoned by reckless dumping of sewage and toxic industrial wastes, the air of our cities is filthy and dangerous to breathe from the belching of uncontrolled products from combustion of coal, coke, oil, and gasoline. Our towns are girdled with wreckage and the debris of our toys—our automobiles and our packaged pleasures. Through uninhibited spraying against one enemy we have destroyed the natural balances our survival requires. All these evils can and must be overcome if America and Americans are to survive; but many of us still conduct ourselves as our ancestors did, stealing from the future for our clear and present profit. 2

Since the river-polluters and the air-poisoners are not criminal or even bad people, we must presume that they are heirs to the early conviction that sky and water are unowned and that they are limitless. In the light of our practices here at home it is very interesting to me to read of the care taken with the carriers of our probes into space to make utterly sure that they are free of pollution of any kind. We would not think of doing to the moon what we do every day to our own dear country. 3

When the first settlers came to America and dug in on the coast, they huddled in defending villages hemmed in by the sea on one side and by endless forests on the other, by Red Indians and, most frightening, the mystery of an unknown land extending nobody knew how far. And for a time very few cared or dared to find out. Our first Americans organized themselves and lived in a state of military alertness; every community built its blockhouse for defense. By law the men went armed and were required to keep their weapons ready and available. Many of them wore armor, made here or imported; on the East Coast, they wore the cuirass and helmet, and the Spaniards on the West Coast wore both steel armor and heavy leather to turn arrows. 4

On the East Coast, and particularly in New England, the colonists 5
farmed meager lands close to their communities and to safety. Every man was permanently on duty for the defense of his family and his village; even the hunting parties went into the forest in force, rather like raiders than hunters, and their subsequent quarrels with the Indians, resulting in forays and even massacres, remind us that the danger was very real. A man took his gun along when he worked the land, and the women stayed close to their thick-walled houses and listened day and night for the signal of alarm. The towns they settled were permanent, and most of them exist today with their records of Indian raids, of slaughter, of scalpings, and of punitive counter-raids. The military leader of the community became the chief authority in time of trouble, and it was a long time before danger receded and the mystery could be explored.

After a time, however, brave and forest-wise men drifted westward 6
to hunt, to trap, and eventually to bargain for the furs which were the first precious negotiable wealth America produced for trade and export. Then trading posts were set up as centers of collection and the exploring men moved up and down the rivers and crossed the mountains, made friends for mutual profit with the Indians, learned the wilderness techniques, so that these explorer-traders soon dressed, ate, and generally acted like the indigenous people around them. Suspicion lasted a long time, and was fed by clashes sometimes amounting to full-fledged warfare; but by now these Americans attacked and defended as the Indians did.

For a goodly time the Americans were travelers, moving about the 7
country collecting its valuables, but with little idea of permanence; their roots and their hearts were in the towns and the growing cities along the eastern edge. The few who stayed, who lived among the Indians, adopted their customs and some took Indian wives and were regarded as strange and somehow treasonable creatures. As for their half-breed children, while the tribe sometimes adopted them they were unacceptable as equals in the eastern settlements.

Then the trickle of immigrants became a stream, and the popula- 8
tion began to move westward—not to grab and leave but to settle and live, they thought. The newcomers were of peasant stock, and they had their roots in a Europe where they had been landless, for the possession of land was the requirement and the proof of a higher social class than they had known. In America they found beautiful and boundless land for the taking—and they took it.

It is little wonder that they went land-mad, because there was so much 9
of it. They cut and burned the forests to make room for crops; they abandoned their knowledge of kindness to the land in order to maintain its usefulness. When they had cropped out a piece they moved on, raping the country like invaders. The topsoil, held by roots and freshened by leaf-fall, was left helpless to the spring freshets, stripped and eroded with the naked bones of clay and rock exposed. The destruction of the forests changed the rainfall, for the searching clouds could find no green and beckoning woods to draw them on and milk them. The merciless nine-

teenth century was like a hostile expedition for loot that seemed limitless. Uncountable buffalo were killed, stripped of their hides, and left to rot, a reservoir of permanent food supply eliminated. More than that, the land of the Great Plains was robbed of the manure of the herds. Then the plows went in and ripped off the protection of the buffalo grass and opened the helpless soil to quick water and slow drought and the mischievous winds that roamed through the Great Central Plains. There has always been more than enough desert in America; the new settlers, like overindulged children, created even more.

The railroads brought new hordes of land-crazy people, and the 10
new Americans moved like locusts across the continent until the western sea put a boundary to their movements. Coal and copper and gold drew them on; they savaged the land, gold-dredged the rivers to skeletons of pebbles and debris. An aroused and fearful government made laws for the distribution of public lands—a quarter section, one hundred and sixty acres, per person—and a claim had to be proved and improved; but there were ways of getting around this, and legally. My own grandfather proved out a quarter section for himself, one for his wife, one for each of his children, and, I suspect, acreage for children he hoped and expected to have. Marginal lands, of course, suitable only for grazing, went in larger pieces. One of the largest land-holding families in California took its richest holdings by a trick: By law a man could take up all the swamp or water-covered land he wanted. The founder of this great holding mounted a scow on wheels and drove his horses over thousands of acres of the best bottom land, then reported that he had explored it in a boat, which was true, and confirmed his title. I need not mention his name; his descendants will remember.

Another joker with a name still remembered in the West worked out 11
a scheme copied many times in after years. Proving a quarter section required a year of residence and some kind of improvement—a fence, a shack—but once the land was proved the owner was free to sell it. This particular princely character went to the stews and skid rows of the towns and found a small army of hopeless alcoholics who lived for whiskey and nothing else. He put these men on land he wanted to own, grubstaked them and kept them in cheap liquor until the acreage was proved, then went through the motions of buying it from his protégés and moved them and their one-room shacks on sled runners to new quarter sections. Bums of strong constitution might prove out five or six homesteads for this acquisitive hero before they died of drunkenness.

It was full late when we began to realize that the continent did not 12
stretch out to infinity; that there were limits to the indignities to which we could subject it. Engines and heavy mechanical equipment were allowing us to ravage it even more effectively than we had with fire, dynamite, and gang plows. Conservation came to us slowly, and much of it hasn't arrived yet. Having killed the whales and wiped out the sea otters and most of the beavers, the market hunters went to work on game birds; ducks and quail were decimated, and the passenger pigeon elimi-

nated. In my youth I remember seeing a market hunter's gun, a three-gauge shotgun bolted to a frame and loaded to the muzzle with shingle nails. Aimed at a lake and the trigger pulled with a string, it slaughtered every living thing on the lake. The Pacific Coast pilchards were once the raw material for a great and continuing industry. We hunted them with aircraft far at sea until they were gone and the canneries had to be closed. In some of the valleys of the West, where the climate makes several crops a year available, which the water supply will not justify, wells were driven deeper and deeper for irrigation, so that in one great valley a million acre feet more of water was taken out than rain and melting snow could replace, and the water table went down and a few more years may give us a new desert.

The great redwood forests of the western mountains early attracted attention. These ancient trees, which once grew everywhere, now exist only where the last Ice Age did not wipe them out. And they were found to have value. The Sempervirens and the Gigantea, the two remaining species, make soft, straight-grained timber. They are easy to split into planks, shakes, fenceposts, and railroad ties, and they have a unique virtue: they resist decay, both wet and dry rot, and an inherent acid in them repels termites. The loggers went through the great groves like a barrage, toppling the trees—some of which were two thousand years old—and leaving no maidens, no seedlings or saplings on the denuded hills. 13

Quite a few years ago when I was living in my little town on the coast of California a stranger came in and bought a small valley where the Sempervirens redwoods grew, some of them three hundred feet high. We used to walk among these trees, and the light colored as though the great glass of the Cathedral at Chartres had strained and sanctified the sunlight. The emotion we felt in this grove was one of awe and humility and joy; and then one day it was gone, slaughtered, and the sad wreckage of boughs and broken saplings left like nonsensical spoilage of the battle-ruined countryside. And I remember that after our rage there was sadness, and when we passed the man who had done this we looked away, because we were ashamed for him. 14

From early times we were impressed and awed by the fantastic accidents of nature, like the Grand Canyon and Yosemite and Yellowstone Park. The Indians had revered them as holy places, visited by the gods, and all of us came to have somewhat the same feeling about them. Thus we set aside many areas of astonishment as publicly owned parks; and though this may to a certain extent have been because there was no other way to use them as the feeling of preciousness of the things we had been destroying grew in Americans, more and more areas were set aside as national and state parks, to be looked at but not injured. Many people loved and were in awe of the redwoods; societies and individuals bought groves of these wonderful trees and presented them to the state for preservation. 15

No longer do we Americans want to destroy wantonly, but our new-found sources of power—to take the burden of work from our shoul- 16 ders, to warm us, and cool us, and give us light, to transport us quickly, and to make the things we use and wear and eat—these power sources spew pollution on our country, so that the rivers and streams are becoming poisonous and lifeless. The birds die for the lack of food; a noxious cloud hangs over our cities that burns our lungs and reddens our eyes. Our ability to conserve has not grown with our power to create, but this slow and sullen poisoning is no longer ignored or justified. Almost daily, the pressure of outrage among Americans grows. We are no longer content to destroy our beloved country. We are slow to learn; but we learn. When a superhighway was proposed in California which would trample the redwood trees in its path, an outcry arose all over the land, so strident and fierce that the plan was put aside. And we no longer believe that a man, by owning a piece of America, is free to outrage it.

But we are an exuberant people, careless and destructive as active children. We make strong and potent tools and then have to use them to prove that they exist. Under the pressure of war we finally made the atom bomb, and for reasons which seemed justifiable at the time we dropped it on two Japanese cities—and I think we finally frightened ourselves. In such things, one must consult himself because there is no other point of reference. I did not know about the bomb, and certainly I had nothing to do with its use, but I am horrified and ashamed; and nearly everyone I know feels the same thing. And those who loudly and angrily justify Hiroshima and Nagasaki—why, they must be the most ashamed of all. 17

COMPREHENSION

1. What is Steinbeck's purpose in writing this essay? State his thesis in your own words.
2. According to Steinbeck, how did the American attitude toward the land evolve?
3. Does Steinbeck think that the American attitude toward the land can be changed? Cite evidence from the essay to support your answer.

RHETORIC

1. Analyze Steinbeck's use of figurative language in paragraphs 1, 2, 9, and 14.
2. Locate images and vocabulary relating to "rape" and destruction in the essay. What is the relevance of this motif to the development of Steinbeck's thesis?
3. How does Steinbeck use examples in paragraphs 1 and 2 to establish the subject and thesis of his essay?
4. Analyze the relationship between the patterns of description and example in the essay. What types of illustration does Steinbeck employ? How does

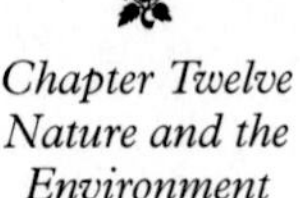

he achieve concreteness through examples? Where does he employ extended example? Does he use examples subjectively or objectively? Explain.

5. How does Steinbeck employ process analysis to highlight his thesis?
6. Explain the relationship between paragraph 16 and paragraph 17 in the essay.

WRITING

1. Analyze the way in which description and figurative language advance Steinbeck's thesis.
2. Write an essay entitled "Americans and the Land," using examples to support your thesis.
3. Write an essay on the relationship between ecology and the state of civilization.

CLASSIC AND CONTEMPORY

HENRY DAVID THOREAU Henry David Thoreau (1817–1862), author of the masterpiece *Walden* (1854), is one of the most important figures in American thought and literature. A social and political activist, he opposed the Mexican War, protested slavery, and refused to pay his poll taxes. As a naturalist, he believed in the preeminence of individualism and nature over technology, materialism, and nationalism. In 1845, Thoreau went to live at Walden Pond, "living deep and sucking out all the marrow of life." *Walden*, describing his life at the pond, is one of the most challenging, exuberant, and innovative works of American literature. This account from Thoreau's masterpiece, tracing the construction of his dwelling, reflects his preoccupation with economy, natural process, and self-reliance.

HENRY DAVID THOREAU

Economy

Near the end of March, 1845, I borrowed an axe and went down to the 1
woods by Walden Pond, nearest to where I intended to build my house, and began to cut down some tall arrowy white pines, still in their youth, for timber. It is difficult to begin without borrowing, but perhaps it is the most generous course thus to permit your fellow-men to have an interest in your enterprise. The owner of the axe, as he released his hold on it, said that it was the apple of his eye; but I returned it sharper than I received it. It was a pleasant hillside where I worked, covered with pine woods, through which I looked out on the pond, and a small open field in the woods where pines and hickories were springing up. The ice in the pond was not yet dissolved, though there were some open spaces, and it was all dark colored and saturated with water. There were some slight flurries of snow during the days that I worked there; but for the most part when I came out onto the railroad, on my way home, its yellow sand heap stretched away gleaming in the hazy atmosphere, and the rails shone in the spring sun, and I heard the lark and pewee and other birds already come to commence another year with us. They were pleasant spring days, in which the winter of man's discontent was thawing as well as the earth, and the life that had lain torpid began to stretch itself. One day, when my axe had come off and I had cut a green hickory for a wedge, driving it with a stone, and had placed the whole to soak in a pond hole in order to swell the wood, I saw a striped snake run into the water, and he lay on the bottom, apparently without inconvenience, as long as I stayed there, or more than a quarter of an hour; perhaps be-

cause he had not yet fairly come out of the torpid state. It appeared to me that for a like reason men remain in their present low and primitive condition; but if they should feel the influence of the spring of springs arousing them, they would of necessity rise to a higher and more ethereal life. I had previously seen the snakes in frosty mornings in my path with portions of their bodies still numb and inflexible, waiting for the sun to thaw them. On the 1st of April it rained and melted the ice, and in the early part of the day, which was very foggy, I heard a stray goose groping about over the pond and cackling as if lost, or like the spirit of the fog.

So I went on for some days cutting and hewing timber, and also 2
studs and rafters, all with my narrow axe, not having many communicable or scholar-like thoughts, singing to myself.

> Men say they know many things;
> But lo! they have taken wings—
> The arts and sciences,
> And a thousand appliances;
> The wind that blows
> Is all that anybody knows.

I hewed the main timber six inches square, most of the studs on two sides only, and the rafters and floor timbers on one side, leaving the rest of the bark on, so that they were just as straight and much stronger than sawed ones. Each stick was carefully mortised or tenoned by its stump, for I had borrowed other tools by this time. My days in the woods were not very long ones; yet I usually carried my dinner of bread and butter, and read the newspaper in which it was wrapped, at noon, sitting amid the green pine boughs which I had cut off, and to my bread was imparted some of their fragrance, for my hands were covered with a thick coat of pitch. Before I had done I was more the friend than the foe of the pine tree, though I had cut down some of them, having become better acquainted with it. Sometimes a rambler in the wood was attracted by the sound of my axe, and we chatted pleasantly over the chips which I had made.

By the middle of April, for I made no haste in my work, but rather 3
made the most of it, my house was framed and ready for the raising. I had already bought the shanty of James Collins, an Irishman who worked on the Fitchburg Railroad, for boards. James Collins' shanty was considered an uncommonly fine one. When I called to see it he was not at home. I walked about the outside, at first unobserved from within, the window was so deep and high. It was of small dimensions, with a peaked cottage roof, and not much else to be seen, the dirt being raised five feet all around as if it were a compost heap. The roof was the soundest part, though a good deal warped and made brittle by the sun. Doorsill there was none, but a perennial passage for the hens under the door board. Mrs. C. came to the door and asked me to view it from the inside. The hens were driven in by my approach. It was dark, and had a dirt floor for the most part, dank, clammy, and aguish, only here

a board and there a board which would not bear removal. She lighted a lamp to show me the inside of the roof and the walls, and also that the board floor extended under the bed, warning me not to step into the cellar, a sort of dust hole two feet deep. In her own words, they were "good boards overhead, good boards all around, and a good window"—of two whole squares originally, only the cat had passed out that way lately. There was a stove, a bed, and a place to sit, an infant in the house where it was born, a silk parasol, gilt-framed looking-glass, and a patent new coffee-mill nailed to an oak sapling, all told. The bargain was soon concluded, for James had in the meanwhile returned. I to pay four dollars and twenty-five cents tonight, he to vacate at five tomorrow morning, selling to nobody else meanwhile: I to take possession at six. It were well, he said, to be there early, and anticipate certain indistinct but wholly unjust claims on the score of ground rent and fuel. This he assured me was the only encumbrance. At six I passed him and his family on the road. One large bundle held their all—bed, coffee-mill, looking-glass, hens—all but the cat; she took to the woods and became a wild cat and, as I learned afterward, trod in a trap set for woodchucks, and so became a dead cat at last.

I took down this dwelling the same morning, drawing the nails, and 4
removed it to the pond side by small cartloads, spreading the boards on the grass there to bleach and warp back again in the sun. One early thrush gave me a note or two as I drove along the woodland path. I was informed treacherously by a young Patrick that neighbor Seeley, an Irishman, in the intervals of the carting, transferred the still tolerable, straight, and drivable nails, staples, and spikes to his pocket, and then stood when I came back to pass the time of day, and look freshly up, unconcerned, with spring thoughts, at the devastation; there being a dearth of work, as he said. He was there to represent spectatordom, and help make this seemingly insignificant event one with the removal of the gods of Troy.

I dug my cellar in the side of a hill sloping to the south, where a 5
woodchuck had formerly dug his burrow, down through sumach and blackberry roots, and the lowest stain of vegetation, six feet square by seven deep, to a fine sand where potatoes would not freeze in any winter. The sides were left shelving, and not stoned; but the sun having never shone on them, the sand still keeps its place. It was but two hours' work. I took particular pleasure in this breaking of ground, for in almost all latitudes men dig into the earth for an equable temperature. Under the most splendid house in the city is still to be found the cellar where they store their roots as of old, and long after the superstructure had disappeared posterity remark its dent in the earth. The house is still but a sort of porch at the entrance of a burrow.

At length, in the beginning of May, with the help of some of my 6
acquaintances, rather to improve so good an occasion for neighborliness than from any necessity, I set up the frame of my house. No man was ever more honored in the character of his raisers than I. They are destined, I trust, to assist at the raising of loftier structures one day. I

began to occupy my house on the 4th of July, as soon as it was boarded and roofed, for the boards were carefully feather-edged and lapped, so that it was perfectly impervious to rain, but before boarding I laid the foundation of a chimney at one end, bringing two cartloads of stones up the hill from the pond in my arms. I built the chimney after my hoeing in the fall, before a fire became necessary for warmth, doing my cooking in the meanwhile out of doors on the ground, early in the morning: which mode I still think is in some respects more convenient and agreeable than the usual one. When it stormed before my bread was baked, I fixed a few boards over the fire, and sat under them to watch my loaf, and passed some pleasant hours in that way. In those days, when my hands were much employed, I read but little, but the least scraps of paper which lay on the ground, my holder, or tablecloth, afforded me as much entertainment, in fact answered the same purpose as the Iliad.

COMPREHENSION

1. Explain the process by which Thoreau builds his house. What are the main steps in this process?
2. What is Thoreau's attitude toward economy in this selection? Which of the details Thoreau has included most successfully reveal this attitude?
3. Compare Thoreau's evocation of place in this essay with Ehrlich's presentation of place in "Wyoming: The Solace of Open Spaces." Are the two authors addressing readers in the same way? Justify your response.

RHETORIC

1. In paragraph 1, what connotation does the author develop for the word *borrowing?* How do words related to economics serve as a motif in the essay?
2. What is the analogy in paragraph 1?
3. How does Thoreau use process analysis? Why is this rhetorical technique reinforced by the natural processes depicted in the essay?
4. How does Thoreau particularize the generalizations he makes in the essay?
5. What is the tone of the essay? Does an implied thesis for the essay emerge? Justify your answer.
6. What is the relationship of the last two sentences in paragraph 6 to the rest of the selection?

WRITING

1. Analyze Thoreau's poem in paragraph 2. Identify the poem's theme. Then write a brief essay explaining its relevance to "Economy."
2. Using Thoreau's method, write an essay in which you trace the process of building or creating something that was important to you.
3. Write a letter to the editor of your college newspaper arguing the need to economize in some aspect of personal or public life. Refer to Thoreau in this letter.

SUE HUBBELL Sue Hubbell (1935–) once managed a bookstore in New York. She has also worked as a librarian and as a commercial beekeeper, an occupation from which she still makes a living. Hubbell was born in Michigan, attended Swarthmore College and the University of Michigan, and earned her M.S. from Drexel University in 1963. In 1986 she published *A Country Year: Living the Questions,* in which she reflects on her experiences with nature in the Ozarks, where she lives. In a selection from that work, Hubbell recounts her struggle to live self-sufficiently in nature without alienating her neighbors.

SUE HUBBELL

Felling Trees

I was out in the woods early in the morning cutting firewood for the winter. I do that every day this time of year. For an hour or two I cut wood, load it into the pickup and carry it back to my cabin and stack it. It isn't such a tiring job when I do a bit of it each day, before it gets hot, and I like being out there at that hour, when the woods are fresh and fragrant. 1

This morning I finished sawing up a tree from the place where I had been cutting for the past week. In the process I lost my screwrench, part screwdriver, part wrench, that I use to make adjustments on my chain saw. I shouldn't carry it in my pocket, but the chain had been loose; I had tightened it and had not walked back to the truck to put the wrench away. Scolding myself for being so careless, I began looking for another tree to cut and found a big one that had recently died. 2

I like to cut the dead trees from my woodlot, leaving the ones still alive to flourish, but this one was bigger than I feel comfortable about felling. I've been running a chain saw and cutting my own firewood for six years now, but I am still awed by the size and weight of a tree as it crashes to the ground. I have to nerve myself to cut the really big ones. I wanted this tree to fall onto a stretch of open ground that was free of other trees and brush, so I cut a wedge-shaped notch on that side of it. The theory is that the tree, thus weakened, will fall slowly on the side of the notch when the serious cut, slightly above the notch on the other side, is made. The trouble is that trees, particularly dead ones that may have rot on the inside, do not know the theory and may fall in an unexpected direction. That is the way accidents happen. 3

I was aware of that and was scared, besides, to be cutting down such a big tree; as a result, perhaps, I cut too timid a wedge. I started sawing through on the other side, keeping an eye on the treetop to detect the characteristic tremble of a tree about to fall. I did not have time to jam the plastic wedge in my back pocket into the cut to hold it open because the tree began to sway and started to fall in my direction. I killed the engine on the saw and jumped out of the way. 4

There was no danger, however. Directly in back of where I had been standing were a number of other trees, which was why I had 5

wanted to have the dead one fall the other way, and as it started down, its top branches snagged. I had sawed completely through the tree, but now the butt end had trapped the saw against the stump. I had cut what is descriptively called a widow maker. If I had been cutting with someone else, we could have used the second saw to free mine and perhaps brought the tree down, but it is dangerous and I don't like to do it. I couldn't even free my saw by taking it apart, for I had lost my screwrench, so I drove back to the barn, gathered up the tools I needed, a socket wrench, chains and a portable winch known as a come-along.

The day was warming and I was sweating by the time I got back to the woods, but I was determined to repair the botch I had made. Using the socket wrench, I removed the bar and chain from the saw and set the saw body aside. The weight of the saw gone, I worked the bar and chain free from under the butt of the tree. Then I spat and drank ice water from my thermos and figured out how I was going to pull down the tree with chain and winch. 6

The come-along is a cheery, sensible tool for a woman. It has a big hook at one end and a hook connected to a steel cable at the other. The cable is wound around a ratchet gear operated by a long handle to give leverage. It divides a heavy job into small, manageable bits that require no more than female strength, and I have used it many times to pull my pickup free from a mudhole. I decided that if I wound a chain around the butt of the widow maker and another chain around a nearby standing tree and connected the two with the come-along, I might be able to winch the felled tree to the ground. I attached the chains and come-along appropriately and began. Slowly, with each pump of the handle against the ratchet gear, the tree sank to the ground. The sun was high, the heat oppressive, and my sweatshirt was soaked with sweat, so I decided to leave the job of cutting up the tree to firewood lengths until tomorrow. I gathered up my tools and, in the process, found the screwrench almost hidden in leaf mold. 7

I am good friends with a woman who lives across the hollow. She and her husband sell cordwood to the charcoal factory in town. Her husband cuts the logs because a chain saw, in the Ozarks, is regarded as a man's tool, and she helps him load and unload the logs. Even though the wood is going to be turned into charcoal, it is traditional to cut it to four-foot lengths. A four-foot oak log is heavy; a strong man can lift it, but a woman has to use all her strength to do her part. My friend returns from her mornings sick with exhaustion, her head throbbing. She and I talk sometimes about how it would be if women were the woodcutters: the length would be less than four feet. Having to do work beyond her strength makes my friend feel weak, ineffectual, dependent and cross. 8

My friend, and other Ozark women, often ask me curiously about my chain saw. Most people out here heat with wood, and if families in the suburbs quarrel about taking out the garbage, here the source of squabbles is getting enough firewood cut early in the year so that it can season. Women usually help by carrying the cut wood to the truck, but 9 it is the men who cut the wood, and since the women think they cannot cut it, they frequently worry and sometimes nag about it.

My female Ozark friends envy me having my firewood supply under my own control, and they are interested when I tell them that they have had the hardest part of the job anyway, carrying the wood to the trucks. Cutting the wood into lengths with the chain saw is not hard work, although it does require some skill. So far, however, my friends have not taken up my offer to come over so that I can give them a lesson in using a chain saw. Forty years ago chain saws were heavy and certainly beyond the strength of a woman to use; today they are much improved and light. My saw is a small, light one, but with its 16-inch bar it is big enough to cut any tree I want to fell.

I know that feeling of helplessness and irritation that my friends have, 11
for that is the way I used to be. Like many women my age, I would stand back and let a man change a flat tire. I could press a button on a washing machine but not fix the machine if something failed. I felt uneasy with tools other than a needle, a typewriter or kitchen utensils.

When I began living here alone I had to learn how to break down 12
work into parcels that I could perform with my strength and I had to learn to use tools that I had never used and use them easily. Either that, or I would have had to leave. It was the hardest schooling I've ever taken but the most exhilarating. When there were Things in the world too heavy to move where I wanted them to be and too mysterious to be kept doing what I wanted them to do, I was filled with dissatisfaction and petulance. Those Things controlled me.

I prefer it the other way around. 13

COMPREHENSION

1. What does felling trees represent to the writer?
2. What points does Hubbell make about outdoor life? What is of particular concern to her Ozark community?
3. What do we learn about the division of labor between men and women in the essay? Does it seem to be traditional or modern in nature? How does Hubbell relate to the other women in the community?

RHETORIC

1. What is the main idea of the essay? At what point does it become clear? What does she accomplish in the sections that precede her thesis? Is this an effective technique? Why, or why not?
2. Does Hubbell employ abstract or concrete language in her piece? Why is this a good choice for her subject and audience?
3. How does the writer's language help set up a mood and evoke a sense of place? Cite specific words or phrases that are especially powerful
4. What is the tone of the essay? What in the writer's style indicates this?
5. How does the author use process analysis in her essay? How does it work with the narration to strengthen her point?

6. Why does Hubbell end her essay as she does? What point is she making with her final sentence? Is this indicative of her attitude? How does the conclusion reinforce the rest of the piece?

WRITING

1. Write a process analysis essay describing, in detail, a difficult task you have accomplished. Consider why the task was so hard, why it had to be done, and how you felt after it was finished.
2. Consider "women's work" in a rural community. Does the nature of the work itself dictate the division of labor, or are there other factors to consider? How does city life affect the nature of working women? Consider these questions in an essay, using your own observations or research.
3. How does city living blunt people's perceptions of and responses to nature? Use Hubbell's and Walker's essays to answer this question.

CLASSIC AND CONTEMPORARY: QUESTIONS FOR COMPARISON

1. Compare and contrast Thoreau's and Hubbell's essays, considering these factors: the work they're undertaking, their relationship to others in the community, the way they choose to tell their stories. What conclusions can we form about the writers' lives and priorities based on the information and ideas expressed in their essays?
2. Define what Thoreau meant by *economy,* and explain its relevance to Hubbell's lifestyle and opinions. How do you think Hubbell might respond to Thoreau's ideas and circumstances?
3. Compare the language used by the writers. Is there anything about Thoreau's syntax that dates his essay? How modern does Hubbell's language appear in comparison? How do they evoke a sense of place through their writing? How is humor used or not used in both essays? How do the writers reveal their attitudes toward nature by their words?

CONNECTIONS

1. Using support from the works of Steinbeck, Carson, and others, write a causal-analysis essay tracing our relationship to the land. To what extent has history, greed, and fear helped to shape our attitude? Can this attitude be changed? How?
2. Compare the essays of Thoreau and Oates. Considering her objections to nature writers, how would Oates respond to his work? How would she critique his tone, content, and language? What about his essay might she applaud? Use the works of both writers to support your view.
3. Write a letter to the Op-Ed page of a newspaper objecting to a governmental ruling harmful to the environment. State the nature of the policy, its possible dangers, and your reasons for opposing it. Use support from any of the writers in this section. Extra reading or research may be necessary.
4. Consider why we fear nature. Why do we consider it an enemy, alien, something to be controlled or destroyed? How would Steinbeck, Oates, and Walker respond to this question? Do you agree or disagree with them?
5. Both Steinbeck and Ehrlich use historical data and description to explore our relationship to the land. How do they approach their subject in terms of language, attitude, and style?
6. Choose an author in this section whose essay, in your opinion, romanticized nature. Compare his or her attitude to that of a writer with a more pragmatic approach to the subject. Compare the two views, and specify the elements in their writing that contribute to the overall strength of their arguments.
7. Thoreau and Hubbell both use process analysis in their essays to convey their messages. Which essay do you feel makes a stronger, more effective point? What about the language and content make it relevant in today's world?
8. Write an essay entitled "Nature's Revenge" in which you examine the consequences of environmental abuse. Consider the short- as well as the long-term effects on the quality of life. Use support from any writer in this section to support your opinion.
9. Write specifically about our relationship to other living creatures on our planet. Is it one of exploitation, cooperation, tyranny? How does this relationship influence how we treat each other? Explore the answers to these question in an essay. Use the works of Walker, Oates, Steinbeck, and Eiseley to support your thesis.

CHAPTER THIRTEEN

Science, Medicine, and Mathematics

Contrary to popular assumptions, contemporary science and mathematics are not dry subjects but, rather, bodies of specialized knowledge concerned with the great "how" and "why" questions of our time. In fact, we are currently in the midst of a whole series of scientific revolutions that will radically transform our lives as we move toward the twenty-first century. The essential problem for humankind is to make sense of all this revolutionary scientific and mathematical knowledge, invest it with value, and make it serve our cultural and global needs.

As you will see in the essays assembled for this chapter, human beings are always the ultimate subject of scientific investigation. Science and mathematics attempt to understand the physical, biological, and chemical events that shape our lives. Whenever we switch on a light or turn on a computer, take an aspirin or start the car, we see that science has intervened effectively in our lives. Often the specialized knowledge of science forces us to make painful decisions. As Deborah Salazar admits in her highly personal essay, "My Abortion," science can provide powerful options for us, but it doesn't simplify the ethical choices that we continually have to make.

The technology of science thus affects everyday decisions as well as the larger contours of culture. Nowhere is the impact of science more apparent than in medicine. As Isaac Asimov and Stephen Jay Gould observe in their essays on cholesterol and AIDS, medical science exists to serve us, to help us with our common dilemmas. At the same time, medical science reminds us that despite advances, we are still mortal. Even as knowledge flows from research laboratories, these mortal paradoxes tend to perplex and goad us as we seek scientific solutions to the complex problems of our era.

Science and mathematics, as specialized bodies of knowledge, can send contradictory messages (for example, Bertrand Russell tells us that there is "supreme beauty" in mathematics while we learn from another author that women are often denied access to this body of knowledge) because science and mathematics are socially constructed and reflect the contours of culture. How we manage the revolution in science—how we harness nuclear weapons or solve the ravages of AIDS—will determine the health of civilization in the next century.

Previewing the Chapter

As you read the essays in this chapter and respond to them in discussion and writing, consider the following questions:

- Does the author take a personal or an objective approach to the subject? What is the effect?
- What area of scientific or mathematical inquiry does the writer focus on?
- What scientific conflicts arise in the course of the essay?
- Is the writer a specialist, a lay person, a journalist, or a commentator? How does the background of the writer affect the tone of the essay?
- What assumptions does the author make about his or her audience? How much specialized knowledge must you bring to the essay?
- How do social issues enter into the author's presentation?
- What gender issues are raised by the author?
- How have your perceptions of the author's topic been changed or enhanced? What new knowledge have you gained? Does the writer contradict any of your assumptions or beliefs?
- Is the writer optimistic or pessimistic about the state of mathematics or science? How do you know?

PERRI KLASS Perri Klass (1958–) is a novelist, short-story writer, essayist, and pediatrician. Born in Trinidad, Klass earned her medical degree at Harvard in 1986 and has been a research fellow at Boston City Hospital since 1990. Klass wrote the "Hers" column in the *New York Times* in 1984 and continues to contribute to that newspaper. Her books include *Recombinations* (1985) and *Other Women's Children* (1990), both novels; and *A Not Entirely Benign Procedure: Four Years as a Medical Student* (1987), a collection of essays recounting her experiences. In the following selection, written in 1984, Klass writes about trying to maintain an emotional balance and a sense of professionalism in the male-dominated world of medicine.

PERRI KLASS

A Long and Difficult Night in the Hospital

It had been a long and difficult night in the hospital. I had had only two hours of sleep, and toward morning a young patient had died of cancer. I was sitting in the nurses' coffee room, staring into space, when the intern, who had had no sleep at all and who had been responsible for everything on the ward, came in and found me. 1

"Are you O.K.?" he asked, and I promptly burst into tears. 2

And then I lied. I told the intern that I was crying for the young woman who had died, whose parents were sitting by her bed, dazed and saddened by the ending of a long and terrible ordeal. I said I was crying for the patient and for her parents, but I knew that in large part I was crying for myself. I was crying because I hadn't slept much, and because I had a long day in front of me in which I would be put on the spot and have my ignorance revealed again and again, a day throughout which I would feel tired and sick and heavy-headed and inadequate. And also, of course, because a young woman had died. It was embarrassing enough to be crying in front of the intern; the least I could do was pretend my motives were purely sympathetic and altruistic rather than substantially mixed with self-pity. 3

The prospect of crying in the hospital haunts many women I met, medical students like me, and interns as well. It seems to hover on the edge of our minds as something we are likely to do, something we must not do because it will confirm all the most clichéd objections to women as doctors. Crying will compromise our professionalism as well as our strength. Actually, before I started my clinical clerkship in the hospital, it never occurred to me to think of myself as someone who cried in public. 4

5 But it turned out that I cried frequently and helplessly in the hospital. My very first week there, I discovered that there was one particular room I could not enter on morning rounds without tears starting to slide down my face. The rooms were decorated with large prints of Impressionist paintings, and that particular room had a Mary Cassatt painting, a woman holding a child. I had suddenly found myself working over a hundred hours a week, spending every third night in the hospital, and I missed my baby badly. I simply could not look at that painting.

6 I cried for the patients. I cried after a man talked to me for fifteen minutes about what a vigorous, lively, intelligent person his wife had been before her stroke, and then took my hand, called me "doctor," and begged me to hold out some hope that she would be that way again.

7 I cried because I forgot to do things. I cried because I didn't know how to do things. I cried because I did things, only to find out they were unnecessary. In fact, looking back on those first couple of weeks in the hospital, it seems to me I was always ducking into bathrooms to sniffle into paper towels and splash cold water on my face. I cried, but I took great care not to be seen at it.

8 I have come to realize that I was not the only one crying. A friend told me about crying because a patient was dying and she could do nothing to help and everyone kept saying it was a "fascinating case." An intern told me about crying because one night when she was swamped she asked a more senior doctor for help, only to be told off the next day because asking for help was a confession of weakness. Perhaps we cry because we are in a harsh environment that offers us little comfort and in which we frequently find ourselves unable to offer comfort to others.

9 I brought up the subject with a couple of male students. No, they said, of course they got upset, and frustrated and unhappy, but it hadn't gotten so bad they actually *cried.* This may simply reflect the much remarked-on truth that men are slower to tears than women in this society. It may also suggest that the hospital is still a male environment, the medical hierarchy created by generations of male doctors, and maybe it all seems a little more comfortable to male students. Or again, maybe they were lying, just too ashamed of those tearful moments in the bathroom and the weakness they implied.

10 I cried so easily last summer because some of my protection was stripped away. Working in the hospital, even as a student with very limited responsibility, I was constantly on the line. Did you do this? Why not? What would have been the right thing to have done? What are the possible consequences of what you didn't do? Precisely because I was a student, I was questioned regularly by any number of people, some of whom were under tremendous pressure themselves, and not inclined to make allowances for my greenness.

11 The steady tension, the fear of making a mistake and the mistakes that inevitably do get made can raise the emotional pitch much too high for

comfort. In addition, I was sleep-deprived and deprived of any time for my family or friends, for anything that might have mitigated the intensity.

12 And finally, the hospital is a place where all sorts of emotions are visible. I saw people mourning and people screaming with pain, people crying with terror and people dying. It's hard to say exactly what effect it has, this everyday drama and melodrama, but perhaps it led me to exaggerate my emotional responses to the tiny dramas of my own life: Will I get three hours of sleep tonight or only two? Will I remember what I read last night about heart disease when they quiz me this morning?

13 It is easy to lose your sense of proportion in the hospital. In fact, it is hard to know what proportion means in a place where people are struggling for their lives, or living with tremendous pain. The medical student, like the intern, tries to maintain both balance and compassion on a schedule that allows for little rest and no relief. And frequently she runs the risk of being overwhelmed, by sorrow for others, by tired hopelessness about her own competence, or by helpless anger at doctors whose idea of teaching involves constant tests of strength and occasional humiliation.

14 I wish I had been telling the whole truth when I said I was crying for the patient who died that night. I can accept my own compassion much more easily than I can accept the mixture of disorientation, inadequacy and self-pity that was actually behind most of my crying in the hospital. And yet, I suppose, accepting those less than nobly sensitive motives is also a necessary step toward acknowledging my own human limitations. Those limitations, after all, even in this age of technological health care, are also in some sense the limitations of the medical profession, whether or not it cares to admit them.

COMPREHENSION

1. What kinds of pressure does Klass, as well as other interns, face daily in the hospital? How does her gender contribute to the stress of her job?
2. Why is Klass reluctant to admit she cries regularly? Why is crying seen as a weakness, particularly in that setting?
3. What does Klass mean by the "limitations of the medical profession" in her conclusion?

RHETORIC

1. Why has Klass written this essay? Does it have a thesis?
2. What impact does Klass's first sentence have? How does the accumulation of details help support the topic sentence? How does the paragraph work to set up the mood of the essay?
3. Is this essay strictly narrative? What other elements contribute to its structure? Cite specific evidence from the piece.
4. Examine the writer's use of repetition in paragraphs 6 and 7. Why is it effective?

5. Why does Klass shift the focus of her essay in paragraphs 12, 13, and 14? How do transitions serve to show this change in focus?
6. How does the conclusion add unity to the essay? What is the function of the last sentence? Does it refer to anything already stated? What was Klass's purpose in ending her essay this way?

WRITING

1. Write an essay analyzing the role of sexual stereotyping in the medical field. How can stereotyping affect the quality of treatment, the doctors, and the patients they treat?
2. Why do people cry? Do men and women cry about the same things? Do men cry as much as women? Why, or why not? What is positive about crying? What is negative? Do you cry? Why? Consider these questions in an essay entitled "Crying."

DEBORAH SALAZAR Deborah Salazar was born in Ecuador but grew up in Denhem Springs, Louisiana, and attended Louisiana State University, where she received her Masters in Fine Arts. Salazar's poetry has been published in many literary magazines. In this essay, which appeared in *Harper's* in 1990, Salazar offers an ostensibly objective account of her abortion, describing a medical procedure that readers themselves must make final judgments upon.

DEBORAH SALAZAR

My Abortion

The procedure itself was the easiest part. A friend had told me to close my eyes and think about anything, think about Donald Duck—sweet and useless advice, I thought at the time—but when I heard the machine come on and the doctor say, "The cervix is slanted at a right angle, this could be a problem; okay, honey, *relax,*" I thought, Donald Duck, Donald Duck, Donald Duck, Donald Duck. I will never be able to watch another Donald Duck cartoon without thinking about my abortion, but I went through the experience feeling pretty calm and entitled. Twenty-seven years old and pregnant for the first time in my life. God bless America, I thought, I sure as hell want a cheap, legal, safe abortion. 1

After I learned that I was pregnant, I started practicing a necessary detachment. The Supreme Court was due to hand down its *Webster* decision any day, and the usual mobs of protesters around women's clinics were doubling in size. I got up before dawn on the fifteenth of June and packed a paper bag with a sweater and socks (because the re- 2 ceptionist said it would be cold inside the clinic) and maxi pads. I wanted to get there as soon as the doors opened, before most of the cross-waving, sign-carrying, chanting, singing protesters showed up. When I pulled into the clinic parking lot with my friend Beth, I saw only two people standing on the curb: a woman, dressed all in black, and a man. As we got closer, I saw that the woman was about my age, with straight black hair and pale eyes turned skyward. She was moaning the words, "Don't kill me, Mommy, don't kill me."

The man and the woman followed our car until it stopped at the door. I stepped out, and the man stood in front of me. He was tall, wearing a suit and tie and singing, "Jesus loves the little children." I laughed in his face. Strange. Three years ago I had worked as a volunteer escort at this very clinic, and I'd always been so solemn with these people. I never would've expected to laugh today. The man obviously hadn't expected me to laugh either. He got angry. "Lesbian!" he called after me as I walked into the clinic. "You're a lesbian. That's why you hate babies!" A tall young man wearing an official clinic-escort T-shirt was standing at the threshold. "Sorry about this," he muttered as I passed by. I was still laughing. "I wish I were a lesbian," I said a little hysterically. "I wouldn't be pregnant." And then I was inside the clinic. 3

I knew the routine. I took my forms and my plastic cup. I went directly to the bathroom. I could hear the protesters while I was in the bathroom. I could hear them the whole time I was in the clinic. The chanting was discontinuous, but it was louder every time it started up. "Murderers! Murderers!" I could hear them in the dressing room, in the weigh-in room, in counseling, in recovery, although I don't remember if I heard them in the procedure room itself. I was told later that my encounter with the protesters had been relatively undramatic: one escort said that these days he was seeing protesters trying to hold car doors shut while women fought to get out. 4

After I turned in my urine cup, I sat back in the waiting room and started filling out forms. One of them was a personal questionnaire that included the question, "What method of birth control were you using at the time you got pregnant?" I thought about lying for a second before I checked the box beside "none." One of the protesters outside had started playing a tape of a baby crying. I signed my name over and over. Yes, I understand the risks involved, yes, I understand that the alternatives to abortion are birth and adoption. I wanted to do more—I wanted to fill out a page or so explaining why I had chosen to do this. I wanted to explain to someone that I was a responsible person; you see, ladies and gentlemen, I never had sex without condoms unless I was having my period; I got pregnant during my period, isn't there something I could sign swearing to that? I had a three-day affair with a friend, I'm broke and unemployed, I can't give up a baby for adoption, I can't afford to be pregnant while I look for a job. 5

In counseling, I was asked why I'd gone off the pill, and I didn't hesitate to respond, "I can get rid of an accidental pregnancy. I can't get rid 6 of cancer.” In the lounge room where I sat in my dressing gown before going in to see the doctor, there was a tiny television (Pee-wee Herman was on) and a table with magazines (*Cosmopolitan, Vogue, American Baby*). The room was already filled to capacity, all twelve chairs taken, when the little bowhead came in. She couldn’t have been more than seventeen, wearing only her gown and a very big white satin bow in her hair. She was a beauty. She looked like she belonged on a homecoming float. She had been crying. “I hate them,” she announced, dropping her shopping bag of clothes on the floor. “They don’t have to say the things they say. Makes me want to go out there and shoot them with a gun.”

“You can’t hear them that well in here, honey,” one of the older
women said. “You can watch the cartoons.” 7

“You know what one of them called my mama?” the beauty said.
“Called her a slut, an unchristian woman. My mama yelled back that I 8
got raped by a priest, that’s how come I’m here.” Stares. The bowhead picked up her shopping bag and leaned against the wall. She spoke again in a quieter voice. “I didn’t really get raped by a priest. My mama just said that.”

The doctor was late that morning. Outside, the chants were getting
louder, competing with Pee-wee Herman, who was on full blast. The 9
protesters were singing a hymn when my name was called. I walked down a short hallway in my bare feet, and then liquid Valium injected directly into my left arm made everything after that feel like it was taking place on another planet. I remember that the doctor was wearing a dark red surgical outfit and that it looked pretty gruesome—I wished he’d worn the traditional pale blue or green. I remember that the Valium made me want to laugh and I didn’t want to laugh because I was afraid I’d wiggle, and I’d been warned *not* to wiggle unless I wanted my uterus perforated. I’d been at the clinic six hours already, preparing for this little operation that would take only five minutes. I remember that after the machine came on, it seemed like less than five minutes. I remember that it hurt and that I was amazed at how empty, relieved, and not pregnant I felt as soon as it was over. The cramps that followed were painful but not terribly so; I could feel my uterus contracting, trying to collapse back to its former size. I was led by a nurse into a dark room, where I sat on a soft mat in a soft chair and bled for a while. I closed my eyes. The woman in the next seat was sobbing softly. I knew it was the blond with the white bow in her hair. I reached over and took her hand in mine. The Valium made me feel as though we were both wearing gloves. Her hand was so still I wondered if she knew I was there, but the sobbing grew softer and softer and eventually it just stopped.

COMPREHENSION

1. How would you describe the writer’s state of mind during the abortion procedure?
2. Why does the narrator choose to have an abortion?
3. How would you describe the atmosphere outside the clinic?

RHETORIC

1. How would you describe the author's tone in the essay? Are there any indications of Salazar's feelings about the event?
2. Why does Salazar use dialogue in her essay? What impact does its use have on the narrative? Find especially powerful uses of dialogue in the essay to support your views.
3. Cite specific use of descriptive details and figurative language. How does their use enrich the atmosphere in the story?
4. Why has the writer chosen narrative to explore her topic? What makes it an effective choice?
5. How does Salazar organize her essay? What transitional words contribute to the structure of the piece?
6. Examine Salazar's final paragraph. How does it function as a conclusion? How does it serve to unify the essay?

WRITING

1. Pretend to be one of the protesters outside the abortion clinic. If you had a chance to approach Salazar quietly and discuss her decision with her, how would you do it? What would you say to her about the morality of her actions? Develop this idea in a brief essay.
2. Write a descriptive narrative about a visit you made to a clinic. What was your medical problem? What procedure did you have done? What was the experience like? Describe the atmosphere and the people around you in detail to evoke a sense of place.
3. In an argumentation essay, express your own views on abortion. Do you consider it immoral? Necessary in certain cases? What are the alternatives to abortion? Be sure to include opposing viewpoints in your argument.

LEWIS THOMAS Lewis Thomas (1913–) is past president of the Memorial Sloan-Kettering Cancer Center. He first came to public attention when his collection of essays, *Lives of a Cell* (1974), appeared. Because of his eloquent capacity to extract metaphors from the discoveries of modern biology and because of his optimism, Thomas's essays have attracted a large and enthusiastic following. Another collection of his essays, *The Medusa and the Snail,* was published in 1979. Thomas can discover an almost magical value in the most humble activities, as the essay below demonstrates.

LEWIS THOMAS

On Societies as Organisms

1 Viewed from a suitable height, the aggregating clusters of medical scientists in the bright sunlight of the boardwalk at Atlantic City, swarmed there from everywhere for the annual meetings, have the look of assemblages of social insects. There is the same vibrating, ionic movement, interrupted by the darting back and forth of jerky individuals to touch antennae and exchange small bits of information; periodically, the mass casts out, like a trout-line, a long single file unerringly toward Child's. If the boards were not fastened down, it would not be a surprise to see them put together a nest of sorts.

2 It is permissible to say this sort of thing about humans. They do resemble, in their most compulsively social behavior, ants at a distance. It is, however, quite bad form in biological circles to put it the other way round, to imply that the operation of insect societies has any relation at all to human affairs. The writers of books on insect behavior generally take pains, in their prefaces, to caution that insects are like creatures from another planet, that their behavior is absolutely foreign, totally unhuman, unearthly, almost unbiological. They are more like perfectly tooled but crazy little machines, and we violate science when we try to read human meanings in their arrangements.

3 It is hard for a bystander not to do so. Ants are so much like human beings as to be an embarrassment. They farm fungi, raise aphids as livestock, launch armies into wars, use chemical sprays to alarm and confuse enemies, capture slaves. The families of weaver ants engage in child labor, holding their larvae like shuttles to spin out the thread that sews the leaves together for their fungus gardens. They exchange information ceaselessly. They do everything but watch television.

4 What makes us most uncomfortable is that they, and the bees and termites and social wasps, seem to live two kinds of lives: they are individuals, going about the day's business without much evidence of thought for tomorrow, and they are at the same time component parts, cellular elements, in the huge, writhing, ruminating organism of the Hill, the nest, the hive. It is because of this aspect, I think, that we most wish for them to be something foreign. We do not like the notion that there can be collective societies with the capacity to behave like organisms. If such things exist, they can have nothing to do with us.

5 Still, there it is. A solitary ant, afield, cannot be considered to have much of anything on his mind; indeed, with only a few neurons strung together by fibers, he can't be imagined to have a mind at all, much less a thought. He is more like a ganglion on legs. Four ants together, or ten, encircling a dead moth on a path, begin to look more like an idea.

They fumble and shove, gradually moving the food toward the Hill, but as though by blind chance. It is only when you watch the dense mass of thousands of ants, crowded together around the Hill, blackening the ground, that you begin to see the whole beast, and now you observe it thinking, planning, calculating. It is an intelligence, a kind of live computer, with crawling bits for its wits.

At a stage in the construction, twigs of certain size are needed, and all the members forage obsessively for twigs of just this size. Later, when outer walls are to be finished, thatched, the size must change, and as though given new orders by telephone, all the workers shift the search to the new twigs. If you disturb the arrangement of a part of the Hill, hundreds of ants will set it vibrating, shifting, until it is put right again. Distant sources of food are somehow sensed, and long lines, like tentacles, reach out over the ground, up over walls, behind boulders, to fetch it in. 6

Termites are even more extraordinary in the way they seem to accumulate intelligence as they gather together. Two or three termites in a chamber will begin to pick up pellets and move them from place to place, but nothing comes of it; nothing is built. As more join in, they seem to reach a critical mass, a quorum, and the thinking begins. They place pellets atop pellets, then throw up columns and beautiful, curving, symmetrical arches, and the crystalline architecture of vaulted chambers is created. It is not known how they communicate with each other, how the chains of termites building one column know when to turn toward the crew on the adjacent column, or how, when the time comes, they manage the flawless joining of the arches. The stimuli that set them off at the outset, building collectively instead of shifting things about, may be pheromones released when they reach committee size. They react as if alarmed. They become agitated, excited, and then they begin working, like artists. 7

Bees live lives of organisms, tissues, cells, organelles, all at the same time. The single bee, out of the hive retrieving sugar (instructed by the dancer: "south-southeast for seven hundred meters, clover—mind you make corrections for the sundrift") is still as much a part of the hive as if attached by a filament. Building the hive, the workers have the look of embryonic cells organizing a developing tissue; from a distance they are like the viruses inside of a cell, running off row after row of symmetrical polygons as though laying down crystals. When the time for swarming comes, and the old queen prepares to leave with her part of the population, it is as though the hive were involved in mitosis. There is an agitated moving of bees back and forth, like granules in cell sap. They distribute themselves in almost precisely equal parts, half to the departing queen, half to the new one. Thus, like an egg, the great, hairy, black and golden creature splits in two, each with an equal share of the family genome. 8

The phenomenon of separate animals joining up to form an organism is not unique in insects. Slime-mold cells do it all the time, of course, in each life cycle. At first they are single amebocytes swimming around, eating bacteria, aloof from each other, untouching, voting 9 straight Republican. Then, a bell sounds, and acrasin is released by special cells toward which the others converge in stellate ranks, touch, fuse together, and construct the slug, solid as a trout. A splendid stalk is raised, with a fruiting body on top, and out of this comes the next generation of amebocytes, ready to swim across the same moist ground, solitary and ambitious.

Herring and other fish in schools are at times so closely integrated, their actions so coordinated, that they seem to be functionally a great multi-fish organism. Flocking birds, especially the seabirds nesting on the slopes of offshore islands in Newfoundland, are similarly attached, connected, synchronized. 10

Although we are by all odds the most social of all social animals—more interdependent, more attached to each other, more inseparable in our behavior than bees—we do not often feel our conjoined intelligence. Perhaps, however, we are linked in circuits for the storage, processing, and retrieval of information, since this appears to be the most basic and universal of all human enterprises. It may be our biological function to build a certain kind of Hill. We have access to all the information of the biosphere, arriving as elementary units in the stream of solar photons. When we have learned how these are rearranged against randomness, to make, say, springtails, quantum mechanics, and the late quartets, we may have a clearer notion how to proceed. The circuitry seems to be there, even if the current is not always on. 11

The system of communications used in science should provide a neat, workable model for studying mechanisms of information-building in human society. Ziman, in a recent *Nature* essay, points out, "the invention of a mechanism for the systematic publication of *fragments* of scientific work may well have been the key event in the history of modern science." He continues: 12

> A regular journal carries from one research worker to another the various . . . observations which are of common interest. . . . A typical scientific paper has never pretended to be more than another little piece in a larger jigsaw—not significant in itself but as an element in a grander scheme. *This technique, of soliciting many modest contributions to the store of human knowledge, has been the secret of Western science since the seventeenth century, for it achieves a corporate, collective power that is far greater than any one individual can exert.* [italics mine]

With some alteration of terms, some toning down, the passage could describe the building of a termite nest. 13

It is fascinating that the word "explore" does not apply to the searching aspect of the activity, but has its origins in the sounds we make while engaged in it. We like to think of exploring in science as a lonely, meditative business, and so it is in the first stages, but always, sooner or later, before the enterprise reaches completion, as we explore, we call to each other, communicate, publish, send letters to the editor, present papers, cry out on finding. 14

COMPREHENSION

1. In this essay, does Thomas write for a specialized or for a general audience? Explain your answer.
2. Describe the insects that Thomas says have humanlike behavior. What is his thesis?
3. Why do writers of books about insects avoid using personification in their descriptions? Why does Thomas purposely use it?

RHETORIC

1. Thomas tends to use words that are not generally used. Define *genome, ionic, amebocytes, mitosis, acrasin, ganglion, stellate,* and *organism.*
2. Thomas uses metaphors frequently and imaginatively. List seven metaphors in the essay, and describe how they are used. Compare his use of metaphor to that of Virginia Woolf in "The Death of the Moth" (Chapter 10).
3. Paragraph 4 is crucial to the organization of the essay. What two methods of classification does it introduce?
4. What is the difference between solitary and collective behavior among the social insects? Thomas compares this behavior to certain kinds of human behavior. What are the details of this comparison?
5. According to your dictionary, what is the etymology of the word *explore?* How does Thomas use this etymology?
6. Thomas extends his discussion in paragraph 9 beyond insects. What effect does he achieve by doing this?

WRITING

1. Do you find it reassuring or disturbing to compare human behavior to insect behavior? Do you find it difficult to consider human society an organism? Why do you think Thomas finds this encouraging?
2. Divide human behavior into groups (school, sports, business), and compare solitary and collective behavior within one or more groups.
3. Write an essay comparing your pet's behavior to human behavior.
4. Thomas has complained about "how awful the prose is in scientific papers." Evaluate the author's own prose in this essay. Argue for or against its effectiveness.

RICHARD SELZER Richard Selzer (1928–), a surgeon with a full-time practice in New Haven, Connecticut, began writing several hours each night after already establishing a successful medical career. His first book of essays, *Mortal Lessons: Notes on the Art of Surgery* (1974), established him as a prominent essayist specializing in the world of medicine and surgery. Selzer employs his elegant prose style in describing the often tragic, unpleasant, and painful world of medical patients. He is a contributor to popular magazines, and his essays have been collected in several books, among them *Confessions of a Knife* (1979) and *Letters to a Young Doctor* (1982). The following essay demonstrates Selzer's experience and expertise as a surgeon as well as his unique ability to describe the world of medicine in poetic and graceful terms.

RICHARD SELZER

Letter to a Young Surgeon

At this, the start of your surgical internship, it is well that you be told how to behave in an operating room. You cannot observe decorum unless you first know what decorum is. Say that you have already changed into a scrub suit, donned cap, mask and shoe covers. You have scrubbed your hands and been helped into your gown and gloves. Now stand out of the way. Eventually, your presence will be noticed by the surgeon, who will motion you to take up a position at the table. Surgery is not one of the polite arts, as are Quilting and Illuminating Manuscripts. Decorum in the operating room does not include doffing your cap in the presence of nurses. Even the old-time surgeons knew this and operated without removing their hats. 1

The first rule of conversation in the operating room is silence. It is a rule to be broken freely by the Master, for he is engaged in the art of teaching. The forceful passage of bacteria through a face mask during speech increases the contamination of the wound and therefore the possibility of infection in that wound. It is a risk that must be taken. By the surgeon, wittingly, and by the patient, unbeknownst. Say what you will about a person's keeping control over his own destiny, there are some things that cannot be helped. Being made use of for teaching purposes in the operating room is one of them. It is an inevitable, admirable and noble circumstance. Besides, I have placated Fate too long to believe that She would bring on wound infection as the complication of such a high enterprise. 2

Observe the least movement of the surgeon's hands. See how he holds out his hand to receive the scalpel. See how the handle of it rides between his thumb and fingertips. The scalpel is the subtlest of the instruments, transmitting the nervous current in the surgeon's arm to the body of the patient. Too timidly applied, and it turns flabby, lifeless; too much pressure and it turns vicious. See how the surgeon applies the blade to the skin—holding it straight in its saddle lest he undercut and one edge of the incision be thinner than the other edge. The application of knife to flesh proclaims the master and exposes the novice. See the surgeon advancing his hand blindly into the abdomen as though it were a hollow in a tree. He is wary, yet needing to know. Will it be something soft and dead? Or a sudden pain in his bitten finger! 3

4 The point of the knife is called the *tang,* from the Latin word for *touch.* The sharp curving edge is the *belly* of the blade. The tang is for assassins, the belly for surgeons. Enough! You will not hold this knife for a long time. Do not be impatient for it. Nor reckon the time. Ripen only. Over the course of your training you will be given ever more elaborate tasks to perform. But for now, you must watch and wait. Excessive ego, arrogance and self-concern in an intern are out of place, as they preclude love for the patient on the table. There is no room for clever disobedience here. For the knife is like fire. The small child yearns to do what his father does, and he steals matches from the man's pocket. The fire he lights in his hiding place is beautiful to him; he toasts marshmallows in it. But he is just as likely to be burned. And reverence for the teacher is essential to the accumulation of knowledge. Even a bad surgeon will teach if only by the opportunity to see what not to do.

5 You will quickly come to detect the difference between a true surgeon and a mere product of the system. Democracy is not the best of all social philosophies in the selection of doctors for training in surgery. Anyone who so desires, and who is able to excel academically and who is willing to undergo the harsh training, can become a surgeon whether or not he is fit for the craft either manually or by temperament. If we continue to award licenses to the incompetent and the ill-suited, we shall be like those countries where work is given over not to those who can do it best, but to those who need it. That offers irritation enough in train stations; think of the result in airplane cockpits or operating rooms. Ponder long and hard upon this point. The mere decision to be a surgeon will not magically confer upon you the dexterity, compassion and calmness to do it.

6 Even on your first day in the operating room, you must look ahead to your last. An old surgeon who has lost his touch is like an old lion whose claws have become blunted, but not the desire to use them. Knowing when to quit and retire from the consuming passion of your life is instinctive. It takes courage to do it. But do it you must. No consideration of money, power, fame or fear of boredom may give you the slightest pause in laying down your scalpel when the first flagging of energy, bravery or confidence appears. To withdraw gracefully is to withdraw in a state of grace. To persist is to fumble your way to injury and ignominy.

7 Do not be dismayed by the letting of blood, for it is blood that animates this work, distinguishes it from its father, Anatomy. Red is the color in which the interior of the body is painted. If an operation be thought of as a painting in progress, and blood red the color of the brush, it must be suitably restrained and attract no undue attention; yet any insufficiency of it will increase the perishability of the canvas. Surgeons are of differing stripes. There are those who are slow and methodical, obsessive beyond all reason. These tortoises operate in a field as bloodless as a cadaver. Every speck of tissue in its proper place, every nerve traced out and brushed clean so that a Japanese artist could render it down to the dendrites. Should the contents of a single capil-

lary be inadvertently shed, the whole procedure comes to a halt while Mr. Clean irrigates and suctions and mops and clamps and ties until once again the operative field looks like Holland at tulip time. Such a surgeon tells time not by the clock but by the calendar. For this, he is ideally equipped with an iron urinary bladder which he has disciplined to contract no more than once a day. To the drop-in observer, the work of such a surgeon is faultless. He gasps in admiration at the still life on the table. Should the same observer leave and return three hours later, nothing will have changed. Only a few more millimeters of perfection.

Then there are the swashbucklers who crash through the underbrush waving a machete, letting tube and ovary fall where they may. This surgeon is equipped with gills so that he can breathe under blood. You do not set foot in his room without a slicker and boots. Seasoned nurses quake at the sight of those arms, elbow-deep and *working.* It is said that one such surgeon entertained the other guests at a department Christmas party by splenectomizing a cat in thirty seconds from skin to skin. 8

Then there are the rest of us who are neither too timid nor too brash. We are just right. And now I shall tell you a secret. To be a good surgeon does not require immense technical facility. Compared to a violinist it is nothing. The Japanese artist, for one, is skillful at double brushing, by which technique he lays on color with one brush and shades it off with another, both brushes being held at the same time and in the same hand, albeit with different fingers. Come to think of it, a surgeon, like a Japanese artist, ought to begin his training at the age of three, learning to hold four or five instruments at a time in the hand while suturing with a needle and thread held in the teeth. By the age of five he would be able to dismantle and reconstruct an entire human body from calvarium to calcaneus unassisted and in the time it would take one of us to recite the Hippocratic Oath. A more obvious advantage of this baby surgeon would be his size. In times of difficulty he could be lowered whole into the abdomen. There, he would swim about, repair the works, then give three tugs on a rope and . . . Presto! Another gallbladder bites the dust. 9

In the absence of any such prodigies, each of you who is full-grown must learn to exist in two states—Littleness and Bigness. In your littleness you descend for hours each day through a cleft in the body into a tiny space that is both your workshop and your temple. Your attention in Lilliput is total and undistracted. Every artery is a river to be forded or dammed, each organ a mountain to be skirted or moved. At last, the work having been done, you ascend. You blink and look about at the vast space peopled by giants and massive furniture. Take a deep breath . . . and you are Big. Such instantaneous hypertrophy is the process by which a surgeon reenters the outside world. Any breakdown in this resonance between the sizes causes the surgeon to live in a Renaissance painting where the depth perception is so bad. 10

Nor ought it to offend you that, a tumor having been successfully removed, and the danger to the patient having been circumvented, the very team of surgeons that only moments before had been a model of 11 discipline and deportment comes loose at the seams and begins to wobble. Jokes are told, there is laughter, a hectic gaiety prevails. This is in no way to be taken as a sign of irreverence or callousness. When the men of the Kalahari return from the hunt with a haunch of zebra, the first thing everybody does is break out in a dance. It is a rite of thanksgiving. There will be food. They have made it safely home.

Man is the only animal capable of tying a square knot. During the course of an operation you may be asked by the surgeon to tie a knot. As drawing and coloring are the language of art, incising, suturing and knot tying are the grammar of surgery. A facility in knot tying is gained only by tying ten thousand of them. When the operation is completed, take home with you a package of leftover sutures. Light a fire in the fireplace and sit with your lover on a rug in front of the fire. Invite her to hold up her index finger, gently crooked in a gesture of beckoning. Using her finger as a strut, tie one of the threads about it in a square knot. Do this one hundred times. Now make a hundred grannies. Only then may you permit yourself to make love to her. This method of learning will not only enable you to master the art of knot tying, both grannies and square, it will bind you, however insecurely, to the one you love. 12

To do surgery without a sense of awe is to be a dandy—all style and no purpose. No part of the operation is too lowly, too menial. Even when suturing the skin at the end of a major abdominal procedure, you must operate with piety, as though you were embellishing a holy reliquary. The suturing of the skin usually falls to the lot of the beginning surgeon, the sights of the Assistant Residents and Residents having been firmly set upon more biliary, more gastric glories. In surgery, the love of inconsiderable things must govern your life—ingrown toenails, thrombosed hemorrhoids, warts. Never disdain the common ordinary ailment in favor of the exotic or rare. To the patient every one of his ailments is unique. One is not to be amused or captivated by disease. Only to a woodpecker is a wormy tree more fascinating than one uninhabited. There is only absorption in your patient's plight. To this purpose, willingly accept the smells and extrusions of the sick. To be spattered with the phlegm, vomitus and blood of suffering is to be badged with the highest office. 13

The sutured skin is all of his operation that the patient will see. It is your signature left upon his body for the rest of his life. For the patient, it is the emblem of his suffering, a reminder of his mortality. Years later, he will idly run his fingers along the length of the scar, and he will hush and remember. The good surgeon knows this. And so he does not overlap the edges of the skin, makes no dog-ears at the corners. He does not tie the sutures too tightly lest there be a row of permanent crosshatches. (It is not your purpose to construct a ladder upon which a touring louse could climb from pubis to navel and back.) The good surgeon does not pinch the skin with forceps. He leaves the proper distance between the sutures. He removes the sutures at the earliest possible date, and he uses sutures of the finest thread. All these things he 14 does and does not do out of reverence for his craft and love for his patient. The surgeon who does otherwise ought to keep his hands in his pockets. At the end of the operation, cholecystectomy, say, the surgeon may ask you to slit open the gallbladder so that everyone in the room might examine the stones. Perform even this cutting with reverence as though the organ were still within the patient's body. You cut, and notice how the amber bile runs out, leaving a residue of stones. Faceted, shiny, they glisten. Almost at once, these wrested dewy stones surrender their warmth and moisture; they grow drab and dull. The descent from jewel to pebble takes place before your eyes.

Deep down, I keep the vanity that surgery is the red flower that 15
blooms among the leaves and thorns that are the rest of Medicine. It is Surgery that, long after it has passed into obsolescence, will be remembered as the glory of Medicine. Then men shall gather in mead halls and sing of that ancient time when surgeons, like gods, walked among the human race. Go ahead. Revel in your Specialty; it is your divinity.

It is quest and dream as well. 16

The incision has been made. One expects mauve doves and colored 17
moths to cloud out of the belly in celebration of the longed-for coming. Soon the surgeon is greeted by the eager blood kneeling and offering its services. Tongues of it lap at his feet; flames and plumes hold themselves aloft to light his way. And he follows this guide that flows just ahead of him through rifts, along the edges of cliffs, picking and winding, leaping across chasms, at last finding itself and pooling to wait for him. But the blood cannot wait a moment too long lest it become a blob of coagulum, something annulled by its own puddling. The surgeon rides the patient, as though he were riding a burro down into a canyon. This body is beautiful to him, and he to it—he whom the patient encloses in the fist of his flesh. For months, ever since the first wild mitosis, the organs had huddled like shipwrecks. When would he come? Will he never come? And suddenly, into the sick cellar—fingers of light! The body lies stupefied at the moment of encounter. The cool air stirs the buried flesh. Even the torpid intestine shifts its slow coils to make way.

Now the surgeon must take care. The fatal glissade, once begun, is 18
not to be stopped. Does this world, too, he wonders, roll within the precincts of mercy? The questing dreamer leans into the patient to catch the subtlest sounds. He hears the harmonies of their two bloods, his and the patient's. They sing of death and the beauty of the rose. He hears the playing together of their two breaths. If Pythagoras is right, there is no silence in the universe. Even the stars make music as they move.

Only do not succumb to self-love. I know a surgeon who, having 19
left the room, is certain, beyond peradventure of doubt, that his disembodied radiance lingers on. And there are surgeons of such aristocratic posture that one refrains only with difficulty from slipping them into the nobility. As though they had risen from Mister to Doctor to Professor, then on to Baron, Count, Archduke, then further, to Apostle, Saint. I could go further.

Such arrogance can carry over to the work itself. There was a surgeon in New Haven, Dr. Truffle, who had a penchant for long midline incisions—from sternum to pubis—no matter the need for exposure. Somewhere along the way, this surgeon had become annoyed by the presence of the navel, which, he decided, interrupted the pure line of his slice. Day in, day out, it must be gone around, either to the right or to the left. Soon, what was at first an annoyance became a hated impediment that must be got rid of. Mere circumvention was not enough. And so, one day, having arrived at the midpoint of his downstroke, this surgeon paused to cut out the navel with a neat ellipse of skin before continuing on down to the pubis. Such an elliptical incision when sutured at the close of the operation forms the continuous straight line without which this surgeon could not live. Once having cut out a navel (the first incidental umbilectomy, I suppose, was the hardest) and seeing the simple undeviate line of his closure, he vowed never again to leave a navel behind. Since he was otherwise a good surgeon, and very successful, it was not long before there were thousands of New Haveners walking around minus their belly buttons. Not that this interfered with any but the most uncommon of activities, but to those of us who examined them postoperatively, these abdomens had a blind, bland look. Years later I would happen upon one of these bellies and know at once the author of the incision upon it. Ah, I would say, Dr. Truffle has been here. 20

It is so difficult for a surgeon to remain "unconscious," retaining the clarity of vision of childhood, to know and be secure in his ability, yet be unaware of his talents. It is almost impossible. There are all too many people around him paying obeisance, pandering, catering, beaming, lusting. Yet he must try. 21

It is not enough to love your work. Love of work is a kind of self-indulgence. You must go beyond that. Better to perform endlessly, repetitiously, faithfully, the simplest acts, like trimming the toenails of an old man. By so doing, you will not say *Here I Am,* but *Here It Is.* You will not announce your love but will store it up in the bodies of your patients to carry with them wherever they go. 22

Many times over, you will hear otherwise sensible people say, "You have golden hands," or, "Thanks to you and God, I have recovered." (Notice the order in which the credit is given.) Such ill-directed praise has no significance. It is the patient's disguised expression of relief at having come through, avoided death. It is a private utterance, having nothing to do with you. Still, such words are enough to turn a surgeon's head, if any more turning were needed. 23

Avoid these blandishments at all cost. You are in service to your patients, and a servant should know his place. The world is topsy-turvy in which a master worships his servant. You are a kindly, firm, experienced servant, but a servant still. If any patient of mine were to attempt to bathe my feet, I'd kick over his basin, suspecting that he possessed not so much a genuine sentiment as a conventional one. It is beneath your dignity to serve as an object of veneration or as the foil in an act of 24 contrition. To any such effusion a simple "Thank you" will do. The rest is pride, and everyone knoweth before *what* that goeth.

Alexander the Great had a slave whose sole responsibility was to whisper "Remember, you are mortal" when he grew too arrogant. Perhaps every surgeon should be assigned such a deflator. The surgeon is the mere instrument which the patient takes in his hand to heal himself. An operation, then, is a time of revelation, both physical and spiritual, when, for a little while, the secrets of the body are set forth to be seen, to be touched, and the surgeon himself is laid open to Grace. 25

An operation is a reenactment of the story of Jonah and the Whale. In surgery, the patient is the whale who swallows up the surgeon. Unlike Jonah, however, the surgeon does not cry out *non serviam,* but willingly descends into the sick body in order to cut out of it the part that threatens to kill it. In an operation where the patient is restored to health, the surgeon is spewed out of the whale's body, and both he and his patient are healed. In an operation where the patient dies on the table, the surgeon, although he is rescued from the whale and the sea of blood, is not fully healed, but will bear the scars of his sojourn in the belly of the patient for the rest of his life. 26

COMPREHENSION

1. How do you know that this is not a true letter? Why has Selzer titled it a "letter"?
2. Assuming one did not know the author is a surgeon, what gives the "voice" of the essay its authority?
3. Summarize the advice that Selzer offers the young surgeon. What does he mean when he states, "Revel in your Specialty; it is your divinity" (paragraph 15)?

RHETORIC

1. With paragraph 3, there begins extensive use of the imperative. What impact does it have on the tone of the essay? What relationship does it establish between the writer and the implied reader?
2. How does Selzer make effective use of figurative language in paragraphs 7, 8, and 10?
3. Paragraphs 7, 8, and 9 employ classification. What is Selzer classifying? What transitional device does Selzer use to unify these three paragraphs?
4. Why is there a break after paragraph 11? How does the beginning of paragraph 12 shift the focus of the essay?
5. What is the central image of paragraph 17? How do the various elements in the paragraph contribute to creating the image?
6. In the concluding paragraph, Selzer states, "An operation is a reenactment of the story of Jonah and the Whale." What other paragraphs in the essay reflect this analogy?

WRITING

1. In paragraph 15, Selzer suggests that surgeons are "like gods." Does the profession of surgery warrant this analogy? Why, or why not?
2. Develop a theme that makes a comparison between a profession and something else—for example, "Basketball players are like ballet dancers," "Novelists are like gods," or "Teachers are like parents." Write an essay based on the comparison you have chosen.
3. Write a "letter" to a first-year college student. Instruct the student in what to expect and how to behave in college.

ISAAC ASIMOV Isaac Asimov (1920–1992), a writer and scientist, taught biochemistry at Boston University. He was born in Russia and educated in America. Asimov's works included both scientific textbooks and science fiction, most notably *The Foundation Trilogy* (1951–1953). Asimov was extraordinarily productive, the author of more than a hundred books; his texts on popular science helped to explain difficult concepts for the lay reader. In the essay below, Asimov uses a clear, straightforward style to explain the function of cholesterol.

ISAAC ASIMOV

Cholesterol

Cholesterol is a dirty word these days, and every report that comes out seems to make it worse. A government study of more than 350,000 American men between 35 and 37 years old was reported last month and 80% of them had cholesterol levels of more than 180 milligrams per 100 milliliters of blood. Anything over the 180 mark indicates an increased probability of an early death from heart disease. The higher the measurement the higher the probability. 1

And yet this grinning death mask is not the only face that cholesterol bears. Cholesterol happens to be absolutely essential to animal life. Every animal from the amoeba to the whale (including human beings, of course) possesses cholesterol. The human body is about one-third of 1% cholesterol. 2

The portion of the animal body that is richest in cholesterol is the nervous system. There we encounter masses of nerve cells which, in bulk, have a grayish appearance and are therefore referred to as "gray matter." 3

Each nerve cell has fibers extending from it, including a particularly long one called the "axon" along which electrical impulses travel from 4 nerve cell to nerve cell, coordinating the body and making it possible for us to receive sense-impressions, to respond appropriately and, above all (for human beings), to think.

5 The axon is surrounded by a fatty sheath, which presumably acts as an insulating device that enables the electrical impulse to travel faster and more efficiently. Without its insulating powers, it is possible that nerve cells would "short-circuit" and that the nervous system would not function.

6 The fatty sheath has a whitish appearance so that those portions of the nervous system that are made up of masses of axons are called the "white matter."

7 As it happens, two out of every five molecules in the fatty sheath are cholesterol. Why that should be, we don't know, but the cholesterol cannot be dispensed with. Without it, we would have no nervous system, and without a nervous system, we could neither think nor live.

8 So important is cholesterol that the body has the full power to manufacture it from simpler materials. Cholesterol does not need to be present in the diet at all.

9 The trouble is, though, that if, for any reason, the body has more cholesterol than it needs, there is a tendency to get rid of it by storing it on the inner surface of the blood vessels—especially the coronary vessels that feed the heart. This is "atherosclerosis," and it occurs in men more often than in women. The cholesterol deposits narrow the blood vessels, stiffen and roughen them, make internal clotting easier and, in general, tend to produce heart attacks, strokes and death.

10 Why is that? Why should such a vital substance, without which we could not live, present such a horrible other face? Why haven't we evolved in such a way as not to experience such dangerous cholesterol deposits?

11 One possible answer is that until the coming of modern medicine, human beings did not have a long life span, on the average. Most people, even in comparatively good times, were dead of violence or infectious disease before they were 40, and by that time atherosclerosis had not had time to become truly dangerous.

12 It is only since the average human life span has reached 75, in many parts of the world, that atherosclerosis and other "degenerative diseases" have become of overwhelming importance.

13 What to do? There is the matter of diet, for one thing. Apparently, flooding the body with high-cholesterol items of diet (eggs, bacon, butter and other fatty foods of animal origin) encourages a too-high level of cholesterol in the blood and consequently atherosclerosis.

14 As it happens, plants do not contain cholesterol. They have related compounds, but not cholesterol. Therefore, to cut down on fatty animal food in the diet (the cholesterol is in the fat) and to increase plant food lower the chance of atherosclerosis.

15 In fact, since most primates (apes and monkeys) are much more vegetarian in their diet than human beings, can it be that we have not

yet had time to fully adapt to the kind of carnivorous diet we have grown accustomed to? This is particularly so in prosperous Western countries. People of the Third World countries eat far less meat than Westerners do. They may have troubles of their own, but atherosclerosis, at least, is a minor problem.

We may also develop drugs that interfere with the body's ability to deposit cholesterol in the blood vessels. A new drug called lovastatin has been recently reported to show promising effectiveness in this direction. There is hope.

COMPREHENSION

1. What is cholesterol? Where is it found? What is its function?
2. According to Asimov, what are some of the reasons that humans may have problems with cholesterol?
3. What solutions does Asimov offer?

RHETORIC

1. Comment on Asimov's first sentence. What tone does it establish for the essay? How does the rest of the paragraph support the topic sentence?
2. Does this essay contain a thesis statement? Is it implied or explicit? Where does it appear?
3. What level of language does Asimov use? Is it aimed at the general reader or at a specialized one? Justify your response.
4. How does Asimov use definition in his piece?
5. What technique does Asimov employ in paragraph 10? What is the effect on the structure of the essay? How does it relate to subsequent paragraphs?
6. Critique Asimov's conclusion. How does it serve to unify the information preceding it?

WRITING

1. Write an essay defining another biological or medical term. Consider your intended audience and how technical you want to make the language. Some research will be necessary.
2. Asimov mentions diet in his essay. Write an essay in which you emphasize the importance of diet in maintaining a healthy body. What diet would you recommend? What kinds of food do you eat? What other factors, such as physical exercise, affect health?
3. Research the latest findings about cholesterol. How does this new information disprove or support Asimov's theories? Compare and contrast what you discover with Asimov's essay.

STEPHEN JAY GOULD Stephen Jay Gould (1941–), an acclaimed contemporary science writer, teaches biology, geology, and the history of science at Harvard University. He also writes a monthly column, "This View of Life," for *Natural History* and is the author of *Ever Since Darwin* (1977), *Ontogeny and Phylogeny* (1977), *The Panda's Thumb* (1980), *Wonderful Life* (1989), and *Bully for Brontosaurus* (1991). In this essay, Gould explains in clear, precise language why AIDS is a "natural phenomenon" and warns against viewing it in moral terms.

STEPHEN JAY GOULD

The Terrifying Normalcy of AIDS

Disney's Epcot Center in Orlando, Fla., is a technological tour de force and a conceptual desert. In this permanent World's Fair, American industrial giants have built their versions of an unblemished future. These masterful entertainments convey but one message, brilliantly packaged and relentlessly expressed: progress through technology is the solution to all human problems. G.E. proclaims from Horizons: "If we can dream it, we can do it." A.T.&T. speaks from on high within its giant golf ball: We are now "unbounded by space and time." United Technologies bubbles from the depths of Living Seas: "With the help of modern technology, we feel there's really no limit to what can be accomplished." 1

Yet several of these exhibits at the Experimental Prototype Community of Tomorrow, all predating last year's space disaster, belie their stated message from within by using the launch of the shuttle as a visual metaphor for technological triumph. The Challenger disaster may represent a general malaise, but it remains an incident. The AIDS pandemic, an issue that may rank with nuclear weaponry as the greatest danger of our era, provides a more striking proof that mind and technology are not omnipotent and that we have not canceled our bond to nature. 2

In 1984, John Platt, a biophysicist who taught at the University of Chicago for many years, wrote a short paper for private circulation. At a time when most of us were either ignoring AIDS, or viewing it as a contained and peculiar affliction of homosexual men, Platt recognized that the limited data on the origin of AIDS and its spread in America suggested a more frightening prospect: we are all susceptible to AIDS, and the disease has been spreading in a simple exponential manner. 3

Exponential growth is a geometric increase. Remember the old kiddy problem: if you place a penny on square one of a checkerboard and double the number of coins on each subsequent square—2, 4, 8, 16, 32 . . . —how big is the stack by the sixty-fourth square? The answer: about as high as the universe is wide. Nothing in the external en- 4 vironment inhibits this increase, thus giving to exponential processes their relentless character. In the real, noninfinite world, of course, some limit will eventually arise, and the process slows down, reaches a steady state, or destroys the entire system: the stack of pennies falls over, the bacterial cells exhaust their supply of nutrients.

Platt noticed that data for the initial spread of AIDS fell right on 5
an exponential curve. He then followed the simplest possible procedure of extrapolating the curve unabated into the 1990's. Most of us were incredulous, accusing Platt of the mathematical gamesmanship that scientists call "curve fitting." After all, aren't exponential models unrealistic? Surely we are not all susceptible to AIDS. Is it not spread only by odd practices to odd people? Will it not, therefore, quickly run its short course within a confined group?

Well, hello 1987—worldwide data still match Platt's extrapolated curve. 6
This will not, of course, go on forever. AIDS has probably already saturated the African areas where it probably originated, and where the sex ratio of afflicted people is 1-to-1, male-female. But AIDS still has far to spread, and may be moving exponentially, through the rest of the world. We have learned enough about the cause of AIDS to slow its spread, if we can make rapid and fundamental changes in our handling of that most powerful part of human biology—our own sexuality. But medicine, as yet, has nothing to offer as a cure and precious little even for palliation.

This exponential spread of AIDS not only illuminates its, and our, bi- 7
ology, but also underscores the tragedy of our moralistic misperception. Exponential processes have a definite time and place of origin, an initial point of "inoculation"—in this case, Africa. We didn't notice the spread at first. In a population of billions, we pay little attention when one increases to two, or eight to sixteen, but when one million becomes two million, we panic, even though the *rate* of doubling has not increased.

The infection has to start somewhere, and its initial locus may be 8
little more than an accident of circumstance. For a while, it remains confined to those in close contact with the primary source, but only by accident of proximity, not by intrinsic susceptibility. Eventually, given the power and lability of human sexuality, it spreads outside the initial group and into the general population. And now AIDS has begun its march through our own heterosexual community.

What a tragedy that our moral stupidity caused us to lose precious 9
time, the greatest enemy in fighting an exponential spread, by downplaying the danger because we thought that AIDS was a disease of three irregular groups of minorities: minorities of life style (needle users), of sexual preference (homosexuals) and of color (Haitians). If AIDS had first been imported from Africa into a Park Avenue apartment, we would not have dithered as the exponential march began.

The message of Orlando—the inevitability of technological solutions— 10
is wrong, and we need to understand why.

Our species has not won its independence from nature, and we cannot do all that we can dream. Or at least we cannot do it at the rate required to avoid tragedy, for we are not unbounded from time. Viral diseases are preventable in principle, and I suspect that an AIDS vaccine will one day be produced. But how will this discovery avail us if it takes until the millennium, and by then AIDS has fully run its exponential course and saturated our population, killing a substantial percentage of the human race? A fight against an exponential enemy is primarily a race against time. 11

We must also grasp the perspective of ecology and evolutionary biology and recognize, once we reinsert ourselves properly into nature, that AIDS represents the ordinary workings of biology, not an irrational or diabolical plague with a moral meaning. Disease, including epidemic spread, is a natural phenomenon, part of human history from the beginning. An entire subdiscipline of my profession, paleopathology, studies the evidence of ancient diseases preserved in the fossil remains of organisms. Human history has been marked by episodic plagues. More native peoples died of imported disease than ever fell before the gun during the era of colonial expansion. Our memories are short, and we have had a respite, really, only since the influenze pandemic at the end of World War I, but AIDS must be viewed as a virulent expression of an ordinary natural phenomenon. 12

I do not say this to foster either comfort or complacency. The evolutionary perspective is correct, but utterly inappropriate for our human scale. Yes, AIDS is a natural phenomenon, one of a recurring class of pandemic diseases. Yes, AIDS may run through the entire population, and may carry off a quarter or more of us. Yes, it may make no *biological* difference to Homo sapiens in the long run: there will still be plenty of us left and we can start again. Evolution cares as little for its agents—organisms struggling for reproductive success—as physics cares for individual atoms of hydrogen in the sun. But we care. These atoms are our neighbors, our lovers, our children and ourselves. AIDS is both a natural phenomenon and, potentially, the greatest natural tragedy in human history. 13

The cardboard message of Epcot fosters the wrong attitudes: we must both reinsert ourselves into nature and view AIDS as a natural phenomenon in order to fight properly. If we stand above nature and if technology is all-powerful, then AIDS is a horrifying anomaly that must be trying to tell us something. If so, we can adopt one of two attitudes, each potentially fatal. We can either become complacent, because we believe the message of Epcot and assume that medicine will soon generate a cure, or we can panic in confusion and seek a scapegoat for something so irregular that it must have been visited upon us to teach us a moral lesson. 14

But AIDS is not irregular. It is part of nature. So are we. This should galvanize us and give us hope, not prompt the worst of all responses: a kind of "new-age" negativism that equates natural with what 15 we must accept and cannot, or even should not, change. When we view AIDS as natural, and when we recognize both the exponential property of its spread and the accidental character of its point of entry into America, we can break through our destructive tendencies to blame others and to free ourselves of concern.

16 If AIDS is natural, then there is no message in its spread. But by all that science has learned and all that rationality proclaims, AIDS works by a *mechanism*—and we can discover it. Victory is not ordained by any principle of progress, or any slogan of technology, so we shall have to fight like hell, and be watchful. There is no message, but there is a mechanism.

COMPREHENSION

1. What does Gould mean when he defines AIDS as a "natural phenomenon"? How does the title support this definition?
2. What does Gould mean by "our moral stupidity" in paragraph 9?
3. What connection does Gould make between our reaction to the AIDS crisis and our alienation from nature?

RHETORIC

1. What is Gould's main idea? Where in the essay is it stated?
2. What is the purpose of paragraphs 1 and 2? How do they contribute to Gould's argument? How do they help establish the tone of the essay? What *is* the tone? What is the importance of Epcot Center to Gould's thesis?
3. Gould uses scientific terminology in his essay. Define the words *exponential* in paragraph 3 and *pandemic* and *phenomenon* in paragraph 13. Is this essay intended for a specialized audience? Justify your response.
4. Trace the progression of ideas in paragraphs 2, 3, 4, and 5. What transitions does Gould employ?
5. Does Gould use rhetorical strategies besides argument in his essay? Cite evidence of this.
6. Explain the final sentence in Gould's conclusion. What is its relation to the total paragraph?

WRITING

1. Write an essay in which you expand on Gould's belief that "our moral stupidity" has not only hindered society's recognition of the AIDS threat but continues to impede AIDS research and treatment.
2. Gould states that we must "reinstate ourselves into nature." What does he mean by this? How would this affect the way in which we deal with disease and death in our society? Explore this issue in a brief essay.

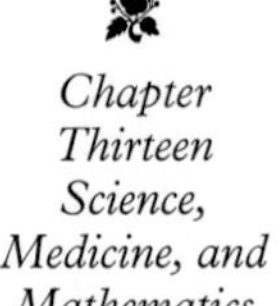

J. B. S. HALDANE John Burdon Sanderson Haldane (1892–1964) was a geneticist, biologist, and writer of science books for the lay reader. His best-known work is *Animal Biology* (1927), written in collaboration with John S. Huxley. He also wrote *Adventures of a Biologist* (1940) and *Everything Has a History* (1951), a collection of essays. Haldane was famous for his ability to explain the abstract, often abstruse, ideas of modern science with concrete examples. "On Being the Right Size," which mixes mathematics and physics with insects and elephants, exemplifies Haldane's skill.

J. B. S. HALDANE

On Being the Right Size

The most obvious differences between different animals are differences of size, but for some reason the zoologists have paid singularly little attention to them. In a large textbook of zoology before me I find no indication that the eagle is larger than the sparrow, or the hippopotamus bigger than the hare, though some grudging admissions are made in the case of the mouse and the whale. But yet it is easy to show that a hare could not be as large as a hippopotamus, or a whale as small as a herring. For every type of animal there is a most convenient size, and a large change in size inevitably carries with it a change of form. 1

Let us take the most obvious of possible cases, and consider a giant man sixty feet high—about the height of Giant Pope and Giant Pagan in the illustrated *Pilgrim's Progress* of my childhood. These monsters were not only ten times as high as Christian, but ten times as wide and ten times as thick, so that their total weight was a thousand times his, or about eighty to ninety tons. Unfortunately the cross sections of their bones were only a hundred times those of Christian, so that every square inch of giant bone had to support ten times the weight borne by a square inch of human bone. As the human thighbone breaks under about ten times the human weight, Pope and Pagan would have broken their thighs every time they took a step. This was doubtless why they were sitting down in the picture I remember. But it lessens one's respect for Christian and Jack the Giant Killer. 2

To turn to zoology, suppose that a gazelle, a graceful little creature with long thin legs, is to become large, it will break its bones unless it does one of two things. It may make its legs short and thick, like the rhinoceros, so that every pound of weight has still about the same area of bone to support it. Or it can compress its body and stretch out its legs obliquely to gain stability, like the giraffe. I mention these two beasts because they happen to belong to the same order as the gazelle, and both are quite successful mechanically, being remarkably fast runners. 3

Gravity, a mere nuisance to Christian, was a terror to Pope, Pagan, 4
and Despair. To the mouse and any smaller animal it presents practically no dangers. You can drop a mouse down a thousand-yard mine shaft; and, on arriving at the bottom, it gets a slight shock and walks away, provided that the ground is fairly soft. A rat is killed, a man is broken, a horse splashes. For the resistance presented to movement by the air is proportional to the surface of the moving object. Divide an animal's length, breadth, and height each by ten; its weight is reduced to a thousandth, but its surface only to a hundredth. So the resistance to falling in the case of the small animal is relatively ten times greater than the driving force.

An insect, therefore, is not afraid of gravity; it can fall without 5
danger, and can cling to the ceiling with remarkably little trouble. It can go in for elegant and fantastic forms of support like that of the daddy-longlegs. But there is a force which is as formidable to an insect as gravitation to a mammal. This is surface tension. A man coming out of a bath carries with him a film of water of about one-fiftieth of an inch in thickness. This weighs roughly a pound. A wet mouse has to carry about its own weight of water. A wet fly has to lift many times its own weight and, as everyone knows, a fly once wetted by water or any other liquid is in a very serious position indeed. An insect going for a drink is in as great danger as a man leaning out over a precipice in search of food. If it once falls into the grip of the surface tension of the water—that is to say, gets wet—it is likely to remain so until it drowns. A few insects, such as waterbeetles, contrive to be unwettable; the majority keep well away from their drink by means of a long proboscis.

Of course tall land animals have other difficulties. They have to 6
pump their blood to greater heights than a man, and therefore, require a larger blood pressure and tougher blood-vessels. A great many men die from burst arteries, especially in the brain, and this danger is presumably still greater for an elephant or a giraffe. But animals of all kinds find difficulties in size for the following reason. A typical small animal, say a microscopic worm or rotifer, has a smooth skin through which all the oxygen it requires can soak in, a straight gut with sufficient surface to absorb its food, and a single kidney. Increase its dimensions tenfold in every direction, and its weight is increased a thousand times, so that if it is to use its muscles as efficiently as its miniature counterpart, it will need a thousand times as much food and oxygen per day and will excrete a thousand times as much of waste products.

Now if its shape is unaltered its surface will be increased only a 7
hundredfold, and ten times as much oxygen must enter per minute through each square millimetre of skin, ten times as much food through each square millimetre of intestine. When a limit is reached to their absorptive powers their surface has to be increased by some special device. For example, a part of the skin may be drawn out into tufts to make gills or pushed in to make lungs, thus increasing the oxygen-

absorbing surface in proportion to the animal's bulk. A man, for example, has a hundred square yards of lung. Similarly, the gut, instead of being smooth and straight, becomes coiled and develops a velvety surface, and other organs increase in complication. The higher animals are not larger than the lower because they are more complicated. They are more complicated because they are larger. Just the same is true of plants. The simplest plants, such as the green algae growing in stagnant water or on the bark of trees, are mere round cells. The higher plants increase their surface by putting out leaves and roots. Comparative anatomy is largely the story of the struggle to increase surface in proportion to volume.

Some of the methods of increasing the surface are useful up to a 8
point, but not capable of a very wide adaptation. For example, while vertebrates carry the oxygen from the gills or lungs all over the body in the blood, insects take air directly to every part of their body by tiny blind tubes called tracheae which open to the surface at many different points. Now, although by their breathing movements they can renew the air in the outer part of the tracheal system, the oxygen has to penetrate the finer branches by means of diffusion. Gases can diffuse easily through very small distances, not many times larger than the average length travelled by a gas molecule between collisions with other molecules. But when such vast journeys—from the point of view of a molecule—as a quarter of an inch have to be made, the process becomes slow. So the portions of an insect's body more than a quarter of an inch from the air would always be short of oxygen. In consequence hardly any insects are much more than half an inch thick. Land crabs are built on the same general plan as insects, but are much clumsier. Yet like ourselves they carry oxygen around in their blood, and are therefore able to grow far larger than any insects. If the insects had hit on a plan for driving air through their tissues instead of letting it soak in, they might well have become as large as lobsters, though other considerations would have prevented them from becoming as large as man.

Exactly the same difficulties attach to flying. It is an elementary 9
principle of aeronautics that the minimum speed needed to keep an aeroplane of a given shape in the air varies as the square root of its length. If its linear dimensions are increased four times, it must fly twice as fast. Now the power needed for the minimum speed increases more rapidly than the weight of the machine. So the larger aeroplane, which weighs sixty-four times as much as the smaller, needs one hundred and twenty-eight times its horsepower to keep up. Applying the same principle to the birds, we find that the limit to their size is soon reached. An angel whose muscles developed no more power weight for weight than those of an eagle or a pigeon would require a breast projecting for about four feet to house the muscles engaged in working its wings, while to economize its weight, its legs would have to be reduced to mere stilts. Actually a large bird such as an eagle or kite does not keep in the air mainly by moving its wings. It is generally to be seen

soaring, that is to say balanced on a rising column of air. And even soaring becomes more and more difficult with increasing size. Were this not the case eagles might be as large as tigers and as formidable to man as hostile aeroplanes.

But it is time that we pass to some of the advantages of size. One of the most obvious is that it enables one to keep warm. All warm-blooded animals at rest lose the same amount of heat from a unit area of skin, for which purpose they need a food-supply proportional to their surface and not to their weight. Five thousand mice weigh as much as a man. Their combined surface and food or oxygen consumption are about seventeen times a man's. In fact a mouse eats about one quarter its own weight of food every day, which is mainly used in keeping it warm. For the same reason small animals cannot live in cold countries. In the arctic regions there are no reptiles or amphibians, and no small mammals. The smallest mammal in Spitzbergen is the fox. The small birds fly away in winter, while the insects die, though their eggs can survive six months or more of frost. The most successful mammals are bears, seals, and walruses.

Similarly, the eye is a rather inefficient organ until it reaches a 11
large size. The back of the human eye on which an image of the outside world is thrown, and which corresponds to the film of a camera, is composed of a mosaic of "rods and cones" whose diameter is little more than a length of an average light wave. Each eye has about a half a million, and for two objects to be distinguishable their images must fall on separate rods or cones. It is obvious that with fewer but larger rods and cones we should see less distinctly. If they were twice as broad two points would have to be twice as far apart before we could distinguish them at a given distance. But if their size were diminished and their number increased we should see no better. For it is impossible to form a definite image smaller than a wave-length of light. Hence a mouse's eye is not a small-scale model of a human eye. Its rods and cones are not much smaller than ours, and therefore there are far fewer of them. A mouse could not distinguish one human face from another six feet away. In order that they should be of any use at all the eyes of small animals have to be much larger in proportion to their bodies than our own. Large animals on the other hand only require relatively small eyes, and those of the whale and elephant are little larger than our own.

For rather more recondite reasons the same general principle holds 12
true of the brain. If we compare the brain-weights of a set of very similar animals such as the cat, cheetah, leopard, and tiger, we find that as we quadruple the body-weight the brain-weight is only doubled. The larger animal with proportionately larger bones can economize on brain, eyes, and certain other organs.

Such are a very few of the considerations which show that for every 13
type of animal there is an optimum size. Yet although Galileo demonstrated the contrary more than three hundred years ago, people still believe that if a flea were as large as a man it could jump a thousand feet

into the air. As a matter of fact the height to which an animal can jump is more nearly independent of its size than proportional to it. A flea can jump about two feet, a man about five. To jump a given height, if we neglect the resistance of the air, requires an expenditure of energy proportional to the jumper's weight. But if the jumping muscles form a constant fraction of the animal's body, the energy developed per ounce of muscle is independent of the size, provided it can be developed quickly enough in the small animal. As a matter of fact an insect's muscles, although they can contract more quickly than our own, appear to be less efficient; as otherwise a flea or grasshopper could rise six feet into the air.

COMPREHENSION

1. According to Haldane, how do people adapt to the problems of their size?
2. What are the effects of size on insects and mice?
3. Explain Haldane's thesis in your own words.

RHETORIC

1. Cite examples of personification in the essay. Why does Haldane use them?
2. Haldane is an adept practitioner of parallel structure. Cite examples of parallel structure in paragraphs 4 and 5.
3. Describe the simple dichotomy Haldane uses to organize his essay.
4. Because Haldane is describing neither a scene nor an event, he can use neither temporal nor spatial transitional devices to make his essay coherent. Identify the transitional devices he employs.
5. Many of Haldane's explanations involve mathematical formulas. Give specific examples of how he helps his reader understand his math.
6. Where does Haldane use hypothetical examples? Why are they effective?

WRITING

1. Based on Haldane's discussion of size, speculate on how the size of a country, of a business, of a family, or of a college might have limits.
2. Write an essay on the effect of size on a human institution.
3. Although explaining mathematical and physical laws is difficult, Haldane is successful. Write an essay in which you try to explain a physical law.

CLASSIC AND CONTEMPORARY

BERTRAND RUSSELL Bertrand Arthur William Russell (1872–1970) was one of the great philosophers, mathematicians, liberal political theorists, and authors of the twentieth century. His works are legion. From his early *Principles of Mathematics* (1903) to *An Inquiry into Meaning and Truth* (1940) and, finally, his three-volume *Autobiography* (1967–1969), Russell demonstrated his multivarious talents as a writer and thinker. He was awarded the Nobel Prize in Literature in 1950. One aspect of Russell's career—his desire to explain science to lay people—is represented in the following essay.

BERTRAND RUSSELL

The Study of Mathematics

In regard to every form of human activity it is necessary that the question should be asked from time to time, What is its purpose and ideal? In what way does it contribute to the beauty of human existence? As respects those pursuits which contribute only remotely, by providing the mechanism of life, it is well to be reminded that not the mere fact of living is to be desired, but the art of living in the contemplation of great things. Still more in regard to those avocations which have no end outside themselves, which are to be justified, if at all, as actually adding to the sum of the world's permanent possessions, it is necessary to keep alive a knowledge of their aims, a clear prefiguring vision of the temple in which creative imagination is to be embodied. 1

Although tradition has decreed that the great bulk of educated men shall know at least the elements of the subject [of mathematics], the reasons for which the tradition arose are forgotten, buried beneath a great rubbish-heap of pedantries and trivialities. To those who inquire as to the purpose of mathematics, the usual answer will be that it facilitates the making of machines, the travelling from place to place, and the victory over foreign nations, whether in war or commerce. If it be objected that these ends—all of which are of doubtful value—are not furthered by the merely elementary study imposed upon those who do not become expert mathematicians, the reply, it is true, will probably be that mathematics trains the reasoning faculties. Yet the very men who make this reply are, for the most part, unwilling to abandon the teaching of definite fallacies, known to be such, and instinctively rejected by the unsophisticated mind of every intelligent learner. And the reasoning faculty itself is generally conceived, by those who urge its cultivation, as merely a means for the avoidance of 2

pitfalls and a help in the discovery of rules for the guidance of practical life. All these are undeniably important achievements to the credit of mathematics; yet it is none of these that entitles mathematics to a place in every liberal education.

Mathematics, rightly viewed, possesses not only truth, but supreme beauty—a beauty cold and austere, like that of sculpture, without appeal to any part of our weaker nature, without the gorgeous trappings of painting or music, yet sublimely pure, and capable of a stern perfection such as only the greatest art can show. The true spirit of delight, the exaltation, the sense of being more than man, which is the touchstone of the highest excellence, is to be found in mathematics as surely as in poetry. What is best in mathematics deserves not merely to be learnt as a task, but to be assimilated as a part of daily thought, and brought again and again before the mind with ever-renewed encouragement. Real life is, to most men, a long second-best, a perpetual compromise between the ideal and the possible; but the world of pure reason knows no compromise, no practical limitations, no barrier to the creative activity embodying in splendid edifices the passionate aspiration after the perfect from which all great work springs. Remote from human passions, remote even from the pitiful facts of nature, the generations have gradually created an ordered cosmos, where pure thought can dwell as in its natural home, and where one, at least, of our nobler impulses can escape from the dreary exile of the actual world. 3

So little, however, have mathematicians aimed at beauty, that hardly anything in their work has had this conscious purpose. Much, owing to irrepressible instincts, which were better than avowed beliefs, has been moulded by an unconscious taste; but much also has been spoilt by false notions of what was fitting. The characteristic excellence of mathematics is only to be found where the reasoning is rigidly logical: the rules of logic are to mathematics what those of structure are to architecture. In the most beautiful work, a chain of argument is presented in which every link is important on its own account, in which there is an air of ease and lucidity throughout, and the premises achieve more than would have been thought possible, by means which appear natural and inevitable. Literature embodies what is general in particular circumstances whose universal significance shines through their individual dress; but mathematics endeavours to present whatever is most general in its purity, without any irrelevant trappings. 4

COMPREHENSION

1. What is Russell's thesis?
2. In this essay, Russell compares and contrasts several disciplines or vocations with mathematics. Of which one does he approve? Of which ones does he disapprove?
3. According to Russell, what are the reasons for studying mathematics?

RHETORIC

1. Identify examples of connotative language in this essay.
2. How many specific details appear in this essay? How does this affect the style of the essay?
3. Describe the structure of this 4-paragraph essay.
4. Why does Russell compare mathematics to the arts? How is mathematics superior?
5. What assumptions about the world of nature and human beings and of the mind underlie the essay?
6. In paragraph 4, what method of definition does Russell use?

WRITING

1. How would you define *beauty,* as Russell uses the word? Does your own idea of beauty differ from Russell's? How is mathematics "beautiful"? Write a brief essay on this topic.
2. Imitate the structure of this essay to organize your definition of *engineering, science,* or *medicine.* Use specific details and examples from the field to clarify your extended definition.
3. Write your own personal essay entitled "My Study of Mathematics."

SUSAN JACOBY Susan Jacoby has worked as an educator and as a reporter for the *Washington Post.* As a free-lance journalist in the Soviet Union (from 1969 to 1971), she produced two books about her experiences. Jacoby now contributes to *The Nation* and *McCall's*; her books include *The Possible She* (1979), a collection of autobiographical essays. In this essay from the *New York Times,* Jacoby examines the reasons why girls are often deficient in math and science.

SUSAN JACOBY

When Bright Girls Decide That Math Is "a Waste of Time"

Susannah, a 16-year-old who has always been an A student in every subject from algebra to English, recently informed her parents that she intended to drop physics and calculus in her senior year of high school and replace them with a drama seminar and a work-study program. She expects a major in art or history in college, she explained, and "any more science or math will just be a waste of my time." 1

Her parents were neither concerned by nor opposed to her decision. "Fine, dear," they said. Their daughter is, after all, an outstanding student. What does it matter if, at age 16, she has taken a step that may limit her understanding of both machines and the natural world for the rest of her life? 2

This kind of decision, in which girls turn away from studies that would give them a sure footing in the world of science and technology, is a self-inflicted female disability that is, regrettably, almost as common today as it was when I was in high school. If Susannah had announced that she had decided to stop taking English in her senior year, her mother and father would have been horrified. I also think they would have been a good deal less sanguine about her decision if she were a boy. 3

In saying that scientific and mathematical ignorance is a self-inflicted female wound, I do not, obviously, mean that cultural expectations play no role in the process. But the world does not conspire to deprive modern women of access to science as it did in the 1930's, when Rosalyn S. Yalow, the Nobel Prize-winning physicist, graduated from Hunter College and was advised to go to work as a secretary because no graduate school would admit her to its physics department. The current generation of adolescent girls—and their parents, bred on old expectations about women's interests—are active conspirators in limiting their own intellectual development. 4

It is true that the proportion of young women in science-related graduate and professional schools, most notably medical schools, has increased significantly in the past decade. It is also true that so few women were studying advanced science and mathematics before the early 1970's that the percentage increase in female enrollment does not yet translate into large numbers of women actually working in science. 5

The real problem is that so many girls eliminate themselves from any serious possibility of studying science as a result of decisions made during the vulnerable period of midadolescence, when they are most likely to be influenced—on both conscious and subconscious levels—by the traditional belief that math and science are "masculine" subjects. 6

During the teen-age years the well-documented phenomenon of "math anxiety" strikes girls who never had any problem handling numbers during earlier schooling. Some men, too, experience this syndrome—a form of panic, akin to a phobia, at any task involving numbers—but women constitute the overwhelming majority of sufferers. The onset of acute math anxiety during the teen-age years is, as Stalin was fond of saying, "not by accident." 7

In adolescence girls begin to fear that they will be unattractive to boys if they are typed as "brains." Science and math epitomize unfeminine braininess in a way that, say, foreign languages do not. High-school girls who pursue an advanced interest in science and math (unless they are students at special institutions like the Bronx High School of Science where everyone is a brain) usually find that they are greatly outnumbered by boys in their classes. They are, therefore, intruding on male turf at a time when their sexual confidence, as well as that of the boys, is most fragile. 8

A 1981 assessment of female achievement in mathematics, based on research conducted under a National Institute for Education grant, found significant differences in the mathematical achievements of 9th and 12th graders. At age 13 girls were equal to or slightly better than boys in tests involving algebra, problem solving and spatial ability; four years later the boys had outstripped the girls. 9

10 It is not mysterious that some very bright high-school girls suddenly decide that math is "too hard" and "a waste of time." In my experience, self-sabotage of mathematical and scientific ability is often a conscious process. I remember deliberately pretending to be puzzled by geometry problems in my sophomore year in high school. A male teacher called me in after class and said, in a baffled tone, "I don't see how you can be having so much trouble when you got straight A's last year in my algebra class."

11 The decision to avoid advanced biology, chemistry, physics and calculus in high school automatically restricts academic and professional choices that ought to be wide open to anyone beginning college. At all coeducational universities women are overwhelmingly concentrated in the fine arts, social sciences and traditionally female departments like education. Courses leading to degrees in science- and technology-related fields are filled mainly by men.

12 In my generation, the practical consequences of mathematical and scientific illiteracy are visible in the large number of special programs to help professional women overcome the anxiety they feel when they are promoted into jobs that require them to handle statistics.

13 The consequences of this syndrome should not, however, be viewed in narrowly professional terms. Competence in science and math does not mean one is going to become a scientist or mathematician any more than competence in writing English means one is going to become a professional writer. Scientific and mathematical illiteracy—which has been cited in several recent critiques by panels studying American education from kindergarten through college—produces an incalculably impoverished vision of human experience.

14 Scientific illiteracy is not, of course, the exclusive province of women. In certain intellectual circles it has become fashionable to proclaim a willed, aggressive ignorance about science and technology. Some female writers specialize in ominous, uninformed diatribes against genetic research as a plot to remove control of childbearing from women, while some well-known men of letters proudly announce that they understand absolutely nothing about computers, or, for that matter, about electricity. This lack of understanding is nothing in which women or men ought to take pride.

15 Failure to comprehend either computers or chromosomes leads to a terrible sense of helplessness, because the profound impact of science on everyday life is evident even to those who insist they don't, won't, can't understand why the changes are taking place. At this stage of history women are more prone to such feelings of helplessness than men because the culture judges their ignorance less harshly and because women themselves acquiesce in that indulgence.

16 Since there is ample evidence of such feelings in adolescence, it is up to parents to see that their daughters do not accede to the old stereotypes about "masculine" and "feminine" knowledge. Unless we want our daughters to share our intellectual handicaps, we had better tell them no, they can't stop taking mathematics and science at the ripe old age of 16.

COMPREHENSION

1. What reasons does Jacoby give for girls' deficiency in math and science?
2. Why does she call it a "self-inflicted disability"?
3. What are the consequences of being math and science illiterate?

RHETORIC

1. Explain the main idea of Jacoby's essay in your own words.
2. Does the writer use abstract or concrete language in her essay? Cite examples to support your response.
3. What technique does Jacoby use in paragraphs 1 and 2? How does it aid in setting up her argument?
4. What rhetorical strategies does the writer use in her essay?
5. How does the use of dialogue aid in developing paragraph 10? What effect does the general use of dialogue have on the writer's point?
6. How is Jacoby's conclusion consistent in tone with the rest of the essay? Does it supply a sense of unity? Why, or why not?

WRITING

1. Write an essay describing a school-related phobia you once had, or continue to have (for example, in math, writing, physical education, biology). Explain where you think that fear came from, how it affected your performance in school, and what you did (or are doing) to cope with the problem.
2. Write an argumentation essay proposing that math and science phobia is not "self-inflicted" but caused primarily by the continued presence of sexism in society.
3. Write an essay about the need for math and science literacy in today's world. Use support from Jacoby's essay.

CLASSIC AND CONTEMPORARY: QUESTIONS FOR COMPARISON

1. How do Russell and Jacoby approach the subject of math? Do they have different priorities? Are they writing for a similar audience? Use examples from both writers to support your ideas.
2. Analyze the language used in the two essays. What is similar or different about the style and diction of the two pieces? Which uses figurative language? Is one essay more accessible to the modern reader? If so, why? How do they each use details?
3. Would Russell's essay inspire the modern young women Jacoby writes about? Why, or why not? What advice would Russell give today's young women about studying math? Do you think in his day Russell advocated the study of math for both boys and girls? Do you think Russell would find fault with Jacoby's pragmatic approach to mathematics?

CONNECTIONS

1. Using the essays of Klass and Selzer, compare and contrast the way in which the hospital environment affects male and female doctors. How might Selzer's advice help to relieve some of the stress Klass felt as a female medical student? How does Selzer's essay confirm some of the observations made by Klass concerning the attitudes of some male doctors at work?
2. How does Haldane's essay on size illustrate the usefulness of mathematics in explaining the world? How does his essay reinforce what Russell calls the "beauty" of mathematics?
3. Compare the essays of Salazar, Klass, and Selzer in their use of figurative language and details to convey the atmosphere of a clinical environment.
4. Using any of the essays in this section, write an essay advancing the need for literacy in math and science. What will society lose if its young people continue to rate low in these subjects?
5. Compare the essays of Thomas and Haldane. What does each have to say about the life and functions of different organisms? How does each use personification, figurative language, and humor to convey information?
6. Consider the treatment of AIDS patients in hospitals today. How might "moral stupidity" affect the way doctors, nurses, and other workers cope with these patients? How might doctor arrogance manifest itself in that situation? Use the works of Klass, Selzer, and Gould to explore this issue.
7. Make a connection between Thomas's views on societies (both human and insect) and Gould's view that "Our species has not won its independence from nature." How alienated are we from other animal societies? What do we share with them? How can we use this knowledge to save ourselves and our planet?

CHAPTER FOURTEEN

Civilization

At the end of the twentieth century, the paroxysms caused by conflicts among peoples, nations, and cultures continue to shake continents. The United States might have emerged from the cold war as the dominant superpower, but numerous local and global threats remain. Woody Allen observes facetiously in "My Speech to the Graduates" that we seem to be at a crossroads in civilization. "One path leads to despair and utter hopelessness. The other, to total extinction." Yet the author also reminds us, perhaps as a whimsical article of faith, that the future holds great promise.

The future of civilization assuredly holds significant peril as well as promise. If by *civilization* we mean the complete absence of barbarism and nonrational behavior in human affairs, coupled with a commitment to harmonious or "civil" conduct within various social realms, then it is clear that we have not attained this ideal state of cultural or world development. At the same time, we have advanced beyond the point in primitive civilization where someone chipped at a stone in order to make a better tool. The *process* of civilization whereby we harness our physical, creative, scientific, political, philosophical, and spiritual resources is well advanced. However, the current state of civilization, as many writers in this final chapter testify, remains ambiguous.

As we consider the course of contemporary civilization, we must contend with the interplay of contradictory forces. We have become increasingly what V. S. Naipaul terms one "universal civilization," but we still have rampant nationalism to deal with. Indeed, we have entered an era of renewed ethnic strife, where a preoccupation with cultural difference seems stronger than the desire for universal civilization. The writers assembled here grapple with these contradictions; they move from

the United States, to Canada, to Europe, to Asia as they search for those constituents of culture that might hasten a civilized world.

The idea of civilization suggests a pluralistic ethos whereby people of diverse backgrounds can maintain cultural identities but also coexist with other cultural representatives in a spirit of tolerance and mutual respect. The wars, upheavals, and catastrophes of this century were spawned by a narrower consciousness, rooted in the various "ism's" that J. B. Priestley alluded to in an earlier essay. Hopefully, as we prepare for a new century, all of us can advance the goal of a universal civilization based on the best that we have been able to create for humankind.

Previewing the Chapter

As you read the essays in this chapter and respond to them in discussion and writing, consider the following questions:

- How does the author define *civilization?* Is this definition stated or implied? Is it broad or narrow? Explain.
- Is the writer hopeful or pessimistic about the state of civilization?
- What values does the author seem to think are necessary to advance the idea of civilization?
- Do you find the author's tone to be objective or subjective?
- Which areas of knowledge—for example, history, philosophy, political science—does the author bring to bear on the subject?
- Do you agree or disagree with the author's view of the contemporary state of civilization?
- What essays in previous chapters inform your understanding of the selections in this chapter?
- Based on your reading of these essays, how would you define *civilization?* Are you hopeful about the current state of civilization?

MAXINE HONG KINGSTON Maxine Hong Kingston (1940–) has written three books on the Chinese-American experience that have established her as a major contemporary prose stylist. *The Woman Warrior* (1976) and *China Men* (1980) are brilliant explorations of personal and ethnic consciousness. Her newest work, a novel, is entitled *Tripmaster Monkey* (1989). This selection from *China Men* offers a contemporary parable on the perils of cultural difference.

MAXINE HONG KINGSTON

The Wild Man of the Green Swamp

For eight months in 1975, residents on the edge of Green Swamp, Florida, had been reporting to the police that they had seen a Wild Man. When they stepped toward him, he made strange noises as in a foreign language and ran back into the saw grass. At first, authorities said the Wild Man was a mass hallucination. Man-eating animals lived in the swamp, and a human being could hardly find a place to rest without sinking. Perhaps it was some kind of a bear the children had seen. 1

In October, a game officer saw a man crouched over a small fire, but as he approached, the figure ran away. It couldn't have been a bear because the Wild Man dragged a burlap bag after him. Also, the fire was obviously man-made. 2

The fish-and-game wardens and the sheriff's deputies entered the swamp with dogs but did not search for long; no one could live in the swamp. The mosquitoes alone would drive him out. 3

The Wild Man made forays out of the swamp. Farmers encountered him taking fruit and corn from the turkeys. He broke into a house trailer, but the occupant came back, and the Wild Man escaped out a window. The occupant said that a bad smell came off the Wild Man. Usually, the only evidence of him were his abandoned campsites. At one he left the remains of a four-foot-long alligator, of which he had eaten the feet and tail. 4

In May a posse made an air and land search; the plane signaled down to the hunters on the ground, who circled the Wild Man. A fish-and-game warden "brought him down with a tackle," according to the news. The Wild Man fought, but they took him to jail. He looked Chinese, so they found a Chinese in town to come translate. 5

The Wild Man talked a lot to the translator. He told him his name. He said he was thirty-nine years old, the father of seven children, who were in Taiwan. To support them, he had shipped out on a Liberian freighter. He had gotten very homesick and asked everyone if he could leave the ship and go home. But the officers would not let him off. They sent messages to China to find out about him. When the ship landed, they took him to the airport and tried to put him on an airplane to some foreign place. Then, he said, the white demons took him to Tampa Hospital, which is for insane people, but he escaped, just walked out and went into the swamp. 6

The interpreter asked how he lived in the swamp. He said he ate snakes, turtles, armadillos, and alligators. The captors could tell how he lived when they opened up his bag, which was not burlap but a pair of pants with the legs knotted. Inside, he had carried a pot, a piece of 7

sharpened tin, and a small club, which he had made by sticking a railroad spike into a section of aluminum tubing.

The sheriff found the Liberian freighter that the Wild Man had 8
been on. The ship's officers said that they had not tried to stop him from going home. His shipmates had decided that there was something wrong with his mind. They had bought him a plane ticket and arranged his passport to send him back to China. They had driven him to the airport, but there he began screaming and weeping and would not get on the plane. So they found him a doctor, who sent him to Tampa Hospital.

Now the doctors at the jail gave him medicine for the mosquito 9
bites, which covered his entire body, and medicine for his stomachache. He was getting better, but after he'd been in jail for three days, the U. S. Border Patrol told him they were sending him back. He became hysterical. That night, he fastened his belt to the bars, wrapped it around his neck, and hung himself.

In the newspaper picture he did not look very wild, being led by the 10
posse out of the swamp. He did not look dirty, either. He wore a checkered shirt unbuttoned at the neck, where his white undershirt showed; his shirt was tucked into his pants; his hair was short. He was surrounded by men in cowboy hats. His fingers stretching open, his wrists pulling apart to the extent of the handcuffs, he lifted his head, his eyes screwed shut, and cried out.

There was a Wild Man in our slough too, only he was a black man. 11
He wore a shirt and no pants, and some mornings when we walked to school, we saw him asleep under the bridge. The police came and took him away. The newspaper said he was crazy; it said the police had been on the lookout for him for a long time, but we had seen him every day.

COMPREHENSION

1. Why is Hong Kingston recounting this tale?
2. What is the connection between the Wild Man in the Swamp and the homeless black man at the end of the narrative?
3. Do you believe either man is actually crazy? Does the author? What is the nature of their insanity?

RHETORIC

1. What is Hong Kingston's tone in this essay? Are there any clues in the narrative? How does the writer's use of language complement the tone?
2. What journalistic technique does Hong Kingston use to structure her introductory paragraph? How does it influence the rest of the essay?
3. Examine the writer's use of detail. How does its use enhance the story?
4. How does the writer's use of transitional phrases add an element of suspense to the narrative? How do they aid in structuring the essay?

5. Is this narrative a parable? Why, or why not?
6. What impact does the final paragraph have? What point is the writer making? How does the paragraph's final sentence aid in understanding the narrative?

WRITING

1. In a brief essay, analyze what Hong Kingston is saying about the state of homelessness. What is the difference between the Chinese Wild Man and the man in the writer's neighborhood? What ironic overtones do their situations have?
2. Write an essay in which you define the concept of "home." What does it mean? How does it shape a person's identity? Can a person be truly at home anywhere? What are the consequences of not having a home?
3. Compare and contrast Hong Kingston's story of the Wild Man with the thoughts and observations of Baldwin in "Stranger in the Village." What are the similarities and the differences between the two situations?

RUTH PRAWER JHABVALA Ruth Prawer Jhabvala (1927–) has long been associated with the Merchant-Ivory team of filmmakers, who specialize in translating literary works onto the screen. Jhabvala, born in Germany, also lived in India for many years before coming to the United States in 1975. Along with screenplays for *A Room with a View* (1985), for which she won an Academy Award, and *Howard's End* (1992), she has written fiction including *Heat and Dust* (1975) and *Out of India: Selected Stories* (1986). In this narrative essay from the latter, Jhabvala tells of her struggles to accept the spiritually demanding conditions of life in India.

RUTH PRAWER JHABVALA

Myself in India

I have lived in India for most of my adult life. My husband is Indian and so are my children. I am not, and less so every year. 1

India reacts very strongly on people. Some loathe it, some love it, most do both. There is a special problem of adjustment for the sort of people who come today, who tend to be liberal in outlook and have been educated to be sensitive and receptive to other cultures. But it is not always easy to be sensitive and receptive to India: There comes a point where you have to close up in order to protect yourself. The place is very strong and often proves too strong for European nerves. There is a cycle that Europeans—by Europeans I mean all Westerners, 2 including Americans—tend to pass through. It goes like this: first stage, tremendous enthusiasm—everything Indian is marvelous; second stage, everything Indian not so marvelous; third stage, everything Indian abominable. For some people it ends there, for others the cycle renews itself and goes on. I have been through it so many times that now I think of myself as strapped to a wheel that goes round and round and sometimes I'm up and sometimes I'm down. When I meet other Europeans, I can usually tell after a few moments' conversation at what stage of the cycle they happen to be. Everyone likes to talk about India, whether they happen to be loving or loathing it. It is a topic on which a lot of things can be said, and on a variety of aspects—social, economic, political, philosophical: It makes fascinating viewing from every side.

However, I must admit that I am no longer interested in India. 3
What I am interested in now is myself in India—which sometimes, in moments of despondency, I tend to think of as my survival in India. I had better say straightaway that the reason I live in India is that my strongest human ties are here. If I hadn't married an Indian, I don't think I would ever have come here for I am not attracted—or used not to be attracted—to the things that usually bring people to India. I know I am the wrong type of person to live here. To stay and endure, one should have a mission and a cause, to be patient, cheerful, unselfish, strong. I am a central European with an English education and a deplorable tendency to constant self-analysis. I am irritable and have weak nerves.

The most salient fact about India is that it is very poor and very 4
backward. There are so many other things to be said about it but this must remain the basis of all of them. We may praise Indian democracy, go into raptures over Indian music, admire Indian intellectuals—but whatever we say, not for one moment should we lose sight of the fact that a very great number of Indians never get enough to eat. Literally that: From birth to death they never for one day cease to suffer from hunger. *Can* one lose sight of that fact? God knows, I've tried. But after seeing what one has to see here every day, it is not really possible to go on living one's life the way one is used to. People dying of starvation in the streets, children kidnapped and maimed to be sent out as beggars—but there is no point in making a catalog of the horrors with which one lives, *on* which one lives, as on the back of an animal. Obviously, there has to be some adjustment.

There are several ways. The first and best is to be a strong person 5
who plunges in and does what he can as a doctor or social worker. I often think that perhaps this is the only condition under which Europeans have any right to be here. I know several people like that. They are usually attached to some mission. They work very hard and stay very cheerful. Every few years they are sent on home leave. Once I met such a person—a woman doctor—who had just returned from her first home leave after being out here for twelve years. I asked her: But what does it feel like to go back after such a long time? How do you manage to adapt yourself? She didn't understand. This question, which

was of such tremendous import to me—how to adapt oneself to the differences between Europe and India—didn't mean a thing to her. It simply didn't matter. And she was right, for in view of the things she sees and does every day, the delicate nuances of one's own sensibilities are best forgotten.

Another approach to India's basic conditions is to accept them. This seems to be the approach favored by most Indians. Perhaps it has something to do with their belief in reincarnation. If things are not to your liking in this life, there is always the chance that in your next life everything will be different. It appears to be a consoling thought for both rich and poor. The rich man stuffing himself on pilau can do so with an easy conscience because he knows he has earned this privilege by his good conduct in previous lives; and the poor man can watch him with some degree of equanimity, for he knows that next time around it may well be *he* who will be digging into that pilau while the other will be crouching outside the door with an empty stomach. However, this path of acceptance is not open to you if you don't have a belief in reincarnation ingrained within you. And if you don't accept, then what can you do? Sometimes one wants just to run away and go to a place where everyone has enough to eat and clothes to wear and a home fit to live in. But even when you get there, can you ever forget? Having once seen the sights in India, and the way it has been ordained that people must live out their lives, nowhere in the world can ever be all that good to be in again. 6

None of this is what I wanted to say. I wanted to concentrate only on myself in India. But I could not do so before indicating the basis on which everyone who comes here has to live. I have a nice house, I do my best to live in an agreeable way. I shut all my windows, I let down the blinds, I turn on the air-conditioner; I read a lot of books, with a special preference for the great masters of the novel. All the time I know myself to be on the back of this great animal of poverty and backwardness. It is not possible to pretend otherwise. Or rather, one does pretend, but retribution follows. Even if one never rolls up the blinds and never turns off the air-conditioner, something is bound to go wrong. People are not meant to shut themselves up in rooms and pretend there is nothing outside. 7

Now I think I am drawing nearer to what I want to be my subject. Yes, something is wrong: I am not happy this way. I feel lonely, shut in, shut off. It is my own fault. I should go out more and meet people and learn what is going on. All right, so I am not a doctor nor a social worker nor a saint nor at all a good person; then the only thing to do is to try to push that aspect of India out of sight and turn to others. There are many others. I live in the capital, where so much is going on. The winter is one round of parties, art exhibitions, plays, music and dance recitals, visiting European artists: There need never be a dull moment. Yet all my moments are dull. Why? It is my own fault, I know. I can't quite explain it to myself but somehow I have no heart for these things here. Is it because all the time underneath I feel the animal moving? But 8

I have decided to ignore the animal. I wish to concentrate only on modern, Westernized India, and on modern, well-off, cultured Westernized Indians.

Let me try and describe a Westernized Indian woman with whom I 9
ought to have a lot in common and whose company I ought to enjoy. She has been to Oxford or Cambridge or some smart American college. She speaks flawless, easy, colloquial English with a charming lilt of an accent. She has a degree in economics or political science or English literature. She comes from a good family. Her father may have been an I. C. S. officer or some other high-ranking government official; he too was at Oxford or Cambridge, and he and her mother traveled in Europe in prewar days. They have always lived a Western-style life, with Western food and an admiration for Western culture. The daughter now tends rather to frown on this. She feels one should be more deeply Indian, and with this end in view, she wears handloom saris and traditional jewelry and has painted an abnormally large vermilion mark on her forehead. She is interested in Indian classical music and dance. If she is rich enough—she may have married into one of the big Indian business houses—she will become a patroness of the arts and hold delicious parties on her lawn on summer nights. All her friends are there—and she has so many, both Indian and European, all interesting people—and trays of iced drinks are carried around by servants in uniform and there is intelligent conversation and then there is a superbly arranged buffet supper and more intelligent conversation, and then the crown of the evening: a famous Indian maestro performing on the sitar. The guests recline on carpets and cushions on the lawn. The sky sparkles with stars and the languid summer air is fragrant with jasmine. There are many pretty girls reclining against bolsters; their faces are melancholy, for the music is stirring their hearts, and sometimes they sigh with yearning and happiness and look down at their pretty toes (adorned with a tiny silver toe ring) peeping out from under the sari. Here is Indian life and culture at its highest and best. Yet, with all that, it need not be thought that our hostess has forgotten her Western education. Not at all. In her one may see the best of East and West combined. She is interested in a great variety of topics and can hold her own in any discussion. She loves to exercise her emancipated mind, and whatever the subject of conversation—economics, or politics, or literature, or film—she has a well-formulated opinion on it and knows how to express herself. How lucky for me if I could have such a person for a friend! What enjoyable, lively times we two could have together!

In fact, my teeth are set on edge if I have to listen to her for more 10
than five minutes—yes, even though everything she says is so true and in line with the most advanced opinions of today. But when she says it, somehow, even though I know the words to be true, they ring completely false. It is merely lips moving and sounds coming out: It doesn't mean anything, nothing of what she says (though she says it with such conviction, skill, and charm) is of the least importance to her. She is only making conversation in the way she knows educated women have

to make conversation. And so it is with all of them. Everything they say, all that lively conversation around the buffet table, is not prompted by anything they really feel strongly about but by what they think they ought to feel strongly about. This applies not only to subjects that are naturally alien to them—for instance, when they talk oh so solemnly! and with such profound intelligence! of Godard and Becket and ecology—but when they talk about themselves too. They know modern India to be an important subject and they have a lot to say about it: But though they themselves *are* modern India, they don't look at themselves, they are not conditioned to look at themselves except with the eyes of foreign experts whom they have been taught to respect. And while they are fully aware of India's problems and are up on all the statistics and all the arguments for and against nationalization and a socialistic pattern of society, all the time it is as if they were talking about some *other* place—as if it were a subject for debate—an abstract subject—and not a live animal actually moving under their feet.

But if I have no taste for the company of these Westernized Indians, 11
then what else is there? Other Indians don't really have a social life, not in our terms; the whole conception of such a life is imported. It is true that Indians are gregarious insofar as they hate to be alone and always like to sit together in groups; but these groups are clan-units—it is the family, or clan members, who gather together and enjoy each other's company. And again, their conception of enjoying each other's company is different from ours. For them it is enough just to *be* together; there are long stretches of silence in which everyone stares into space. From time to time there is a little spurt of conversation, usually on some commonplace everyday subject as rising prices, a forthcoming marriage, or a troublesome neighbor. There is no attempt at exercising the mind or testing one's wits against those of others: The pleasure lies only in having other familiar people around and enjoying the air together and looking forward to the next meal. There is actually something very restful about this mode of social intercourse, and certainly holds more pleasure than the synthetic social life led by Westernized Indians. It is also more adapted to the Indian climate, which invites one to be absolutely relaxed in mind and body, to do nothing, to think nothing, just to feel, to *be*. I have in fact enjoyed sitting around like that for hours on end. But there is something in me that after some time revolts against such lassitude. I can't just *be!* Suddenly I jump up and rush away out of that contented circle. I want to do something terribly difficult like climbing a mountain or reading the *Critique of Pure Reason.* I feel tempted to bang my head against the wall as if to wake myself up. Anything to prevent myself from being sucked down into the bog of passive, intuitive being. I feel I cannot, I must not allow myself to live this way.

Of course there are other Europeans more or less in the same situ- 12
ation as myself. For instance, other women married to Indians. But I hesitate to seek them out. People suffering from the same disease do not usually make good company for one another. Who is to listen to

whose complaints? On the other hand, with what enthusiasm I welcome visitors from abroad. Their physical presence alone is a pleasure to me. I love to see their fresh complexions, their red cheeks that speak of wind and rain; and I like to see their clothes and their shoes, to admire the texture of these solid European materials and the industrial skills that have gone into making them. I also like to hear the way in which these people speak. In some strange way their accents, their intonations are redolent to me of the places from which they have come, so that as voices rise and fall I hear in them the wind stirring in English trees or a mild brook murmuring through a summer wood. And apart from these sensuous pleasures, there is also the pleasure of hearing what they have to say. I listen avidly to what is said about people I know or have heard of and about new plays and restaurants and changes and fashions. However, neither the subject nor my interest in it is inexhaustible; and after that, it is my turn. What about India? Now they want to hear, but I don't want to say. I feel myself growing sullen. I don't want to talk about India. There is nothing I can tell them. There is nothing they would understand. However, I do begin to talk, and after a time even to talk with passion. But everything I say is wrong. I listen to myself with horror; they too listen with horror. I want to stop and reverse, but I can't. I want to cry out, this is not what I mean! You are listening to me in entirely the wrong context! But there is no way of explaining the context. It would take too long, and anyway what is the point? It's such a small, personal thing. I fall silent. I have nothing more to say. I turn my face and want them to go away.

So I am back again alone in my room with the blinds drawn and the 13
air-conditioner on. Sometimes, when I think of my life, it seems to have contracted to this one point and to be concentrated in this one room, and it is always a very hot, very long afternoon when the air-conditioner has failed. I cannot describe the *oppression* of such afternoons. It is a physical oppression—heat pressing down on me and pressing in the walls and the ceiling and congealing together with time that has stood still and will never move again. And it is not only those two—heat and time—that are laying their weight on me but behind them, or held within them, there is something more, which I can only describe as the whole of India. This is hyperbole, but I need hyperbole to express my feelings about those countless afternoons spent over what now seem to me countless years in a country for which I was not born. India swallows me up and now it seems to me that I am no longer in my room but in the white-hot city streets under a white-hot sky; people cannot live in such heat, so everything is deserted—no, not quite, for here comes a smiling leper in a cart being pushed by another leper; there is also the carcass of a dog and vultures have swooped down on it. The river has dried up and stretches in miles of flat cracked earth; it is not possible to make out where the river ceases and the land begins, for this too is as flat, as cracked, as dry as the riverbed and stretches on forever. Until we come to a jungle in which wild beasts live, and then there are ravines

and here live outlaws with the hearts of wild beasts. Sometimes they make raids into the villages and they rob and burn and mutilate and kill for sport. More mountains and these are very, very high, and now it is no longer hot but terribly cold, we are in snow and ice and here is Mount Kailash on which sits Siva the Destroyer wearing a necklace of human skulls. Down in the plains they are worshiping him. I can see them from here—they are doing something strange—what is it? I draw nearer. Now I can see. They are killing a boy. They hack him to pieces and now they bury the pieces into the foundations dug for a new bridge. There is a priest with them who is quite naked except for ash smeared all over him; he is reciting some holy verses over the foundations, to bless and propitiate.

I am using these exaggerated images in order to give some idea of 14
how intolerable India—the idea, the sensation of it—can become. A point is reached where one must escape, and if one can't do so physically, then some other way must be found. And I think it is not only Europeans but Indians too who feel themselves compelled to seek refuge from their often unbearable environment. Here perhaps less than anywhere else is it possible to believe that this world, this life, is all there is for us, and the temptation to write it off and substitute something more satisfying becomes overwhelming. This brings up the question whether religion is such a potent force in India because life is so terrible, or is it the other way around—is life so terrible because, with the eyes of the spirit turned elsewhere, there is no incentive to improve its quality? Whichever it is, the fact remains that the eyes of the spirit *are* turned elsewhere, and it really is true that God seems more present in India than in other places. Every morning I wake up at 3 A.M. to the sound of someone pouring out his spirit in devotional song; and then at dawn the temple bells ring, and again at dusk, and conch shells are blown, and there is the smell of incense and of the slightly overblown flowers that are placed at the feet of smiling, pink-cheeked idols. I read in the papers that the Lord Krishna has been reborn as the son of a weaver woman in a village somewhere in Madhya Pradesh. On the banks of the river there are figures in meditation and one of them may turn out to be the teller in your bank who cashed your check just a few days ago; now he is in the lotus pose and his eyes are turned up and he is in ecstasy. There are ashrams full of little old half-starved widows who skip and dance about, they giggle and play hide-and-seek because they are Krishna's milkmaids. And over all this there is a sky of enormous proportions—so much larger than the earth on which you live, and often so incredibly beautiful, an unflawed unearthly blue by day, all shining with stars at night, that it is difficult to believe that something grand and wonderful beyond the bounds of human comprehension does not emanate from there.

I love listening to Indian devotional songs. They seem pure like 15
water drawn from a well; and the emotions they express are both beautiful and easy to understand because the imagery employed is so human. The soul crying out for God is always shown as the beloved

yearning for the lover in an easily recognizable way ("I wait for Him. Do you hear His step? He has come."). I feel soothed when I hear such songs and all my discontentment falls away. I see that everything I have been fretting about is of no importance at all because all that matters is this promise of eternal bliss in the Lover's arms. I become patient and good and feel that everything is good. Unfortunately this tranquil state does not last for long, and after a time it again seems to me that nothing is good and neither am I. Once somebody said to me: "Just see, how sweet is the Indian soul that can see God in a cow!" But when I try to assume this sweetness, it turns sour: For, however much I may try to fool myself, whatever veils I may try, for the sake of peace of mind, to draw over my eyes, it is soon enough clear to me that the cow *is* a cow, and a very scrawny, underfed, diseased one at that. And then I feel that I want to keep this knowledge, however painful it is, and not exchange it for some other that may be true for an Indian but can never quite become that for me.

And here, it seems to me, I come to the heart of my problem. To 16
live in India and be at peace, one must to a very considerable extent become Indian and adopt Indian attitudes, habits, beliefs, assume if possible an Indian personality. But how is this possible? And even if it were possible—without cheating oneself—would it be desirable? Should one want to try to become something other than what one is? I don't always say no to this question. Sometimes it seems to me how pleasant it would be to say yes and give in and wear a sari and be meek and accepting and see God in a cow. Other times it seems worthwhile to be defiant and European and—all right, be crushed by one's environment, but all the same have made some attempt to remain standing. Of course, this can't go on indefinitely and in the end I'm bound to lose—if only at the point where my ashes are immersed in the Ganges to the accompaniment of Vedic hymns, and then who will say that I have not truly merged with India?

I do sometimes go back to Europe. But after a time I get bored 17
there and want to come back here. I also find it hard now to stand the European climate. I have got used to intense heat and seem to need it.

COMPREHENSION

1. Does Jhabvala truly hate India? What evidence suggests the opposite?
2. What is it about India that makes it "too strong for European nerves"? What does this suggest about European sensibilities?
3. How does Jhabvala describe the Indian character?

RHETORIC

1. Comment on Jhabvala's animal metaphor. Is it a suitable one for India? Cite other uses of figurative language in the essay. How does the language evoke a sense of place? Why is this important to the writer's purposes?

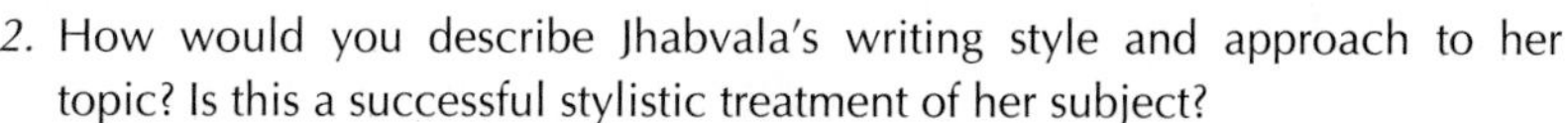

2. How would you describe Jhabvala's writing style and approach to her topic? Is this a successful stylistic treatment of her subject?
3. How do the topic sentences of paragraphs 7 and 8 reveal the writer's state of mind? Why does she use this device? What response is she trying to elicit?
4. Jhabvala employs numerous rhetorical strategies to develop her essay. Identify key passages that reflect these strategies.
5. How does Jhabvala's juxtaposition of opposites reflect her attitude in paragraph 10? How does this technique lend force to the thesis of the essay?
6. Is Jhabvala's conclusion satisfying? Why, or why not? How does it relate to the content of the essay and the author's thesis?

WRITING

1. In paragraph 7 of her essay, Jhabvala states: "People are not meant to shut themselves up in rooms and pretend there is nothing outside." Write an essay in which you agree or disagree with this opinion. Consider the problems outside your door, both national and global. Can you ignore them? How? On the other hand, is it your duty to try to remedy these problems? Is it ever necessary to escape?
2. Jhabvala attributes the Indian character to the belief in reincarnation. What is reincarnation? In a research paper, examine the teachings of this belief. Use the information you gather to comment on the validity of Jhabvala's remarks.
3. Write a personal narrative similar to Jhabvala's in which you examine and analyze your feelings about the country in which you were born or raised. What ambivalent feelings do you have about the place, if any? How does it feel to be a product of a particular culture? What effect has it had on your identity or your sense of the world?

ISHMAEL REED Ishmael Reed (1938–), an American novelist and poet, is the founder and editor (along with Al Young) of *Quilt* magazine, begun in 1981. In his writing, Reed uses a combination of standard English, black dialect, and slang to satirize American society. He believes that African Americans must move away from identification with Europe in order to rediscover their African qualities. Reed's books include *Flight to Canada* (1976), *The Terrible Twos* (1982), and *The Terrible Threes* (1989). In addition, he has written volumes of verse, including *Secretary to the Spirits* (1975), and a play, *Hell Hath No Fury* (1960). In the following essay from *Writin' Is Fightin',* Reed seeks to debunk the myth of the European ideal and argues for a universal definition of *culture.*

ISHMAEL REED

America: The Multinational Society

At the annual Lower East Side Jewish Festival yesterday, a Chinese woman ate a pizza slice in front of Ty Thuan Duc's Vietnamese grocery store. Beside her a Spanish-speaking family patronized a cart with two signs: "Italian Ices" and "Kosher by Rabbi Alper." And after the pastrami ran out, everybody ate knishes. —*New York Times,* June 23, 1983

On the day before Memorial Day, 1983, a poet called me to describe a city he had just visited. He said that one section included mosques, built by the Islamic people who dwelled there. Attending his reading, he said, were large numbers of Hispanic people, forty thousand of whom lived in the same city. He was not talking about a fabled city located in some mysterious region of the world. The city he'd visited was Detroit. 1

A few months before, as I was leaving Houston, Texas, I heard it announced on the radio that Texas's largest minority was Mexican American, and though a foundation recently issued a report critical of bilingual education, the taped voice used to guide the passengers on the air trams connecting terminals in Dallas Airport is in both Spanish and English. If the trend continues, a day will come when it will be difficult to travel through some sections of the country without hearing commands in both English and Spanish; after all, for some western states, Spanish was the first written language and the Spanish style lives on in the western way of life. 2

Shortly after my Texas trip, I sat in an auditorium located on the campus of the University of Wisconsin at Milwaukee as a Yale professor—whose original work on the influence of African cultures upon those of the Americas has led to his ostracism from some monocultural intellectual circles—walked up and down the aisle, like an old-time southern evangelist, dancing and drumming the top of the lectern, illustrating his points before some serious Afro-American intellectuals and artists who cheered and applauded his performance and his mastery of information. The professor was "white." After his lecture, he joined a group of Milwaukeeans in a conversation. All of the participants spoke Yoruban, though only the professor had ever traveled to Africa. 3

One of the artists told me that his paintings, which included African and Afro-American mythological symbols and imagery, were hanging in the local McDonald's restaurant. The next day I went to McDonald's and snapped pictures of smiling youngsters eating hamburgers below paintings that could grace the walls of any of the coun- 4

try's leading museums. The manager of the local McDonald's said, "I don't know what you boys are doing, but I like it," as he commissioned the local painters to exhibit in his restaurant.

Such blurring of cultural styles occurs in everyday life in the United States to a greater extent than anyone can imagine and is probably more prevalent than the sensational conflict between people of different backgrounds that is played up and often encouraged by the media. The result is what the Yale professor, Robert Thompson, referred to as a cultural bouillabaisse, yet members of the nation's present educational and cultural Elect still cling to the notion that the United States belongs to some vaguely defined entity they refer to as "Western civilization," by which they mean, presumably, a civilization created by the people of Europe, as if Europe can be viewed in monolithic terms. Is Beethoven's Ninth Symphony, which includes Turkish marches, a part of Western civilization, or the late nineteenth- and twentieth-century French paintings, whose creators were influenced by Japanese art? And what of the cubists, through whom the influence of African art changed modern painting, or the surrealists, who were so impressed with the art of the Pacific Northwest Indians that, in their map of North America, Alaska dwarfs the lower forty-eight in size?

Are the Russians, who are often criticized for their adoption of 6
"Western" ways by Tsarist dissidents in exile, members of Western civilization? And what of the millions of Europeans who have black African and Asian ancestry, black Africans having occupied several countries for hundreds of years? Are these "Europeans" members of Western civilization, or the Hungarians, who originated across the Urals in a place called Greater Hungary, or the Irish, who came from the Iberian Peninsula?

Even the notion that North America is part of Western civilization 7
because our "system of government" is derived from Europe is being challenged by Native American historians who say that the founding fathers, Benjamin Franklin especially, were actually influenced by the system of government that had been adopted by the Iroquois hundreds of years prior to the arrival of large numbers of Europeans.

Western civilization, then, becomes another confusing category like 8
Third World, or Judeo-Christian culture, as man attempts to impose his small-screen view of political and cultural reality upon a complex world. Our most publicized novelist recently said that Western civilization was the greatest achievement of mankind, an attitude that flourishes on the street level as scribbles in public restrooms: "White Power," "Niggers and Spics Suck," or "Hitler was a prophet," the latter being the most telling, for wasn't Adolph Hitler the archetypal monoculturalist who, in his pigheaded arrogance, believed that one way and one blood was so pure that it had to be protected from alien strains at all costs? Where did such an attitude, which has caused so much misery and depression in our national life, which has tainted even our noblest achievements, begin? An attitude that caused the incarceration of Japanese-American citizens during World War II, the persecution of

Chicanos and Chinese Americans, the near-extermination of the Indians, and the murder and lynchings of thousands of Afro-Americans.

Virtuous, hardworking, pious, even though they occasionally would wander off after some fancy clothes, or rendezvous in the woods with the town prostitute, the Puritans are idealized in our schoolbooks as "a hardy band" of no-nonsense patriarchs whose discipline razed the forest and brought order to the New World (a term that annoys Native American historians). Industrious, responsible, it was their "Yankee ingenuity" and practicality that created the work ethic. They were simple folk who produced a number of good poets, and they set the tone for the American writing style, of lean and spare lines, long before Hemingway. They worshiped in churches whose colors blended in with the New England snow, churches with simple structures and ornate lecterns. 9

The Puritans were a daring lot, but they had a mean streak. They hated the theater and banned Christmas. They punished people in a cruel and inhuman manner. They killed children who disobeyed their parents. When they came in contact with those whom they considered heathens or aliens, they behaved in such a bizarre and irrational manner that this chapter in the American history comes down to us as a late-movie horror film. They exterminated the Indians, who taught them how to survive in a world unknown to them, and their encounter with the calypso culture of Barbados resulted in what the tourist guide in Salem's Witches' House refers to as the Witchcraft Hysteria. 10

The Puritan legacy of hard work and meticulous accounting led to the establishment of a great industrial society; it is no wonder that the American industrial revolution began in Lowell, Massachusetts, but there was the other side, the strange and paranoid attitudes toward those different from the Elect. 11

The cultural attitudes of that early Elect continue to be voiced in everyday life in the United States: the president of a distinguished university, writing a letter to the *Times,* belittling the study of African civilizations; the television network that promoted its show on the Vatican art with the boast that this art represented "the finest achievements of the human spirit." A modern up-tempo state of complex rhythms that depends upon contacts with an international community can no longer behave as if it dwelled in a "Zion Wilderness" surrounded by beasts and pagans. 12

When I heard a schoolteacher warn the other night about the invasion of the American educational system by foreign curriculums, I wanted to yell at the television set, "Lady, they're already here." It has already begun because the world is here. The world has been arriving at these shores for at least ten thousand years from Europe, Africa, and Asia. In the late nineteenth and early twentieth centuries, large numbers of Europeans arrived, adding their cultures to those of the European, African, and Asian settlers who were already here, and recently millions have been entering the country from South America 13 and the Caribbean, making Yale Professor Bob Thompson's bouillabaisse richer and thicker.

One of our most visionary politicians said that he envisioned a time when the United States could become the brain of the world, by which he meant the repository of all of the latest advanced information systems. I thought of that remark when an enterprising poet friend of mine called to say that he had just sold a poem to a computer magazine and that the editors were delighted to get it because they didn't carry fiction or poetry. Is that the kind of world we desire? A humdrum homogeneous world of all brains but no heart, no fiction, no poetry; a world of robots with human attendants bereft of imagination, of culture? Or does North America deserve a more exciting destiny? To become a place where the cultures of the world crisscross. This is possible because the United States is unique in the world: The world is here.

COMPREHENSION

1. Why does Reed believe that the notion of Western or European civilization is fallacious?
2. According to Reed, what are the origins of our monoculturalist view?
3. What are the dangers of such a narrow view? What historical examples does Reed allude to?

RHETORIC

1. How do paragraphs 1 to 4 help set the stage for Reed's discourse? Does this section contain Reed's thesis?
2. Does the computer analogy in Reed's conclusion work? Do his rhetorical questions underscore the thesis?
3. Comment on the author's extensive use of details and examples. How do they serve to support his point? Which examples are especially illuminating? Why?
4. What kind of humor does Reed use in his essay? Does its use contribute to the force of his essay? Why, or why not?
5. Is Reed's reasoning inductive or deductive? Justify your answer.
6. How does Reed employ definitions to structure his essay?

WRITING

1. Write an essay arguing that a multinational society is often riddled with complex problems. What are some of the drawbacks or disadvantages of such a society? What causes these conflicts? Explore these issues in your writing.
2. How does America's insistence that it is a European country affect its dealings with other nations? How does it influence the way it treats its own citizens? Explore these questions in a causal-analysis essay, using support from Reed.

3. Write an essay in which you consider how a multinational United States affects you on a day-to-day basis. How does it enrich your life or the life of the country? Use specific examples and details to support your opinion.

V. S. NAIPAUL V. S. Naipaul (1932–), whose given name is Vidiadhari Surajprasad, is a West-Indian novelist and essayist who has lived in England since 1950. His parents were Hindus, but Naipaul was educated in Trinidad and at Oxford. Naipaul's work reflects his inner conflicts about his dual heritage and offers an ironic view of life. His novels, including *A House for Mr. Biswas* (1961) and *Guerillas* (1975), demonstrate his elegant prose, while *Among the Believers: An Islamic Journey* (1981) and *India: A Million Mutinies Now* (1990) offer penetrating nonfictional analyses. In the following essay from *The New York Times,* Naipaul explores the efforts to achieve an international community and confronts issues of ethnic identity.

V. S. NAIPAUL

Our Universal Civilization

I never formulated the idea of the universal civilization until 11 years ago, when I traveled for many months in a number of non-Arab Muslim countries—Iran, Indonesia, Malaysia and Pakistan—to try to understand what had driven them to their rage. That Muslim rage was just beginning to be apparent. 1

I thought I would be traveling among people who would be like the people of my own community, the Trinidad Indian community. A large portion of Indians were Muslims; we both had a similar 19th century imperial or colonial history. But it wasn't like that. 2

Despite the history we had in common, I had traveled a different way. Starting with the Hindu background of the instinctive, ritualized life; growing up in the unpromising conditions of colonial Trinidad; I had gone through many stages of knowledge and self-knowledge. I had been granted the ideas of inquiry and the tools of scholarship. I could carry four or five or six different cultural ideas in my head. Now, traveling among non-Arab Muslims, I found myself among a colonized people who had been stripped by their faith of all that expanding cultural and historical knowledge of the world that I had been growing into on the other side of the world. 3

Before I began my journey—while the Shah still ruled—there had appeared in the United States a small novel, *Foreigner*, by Nahid Rachlin, a young Iranian woman, that in its subdued, unpolitical way foreshadowed the hysteria that was to come. The central figure is a 4 young Iranian woman who does research work in Boston as a biologist. She is married to an American, and she might seem well adapted.

But when she goes back on a holiday to Teheran, she begins to feel lost. She reflects on her time in the United States. It is not a time of clarity; she sees it now to be a time of emptiness. She has never been in control. We can see that she was not prepared for the movement out of the shut-in Iranian world—where the faith was the complete way, filled everything, left no spare corner of the mind or will or soul—to the other world where it was necessary to be an individual and responsible; where people developed vocations and were stirred by ambition and achievement, and believed in perfectibility.

In her distress, she falls ill. She goes to a hospital. The doctor understands her unhappiness. He tells the young woman that her pain comes from an old ulcer. "What you have," he says in his melancholy, seductive way, "is a Western disease." And the research biologist arrives at a decision. She will give up that Boston-imposed life of the intellect and meaningless work; she will stay in Iran and put on the veil. 6

Immensely satisfying, that renunciation. But it is intellectually flawed: it assumes that there will continue to be people striving out there, in the stressed world, making drugs and medical equipment, to keep the Iranian doctor's hospital going. 7

Again and again, on my Islamic journey in 1979, I found a similar unconscious contradiction in people's attitudes. I remember especially a newspaper editor in Teheran. His paper had been at the heart of the revolution. In the middle of 1979 it was busy, in a state of glory. Seven months later, when I went back to Teheran, it had lost its heart; the once busy main room was empty; all but two of the staff had disappeared. The American Embassy had been seized; a financial crisis had followed; many foreign firms had closed down; advertising had dried up; the newspaper editor could hardly see his way ahead; every issue of the paper lost money; the editor, it might be said, had become as much a hostage as the diplomats. 8

He also, as I now learned, had two sons of university age. One was studying in the United States; the other had applied for a visa, but then the hostage crisis had occurred. This was news to me—that the United States should have been so important to the sons of one of the spokesmen of the Islamic revolution. I told the editor I was surprised. He said, speaking especially of the son waiting for the visa, "It's his future." 9

Emotional satisfaction on one hand; thought for the future on the other. The editor was as divided as nearly everyone else. 10

One of Joseph Conrad's earliest stories of the East Indies, from the 1890's, was about a local raja or chieftain, a murderous man, a Muslim (though it is never explicitly said), who, in a crisis, having lost his magical counselor, swims out one night to one of the English merchant ships in the harbor to ask the sailors, representatives of the immense power that had come from the other end of the world, for an amulet, a magical charm. The sailors are at a loss; but then someone among them gives the raja a British coin, a sixpence commemorating Queen 11

Victoria's Jubilee; and the raja is well pleased. Conrad didn't treat the story as a joke; he loaded it with philosophical implications for both sides, and I feel now that he saw truly.

In the 100 years since that story, the wealth of the world has grown, power has grown, education has spread; the disturbance, the "philosophical shriek" of men at the margin (to use Conrad's words), has been amplified. The division in the revolutionary editor's spirit, and the renunciation of the fictional biologist, both contain a tribute—unacknowledged, but all the more profound—to the universal civilization. Simple charms alone cannot be acquired from it; other, difficult things come with it as well: ambition, endeavor, individuality. 12

The universal civilization has been a long time in the making. It wasn't always universal; it wasn't always as attractive as it is today. The expansion of Europe gave it for at least three centuries a racial taint, which still causes pain. 13

In Trinidad I grew up in the last days of that kind of racialism. And that, perhaps, has given me a greater appreciation of the immense changes that have taken place since the end of the war, the extraordinary attempt to accommodate the rest of the world, and all the currents of that world's thought. 14

Because my movement within this civilization has been from Trinidad to England, from the periphery to the center, I may have felt certain of its guiding principles more freshly than people to whom these things were everyday. One such realization—I suppose I have sensed it most of my life, but I have understood it philosophically only during the preparation of this talk—has been the beauty of the idea of the pursuit of happiness. Familiar words, easy to take for granted; easy to misconstrue. 15

This idea of the pursuit of happiness is at the heart of the attractiveness of the civilization to so many outside it or on its periphery. I find it marvelous to contemplate to what an extent, after two centuries, and after the terrible history of the earlier part of this century, the idea has come to a kind of fruition. It is an elastic idea; it fits all men. It implies a certain kind of society, a certain kind of awakened spirit. I don't imagine my father's Hindu parents would have been able to understand the idea. So much is contained in it: the idea of the individual, responsibility, choice, the life of the intellect, the idea of vocation and perfectibility and achievement. It is an immense human idea. It cannot be reduced to a fixed system. It cannot generate fanaticism. But it is known to exist, and because of that, other more rigid systems in the end blow away. 16

COMPREHENSION

1. What does Naipaul mean by "universal civilization"?
2. What are the differences between Naipaul's Muslims and the ones he encounters in his travels? What factors does the author cite to explain those differences?
3. What conflicts do the non-Arab Muslims face in a universal civilization?

RHETORIC

1. What is Naipaul's thesis? Where does it appear?
2. In paragraph 8, how does the author structure his example? Comment on his choice of punctuation and his ordering of events.
3. How does Naipaul use other literary sources to structure the essay? How do they serve to amplify his points?
4. How does Naipaul employ comparative analysis and definition? Is his overall approach deductive or inductive? Explain your views.
5. Cite uses of parallel structure in Naipaul's essay. How is it used?
6. The author introduces and expands on the theme of "the pursuit of happiness" in his conclusion. Is there any hint to the reader that it's an important issue for Naipaul before it's mentioned? What is the purpose of placing it in the final paragraphs?

WRITING

1. In an essay, develop Naipaul's remark: "I could carry four or five or six cultural ideas around in my head." What does the writer mean by this? How can such an attitude enhance a person's perception of the world? Can most people make the same claim? Do you feel that your own perspective is broad or narrow?
2. Write an essay exploring the meaning of "the pursuit of happiness." Is it a concept that most Americans and other Westerners take for granted? What does it mean? Can it be abused?
3. In a brief essay using Naipaul's observations as support, explore the role of religion in defining a country's philosophy and customs. How can religion narrow a country's global vision?

JAMES BALDWIN James Baldwin (1924–1988), a major American essayist, novelist, short-story writer, and playwright, was born and grew up in Harlem. He won a Eugene Saxon Fellowship and lived in Europe from 1948 to 1956. Always an activist in civil-rights causes, Baldwin focused in his essays and fiction on the black search for identity in modern America and on the myth of white superiority. Among his principal works are *Go Tell It on the Mountain* (1953), *Notes of a Native Son* (1955), *Giovanni's Room* (1956), *Nobody Knows My Name* (1961), *Another Country* (1962), and *If Beale Street Could Talk* (1974). One of the finest contemporary essayists, Baldwin had a rare talent for portraying the deepest concerns about civilization in an intensely personal style, as the following essay indicates.

JAMES BALDWIN

Stranger in the Village

From all available evidence no black man had ever set foot in this tiny Swiss village before I came. I was told before arriving that I would probably be a "sight" for the village; I took this to mean that people of my complexion were rarely seen in Switzerland, and also that city people are always something of a "sight" outside of the city. It did not occur to me—possibly because I am an American—that there could be people anywhere who had never seen a Negro. 1

It is a fact that cannot be explained on the basis of the inaccessibility of the village. The village is very high, but it is only four hours from Milan and three hours from Lausanne. It is true that it is virtually unknown. Few people making plans for a holiday would elect to come here. On the other hand, the villagers are able, presumably, to come and go as they please—which they do: to another town at the foot of the mountain, with a population of approximately five thousand, the nearest place to see a movie or go to the bank. In the village there is no movie house, no bank, no library, no theater; very few radios, one jeep, one station wagon; and, at the moment, one typewriter, mine, an invention which the woman next door to me here had never seen. There are about six hundred people living here, all Catholic—I conclude this from the fact that the Catholic church is open all year round, whereas the Protestant chapel, set off on a hill a little removed from the village, is open only in the summertime when the tourists arrive. There are four or five hotels, all closed now, and four or five *bistros,* of which, however, only two do any business during the winter. These two do not do a great deal, for life in the village seems to end around nine or ten o'clock. There are a few stores, butcher, baker, *épicerie,* a hardware store, and a money-changer—who cannot change travelers' checks, but must send them down to the bank, an operation which takes two or three days. There is something called the *Ballet Haus,* closed in the winter and used for God knows what, certainly not ballet, during the summer. There seems to be only one schoolhouse in the village, and this for the quite young children; I suppose this to mean that their older brothers and sisters at some point descend from these mountains in order to complete their education—possibly, again, to the town just below. The landscape is absolutely forbidding, mountains towering on all four sides, ice and snow as far as the eye can reach. In this white wilderness, men and women and children move all day, carrying washing, wood, buckets of milk or water, sometimes skiing on Sunday afternoons. All week long boys and young men are to be seen shoveling snow off the rooftops, or dragging wood down from the forest in sleds. 2

The village's only real attraction, which explains the tourist season, 3 is the hot spring water. A disquietingly high proportion of these tourists are cripples, or semi-cripples, who come year after year—from other parts of Switzerland, usually—to take the waters. This lends the village, at the height of the season, a rather terrifying air of sanctity, as though it were a lesser Lourdes. There is often something beautiful, there is always something awful, in the spectacle of a person who has lost one of his faculties, a faculty he never questioned until it was gone, and who struggles to recover it. Yet people remain people, on crutches or indeed on deathbeds; and wherever I passed, the first summer I was here, among the native villagers or among the lame, a wind passed with me—of astonishment, curiosity, amusement, and outrage. The first summer I stayed two weeks and never intended to return. But I did return in the winter, to work; the village offers, obviously, no distractions whatever and has the further advantage of being extremely cheap. Now it is winter again, a year later, and I am here again. Everyone in the village knows my name, though they scarcely ever use it, knows that I come from America—though this, apparently, they will never really believe: black men come from Africa—and everyone knows that I am the friend of the son of a woman who was born here, and that I am staying in their chalet. But I remain as much a stranger today as I was the first day I arrived, and the children shout *Neger! Neger!* as I walk along the streets.

It must be admitted that in the beginning I was far too shocked to 4 have any real reaction. In so far as I reacted at all, I reacted by trying to be pleasant—it being a great part of the American Negro's education (long before he goes to school) that he must make people "like" him. This smile-and-the-world-smiles-with-you routine worked about as well in this situation as it had in the situation for which it was designed, which is to say that it did not work at all. No one, after all, can be liked whose human weight and complexity cannot be, or has not been, admitted. My smile was simply another unheard-of phenomenon which allowed them to see my teeth—they did not, really, see my smile and I began to think that, should I take to snarling, no one would notice any difference. All of the physical characteristics of the Negro which had caused me, in America, a very different and almost forgotten pain were nothing less than miraculous—or infernal—in the eyes of the village people. Some thought my hair was the color of tar, that it had the texture of wire, or the texture of cotton. It was jocularly suggested that I might let it all grow long and make myself a winter coat. If I sat in the sun for more than five minutes some daring creature was certain to come along and gingerly put his fingers on my hair, as though he were afraid of an electric shock, or put his hand on my hand, astonished that the color did not rub off. In all of this, in which it must be conceded there was the charm of genuine wonder and in which there was certainly no element of intentional unkindness, there was yet no suggestion that I was human: I was simply a living wonder.

5 I knew that they did not mean to be unkind, and I know it now; it is necessary, nevertheless, for me to repeat this to myself each time I walk out of the chalet. The children who shout *Neger!* have no way of knowing the echoes this sound raises in me. They are brimming with good humor and the more daring swell with pride when I stop to speak with them. Just the same, there are days when I cannot pause and smile, when I have no heart to play with them; when, indeed, I mutter sourly to myself, exactly as I muttered on the streets of a city these children have never seen, when I was no bigger than these children are now: *Your* mother *was a nigger.* Joyce is right about history being a nightmare—but it may be the nightmare from which no one *can* awaken. People are trapped in history and history is trapped in them.

6 There is a custom in the village—I am told it is repeated in many villages—of "buying" African natives for the purpose of converting them to Christianity. There stands in the church all year round a small box with a slot for money, decorated with a black figurine, and into this box the villagers drop their francs. During the *carnaval* which precedes Lent, two village children have their faces blackened—out of which bloodless darkness their blue eyes shine like ice—and fantastic horsehair wigs are placed on their blond heads; thus disguised, they solicit among the villagers for money for the missionaries in Africa. Between the box in the church and the blackened children, the village "bought" last year six or eight African natives. This was reported to me with pride by the wife of one of the *bistro* owners and I was careful to express astonishment and pleasure at the solicitude shown by the village for the souls of black folk. The *bistro* owner's wife beamed with a pleasure far more genuine than my own and seemed to feel that I might now breathe more easily concerning the souls of at least six of my kinsmen.

7 I tried not to think of these so lately baptized kinsmen, of the price paid for them, or the peculiar price they themselves would pay, and said nothing about my father, who having taken his own conversion too literally never, at bottom, forgave the white world (which he described as heathen) for having saddled him with a Christ in whom, to judge at least from their treatment of him, they themselves no longer believed. I thought of white men arriving for the first time in an African village, strangers there, as I am a stranger here, and tried to imagine the astounded populace touching their hair and marveling at the color of their skin. But there is a great difference between being the first white man to be seen by Africans and being the first black man to be seen by whites. The white man takes the astonishment as tribute, for he arrives to conquer and to convert the natives, whose inferiority in relation to himself is not even to be questioned; whereas I, without a thought of conquest, find myself among a people whose culture controls me, has even, in a sense, created me, people who have cost me more in anguish and rage than they will ever know, who yet do not even know of my existence. The astonishment with which I might have greeted them, should they have stumbled into my African village a few hundred years ago, might have rejoiced their hearts. But

the astonishment with which they greet me today can only poison mine.

And this is so despite everything I may do to feel differently, despite my friendly conversations with the *bistro* owner's wife, despite their three-year-old son who has at last become my friend, despite the *saluts* and *bonsoirs* which I exchange with people as I walk, despite the fact that I know that no individual can be taken to task for what history is doing, or has done. I say that the culture of these people controls me—but they can scarcely be held responsible for European culture. America comes out of Europe, but these people have never seen America nor have most of them seen more of Europe than the hamlet at the foot of their mountain. Yet they move with an authority which I shall never have; and they regard me, quite rightly, not only as a stranger in their village but as a suspect latecomer, bearing no credentials, to everything they have—however unconsciously—inherited.

9 For this village, even were it incomparably more remote and incredibly more primitive, is the West, the West onto which I have been so strangely grafted. These people cannot be, from the point of view of power, strangers anywhere in the world; they have made the modern world, in effect, even if they do not know it. The most illiterate among them is related, in a way that I am not, to Dante, Shakespeare, Michelangelo, Aeschylus, Da Vinci, Rembrandt, and Racine; the cathedral at Chartres says something to them which it cannot say to me, as indeed would New York's Empire State Building, should anyone here ever see it. Out of their hymns and dances come Beethoven and Bach. Go back a few centuries and they are in their full glory—but I am in Africa, watching the conquerors arrive.

10 The rage of the disesteemed is personally fruitless, but it is also absolutely inevitable; this rage, so generally discounted, so little understood even among the people whose daily bread it is, is one of the things that makes history. Rage can only with difficulty, and never entirely, be brought under the domination of the intelligence and is therefore not susceptible to any arguments whatever. This is a fact which ordinary representatives of the *Herrenvolk,* having never felt this rage and being unable to imagine it, quite fail to understand. Also, rage cannot be hidden, it can only be dissembled. This dissembling deludes the thoughtless, and strengthens rage and adds, to rage, contempt. There are, no doubt, as many ways of coping with the resulting complex of tensions as there are black men in the world, but no black man can hope ever to be entirely liberated from this internal warfare—rage, dissembling, and contempt having inevitably accompanied his first realization of the power of white men. What is crucial here is that, since white men represent in the black man's world so heavy a weight, white men have for black men a reality which is far from being reciprocal; and hence all black men have toward all white men an attitude which is designed, really, either to rob the white man of the jewel of his naïveté, or else to make it cost him dear.

The black man insists, by whatever means he finds at his disposal, that the white man cease to regard him as an exotic rarity and recognize him as a human being. This is a very charged and difficult moment, for there is a great deal of will power involved in the white man's naïveté. Most people are not naturally reflective any more than they are naturally malicious, and the white man prefers to keep the black man at a certain human remove because it is easier for him thus to preserve his simplicity and avoid being called to account for crimes committed by his forefathers, or his neighbors. He is inescapably aware, nevertheless, that he is in a better position in the world than black men are, nor can he quite put to death the suspicion that he is hated by black men therefore. He does not wish to be hated, neither does he wish to change places, and at this point in his uneasiness he can scarcely avoid having recourse to those legends which white men have created about black men, the most usual effect of which is that the white man finds himself enmeshed, so to speak, in his own language which describes hell, as well as the attributes which lead one to hell, as being as black as night. 11

Every legend, moreover, contains its residuum of truth, and the root function of language is to control the universe by describing it. It is of quite considerable significance that black men remain, in the imagination, and in overwhelming numbers in fact, beyond the disciplines of salvation; and this despite the fact the West has been "buying" African natives for centuries. There is, I should hazard, an instantaneous necessity to be divorced from this so visibly unsaved stranger, in whose heart, moreover, one cannot guess what dreams of vengeance are being nourished; and, at the same time, there are few things on earth more attractive than the idea of the unspeakable liberty which is allowed the unredeemed. When, beneath the black mask, a human being begins to make himself felt one cannot escape a certain awful wonder as to what kind of human being it is. What one's imagination makes of other people is dictated, of course, by the laws of one's own personality and it is one of the ironies of black-white relations that, by means of what the white man imagines the black man to be, the black man is enabled to know who the white man is. 12

I have said, for example, that I am as much a stranger in this village today as I was the first summer I arrived, but this is not quite true. The villagers wonder less about the texture of my hair than they did then, and wonder rather more about me. And the fact that their wonder now exists on another level is reflected in their attitudes and in their eyes. There are the children who make those delightful, hilarious, sometimes astonishingly grave overtures of friendship in the unpredictable fashion of children; other children, having been taught that the devil is a black man, scream in genuine anguish as I approach. Some of the older women never pass without a friendly greeting, never pass, indeed, if it seems that they will be able to engage me in conversation; other women look down or look away or rather contemptuously smirk. Some of the men drink with me and suggest that I learn how to ski—partly, I gather, 13 because they cannot imagine what I would look like on skis—and want to know if I am married, and ask questions about my *métier.* But some of the men have accused *le sale négre*—behind my back—of stealing wood and there is already in the eyes of some of them that peculiar, intent, paranoiac malevolence which one sometimes surprises in the eyes of American white men when, out walking with their Sunday girl, they see a Negro male approach.

There is a dreadful abyss between the streets of this village and the streets of the city in which I was born, between the children who shout *Neger!* today and those who shouted *Nigger!* yesterday—the abyss is experience, the American experience. The syllable hurled behind me today expresses, above all, wonder: I am a stranger here. But I am not a stranger in America and the same syllable riding on the American air expresses the war my presence has occasioned in the American soul. 14

For this village brings home to me this fact: that there was a day, and not really a very distant day, when Americans were scarcely Americans at all but discontented Europeans, facing a great unconquered continent and strolling, say, into a marketplace and seeing black men for the first time. The shock this spectacle afforded is suggested, surely, by the promptness with which they decided that these black men were not really men but cattle. It is true that the necessity on the part of the settlers of the New World of reconciling their moral assumptions with the fact—and the necessity—of slavery enhanced immensely the charm of this idea, and it is also true that this idea expresses, with a truly American bluntness, the attitude which to varying extents all masters have had toward all slaves. 15

But between all former slaves and slave-owners and the drama which begins for Americans over three hundred years ago at Jamestown, there are at least two differences to be observed. The American Negro slave could not suppose, for one thing, as slaves in past epochs had supposed and often done, that he would ever be able to wrest the power from his master's hands. This was a supposition which the modern era, which was to bring about such vast changes in the aims and dimensions of power, put to death; it only begins, in unprecedented fashion, and with dreadful implications, to be resurrected today. But even had this supposition persisted with undiminished force, the American Negro slave could not have used it to lend his condition dignity, for the reason that this supposition rests on another: that the slave in exile yet remains related to his past, has some means—if only in memory—of revering and sustaining the forms of his former life, is able, in short, to maintain his identity. 16

This was not the case with the American Negro slave. He is unique among the black men of the world in that his past was taken from him, almost literally, at one blow. One wonders what on earth the first slave found to say to the first dark child he bore. I am told that there are Haitians able to trace their ancestry back to African kings, but any American Negro wishing to go back so far will find his journey through time abruptly arrested by the signature on the bill of sale which served 17

as the entrance paper for his ancestor. At the time—to say nothing of the circumstances—of the enslavement of the captive black man who was to become the American Negro, there was not the remotest possibility that he would ever take power from his master's hands. There was no reason to suppose that his situation would ever change, nor was there, shortly, anything to indicate that his situation had ever been different. It was his necessity, in the words of E. Franklin Frazier, to find a "motive for living under American culture or die." The identity of the American Negro comes out of this extreme situation, and the evolution of this identity was a source of the most intolerable anxiety in the minds and the lives of his masters.

For the history of the American Negro is unique also in this: that 18
the question of his humanity, and of his rights therefore as a human being, became a burning one for several generations of Americans, so burning a question that it ultimately became one of those used to divide the nation. It is out of this argument that the venom of the epithet *Nigger!* is derived. It is an argument which Europe has never had, and hence Europe quite sincerely fails to understand how or why the argument arose in the first place, why its effects are so frequently disastrous and always so unpredictable, why it refuses until today to be entirely settled. Europe's black possessions remained—and do remain—in Europe's colonies, at which remove they represented no threat whatever to European identity. If they posed any problem at all for the European conscience, it was a problem which remained comfortingly abstract: in effect, the black man, *as a man,* did not exist for Europe. But in America, even as a slave, he was an inescapable part of the general social fabric and no American could escape having an attitude toward him. Americans attempt until today to make an abstraction of the Negro, but the very nature of these abstractions reveals the tremendous effects the presence of the Negro has had on the American character.

When one considers the history of the Negro in America it is of the 19
greatest importance to recognize that the moral beliefs of a person, or a people, are never really as tenuous as life—which is not moral—very often causes them to appear; these create for them a frame of reference and a necessary hope, the hope being that when life has done its worst they will be enabled to rise above themselves and to triumph over life. Life would scarcely be bearable if this hope did not exist. Again, even when the worst has been said, to betray a belief is not by any means to have put oneself beyond its power; the betrayal of a belief is not the same thing as ceasing to believe. If this were not so there would be no moral standards in the world at all. Yet one must also recognize that morality is based on ideas and that all ideas are dangerous—dangerous because ideas can only lead to action and where the action leads no man can say. And dangerous in this respect: that confronted with the impossibility of becoming free of them, one can be driven to the most inhuman excesses. The ideas on which American beliefs are based are not, though Americans often seem to think so, ideas which originated in America. They came out of Europe. And the establishment of

democracy on the American continent was scarcely as radical a break with the past as was the necessity, which Americans faced, of broadening this concept to include black men.

This was, literally, a hard necessity. It was impossible, for one thing, 20
for Americans to abandon their beliefs, not only because these beliefs alone seemed able to justify the sacrifices they had endured and the blood that they had spilled, but also because these beliefs afforded them their only bulwark against a moral chaos as absolute as the physical chaos of the continent it was their destiny to conquer. But in the situation in which Americans found themselves, these beliefs threatened an idea which, whether or not one likes to think so, is the very warp and woof of the heritage of the West, the idea of white supremacy.

Americans have made themselves notorious by the shrillness and 21
the brutality with which they have insisted on this idea, but they did not invent it; and it has escaped the world's notice that those very excesses of which Americans have been guilty imply a certain, unprecedented uneasiness over the idea's life and power, if not, indeed, the idea's validity. The idea of white supremacy rests simply on the fact that white men are the creators of civilization (the present civilization, which is the only one that matters; all previous civilizations are simply "contributions" to our own) and are therefore civilization's guardians and defenders. Thus it was impossible for Americans to accept the black man as one of themselves, for to do so was to jeopardize their status as white men. But not so to accept him was to deny his human reality, his human weight and complexity, and the strain of denying the overwhelmingly undeniable forced Americans into rationalizations so fantastic that they approached the pathological.

At the root of the American Negro problem is the necessity of the 22
American white man to find a way of living with the Negro in order to be able to live with himself. And the history of this problem can be reduced to the means used by Americans—lynch law and law, segregation and legal acceptance, terrorization and concession—either to come to terms with this necessity, or to find a way around it, or (most usually) to find a way of doing both these things at once. The resulting spectacle, at once foolish and dreadful, led someone to make the quite accurate observation that "the Negro-in-America is a form of insanity which overtakes white men."

In this long battle, a battle by no means finished, the unforeseeable 23
effects of which will be felt by many future generations, the white man's motive was the protection of his identity; the black man was motivated by the need to establish an identity. And despite the terrorization which the Negro in America endured and endures sporadically until today, despite the cruel and totally inescapable ambivalence of his status in his country, the battle for his identity has long ago been won. He is not a visitor to the West, but a citizen there, an American; as American as the Americans who despise him, the Americans who fear him, the Americans who love him—the Americans who became less than themselves, or rose to be greater than themselves by virtue of the fact that

the challenge he represented was inescapable. He is perhaps the only black man in the world whose relationship to white men is more terrible, more subtle, and more meaningful than the relationship of bitter possessed to uncertain possessor. His survival depended, and his development depends, on his ability to turn his peculiar status in the Western world to his own advantage and, it may be, to the very great advantage of that world. It remains for him to fashion out of his experience that which will give him sustenance, and a voice.

The cathedral at Chartres, I have said, says something to the people of this village which it cannot say to me; but it is important to understand that this cathedral says something to me which it cannot say to them. Perhaps they are struck by the power of the spires, the glory of the windows; but they have known God, after all, longer than I have known him, and in a different way, and I am terrified by the slippery bottomless well to be found in the crypt, down which heretics were hurled to death, and by the obscene, inescapable gargoyles jutting out of the stone and seeming to say that God and the devil can never be divorced. I doubt that the villagers think of the devil when they face a cathedral because they have never been identified with the devil. But I must accept the status which myth, if nothing else, gives me in the West before I can hope to change the myth. 24

Yet, if the American Negro has arrived at his identity by virtue of the absoluteness of his estrangement from his past, American white men still nourish the illusion that there is some means of recovering the European innocence, of returning to a state in which black men do not exist. This is one of the greatest errors Americans can make. The identity they fought so hard to protect has, by virtue of that battle, undergone a change: Americans are as unlike any other white people in the world as it is possible to be. I do not think, for example, that it is too much to suggest that the American vision of the world—which allows so little reality, generally speaking, for any of the darker forces in human life, which tends until today to paint moral issues in glaring black and white—owes a great deal to the battle waged by Americans to maintain between themselves and black men a human separation which could not be bridged. It is only now beginning to be borne in on us—very faintly, it must be admitted, very slowly, and very much against our will—that this vision of the world is dangerously inaccurate, and perfectly useless. For it protects our moral high-mindedness at the terrible expense of weakening our grasp of reality. People who shut their eyes to reality simply invite their own destruction, and anyone who insists on remaining in a state of innocence long after that innocence is dead turns himself into a monster. 25

The time has come to realize that the interracial drama acted out on the American continent has not only created a new black man, it has created a new white man, too. No road whatever will lead Americans back to the simplicity of this European village where white men still have the luxury of looking on me as a stranger. I am not, really, a stranger any longer for any American alive. One of the things that distinguishes Americans from other people is that no other people has 26 ever been so deeply involved in the lives of black men, and vice versa. This fact faced, with all its implications, it can be seen that the history of the American Negro problem is not merely shameful, it is also something of an achievement. For even when the worst has been said, it must also be added that the perpetual challenge posed by this problem was always, somehow, perpetually met. It is precisely this black-white experience which may prove of indispensable value to us in the world we face today. This world is white no longer, and it will never be white again.

COMPREHENSION

1. According to Baldwin, what distinguishes Americans from other people? What is his purpose in highlighting these differences?
2. What connections between Europe, Africa, and America emerge from this essay? What is the relevance of the Swiss village to this frame of reference?
3. In the context of the essay, explain what Baldwin means by his statement, "People are trapped in history and history is trapped in them" (paragraph 5).

RHETORIC

1. Analyze the effect of Baldwin's repetition of "there is" and "there are" constructions in paragraph 2. What does the parallelism at the start of paragraph 8 accomplish? Locate other examples of parallelism in the essay.
2. Analyze the image of winter in paragraph 3 and its relation to the rest of the essay.
3. Where in the essay is Baldwin's complex thesis condensed for the reader? What does this placement of thesis reveal about the logical method of development in the essay?
4. How does Baldwin create his introduction? What is the focus? What key motifs does the author present that will inform the rest of the essay? What is the relationship of paragraph 5 to paragraph 6?
5. What paragraphs constitute the second section of the essay? What example serves to unify this section? What major shift in emphasis occurs in the third part of the essay? Explain the cathedral of Chartres as a controlling motif between these two sections.
6. What comparisons and contrasts help to structure and unify the essay?

WRITING

1. Examine the paradox implicit in Baldwin's statement in the last paragraph that the American Negro problem is "something of an achievement."
2. Write an essay on civilization based on the last sentence in Baldwin's essay: "This world is white no longer, and it will never be white again."
3. Describe a time when you felt yourself a "stranger" in a certain culture.
4. In a comparative essay, analyze "Stranger in the Village" and Wright's "The Library Card" in Chapter 4.

WOODY ALLEN Allen Stewart Konigsberg (1935–), legally renamed Heywood Allen and known popularly as Woody Allen, is a comedian, actor, director, and writer for television, film, drama, and such national publications as *Playboy, The New Yorker,* and *Esquire.* His notable screenplays *Manhattan* (1979), *Zelig* (1984), *Hannah and Her Sisters* (1986), *Crimes and Misdemeanors* (1989), and *Annie Hall* (1977), a film that won the Academy Award, with Allen also taking honors for best director and, with Marshall Brickman, for best original screenplay. Allen's books, demonstrating the same comic genius as his best films, include *Getting Even* (1971), *Without Feathers* (1975), and *Side Effects* (1980). This essay is a parody of one graduation ritual as well as a satire on present civilization.

WOODY ALLEN

My Speech to the Graduates

More than any other time in history, mankind faces a crossroads. One path leads to despair and utter hopelessness. The other, to total extinction. Let us pray we have the wisdom to choose correctly. I speak, by the way, not with any sense of futility, but with a panicky conviction of the absolute meaninglessness of existence which could easily be misinterpreted as pessimism. It is not. It is merely a healthy concern for the predicament of modern man. (Modern man is here defined as any person born after Nietzche's edict that "God is dead," but before the hit recording "I Wanna Hold Your Hand.") This "predicament" can be stated in one of two ways, though certain linguistic philosophers prefer to reduce it to a mathematical equation where it can be easily solved and even carried around in the wallet. 1

Put in its simplest form, the problem is: How is it possible to find meaning in a finite world given my waist and shirt size? This is a very difficult question when we realize that science has failed us. True, it has conquered many diseases, broken the genetic code, and even placed human beings on the moon, and yet when a man of 80 is left in a room with two 18-year-old cocktail waitresses nothing happens. Because the real problems never change. After all, can the human soul be glimpsed through a microscope? Maybe—but you'd definitely need one of those very good ones with two eyepieces. We know that the most advanced computer in the world does not have a brain as sophisticated as that of an ant. True, we could say that of many of our relatives but we only have to put up with them at weddings or special occasions. Science is something we depend on all the time. If I develop a pain in the chest I must take an X-ray. But what if the radiation from the X-ray causes me deeper problems? Before I know it, I'm in for surgery. Naturally, while 2

they're giving me oxygen an intern decides to light up a cigarette. The next thing you know I'm rocketing over the World Trade Center in bedclothes. Is this science? True, science has taught us how to pasteurize cheese. And true, this can be fun in mixed company—but what of the H-bomb? Have you ever seen what happens when one of those things falls off a desk accidentally? And where is science when one ponders the eternal riddles? How did the cosmos originate? How long has it been around? Did matter begin with an explosion or by the word of God? And if by the latter, could He not have begun it just two weeks earlier to take advantage of some of the warmer weather? Exactly what do we mean when we say man is mortal? Obviously it's not a compliment.

Religion, too, has unfortunately let us down. Miguel de Unamuno writes blithely of the "eternal persistence of consciousness," but that is no easy feat. Particularly when reading Thackeray. I often think how comforting life must have been for early man because he believed in a powerful, benevolent Creator who looked after all things. Imagine his disappointment when he saw his wife putting on weight. Contemporary man, of course, has no such peace of mind. He finds himself in the midst of a crisis of faith. He is what we fashionably call "alienated." He has seen the ravages of war, he has known natural catastrophes, he has been to singles bars. My good friend Jacques Monod spoke often of the randomness of the cosmos. He believed everything in existence occurred by pure chance with the possible exception of his breakfast, which he felt certain was made by his housekeeper. Naturally belief in a divine intelligence inspires tranquillity. But this does not free us from our human responsibilities. Am I my brother's keeper? Yes. Interestingly, in my case I share that honor with the Prospect Park Zoo. Feeling godless then, what we have done is made technology God. And yet can technology really be the answer when a brand new Buick, driven by my close associate, Nat Persky, winds up in the window of Chicken Delight causing hundreds of customers to scatter? My toaster has never once worked properly in four years. I follow the instructions and push two slices of bread down in the slots and seconds later they rifle upward. Once they broke the nose of a woman I loved very dearly. Are we counting on nuts and bolts and electricity to solve our problems? Yes, the telephone is a good thing—and the refrigerator—and the air conditioner. But not every air conditioner. Not my sister Henny's, for instance. Hers makes a loud noise and still doesn't cool. When the man comes over to fix it, it gets worse. Either that or he tells her she needs a new one. When she complains, he says not to bother him. This man is truly alienated. Not only is he alienated but he can't stop smiling. 3

The trouble is, our leaders have not adequately prepared us for a mechanized society. Unfortunately our politicians are either incompetent or corrupt. Sometimes both on the same day. The Government is unresponsive to the needs of the little man. Under five-seven, it is impossible to get your Congressman on the phone. I am not denying that democracy is still the finest form of government. In a democracy at 4

least, civil liberties are upheld. No citizen can be wantonly tortured, imprisoned, or made to sit through certain Broadway shows. And yet this is a far cry from what goes on in the Soviet Union. Under their form of totalitarianism, a person merely caught whistling is sentenced to 30 years in a labor camp. If, after 15 years, he still will not stop whistling they shoot him. Along with this brutal fascism we find its handmaiden, terrorism. At no other time in history has man been so afraid to cut into his veal chop for fear that it will explode. Violence breeds more violence and it is predicted that by 1990 kidnapping will be the dominant mode of social interaction. Overpopulation will exacerbate problems to the breaking point. Figures tell us there are already more people on earth than we need to move even the heaviest piano. If we do not call a halt to breeding, by the year 2000 there will be no room to serve dinner unless one is willing to set the table on the heads of strangers. Then they must not move for an hour while we eat. Of course energy will be in short supply and each car owner will be allowed only enough gasoline to back up a few inches.

Instead of facing these challenges we turn to distractions like drugs 5
and sex. We live in far too permissive a society. Never before has pornography been this rampant. And those films are lit so badly! We are a people who lack defined goals. We have never learned to love. We lack leaders and coherent programs. We have no spiritual center. We are adrift in the cosmos wreaking monstrous violence on one another out of frustration and pain. Fortunately, we have not lost our sense of proportion. Summing up, it is clear the future holds great opportunities. It also holds pitfalls. The trick will be to avoid the pitfalls, seize the opportunities, and get back home by six o'clock.

COMPREHENSION

1. For what purpose does Allen adopt a comic tone? How does this tone suit his audience?
2. Explain the author's comic attitude toward science, religion, and politics. What specific subjects does he ridicule?
3. Beneath the surface of comedy in the essay, we can infer that Allen is concerned with the modern "predicament." Cite examples to support this judgment.

RHETORIC

1. What purpose does the author's allusion to Nietzche, Unamuno, and Monod serve?
2. Does the author use understatement or overstatement in his ironic language? Explain by reference to the essay.
3. What is the relationship of the title to the substance of the essay? Does the author, in his introduction, give any appearance of writing seriously? How

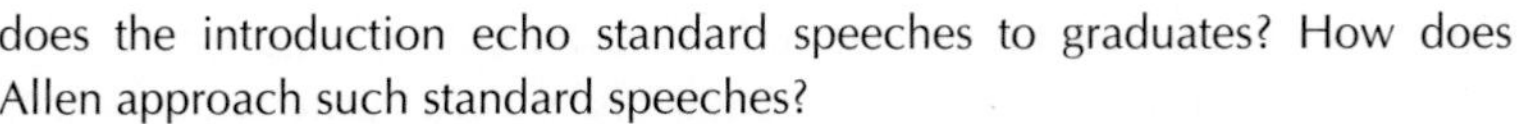

does the introduction echo standard speeches to graduates? How does Allen approach such standard speeches?

4. What role does logic, either inductive or deductive, play within the pattern of the essay?
5. In what manner does the pattern of cause and effect heighten the irony in the essay?
6. Examine the substance and structure of Allen's "summing up" in the last paragraph.

WRITING

1. Does Allen's variety of humor seem too slapstick or too strained? Explain in a brief essay.
2. Write your own comic speech to the graduates.
3. Satirize one aspect of contemporary college life.

MARTIN LUTHER KING, JR. Martin Luther King, Jr. (1929–1968) was born in Atlanta, Georgia, and earned degrees from Moorehouse College, Crozer Theological Seminary, Boston University, and Chicago Theological Seminary. As a Baptist clergyman, civil-rights leader, founder and president of the Southern Christian Leadership Council, and, in 1964, Nobel Peace Prize winner, King was a celebrated advocate of nonviolent resistance to achieve equality and racial integration in the world. King was a gifted orator and a highly persuasive writer. His books include *Letter from Birmingham City Jail* (1963), *Why We Can't Wait* (1964), *Stride Toward Freedom* (1958), *Strength to Love* (1963), and *Where Do We Go from Here: Chaos or Community?* (1967), a book published shortly before he was assassinated on April 4, 1968, in Memphis, Tennessee. In "The World House," a section from his last book, King uses analogy to promote his long-standing vision of a peaceful and united world civilization.

MARTIN LUTHER KING, JR.

The World House

Some years ago a famous novelist died. Among his papers was found a list of suggested plots for future stories, the most prominently underscored being this one: "A widely separated family inherits a house in which they have to live together." This is the great new problem of mankind. We have inherited a large house, a great "world house" in which we have to live together—black and white, Easterner and Westerner, Gentile and Jew, Catholic and Protestant, Moslem and 1

Hindu—a family unduly separated in ideas, culture and interest, who, because we can never again live apart, must learn somehow to live with each other in peace.

2 However deeply American Negroes are caught in the struggle to be at last at home in our homeland of the United States, we cannot ignore the larger world house in which we are also dwellers. Equality with whites will not solve the problem of either whites or Negroes if it means equality in a world society stricken by poverty and in a universe doomed to extinction by war.

3 All inhabitants of the globe are now neighbors. This world-wide neighborhood has been brought into being largely as a result of the modern scientific and technological revolutions. The world of today is vastly different from the world of just one hundred years ago. A century ago Thomas Edison had not yet invented the incandescent lamp to bring light to many dark places of the earth. The Wright brothers had not yet invented that fascinating mechanical bird that would spread its gigantic wings across the skies and soon dwarf distance and place time in the service of man. Einstein had not yet challenged an axiom and the theory of relativity had not yet been posited.

4 Human beings, searching a century ago as now for better understanding, had no television, no radios, no telephones and no motion pictures through which to communicate. Medical science had not yet discovered the wonder drugs to end many dread plagues and diseases. One hundred years ago military men had not yet developed the terrifying weapons of warfare that we know today—not the bomber, an airborne fortress raining down death; nor napalm, that burner of all things and flesh in its path. A century ago there were no skyscraping buildings to kiss the stars and no gargantuan bridges to span the waters. Science had not yet peered into the unfathomable ranges of interstellar space, nor had it penetrated oceanic depths. All these new inventions, these new ideas, these sometimes fascinating and sometimes frightening developments came later. Most of them have come within the past sixty years, sometimes with agonizing slowness, more characteristically with bewildering speed, but always with enormous significance for our future.

5 The years ahead will see a continuation of the same dramatic developments. Physical science will carve new highways through the stratosphere. In a few years astronauts and cosmonauts will probably walk comfortably across the uncertain pathways of the moon. In two or three years it will be possible, because of the new supersonic jets, to fly from New York to London in two and one-half hours. In the years ahead medical science will greatly prolong the lives of men by finding a cure for cancer and deadly heart ailments. Automation and cybernation will make it possible for working people to have undreamed-of amounts of leisure time. All this is a dazzling picture of the furniture, the workshop, the spacious rooms, the new decorations and the architectural pattern of the large world house in which we are living.

6 Along with the scientific and technological revolution, we have also

witnessed a world-wide freedom revolution over the last few decades. The present upsurge of the Negro people of the United States grows out of a deep and passionate determination to make freedom and equality a reality "here" and "now." In one sense the civil rights movement in the United States is a special American phenomenon which must be understood in the light of American history and dealt with in terms of the American situation. But on another and more important level, what is happening in the United States today is a significant part of a world development.

We live in a day, said the philosopher Alfred North Whitehead, 7
"when civilization is shifting its basic outlook; a major turning point in history where the pre-suppositions on which society is structured are being analyzed, sharply challenged, and profoundly changed." What we are seeing now is a freedom explosion, the realization of "an idea whose time has come," to use Victor Hugo's phrase. The deep rumbling of discontent that we hear today is the thunder of disinherited masses, rising from dungeons of oppression to the bright hills of freedom. In one majestic chorus the rising masses are singing, in the words of our freedom song, "Ain't gonna let nobody turn us around." All over the world like a fever, freedom is spreading in the widest liberation movement in history. The great masses of people are determined to end the exploitation of their races and lands. They are awake and moving toward their goal like a tidal wave. You can hear them rumbling in every village street, on the docks, in the houses, among the students, in the churches and at political meetings. For several centuries the direction of history flowed from the nations and societies of Western Europe out into the rest of the world in "conquests" of various sorts. That period, the era of colonialism, is at an end. East is moving West. The earth is being redistributed. Yes, we are "shifting our basic outlooks."

These developments should not surprise any student of history. 8
Oppressed people cannot remain oppressed forever. The yearning for freedom eventually manifests itself. The Bible tells the thrilling story of how Moses stood in Pharaoh's court centuries ago and cried, "Let my people go." This was an opening chapter in a continuing story. The present struggle in the United States is a later chapter in the same story. Something within has reminded the Negro of his birthright of freedom, and something without has reminded him that it can be gained. Consciously or unconsciously, he has been caught up by the spirit of the times, and with his black brothers of Africa and his brown and yellow brothers in Asia, South America and the Caribbean, the United States Negro is moving with a sense of great urgency toward the promised land of racial justice.

Nothing could be more tragic than for men to live in these revolu- 9
tionary times and fail to achieve the new attitudes and the new mental outlooks that the new situation demands. In Washington Irving's familiar story of Rip Van Winkle, the one thing that we usually remember is that Rip slept twenty years. There is another important point, however, that is almost always overlooked. It was the sign on the inn in the little

town on the Hudson from which Rip departed and scaled the mountain for his long sleep. When he went up, the sign had a picture of King George III of England. When he came down, twenty years later, the sign had a picture of George Washington. As he looked at the picture of the first President of the United States, Rip was confused, flustered and lost. He knew not who Washington was. The most striking thing about this story is not that Rip slept twenty years, but that he slept through a revolution that would alter the course of human history.

One of the great liabilities of history is that all too many people fail 10
to remain awake through great periods of social change. Every society has its protectors of the status quo and its fraternities of the indifferent who are notorious for sleeping through revolutions. But today our very survival depends on our ability to stay awake, to adjust to new ideas, to remain vigilant and to face the challenge of change. The large house in which we live demands that we transform this world-wide neighborhood into a world-wide brotherhood. Together we must learn to live as brothers or together we will be forced to perish as fools.

We must work passionately and indefatigably to bridge the gulf be- 11
tween our scientific progress and our moral progress. One of the great problems of mankind is that we suffer from a poverty of the spirit which stands in glaring contrast to our scientific and technological abundance. The richer we have become materially, the poorer we have become morally and spiritually.

Every man lives in two realms, the internal and the external. The in- 12
ternal is that realm of spiritual ends expressed in art, literature, morals and religion. The external is that complex of devices, techniques, mechanisms and instrumentalities by means of which we live. Our problem today is that we have allowed the internal to become lost in the external. We have allowed the means by which we live to outdistance the ends for which we live. So much of modern life can be summarized in that suggestive phrase of Thoreau: "Improved means to an unimproved end." This is the serious predicament, the deep and haunting problem, confronting modern man. Enlarged material powers spell enlarged peril if there is not proportionate growth of the soul. When the external of man's nature subjugates the internal, dark storm clouds begin to form.

Western civilization is particularly vulnerable at this moment, for our 13
material abundance has brought us neither peace of mind nor serenity of spirit. An Asian writer has portrayed our dilemma in candid terms:

> You call your thousand material devices "labor-saving machinery," yet you are forever "busy." With the multiplying of your machinery you grow increasingly fatigued, anxious, nervous, dissatisfied. Whatever you have, you want more; and wherever you are you want to go somewhere else . . . your devices are neither time-saving nor soul-saving machinery. They are so many sharp spurs which urge you on to invent more machinery and to do more business.*

*Abraham Mitrie Rihbany, *Wise Men from the East and from the West,* Houghton, Mifflin, 1922.

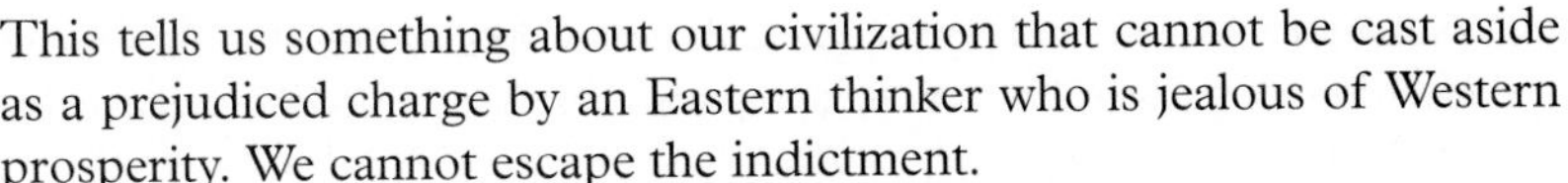

This tells us something about our civilization that cannot be cast aside as a prejudiced charge by an Eastern thinker who is jealous of Western prosperity. We cannot escape the indictment.

This does not mean that we must turn back the clock of scientific progress. No one can overlook the wonders that science has wrought for our lives. The automobile will not abdicate in favor of the horse and buggy, or the train in favor of the stagecoach, or the tractor in favor of the hand plow, or the scientific method in favor of ignorance and superstition. But our moral and spiritual "lag" must be redeemed. When scientific power outruns moral power, we end up with guided missiles and misguided men. When we foolishly minimize the internal of our lives and maximize the external, we sign the warrant for our own day of doom.

Our hope for creative living in this world house that we have inher- 15
ited lies in our ability to re-establish the moral ends of our lives in personal character and social justice. Without this spiritual and moral reawakening we shall destroy ourselves in the misuse of our own instruments.

COMPREHENSION

1. What does the author mean by the concept of a "world house"? How is the modern era drawing the peoples of the world together? How does King explain the dangers confronting the world house? What is his proposal for "creative living"?
2. According to King, what are the two "realms" that we live in? How are these realms reflected in the content of this selection?
3. Explain the connection that King draws between oppression, freedom, and revolution.

RHETORIC

1. King, a compelling preacher and speaker (see his "I Have a Dream" speech in Chapter 6, a contemporary classic delivered in 1963 at the end of the March on Washington), often delivered his prose in biblical and oratorical rhythms. Find three examples of rhythmical, carefully balanced cadences in this essay, and explain their effect. Compare these rhythms with those in "I Have a Dream."
2. A second characteristic of King's oratorical and literary style is his fondness for figurative language. Locate and identify five examples of figurative language.
3. What is King's thesis? How does the key rhetorical strategy of analogy help to advance it? What minor analogies exist in the essay?
4. Describe King's relationship with his reading audience. Identify words and phrases that clarify this relationship. Why, for example, does the author use the pronoun *we?*
5. How do the first and last paragraphs serve as a frame for this selection? How effective are they? Why?

6. What argumentative and persuasive techniques do you detect in this essay? How does King use illustration, comparison, and contrast to advance his proposition?

WRITING

1. Comment on the relevance of King's analogy to the 1990s.
2. Write a paper on "the world house," using contemporary events, quotations from authorities, and your own ideas about today's conflicts to frame the analogy.
3. Using Whitehead's quotation (paragraph 7) as a guide, develop an argumentative essay on whether we are at a turning point in civilization.

CLASSIC AND CONTEMPORARY

OLIVER GOLDSMITH Oliver Goldsmith (1730–1774), the son of an Anglican curate, was an Anglo-Irish essayist, poet, novelist, dramatist, and journalist. His reputation as an enduring figure in English literature is based on his novel, *The Vicar of Wakefield* (1766); his play, *She Stoops to Conquer* (1773); his major peom, *The Deserted Village* (1770); and the essays and satiric letters collected in *The Bee* (1759) and *The Citizen of the World* (1762). In this essay, Goldsmith argues quietly for a new type of citizen, one who can transcend the xenophobia governing national behavior.

OLIVER GOLDSMITH

National Prejudices

As I am one of that sauntering tribe of mortals, who spend the greatest part of their time in taverns, coffee houses, and other places of public resort, I have thereby an opportunity of observing an infinite variety of characters, which, to a person of a contemplative turn, is a much higher entertainment than a view of all the curiosities of art or nature. In one of these, my late rambles, I accidentally fell into the company of half a dozen gentlemen, who were engaged in a warm dispute about some political affair; the decision of which, as they were equally divided in their sentiments, they thought proper to refer to me, which naturally drew me in for a share of the conversation. 1

Amongst a multiplicity of other topics, we took occasion to talk of the different characters of the several nations of Europe; when one of the gentlemen, cocking his hat, and assuming such an air of importance as if he had possessed all the merit of the English nation in his own person, declared that the Dutch were a parcel of avaricious wretches; the French a set of flattering sycophants; that the Germans were drunken sots, and beastly gluttons; and the Spaniards proud, haughty, and surly tyrants; but that in bravery, generosity, clemency, and in every other virtue, the English excelled all the rest of the world. 2

This very learned and judicious remark was received with a general smile of approbation by all the company—all, I mean, but your humble servant; who, endeavoring to keep my gravity as well as I could, and reclining my head upon my arm, continued for some time in a posture of affected thoughtfulness, as if I had been musing on something else, and did not seem to attend to the subject of conversation; hoping by these means to avoid the disagreeable necessity of explaining myself, and thereby depriving the gentleman of his imaginary happiness. 3

But my pseudo-patriot had no mind to let me escape so easily. Not satisfied that his opinion should pass without contradiction, he was determined to have it ratified by the suffrage of every one in the company; for which purpose addressing himself to me with an air of inexpressible confidence, he asked me if I was not of the same way of thinking. As I am never forward in giving my opinion, especially when I have reason to believe that it will not be agreeable; so, when I am obliged to give it, I always hold it for a maxim to speak my real sentiments. I therefore told him that, for my own part, I should not have ventured to talk in such a peremptory strain, unless I had made the tour of Europe, and examined the manners of these several nations with great care and accuracy: that, perhaps, a more impartial judge would not scruple to affirm that the Dutch were more frugal and industrious, the French more temperate and polite, the Germans more hardy and patient of labour and fatigue, and the Spaniards more staid and sedate, than the English; who, though undoubtedly brave and generous, were at the same time rash, headstrong, and impetuous; too apt to be elated with prosperity, and to despond in adversity. 4

I could easily perceive that all the company began to regard me with a jealous eye before I had finished my answer, which I had no sooner done, than the patriotic gentleman observed, with a contemptuous sneer, that he was greatly surprised how some people could have the conscience to live in a country which they did not love, and to enjoy the protection of a government, to which in their hearts they were inveterate enemies. Finding that by this modest declaration of my sentiments I had forfeited the good opinion of my companions, and given them occasion to call my political principles in question, and well knowing that it was in vain to argue with men who were so very full of themselves, I threw down my reckoning and retired to my own lodgings, reflecting on the absurd and ridiculous nature of national prejudice and prepossession. 5

Among all the famous sayings of antiquity, there is none that does greater honour to the author, or affords greater pleasure to the reader (at least if he be a person of a generous and benevolent heart), than that of the philosopher, who, being asked what "countryman he was," replied, that he was, "a citizen of the world."—How few are there to be found in modern times who can say the same, or whose conduct is consistent with such a profession!—We are now become so much Englishmen, Frenchmen, Dutchmen, Spaniards, or Germans, that we are no longer citizens of the world; so much the natives of one particular spot, or members of one petty society, that we no longer consider ourselves as the general inhabitants of the globe, or members of that grand society which comprehends the whole human kind. 6

Did these prejudices prevail only among the meanest and lowest of the people, perhaps they might be excused, as they have few, if any, opportunities of correcting them by reading, travelling, or conversing with foreigners; but the misfortune is, that they infect the minds, and influence the conduct, even of our gentlemen; of those, I mean, who have 7 every title to this appellation but an exemption from prejudice, which however, in my opinion, ought to be regarded as the characteristical mark of a gentleman; for let a man's birth be ever so high, his station ever so exalted, or his fortune ever so large, yet if he is not free from national and other prejudices, I should make bold to tell him, that he had a low and vulgar mind, and had no just claim to the character of a gentleman. And in fact, you will always find that those are most apt to boast of national merit, who have little or no merit of their own to depend on; than which, to be sure, nothing is more natural: the slender vine twists around the sturdy oak, for no other reason in the world but because it has not strength sufficient to support itself.

Should it be alleged in defense of national prejudice, that it is the natural and necessary growth of love to our country, and that therefore the former cannot be destroyed without hurting the latter, I answer, that this is a gross fallacy and delusion. That it is the growth of love to our country, I will allow; but that it is the natural and necessary growth of it, I absolutely deny. Superstition and enthusiasm too are the growth of religion; but who ever took it in his head to affirm that they are the necessary growth of this noble principle? They are, if you will, the bastard sprouts of this heavenly plant, but not its natural and genuine branches, and may safely enough be lopped off, without doing any harm to the parent stock; nay, perhaps, till once they are lopped off, this goodly tree can never flourish in perfect health and vigour. 8

Is it not very possible that I may love my own country, without hating the natives of other countries? that I may exert the most heroic bravery, the most undaunted resolution, in defending its laws and liberty, without despising all the rest of the world as cowards and poltroons? Most certainly it is; and if it were not—But why need I suppose what is absolutely impossible?—But if it were not, I must own, I should prefer the title of the ancient philosopher, viz. a citizen of the world, to that of an Englishman, a Frenchman, a European, or to any other appellation whatever. 9

COMPREHENSION

1. Why does Goldsmith maintain that he is "a citizen of the world"? According to the author, could such an individual also be a patriot? Explain.
2. What connection does Goldsmith make between national prejudices and the conduct of gentlemen? Why does he allude to the manners of gentlemen?
3. Compare and contrast Goldsmith's observations with those of Priestley in "Wrong Ism" (Chapter 6).

RHETORIC

1. Locate in the essay examples of the familiar style in writing. What is the relationship between this style and the tone and substance of the essay?
2. Explain the metaphors at the end of paragraphs 7 and 8.

3. What is the relevance of the introductory narrative, with its description of characters, to the author's declaration of thesis? Where does the author state his proposition concerning national prejudices?
4. Analyze the function of classification and contrast in paragraphs 2 to 5. How does the entire essay serve as a pattern of definition?
5. Examine the pattern of reasoning involved in the author's presentation of his argument in the essay, notably in paragraphs 6 to 8. What appeals to emotion and to reason does he make?
6. Assess the rhetorical effectiveness of Goldsmith's concluding paragraph.

WRITING

1. Why has it been difficult to eliminate the problem that Goldsmith posed in 1762? Are we better able today to function as citizens of the world? In what ways? What role does the United Nations play in this issue? What factors contribute to a new world citizenry? Explore these questions in an essay.
2. Write an argumentative essay on the desirability of world government or on the need to be a citizen of the world.
3. Write a paper on contemporary national prejudices—from the viewpoint of an ingenious foreigner.

MARGARET ATWOOD Margaret Atwood (1939–) is a Canadian-born poet, novelist, short-story writer, and critic whose work explores the role of personal consciousness in a troubled world. While her second collection of poems, *The Circle Game* (1966), brought her recognition, she is also well known for her novels, which include *Surfacing* (1973), *Life before Man* (1979), *The Handmaid's Tale* (1986), and *Cat's Eye* (1988). Atwood is interested in the complexities of language, and her subjects range from the personal to the global. In the following piece from *Mother Jones Magazine,* Atwood draws a provocative parallel between male behavior and the American influence in Canada.

MARGARET ATWOOD

Canadians: What Do They Want?

Last month, during a poetry reading, I tried out a short prose poem called "How to Like Men." It began by suggesting that one start with the feet. Unfortunately, the question of jackboots soon arose, and things went on from there. After the reading I had a conversation with a young man who thought I had been unfair to men. He wanted men to be liked totally, not just from the heels to the knees, and not just as individuals but as a group; and he thought it negative and inegalitarian of me to have alluded to war and rape. I pointed out that as far as any of us knew these were two activities not widely engaged in by women, but he was still upset. "We're both in this together," he protested. I admit- 1 ted that this was so; but could he, maybe, see that our relative positions might be a little different.

This is the conversation one has with Americans, even, uh, *good* 2
Americans, when the dinner-table conversation veers round to Canadian-American relations. "We're in this together," they like to say, especially when it comes to continental energy reserves. How do you *explain* to them, as delicately as possible, why they are not categorically beloved? It gets like the old Lifebuoy ads: even their best friends won't tell them. And Canadians are supposed to be their best friends, right? Members of the family?

Well, sort of. Across the river from Michigan, so near and yet so far, 3
there I was at the age of eight, reading *their* Donald Duck comic books (originated however by one of *ours*; yes, Walt Disney's parents were Canadian) and coming at the end to Popsicle Pete, who promised me the earth if only I would save wrappers, but took it all away from me again with a single asterisk: Offer Good Only in the United States. Some cynical members of the world community may be forgiven for thinking that the same asterisk is there, in invisible ink, on the Constitution and the Bill of Rights.

But quibbles like that aside, and good will assumed, how does one 4
go about liking Americans? Where does one begin? Or, to put it another way, why did the Canadian women lock themselves in the john during a '70s, "international" feminist conference being held in Toronto? Because the American sisters were being "imperialist," that's why.

But then, it's always a little naive of Canadians to expect that 5
Americans, of whatever political stamp, should stop being imperious. How can they? The fact is that the United States is an empire and Canada is to it as Gaul was to Rome.

It's hard to explain to Americans what it feels like to be a Canadian. 6
Pessimists among us would say that one has to translate the experience into their own terms and that this is necessary because Americans are incapable of thinking in any other terms—and this in itself is part of the problem. (Witness all those draft dodgers who went into culture shock when they discovered to their horror that Toronto was not Syracuse.)

Here is a translation: Picture a Mexico with a population ten times 7
larger than that of the United States. That would put it at about two billion. Now suppose that the official American language is Spanish, that 75 percent of the books Americans buy and 90 percent of the movies they see are Mexican, and that the profits flow across the border to Mexico. If an American does scrape it together to make a movie, the Mexicans won't let him show it in the States, because they own the distribution outlets. If anyone tries to change this ratio, not only the Mexicans but many fellow Americans cry "National chauvinism," or, even more effectively, "National socialism." After all, the American public prefers the Mexican product. It's what they're used to.

Retranslate and you have the current American-Canadian picture. 8
It's changed a little recently, not only on the cultural front. For instance, Canada, some think a trifle late, is attempting to regain control of its

own petroleum industry. Americans are predictably angry. They think of Canadian oil as *theirs*.

"What's mine is yours," they have said for years, meaning exports: "What's yours is mine" means ownership and profits. Canadians are supposed to do retail buying, not controlling, or what's an empire for? One could always refer Americans to history, particularly that of their own revolution. They objected to the colonial situation when they themselves were a colony; but then, revolution is considered one of a very few homegrown American products that definitely are not for export. 9

Objectively, one cannot become too self-righteous about this state of affairs. Canadians owned lots of things, including their souls, before World War II. After that they sold, some say because they had put too much into financing the war, which created a capital vacuum (a position they would not have been forced into if the Americans hadn't kept out of the fighting for so long, say the sore losers). But for whatever reason, capital flowed across the border in the '50s, and Canadians, traditionally sock-under-the-mattress hoarders, were reluctant to invest in their own country. Americans did it for them and ended up with a large part of it, which they retain to this day. In every sellout there's a seller as well as a buyer, and the Canadians did a thorough job of trading their birthright for a mess. 10

That's on the capitalist end, but when you turn to the trade union side of things you find much the same story, except that the sellout happened in the '30s under the banner of the United Front. Now Canadian workers are finding that in any empire the colonial branch plants are the first to close, and what could be a truly progressive labor movement has been weakened by compromised bargains made in international union headquarters south of the border. 11

Canadians are sometimes snippy to Americans at cocktail parties. They don't like to feel owned and they don't like having been sold. But what really bothers them—and it's at this point that the United States and Rome part company—is the wide-eyed innocence with which their snippiness is greeted. 12

Innocence becomes ignorance when seen in the light of international affairs, and though ignorance is one of the spoils of conquest—the Gauls always knew more about the Romans than the Romans knew about them—the world can no longer afford America's ignorance. Its ignorance of Canada, though it makes Canadians bristle, is a minor and relatively harmless example. More dangerous is the fact that individual Americans seem not to know that the United States is an imperial power and is behaving like one. They don't want to admit that empires dominate, invade and subjugate—and live on the proceeds—or, if they do admit it, they believe in their divine right to do so. The export of divine right is much more harmful than the export of Coca-Cola, though they may turn out to be much the same thing in the end. 13

Other empires have behaved similarly (the British somewhat better, Genghis Khan decidedly worse); but they have not expected to be *liked* for it. It's the final Americanism, this passion for being liked. Alas, 14

many Americans are indeed likable; they are often more generous, more welcoming, more enthusiastic, less picky and sardonic than Canadians, and it's not enough to say it's only because they can afford it. Some of that revolutionary spirit still remains: the optimism, the eighteenth-century belief in the fixability of almost anything, the conviction of the possibility of change. However, at cocktail parties and elsewhere one must be able to tell the difference between an individual and a foreign policy. Canadians can no longer afford to think of Americans as only a spectator sport. If Reagan blows up the world, we will unfortunately be doing more than watching it on television. "No annihilation without representation" sounds good as a slogan, but if we run it up the flagpole, who's going to salute?

We *are* all in this together. For Canadians, the question is how to 15
survive it. For Americans there is no question, because there does not have to be. Canada is just that vague, cold place where their uncle used to go fishing, before the lakes went dead from acid rain.

How do you like Americans? Individually, it's easier. Your average 16
American is no more responsible for the state of affairs than your average man is for war and rape. Any Canadian who is so narrow-minded as to dislike Americans merely on principle is missing out on one of the good things in life. The same might be said, to women, of men. As a group, as a foreign policy, it's harder. But if you like men, you can like Americans. Cautiously. Selectively. Beginning with the feet. One at a time.

COMPREHENSION

1. Atwood makes a connection between men and an imperialistic America. How does the title help expand this link? Is this thread woven into the total essay?
2. How has Canada's sometimes reluctant connection to the United States imperiled its sense of identity? How does America's attitude continue to worsen the problem?
3. How does Atwood define the American character?

RHETORIC

1. Who is Atwood's intended audience? Does she expect a sympathetic reader? An antagonist? What in her language and approach suggest the answer to these questions?
2. Describe Atwood's tone in the essay. Provide evidence from her writing.
3. How does the comparative method serve to unify this essay? What points of comparison does Atwood draw?
4. What historical analogy recurs in Atwood's essay? How does it strengthen Atwood's contention? Why does she choose not to recount the event?

5. Comment on the writer's use of generalization in her essay. Cite an example of this, and critique Atwood's support of it.
6. How does Atwood bring the reader back to her original point? What effect do the final phrases in her conclusion have on the reader?

WRITING

1. Write a rebuttal essay defending America's forays into other countries. List the ways in which America has benefited Canada and other countries it has formed bonds with. How has American "imperialism" raised these countries' economy and standard of living? Use Atwood's article as it applies. Some research may be necessary.
2. Write an essay entitled "What's Wrong with Nationalism?" You may treat the topic in a tongue-in-cheek fashion, or you may approach it seriously.
3. Is America's influence on Canada's national identity and culture an example of Reed's "multinational society"? Explore this question in a brief essay. Use support from both essays.

CLASSIC AND CONTEMPORARY: QUESTIONS FOR COMPARISON

1. In his essay, Goldsmith argues against nationalism and professes to be a "citizen of the world." How does Atwood feel about the issue of nationalism? How do their arguments differ? Are they on the same side? Discuss how they approach the subject in their essays. Use examples from both to support your opinion.
2. Examine the language used by the two writers. How do they use figurative language? Who is the intended audience for each essay? How does the language used in each reflect this? Discuss the writing styles used, including vocabulary and syntax. Cite examples to support your responses.
3. Both writers use humor in their writing. What kind of humor does each use? Provide examples of humor in each essay, and consider how effectively it is used.

CONNECTIONS

1. How does a country maintain a strong sense of self and still remain open to outside influences? Is a national identity crucial to a country's survival? Use the opinions of Atwood, Reed, Naipaul, or Jhabvala to address the question.
2. In his essay, Naipaul expresses his belief that Muslims have been "stripped by their faith." How do his views of religion as an impediment to a "universal civilization" clash with Martin Luther King's overtly religious approach to the issue? Use support from both writers to compare and contrast their points of view.
3. Compare America's involvement in Canada's cultural and economic life to that of Europe's in India. What are the advantages and disadvantages of such a relationship?
4. How does Baldwin's contention that there is no longer a home to which the American white man can return illustrate Reed's rejection of the concept of a Western civilization?
5. Is there such a thing as a "national character," something that distinguishes an Indian from a European, an American from a Canadian? What factors contribute to this identification with country? Use the works of Jhabvala, Naipaul, and Atwood to explore this issue.
6. Although Woody Allen's essay uses a satirical approach to global problems, what concerns does he share with the other writers in this section?
7. Use the essays of Goldsmith, Naipaul, and King to explore the dangers of nationalism to a country's relation to its own people and the larger world. What are the consequences of a "monoculturalist" outlook?
8. Compare Baldwin's belief that the African American has only one home with King's dreams of a "world house." Have we yet achieved an "American House"? Where do the two writers come together on issues? Where do they differ?
9. Based on your reading of the essays in this chapter and throughout the anthology, write an extended definition of the term *civilization.*
10. Argue for or against the proposition that we are becoming a "one-world" civilization. Refer to the essays in this chapter to support your position.

Glossary of Terms

Abstract/concrete patterns of language reflect an author's word choice. Abstract words (for example, *wisdom, power, beauty*) refer to general ideas, qualities, or conditions. Concrete words name material objects and items associated with the five senses—words like *rock, pizza,* and *basketball.* Both abstract and concrete language are useful in communicating ideas. Generally you should not be too abstract in writing. It is best to employ concrete words, naming things that can be seen, touched, smelled, heard, or tasted in order to support generalizations, topic sentences, or more abstract ideas.

Acronym is a word formed from the first or first few letters of several words, as in OPEC (Organization of Petroleum Exporting Countries).

Action in narrative writing is the sequence of happenings or events. This movement of events may occupy just a few minutes or extend over a period of years or centuries.

Alliteration is the repetition of initial consonant sounds in words placed closely next to each other, as in "what a *t*ale of *t*error now their *t*urbulency *t*ells." Prose that is highly rhythmical or "poetic" often makes use of this method.

Allusion is a literary, biographical, or historical reference, whether real or imaginary. It is a "figure of speech" (a fresh, useful comparison) employed to illuminate an idea. A writer's prose style can be made richer through this economical method of evoking an idea or emotion, as in E. M. Forster's biblical allusion in this sentence: "Property produces men of weight, and it was a man of weight who failed to get into the Kingdom of Heaven."

Analogy is a form of comparison that uses a clear illustration to explain a difficult idea or function. It is unlike a formal comparison in that its subjects of comparison are from different categories or areas. For example, an analogy likening "division of labor" to the activity of bees in a hive makes the first concept more concrete by showing it to the reader through the figurative comparison with the bees. Analogy in exposition can involve a few sentences, a paragraph or set of paragraphs, or an entire essay. Analogies can also be used in argumentation to heighten an appeal to emotion, but they cannot actually *prove* anything.

Analysis is a method of exposition in which a subject is broken up into its parts so as to explain their nature, function, proportion, or relationship. Analysis thus explores connections and processes within the context of a given subject. (See *Causal Analysis* and *Process Analysis.*)

Anecdote is a brief, engaging account of some happening, often historical, biographical, or personal. As a technique in writing, anecdote is especially effective in creating interesting essay introductions and also in illuminating abstract concepts in the body of the essay.

Antecedent in grammar refers to the word, phrase, or clause to which a pronoun refers. In writing, antecedent also refers to any happening or thing that is prior to another, or to anything that logically precedes a subject.

Antithesis is the balancing of one idea or term against another for emphasis.

Antonym is a word whose meaning is opposite to that of another word.

Aphorism is a short, pointed statement expressing a general truism or idea in an original or imaginative way. Marshall McLuhan's statement that "the medium is the message" is a well-known contemporary aphorism.

Archaic language is vocabulary or usage that belongs to an early period and is old-fashioned today. A word like *thee* for *you* would be an archaism still in use in certain situations.

Archetypes are special images or symbols that, according to Carl Jung, appeal to the total racial or cultural understanding of a people. Such images or symbols as the mother archetype, the cowboy in American film, a sacred mountain, or spring as a time of renewal tend to trigger the "collective unconscious" of the human race.

Argumentation is a formal variety of writing that offers reasons for or against something. Its goal is to persuade or convince the reader through logical reasoning and carefully controlled emotional appeal. Argumentation as a formal mode of writing contains many properties that distinguish it from exposition. (See *Assumption, Deduction, Evidence, Induction, Logic, Persuasion, Proposition,* and *Refutation.*)

Assonance defined generally is likeness or rough similarity of sound. Its specific definition is a partial rhyme in which the stressed vowel sounds are alike but the consonant sounds are unlike, as in *late* and *make*. Although more common to poetry, assonance can also be detected in highly rhythmic prose.

Assumption in argumentation is anything taken for granted or presumed to be accepted by the audience and therefore unstated. Assumptions in argumentative writing can be dangerous because the audience might not always accept the idea implicit in them. (See *Begging the Question.*)

Audience is that readership toward which an author directs his or her essay. In composing essays, writers must acknowledge the nature of their expected readers—whether specialized or general, minimally educated or highly educated, sympathetic or unsympathetic toward the writer's opinions, and so forth. Failure to focus on the writer's true audience can lead to confusions in language and usage, presentation of inappropriate content, and failure to appeal to the expected reader.

Balance in sentence structure refers to the assignment of equal treatment in the arrangement of coordinate ideas. It is often used to heighten a contrast of ideas.

Begging the question is an error or fallacy in reasoning and argumentation in which the writer assumes as a truth something for which evidence or proof is actually needed.

Causal analysis is a form of writing that examines causes and effects of events or conditions as they relate to a specific subject. Writers can investigate the causes of a particular effect or the effects of a particular cause or combine both methods. Basically, however, causal analysis looks for connections between things and reasons behind them.

Characterization especially in narrative or descriptive writing is the creation of people involved in the action. Authors use techniques of dialogue, description, reportage, and observation in attempting to present vivid and distinctive characters.

Chronology or chronological order is the arrangement of events in the order in which they happened. Chronological order can be used in such diverse narrative situations as history, biography, scientific process, and personal account. Essays that are ordered by chronology move from one step or point to the next in time.

Cinematic technique in narration, description, and occasionally exposition is the conscious application of film art to the development of the contemporary essay. Modern writers often are aware of such film techniques as montage (the process of cutting and arranging film so that short scenes are presented in rapid succession), zoom (intense enlargement of subject), and various forms of juxtaposition, using these methods to enhance the quality of their essays.

Classification is a form of exposition in which the writer divides a subject into categories and then groups elements in each of those categories according to their relationships to each other. Thus a writer

using classification takes a topic, divides it into several major groups, and then often subdivides these groups, moving always from larger categories to smaller ones.

Cliché is an expression that once was fresh and original but has lost much of its vitality through overuse. Because terms like "as quick as a wink" and "blew her stack" are trite or common today, they should be avoided in writing.

Climactic ordering is the arrangement of a paragraph or essay so that the most important items are saved for last. The effect is to build slowly through a sequence of events or ideas to the most critical part of the composition.

Coherence is a quality in effective writing that results from the careful ordering of each sentence in a paragraph and each paragraph in the essay. If an essay is coherent, each part will grow naturally and logically from those parts that come before it. Following careful chronological, logical, spatial, or sequential order is the most natural way to achieve coherence in writing. The main devices used in achieving coherence are transitions, which help to connect one thought with another.

Colloquial language is conversational language used in certain types of informal and narrative writing but rarely in essays, business writing, or research writing. Expressions like "cool," "pal," or "I can dig it" often have a place in conversational settings. However, they should be used sparingly in essay writing for special effects.

Comparison/contrast as an essay pattern treats similarities and differences between two subjects. Any useful comparison involves two items from the same class. Moreover, there must be a clear reason for the comparison or contrast. Finally, there must be a balanced treatment of the various comparative or contrasting points between the two subjects.

Conclusions are the endings of essays. Without a conclusion, an essay would be incomplete, leaving the reader with the feeling that something important has been left out. There are numerous strategies for conclusions available to writers: summarizing main points in the essay, restating the main idea, using an effective quotation to bring the essay to an end, offering the reader the climax to a series of events, returning to the beginning and echoing it, offering a solution to a problem, emphasizing the topic's significance, or setting a new frame of reference by generalizing from the main thesis. A conclusion should end the essay in a clear, convincing, or emphatic way.

Concrete (See *Abstract/concrete*.)

Conflict in narrative writing is the clash or opposition of events, characters, or ideas that makes the resolution of action necessary.

Connotation/denotation are terms specifying the way a word has meaning. Connotation refers to the "shades of meaning" that a word might have because of various emotional associations it calls up for writers and readers alike. Words like *patriotism, pig,* and *rose* have strong con-

notative overtones to them. Denotation refers to the "dictionary" definition of a word—its exact meaning. Good writers understand the connotative and denotative value of words and must control the shades of meaning that many words possess.

Context is the situation surrounding a word, group of words, or sentence. Often the elements coming before or after a certain confusing or difficult construction will provide insight into the meaning or importance of that item.

Coordination in sentence structure refers to the grammatical arrangement of parts of the same order or equality in rank.

Declarative sentences make a statement or assertion.

Deduction is a form of logic that begins with a generally stated truth or principle and then offers details, examples, and reasoning to support the generalization. In other words, deduction is based on reasoning from a known principle to an unknown principle, from the general to the specific, or from a premise to a logical conclusion. (See *Syllogism.*)

Definition in exposition is the extension of a word's meaning through a paragraph or an entire essay. As an extended method of explaining a word, this type of definition relies on other rhetorical methods, including detail, illustration, comparison and contrast, and anecdote.

Denotation (See *Connotation/denotation.*)

Description in the prose essay is a variety of writing that uses details of sight, sound, color, smell, taste, and touch to create a word picture and to explain or illustrate an idea.

Development refers to the way a paragraph or essay elaborates or builds upon a topic or theme. Typical development proceeds either from general illustrations to specific ones or from one generalization to another. (See *Horizontal/vertical.*)

Dialogue is the reproduction of speech or conversation between two or more persons in writing. Dialogue can add concreteness and vividness to an essay and can also help to reveal character. A writer who reproduces dialogue in an essay must use it for a purpose and not simply as a decorative device.

Diction is the manner of expression in words, choice of words, or wording. Writers must choose vocabulary carefully and precisely to communicate a message and also to address an intended audience effectively; this is good diction.

Digression is a temporary departure from the main subject in writing. Any digression in the essay must serve a purpose or be intended for a specific effect.

Discourse (forms of) relates conventionally to the main categories of writing—narration, description, exposition, and argumentation. In practice, these forms of discourse often blend or overlap. Essayists seek the ideal fusion of forms of discourse in the treatment of their subject.

Division is that aspect of classification in which the writer divides some large subject into categories. Division helps writers to split large and potentially complicated subjects into parts for orderly presentation and discussion.

Dominant impression in description is the main impression or effect that writers attempt to create for their subject. It arises from an author's focus on a single subject and from the feelings the writer brings to that subject.

Editorialize is to express personal opinions about the subject of the essay. An editorial tone can have a useful effect in writing, but at other times an author might want to reduce editorializing in favor of a better balanced or more objective tone.

Effect is a term used in causal analysis to describe the outcome or expected result of a chain of happenings.

Emphasis indicates the placement of the most important ideas in key positions in the essay. As a major principle, emphasis relates to phrases, sentences, paragraphs—the construction of the entire essay. Emphasis can be achieved by repetition, subordination, careful positioning of thesis and topic sentences, climactic ordering, comparison and contrast, and a variety of other methods.

Episodic relates to that variety of narrative writing that develops through a series of incidents or events.

Essay is the name given to a short prose work on a limited topic. Essays take many forms, ranging from personal narratives to critical or argumentative treatments of a subject. Normally an essay will convey the writer's personal ideas about the subject.

Etymology is the origin and development of a word—tracing a word back as far as possible.

Evidence is material offered to support an argument or a proposition. Typical forms of evidence are facts, details, and expert testimony.

Example is a method of exposition in which the writer offers illustrations in order to explain a generalization or a whole thesis. (See *Illustration.*)

Exclamatory sentences in writing express surprise or strong emotion.

Expert testimony as employed in argumentative essays and in expository essays is the use of statements by authorities to support a writer's position or idea. This method often requires careful quotation and acknowledgment of sources.

Exposition is a major form of discourse that informs or explains. Exposition is the form of expression required in much college writing, for it provides facts and information, clarifies ideas, and establishes meaning. The primary methods of exposition are illustration, comparison and contrast, analogy, definition, classification, causal analysis, and process analysis (see entries).

Extended metaphor is a figurative comparison that is used to structure a significant part of the composition or the whole essay. (See *Figurative language* and *metaphor.*)

Fable is a form of narrative containing a moral that normally appears clearly at the end.

Fallacy in argumentation is an error in logic or the reasoning process. Fallacies occur because of vague development of ideas, lack of awareness on the part of writers of the requirements of logical reasoning, or faulty assumptions about the proposition.

Figurative language as opposed to literal language is a special approach to writing that departs from what is typically a concrete, straightforward style. It is the use of vivid, imaginative statements to illuminate or illustrate an idea. Figurative language adds freshness, meaning, and originality to a writer's style. Major figures of speech include allusion, hyperbole, metaphor, personification, and simile (see entries).

Flashback is a narrative technique in which the writer begins at some point in the action and then moves into the past in order to provide crucial information about characters and events.

Foreshadowing is a technique that indicates beforehand what is to occur at a later point in the essay.

Frame in narration and description is the use of a key object or pattern—typically at the start and end of the essay—that serves as a border or structure to contain the substance of the composition.

General/specific words are the basis of writing, although it is wise in college composition to keep vocabulary as specific as possible. General words refer to broad categories and groups, whereas specific words capture with force and clarity the nature of a term. General words refer to large classes, concepts, groups, and emotions; specific words are more particular in providing meanings. The distinction between general and specific language is always a matter of degree.

Generalization is a broad idea or statement. All generalizations require particulars and illustrations to support them.

Genre is a type or form of literature—for example, short fiction, novel, poetry, drama.

Grammatical structure is a systematic description of language as it relates to the grammatical nature of a sentence.

Horizontal/vertical paragraph and essay development refers to the basic way a writer moves either from one generalization to another in a carefully related series of generalizations (horizontal) or from a generalization to a series of specific supporting examples (vertical).

Hortatory style is a variety of writing designed to encourage, give advice, or urge to good deeds.

Hyperbole is a form of figurative language that uses exaggeration to overstate a position.

Hypothesis is an unproven theory or proposition that is tentatively accepted to explain certain facts. A working hypothesis provides the basis for further investigation or argumentation.

Hypothetical examples are illustrations in the form of assumptions that are based on the hypothesis. As such, they are conditional rather than absolute or certain facts.

Identification as a method of exposition refers to focusing on the main subject of the essay. It involves the clear location of the subject within the context or situation of the composition.

Idiomatic language is the language or dialect of a people, region, or class—the individual nature of a language.

Ignoring the question in argumentation is a fallacy that involves the avoidance of the main issue by developing an entirely different one.

Illustration is the use of one or more examples to support an idea. Illustration permits the writer to support a generalization through particulars or specifics.

Imagery is clear, vivid description that appeals to our sense of sight, smell, touch, sound, or taste. Much imagery exists for its own sake, adding descriptive flavor to an essay. However, imagery (especially when it involves a larger pattern) can also add meaning to an essay.

Induction is a method of logic consisting of the presentation of a series of facts, pieces of information, or instances in order to formulate or build a likely generalization. The key is to provide prior examples before reaching a logical conclusion. Consequently, as a pattern of organization in essay writing, the inductive method requires the careful presentation of relevant data and information before the conclusion is reached at the end of the paper.

Inference involves arriving at a decision or opinion by reasoning from known facts or evidence.

Interrogative sentences are sentences that ask or pose a question.

Introduction is the beginning or opening of an essay. The introduction should alert the reader to the subject by identifying it, set the limits of the essay, and indicate what the thesis (or main idea) will be. Moreover, it should arouse the reader's interest in the subject. Among the devices available in the creation of good introductions are making a simple statement of thesis; giving a clear, vivid description of an important setting; posing a question or series of questions; referring to a relevant historical event; telling an anecdote; using comparison and contrast to frame the subject; using several examples to reinforce the statement of the subject; and presenting a personal attitude about a controversial issue.

Irony is the use of language to suggest the opposite of what is stated. Writers use irony to reveal unpleasant or troublesome realities that exist in life or to poke fun at human weaknesses and foolish attitudes. In an

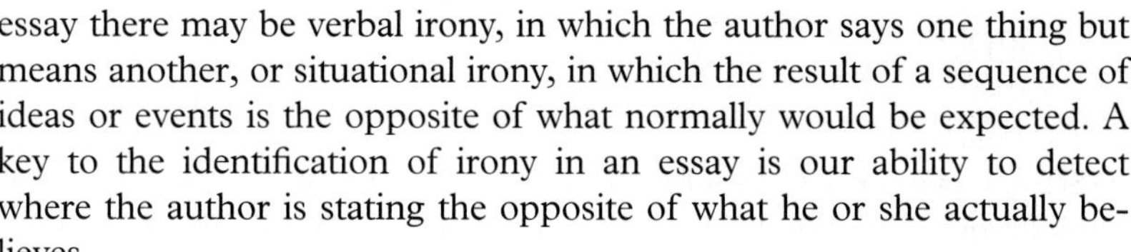

essay there may be verbal irony, in which the author says one thing but means another, or situational irony, in which the result of a sequence of ideas or events is the opposite of what normally would be expected. A key to the identification of irony in an essay is our ability to detect where the author is stating the opposite of what he or she actually believes.

Issue is the main question upon which an entire argument rests. It is the idea that the writer attempts to prove.

Jargon is the use of special words associated with a specific area of knowledge or a particular profession. Writers who employ jargon either assume that readers know specialized terms or take care to define terms for the benefit of the audience.

Juxtaposition as a technique in writing or essay organization is the placing of elements—either similar or contrasting—close together; positioning them side by side in order to illuminate the subject.

Levels of language refer to the kinds of language used in speaking and writing. Basically there are three main levels of language—formal, informal, and colloquial. Formal English, used in writing or speech, is the type of English employed to address special groups and professional people. Informal English is the sort of writing found in newspapers, magazines, books, and essays. It is popular English for an educated audience but still more formal than conversational English. Finally, colloquial English is spoken (and occasionally written) English used in conversations with friends, employees, and peer group members; it is characterized by the use of slang, idioms, ordinary language, and loose sentence structure.

Linear order in paragraph development means the clear line of movement from one point to another.

Listing is a simple technique of illustration in which facts or examples are used in order to support a topic or generalization.

Logic as applied to essay writing is correct reasoning based on induction or deduction. The logical basis of an essay must offer reasonable criteria or principles of thought, present these principles in an orderly manner, avoid faults in reasoning, and result in a complete and satisfactory outcome in the reasoning process.

Metaphor is a type of figurative language in which an item from one category is compared briefly and imaginatively with an item from another area. Writers use such implied comparisons to assign meaning in a fresh, vivid, and concrete way.

Metonymy is a figure of language in which a thing is not designated by its own name but by another associated with or suggested by it, as in "The Supreme Court has decided" (meaning that the judges of the Supreme Court have decided).

Mood is the creation of atmosphere in descriptive writing.

Motif in an essay is any series of components that can be detected as a pattern. For example, a particular detail, idea, or image can be elaborated upon or designed so as to form a pattern or motif in the essay.

Myth in literature is a traditional story or series of events explaining some basic phenomenon of nature; the origin of humanity; or the customs, institutions, and religious rites of a people. Myth often relates to the exploits of gods, goddesses, and heroes.

Narration as a form of essay writing is the presentation of a story in order to illustrate an idea.

Non sequitur in argumentation is a conclusion or inference that does not follow from the premises or evidence on which it is based. The *non sequitur* thus is a type of logical fallacy.

Objective/subjective writing refers to the attitude that writers take toward their subject. When writers are objective, they try not to report their personal feelings about the subject; they attempt to be detached, impersonal, and unbiased. Conversely, subjective writing reveals an author's personal attitudes and emotions. For many varieties of college writing, such as business or laboratory reports, term papers, and literary analyses, it is best to be as objective as possible. But for many personal essays in composition courses, the subjective touch is fine. In the hands of skilled writers, the objective and subjective tones often blend.

Onomatopoeia is the formation of a word by imitating the natural sound associated with the object or action, as in *buzz* or *click*.

Order is the arrangement of information or materials in an essay. The most common ordering techniques are *chronological order* (time in sequence); *spatial order* (the arrangement of descriptive details); *process order* (a step-by-step approach to an activity); *deductive order* (a thesis followed by information to support it); and *inductive order* (evidence and examples first, followed by the thesis in the form of a conclusion). Some rhetorical patterns such as comparison and contrast, classification, and argumentation require other ordering methods. Writers should select those ordering principles that permit them to present materials clearly.

Overstatement is an extravagant or exaggerated claim or statement.

Paradox is a statement that seems to be contradictory but actually contains an element of truth.

Paragraph is a unit in an essay that serves to present and examine one aspect of a topic. Composed normally of a group of sentences (one-sentence paragraphs can be used for emphasis or special effect), the paragraph elaborates an idea within the larger framework of the essay and the thesis unifying it.

Parallelism is a variety of sentence structure in which there is "balance" or coordination in the presentation of elements. "I came, I saw, I conquered" is a standard example of parallelism, presenting both pronouns and verbs in a coordinated manner. Parallelism can appear in a sentence, a group of sentences, or an entire paragraph.

Paraphrase as a literary method is the process of rewording the thought or meaning expressed in something that has been said or written before.

Parenthetical refers to giving qualifying information or explanation. This information normally is marked off or placed within parentheses.

Parody is ridiculing the language or style of another writer or composer. In parody, a serious subject tends to be treated in a nonsensical manner.

Periphrasis is the use of many words where one or a few would do; it is a roundabout way of speaking or writing.

Persona is the role or characterization that writers occasionally create for themselves in a personal narrative.

Personification is giving an object, thing, or idea lifelike or human characteristics, as in the common reference to a car as "she." Like all forms of figurative language, personification adds freshness to description and makes ideas vivid by setting up striking comparisons.

Persuasion is the form of discourse, related to argumentation, that attempts basically to move a person to action or to influence an audience toward a particular belief.

Point of view is the angle from which a writer tells a story. Many personal and informal essays take the *first-person* (or "I") point of view, which is natural and fitting for essays in which the author wants to speak in a familiar way to the reader. On the other hand, the *third-person* point of view ("he," "she," "it," "they") distances the reader somewhat from the writer. The third-person point of view is useful in essays in which the writers are not talking exclusively about themselves but about other people, ideas, and events.

Post hoc, ergo propter hoc in logic is the fallacy of thinking that a happening that follows another must be its results. It arises from a confusion about the logical causal relationship.

Process analysis is a pattern of writing that explains in a step-by-step way how something is done, how it is put together, how it works, or how it occurs. The subject can be a mechanical device, a product, an idea, a natural phenomenon, or a historical sequence. However, in all varieties of process analysis, the writer traces all important steps, from beginning to end.

Progression is the forward movement or succession of acts, events, or ideas presented in an essay.

Proportion refers to the relative emphasis and length given to an event, idea, time, or topic within the whole essay. Basically, in terms of proportion the writer gives more emphasis to a major element than to a minor one.

Proposition is the main point of an argumentative essay—the statement to be defended, proven, or upheld. It is like a *thesis* (see entry) except that it presents an idea that is debatable or can be disputed. The *major proposition* is the main argumentative point; *minor propositions* are the reasons given to support or prove the issue.

Purpose is what the writer wants to accomplish in an essay. Writers having a clear purpose will know the proper style, language, tone, and materials to utilize in designing an effective essay.

Refutation in argumentation is a method by which you recognize and deal effectively with the arguments of your opponents. Your own argument will be stronger if you refute—prove false or wrong—all opposing arguments.

Repetition is a simple method of achieving emphasis by repeating a word, phrase, or idea.

Rhetoric is the art of using words effectively in speaking or writing. It is also the art of literary composition, particularly in prose, including both figures of speech and such strategies as comparison and contrast, definition, and analysis.

Rhetorical question is a question asked only to emphasize a point, introduce a topic, or provoke thought, but not to elicit an answer.

Rhythm in prose writing is a regular recurrence of elements or features in sentences, creating a patterned emphasis, balance, or contrast.

Sarcasm is a sneering or taunting attitude in writing, designed to hurt by evaluating or criticizing. Basically, sarcasm is a heavy-handed form of irony (see entry). Writers should try to avoid sarcastic writing and to use more acceptable varieties of irony and satire to criticize their subject.

Satire is the humorous or critical treatment of a subject in order to expose the subject's vices, follies, stupidities, and so forth. The *intention* of such satire is to reform by exposing the subject to comedy or ridicule.

Sensory language is language that appeals to any of the five senses—sight, sound, touch, taste, or feel.

Sentimentality in prose writing is the excessive display of emotion, whether intended or unintended. Because sentimentality can distort the true nature of a situation or idea, writers should use it cautiously, or not at all.

Series as a technique in prose is the presentation of several items, often concrete details or similar parts of grammar such as verbs or adjectives, in rapid sequence.

Setting in narrative and descriptive writing is the time, place, environment, background, or surroundings established by an author.

Simile is a figurative comparison using "like" or "as."

Slang is a kind of language that uses racy or colorful expressions associated more often with speech than with writing. It is colloquial English and should be used in essay writing only to reproduce dialogue or to create a special effect.

Spatial order in descriptive writing is the careful arrangement of details or materials in space—for example, from left to right, top to bottom, or near to far.

Specific words (See *General/specific words.*)

Statistics are facts or data of a numerical kind, assembled and tabulated to present significant information about a given subject. As a technique of illustration, statistics can be useful in analysis and argumentation.

Style is the specific or characteristic manner of expression, execution, construction, or design of an author. As a manner or mode of expression in language, it is the unique way each writer handles ideas. There are numerous stylistic categories—literary, formal, argumentative, satiric—but ultimately no two writers have the same style.

Subjective (See *Objective/subjective.*)

Subordination in sentence structure is the placing of a relatively less important idea in an inferior grammatical position to the main idea. It is the designation of a minor clause that is dependent upon a major clause.

Syllogism is an argument or form of reasoning in which two statements or premises are made and a logical conclusion drawn from them. As such, it is a form of deductive logic—reasoning from the general to the particular. The *major premise* presents a quality of class ("All writers are mortal."). The *minor premise* states that a particular subject is a member of that class ("Ernest Hemingway was a writer."). The conclusion states that the qualities of the class and the member of the class are the same ("Hemingway was mortal.").

Symbol is something—normally a concrete image—that exists in itself but also stands for something else or has greater meaning. As a variety of figurative language, the symbol can be a strong feature in an essay, operating to add depth of meaning and even to unify the composition.

Synonym is a word that means roughly the same as another word. In practice, few words are exactly alike in meaning. Careful writers use synonyms to vary word choice without ever moving too far from the shade of meaning intended.

Theme is the central idea in an essay; it is also termed the *thesis.* Everything in an essay should support the theme in one way or another.

Thesis is the main idea in an essay. The *thesis sentence,* appearing early in the essay (normally somewhere in the first paragraph) serves to convey the main idea to the reader in a clear and emphatic manner.

Tone is the writer's attitude toward his or her subject or material. An essay writer's tone may be objective, subjective, comic, ironic, nostalgic, critical, or a reflection of numerous other attitudes. Tone is the "voice" that writers give to an essay.

Topic sentence is the main idea that a paragraph develops. Not all paragraphs contain topic sentences; often the topic is implied.

Transition is the linking of ideas in sentences, paragraphs, and larger segments of an essay in order to achieve *coherence* (see entry). Among the most common techniques to achieve smooth transitions are: (1) repeating a key word or phrase; (2) using a pronoun to refer back to a key word or phrase; (3) relying on traditional connectives such as *thus, however, moreover, for example, therefore, finally,* and *in conclusion*; (4) using parallel structure (see *Parallelism*); and (5) creating a sentence or paragraph that serves as a bridge from one part of an essay to another. Transition is best achieved when a writer presents ideas and details carefully and in logical order.

Understatement is a method of making a weaker statement than is warranted by truth, accuracy, or importance.

Unity is a feature in an essay whereby all material relates to a central concept and contributes to the meaning of the whole. To achieve a unified effect in an essay, the writer must design an effective introduction and conclusion, maintain consistent tone or point of view, develop middle paragraphs in a coherent manner, and above all stick to the subject, never permitting unimportant or irrelevant elements to enter.

Usage is the way in which a word, phrase, or sentence is used to express a particular idea; it is the customary manner of using a given language in speaking or writing.

Vertical (See *Horizontal/vertical.*)

Acknowledgments

McGraw-Hill wishes to thank the copyright owners for permission to reprint the following copyrighted works.

Chinua Achebe, "The Igbo World and Its Art" from *Hopes and Impediments.* Copyright © 1988 by Chinua Achebe. Reprinted by permission of Doubleday, a division of Bantam Doubleday Dell Publishing Group, Inc., and Harold Ober Associates.

Woody Allen, "My Speech to the Graduates" from *Side Effects.* Copyright © 1980 by Woody Allen. Reprinted by permission of Random House, Inc.

Julia Alvarez, "Hold the Mayonnaise" from "Hers," *The New York Times,* January 12, 1992. Copyright © 1992 by Julia Alvarez. Reprinted by permission of Susan Bergholz Literary Services, New York.

Maya Angelou, "Graduation" and "Momma, the Dentist, and Me" from *I Know Why the Caged Bird Sings.* Copyright © 1969 by Maya Angelou. Reprinted by permission of Random House, Inc.

Isaac Asimov, "Cholesterol" from *Los Angeles Times.* Copyright © 1986 by Isaac Asimov. Reprinted by permission of Ralph M. Vicinanza, Ltd., New York.

Margaret Atwood, "Canadians: What Do They Want?" from *Mother Jones Magazine.* Copyright © 1982 Foundation for National Progress. Reprinted by permission of Mother Jones Magazine and Phoebe Larmore Literary Agency.

Margaret Atwood, "The Female Body" from *Michigan Quarterly Review.* Reprinted by permission of Coach House Press, Toronto.

James Baldwin, "Stranger in the Village" from *Notes of a Native Son.* Copyright © 1955, renewed 1983 by James Baldwin. Reprinted by permission of Beacon Press.

Imamu Amiri Baraka, "Soul Food" from *Home: Social Essays.* Copyright © 1962, 1963, 1966 by the author. Reprinted by permission of William Morrow & Company, Inc., Publishers, and Sterling Lord Literistic, Inc.

Dave Barry, "Red, White, and Beer" from *Dave Barry's Greatest Hits.* Copyright © 1988 by Dave Berry. Reprinted by permission of the author.

Ruth Benedict, "Periodic Worship of the Zumis" in *Patterns of Culture.* Copyright 1934, renewed © 1961 by Ruth Benedict Valentine. Reprinted by permission of Houghton Mifflin Company. All rights reserved.

Carol Bly, "Getting Tired" from *Letters from the Country.* Copyright © 1981 by Carol Bly. Reprinted by permission of HarperCollins Publishers, Inc.

Martin Buber, "The Third Leg of the Table" from *A Believing Humanism: My Testament 1902–1965.* Copyright 1926, 1927 by Martin Buber. English translation copyright © 1967 by Marurice Friedman. Reprinted by permission of Georges Borchardt, Inc.

Rachel Carson, "The Obligation to Endure" from *Silent Spring.* Copyright © 1962 by Rachel L. Carson, renewed 1990 by Roger Christie. Reprinted by permission of Houghton Mifflin Company. All rights reserved.

Bruce Catton, "Grant and Lee: A Study in Contrasts" from *The American Story,* edited by Earl Schenk Miers, Channel Press, 1956. Reprinted by permission of the U.S. Capitol Historical Society.

Sandra Cisneros, "Only Daughter" from *Glamour,* November 1990. Copyright © 1990 by Sandra Cisneros. Reprinted by permission of Susan Bergholz Literary Services, New York.

Samuel Clemens (Mark Twain), "A Boy's Life" from *The Autobiography of Mark Twain.* Copyright © 1927, © 1959 by The Mark Twain Company; copyright 1924, 1952 by Clara Clemens Samossoud. Copyright © 1959 by Charles Neider. Reprinted by permission of HarperCollins Publishers, Inc.

Michelle Cliff, "A Journey into Speech" from *The Land of Look Behind.* Copyright © 1985 by Michelle Cliff. Reprinted by permission of Firebrand Books, Ithaca, New York 14850.

Judith Ortiz Cofer. "Silent Dancing" from *Silent Dancing* (Houston: Arte Publico Press-University of Houston, 1990). Originally published in *Georgia Review,* 1991. Reprinted by permission of the publisher.

Robert Coles, "I Listen to My Parents and Wonder What They Believe." Appeared in *Redbook* magazine, February 1980. Reprinted by permission of the author.

Joan Didion, "The Cuban Presence" from *Miami.* Reprinted by permission of Simon & Schuster.

Joan Didion, "Georgia O'Keefe" from *The White Album.* Copyright © 1968, 1976, 1979, 1989 by Joan Didion. Reprinted by permission of Farrar Straus and Giroux, Inc. "On Keeping a Notebook" from *Slouching Towards Bethlehem.* Copyright © 1966, 1968 by Joan Didion. Reprinted by permission of Farrar, Straus and Giroux, Inc. "On Morality" from *Slouching Towards Bethlehem.* Copyright © 1965, 1968 by Joan Didion. Reprinted by permission of Farrar, Straus and Giroux, Inc.

Annie Dillard, "Death of a Moth" Copyright © 1976 by Annie Dillard. Reprinted by permission of the author and BCG, Inc.

Michael Dorris, "For the Indians No Thanksgiving" and "What Men are Missing." Copyright © 1988 by Michael Dorris. Reprinted by permission of the author.

Dinesh D'Souza, "Bogus Multiculturalism" from *American Educator,* Winter 1991. Reprinted by permission of the American Federation of Teachers.

Audrey Edwards, "Fighting Racism on Campus" from *Connections,* Winter 1992. Reprinted by permission of American Express.

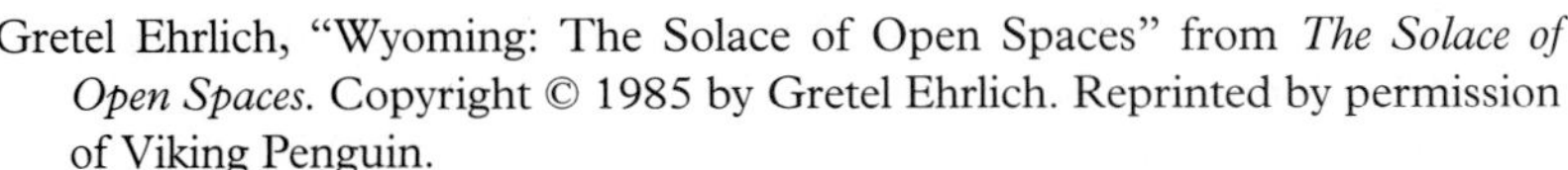

Gretel Ehrlich, "Wyoming: The Solace of Open Spaces" from *The Solace of Open Spaces.* Copyright © 1985 by Gretel Ehrlich. Reprinted by permission of Viking Penguin.

Loren Eiseley, "How Natural Is Natural?" from *The Firmament of Time.* Copyright © 1960 by Loren Eiseley. Copyright © 1960 by The Trustees of The University of Pennsylvania. Reprinted by permission of Atheneum Publishers, an imprint of Macmillan Publishing Company.

Rosario Ferre, "The Writer's Kitchen" from *Lives on the Line: Testimonies of Contemporary Latin Writers,* edited by Doris Meyer. Copyright © 1988 Regents of the University of California. Reprinted by permission of the University of California Press.

E. M. Forster, "My Wood" from *Abinger Harvest.* Copyright 1936 and renewed © 1964 by Edward Morgan Forster. Reprinted by permission of Harcourt Brace & Company, Inc. and The Society of Authors.

Sigmund Freud, "Libidinal Types" from *International Journal of Psycho-Analysis,* 13:277–280. Copyright © 1932 Institute of Psycho-Analysis. Reprinted by permission of the International Journal of Psycho-Analysis and A. W. Freud et al.

Henry Louis Gates, Jr., "Delusions of Grandeur" from *Sports Illustrated,* volume 75, no. 8 (August 18, 1991). Copyright © 1991 by Henry Louis Gates, Jr. Reprinted by permission of Brandt & Brandt Literary Agents, Inc.

Ellen Goodman, "Being a Secretary Can Be Hazardous to Your Health" from *At Large.* Copyright © 1981 by The Washington Post Company. Reprinted by permission of Summit Books, a division of Simon & Schuster, Inc.

Mary Gordon, "More Than Just a Shrine: Paying Homage to the Ghosts of Ellis Island" from *Good Boys and Dead Girls.* Copyright © 1985 by The New York Times Company. Reprinted by permission.

Stephen Jay Gould, "The Terrifying Normalcy of AIDS." Reprinted by permission of the author.

Francine du Plessix Gray, "In Praise of Idleness" in *Harper's,* April 1990. Copyright © 1990 by Francine du Plessix Gray. Reprinted by permission of Georges Borchardt, Inc., for the author.

Shusha Guppy, "Ramadan" from *The Blindfold Horse.* Copyright © 1988 by Shusha Guppy. Reprinted by permission of Beacon Press.

J. B. S. Haldane, "On Being the Right Size" from *Possible Worlds.* Copyright 1928 by Harper & Row, Publishers, Inc., renewed © 1965 by J. B. S. Haldane. Reprinted by permission of HarperCollins Publishers, Inc., the author's estate, and Chatto and Windus, Ltd.

Vaclav Havel, "The Revolution Has Just Begun," from *Time* magazine, March 5, 1990. Copyright © 1990 The Time Inc. Magazine Company. Reprinted by permission.

S. I. Hayakawa, "Words and Children," from *Through the Communication Barrier.* Reprinted by permission of the author.

Sue Hubbell, "Felling Trees" from *The New York Times,* 1984. Copyright © 1984 by Sue Hubbell. Reprinted by permission of Darhansoff & Verrill Literary Agency.

Langston Hughes, "Salvation" from *The Big Sea.* Copyright 1940 by Langston Hughes, renewed © 1968 by Arna Bontemps and George Houston Bass. Reprinted by permission of Hill and Wang, a division of Farrar, Straus and Giroux, Inc.

Pico Iyer, "Vietnam: A Delicate Innocence" from *Condé Nast Traveler,* January 1992. Reprinted by permission of the author.

Susan Jacoby, "When Bright Girls Decide That Math Is 'a Waste of Time'," *The New York Times,* June 2, 1983. Copyright © 1983 by Susan Jacoby. Reprinted by permission of Georges Borchardt, Inc., for the author.

Ruth Prawer Jhabvala, "Myself in India" from *Out of India: Selected Stories.* Copyright © 1986 by Ruth Prawer Jhabvala. Reprinted by permission of William Morrow & Company, Inc.

Jamaica Kincaid, "Antigua: A Small Place" from *A Small Place.* Copyright © 1988 by Jamaica Kincaid. Reprinted by permission of Farrar, Straus and Giroux, Inc.

Coretta Scott King, "The Death Penalty Is a Step Back." Copyright © 1981 Coretta Scott King. Reprinted by arrangement with Coretta Scott King, c/o Joan Daves Agency as agent for the Proprietor.

Martin Luther King, Jr., "I Have a Dream." Copyright © 1963 by Dr. Martin Luther King, Jr., renewed 1991 by Coretta Scott King. Reprinted by arrangement with the Heirs of the Estate of Martin Luther King, Jr., c/o Joan Daves Agency as agent for the Proprietor. "The World House" from *Where Do We Go From Here: Chaos or Community?* (New York: Harper, 1967). Copyright © 1967 by Dr. Martin Luther King., Jr. Reprinted by arrangement with the Heirs of the Estate of Martin Luther King, Jr., c/o Joan Daves Agency as agent for the Proprietor.

Maxine Hong Kingston, "The Woman Warrior" from *The Woman Warrior: Memoirs of a Girlhood among Ghosts.* Copyright © 1975, 1976 by Maxine Hong Kingston. Reprinted by permission of Alfred A. Knopf, Inc. "The Wild Man of the Green Swamp" from *China Men.* Copyright © 1980 by Maxine Hong Kingston. Reprinted by permission of Alfred A. Knopf, Inc.

Perri Klass, "A Long and Difficult Night in the Hospital" from *A Not Entirely Benign Procedure: Four Years as a Medical Student.* Copyright © 1987 by Perri Klass. Reprinted by permission of The Putnam Berkeley Publishing Group.

Joseph Wood Krutch, "The New Immorality" from *Saturday Review* magazine, July 30, 1960. Reprinted by permission.

John Lame Deer, "Green Frog Skin" from *Lame Deer: Seeker of Visions* by John Lame Deer and Richard Erdoes. Copyright © by John Lame Deer and Richard Erdoes. Reprinted by permission of Simon & Schuster, Inc.

Margaret Laurence, "Where the World Began," from *Heart of a Stranger.* © 1976 by Margaret Laurence. Reprinted with the permission of New End Inc.

D. H. Lawrence, "Sex versus Loveliness" from *Phoenix II: Uncollected Papers of D. H. Lawrence,* edited by Roberts and Moore. Copyright © 1959, 1963, 1968 by the Estate of Frieda Lawrence Ravagli. Reprinted by permission of Viking Penguin, a division of Penguin Books USA Inc. "Why the Novel Matters" from *Phoenix: The Posthumous Papers of D. H. Lawrence,* edited by Edward McDonald. Copyright 1936 by Frieda Lawrence, renewed © 1964 by the Estate of Frieda Lawrence Ravagli. Reprinted by permission of Viking Penguin, a division of Penguin Books USA Inc.

Mary Leakey, "Footprints in the Ashes of Time" from *National Geographic Magazine.* April 1979. Copyright 1979 by National Geographic Magazine. Reprinted by permission of the author.

Doris Lessing, "Being Prohibited" in *A Small Personal Voice,* edited by Paul Schlueter. Reprinted by permission of Alfred A. Knopf, Inc.

C. S. Lewis, "The Rival Conceptions of God" from *Mere Christianity.* Copyright 1942, 1945, 1952 by Macmillan Publishing Company. Reprinted by permission of HarperCollins Publishers, Ltd.

Barry Lopez, "Mapping the Real Geography." All rights reserved.

Marya Mannes, "How Do You Know It's Good?" from *Glamour* magazine, November 1962. Copyright © 1962 by Marya Mannes. Reprinted by permission of David J. Blow.

Mary McCarthy, "Names" from *Memories of a Catholic Girlhood.* Copyright © 1957, 1985 by Mary McCarthy. Reprinted by permission of Harcourt Brace & Company.

Carson McCullers, "Home for Christmas" from *The Mortgaged Heart.* Copyright 1940, 1941, 1942, 1945, 1954, © 1956, 1959, 1963, 1967, 1971 by Floria V. Lasky, Executrix of the Estate of Carson McCullers. Copyright 1936, 1952, © 1955, 1957, 1963 by Carson McCullers. Reprinted by permission of Houghton Mifflin Company.

John McPhee, "Travels in Georgia" from *Pieces of the Frame.* Copyright © 1963, 1969, 1970, 1971, 1972, 1973, 1974, 1975 by John McPhee. Reprinted by permission of Farrar, Straus and Giroux, Inc.

Margaret Mead, "New Superstitions for Old" from *A Way of Seeing.* Copyright © 1962, 1970 by Margaret Mead. Reprinted by permission of William Morrow & Company, Inc., Publishers.

Jessica Mitford, excerpt from *The American Way of Death.* Copyright © 1978 by Jessica Mitford. Reprinted by permission of the author.

Ann Grace Mojtabai, "Polygamy" from *The New York Times,* June 5, 1980. Copyright © 1980 by The New York Times Company. Reprinted by permission.

N. Scott Momaday, "The Way to Rainy Mountain" from *The Way to Rainy Mountain.* Copyright © 1969 by the University of New Mexico Press. First published in *The Reporter,* 26 January 1967. Reprinted by permission of the University of New Mexico Press. "Sacred and Ancestral Ground" in *The Sophisticated Traveler,* March 13, 1988. Copyright © 1988 by The New York Times Company. Reprinted by permission.

Bharati Mukherjee, "A Four-Hundred-Year-Old Woman" from *Critical Fictions,* edited by Philimena Mariani. Copyright 1991 by Bharati Mukherjee. Reprinted by permission of The Elaine Markson Agency and the author.

Vladimir Nabokov, "Philistines and Philistinism" from *Lectures on Russian Literature.* Copyright © 1981 by the Estate of Vladimir Nabokov. Reprinted by permission of Harcourt Brace & Company.

V. S. Naipaul, "Our Universal Civilization" in *The New York Times,* November 5, 1990. Copyright © 1990 by The New York Times Company. Reprinted by permission.

Pablo Neruda, "The Odors of Homecoming" from *Passions and Impressions.* English tranlation copyright © 1980, 1981, 1983 by Farrar, Straus and Giroux, Inc. Reprinted by permission.

Joyce Carol Oates, "Against Nature" from *Ontario Review.* Copyright © 1986 by Ontario Review Press, Inc. Reprinted by permission of John Hawkins & Associates, Inc.

George Orwell, "Shooting an Elephant" from *Shooting an Elephant and Other Essays.* Copyright 1950 by Sonia Brownell Orwell and renewed © 1978 by Sonia Pitt-Rivers. Reprinted by permission of Harcourt Brace & Company, the estate of the late Sonia Brownell Orwell, and Martin Secker & Warburg, Ltd. "Politics and the English Language" from *Shooting an Elephant and other Essays.* Copyright 1946 by Sonia Brownell Orwell and renewed © 1974 by Sonia Pitt Orwell. Reprinted by permission of Harcourt Brace & Company, the estate of the late Sonia Brownell Orwell, and Martin Secker & Warburg, Ltd.

Anna Quindlen, "Sex Ed" from *Living Out Loud.* Copyright © 1986 by Anna Quindlen. Reprinted by permission of Random House, Inc.

Octavio Paz, "Walt Whitman" from *On Poets and Others.* Copyright © 1986 by Octavio Paz. Translation copyright © 1986 by Seaver Books. Reprinted from *On Poets and Others* by Octavio Paz, translated from the Spanish by Michael Schmidt, published by Seaver Books, New York, New York. Reprinted by permission of Seaver Books and Carcanet Press, Ltd.

Sylvia Plath, "A Comparison" from *Johnny Panic and the Bible of Dreams.* Copyright © 1962 by Sylvia Plath. Copyright © 1962, 1977 by Ted Hughes. Reprinted by permission of HarperCollins Publishers, Inc., and Olwyn Hughes Literary Agency.

Letty Cottin Pogrebin, "Superstitious Minds" from "Person to Person" column, *Ms.* magazine, February 1988. Copyright © 1988 by Letty Cottin Pogrebin. Reprinted by permission of the author.

J. B. Priestly, "Wrong Ism" from *Essays of Five Decades.* Copyright © 1966 by J. B. Priestly. Reprinted by permission of the Peters Fraser & Dunlop Group, Ltd.

Santha Rama Rau, "By Any Other Name" from *Gifts of Passage.* Copyright 1951 by Vasanthi Rama Rau Bowers. Originally appeared in *The New Yorker.* Reprinted by permission of HarperCollins Publishers, Inc.

Ishmael Reed, "America: The Multinational Society" from *Writin' Is Fightin': Thirty-Seven Years of Boxing on Paper.* Copyright © 1983 by Ishmael Reed.

Adrienne Rich, "The Anger of a Child" from *Of Woman Born: Motherhood as Experience and Institution.* Copyright © 1976 by W. W. Norton & Company. Reprinted by permission.

Richard Rodriguez, "The Lonely Good Company of Books" and "Los Pobres" from *Hunger of Memory.* Copyright © 1982 by Richard Rodriguez. Reprinted by permission of David R. Godine, Publisher.

Bertrand Russell, "Knowledge and Wisdom" from *Portraits from Memory.* Copyright 1951, 1952, 1953, © 1956 by Bertrand Russell. Reprinted by permission of Unwin Hyman, a division of HarperCollins Publishers, Ltd. "The Study of Mathematics" from *Mysticism and Logic.* Copyright 1929 by Allen & Unwin, Ltd. Reprinted by permission of Unwin Hyman, a division of HarperCollins publishers, Ltd.

Deborah Salazar, "My Abortion" from *Exquisite Corpse,* October-December 1989. Reprinted by permission of *Exquisite Corpse.*

Richard Selzer, "Letter to a Young Surgeon" from *Letters to a Young Doctor.* Copyright © 1982 by David Goldmand and Janet Selzer, Trustees. Reprinted by permission of Simon & Schuster, Inc.

Charles Simic, "Reading Philosophy at Night" from *Wonderful Worlds, Silent Truths.* Copyright © 1987 by Charles Simic. First published in *Antaeus* 59, Fall 1987. Reprinted by permission of the University of Michigan Press.

Isaac Bashevis Singer, "Why the Geese Shrieked" from *A Day of Pleasure.* Copyright © 1963, 1965, 1966, 1969 by Isaac Bashevis Singer. Reprinted by permission of Farrar, Straus and Giroux, Inc.

Susan Sontag, "Beauty" from *Women's Beauty: Put-Down or Power Source?*

Copyright © 1975 by Susan Sontag. Reprinted by permission of Farrar, Straus and Giroux, Inc.

Gary Soto, "Looking for Work" from *Living up the Street: Narrative Recollections.* Reprinted by permission of Strawberry Hill Press.

Thomas Sowell, "We're Not Really Equal" from *Newsweek,* September 7, 1981. Reprinted by permission of the author.

Wole Soyinka, excerpt from *Ake: The Years of Childhood.* Reprinted by permission of Random House.

John Steinbeck, "Americans and the Land" from *America and Americans.* Copyright © 1966 by John Steinbeck. Reprinted by permission of Viking Penguin, a division of Penguin Books USA Inc.

Gloria Steinem, "Erotica and Pornography" from *Outrageous Acts and Everyday Rebellions.* Copyright © 1983 by East Toledo Productions, Inc. Reprinted by permission of Henry Holt and Company, Inc.

Ronald Takaki, "Roots" in *Strangers from a Different Shore.* Copyright © 1989 by Ronald Takaki. Reprinted by permission of Little, Brown and Company.

Amy Tan, "The Language of Discretion" from *The State of the Language,* edited by Christopher Ricks and Leonard Michaels. Reprinted by permission of the University of California Press and the Sandra Dijkstra Literary Agency.

Paul Theroux, "Being a Man" from *Sunrise with Seamonsters: Travels and Discoveries.* Copyright © 1985 by Cape Code Scriveners Co. Reprinted by permission of Houghton Mifflin Company.

Lewis Thomas, "Notes on Punctuation" from *The Medusa and the Snail.* Copyright © 1979 by Lewis Thomas. Reprinted by permission of Viking Penguin, a division of Penguin Books USA Inc. "On Societies as Organisms" from *The Lives of a Cell.* Copyright © 1971 by the Massachusetts Medical Society. Reprinted by permission of Viking Penguin, a division of Penguin Books USA Inc.

Barbara Tuchman, "An Inquiry into the Persistence of Unwisdom in Government" from *Esquire* May 1980. Copyright © 1980 by Barbara Tuchman. Reprinted by permission of Russell & Volkening as agents for the author.

Alice Walker, "Beauty: When the Other Dancer Is the Self" from *In Search of Our Mothers' Gardens: Womanist Prose.* Copyright © 1976 by Alice Walker. Reprinted by permission of Harcourt Brace & Company. "Saving the Life That Is Your Own: The Importance of Models in the Artist's Life" from *In Search of Our Mothers' Gardens: Womanist Prose.* Copyright © 1983 by Alice Walker. Reprinted by permission of Harcourt Brace & Company. "Am I Blue?" from *Living by the Word: Selected Writings 1973–1987.* Copyright © 1987 by Alice Walker. Reprinted by permission of Harcourt Brace & Company.

Eudora Welty, "One Writer's Beginnings" from *One Writer's Beginnings.* Copyright © 1983, 1984 by Eudora Welty. Reprinted by permission of Harvard University Press.

E. B. White, "Education" from *One Man's Meat.* Copyright 1939, © 1967, by E. B. White. Reprinted by permission of HarperCollins Publishers, Inc. "Here Is New York" from *Here Is New York.* Copyright 1949 by E. B. White. Reprinted by permission of HarperCollins Publishers, Inc. "Once More to the Lake" from *Essays of E. B. White.* Copyright 1941, © 1969 by E. B. White. Reprinted by permission of HarperCollins Publishers, Inc.

Jade Snow Wong, "Pilgrims from the Orient" from *The Immigrant Experience,*

edited by Thomas Wheeler. Reprinted by permission of The Dial Press, a division of Bantam Doubleday Dell Publishing Group, Inc.

Virginia Woolf, "The Death of the Moth" and "Professions for Women" from *The Death of The Moth and Other Essays.* Copyright 1942 by Harcourt Brace and Company, renewed © 1970 by Marjorie R. Parsons, Executrix. Reprinted by permission Harcourt Brace & Company and Chatto & Windus, Ltd.

Richard Wright, "The Library Card" from *Black Boy.* Copyright 1937, 1942, 1944, 1945 by Richard Wright. Reprinted by permission of HarperCollins Publishers, Inc.

Index